D0472898

Inequality in the United States: A Reader

Inequality in the United States: A Reader

John Brueggemann
Skidmore College

Allyn & Bacon

Boston   Columbus   Indianapolis   New York   San Francisco   Upper Saddle River
Amsterdam   Cape Town   Dubai   London   Madrid   Milan   Munich   Paris   Montreal   Toronto
Delhi   Mexico City   São Paulo   Sydney   Hong Kong   Seoul   Singapore   Taipei   Tokyo

Publisher: Karen Hanson
Editorial Assistant: Christine Dore
Executive Marketing Manager: Kelly May
Marketing Assistant: Janeli Bitor
Production Assistant: Caitlin Smith
Production Manager: Meghan DeMaio
Creative Director: Jayne Conte
Cover Designer: Suzanne Behnke
Cover Design: © Elwynn/Fotolia
Editorial Production and Composition Service: PreMediaGlobal/Paul Smith
Printer/Binder/Cover Printer: R.R. Donnelley & Sons

Credits and acknowledgements borrowed from other sources and reproduced, with permission, in this textbook appear on appropriate page within text.

Library of Congress Cataloging-in-Publication Data

Inequality in the United States : a reader / [edited by] John Brueggemann.
    p. cm.
  Includes index.
  ISBN-13: 978-0-205-62778-3
  ISBN-10: 0-205-62778-1
  1. Equality—United States.   2. Social problems—United States.   3. Social classes—United States.
4. Racism—United States.   5. Poverty—United States.   6. Sex discrimination—United States.
7. United States—Race relations.   8. United States—Social conditions.   9. United States—Economic conditions.
I. Brueggemann, John, 1965–
  HN90.S6I53 2012
  305.0973—dc22

                  2010054562

Copyright © 2012 Pearson Education, Inc., publishing as Allyn & Bacon, 75 Arlington Street, Suite 300, Boston, MA 02116. All rights reserved. Manufactured in the United States of America. This publication is protected by Copyright, and permission should be obtained from the publisher prior to any prohibited reproduction, storage in a retrieval system, or transmission in any form or by any means, electronic, mechanical, photocopying, recording, or likewise. To obtain permission(s) to use material from this work, please submit a written request to Pearson Higher Education, Rights and Contracts Department, 501 Boylston Street, Suite 900, Boston, MA 02116, or fax your request to 617-671-3447.

Many of the designations by manufacturers and seller to distinguish their products are claimed as trademarks. Where those designations appear in this book, and the publisher was aware of a trademark claim, the designations have been printed in initial caps or all caps.

10 9 8 7 6 5 4 3 2 1 [DOH] 15 14 13 12 11

Allyn & Bacon
is an imprint of

www.pearsonhighered.com

ISBN-10:   0-205-62778-1
ISBN-13: 978-0-205-62778-3

CONTENTS

ACKNOWLEDGMENTS

This project would not have been possible without the assistance of numerous people. It is my pleasure to thank them here.

Jeff Lasser and Karen Hanson of Pearson have been helpful and supportive throughout the process. Shannon Foreman of Omegatype Typography, Inc. did the important work of securing copyright permissions. Paul Smith of PreMediaGlobal did a wonderful job of copy editing.

I am grateful for institutional support I received from various administrators at Skidmore College, especially Paty Rubio, Muriel Poston, Susan Kress and Phillip Glotzbach. I want to thank the Quadracci family as well for its endowment of the Quadracci Chair in Social Responsibility.

As always, Linda Santagato provided wonderful clerical support in the Department of Sociology, Anthropology and Social Work. It has been my pleasure to work with several able teaching assistants. Tiana Olewnick and Willa Jones contributed valuable labor at various stages. Sarah Rosenblatt was especially helpful in editing and assembling the reader.

I am fortunate to have received suggestions from a number of other scholars and friends, who guided me to relevant readings, examples and ideas. They include Kate Berheide, Irene Browne, Kristie Ford, Bill Fox, Rory McVeigh, Lisa Meyer, Joya Misra, Rik Scarce, and Susan Walzer. I appreciate the contributions of all the people listed above who helped with the completion of this project.

There are three other people to whom I owe a special debt of gratitude. Vinnie Roscigno has been a supportive, generous and engaged colleague for years. I am thankful for his insights and inspiration. Cliff Brown and I have collaborated together one way or another for over two decades, through college, graduate school, and professional work in our field. For me, it has been an enormously edifying partnership. Finally, I want to acknowledge my mentor, Terry Boswell (1955–2006). It was in his graduate seminar, Social Stratification, that I first developed an interest in the matters taken up in this reader. I am truly fortunate to have known him as a teacher and friend.

INTRODUCTION

"Why do poor people whine about what someone else should do for them instead of going out and getting a job?" "Why do liberals want government to give out charity to lazy people?" "How can white people act like they don't know racism is everywhere?" "Why are conservatives so heartless?" Such messages can be heard every day in America as a subtext under the thinly veiled theater of breezy public conversation or the evening news. As intense as the dispute about social inequality is today, though, it is not new. Sociologists have been exploring these kinds of issues for some two hundred years.

The early sociologists, scholars such as Karl Marx, Emile Durkheim, and Max Weber, studied a broad range of issues. They wanted to understand what it meant for society to develop radically new economic, political, organizational, and cultural capacities. At the center of their analyses, though, were basic questions about inequality. Why are some people rich and some poor? What sorts of people gain real power? How do we decide who has status? Why do certain people have greater access to resources and opportunities? What kinds of uneven access are fair? What kinds are unjust? They sought coherent, robust answers to these and many other questions.

For a long time the answer to most questions in sociology was modernization. Why is our economy structured the way it is? What makes society hold together in the way that it does? Why are many organizations so bureaucratic? What accounts for changes in the family, religion, medicine, and education? And what distinguishes western society from other parts of the world? The answer in each case involved modernization. As with many sociological terms, the real insights were revealed in the unpacking of this important concept.

The topic preoccupied the founders of sociology because the forces of modernization were profoundly important and relatively new during their era. Industrial technology, complex division of labor, rational law, democratic ideals, urbanization,

new forms of transportation and communication all contributed to the rise of modern society in complicated, lasting ways. Few boundaries are more decisive for a society than whether it is modern or pre-modern. This was one of the insights Marx, Durkheim, and Weber uncovered as all the changes unfolded around them during the modernization of western society.

A few years before August Comte first used the term "sociology" in the early 18th century, another group of founders were eagerly paying attention to similar issues but with an eye toward a different objective. As much a product of the Enlightenment as the early sociologists, the Founding Fathers of the United States also believed in the promise of reason and progress. In seeking to establish a society with unprecedented freedom and equality amidst the turmoil of modernization, the Founding Fathers grappled with issues of inequality as well.

In some sense modernization gave birth to both the new nation-state and the new discipline. The issue of social inequality was important in each case because how we make the things we need to survive, how they are distributed, and who controls those processes—paramount issues for both sets of founders—were revolutionized during modernization.

The growth of industry, cities, opportunity, individualism, and a host of other modernizing developments brought into question what the average person could expect out of life. Free market capitalism reduced the level of material scarcity compared to previous eras and diminished the importance of traditional bases of social identity (e.g., caste, clan, tribe). But it also escalated individual competition and isolation. In the context of these changes, American leaders wrestled with the gap between our nation's stated ideals of freedom and equality and the reality of systemic inequality. Having waged a revolution against a monarchy, the Founding Fathers, who were almost all affluent, Christian, white men of

European ancestry, struggled to negotiate the goals of liberty, order, and retaining their own privilege.

As sociologists sought to understand inequality in the context of modernization, the starting point was social class. "The history of all hitherto existing society is the history of class struggles," Karl Marx declared. For the founding generations of the new republic, the main challenge was the "American dilemma" of race. A nation organized around inalienable rights was built on the stolen resources of Native Americans and the forced labor of Africans. Members of the first Constitutional Congress were deeply divided about how to handle the issue of slavery in particular. Over time the barely hidden connections between class and race became explicit topics for sociologists and American leaders. And, there were other sources of domination always present that were integral to modern society but not yet explicitly taken up in public discourse. For instance, the deeply gendered culture of the United States remained wholly taken for granted until the middle of the 19th century when the suffrage movement began.

In responding to the central question of "who gets what?," sociologists have often looked to institutions and culture, that is to different aspects of society, for answers. More mainstream (non-sociological) analysts in American discourse, including scholars and political leaders, have often emphasized individualistic factors such as ambition and ability. In short, the debate about inequality is deeply sociological and deeply American, but there has ever been a fundamental tension between the defining sociological analyses and the dominant mainstream perspectives on the key issues.

As a society, we have always been interested in and divided by the question of who *deserves* what? This was true at every defining moment in our nation's history—1776, 1865, 1929, 1945, 1968, for example—just as it is today. In contemporary society, the question of how resources will be distributed permeates almost every political or moral dispute. Of course this includes publicly debated issues like taxation, welfare, health care, education, the environment, and military spending. But this question also relates to challenges we talk about less frequently with explicit connections

to resources, topics like division of labor in the family, consumption, recreation and leisure, art, religion, and so on. Indeed, it is difficult to think of an important social issue that is not integrally tied to questions about the resources and opportunities people will have in their lives.

For all these reasons, as important and interconnected as it is in many times and places, the topic of social stratification has special significance for contemporary America. This volume is intended to provide an introduction to the themes of inequality mentioned here. It begins where most sociological discourse about inequality begins, with Karl Marx. It then considers the main categories established in the durable framework introduced by the other preeminent pioneer in the sociological study of inequality, Max Weber. Partly in response to Marx's writing, which emphasized the primacy of social class, Weber wrote his essay, "Class, Status, Party," in which he argued that other dimensions of stratification are at times also very important. He described caste as the main exemplar of "status-honor." Other sociologists subsequently made good use of Weber's concept of status to explain the dynamics of gender, sexuality, and other subjectively constructed social categories. Weber suggested that his final dimension, "party," would be the most important one in modern western society. Parties, which include any group of people who organize together in pursuit of some common goal, play an increasingly important role in societies highly structured with legal-rational bureaucracy.

Some of the voices in this volume are influenced by the third founding father of sociology, Emile Durkheim. That he had little to say about structured inequality reflects his premise that society operates like a body with different parts that are necessarily both valuable and unequal in their significance. The inequality is inevitable, functional, and therefore, for Durkheim at least, not worth belaboring. Kingsley Davis and Wilbert Moore explicitly link Durkheim's functionalism to inequality in an article included here.

Many scholars have built on, criticized, and extended the study of inequality based on these foundational perspectives. One echo of Weber's disagreement with Marx is the post-modern critique of classic sociology, which has revealed the fluid interaction of social forces previously considered separate. According to this assessment, the order, coherence, and progress imagined in culture, art, literature, and social theory of the modern period is at least problematic if not untenable. From a sociological perspective, this means that no single framework or "grand theory" can account for the dynamic, multifaceted forces alive in the social world. In addition, different people have distinctive stories to tell and varied ways of seeing things, a reality that scholars themselves are not able to fully elude.

Well before mainstream sociology recognized this challenge, W. E. B. DuBois articulated how important the standpoint of a person is and the imperative of nevertheless trying to assess empirical patterns.

> I do not for a moment doubt that my Negro descent and narrow group culture have in many cases predisposed me to interpret my facts too favorably for my race; but there is little danger of long misleading here, for the champions of white folk are legion. The Negro has long been the clown of history; the football of anthropology; and the slave of industry. I am trying to show here why these attitudes can no longer be maintained. I realize that the truth of history lies not in the mouths of partisans but rather in the calm Science that sits between. Her cause I seek to serve, and wherever I fail, I am at least paying Truth the respect of earnest effort (2007 [1939], p. xxxi).

As DuBois's sensibility spread, especially during recent decades, social research has revealed new ways of understanding inequality, not just in varied settings but through multiple lenses. New streams of scholarship have illuminated the connections between identity and institutional resources. The ways we think about ourselves and others are patterned into systems of domination and exclusion.

Another important development in recent decades is the intensification of different forms of inequality. There has certainly been a great deal of progress on many fronts since the middle of the 20th century, most notably more egalitarian practices related to race and gender. But the rate of change has slowed a great deal. And in the last 30 years, certain forms of stratification, especially economic inequality, have actually become much more extreme.

In this collection of writings, I seek to illuminate these patterns and the debates about them by sharing the insights and tensions of multiple views. While I have mentioned a few central themes in the discourse, there are really many facets to any serious consideration of inequality, and much more material than could be contained in one volume. This includes substantive topics such as class, race, ethnicity, gender, sexuality, and power. The readings in this book try to account for the bases of these forces and the implications of them, that is: where do they come from and what are their implications? To answer such questions, we must pay attention to the institutional contexts and ideological understandings of these dimensions. We find systematic inequality fostered in foundational institutions like the economy, government, and the family. And we see it attached to new issues unfamiliar to previous generations, such as "environmental discrimination" and digital technology.

In sum, students of inequality will find in these pages a variety of approaches and viewpoints that do not line up neatly next to one another. Classic theories are contrasted by postmodern appraisals. Quantitative research is complemented by qualitative research. Some scholars suggest that class is of preeminent importance, others say race. Many others claim that social inequality is more complicated than such conclusions. And still others hold that individuals are much more important than any social categories in determining their own destiny. This is not to say that all the assertions included in this volume should be taken at face value or treated as having equal value. But all of the writings herein have served as important guideposts in the study of and debate about social inequality.

Each part of this volume is preceded by a brief introduction that provides a short overview of what follows. Part I includes classic statements from Marx, Weber, and other influential writers, mostly from the 19th and early 20th centuries, who have set the terms for the scholarly investigations and debates that followed. The main topics for the next three parts are drawn from Weber's essay, but with attention to how each issue has been influential and analyzed in more recent scholarship.

Part II focuses on different aspects of class inequality. Part III includes writings about status, with two clusters of topics related to race and ethnicity (Section A) as well as gender and sexuality (Section B). Part IV covers Weber's third category of party, with emphasis on power and ideology.

The final part is organized around the recognition that empirical reality is messier than the conventional categories in the study of stratification. People do not live their lives simply defined as a proletarian, a white person, or a woman, for example. Rather, they are beholden to numerous social categories that contribute to their experience in the world. Part V explores this complexity by focusing on the "intersections" of social categories.

The substantive body of this text is followed by an appendix with data related to various trends in the study of social inequality. Throughout these readings I have made minor editorial changes in an effort to eliminate typographical errors in the original versions and reduce confusing references in excerpts to subsequent sections or chapters not included here.

At the end of this volume, readers will find an Appendix, which summarizes a number of quantitative patterns related to inequality in contemporary American society.

INSTRUCTOR RESOURCES

Instructor's Manual and Test Bank (ISBN 020562779X): This supplement offers an overview for each reading followed by essay, multiple choice, and true/false questions. The Instructor's Manual and Test Bank is available to adopters at www.pearsonhighered.com.

MyTest (ISBN 0205054714): This computerized software allows instructors to create their own personalized exams, to edit any or all of the existing test questions, and to add new questions. Other special features of this program include random generation of test questions, creation of alternate versions of the same test, scrambling question sequence, and test preview before printing. For easy access, this software is available at www.pearsonhighered.com.

Foundations

INTRODUCTION

"The question to be answered next is: 'what makes a class?' " Karl Marx had much to say about social class, but never answered his own question very clearly. The third and final volume of his masterpiece, *Capital*, ends a few lines later with a cryptic note from Marx's long-time collaborator, Frederick Engels: "At this point the manuscript breaks off.— F.E." Marx and Engels mentioned several of their arguments in "The Manifesto of the Communist Party" (published in 1848) that they developed more fully in subsequent writings. One of them is that the class that controls an economic system is the one which dominates its most important tools, or "means of production." In capitalism, the bourgeoisie builds up profitable property. Members of the proletariat are forced to sell their labor to those who own the capital. Marx and Engels expected society to become split between capitalists and workers. This increasing polarization is also facilitated by the processes of exploitation and alienation.

Max Weber thought that in addition to Marx's emphasis on property, skills were significant in determining social class. This was especially important as middle classes became more prevalent (not less, as Marx and Engels expected). As suggested in the title of his essay, "Class, Status, Party," Weber also thought there were other important dimensions of social stratification. This includes culturally constructed categories such as ethnicity, that is, "status groups." It also includes groups organized for some political goal, or "parties," which Weber thought would become the most important dimension of stratification in a modern society governed by rational law like our own.

Three years younger than Weber, W.E.B. Du Bois was influenced by lectures delivered by the great German intellectual during his studies at the University of Berlin from 1892 to 1894. Later when Du Bois published *The Souls of Black Folk* in 1905, he received a letter from Weber expressing admiration and congratulations (see David Levering Lewis, *W. E. B. Du Bois: Biography of a Race 1868–1919*, p. 277). In the first essay from that book, "Of Our Spiritual Strivings," Du Bois's idea of "double-consciousness" describes the experience of the "American Negro" belonging fully neither in America nor in Africa. But the idea would resonate with marginalized peoples in various social circumstances. Du Bois elaborated further on the basis of racial identity in "The Conservation of Races," underscoring its fundamentally sociological character (in contrast to primarily biological or theological explanations).

Anticipating Du Bois's notion of "twoness" by a few years, Anna Julia Cooper portrays the complex consciousness of black, southern women in the context of higher education in *A Voice from the South*, which was published just as DuBois was sitting in Weber's lecture hall in Germany. Cooper's perspective shares and complicates Du Bois's view that the significance and character of different social institutions depend greatly on one's standpoint.

The perspective of another pioneer in sociology, Emile Durkheim, is also represented among these foundational texts in the work of Kingsley Davis and Wilbert Moore. Advancing a view that is frankly less common among sociologists today but quite popular among lay people, Davis and Moore argue in "Some Principles of Stratification," that systematic social inequality allows the most able and hard-working members of society to find their way to important jobs. The social hierarchy in terms of pay and status that exists among different occupations is therefore highly functional for society. Each of the writings in this first part provides the foundations for much of what followed in the study of stratification, as well as the parameters of debate in public and scholarly discourse.

1

Excerpts from "The Manifesto of the Communist Party"

KARL MARX AND FREDERICK ENGELS

A specter is haunting Europe—the specter of Communism. All the powers of old Europe have entered into a holy alliance to exorcise this specter: Pope and Czar, Metternich and Guizot, French Radicals and German police-spies.

Where is the party in opposition that has not been decried as communistic by its opponents in power? Where is the Opposition that has not hurled back the branding reproach of Communism, against the more advanced opposition parties, as well as against its reactionary adversaries?

Two things result from this fact:

  I. Communism is already acknowledged by all European powers to be itself a power.

 II. It is high time that Communists should openly, in the face of the whole world, publish their views, their aims, their tendencies, and meet this nursery tale of the specter of Communism with a manifesto of the party itself.

To this end, Communists of various nationalities have assembled in London, and sketched the following manifesto, to be published in the English, French, German, Italian, Flemish, and Danish languages.

I   Bourgeois and Proletarians

The history of all hitherto existing society is the history of class struggles.

Freeman and slave, patrician and plebeian, lord and serf, guild-master and journeyman, in a word, oppressor and oppressed, stood in constant opposition to one another, carried on an uninterrupted, now hidden, now open fight, a fight that each time ended, either in a revolutionary reconstitution of society at large, or in the common ruin of the contending classes.

From Karl Marx and Frederick Engels, *The Manifesto of the Communist Party* (New York: International Publishers). Copyright 1948. Reprinted with permission.

In the earlier epochs of history, we find almost everywhere a complicated arrangement of society into various orders, a manifold gradation of social rank. In ancient Rome we have patricians, knights, plebeians, slaves; in the Middle Ages, feudal lords, vassals, guild-masters, journeymen, apprentices, serfs; in almost all of these classes, again, subordinate gradations.

The modern bourgeois society that has sprouted from the ruins of feudal society, has not done away with class antagonisms. It has but established new classes, new conditions of oppression, new forms of struggle in place of the old ones.

Our epoch, the epoch of the bourgeoisie, possesses, however, this distinctive feature: It has simplified the class antagonisms. Society as a whole is more and more splitting up into two great hostile camps, into two great classes directly facing each other—bourgeoisie and proletariat.

From the serfs of the Middle Ages sprang the chartered burghers of the earliest towns. From these burgesses the first elements of the bourgeoisie were developed.

The discovery of America, the rounding of the Cape, opened up fresh ground for the rising bourgeoisie. The East Indian and Chinese markets, the colonization of America, trade with the colonies, the increase in the means of exchange and in commodities generally, gave to commerce, to navigation, to industry, an impulse never before known, and thereby, to the revolutionary element in the tottering feudal society, a rapid development.

The feudal system of industry, in which industrial production was monopolized by closed guilds, now no longer sufficed for the growing wants of the new markets. The manufacturing system took its place. The guild-masters were pushed aside by the manufacturing middle class; division of labor between the different corporate guilds vanished in the face of division of labor in each single workshop.

Meantime the markets kept ever growing, the demand ever rising. Even manufacture no longer sufficed. Thereupon, steam and machinery revolutionized industrial production. The place of manufacture was taken by the giant, modern industry, the place of the industrial middle class, by industrial millionaires—the leaders of whole industrial armies, the modern bourgeois.

Modern industry has established the world market, for which the discovery of America paved the way. This market has given an immense development to commerce, to navigation, to communication by land. This development has, in its turn, reacted on the extension of industry; and in proportion as industry, commerce, navigation, railways extended, in the same proportion the bourgeoisie developed, increased its capital, and pushed into the background every class handed down from the Middle Ages.

We see, therefore, how the modern bourgeoisie is itself the product of a long course of development, of a series of revolutions in the modes of production and of exchange.

Each step in the development of the bourgeoisie was accompanied by a corresponding political advance of that class. An oppressed class under the sway of the feudal nobility, it became an armed and self-governing association in the medieval commune; here independent urban republic (as in Italy and Germany), there taxable "third estate" of the monarchy (as in France); afterwards, in the period of manufacture proper, serving either the semi-feudal or the absolute monarchy as a counterpoise against the nobility, and, in fact, cornerstone of the great monarchies in general—the bourgeoisie has at last, since the establishment of modern industry and of the world market, conquered for itself, in the modern representative state, exclusive political sway. The executive of the modern state is but a committee for managing the common affairs of the whole bourgeoisie.

The bourgeoisie has played a most revolutionary role in history.

The bourgeoisie, wherever it has got the upper hand, has put an end to all feudal, patriarchal, idyllic relations. It has pitilessly torn asunder the motley feudal ties that bound man to his "natural superiors," and has left no other bond between man and man than naked self-interest, than callous "cash payment." It has drowned the most heavenly ecstasies of religious fervor, of chivalrous enthusiasm, of philistine sentimentalism, in the icy water of egotistical calculation. It has resolved personal worth into exchange value and in place of the numberless indefeasible chartered freedoms, has set up that single, unconscionable freedom—Free Trade. In one word, for exploitation, veiled by religious and political illusions, it has substituted naked, shameless, direct, brutal exploitation.

The bourgeoisie has stripped of its halo every occupation hitherto honored, and looked up to with reverent awe. It has converted the physician, the lawyer, the priest, the poet, the man of science, into its paid wage-laborers.

The bourgeoisie has torn away from the family its sentimental *veil,* and has reduced the family relation to a mere money relation.

The bourgeoisie has disclosed how it came to pass that the brutal display of vigor in the Middle Ages, which reactionaries so much admire, found its fitting complement in the most slothful indolence. It has been the first to show what man's activity can bring about. It has accomplished wonders far surpassing Egyptian pyramids, Roman aqueducts, and Gothic cathedrals; it has conducted expeditions that put in the shade all former migrations of nations and crusades.

The bourgeoisie cannot exist without constantly revolutionizing the instruments of production, and thereby the relations of production, and with them the whole relations of society. Conservation of the old modes of production in unaltered form, was, on the contrary, the first condition of existence for all earlier industrial classes. Constant revolutionizing of production, uninterrupted disturbance of all social conditions, everlasting uncertainty and agitation distinguish the bourgeois epoch from all earlier ones. All fixed, fast-frozen relations, with their train of ancient and venerable prejudices and opinions, are swept away, all new-formed ones become antiquated before they can ossify. All that is solid melts into air, all that is holy is profaned, and man is at last compelled to face with sober senses his real conditions of life and his relations with his kind.

The need of a constantly expanding market for its products chases the bourgeoisie over the whole surface of the globe. It must nestle everywhere, settle everywhere, establish connections everywhere.

The bourgeoisie has through its exploitation of the world market given a cosmopolitan character to production and consumption in every country. To the great chagrin of reactionaries, it has drawn from under the feet of industry the national ground on which it stood. All old-established national industries have been destroyed or are daily being destroyed. They are dislodged by new industries, whose introduction becomes a life and death question for all civilized nations, by industries that no longer work up indigenous raw material, but raw material drawn from the remotest zones; industries whose products are consumed, not only at home, but in every corner of the globe. In place of the old wants, satisfied by the production of the country, we find new wants, requiring for their satisfaction the products of distant lands and climes. In place of the old local and national seclusion and self-sufficiency, we have intercourse in every direction, universal inter-dependence of nations. And as in material, so also in intellectual production. The intellectual creations of individual nations become common property. National one-sidedness and narrow-mindedness become more and more impossible, and from the numerous national and local literatures there arises a world literature.

The bourgeoisie, by the rapid improvement of all instruments of production, by the immensely facilitated means of communication, draws all nations, even the most barbarian, into civilization. The cheap prices of its commodities are the heavy artillery with which it batters down all Chinese walls, with which it forces the barbarians' intensely obstinate hatred of foreigners to capitulate. It compels all nations, on pain of extinction, to adopt the bourgeois mode of production; it compels them to introduce what it calls civilization into their midst, i.e., to become bourgeois themselves. In a word, it creates a world after its own image.

The bourgeoisie has subjected the country to the rule of the towns. It has created enormous cities, has greatly increased the urban population as compared with the rural, and has thus rescued a considerable part of the population from the idiocy of rural life. Just as it has made the country dependent on the towns, so it has made barbarian and semi-barbarian countries dependent on the civilized ones, nations of peasants on nations of bourgeois, the East on the West.

More and more the bourgeoisie keeps doing away with the scattered state of the population, of the means of production, and of property. It has agglomerated population, centralized means of production, and has concentrated property in a few hands. The necessary consequence of this was political centralization. Independent, or but loosely connected provinces, with separate interests, laws, governments, and systems of taxation, became lumped together into one nation, with one government, one code of laws, one national class interest, one frontier, and one customs tariff.

The bourgeoisie, during its rule of scarce one hundred years, has created more massive and more colossal productive forces than have all preceding generations together. Subjection of nature's forces to man, machinery, application of chemistry to industry and agriculture, steam-navigation, railways, electric telegraphs, clearing of whole continents for cultivation, canalization of rivers, whole populations conjured out of the ground—what earlier century had even a presentiment that such productive forces slumbered in the lap of social labor?

We see then that the means of production and of exchange, which served as the foundation for the growth of the bourgeoisie, were generated in feudal society. At a certain stage in the development of these means of production and of exchange, the conditions under which feudal society produced and exchanged, the feudal organization of agriculture and manufacturing industry, in a word, the feudal relations of property became no longer compatible with the already developed productive forces; they became so many fetters. They had to be burst asunder; they were burst asunder.

Into their place stepped free competition, accompanied by a social and political constitution adapted to it, and by the economic and political sway of the bourgeois class.

A similar movement is going on before our own eyes. Modern bourgeois society with its relations of production, of exchange and of property, a society that has conjured up such gigantic means of production and of exchange, is like the sorcerer who is no longer able to control the powers of the nether world whom he has called up by his spells. For many a decade past the history of industry and commerce is but the history of the revolt of modern productive forces against modern conditions of production, against the property relations that are the conditions for the existence of the bourgeoisie and of its rule. It is enough to mention the commercial crises that by their periodical return put the existence of the entire bourgeois society on trial, each time more threateningly. In these crises a great part not only of the existing products, but also of the previously created productive forces, are periodically destroyed. In these crises there breaks out an epidemic that, in all earlier epochs, would have seemed an absurdity—the epidemic of over-production. Society suddenly finds itself put back into a state of momentary barbarism; it appears as if a famine, a universal war of devastation had cut off the supply of every means of subsistence; industry and commerce seem to be destroyed. And why? Because there is too much civilization, too much means of subsistence, too much industry, too much commerce. The productive forces at the disposal of society no longer tend to further the development of the conditions of bourgeois property; on the contrary, they have become too powerful for these conditions, by which they are fettered, and no sooner do they overcome these fetters than they bring disorder into the whole of bourgeois society, endanger the existence of bourgeois property. The conditions of bourgeois society are too narrow to comprise the wealth created by them. And how does the bourgeoisie get over these crises? On the one hand, by enforced destruction of a mass of productive forces; on the other, by the conquest of new markets, and by the more thorough exploitation of the old ones. That is to say, by paving the way for more extensive and more destructive crises, and by diminishing the means whereby crises are prevented.

The weapons with which the bourgeoisie felled feudalism to the ground are now turned against the bourgeoisie itself.

But not only has the bourgeoisie forged the weapons that bring death to itself; it has also called into existence the men who are to wield those weapons—the modern working class—the proletarians.

In proportion as the bourgeoisie, i.e., capital, is developed, in the same proportion is the proletariat, the modern working class, developed—a class of laborers, who live only so long as they find work, and who find work only so long as their labor increases capital. These laborers, who must sell themselves piecemeal, are a commodity, like every other article of commerce, and are consequently exposed to all the vicissitudes of competition, to all the fluctuations of the market.

Owing to the extensive use of machinery and to division of labor, the work of the proletarians has lost all individual character, and, consequently, all charm for the workman. He becomes an appendage of the machine, and it is only the most simple, most monotonous, and most easily acquired knack, that is required of him. Hence, the cost of production of a workman is restricted, almost entirely, to the means of subsistence that he requires for his maintenance, and for the propagation of his race. But the price of a commodity, and therefore also of labor, is equal to its cost of production. In proportion, therefore, as the repulsiveness of the work increases, the wage decreases. Nay more, in proportion as the use of machinery and division of labor increases, in the same proportion the burden of toil also increases, whether by prolongation of the working hours, by increase of the work exacted in a given time, or by increased speed of the machinery, etc.

Modern industry has converted the little workshop of the patriarchal master into the great factory of the industrial capitalist. Masses of laborers, crowded into the factory, are organized like soldiers. As privates of the industrial army they are placed under the command of a perfect hierarchy of officers and sergeants. Not only are they slaves of the bourgeois class, and of the bourgeois state; they are daily and hourly enslaved by the machine, by the over-looker, and, above all, by the individual bourgeois manufacturer himself. The more openly this despotism proclaims gain to be its end and aim, the more petty, the more hateful and the more embittering it is.

The less the skill and exertion of strength implied in manual labor, in other words, the more modern industry develops, the more is the labor of men superseded by that of women. Differences of age and sex have no longer any distinctive social validity for the working class. All are instruments of labor, more or less expensive to use, according to their age and sex.

No sooner has the laborer received his wages in cash, for the moment escaping exploitation by the manufacturer, than he is set upon by the other portions of the bourgeoisie, the landlord, the shopkeeper, the pawnbroker, etc.

The lower strata of the middle class—the small tradespeople, shopkeepers and retired tradesmen generally, the handicraftsmen and peasants—all these sink gradually into the proletariat, partly because their diminutive capital does not suffice for the scale on which modern industry is carried on, and is swamped in the competition with the large capitalists, partly because their specialized skill is rendered worthless by new methods of production. Thus the proletariat is recruited from all classes of the population.

The proletariat goes through various stages of development. With its birth begins its struggle with the bourgeoisie. At first the contest is carried on by individual laborers, then by the work people of a factor, then by the operatives of one trade, in one locality, against the individual bourgeois who directly exploits them. They direct their attacks not against the bourgeois conditions of production, but against the instruments of production themselves; they destroy imported wares that compete with their labor, they smash machinery to pieces, they set factories ablaze, they seek to restore by force the vanished status of the workman of the Middle Ages.

At this stage the laborers still form an incoherent mass scattered over the whole country, and broken up by their mutual competition. If anywhere they unite to form more compact bodies, this is not yet the consequence of their own active union, but of the union of the bourgeoisie, which class, in order to attain its own political ends, is compelled to set the whole proletariat in motion, and is moreover still able to do so for a time. At this stage, therefore, the proletarians do not fight their enemies, but the enemies of their enemies, the remnants of absolute monarchy, the landowners, the non-industrial bourgeois, the petty bourgeoisie. Thus the whole historical movement is concentrated in the hands of the bourgeoisie; every victory so obtained is a victory for the bourgeoisie.

But with the development of industry the proletariat not only increases in number; it becomes concentrated in greater masses, its strength grows, and it feels that strength more. The various interests and conditions of life within the ranks of the proletariat are more and more equalized, in proportion as machinery obliterates all distinctions of labor and nearly everywhere reduces wages to the same low level. The growing competition among the bourgeois, and the resulting commercial crises, make the wages of the workers ever more fluctuating. The unceasing improvement of machinery, ever more rapidly developing, makes their livelihood more and more precarious; the collisions between individual workmen and individual bourgeois take more and more the character of collisions between two classes. Thereupon the workers begin to form combinations (trade unions) against the bourgeoisie; they club together in order to keep up the rate of wages; they found permanent associations in order to make provision beforehand for these occasional revolts. Here and there the contest breaks out into riots.

Now and then the workers are victorious, but only for a time. The real fruit of their battles lies, not in the immediate result, but in the ever expanding union of the workers. This union is furthered by the improved means of communication which are created by modern industry, and which place the workers of different localities in contact with one another. It was just this contact that was needed to centralize the numerous local struggles, all of the same character, into one national struggle between classes. But every class struggle is a political struggle. And that union, to attain which the burghers of the Middle Ages, with their miserable highways, required centuries, the modern proletarians, thanks to railways, achieve in a few years.

This organization of the proletarians into a class, and consequently into a political party is continually being upset again by the competition between the workers themselves. But it ever rises up again, stronger, firmer, mightier. It compels legislative recognition of particular interests of the workers, by taking advantage of the divisions among the bourgeoisie itself. Thus the ten-hour bill in England was carried.

Altogether, collisions between the classes of the old society further the course of development of the proletariat in many ways. The bourgeoisie finds itself involved in a constant battle. At first with the aristocracy; later on, with those portions of the bourgeoisie itself whose interests have become antagonistic to the progress of industry; at all times with the bourgeoisie of foreign countries. In all these battles it sees itself compelled to appeal to the proletariat, to ask for its help, and thus, to drag it into the political arena. The bourgeoisie itself, therefore, supplies the proletariat with its own elements of political and general education, in other words, it furnishes the proletariat with weapons for fighting the bourgeoisie.

Further, as we have already seen, entire sections of the ruling classes are, by the advance of industry precipitated into the proletariat, or are at least threatened in their conditions of existence. These also supply the proletariat with fresh elements of enlightenment and progress.

Finally, in times when the class struggle nears the decisive hour, the process of dissolution going on within the ruling class, in fact within the whole range of old society, assumes such a violent, glaring character, that a small section of the ruling class cuts itself adrift, and joins the revolutionary class, the class that holds the future in its hands. Just as, therefore, at an earlier period, a section of the nobility went over to the bourgeoisie, so now a portion of the bourgeoisie goes over to the proletariat, and in particular, a portion of the bourgeois ideologists, who have raised themselves to the level of comprehending theoretically the historical movement as a whole.

Of all the classes that stand face to face with the bourgeoisie today, the proletariat alone is a really revolutionary class. The other classes decay and finally disappear in the face of modern industry; the proletariat is its special and essential product.

The lower middle class, the small manufacturer, the shopkeeper, the artisan, the peasant, all these fight against the bourgeoisie, to save from extinction their existence as fractions of the middle class. They are therefore not revolutionary, but conservative. Nay more, they are reactionary, for they try to roll back the wheel of history. If by chance they are revolutionary, they are so only in view of their impending transfer into the proletariat; they thus defend not their present, but their future interests; they desert their own standpoint to adopt that of the proletariat.

The "dangerous class," the social scum (*Lumpenproletariat*), that passively rotting mass thrown off by the lowest layers of old society, may, here and there, be swept into the movement by a proletarian revolution; its conditions of life, however, prepare it far more for the part of a bribed tool of reactionary intrigue.

The social conditions of the old society no longer exist for the proletariat. The proletarian is without property; his relation to his wife and children has no longer anything in common with bourgeois family relations; modern industrial labor, modern subjection to capital, the same in England as in France, in America as in Germany, has stripped him of every trace of national character. Law, morality, religion, are to him so many bourgeois prejudices, behind which lurk in ambush just as many bourgeois interests.

All the preceding classes that got the upper hand sought to fortify their already acquired status by subjecting society at large to their conditions of appropriation. The proletarians cannot become masters of the productive forces of society, except by abolishing their own previous mode of appropriation, and thereby also every other previous mode of appropriation. They have nothing of their own to secure and to fortify; their mission is to destroy all previous securities for, and insurances of, individual property.

All previous historical movements were movements of minorities, or in the interest of minorities. The proletarian movement is in the self-conscious, independent movement of the immense majority, in the interest of the immense majority. The proletariat the lowest stratum of our present society, cannot stir, cannot raise itself up, without the whole superincumbent strata of official society being sprung into the air.

Though not in substance, yet in form, the struggle of the proletariat with the bourgeoisie is at first a national struggle. The proletariat of each country must, of course, first of all settle matters with its own bourgeoisie.

In depicting the most general phases of the development of the proletariat, we traced the more or less veiled civil war, raging within existing society, up to the point where that war breaks out into open revolution, and where the violent overthrow of the bourgeoisie lays the foundation for the sway of the proletariat.

Hitherto, every form of society has been based, as we have already seen, on the antagonism of oppressing and oppressed classes. But in order to oppress a class, certain conditions must be assured to it under which it can, at least, continue its lavish existence. The serf, in the period of serfdom, raised himself to membership in the commune, just as the petty bourgeois, under the yoke of feudal absolutism, managed to develop into a bourgeois. The modern laborer, on the contrary, instead of rising with the progress of industry, sinks deeper and deeper below the conditions of existence of his own class. He becomes a pauper, and pauperism develops more rapidly than population and wealth. And here it becomes evident, that the bourgeoisie is unfit any longer to be the ruling class in society, and to impose its conditions of existence upon society as an overriding law. It is unfit to rule because it is incompetent to assure an existence to its slave within his slavery, because it cannot help letting him sink into such a state, that it has to feed him, instead of being fed by him. Society can no longer live under this bourgeoisie, in other words, its existence is no longer compatible with society.

The essential condition for the existence and sway of the bourgeois class, is the formation and augmentation of capital; the condition for capital is wage-labor. Wage-labor rests exclusively on competition between the laborers. The advance of industry, whose involuntary promoter is the bourgeoisie, replaces the isolation of the laborers, due to competition, by their revolutionary combination, due to association. The development of modern industry, therefore, cuts from under its feet the very foundation on which the bourgeoisie produces and appropriates products. What the bourgeoisie therefore produces, above all, are its own grave-diggers. Its fall and the victory of the proletariat are equally inevitable.

II Proletarians and Communists

In what relation do the Communists stand to the proletarians as a whole?

The Communists do not form a separate party opposed to other working-class parties.

They have no interests separate and apart from those of the proletariat as a whole.

They do not set up any sectarian principles of their own, by which to shape and mould the proletarian movement.

The Communists are distinguished from the other working-class parties by this only:

1. In the national struggles of the proletarians of the different countries, they point out and bring to the front the common interests of the entire proletariat, independently of all nationality.

2. In the various stages of development which the struggle of the working class against the bourgeoisie has to pass through, they always and everywhere represent the interests of the movement as a whole.

The Communists, therefore, are on the one hand, practically, the most advanced and resolute section of the working-class parties of every country, that section which pushes forward all others; on the other hand, theoretically, they have over the great mass of the proletariat the advantage of clearly understanding the line of march, the conditions, and the ultimate general results of the proletarian movement.

The immediate aim of the Communists is the same as that of all the other proletarian parties: Formation of the proletariat into a class, overthrow of bourgeois supremacy, conquest of political power by the proletariat.

The theoretical conclusions of the Communists are in no way based on ideas or principles that have been invented, or discovered, by this or that would-be universal reformer.

They merely express, in general terms, actual relations springing from an existing class struggle, from a historical movement going on under our very eyes. The abolition of existing property relations is not at all a distinctive feature of Communism.

All property relations in the past have continually been subject to historical change consequent upon the change in historical conditions.

The French Revolution, for example, abolished feudal property in favor of bourgeois property.

The distinguishing feature of Communism is not the abolition of property generally, but the abolition of bourgeois property. But modern bourgeois private property is the final and most complete expression of the system of producing and appropriating products that is based on class antagonisms, on the exploitation of the many by the few.

In this sense, the theory of the Communists may be summed up in the single sentence: Abolition of private property.

We Communists have been reproached with the desire of abolishing the right of personally acquiring property as the fruit of a man's own labor, which property is alleged to be the groundwork of all personal freedom, activity, and independence.

Hard-won, self-acquired, self-earned property! Do you mean the property of the petty artisan and of the small peasant, a form of property that preceded the bourgeois form? There is no need to abolish that; the development of industry has to a great extent already destroyed it, and is still destroying it daily.

Or do you mean modern bourgeois private property?

But does wage-labor create any property for the laborer? Not a bit. It creates capital, i.e., that kind of property which exploits wage-labor, and which cannot increase except upon condition of begetting a new supply of wage-labor for fresh exploitation. Property, in its present form, is based on the antagonism of capital and wage-labor. Let us examine both sides of this antagonism.

To be a capitalist, is to have not only a purely personal, but a social *status* in production. Capital is a collective product, and only by the united action of many members, nay, in the last resort, only by the united action of all members of society can it be set in motion.

Capital is therefore not a personal, it is a social power.

When, therefore, capital is converted into common property, into the property of all members of society, personal property is not thereby transformed into social property. It is only the social character of the property that is changed. It loses its class character.

Let us now take wage-labor.

The average price of wage-labor, is the minimum wage, i.e., that quantum of the means of subsistence which is absolutely requisite to keep the laborer in bare existence as a laborer. What, therefore, the wage-laborer appropriates by means of his labor, merely suffices to prolong and reproduce a bare existence. We by no means intend to abolish this personal appropriation of the products of labor, an appropriation that is made for the maintenance and reproduction of human life, and that leaves no surplus wherewith to command the labor of others. All that we want to do away with is the miserable character of this appropriation, under which the laborer lives merely to increase capital, and is allowed to live only insofar as the interest of the ruling class requires it.

In bourgeois society, living labor is but a means to increase accumulated labor. In Communist society, accumulated labor is but a means to widen, to enrich, to promote the existence of the laborer.

In bourgeois society, therefore, the past dominates the present; in Communist society, the present dominates the past. In bourgeois society capital is independent and has individuality, while the living person is dependent and has no individuality.

And the abolition of this state of things is called by the bourgeois, abolition of individuality and freedom! And rightly so. The abolition of bourgeois individuality, bourgeois independence, and bourgeois freedom is undoubtedly aimed at.

By freedom is meant, under the present bourgeois conditions of production, free trade, free selling and buying.

But if selling and buying disappears, free selling and buying disappears also. This talk about free selling and buying, and all the other "brave words" of our bourgeoisie about freedom in general, have a meaning, if any, only in contrast with restricted selling and buying, with the fettered traders of the Middle Ages, but have no meaning when opposed to the Communist abolition of buying and selling, of the bourgeois conditions of production, and of the bourgeoisie itself.

You are horrified at our intending to do away with private property. But in your existing society, private property is already done away with for nine-tenths of the population; its existence for the few is solely due to its nonexistence in the hands of those nine-tenths. You reproach us, therefore, with intending to do away with a form

of property, the necessary condition for whose existence is the nonexistence of any property for the immense majority of society.

In a word, you reproach us with intending to do away with your property. Precisely so; that is just what we intend.

From the moment when labor can no longer be converted into capital, money, or rent, into a social power capable of being monopolized, i.e., from the moment when individual property can no longer be transformed into bourgeois property, into capital, from that moment, you say, individuality vanishes.

You must, therefore, confess that by "individual" you mean no other person than the bourgeois, than the middle-class owner of property. This person must, indeed, be swept out of the way, and made impossible.

Communism deprives no man of the power to appropriate the products of society; all that it does is to deprive him of the power to subjugate the labor of others by means of such appropriation.

It has been objected, that upon the abolition of private property all work will cease, and universal laziness will overtake us.

According to this, bourgeois society ought long ago to have gone to the dogs through sheer idleness; for those of its members who work, acquire nothing, and those who acquire anything, do not work. The whole of this objection is but another expression of the tautology: There can no longer be any wage-labor when there is no longer any capital.

All objections urged against the Communist mode of producing and appropriating material products have, in the same way, been urged against the Communist modes of producing and appropriating intellectual products. Just as, to the bourgeois, the disappearance of class property is the disappearance of production itself, so the disappearance of class culture is to him identical with the disappearance of all culture.

That culture, the loss of which he laments, is, for the enormous majority, a mere training to act as a machine.

But don't wrangle with us so long as you apply, to our intended abolition of bourgeois property, the standard of your bourgeois notions of freedom, culture, law, etc. Your very ideas are but the outgrowth of the conditions of your bourgeois production and bourgeois property, just as your jurisprudence is but the will of your class made into a law for all, a will whose essential character and direction are determined by the economic conditions of existence of your class.

The selfish misconception that induces you to transform into eternal laws of nature and of reason, the social forms springing from your present mode of production and form of property—historical relations that rise and disappear in the progress of production—this misconception you share with every ruling class that has preceded you. What you see clearly in the case of ancient property, what you admit in the case of feudal property, you are of course forbidden to admit in the case of your own bourgeois form of property. . . .

The Communists are further reproached with desiring to abolish countries and nationality.

The workingmen have no country. We cannot take from them what they have not got. Since the proletariat must first of all acquire political supremacy, must rise to be the leading class of the nation, must constitute itself *the* nation, it is, so far, itself national, though not in the bourgeois sense of the word.

National differences and antagonisms between peoples are vanishing gradually from day to day, owing to the development of the bourgeoisie, to freedom of commerce, to the world market, to uniformity in the mode of production and in the conditions of life corresponding thereto.

The supremacy of the proletariat will cause them to vanish still faster. United action, of the leading civilized countries at least, is one of the first conditions for the emancipation of the proletariat.

In proportion as the exploitation of one individual by another is put an end to, the exploitation of one nation by another will also be put an end to. In proportion as the antagonism between classes within the nation vanishes, the hostility of one nation to another will come to an end.

The charges against Communism made from a religious, a philosophical, and, generally, from an ideological standpoint, are not deserving of serious examination.

Does it require deep intuition to comprehend that man's ideas, views, and conceptions, in one word, man's consciousness, changes with every change in the conditions of his material existence, in his social relations and in his social life?

What else does the history of ideas prove, than that intellectual production changes its character in proportion as material production is changed? The ruling ideas of each age have ever been the ideas of its ruling class.

When people speak of ideas that revolutionize society, they do but express the fact that within the old society the elements of a new one have been created, and that the dissolution of the old ideas keeps even pace with the dissolution of the old conditions of existence.

When the ancient world was in its last throes, the ancient religions were overcome by Christianity. When Christian ideas succumbed in the 18th century to rationalist ideas, feudal society fought its death-battle with the then revolutionary bourgeoisie. The ideas of religious liberty and freedom of conscience, merely gave expression to the sway of free competition within the domain of knowledge.

"Undoubtedly," it will be said, "religion, moral, philosophical, and juridical ideas have been modified in the course of historical development. But religion, morality, philosophy, political science, and law, constantly survived this change."

"There are, besides, eternal truths, such as Freedom, Justice, etc., that are common to all states of society. But Communism abolishes eternal truths, it abolishes all religion, and all morality, instead of constituting them on a new basis; it therefore acts in contradiction to all past historical experience."

What does this accusation reduce itself to? The history of all past society has consisted in the development of class antagonisms, antagonisms that assumed different forms at different epochs.

But whatever form they may have taken, one fact is common to all past ages, viz., the exploitation of one part of society by the other. No wonder, then, that the social consciousness of past ages, despite all the multiplicity and variety it displays, moves within certain common forms, or general ideas, which cannot completely vanish except with the total disappearance of class antagonisms.

The Communist revolution is the most radical rupture with traditional property relations; no wonder that its development involves the most radical rupture with traditional ideas.

But let us have done with the bourgeois objections to Communism.

We have seen above, that the first step in the revolution by the working class, is to raise the proletariat to the position of ruling class, to establish democracy.

The proletariat will use its political supremacy to wrest, by degrees, all capital from the bourgeoisie, to centralize all instruments of production in the hand of the state, i.e., of the proletariat organized as the ruling class; and to increase the total of productive forces as rapidly as possible.

Of course, in the beginning, this cannot be effected except by means of despotic inroads on the rights of property, and on the conditions of bourgeois production; by means of measures, therefore, which appear economically insufficient and untenable, but which, in the course of the movement, outstrip themselves, necessitate further inroads upon the old social order, and are unavoidable as a means of entirely revolutionizing the mode of production.

These measures will of course be different in different countries.

Nevertheless in the most advanced countries, the following will pretty generally applicable.

1. Abolition of property in land and application of all rents of land to public purposes.

2. A heavy progressive or graduated income tax.

3. Abolition of all right of inheritance.

4. Confiscation of the property of all emigrants and rebels.

5. Centralization of credit in the hands of the state, by means of a national bank with state capital and an exclusive monopoly.

6. Centralization of the means of communication and transport in the hands of the state.

7. Extension of factories and instruments of production owned by the state; the bringing into cultivation of waste lands, and the improvement of the soil generally in accordance with a common plan.

8. Equal obligation of all to work. Establishment of industrial armies, especially for agriculture.

9. Combination of agriculture with manufacturing industries; gradual abolition of the distinction between town and country, by a more equable distribution of the population over the country.

10. Free education for all children in public schools. Abolition of child factory labor in its present form. Combination of education with industrial production, etc.

When, in the course of development, class distinctions have disappeared, and all production has been concentrated in the hands of a vast association of the whole nation, the public power will lose its political character. Political power, properly so called, is merely the organized power of one class for oppressing another. If the proletariat during its contest with the bourgeoisie is compelled, by the force of circumstances, to organize itself as a class; if, by means of a revolution, it makes itself the ruling class, and, as such sweeps away by force the old conditions of production, then it will, along with these conditions, have swept away the conditions for the existence of class antagonisms, and of classes generally, and will thereby have abolished its own supremacy as a class.

In place of the old bourgeois society, with its classes and class antagonisms, we shall have an association, in which the free development of each is the condition for the free development of all. . . .

2

Excerpts from "Class, Status, Party"

MAX WEBER

Law exists when there is a probability that an order will be upheld by a specific staff of men who will use physical or psychical compulsion with the intention of obtaining conformity with the order, or of inflicting sanctions for infringement of it.* The structure of every legal order directly influences the distribution of power, economic or otherwise, within its respective community. This is true of all legal order and not only that of the state. In general, we understand by 'power' the chance of a man or of a number of men to realize their own will in a communal action even against the resistance of others who are participating in the action.

'Economically conditioned' power is not, of course, identical with 'power' as such. On the contrary, the emergence of economic power may be consequence of power existing on other grounds. Man does not strive for power only in order to enrich himself economically. Power, including economic power, may be valued 'for its own sake.' Very frequently the striving for power is also conditioned by the social 'honor' it entails. Not all power, however, entails social honor: The typical American Boss, as well as the typical big speculator, deliberately relinquishes social honor. Quite generally, 'mere economic' power, and especially 'naked' money power, is by no means a recognized basis of social honor. Nor is power the only basis of social honor. Indeed, social honor, or prestige, may even be the basis of political or economic power, and or very frequently has been. Power, as well as honor, may be guaranteed by the legal order, but, at least normally, it is not their primary source. The legal order is rather an additional factor that enhances the chance to hold power or honor; but it cannot always secure them.

The way in which social honor is distributed in a community between typical groups participating in this distribution we may call the 'social order.' The social order and the economic order are, of course, similarly related to the 'legal order.' However, the social and the economic order are not identical. The economic order is for us merely the way in which economic goods and services

---

*Wirtschaft und Gesellschaft, part III, chap. 4, pp. 631–40. The first sentence in paragraph one and the several definitions in this chapter which are in brackets do not appear in the original text. They have been taken from other contexts of Wirtschaft und Gesellschaft.

are distributed and used. The social order is of course conditioned by the economic order to high degree, and in its turn reacts upon it.

Now: 'classes,' 'status groups,' and 'parties' are phenomena of the distribution of power within a community.

Determination of Class-Situation by Market-Situation

In our terminology, 'classes' are not communities; they merely represent possible, and frequent, bases for communal action. We may speak of a 'class' when (1) a number of people have in common a specific causal component of their life chances, in so far as (2) this component is represented exclusively by economic interests in the possession of goods and opportunities for income, and (3) is represented under the conditions of the commodity or labor markets. [These points refer to 'class situation,' which we may express more briefly as the typical chance for a supply of goods, external living conditions, and personal life experiences, in so far as this chance is determined by the amount and kind of power, or lack of such, to dispose of goods or skills for the sake of income in a given economic order. The term 'class' refers to any group of people that is found in the same class situation.]

It is the most elemental economic fact that the way in which the disposition over material property is distributed among a plurality of people, meeting competitively in the market for the purpose of exchange, in itself creates specific life chances. According to the law of marginal utility this mode of distribution excludes the non-owners from competing for highly valued goods; it favors the owners and, in fact, gives to them a monopoly to acquire such goods. Other things being equal, this mode of distribution monopolizes the opportunities for profitable deals for all those who, provided with goods, do not necessarily have to exchange them. It increases, at least generally, their power in price wars with those who, being property less, have nothing to offer but their services in native form or goods in a form constituted through their own labor, and who above all are compelled to get rid of these products in order barely to subsist. This mode of distribution gives to the propertied a monopoly on the possibility of transferring property from the sphere of use as a 'fortune,' to the sphere of 'capital goods'; that is, it gives them the entrepreneurial function and all chances to share directly or indirectly in returns on capital. All this holds true within the area in which pure market conditions prevail. 'Property' and 'lack of property' are, therefore, the basic categories of all class situations. It does not matter whether these two categories become effective in price wars or in competitive struggles.

Within these categories, however, class situations are further differentiated: on the one hand, according to the kind of property that is usable for returns; and, on the other hand, according to the kind of services that can be offered in the market. Ownership of domestic buildings; productive establishments; warehouse; stores; agriculturally usable land, large and small holdings—quantitative differences with possibly qualitative consequences—ownership of mines; cattle; men (slaves); disposition over mobile instruments of production, or capital goods of all sorts, especially money or objects that can be exchanged for money easily and at a any time; disposition over products of one's own labor or of others' labor differing according to their various distances from consumability; disposition over transferable monopolies of any kind—all these distinction differentiate the class situations of the propertied just as does the 'meaning' which they can and do give to the utilization of property, especially to property which has money equivalence. Accordingly, the propertied, for instance, may belong to the class of rentiers or to the class of entrepreneurs.

Those who have no property but who offer services are differentiated just as much according to their kinds of services as according to the way in which they make use of these services, in a continuous or discontinuous relation to a recipient. But always this is the generic connotation of the concept of class: that the kind of chance in the *market* is the decisive moment which presents a common condition for the individual's fate. 'Class situation' is, in this sense, ultimately 'market situation.' The effect of naked possession *per se,* which among cattle breeders gives the non-owning slave or serf into the power of cattle owner, is only a forerunner of real 'class' formation. However, in the cattle loan and in the naked severity of the law of debts in such communities, for the first time mere 'possession' as such emerges as decisive for the fate of the individual. This is very much in contrast to the agricultural communities based on labor. The creditor-debtor relation becomes the basis of 'class situations' only in those cities where a 'credit market,' however primitive, with rates of interest increasing according to the extent of dearth and a factual monopolization of credits, is developed by a plutocracy. Therewith 'class struggles' begin.

Those men whose fate is not determined by the chance of using goods or services for themselves on the market, e.g. slaves, are not, however, a 'class' in the technical sense of the term. They are, rather, a 'status group.'

Communal Action Flowing from Class Interest

According to our terminology, the factor that creates 'class' is unambiguously economic interest, and indeed, only those interests involved in the existence of the 'market.' Nevertheless, the concept of 'class-interest' is an ambiguous one: even as an empirical concept it is ambiguous as soon as one understands by it something other than the factual direction of interests following with a certain probability from the class situation for a certain 'average' of those people subjected to the class situation. The class situation and other circumstances remaining the same, the direction in which the individual worker, for instance, is likely to pursue his interests may vary widely, according to whether he is constitutionally qualified for the task at hand to a high, to an average, or to a low degree. In the same way, the direction of interests may vary according to whether or not a *communal* action of a larger or smaller portion of those commonly affected by the 'class situation,' or even an association among them, e.g. a 'trade union,' has grown out of the class situation from which the individual may or may not expect promising results. [Communal action refers to that action which is oriented to the feeling of the actors that they belong together. Societal action, on the other

hand, is oriented to a rationally motivated adjustment of interests.] The rise of societal or even of communal action from a common class situation is by no means a universal phenomenon.

The class situation may be restricted in its effects to the generation of essentially *similar* reactions, that is to say, within our terminology, of 'mass actions.' However, it may not have even this result. Furthermore, often merely an amorphous communal action emerges. For example, the 'murmuring' of the workers known in ancient oriental ethics: the moral disapproval of the work-master's conduct, which in its practical significance was probably equivalent to an increasingly typical phenomenon of precisely the latest industrial development, namely, the 'slow down' (the deliberate limiting of work effort) of laborers by virtue of tacit agreement. The degree in which 'communal action' and possibly 'societal action' emerges from the 'mass actions' of the members of a class is linked to general cultural conditions, especially to those of an intellectual sort. It is also linked to the extent of the contrasts that have already evolved, and is especially linked to the *transparency* of the connections between the causes and the consequences of the 'class situation.' For however different life chances may be, this fact in itself, according to all experience, by no means gives birth to 'class action' (communal action by the members of a class). The fact of being conditioned and the results of the class situation must be distinctly recognizable. For only then the contrast of life chances can be felt not as an absolutely given fact to be accepted, but as a resultant from either (1) the given distribution of property, or (2) the structure of the concrete economic order. It is only then that people may react against the class structure not only through acts of an intermittent and irrational protest, but in the form of rational association. There have been 'class situations' of the first category (1), of a specifically naked and transparent sort, in the urban centers of Antiquity and during the Middle Ages; especially then, when great fortunes were accumulated by factually monopolized trading in industrial products of these localities or in foodstuffs. Furthermore, under certain circumstances, in the rural economy of the most diverse periods, when agriculture was increasingly exploited in a profit-making manner. The most important historical example of the second category (2) is the class situation of the modern 'proletariat.'

Types of 'Class Struggle'

Thus every class may be the carrier of any one of the possibly innumerable forms of 'class action,' but this is not necessarily so. In any case, a class does not in itself constitute a community. To treat 'class' conceptually as having the same value as 'community' leads to distortion. That men in the same class situation regularly react in mass actions to such tangible situations as economic ones in the direction of those interests that are most adequate to their average number is an important and after all simple fact for the understanding of historical events. Above all, this fact must not lead to that kind of pseudo-scientific operation with the concepts of 'class' and 'class interests' so frequently found these days, and which has found its most classic expression in the statement of a talented author, that the individual may be in error concerning his interests but that the 'class' is 'infallible' about its interests. Yet, if classes as such are not communities nevertheless class situations emerge only on the basis of communalization. The communal action that brings forth class situations, however, is not basically action between members of the identical class; it is an action between members of different classes. Communal actions that directly determine the class situation of the worker and the entrepreneur are: the labor market, the commodities market, and the capitalistic enterprise. But, in its turn, the existence of a capitalistic enterprise presupposes that a very specific communal action exists and that it is specifically structured to protect the possession of goods *per se,* and especially the power of individuals to dispose in principle freely, over the means of production. The existence of a capitalistic enterprise is preconditioned by a specific kind of 'legal order.' Each kind of class situation, and above all when it rests upon the power of property *per se,* will become most clearly efficacious when all other determinants of reciprocal relations are, as far as possible, eliminated in their significance. It is

in this way that the utilization of the power of property the market obtains its sovereign importance.

Now 'status groups' hinder strict carrying through of the sheer market principle. In the present context they are of interest to us only from this one point of view. Before we briefly consider them, note that not much of a general nature can be said about the more specific kinds of antagonism between 'classes' (in our meaning of the term). The great shift, which has been going on continuously in the past, and up to our times, may be summarized, although at the cost of some precision: the struggle in which class situations are effective has progressively shifted from consumption credit toward, first, competitive struggles in the commodity market and, then, toward price wars on the labor market. The 'class struggles' of antiquity—to the extent that they were genuine class struggles and not struggles between status groups—were initially carried on by indebted peasants and perhaps also by artisans threatened by debt bondage and struggling against urban creditors. For debt bondage is the normal result of the differentiation of wealth in commercial cities, especially in seaport cities. A similar situation has existed among cattle breeders. Debt relationships as such produced class action up to the time of Cataline. Along with this, and with an increase in provision of grain for the city by transporting it from the outside, the struggle over the means of sustenance emerged. It centered in the first place around the provision of bread and the determination of the price of bread. It lasted throughout antiquity and the entire Middle Ages. The propertyless as such flocked together against those who actually and supposedly were interested in the dearth of bread. This fight spread until it involved all those commodities essential to the way of life and to handicraft production. There were only incipient discussions of wage disputes in antiquity and in the Middle Ages. But they have been slowly increasing up into modern times. In the earlier periods they were completely secondary to slave rebellions as well as to fights in the commodity market.

The propertyless of antiquity and of the Middle Ages protested against monopolies, preemption, forestalling, and the withholding of goods from the market in order to raise prices. Today the central issue is the determination of the price of labor.

This transition is represented by the fight for access to the market and for the determination of the price of products. Such fights went on between merchants and workers in the putting-out system of domestic handicraft during the transition to modern times. Since it is quite a general phenomenon we must mention here that the class antagonisms that are conditioned through the market situation are usually most bitter between those who actually and directly participate as opponents in price wars. It is not the rentier, the share-holder, and the banker who suffer the ill will of the worker, but almost exclusively the manufacturer and the business executives who are the direct opponents of workers in price wars. This is so in spite of the fact that it is precisely the cash boxes of the rentier, the share-holder, and the banker into which the more or less 'unearned' gains flow, rather than into the pockets of the manufacturers or of the business executives. This simple state of affairs has very frequently been decisive for the role the class situation has played in the formation of political parties. For example, it has made possible the varieties of patriarchal socialism and the frequent attempts—formerly, at least—of threatened status groups to form alliances with the proletariat against the 'bourgeoisie.'

Status Honor

In contrast to classes, *status groups* are normally communities. They are, however, often of an amorphous kind. In contrast to the purely economically 'class situation' we wish to designate as 'status situation every typical component of the life fate of men that is determined by a specific, positive or negative, social estimation of *honor*. This honor may be connected with any quality shared by a plurality, and, of course, it can be knit to a class situation: class distinctions are linked in the most varied ways with status distinctions. Property as such is not always recognized as a status qualification, but in the long run it is, and with extraordinary regularity. In the subsistence economy of the organized neighborhood, very often the richest man is simply the chieftain. However, this often means only an honorific preference. For example, in the so-called

pure modern 'democracy,' that is, one devoid of any expressly ordered status privileges for individuals, it may be that only the families coming under approximately the same tax class dance with one another. This example is reported of certain smaller Swiss cities. But status honor need not necessarily be linked with a 'class situation.' On the contrary, it normally stands in sharp opposition to the pretensions of sheer property.

Both propertied and propertyless people can belong to the same status group, and frequently they do with very tangible consequences. This 'equality' of social esteem may, however, in the long run become quite precarious. The 'equality' of status among the American 'gentlemen,' for instance, is expressed by the fact that outside the subordination determined by the different functions of 'business,' it would be considered strictly repugnant—wherever the old tradition still prevails—if even the richest 'chief,' while playing billiards or cards in his club in the evening, would not treat his 'clerk' as in every sense fully his equal in birthright. It would be repugnant if the American 'chief' would bestow upon his 'clerk' the condescending 'benevolence' marking a distinction of 'position,' which the German chief can never dissever from his attitude. This is one of the most important reasons why in America the German 'clubby-ness' has never been able to attain the attraction that the American clubs have.

Guarantees of Status Stratification

In content, status honor is normally expressed by the fact that above all else a specific *style of life* can be expected from all those who wish to belong to circle. Linked with this expectation are restrictions on 'social' (that is, intercourse which is not subservient to economic or any other of business's 'functional' purposes). These restrictions may confine normal marriages to within the status circle and may lead to complete endogamous closure. As soon as there is not a mere individual and socially irrelevant imitation of another style of life, but an agreed-upon communal action of this closing character, the 'status' development is under way.

In its characteristic form, stratification by 'status groups' on the basis of conventional styles of life evolves at the present time in the United States out of the traditional democracy. For example, only the resident of a certain street ('the street') is considered as belonging to 'society,' is qualified for social intercourse, and is visited and invited. Above all, this differentiation evolves in such a way as to make for strict submission to the fashion that is dominant at a given time in society. This submission to fashion also exists among men in America to a degree unknown in Germany. Such submission is considered to be an indication of the fact that a given man *pretends* to qualify as a gentleman. This submission decides, at least *prima facie,* that he will be treated as such. And this recognition becomes just as important for his employment chances in 'swank' establishments, and above all, for social intercourse and marriage with 'esteemed' families, as the qualification for dueling among Germans in the Kaiser's day. As for the rest: certain families resident for a long time, and, of course, correspondingly wealthy, e.g. 'F. F. V., i.e. First Families of Virginia,' or the actual or alleged descendants of the 'Indian Princess' Pocahontas, of the Pilgrim fathers, or of the Knickerbockers, the members of almost inaccessible sects and all sorts of circles setting themselves apart by means of any other characteristics and badges . . . all these elements usurp 'status' honor. The development of status is essentially a question of stratification resting upon usurpation. Such usurpation is the normal origin of almost all status honor. But the road from this purely conventional situation to legal privilege, positive or negative, is easily traveled as soon as a certain stratification of the social order has in fact been 'lived in' and has achieved stability by virtue of a stable distribution of economic power.

'Ethnic' Segregation and 'Caste'

Where the consequences have been realized to their full extent, the Status group evolves into a closed 'caste.' status distinctions are then guaranteed not merely by conventions and laws, but also by *rituals.* This occurs in such a way that every physical contact with a member of any caste that is considered to be 'lower' by the members of a 'higher' caste is considered as making for a ritualistic impurity and to be a stigma which must be expiated by a religious act. Individual castes develop quite distinct cults and gods.

In general, however, the status structure reaches such extreme consequences only where there are underlying differences which are held to be 'ethnic.' The 'caste' is, indeed, the normal form in which ethnic communities usually live side by side in a 'societalized' manner. These ethnic communities believe in blood relationship and exclude exogamous marriage and social intercourse. Such a caste situation is part of the phenomenon of 'pariah' people and is found all over the world. These people form communities, acquire specific occational traditions of handicrafts or of other arts and cultivate a belief in their ethnic community. They live in a 'diaspora' strictly segregated from all personal intercourse, except that of an unavoidable sort, and their situation is legally precarious. Yet, by virtue of their economic indispensability, they are tolerated, indeed, frequently privileged, and they live in interspersed political communities. The Jews are the most impressive historical example.

A 'status' segregation grown into a 'caste' differs in its structure from a mere 'ethnic' segregation: the caste structure transforms the horizontal and unconnected coexistences of ethnically segregated groups into a vertical social system of super and subordination. Correctly formulated: a comprehensive societalization integrates the ethically divided communities into specific political and communal action. In their consequences they differ precisely in this way: ethnic coexistences condition a mutual repulsion and disdain but allow each ethnic community to consider its own honor as the highest one; the caste structure brings about social subordination and an acknowledgment of 'more honor' in favor of the privileged caste and status groups. This is due to the fact that in the caste structure ethnic distinctions as such have become 'functional' distinctions within the political societalization (warriors, priests, artisans that are politically important for war and for building, and so on). But even pariah people who are most despised are usually apt to continue cultivating in some manner that which is equally peculiar to ethnic and to status communities: the belief in their own specific 'honor.' This is the case with the Jews.

Only with the negatively privileged status groups does the 'sense of dignity' take a specific deviation. A sense of dignity is the precipitation in individuals of social honor and of conventional demands which a positively privileged status group raises for the deportment of its members. The sense of dignity that characterizes positively privileged status groups is naturally related to their 'being' which does not transcend itself, that is, it is to their 'beauty and excellence' . . . . Their kingdom is 'of this world.' They live for the present and by exploiting their great past. The sense of dignity of the negatively privileged strata naturally refers to a future lying beyond the present whether it is of this life or of another. In other words, it must be nurtured by the belief in a providential 'mission' and by a belief in a specific honor before God. The 'chosen people's' dignity is nurtured by a belief either that in the beyond 'the last will be the first,' or that in this life a Messiah will appear to bring forth into the light of the world which has cast them out the hidden honor of the pariah people. This simple state of affairs, and not the 'resentment' which is so strongly emphasized in Nietzsche's much admired construction in the *Genealogy of Morals,* is the source of the religiosity cultivated by pariah status groups. In passing, we may note that resentment may be accurately applied only to a limited extent; for one of Nietzsche's main examples, Buddhism, it is not at all applicable.

Incidentally, the development of status groups from ethnic segregations is by no means the normal phenomenon. On the contrary, since objective 'racial differences' are by no means basic to every subjective sentiment of an ethnic community, the ultimately racial foundation of status structure is rightly and absolutely a question of the concrete individual case. Very frequently a status group is instrumental in the production of a thoroughbred anthropological type. Certainly a status group is to a high degree effective in producing extreme types, for they select personally qualified individuals (e.g. the Knighthood selects those who are fit for warfare, physically and psychically). But selection is far from being the only, or the predominant way in which status groups are formed: Political membership or

class situation has at all times been at least as frequently decisive. And today the class situation is by far the predominant factor, for of course the possibility of a style of life expected for members of a status group is usually conditioned economically.

Status Privileges

For all practical purposes, stratification by status goes hand in hand with a monopolization of idea and material goods or opportunities, in a manner we have come to know as typical. Besides the specific status honor, which always rests upon distance and exclusiveness, we find all sorts of material monopolies. Such honorific preferences may consist of the privilege of wearing special costumes, of eating special dishes taboo to others, of carrying arms—which is most obvious in its consequences—the right to pursue certain non-professional dilettante artistic practices, e.g. to play certain musical instruments. Of course, material monopolies provide the most effective motives for the exclusiveness of a status group; although, in themselves, they are rarely sufficient, almost always they come into play to some extent. Within a status circle there is the question of intermarriage: the interest of the families in the monopolization of potential bridegrooms is at least of equal importance and is parallel to the interest in the monopolization of daughters. The daughters of the circle must be provided for. With an increased inclosure of the status group, the conventional preferential opportunities for special employment grow into a legal monopoly of special offices for the members. Certain goods become objects for monopolization by status groups. In the typical fashion these include 'entailed estates' and frequently also the possessions of serfs or bondsmen and, finally, special trades. This monopolization occurs positively when the status group is exclusively entitled to own and to manage them; and negatively when, in order to maintain its specific way of life, the status group must *not* own and manage them.

The decisive role of a 'style of life' in status 'honor' means that status groups are the specific bearers of all 'conventions.' In whatever way it may be manifest, all 'stylization' of life either originates in status groups or is at least conserved by them. Even if the principles of status conventions differ greatly, they reveal certain typical traits, especially among those strata which are most privileged. Quite generally, among privileged status groups there is a status disqualification that operates against the performance of common physical labor. This disqualification is now 'setting in' in America against the old tradition of esteem for labor. Very frequently every rational economic pursuit, and especially 'entrepreneurial activity,' is looked upon as a disqualification of status. Artistic and literary activity is also considered as degrading work as soon as it is exploited for income, or at least when it is connected with hard physical exertion. An example is the sculptor working like a mason in his dusty smock as over against the painter in his salon-like 'studio' and those forms of musical practice that are acceptable to the status group.

Economic Conditions and Effects of Status Stratification

The frequent disqualification of the gainfully employed as such is a direct result of the principle of status stratification peculiar to the social order, and of course, of this principle's opposition to a distribution of power which is regulated exclusively through the market. These two factors operate along with various individual ones, which will be touched upon below.

We have seen above that the market and its processes 'knows no personal distinctions': 'functional' interests dominate it. It knows nothing of 'honor.' The status order means precisely the reverse, viz.: stratification in terms of 'honor' and of styles of life peculiar to status groups as such. If mere economic acquisition and naked economic power still bearing the stigma of its extra-status origin could bestow upon anyone who has won it the same honor as those who are interested in status by virtue of style of life claim for themselves, the status order would be threatened at its very root. This is the more so as, given equality of status honor, property *per se* represents an addition even if it is not overtly acknowledged to be such.

Yet if such economic acquisition and power gave the agent any honor at all, his wealth would result in his attaining more honor than those who successfully claim honor by virtue of style of life. Therefore all groups having interests in the status order react with special sharpness precisely against the pretensions of purely economic acquisition. In most cases they react the more vigorously the more they feel themselves threatened. Calderon's respectful treatment of the peasant, for instance, as opposed to Shakespeare simultaneous and ostensible disdain of the *canaille* illustrates the different way in which a firmly structured status order reacts as compared with a status order that has become economically precarious. This is an example of a state of affairs that recurs everywhere. Precisely because of the rigorous reactions against the claims of property *per se,* the 'parvenu' is never accepted, personally and without reservation, by the privileged status groups, no matter how completely his style of life has been adjusted to theirs. They will only accept his descendants who have been educated in the conventions of their status group and who have never besmirched its honor by their own economic labor.

As to the general *effect* of the status order, only one consequence can be stated, but it is a very important one: the hindrance of the free development of the market occurs first for those goods which status groups directly withheld from free exchange by monopolization. This monopolization may be effected either legally or conventionally. For example, in many Hellenic cities during the epoch of status groups, and also originally in Rome, the inherited estate (as is shown by the old formula for indiction against spendthrifts) was monopolized just as were the estates of knights, peasants, priests, and especially the clientele of the craft and merchant guilds. The market is restricted, and the power of naked property *per se,* which gives its stamp to 'class formation,' is pushed into the background. The results of this process can be most varied. Of course, they do not necessarily weaken the contrasts in the economic situation. Frequently they strengthen these contrasts, and in any case, where stratification by status permeates a community as strongly as was the case in all political communities of antiquity and of the

Middle Ages, one can never speak of a genuinely free market competition as we understand it today. There are wider effects than this direct exclusion of special goods from the market. From the contrariety between the status order and the purely economic order mentioned above, it follows that in most instances the notion of honor peculiar to status absolutely abhors that which is essential to the market: higgling. Honor abhors higgling among peers and occasionally it taboos higgling for the members of a status group in general. Therefore, everywhere some status groups, and usually the most influential, consider almost any kind of overt participation in economic acquisition as absolutely stigmatizing.

With some over-simplification, one might thus say that 'classes' are stratified according to their relations to the production and acquisition of goods; whereas 'status groups' are stratified according to the principles of their *consumption* of goods as represented by special 'styles of life.'

An 'occupational group' is also a status group. For normally, it successfully claims social honor only by virtue of the special style of life which may be determined by it. The differences between classes and status groups frequently overlap. It is precisely those status communities most strictly segregated in terms of honor (viz. the Indian castes) who today show, although within very rigid limits, a relatively high degree of indifference to pecuniary income. However, the Brahmins seek such income in many different ways.

As to the general economic conditions making for the predominance of stratification by 'status,' only very little can be said. When the bases of the acquisition and distribution of goods are relatively stable, stratification by status is favored. Every technological repercussion and economic transformation threatens stratification by status and pushes the class situation into the foreground. Epochs and countries in which the naked class situation is of predominant significance are regularly the periods of technical and economic transformations. And every slowing down of the shifting of economic stratifications leads, in due course, to the growth of status structures and makes for a resuscitation of the important role of social honor.

Parties

Whereas the genuine of 'classes' is within the economic order, the place of 'status groups' is within the sphere of distribution of 'honor.' From within these spheres, classes and status group influence one another and they influence the legal order and are in turn influenced by it. But 'parties live in a house of 'power.'

Their action is oriented toward the acquisition of social 'power,' that is to say, toward influencing a communal action no matter what its content may be. In principle, parties may exist in a social 'club' as well as in 'state.' As over against the actions of classes and status groups, for which this is not necessarily the case, the communal actions of 'parties' always mean a societalization. For party actions are always directed toward a goal which is striven for in planned manner. This goal may be a 'cause' (the party may aim at realizing a program for ideal or material purposes), or the goal may be 'personal' (sinecures, power, and from these, honor for the leader and the followers of the party). Usually the party action aims at all these simultaneously. Parties are, therefore, only possible within communities that are societalized, that is which have some rational order and a staff of persons available who are ready to enforce it. For parties aim precisely at influencing this staff, and if possible, to recruit it from party followers.

In any individual case, parties may represent interests determined through 'class situation' or 'status situation,' and they may recruit their following respectively from one or the other. But they need be neither purely 'class' nor purely 'status' parties. In most cases they are partly class parties and partly status parties, but sometimes they are neither. They may represent ephemeral or enduring structures. Their means of attaining power may be quite varied, ranging from naked violence of any sort to canvassing for votes with coarse or subtle means: money, social influence, the force of speech, suggestions clumsy hoax, and so on to the rougher or more artful tactics of obstruction in parliamentary bodies.

The sociological structure of parties differs in a basic way according to the kind of communal action which they struggle to influence. Parties also differ according to whether or not the community is stratified by status or by classes. Above all else, they vary according to the structure of domination within the community. For their leaders normally deal with the conquest of a community. They are, in the general concept which is maintained here, not only products of specially modern forms of domination. We shall also designate as parties the ancient and medieval 'parties,' despite the fact that their structure differs basically from the structure of modern parties. By virtue of these structural differences of domination it is impossible to say anything about the structure of parties without discussing the structural forms of social domination *per se*. Parties, which are always structures struggling for domination, are very frequently organized in a very strict 'authoritarian' fashion . . .

Concerning 'classes,' 'status groups,' and 'parties,' it must be said in general that they necessarily presuppose a comprehensive societalization, and especially a political framework of communal action, within which they operate. This does not mean that parties would be confined by the frontiers of any individual political community. On the contrary, at all times it has been the order of the day that the societalization (even when it aims at the use of military force in common) reaches beyond the frontiers of politics. This has been the case in the solidarity of interests among the Oligarchs and among the democrats in Hellas, among the Guelfs and among Ghibellines in the Middle Ages and within the Calvinist party during the period of religious struggles. It has been the case up to the solidarity of the landlords (international congress of agrarian landlords), and has continued among princes (holy alliance, Karlsbad decrees), socialist workers, conservatives (the longing of Prussian conservatives for Russian intervention in 1850). But their aim is not necessarily the establishment of new international political, i.e. *territorial*, dominion. In the main they aim to influence the existing dominion.*

----

*The posthumously published text breaks off here. We omit an incomplete sketch of types of 'warrior estates.'

3

Excerpts from
The Souls of Black Folk

W.E.B. DuBois

Between me and the other world there is ever an unasked question: unasked by some through feelings of delicacy; by others through the difficulty of rightly framing it. All, nevertheless, flutter round it. They approach me in a half-hesitant sort of way, eye me curiously or compassionately and then, instead of saying directly, How does it feel to be a problem? they say, I know an excellent colored man in my town; or, I fought at Mechanicsville; or, Do not these Southern outrages make your blood boil? At these I smile, or am interested, or reduce the boiling to a simmer, as the occasion may require. To the real question, How does it feel to be a problem? I answer seldom a word.

And yet, being a problem is a strange experience, peculiar even for one who has never been anything else, save perhaps in babyhood and in Europe. It is in the early days of rollicking boyhood that the revelation first bursts upon one, all in a day, as it were. I remember well when the shadow swept across me. I was a little thing, away up in the hills of New England, where the dark Housatonic winds between Hoosac and Taghkanic to the sea. In a wee wooden schoolhouse, something put it into the boys' and girls' heads to buy gorgeous visiting-cards— ten cents a package—and exchange. The exchange was merry, till one girl, a tall newcomer, refused my card,—refused it peremptorily, with a glance. Then it dawned upon me with a certain suddenness that I was different from the others; or like, mayhap, in heart and life and longing, but shut out from their world by a vast veil. I had thereafter no desire to tear down to creep through; I held all beyond it in common contempt, and lived above it in a region of blue sky and great wandering shadows. That sky was bluest when I could beat my mates at examination-time, or beat them at a foot-race, or even beat their stringy heads. Alas, with the years all this fine contempt began to fade; for the words I longed for, and all their dazzling opportunities, were theirs, not mine. But they should not keep these prizes, I said; some, all, I would wrest from them. Just how I would do it I could never decide: by reading law, by healing the sick, by telling the wonderful tales that swam in my head,—some way. With other black boys the strife was not so fiercely sunny: their youth shrunk into tasteless sycophancy, or into silent hatred of the pale world about them and mocking distrust of every-thing white; or wasted itself in a bitter cry, Why did God make me an outcast and a stranger in mine own house? The shades of the prison-house closed round about us all: walls strait and stubborn to the whitest, but relentlessly narrow, tall, and unscalable to sons of night who must plod darkly on in resignation, or beat unavailing palms against the stone, or steadily, half hopelessly, watch the streak of blue above.

After the Egyptian and Indian, the Greek and Roman, the Teuton and Mongolian, the Negro is a sort of seventh son, born with a veil, and gifted with second-sight in this American world,—a world which yields him no true self consciousness, but only lets him see himself through the revelation of the other world. It is a peculiar sensation, this double-consciousness, this sense of always looking at one's self through eyes of others, of measuring one's soul by the tape of a world that looks on in amused contempt and pity. One ever feels his twoness,—an American, a Negro; two souls, two thoughts, two unreconciled strivings; two warring ideals in one dark body, whose dogged strength alone keeps it from being torn asunder.

The history of the American Negro is the history of this strife,—this longing to attain self-conscious manhood, to merge his double self into a better and truer self. In this merging he wishes neither of the older selves to be lost. He would not Africanize America, for America has too much to teach the world and Africa. He would not bleach his Negro soul in a flood of white Americanism, for he knows that Negro blood has a message for the world. He simply wishes to make it possible for a man to be both a Negro and an American, without being cursed and spit upon by his fellows, without having the doors of opportunity closed roughly in his face.

This, then, is the end of his striving: to be a coworker in the kingdom of culture, to escape both death and isolation, to husband and use his best powers and his latent genius. These powers of body and mind have in the past been strangely wasted, dispersed, or forgotten. The shadow of a mighty Negro past flits through the tale of Ethiopia the Shadowy and of Egypt the Sphinx. Through history, the powers of single black men flash here and there like falling stars, and die sometimes before the world has rightly gauged their brightness. Here in America, in the few days since Emancipation, the

black man's turning hither and thither in hesitant and doubtful striving has often made his very strength to lose effectiveness, to seem like absence of power, like weakness. And yet it is not weakness,—it is the contradiction of double aims. The double-aimed struggle of the black artisan on the one hand to escape white contempt for a nation of mere hewers of wood and drawers of water, and on the other hand to plough and nail and dig for a poverty-stricken horde—could only result in making him a poor craftsman, for he had but half a heart in either cause. By the poverty and ignorance of his people, the Negro minister or doctor was tempted toward quackery and demagogy; and by the criticism of the other world, toward ideals that made him ashamed of his lowly tasks. The would-be black *savant* was confronted by the paradox that the knowledge his people needed was a twice-told tale to his white neighbors, while the knowledge which would teach the white world was Greek to his own flesh and blood. The innate love of harmony and beauty that set the ruder souls of his people a-dancing and a-singing raised but confusion and doubt in the soul of the black artist; for the beauty revealed to him was the soul-beauty of a race which his larger audience despised, and he could not articulate the message of another people. This waste of double aims, this seeking to satisfy two unreconciled ideals, has wrought sad havoc with the courage and faith and deeds of ten thousand thousand people,—has sent them often wooing false gods and invoking false means of salvation, and at times has even seemed about to make them ashamed of themselves.

Away back in the days of bondage they thought to see in one divine event the end of all doubt and disappointment; few men ever worshipped Freedom with half such unquestioning faith as did the American Negro for two centuries. To him, so far as he thought and dreamed, slavery was indeed the sum of all villainies, the cause of all sorrow, the root of all prejudice; Emancipation was the key to a promised land of sweeter beauty than ever stretched before the eyes of wearied Israelites. In song and exhortation swelled one refrain—Liberty; in his tears and curses the God he implored had Freedom in his right hand. At last it came,—suddenly, fearfully, like a dream. With one wild carnival of blood and passion came the message in his own plaintive cadences:—

> *"Shout, O children!*
> *Shout, you're free!*
> *For God has bought your liberty!"*

Years have passed away since then,—ten, twenty, forty; forty years of national life, forty years of renewal and development, and yet the swarthy spectre sits in its accustomed seat at the Nation's feast. In vain do we cry to this our vastest social problem:—

> *"Take any shape but that, and*
> *my firm nerves*
> *Shall never tremble?"*

The Nation has not yet found peace from its sins; the freedman has not yet found in freedom his promised land. Whatever of good may have come in these years of change, the shadow of a deep disappointment rests upon the Negro people,—a disappointment all the more bitter because the unattained ideal was unbounded save by the simple ignorance of a lowly people.

The first decade was merely a prolongation of the vain search for freedom, the boon that seemed ever barely to elude their grasp,—like a tantalizing will-o'-the-wisp, maddening and misleading the headless host. The holocaust of war, the terrors of the Ku-Klux Klan, the lies of carpet-baggers, the disorganization of industry, and the contradictory advice of friends and foes, left the bewildered serf with no new watchword beyond the old cry for freedom. As the time flew, however, he began to grasp a new idea. The ideal of liberty demanded for its attainment powerful means, and these the Fifteenth Amendment gave him. The ballot, which before he had looked upon as a visible sign of freedom, he now regarded as the chief means of gaining and perfecting the liberty with which war had partially endowed him. And why not? Had not votes made war and emancipated millions? Had not votes enfranchised the freedmen? Was anything impossible to a power that had done all this? A million black men started with renewed zeal to vote themselves into the kingdom. So the decade flew away, the revolution of 1876 came, and left the half-free serf weary, wondering, but still inspired. Slowly but steadily, in the following years, a new vision began gradually to replace the dream of political power,—a powerful movement, the rise of another ideal to guide the unguided, another pillar of fire by night after a clouded day. It was the ideal of "book-learning"; the curiosity, born of compulsory ignorance, to know and test the power of the cabalistic letters of the white man, the longing to know. Here at last seemed to have been discovered the mountain path to Canaan; longer than the highway of Emancipation and law, steep and rugged, but straight, leading to heights high enough to overlook life.

Up the new path the advance guard toiled, slowly, heavily, doggedly; only those who have watched and guided the faltering feet, the misty minds, the dull understandings, of the dark pupils of these schools know how faithfully, how piteously, this people strove to learn. It was weary work. The cold statistician wrote down the inches of progress here and there, noted also where here and there a foot had slipped or some one had fallen. To the tired climbers, the horizon was ever dark, the mists were often cold, the Canaan was always dim and far away. If, however, the vistas disclosed as yet no goal, no resting-place, little but flattery and criticism, the journey at least gave leisure for reflection and self-examination; it changed the child of Emancipation to the youth with dawning self-consciousness, self-realization, self-respect. In those sombre forests of his striving his own soul rose before him, and he saw himself,—darkly as through a veil; and yet he saw in himself some faint revelation of his power, of his mission. He began to have a dim feeling that, to attain his place in the world, he must be himself, and not another. For the first time he sought to analyze the burden he bore upon his back, that dead-weight of social degradation partially masked behind a half-named Negro problem. He felt his poverty; without a cent, without a home, without land, tools, or savings, he had entered into competition with rich, landed, skilled neighbors. To be a poor man is hard, 'but to be a poor race in a land of dollars is the very bottom of hardships. He felt the weight of his ignorance,—not simply of letters, but of life, of business, of the humanities; the accumulated sloth and shirking and awkwardness of decades and centuries shackled his hands and feet. Nor was his burden all poverty and ignorance. The red stain of bastardy, which two centuries of systematic legal defilement of Negro women had stamped upon his race, meant not only the loss of ancient African chastity, but also the hereditary weight of a mass of corruption from white adulterers, threatening almost the obliteration of the Negro home.

A people thus handicapped ought not to be asked to race with the world, but rather allowed to give all its time and thought to its own social problems. But alas! while sociologists gleefully count his bastards and his prostitutes, the very soul of the toiling, sweating black man is darkened by the shadow of a vast despair. Men call the shadow prejudice, and learnedly explain it as the natural defence of culture against barbarism, learning against ignorance, purity against crime, the "higher" against the "lower" races. To which the Negro cries Amen! and swears that to so much of this strange prejudice as is founded on just homage to civilization, culture, righteousness, and progress, he humbly bows and meekly does obeisance. But before that nameless prejudice that leaps beyond all this he stands helpless, dismayed, and well-nigh speechless; before that personal disrespect and mockery, the ridicule and systematic humiliation, the distortion of fact and wanton license of fancy, the cynical ignoring of the better and the boisterous welcoming of the worse, the all-pervading desire to inculcate disdain for everything black, from Toussaint to the devil,—before this there rises a sickening despair that would disarm and discourage any nation save that black host to whom "discouragement" is an unwritten word.

But the facing of so vast a prejudice could not but bring the inevitable self-questioning, self-disparagement and lowering of ideals which ever accompany repression and breed in an atmosphere of contempt and hate. Whisperings and portents came borne upon the four winds: Lo! we are diseased and dying, cried the dark hosts; we cannot write, our voting is vain; what need of education, since we must always cook and serve? And the Nation echoed and enforced this self-criticism, saying: Be content to be servants, and nothing more; what need of higher culture for half-men? Away with the black man's ballot, by force or fraud,—and behold the suicide of a race! Nevertheless, out of the evil came something of good,—the more careful adjustment of education to real life, the clearer perception of the Negroes' social responsibilities, and the sobering realization of the meaning of progress.

So dawned the time of *Sturm und Drang:* storm and stress to-day rocks our little boat on the mad waters of the world-sea; there is within and without the sound of conflict, the burning of body and rending of soul; inspiration strives with doubt, and faith with vain questionings. The bright ideals of the past,—physical freedom, political power, the training of brains and the training of hands,—all these in turn have waxed and waned, until even the last grows dim and overcast. Are they all wrong,—all false? No, not that, but each alone was over-simple and incomplete, the dreams of a credulous race-childhood, or the fond imaginings of the other world which does not know and does not want to know our power. To be really true, all these ideals must be melted and welded into one. The training of the schools we need to-day more than ever,—the training of deft hands, quick eyes and ears, and above all the broader, deeper, higher culture of gifted minds and pure hearts. The power of the ballot we need in sheer self defence,—else what shall save us from a second slavery? Freedom, too, the long-sought, we still seek,—the freedom of life and limb, the freedom to work and think, the freedom to love and aspire. Work, culture, liberty,—all these we need, not singly but together, not successively but together, each growing and aiding each, and all striving toward that vaster ideal that swims before the Negro people, the ideal of human brotherhood, gained through the unifying ideal of Race; the ideal of fostering and developing the traits and talents of the Negro, not in opposition to or contempt for other races, but rather in large conformity to the greater ideals of the American Republic, in order that some day on American soil two world-races may give each to each those characteristics both so sadly lack. We the darker ones come even now not altogether empty-handed: there are to-day no truer exponents of the pure human spirit of the Declaration of Independence than the American Negroes; there is no true American music but the wild sweet melodies of the Negro slave; the American fairy tales and folk-lore are Indian and African; and, all in all, we black men seem the sole oasis of simple faith and reverence in a dusty desert of dollars and smartness. Will America be poorer if she replace her brutal dyspeptic blundering with light-hearted but determined Negro humility? or her coarse and cruel wit with loving jovial good-humor? or her vulgar music with the soul of the Sorrow Songs?

Merely a concrete test of the underlying principles of the great republic is the Negro Problem, and the spiritual striving of the freedmen's sons is the travail of souls whose burden is almost beyond the measure of their strength, but who bear it in the name of an historic race, in the name of this the land of their fathers' fathers, and in the name of human opportunity.

And now what I have briefly sketched in large outline let me on coming pages tell again in many ways, with loving emphasis and deeper detail, that men may listen to the striving in the souls of black folk.

4

Excerpts from "The Conservation of Races"

W.E.B. DuBois

The American Negro has always felt an intense personal interest in discussions as to the origins and destinies of races: primarily because back of most discussions of race with which he is familiar, have lurked certain assumptions as to his natural abilities, as to his political, intellectual and moral status, which he felt were wrong. He has, consequently, been led to deprecate and minimize race distinctions, to believe intensely that out of one blood God created all nations, and to speak of human brotherhood as though it were the possibility of an already dawning to-morrow.

Nevertheless, in our calmer moments we must acknowledge that human beings are divided into races; that in this country the two most extreme types of the world's races have met, and the resulting problem as to the future relations of these types is not only of intense and living interest to us, but forms an epoch in the history of mankind.

It is necessary, therefore, in planning our movements, in guiding our future development, that at times we rise above the pressing, but smaller questions of separate schools and cars, wage-discrimination and lynch law, to survey the whole question of race in human philosophy and to lay, on a basis of broad knowledge and careful insight, those large lines of policy and higher ideals which may form our guiding lines and boundaries in the practical difficulties of every day. For it is certain that all human striving must recognize the hard limits of natural law, and that any striving, no matter how intense and earnest, which is against the constitution of the world, is vain. The question, then, which we must seriously consider is this: What is the real meaning of Race; what has, in the past, been the law of race development, and what lessons has the past history of race development to teach the rising Negro people?

When we thus come to inquire into the essential difference of races we find it hard to come at once to any definite conclusion. Many criteria of race differences have in the past been proposed, as color, hair, cranial measurements and language. And manifestly, in each of these respects, human beings differ widely. They vary in color, for instance, from the marble-like pallor of the Scandinavian to the rich, dark brown of the Zulu, passing by the creamy Slav, the yellow Chinese, the light brown Sicilian and the brown Egyptian. Men vary, too, in the texture of hair from the obstinately straight hair of the Chinese to the obstinately tufted and frizzled hair of the Bushman. In measurement of heads, again, men vary; from the broad-headed Tartar to the medium-headed European and the narrow-headed Hottentot; or, again in language, from the highly-inflected Roman tongue to the monosyllabic Chinese. All these physical characteristics are patent enough, and if they agreed with each other it would be very easy to classify mankind. Unfortunately for scientists, however, these criteria of race are most exasperatingly intermingled. Color does not agree with texture of hair, for many of the dark races have straight hair; nor does color agree with the breadth of the head, for the yellow Tartar has a broader head than the German; nor, again, has the science of language as yet succeeded in clearing up the relative authority of these various and contradictory criteria. The final word of science, so far, is that we have at least two, perhaps three, great families of human beings—the whites and Negroes, possibly the yellow race. That other races have arisen from the intermingling of the blood of these two. This broad division of the world's races which men like Huxley and Raetzel have introduced as more nearly true than the old five-race scheme of Blumenbach, is nothing more than an acknowledgment that, so far as purely physical characteristics are concerned, the differences between men do not explain all the differences of their history. It declares, as Darwin himself said, that great as is the physical unlikeness of the various races of men their likenesses are greater, and upon this rests the whole scientific doctrine of Human Brotherhood.

Although the wonderful developments of human history teach that the grosser physical differences of color, hair and bone go but a short way toward explaining the different roles which groups of men have played in Human Progress, yet there are differences—subtle, delicate and elusive, though they may be—which have silently but definitely separated men into groups. While these subtle forces have generally followed the natural cleavage of common blood, descent and physical peculiarities, they have at other times swept across and ignored these. At all times, however, they have divided human beings into races, which, while they perhaps transcend scientific definition, nevertheless, are clearly defined to the eye of the Historian and Sociologist.

If this be true, then the history of the world is the history, not of individuals, but of groups, not of nations, but of races, and he who ignores or seeks to override the race idea in human history ignores and overrides the central thought of all history. What, then, is a race? It is a vast family of human beings, generally of common blood and language, always of common history, traditions and impulses, who are both voluntarily and involuntarily striving together for the accomplishment of certain more or less vividly conceived ideals of life.

Turning to real history, there can be no doubt, first, as to the widespread, nay, universal, prevalence of the race idea, the race spirit, the race ideal, and as to its efficiency as the vastest and most ingenious invention for human progress. We, who have been reared and trained under the individualistic philosophy of the Declaration of Independence and the laisser-faire philosophy of Adam Smith, are loath to see and loath to acknowledge this patent fact of human history. We see the Pharaohs, Caesars, Toussaints and Napoleons of history and forget the vast races of which they were but epitomized expressions. We are apt to think in our American impatience, that while it may have been true in the past that closed race groups made history, that here in conglomerate America *nous avons changer tout cela*—we have changed all that, and have no need of this ancient instrument of progress. This assumption of which the Negro people are especially fond, can not be established by a careful consideration of history.

We find upon the world's stage today eight distinctly differentiated races, in the sense in which History tells us the word must be used. They are, the Slavs of eastern Europe, the Teutons of middle Europe, the English of Great Britain and America, the Romance nations of Southern and Western Europe, the Negroes of Africa and America, the Semitic people of Western Asia and Northern

Africa, the Hindoos of Central Asia and the Mongolians of Eastern Asia. There are, of course, other minor race groups, as the American Indians, the Esquimaux and the South Sea Islanders; these larger races, too, are far from homogeneous; the Slav includes the Czech, the Magyar, the Pole and the Russian; the Teuton includes the German, the Scandinavian and the Dutch; the English include the Scotch, the Irish and the conglomerate American. Under Romance nations the widely-differing Frenchman, Italian, Sicilian and Spaniard are comprehended. The term Negro is, perhaps, the most indefinite of all, combining the Mulattoes and Zamboes of America and the Egyptians, Bantus and Bushmen of Africa. Among the Hindoos are traces of widely differing nations, while the great Chinese, Tartar, Corean and Japanese families fall under the one designation—Mongolian.

The question now is: What is the real distinction between these nations? Is it the physical differences of blood, color and cranial measurements? Certainly we must all acknowledge that physical differences play a great part, and that, with wide exceptions and qualifications, these eight great races of to-day follow the cleavage of physical race distinctions; the English and Teuton represent the white variety of mankind; the Mongolian, the yellow; the Negroes, the black. Between these are many crosses and mixtures, where Mongolian and Teuton have blended into the Slav, and other mixtures have produced the Romance nations and the Semites. But while race differences have followed mainly physical race lines, yet no mere physical distinctions would really define or explain the deeper differences—the cohesiveness and continuity of these groups. The deeper differences are spiritual, psychical, differences—undoubtedly based on the physical, but infinitely transcending them. The forces that bind together the Teuton nations are, then, first, their race identity and common blood; secondly, and more important, a common history, common laws and religion, similar habits of thought and a conscious striving together for certain ideals of life. The whole process which has brought about these race differentiations has been a growth, and the great characteristic of this growth has been the differentiation of spiritual and mental differences

between great races of mankind and the integration of physical differences.

The age of nomadic tribes of closely related individuals represents the maximum of physical differences. They were practically vast families, and there were as many groups as families. As the families came together to form cities the physical differences lessened, purity of blood was replaced by the requirement of domicile, and all who lived within the city bounds became gradually to be regarded as members of the group; *i.e.,* there was a slight and slow breaking down of physical barriers. This, however, was accompanied by an increase of the spiritual and social differences between cities. This city became husbandmen, this, merchants, another warriors, and so on. The *ideals of life* for which the different cities struggled were different. When at last cities began to coalesce into nations there was another breaking down of barriers which separated groups of men. The larger and broader differences of color, hair and physical proportions were not by any means ignored, but myriads of minor differences disappeared, and the sociological and historical races of men began to approximate the present division of races as indicated by physical researches. At the same time the spiritual and physical differences of race groups which constituted the nations became deep and decisive. The English nation stood for constitutional liberty and commercial freedom; the German nation for science and philosophy; the Romance nations stood for literature and art, and the other race groups are striving, each in its own way, to develop for civilization its particular message, its particular ideal, which shall help to guide the world nearer and nearer that perfection of human life for which we all long, that "one far off Divine event."

This has been the function of race differences up to the present time. What shall be its function in the future? Manifestly some of the great races of today—particularly the Negro race—have not as yet given to civilization the full spiritual message which they are capable of giving. I will not say that the Negro race has as yet given no message to the world, for it is still a mooted question among scientists as to just how far Egyptian civilization was Negro in its origin; if it was not wholly Negro, it was certainly very closely allied. Be that as it may, however the fact still remains that the full, complete Negro message of the whole Negro race has not as yet been given to the world: that the messages and ideal of the yellow race have not been completed, and that the striving of the mighty Slavs has but begun. The question is, then: How shall this message be delivered; how shall these various ideals be realized? The answer is plain: By the development of these race groups, not as individuals, but as races. For the development of Japanese genius, Japanese literature and art, Japanese spirit, only Japanese, bound and welded together, Japanese inspired by one vast ideal, can work out in its fullness the wonderful message which Japan has for the nations of the earth. For the development of Negro genius, of Negro literature and art, of Negro spirit, only Negroes bound and welded together, Negroes inspired by one vast ideal, can work out in its fullness the great message we have for humanity. We cannot reverse history; we are subject to the same natural laws as other races, and if the Negro is ever to be a factor in the world's history—if among the gaily-colored banners that deck the broad ramparts of civilization is to hang one uncompromising black, then it must be placed there by black hands, fashioned by black heads and hallowed by the travail of 200,000,000 black hearts beating in one glad song of jubilee.

For this reason, the advance guard of the Negro people—the 8,000,000 people of Negro blood in the United States of America—must soon come to realize that if they are to take their just place in the van of Pan-Negroism, then their destiny is *not* absorption by the white Americans. That if in America it is to be proven for the first time in the modern world that not only Negroes are capable of evolving individual men like Toussaint, the Saviour, but are a nation stored with wonderful possibilities of culture, then their destiny is not a servile imitation of Anglo-Saxon culture, but a stalwart originality which shall unswervingly follow Negro ideals.

It may, however, be objected here that the situation of our race in America renders this attitude impossible; that our sole hope of salvation lies in our being able to lose our race identity in the commingled blood of the nation; and that any other course would merely increase the friction of races which we call race prejudice, and against which we have so long and so earnestly fought.

Here, then, is the dilemma, and it is a puzzling one, I admit. No Negro who has given earnest thought to the situation of his people in America has failed, at some time in life, to find himself at these cross-roads; has failed to ask himself at some time: What, after all, am I? Am I an American or am I a Negro? Can I be both? Or is it my duty to cease to be a Negro as soon as possible and be an American? If I strive as a Negro, am I not perpetuating the very cleft that threatens and separates Black and White America? Is not my only possible practical aim the subduction of all that is Negro in me to the American? Does my black blood place upon me any more obligation to assert my nationality than German, or Irish or Italian blood would?

It is such incessant self-questioning and the hesitation that arises from it, that is making the present period a time of vacillation and contradiction for the American Negro; combined race action is stifled, race responsibility is shirked, race enterprises languish, and the best blood, the best talent, the best energy of the Negro people cannot be marshalled to do the bidding of the race. They stand back to make room for every rascal and demagogue who chooses to cloak his selfish deviltry under the veil of race pride.

Is this right? Is it rational? Is it good policy? Have we in America a distinct mission as a race—a distinct sphere of action and an opportunity for race development, or is self-obliteration the highest end to which Negro blood dare aspire?

If we carefully consider what race prejudice really is, we find it, historically, to be nothing but the friction between different groups of people; it is the difference in aim, in feeling, in ideals of two different races; if, now, this difference exists touching territory, laws, language, or even religion, it is manifest that these people cannot live in the same territory without fatal collision; but if, on the other hand, there is substantial agreement in laws, language and religion; if there is a satisfactory adjustment of economic life, then there is no reason why, in the same country and on the same street, two or three great national ideals might not thrive and develop, that man of different races might not strive together for their race ideals as well, perhaps even better, than in isolation. Here, it seems to me, is the reading of the riddle that puzzles so many of us. We are Americans, not only by birth and by citizenship, but by our political ideals, our language, our religion. Farther than that, our Americanism does not go. At that point, we are Negroes, members of a vast historic race that from the very dawn of creation has slept, but half awakening in the dark forests of its African fatherland. We are the first fruits of this new nation, the harbinger of that black to-morrow which is yet destined to soften the whiteness of the Teutonic to-day. We are that people whose subtle sense of song has given America its only American music, its only American fairy tales, its only touch of pathos and humor amid its mad money-getting plutocracy. As such, it is our duty to conserve our physical powers, our intellectual endowments, our spiritual ideals; as a race we must strive by race organization, by race solidarity, by race unity to the realization of that broader humanity which freely recognizes differences in men, but sternly deprecates inequality in their opportunities of development.

For the accomplishment of these ends we need race organizations: Negro colleges, Negro newspapers, Negro business organizations, a Negro school of literature and art, and an intellectual clearing house, for all these products of the Negro mind, which we may call a Negro Academy. Not only is all this necessary for positive advance, it is absolutely imperative for negative defense. Let us not deceive ourselves at our situation in this country. Weighted with a heritage of moral iniquity from our past history, hard pressed in the economic world by foreign immigrants and native prejudice, hated here, despised there and pitied everywhere; our one haven of refuge is ourselves, and but one means of advance, our own belief in our great destiny, our own implicit trust in our ability and worth. There is no power under God's high heaven that can stop the advance of eight thousand thousand honest, earnest, inspired and united people. But—and here is the rub—they *must* be honest, fearlessly criticising their own faults, zealously correcting them; they must be *earnest*. No people that laughs at itself, and ridicules itself, and wishes to God it was anything but itself ever wrote its name in history; it *must* be

inspired with the Divine faith of our black mothers, that out of the blood and dust of battle will march a victorious host, a mighty nation, a peculiar people, to speak to the nations of earth a Divine truth that shall make them free. And such a people must be united; not merely united for the organized theft of political spoils, not united to disgrace religion with whoremongers and wardheelers; not united merely to protest and pass resolutions, but united to stop the ravages of consumption among the Negro people, united to keep black boys from loafing, gambling and crime; united to guard the purity of black women and to reduce that vast army of black prostitutes that is today marching to hell; and united in serious organizations, to determine by careful conference and thoughtful interchange of opinion the broad lines of policy and action for the American Negro.

This, is the reason for being which the American Negro Academy has. It aims at once to be the epitome and expression of the intellect of the black-blooded people of America, the exponent of the race ideals of one of the world's great races. As such, the Academy must, if successful, be

a. Representative in character.
b. Impartial in conduct.
c. Firm in leadership.

It must be representative in character; not in that it represents all interests or all factions, but in that it seeks to comprise something of the *best* thought, the most unselfish striving and the highest ideals. There are scattered in forgotten nooks and corners throughout the land, Negroes of some considerable training, of high minds, and high motives, who are unknown to their fellows, who exert far too little influence. These the Negro Academy should strive to bring into touch with each other and to give them a common mouthpiece.

The Academy should be impartial in conduct; while it aims to exalt the people it should aim to do so by truth—not by lies, by honesty—not by flattery. It should continually impress the fact upon the Negro people that they must not expect to have things done for them—they MUST DO FOR THEMSELVES; that they have on their hands a vast work of self-reformation to do, and that a little less complaint and whining, and a little more dogged work and manly striving would do us more credit and benefit than a thousand Force or Civil Rights bills.

Finally, the American Negro Academy must point out a practical path of advance to the Negro people; there lie before every Negro today hundreds of questions of policy and right which must be settled and which each one settles now, not in accordance with any rule, but by impulse or individual preference; for instance: What should be the attitude of Negroes toward the educational qualification for voters? What should be our attitude toward separate schools? How should we meet discriminations on railways and in hotels? Such questions need not so much specific answers for each part as a general expression of policy, and nobody should be better fitted to announce such a policy than a representative honest Negro Academy.

All this, however, must come in time after careful organization and long conference. The immediate work before us should be practical and have direct bearing upon the situation of the Negro. The historical work of collecting the laws of the United States and of the various States of the Union with regard to the Negro is a work of such magnitude and importance that no body but one like this could think of undertaking it. If we could accomplish that one task we would justify our existence.

In the field of Sociology an appalling work lies before us. First, we must unflinchingly and bravely face the truth, not with apologies, but with solemn earnestness. The Negro Academy ought to sound a note of warning that would echo in every black cabin in the land: *Unless we conquer our present vices they will conquer us;* we are diseased, we are developing criminal tendencies, and an alarmingly large percentage of our men and women are sexually impure. The Negro Academy should stand and proclaim this over the housetops, crying with Garrison: *I will not equivocate, I will not retreat a single inch, and I will be heard.* The Academy should seek to gather about it the talented, unselfish men, the pure and noble-minded women, to fight an army of devils that disgraces our manhood and our womanhood. There does not stand today upon God's earth a race more capable in muscle, in intellect, in morals, than the American Negro, if he will bend his energies in the right direction; if he will

> *Burst his birth's invidious bar*
> *And grasp the skirts of happy chance,*
> *And breast the blows of circumstance,*
> *And grapple with his evil star. . . .*

5

Excerpts from "Woman Versus The Indian"

ANNA JULIA COOPER

In the National Woman's Council convened at Washington in February 1891, among a number of thoughtful and suggestive papers read by eminent women, was one by the Rev. Anna Shaw, bearing the above title.

That Miss Shaw is broad and just and liberal in principle is proved beyond contradiction. Her noble generosity and womanly firmness are unimpeachable. The unwavering stand taken by herself and Miss Anthony in the subsequent color ripple in Wimodaughsis ought to be sufficient to allay forever any doubts as to the pure gold of these two women.

Of Wimodaughsis (which, being interpreted for the uninitiated, is a woman's culture club whose name is made up of the first few letters of the four words wives, mothers, daughters, and sisters) Miss Shaw is president, and a lady from the Blue Grass State *was* secretary.

Pandora's box is opened in the ideal harmony of this modern Eden without an Adam when a colored lady, a teacher in one of our schools, applies for admission to its privileges and opportunities.

The Kentucky secretary, a lady zealous in good works and one who, I can't help imagining, belongs to that estimable class who daily thank the Lord that He made the earth that they may have the job of superintending its rotations, and who really would like to help "elevate" the colored people (in her own way of course and so long as they understand their places) is filled with grief and horror that any persons of Negro extraction should aspire to learn type-writing or languages or to enjoy any other advantages offered in the sacred halls of Wimodaughsis. Indeed, she had not calculated that there were any wives, mothers, daughters, and sisters, except white ones; and she is really convinced that *Whimodaughsis* would sound just as well, and then it need mean just *white mothers, daughters and sisters.* In fact, so far as there is anything in a name, nothing would be lost by omitting for the sake of euphony, from this unique mosaic, the letters that represent wives. *Whimodaughsis* might be a little startling, and on the whole wives would better yield to white; since clearly all women are not wives, while surely all wives are daughters. The daughters therefore could represent the wives and this immaculate assembly for propagating liberal and progressive ideas and disseminating a broad and humanizing culture might be spared the painful possibility of the sight of

35

a black man coming in the future to escort from an evening class this solitary cream-colored applicant. Accordingly the Kentucky secretary took the cream-colored applicant aside, and, with emotions befitting such an epoch-making crisis, told her, "as kindly as she could," that colored people were not admitted to the classes, at the same time refunding the money which said cream-colored applicant had paid for lessons in type-writing.

When this little incident came to the knowledge of Miss Shaw, she said firmly and emphatically, NO. As a minister of the gospel and as a Christian woman, she could not lend her influence to such unreasonable and uncharitable discrimination; and she must resign the honor of president of Wimodaughsis if persons were to be proscribed solely on account of their color.

To the honor of the board of managers, be it said, they sustained Miss Shaw; and the Kentucky secretary, and those whom she succeeded in inoculating with her prejudices, resigned.

'Twas only a ripple,—some bewailing of lost opportunity on the part of those who could not or would not seize God's opportunity for broadening and enlarging their own souls—and then the work flowed on as before.

Susan B. Anthony and Anna Shaw are evidently too noble to be held in thrall by the provincialisms of women who seem never to have breathed the atmosphere beyond the confines of their grandfathers' plantations. It is only from the broad plateau of light and love that one can see petty prejudice and narrow priggishness in their true perspective; and it is on this high ground, as I sincerely believe, these two grand women stand.

As leaders in the woman's movement of today, they have need of clearness of vision as well as firmness of soul in adjusting recalcitrant forces, and wheeling into line the thousand and one none-such, never-to-be-modified, won't-be-dictated-to banners of their somewhat mottled array.

The black woman and the southern woman, I imagine, often get them into the predicament of the befuddled man who had to take singly across a stream a bag of corn, a fox and a goose. There was no one to help, and to leave the goose with the fox was death—with the corn, destruction. To re-christen the animals, the lion could not be induced to lie down with the lamb unless the lamb would take the inside berth.

The black woman appreciates the situation and can even sympathize with the actors in the serio-comic dilemma.

But, may it not be that, as women, the very lessons which seem hardest to master now are possibly the ones most essential for our promotion to a higher grade of work?

We assume to be leaders of thought and guardians of society. Our country's manners and morals are under our tutoring. Our standards are law in our several little worlds. However tenaciously men may guard some prerogatives, they are our willing slaves in that sphere which they have always conceded to be women's. Here, no one dares demur when her fiat has gone forth. The man would be mad who presumed, however inexplicable and past finding out any reason for her action might be, to attempt to open a door in her kingdom officially closed and regally sealed by her.

The American woman of to-day not only gives tone directly to her immediate world, but her tiniest pulsation ripples out and out, down and down, till the outermost circles and the deepest layers of society feel the vibrations. It is pre-eminently an age of organizations. The "leading woman," the preacher, the reformer, the organizer "enthuses" her lieutenants and captains, the literary women, the thinking women, the strong, earnest, irresistible women; these in turn touch their myriads of church clubs, social clubs, culture clubs, pleasure clubs and charitable clubs, till the same lecture has been duly administered to every married man in the land (not to speak of sons and brothers) from the President in the White House to the stone-splitter of the ditches. . . .

The American woman then is responsible for American manners. Not merely the right ascension and declination of the satellites of her own drawing room; but the rising and the setting of the pestilential or life-giving orbs which seem to wander afar in space, all are governed almost wholly through her magnetic polarity. The atmosphere of street cars and parks and boulevards, of cafes and hotels and steamboats is charged and surcharged with her sentiments and restrictions.

Shop girls and serving maids, cashiers and account-ant clerks, scribblers and drummers, whether wage earner, salaried toiler, or proprietress, whether laboring to instruct minds, to save souls, to delight fancies, or to win bread,—the working women of America in whatever station or calling they may be found, are subjects, officers, or rulers of a strong centralized government, and bound together by a system of codes and countersigns, which, though unwritten, forms a network of perfect subordina-tion and unquestioning obedience as marvelous as that of the Jesuits. At the head and center in this regime stands the Leading Woman in the princi-pality. The one talismanic word that plays along the wires from palace to cook-shop, from imperial Congress to the distant plain, is *Caste.* With all her vaunted independence, the American woman of to-day is as fearful of losing caste as a Brahmin in India. That is the law under which she lives, the precepts which she binds as frontlets between her eyes and writes on the door-posts of her homes, the lesson which she instills into her children with their first baby breakfasts, the injunction she lays upon husband and lover with direst penalties attached.

The queen of the drawing room is absolute ruler under this law. Her pose gives the cue. The microscopic angle, at which her penciled brows are elevated, signifies who may be recognized and who are beyond the pale. . . .

Now, am I right in holding the American woman responsible? Is it true that the exponents of woman's advancement, the leaders in woman's thought, the preachers and teachers of all woman's reforms, can teach this nation to be courteous, to be pitiful, having compassion one of another, not rendering evil for in offensiveness, and railing in proportion to the improbability of being struck back; but contrariwise, being *all* of one mind, to love as brethren?

I think so.

It may require some heroic measures, and like all revolutions will call for a determined front and a courageous, unwavering, stalwart heart on the part of the leaders of the reform. . . .

Lately a great national and international movement characteristic of this age and country, a movement based on the inherent right of every soul to its own highest development, I mean the movement making for Woman's full, free, and complete emancipation, has, after much courting, obtained the gracious smile of the Southern woman—I beg her pardon—the Southern *lady.*

She represents blood, and of course could not be expected to leave that out; and firstly and foremostly she must not, in any organization she may deign to grace with her presence, be asked to associate with "these people who were once her slaves."

Now the Southern woman (I may be par-doned, being one myself) was never renowned for her reasoning powers, and it is not surprising that just a little picking will make her logic fall to pieces even here.

In the first place she imagines that because her grandfather had slaves who were black, all the blacks in the world of every shade and tint were once in the position of her slaves. This is as bad as the Irishman who was about to kill a peace-able Jew in the streets of Cork, having just learned that Jews slew his Redeemer. The black race constitutes one-seventh the known popula-tion of the globe; and there are representatives of it here as elsewhere who were never in bondage at any time to any man,—whose blood is as blue and lineage as noble as any, even that of the white lady of the South. That her slaves were black and she despises her slaves, should no more argue antipathy to all dark people and peoples, than that Guiteau, an assassin, was white, and I hate assassins, should make me hate all persons more or less white. The objection shows a want of clear discrimination.

The second fallacy in the objection grows out of the use of an ambiguous middle, as the logicians would call it, or assigning a double signification to the term *"Social equality."*

Civility to the Negro implies social equality. I am opposed to *associating* with dark persons on terms of social equality. Therefore, I abrogate civility to the Negro. This is like

> *Light is opposed to darkness.*
> *Feathers are light.*
> Ergo, *Feathers are opposed to*
> *darkness.*

The "social equality" implied by civility to the Negro is a very different thing from forced association with him socially. Indeed it seems to me that the mere application of a little cold common sense would show that uncongenial social environments could by no means be forced on any one. I do not, and cannot be made to associate with all dark persons, simply on the ground that I am dark; and I presume the Southern lady can imagine some whose faces are white, with whom she would no sooner think of chatting unreservedly than, were it possible, with a veritable 'darkey.' Such things must and will always be left to individual election. No law, human or divine, can legislate for or against them. Like seeks like; and I am sure with the Southern lady's antipathies at their present temperature, she might enter ten thousand organizations besprinkled with colored women without being any more deflected by them than by the proximity of a stone. The social equality scare then is all humbug, conscious or unconscious, I know not which. And were it not too bitter a thought to utter here, I might add that the overtures for forced association in the past history of these two races were not made by the manacled black man, nor by *the silent and suffering black woman!*

When I seek food in a public cafe or apply for first-class accommodations on a railway train, I do so because my physical necessities are identical with those of other human beings of like constitution and temperament, and crave satisfaction. I go because I want food, or I want comfort—not because I want association with those who frequent these places; and I can see no more "social equality" in buying lunch at the same restaurant, or riding in a common car, than there is in paying for dry goods at the same counter or walking on the same street.

The social equality which means forced or unbidden association would be as much deprecated and as strenuously opposed by the circle in which I move as by the most hide-bound Southerner in the land. Indeed I have been more than once annoyed by the inquisitive white interviewer, who, with spectacles on nose and pencil and note-book in hand, comes to get some "points" about *"your people."*

My "people" are just like other people—indeed, too like for their own good. They hate, they love, they attract and repel, they climb or they grovel, struggle or drift, aspire or despair, endure in hope or curse in vexation, exactly like all the rest of unregenerate humanity. Their likes and dislikes are as strong; their antipathies—and prejudices too I fear, are as pronounced as you will find anywhere; and the entrance to the inner sanctuary of their homes and hearts is as jealously guarded against profane intrusion.

What the dark man wants then is merely to live his own life, in his own world, with his own chosen companions, in whatever of comfort, luxury, or emoluments his talent or his money can in an impartial market secure. Has he wealth, he does not want to be forced into inconvenient or unsanitary sections of cities to buy a home and rear his family. Has he art, he does not want to be cabined and cribbed into emulation with the few who merely happen to have his complexion. His talent aspires to study without proscription the masters of all ages and to rub against the broadest and fullest movements of his own day.

Has he religion, he does not want to be made to feel that there is a white Christ and a black Christ, a white Heaven and a black Heaven, a white Gospel and a black Gospel,—but the one ideal of perfect manhood and womanhood, the one universal longing for development and growth, the one desire for being, and being better, the one great yearning, aspiring, outreaching, in all the heartthrobs of humanity in whatever race or clime. . . .

No true artist can allow himself to be narrowed and provincialized by deliberately shutting out any class of facts or subjects through prejudice against externals. And American art, American science, American literature can never be founded in truth, the universal beauty; can never learn to speak a language intelligible in all climes and for all ages, till this paralyzing grip of caste prejudice is loosened from its vitals, and the healthy sympathetic eye is taught to look out on the great universe as holding no favorites and no black beasts, but bearing in each plainest or loveliest feature the handwriting of its God.

And this is why, as it appears to me, woman in her lately acquired vantage ground for speaking an earnest helpful word, can do this country no deeper and truer and more lasting good than by bending all her energies to thus broadening, humanizing, and civilizing her native land. . . .

Miss Shaw is one of the most powerful of our leaders, and we feel her voice should give no uncertain note. Woman should not, even by inference, or for the sake of argument, seem to disparage what is weak. For woman's cause is the cause of the weak; and when all the weak shall have received their due consideration, then woman will have her "rights," and the Indian will have his rights, and the Negro will have his rights, and all the strong will have learned at last to deal justly, to love mercy, and to walk humbly; and our fair land will have been taught the secret of universal courtesy which is after all nothing but the art, the science, and the religion of regarding one's neighbor as one's self, and to do for him as we would, were conditions swapped, that he do for us. . . .

The cause of freedom is not the cause of a race or a sect, a party or a class,—it is the cause of human kind, the very birthright of humanity. Now unless we are greatly mistaken the Reform of our day, known as the Woman's Movement, is essentially such an embodiment, if its pioneers could only realize it, of the universal good. And especially important is it that there is no confusion of ideas among its leaders as to its scope and universality. All mists must be cleared from the eyes of woman if she is to be a teacher of morals and manners: the former strikes its roots in the individual and its training and pruning may be accomplished by classes; but the latter is to lubricate the joints and minimize the friction of society, and it is important and fundamental that there be no chromatic or other aberration when the teacher is settling the point, "Who is my neighbor?"

It is not the intelligent woman vs. the ignorant woman; or the white woman vs. the black, the brown, and the red,—it is not even the cause of woman vs. man. Nay, 'tis woman's strongest vindication for speaking that *the world needs to hear her voice*. It would he subversive of every human interest that the cry of one-half the human family be stifled. Woman in stepping from the pedestal of statue-like inactivity in the domestic shrine, and daring to think and move and speak,—to undertake to

help shape, mold, and direct the thought of her age, is merely completing the circle of the world's vision. Hers is every interest that has lacked an interpreter and a defender. Her cause is linked with that of every agony that has been dumb—every wrong that needs a voice.

It is no fault of man's that he has not been able to see truth from her standpoint. It does credit both to his head and heart that no greater mistakes have, been committed or even wrongs perpetrated while she sat making tatting and snipping paper flowers. Man's own innate chivalry and the mutual interdependence of their interests have insured his treating her cause, in the main at least, as his own. And he is pardonably surprised and even a little chagrined, perhaps, to find his legislation not considered "perfectly lovely" in every respect. But in any case his work is only impoverished by her remaining dumb. The world has had to limp along with the wobbling gait and one-sided hesitancy of a man with one eye. Suddenly the bandage is removed from the other eye and the whole body is filled with light. It sees a circle where before it saw a segment. The darkened eye restored, every member rejoices with it.

What a travesty of its case for this eye to become plaintiff in a suit, *Eye vs. Foot*. "There is that dull clod, the foot, allowed to roam at will, free and untrammeled; while I, the source and medium of light, brilliant and beautiful, am fettered in darkness and doomed to desuetude." The great burly black man, ignorant and gross and depraved, is allowed to vote; while the franchise is withheld from the intelligent and refined, the pure-minded and lofty souled white woman. Even the untamed and untamable Indian of the prairie, who can answer nothing but 'ugh' to great economic and civic questions is thought by some worthy to wield the ballot which is still denied the Puritan maid and the first lady of Virginia.

Is not this hitching our wagon to something much lower than a star? Is not woman's cause broader, and deeper, and grander, than a blue stocking debate or an aristocratic pink tea? Why woman should become plaintiff in a suit versus the Indian, or the Negro or any other race or class who have been crushed under the iron heel of Anglo-Saxon power and selfishness? If the Indian has been wronged and cheated by the puissance of this American government, it is woman's mission to plead with her country to cease to do evil and to pay its honest debts. If the Negro has been deceitfully cajoled or inhumanly cuffed according to selfish expediency or capricious antipathy, let it be woman's mission to plead that he be met as a man and honestly given half the road. If woman's own happiness has been ignored or misunderstood in our country's legislating for bread winners, for rum sellers, for property holders, for the family relations, for any or all the interests that touch her vitally, let her rest her plea, not on Indian inferiority, nor on Negro depravity, but on the obligation of legislators to do for her as they would have others do for them were relations reversed. Let her try to teach her country that every interest in this world is entitled at least to a respectful hearing, that every sentiency is worthy of its own gratification, that a helpless cause should not be trampled down, nor a bruised reed broken; and when the right of the individual is made sacred, when the image of God in human form, whether in marble or in clay, whether in alabaster or in ebony, is consecrated and inviolable, when men have been taught to look beneath the rags and grime, the pomp and pageantry of mere circumstance and have regard unto the celestial kernel uncontaminated at the core,—when race, color, sex, condition are realized to be the accidents, not the substance of life, and consequently as not obscuring or modifying the inalienable title to life, liberty, and pursuit of happiness,—then is mastered the science of politeness, the art of courteous contact, which is naught but the practical application of the principle of benevolence, the back bone and marrow of all religion; then woman's lesson is taught and woman's cause is won—not the white woman nor the black woman nor the red woman, but the cause of every man or woman who has writhed silently under a mighty wrong. The pleading of the American woman for the right and the opportunity to employ the American method of influencing the disposal to be made of herself her property, her children in civil, economic, or domestic relations is thus seen to be based on a principle as broad as human society. . . .

6

Excerpts from "Some Principles of Stratification"

KINGSLEY DAVIS AND WILBERT MOORE

. . . Starting from the proposition that no society is "classless," or unstratified, an effort is made to explain, in functional terms, the universal necessity which calls forth stratification in any social system. Next, an attempt is made to explain the roughly uniform distribution of prestige as between the major types of positions in every society. Since, however, there occur between one society and another great difference in the degree and kind of stratification, some attention is also given to the varieties of social inequality and the variable factors that give rise to them. . . .

Throughout, it will be necessary to keep in mind one thing—namely, that the discussion relates to the system of positions, not to the individuals occupying those positions. It is one thing to ask why different positions carry different degrees of prestige, and quite another to ask how certain individuals get into those positions. Although, as the argument will try to show, both questions are related, it is essential to keep them separate in our thinking. Most of the literature on stratification has tried to answer the second question (particularly with regard to the ease or difficulty of mobility between strata) without tackling the first. The first question, however, is logically prior and, in the case of any particular individual or group, factually prior.

The Function Necessity of Stratification

Curiously, however, the main functional necessity explaining the universal presence of stratification is precisely the requirement faced by any society of placing and motivating individuals in the social structure. As a functioning mechanism a society must somehow distribute its members in social positions and induce them to perform the duties of these positions. It must thus concern itself with motivation at two different levels: to instill in the proper individuals the desire to fill certain positions, and, once in these positions, the desire to perform the duties attached to them. Even though the social order may be relatively static in form, there is a continuous process of metabolism as new individuals are born into it, shift with age, and die off. Their absorption into the positional system must somehow be arranged and motivated. This is true whether the system is competitive or non-competitive. A competitive system gives greater importance to the motivation to achieve positions, whereas a non-competitive system gives perhaps greater importance to the motivation to perform the duties of the positions; but in any system both types of motivation are required.

If the duties associated with the various positions were all equally pleasant to the human organism, all equally important to societal survival and all equally in need of the same ability or talent, it would make no difference who got into which positions, and the problem of social placement would be greatly reduced. But actually it does make a great deal of difference who gets into which positions, not only because some positions are inherently more agreeable than others, but also because some require special talents or training and some are functionally more important than others. Also, it is essential that the duties of the positions be performed with the diligence that their importance requires. Inevitably, then, a society must have, first, some kind of rewards that it can use as inducements, and, second, some way of distributing these rewards differentially according to positions. The rewards and their distribution become a part of the social order, and thus give rise to stratification.

One may ask what kind of rewards a society has at its disposal in distributing its personnel and securing essential services. It has, first of all, the things that contribute to sustenance and comfort. It has, second, the things that contribute to humor and diversion. And it has, finally, the things that contribute to self respect and ego expansion. The last, because of the peculiarly social character of the self, is largely a function of the opinion of others, but it nonetheless ranks in importance with the first two. In any social system all three kinds of rewards must be dispensed differentially according to positions.

In a sense the rewards are "built into" the position. They consist in the "rights" associated with the position, plus what may be called its accompaniments or perquisites. Often the rights, and sometimes the accompaniments, are functionally related to the duties of the position. (Rights as viewed by the incumbent are usually duties as viewed by other members of the community.) However, there may be a host of subsidiary rights and perquisites that are not essential to the function of the position and have only an indirect and symbolic connection with its duties, but which still may be of considerable importance in inducing people to seek the positions and fulfill the essential duties.

If the rights and perquisites of different positions in a society must be unequal, then the society must be stratified, because that is precisely what stratification means. Social inequality is thus an unconsciously evolved device by which societies insure that the most important positions are conscientiously filled by the most qualified persons. Hence every society, no matter how simple or complex, must differentiate persons in terms of both prestige and esteem, and must therefore possess a certain amount of institutionalized inequality.

It does not follow that the amount or type of inequality need be the same in all societies. This is largely a function of factors that will be discussed presently.

The Two Determinants of Positional Rank

Granting the general function that inequality sub serves, one can specify the two factors that determine the relative rank of different positions. In general those positions convey the best reward, and hence have the highest rank, which (a) have the greatest importance for the society and (b) require the greatest training or talent. The first factor concerns function and is a matter of relative significance; the second concerns means and is a matter of scarcity.

Differential Functional Importance

Actually a society does not need to reward positions in proportion to their functional importance. It merely needs to give sufficient reward to them to insure that they will be filled competently. In other words, it must see that less essential positions do not compete successfully with more essential ones. If a position is easily filled, it need not be heavily rewarded, even though important. On the other hand, if it is important but hard to fill, the reward must be high enough to get it filled anyway. Functional importance is therefore a necessary but not a sufficient cause of high rank being assigned to a position.[1]

Differential Scarcity of Personnel

Practically all positions, no matter how acquired, require some form of skill or capacity for performance. This is implicit in the very notion of position, which implies that the incumbent must, by virtue of his incumbency, accomplish certain things.

There are, ultimately, only two ways in which a person's qualifications come about: through inherent capacity or through training. Obviously, in concrete activities both are always necessary, but from a practical standpoint the scarcity may lie primarily in one or the other, as well as in both. Some positions require innate talents of such high degree that the persons who fill them are bound to be rare. In many cases, however, talent is fairly abundant in the population but the training process is so long, costly, and elaborate that relatively few can qualify. Modern medicine, for example, is within the mental capacity of most individuals, but a medical education is so burdensome and expensive that virtually none would undertake it if the position of the M.D. did not carry a reward commensurate with the sacrifice.

If the talents required for a position are abundant and the training easy, the method of acquiring the position may have little to do with its duties. There may be, in fact, a virtually accidental relationship. But if the skills required are scarce by reason of the rarity of talent or the costliness of training, the position, if functionally important, must have an attractive power that will draw the necessary skills in competition with other positions. This means, in effect, that the position must be high in the social scale—must command great prestige, high salary, ample leisure, and the like.

How Variations Are to Be Understood

In so far as there is a difference between one system of stratification and another, it is attributable to whatever factors affect the two determinants of differential reward—namely, functional importance and scarcity of personnel. Positions important in one society may not be important in another,

because the conditions faced by the societies, or their degree of internal development, may be different. The same conditions, in turn, may affect the question of scarcity; for in some societies the stage of development, or the external situation, may wholly obviate the necessity of certain kinds of skill or talent. Any particular system of stratification, then, can be understood as a product of the special conditions affecting the two aforementioned grounds of differential reward.

Major Societal Functions and Stratification

Religion

The reason why religion is necessary is apparently to be found in the fact that human society achieves its unity primarily through the possession by its members of certain ultimate values and ends in common. Although these values and ends are subjective, they influence behavior, and their integration enables the society to operate as a system. Derived neither from inherited nor from external nature, they have evolved as a part of culture by communication and moral pressure. They must, however, appear to the members of the society to have some reality, and it is the role of religious belief and ritual to supply and reinforce this appearance of reality. Through belief and ritual the common ends and values are connected with an imaginary world symbolized by concrete sacred objects, which world in turn is related in a meaningful way to the facts and trials of the individual's life. Through the worship of the sacred objects and the beings they symbolize, and the acceptance of supernatural prescriptions that are at the same time codes of behavior, a powerful control over human conduct is exercised, guiding it along lines sustaining the institutional structure and conforming to the ultimate ends and values.

If this conception of the role of religion is true, one can understand why in every known society the religious activities tend to be under the charge of particular persons, who tend thereby to enjoy greater rewards than the ordinary societal member. Certain of the rewards and special privileges may attach to only the highest religious functionaries, but others usually apply, if such exists, to the entire sacerdotal class.

Moreover, there is a peculiar relation between the duties of the religious official and the special privileges he enjoys. If the supernatural world governs the destinies of men more ultimately than does the real world, its earthly representative, the person through whom one may communicate with the supernatural, must be a powerful individual. He is a keeper of sacred tradition, a skilled performer of the ritual, and an interpreter of lore and myth. He is in such close contact with the gods that he is viewed as possessing some of their characteristics. He is, in short, a bit sacred, and hence free from some of the more vulgar necessities and controls.

It is no accident, therefore, that religious functionaries have been associated with the very highest positions of power, as in theocratic regimes. Indeed, looking at it from this point of view, one may wonder why it is that they do not get *entire* control over their societies. The factors that prevent this are worthy of note.

In the first place, the amount of technical competence necessary for the performance of religious duties is small. Scientific or artistic capacity is not required. Anyone can set himself up as enjoying an intimate relation with deities, and nobody can successfully dispute him. Therefore, the factor of scarcity of personnel does not operate in the technical sense.

One may assert, on the other hand, that religious ritual is often elaborate and religious lore abstruse, and that priestly ministrations require tact, if not intelligence. This is true, but the technical requirements of the profession are for the most part adventitious, not related to the end in the same way that science is related to air travel. The priest can never be free from competition, since the criteria of whether or not one has genuine contact with the supernatural are never strictly clear. It is this competition that debases the priestly position below what might be expected at first glance. That is why priestly prestige is highest in those societies where membership in the profession is rigidly controlled by the priestly guild itself. That is why, in part at least, elaborate devices are utilized to stress the identification of the person with his office—spectacular costume, abnormal conduct, special diet, segregated residence, celibacy, conspicuous leisure, and the like. In fact, the priest is always in danger of becoming somewhat discredited—as happens in a secularized society—because in a world of stubborn fact, ritual and sacred knowledge alone will not grow crops or build houses. Furthermore, unless he is protected by a professional guild, the priest's identification with the supernatural tends to preclude his acquisition of abundant worldly goods.

As between one society and another it seems that the highest general position awarded the priest occurs in the medieval type of social order. Here there is enough economic production to afford a surplus, which can be used to support a numerous and highly organized priesthood; and yet the populace is unlettered and therefore credulous to a high degree. Perhaps the most extreme example is to be found in the Buddhism of Tibet, but others are encountered in the Catholicism of feudal Europe, the Inca regime of Peru, the Brahmanism of India, and the Mayan priesthood of Yucatan. On the other hand, if the society is so crude as to have no surplus and little differentiation, so that every priest must be also a cultivator or hunter, the separation of the priestly status from the others has hardly gone far enough for priestly prestige to mean much. When the priest actually has high prestige under these circumstances, it is because he also performs other important functions (usually political and medical).

In an extremely advanced society built on scientific technology, the priesthood tends to lose status, because sacred tradition and supernaturalism drop into the background. The ultimate values and common ends of the society tend to be expressed in less anthropomorphic ways, by officials who occupy fundamentally political, economic, or educational rather than religious positions. Nevertheless, it is easily possible for intellectuals to exaggerate the degree to which the priesthood in a presumably secular milieu has lost prestige. When the matter is closely examined the urban proletariat, as well as the rural citizenry, proves to be surprisingly god-fearing and priest-ridden. No society has become so completely secularized as to liquidate entirely the belief in transcendental ends and supernatural entities. Even in a secularized society some system must exist for the integration of ultimate values, for their ritualistic expression, and for the emotional adjustments required by disappointment, death, and disaster.

Government

Like religion, government plays a unique and indispensable part in society. But in contrast to religion, which provides integration in terms of sentiments, beliefs, and rituals, it organizes the society in terms of law and authority. Furthermore, it orients the society to the actual rather than the unseen world.

The main functions of government are, internally, the ultimate enforcement of norms, the final arbitration of conflicting interests, and the overall planning and direction of society; and externally, the handling of war and diplomacy. To carry out these functions it acts as the agent of the entire people, enjoys a monopoly of force, and controls all individuals within its territory.

Political action, by definition, implies authority. An official can command because he has authority and the citizen must obey because he is subject to that authority. For this reason stratification is inherent in the nature of political relationships.

So clear is the power embodied in political position that political inequality is sometimes thought to comprise all inequality? But it can be shown that there are other bases of stratification, that the following controls operate in practice to keep political power from becoming complete: (a) The fact that the actual holders of political office, and especially those determining top policy must necessarily be few in number compared to the total population. (b) The fact that the rulers represent the interest of the group rather than of themselves, and are therefore restricted in their behavior by rules and mores designed to enforce this limitation of interest. (c) The fact that the holder of political office has his authority by virtue of his office and nothing else, and therefore any special knowledge, talent, or capacity he may claim is purely incidental, so that he often has to depend upon others for technical assistance.

In view of these limiting factors, it is not strange that the rulers often have less power and prestige than a literal enumeration of their formal rights would lead one to expect.

Wealth, Property, and Labor

Every position that secures for its incumbent a livelihood is, by definition, economically rewarded.

For this reason there is an economic aspect to those positions (e.g. political and religious) the main function of which is not economic. It therefore becomes convenient for the society to use unequal economic returns as a principal means of controlling the entrance of persons into positions and stimulating the performance of their duties. The amount of the economic return therefore becomes one of the main indices of social status.

It should be stressed, however, that a position does not bring power and prestige *because* it draws a high income. Rather, it draws a high income because it is functionally important and the available personnel is for one reason or another scarce. It is therefore superficial and erroneous to regard high income as the cause of a man's power and prestige, just as it is erroneous to think that a man's fever is the cause of his disease.[2]

The economic source of power and prestige is not income primarily, but the ownership of capital goods (including patents, good will, and professional reputation). Such ownership should be distinguished from the possession of consumers' goods, which is an index rather than a cause of social standing. In other words, the ownership of producers' goods is properly speaking, a source of income like other positions, the income itself remaining an index. Even in situations where social values are widely commercialized and earnings are the readiest method of judging social position, income does not confer prestige on a position so much as it induces people to compete for the position. It is true that a man who has a high income as a result of one position may find this money helpful in climbing into another position as well, but this again reflects the effect of his initial, economically advantageous status, which exercises its influence through the medium of money.

In a system of private property in productive enterprise, an income above what an individual spends can give rise to possession of capital wealth. Presumably such possession is a reward for the proper management of one's finances originally and of the productive enterprise later. But as social differentiation becomes highly advanced and yet the institution of inheritance persists, the phenomenon of pure ownership, and reward for pure ownership, emerges. In such a case it is difficult to prove that the position is functionally important or that the scarcity involved is anything other than extrinsic and accidental. It is for this reason, doubtless, that the institution of private property in productive goods becomes more subject to criticism as social development proceeds toward industrialization. It is only this pure, that is, strictly legal and functionless ownership, however, that is open to attack; for some form of active ownership, whether private or public, is indispensable.

One kind of ownership of production goods consists in rights over the labor of others. The most extremely concentrated and exclusive of such rights are found in slavery, but the essential principle remains in serfdom, peonage, encomienda, and indenture. Naturally this kind of ownership has the greatest significance for stratification, because it necessarily entails an unequal relationship.

But property in capital goods inevitably introduces a compulsive element even into the nominally free contractual relationship. Indeed, in some respects the authority of the contractual employer is greater than that of the feudal landlord, inasmuch as the latter is more limited by traditional reciprocities. Even the classical economics recognized that competitors would fare unequally, but it did not pursue this fact to its necessary conclusion that, however it might be acquired, unequal control of goods and services must give unequal advantage to the parties to a contract.

Technical Knowledge

The function of finding means to single goals, without any concern with the choice between goals, is the exclusively technical sphere. The explanation of why positions requiring great technical skill receive fairly high rewards is easy to see, for it is the simplest case of the rewards being so distributed as to draw talent and motivate training. Why they seldom if ever receive the highest rewards is also clear: The importance of technical knowledge from a societal point of view is never as great as the integration of goals, which takes place on the religious, political, and economic levels. Since the technological level is concerned solely with means, a purely technical position must ultimately be subordinate to other positions that are religious, political, or economic in character.

Nevertheless, the distinction between expert and layman in any social order is fundamental, and cannot be entirely reduced to other terms. Methods of recruitment, as well as of reward, sometimes lead to the erroneous interpretation that technical positions are economically determined. Actually, however, the acquisition of knowledge and skill cannot be accomplished by purchase, although the opportunity to learn may be. The control of the avenues of training may inhere as a sort of property right in certain families or classes, giving them power and prestige in consequence. Such a situation adds an artificial scarcity to the natural scarcity of skills and talents. On the other hand, it is possible for an opposite situation to arise. The rewards of technical position may be so great that a condition of excess supply is created, leading to at least temporary devaluation of the rewards. Thus "unemployment in the learned professions" may result in a debasement of the prestige of those positions. Such adjustments and readjustments are constantly occurring in changing societies; and it is always well to bear in mind that the efficiency of a stratified structure may be affected by the modes of recruitment for positions. The social order itself, however, sets limits to the inflation or deflation of the prestige of experts: an over-supply tends to debase the rewards and discourage recruitment or produce revolution, whereas an under-supply tends to increase the rewards or weaken the society in competition with other societies.

Particular systems of stratification show a wide range with respect to the exact position of technically competent persons. This range is perhaps most evident in the degree of specialization. Extreme division of labor tends to create many specialists without high prestige since the training is short and the required native capacity relatively small. On the other hand it also tends to accentuate the high position of the true experts scientists, engineers, and administrators—by increasing their authority relative to other functionally important positions. But the idea of a technocratic social order or a government or priesthood of engineers or social scientists neglects the limitations of knowledge and skills as a basic for performing social functions. To the extent that the social structure is truly specialized the prestige of the technical person must also be circumscribed.

Variation in Stratified Systems

The generalized principles of stratification here suggested form a necessary preliminary to a consideration of types of stratified systems, because it is in terms of these principles that the types must be described. This can be seen by trying to delineate types according to certain modes of variation. For instance, some of the most important modes (together with the polar types in terms of them) seem to be as follows:

a. *The Degree of Specialization.* The degree of specialization affects the fineness and multiplicity of the gradations in power and prestige. It also influences the extent to which particular functions may be emphasized in the invidious system, since a given function cannot receive much emphasis in the hierarchy until it has achieved structural separation from the other functions. Finally, the amount of specialization influences the bases of selection. Polar types: *Specialized, Unspecialized.*

b. *The Nature of the Functional Emphasis.* In general when emphasis is put on sacred matters, a rigidity is introduced that tends to limit specialization and hence the development of technology. In addition, a brake is placed on social mobility, and on the development of bureaucracy. When the preoccupation with the sacred is withdrawn, leaving greater scope for purely secular preoccupations, a great development, and rise in status, of economic and technological positions seemingly takes place. Curiously, a concomitant rise in political position is not likely, because it has usually been allied with the religious and stands to gain little by the decline of the latter. It is also possible for a society to emphasize family functions—as in relatively undifferentiated societies where high mortality requires high fertility and kinship forms the main basis of social organization.

Main types: *Familistic, Authoritarian* (*Theocratic* or sacred, and *Totalitarian* or secular), *Capitalistic.*

c. *The Magnitude of Invidious Differences.* What may be called the amount of social distance between positions, taking into account the entire scale, is something that should lend itself to quantitative measurement. Considerable differences apparently exist between different societies in this regard, and also between parts of the same society. Polar types: *Equalitarian, Inequalitarian.*

d. *The Degree of Opportunity.* The familiar question of the amount of mobility is different from the question of the comparative equality or inequality of rewards posed above, because the two criteria may vary independently up to a point. For instance, the tremendous divergences in monetary income in the United States are far greater than those found in primitive societies, yet the equality of opportunity to move from one rung to the other in the social scale may also be greater in the United States than in a hereditary tribal kingdom. Polar types: *Mobile* (open), *Immobile* (closed).

e. *The Degree of Stratum Solidarity.* Again, the degree of "class solidarity" (or the presence of specific organizations to promote class interests) may vary to some extent independently of the other criteria, and hence is an important principle in classifying systems of stratification. Polar types: *Class organized, Class unorganized.*

External Conditions

What state any particular system of stratification is in with reference to each of these modes of variation depends on two things: (1) its state with reference to the other ranges of variation, and (2) the conditions outside the system of stratification which nevertheless influence that system. Among the latter are the following:

a. *The Stage of Cultural Development.* As the cultural heritage grows, increased specialization becomes necessary, which in turn contributes to the enhancement of mobility, a decline of stratum solidarity, and a change of functional emphasis.

b. *Situation with Respect to Other Societies.* The presence or absence of open conflict with other societies, of free trade relations or cultural diffusion, all influence the class structure to some extent. A chronic state of warfare tends to place emphasis upon the military functions, especially when the opponents are more or less equal. Free trade, on the other hand, strengthens the hand of the trader at the expense of the warrior and priest. Free movement of ideas generally has an equalitarian effect. Migration and conquest create special circumstances.

c. *Size of the Society.* A small society limits the degree to which functional specialization can go, the degree of segregation of different strata, and the magnitude of inequality.

Composite Types

Much of the literature on stratification has attempted to classify concrete systems into a certain number of types. This task is deceptively simple, however, and should come at the end of an analysis of elements and principles, rather than at the beginning. If the preceding discussion has any validity, it indicates that there are a number of modes of variation between different systems, and that any one system is a composite of the society's status with reference to all these modes of variation. The danger of trying to classify whole societies under such rubrics as *caste, feudal,* or *open class* is that one or two criteria are selected and others ignored, the result being an unsatisfactory solution to the problem posed. The present discussion has been offered as a possible approach to the more systematic classification of composite types.

Notes

1. Unfortunately, functional importance is difficult to establish. To use the position's prestige to establish it, as is often unconsciously done, constitutes circular reasoning from our point of view. There are, however, two independent clues; (a) the degree to which a position is functionally unique, there being no other positions that can perform the same function satisfactorily; (b) the degree to which other positions are dependent on the one in question. Both clues are best exemplified in organized systems of positions built around one major function. Thus, in most complex societies the religious, political, economic, and educational functions are handled by distinct structures not easily interchangeable. In addition, each structure possesses many different positions, some clearly dependent on, if not subordinate to, others. In sum, when an institutional nucleus becomes differentiated around one main junction, and at the same time organizes a large portion of the population into its relationships, the *key* positions in it are of the highest functional importance. The absence of such specialization does not prove functional unimportance, for the whole society may be relatively unspecialized; but it is safe to assume that the more important functions receive the first and clearest structural differentiation.

2. The symbolic rather than intrinsic role of income in social stratification has been succinctly summarized by Talcott Parsons, "An Analytical Approach to the Theory of Social Stratification," *American Journal of Sociology.* 45: 841–862, May, 1940.

Excerpts from
Class Counts

ERIK OLIN WRIGHT

Exploitation is a loaded theoretical term, since it suggests a moral condemnation of particular relations and practices, not simply an analytical description. To describe a social relationship as exploitative is to condemn it as both harmful and unjust to the exploited. Yet, while this moral dimension of exploitation is important, the core of the concept revolves around a particular type of *antagonistic interdependence of material interests* of actors within economic relations, rather than the injustice of those relations as such. As I will use the term, class exploitation is defined by three principal criteria:

a. *The material welfare of one group of people causally depends on the material deprivations of another.*
b. *The causal relation in (a) involves the asymmetrical exclusion of the exploited from access to certain productive resources.* Typically this exclusion is backed by force in the form of property rights, but in special cases it may not be.[1]
c. *The causal mechanism which translates exclusion (b) into differential welfare (a) involves the appropriation of the fruits of labor of the exploited by those who control the relevant productive resources.*[2]

This is a fairly complex set of conditions. Condition (a) establishes the antagonism of material interests. Condition (b) establishes that the antagonism is rooted in the way people are situated within the social organization of production. The expression "asymmetrical" in this criterion is meant to exclude "fair competition" from the domain of possible exploitations. Condition (c) establishes the specific mechanism by which the interdependent, antagonistic material interests are generated. The welfare of the exploiter depends upon the *effort* of the exploited, not merely the deprivations of the exploited.[3]

If only the first two of these conditions are met we have what can be called "nonexploitative economic oppression," but not "exploitation." In nonexploitative economic oppression there is no transfer of the fruits of labor from the oppressed to the oppressor; the welfare of the oppressor depends simply on the exclusion of the oppressed from access to certain resources, but not on their effort. In both instances, the inequalities in question are rooted in ownership and control over productive resources.

The crucial difference between exploitation and nonexploitative oppression is that in an exploitative relation, the exploiter *needs* the exploited since the exploiter depends upon the effort of the exploited. In the case of nonexploitative oppression, the oppressors would be happy if the oppressed simply disappeared. Life would have been much easier for the European settlers in North America if the continent had been uninhabited by people.[4] Genocide is thus always a potential strategy for nonexploitative oppressors. It is not an option in a situation of economic exploitation because exploiters require the labor of the exploited for their material well-being. It is no accident that culturally we have the abhorrent saying, "the only good Indian is a dead Indian," but not the saying "the only good worker is a dead worker" or "the only good slave is a dead slave." It makes sense to say "the only good worker is an obedient and conscientious worker," but not "the only good worker is a dead worker." The contrast between North America and South Africa in the treatment of indigenous peoples reflects this difference poignantly: in North America, where the indigenous people were oppressed (by virtue of being coercively displaced from the land) but not exploited, genocide was the basic policy of social control in the face of resistance; in South Africa, where the European settler population heavily depended upon African labor for its own prosperity, this was not an option.

Exploitation, therefore, does not merely define a set of *statuses* of social actors, but a pattern of on-going *interactions* structured by a set of social relations, relations which mutually bind the exploiter and the exploited together. This dependency of the exploiter on the exploited gives the exploited a certain form of power, since human beings always retain at least some minimal control over their own expenditure of effort. Social control of labor which relies exclusively on repression is costly and, except under special circumstances, often fails to generate optimal levels of diligence and effort on the part of the exploited. As a result, there is generally systematic pressure on exploiters to moderate their domination and in one way or another to try to elicit some degree of consent from the exploited, at least in the sense of gaining some level of minimal cooperation from them. Paradoxically perhaps, exploitation is thus a constraining force on the practices of the exploiter. This constraint constitutes a basis of power for the exploited.

People who are oppressed but not exploited also may have some power, but it is generally more precarious. At a minimum oppressed people have the power that comes from the human capacity for physical resistance. However, since their oppressors are not economically constrained to seek some kind of cooperation from them, this resistance is likely very quickly to escalate into quite bloody and violent confrontations. It is for this reason that the resistance of Native Americans to displacement from the land led to massacres of Native Americans by white settlers. The pressure on nonexploitative oppressors to seek accommodation is very weak; the outcomes of conflict therefore tend to become simply a matter of the balance of brute force between enemies. When the oppressed are also exploited, even if the exploiter feels no moral compunction, there will be economic constraints on the exploiter's treatment of the exploited.

Describing the material interests of actors generated by exploitation as antagonistic does not prejudge the moral question of the justice or injustice of the inequalities generated by these antagonisms. One can believe, for example, that it is morally justified to prevent poor people in third world countries from freely coming into the United States and still recognize that there is an objective antagonism of material interests between US citizens and the excluded would-be third world migrants. Similarly, to recognize the capital-labor conflict as involving antagonistic material interests rooted in the appropriation of labor effort does not necessarily imply that capitalist profits are unjust; it simply means that they are generated in a context of inherent conflict.

Nevertheless, it would be disingenuous to claim that the use of the term "exploitation" to designate this form of antagonistic interdependency of material interests is a strictly scientific, technical choice. Describing the appropriation of labor effort as "exploitation" rather than simply a "transfer" adds a sharp moral judgment to the analytical claim. Without at least a thin notion of the moral status of the appropriation, it would be impossible, for example, to distinguish such things as legitimate taxation from exploitation. Taxation involves coercive appropriation, and in many instances there is arguably a conflict of material interests between the taxing authorities and the taxpayer as a private individual. Even under deeply democratic and egalitarian conditions, many people would not voluntarily pay taxes since they would prefer to enhance their personal material interests by free-riding on other people's tax payments. Right-wing libertarians in fact do regard taxation as a form of exploitation because it is a violation of the sanctity of private property rights and thus an unjust, coercive appropriation. The motto "taxation is theft" is equivalent to "taxation is exploitation." The claim that the capitalist appropriation of labor effort from workers is "exploitation," therefore, implies something more than simply an antagonism of material interests between workers and capitalists; it implies that this appropriation is unjust.

While I feel that a good moral case can be made for the kind of radical egalitarianism that provides a grounding for treating capitalist appropriation as unjust, it would take us too far afield here to explore the philosophical justifications for this claim.[5] In any case, for purposes of sociological class analysis, the crucial issue is the recognition of the antagonism of material interests that are linked to class relations by virtue of the appropriation of labor effort, and on this basis I will refer to this as "exploitation." . . .

7.1 Class and Exploitation

Within the Marxist tradition of class analysis, class divisions are defined primarily in terms of the linkage between property relations and exploitation. Slave masters and slaves constitute classes because a particular property relation (property rights in people) generates exploitation (the appropriation of the fruits of labor of the slave by the slave master). Homeowners and the homeless would not constitute "classes" even though they are distinguished by property rights in housing since this division does not constitute a basis for the exploitation of the homeless by homeowners.[6]

In capitalist society, the central form of exploitation is based on property rights in the means of production. These property rights generate three basic classes: *capitalists* (exploiters), who own the means of production and hire workers; *workers* (exploited), who do not own the means of production and sell their labor power to

capitalists; and *petty bourgeois* (neither exploiter nor exploited), who own and use the means of production without hiring others.[7] The Marxist account of how the capital-labor relation generates exploitation is a familiar one: propertyless workers, in order to acquire their means of livelihood, must sell their labor power to people who own the means of production.[8] In this exchange relation, they agree to work for a specified length of time in exchange for a wage which they use to buy their means of subsistence. Because of the power relation between capitalists and workers, capitalists are able to force workers to produce more than is needed to provide them with this subsistence. As a result, workers produce a surplus which is owned by the capitalist and takes the form of profits. Profits, the amount of the social product that is left over after the costs of producing and reproducing all of the inputs (both labor power inputs and physical inputs) have been deducted, constitute an appropriation of the fruits of labor of workers.

Describing this relation as exploitative is a claim about the basis for the inherent conflict between workers and capitalists in the employment relation. It points to the crucial fact that the conflict between capitalists and workers is not simply over the *level of wages,* but over the *amount of work effort* performed for those wages. Capitalists always want workers to expend more effort than workers willingly want to do. As Bowles and Gintis (1990) have argued, "the whistle while you work" level of effort of workers is always suboptimal for capitalists, and thus capitalists have to adopt various strategies of surveillance and control to increase labor effort. While the intensity of overt conflict generated by these relations will vary over time and place, and class compromises may occur in which high levels of cooperation between labor and management take place, nevertheless, this underlying antagonism of material interests remains so long as the relationship remains exploitative.

For some theoretical and empirical purposes, this simple image of the class structure may be sufficient. For example, if the main purpose of an analysis is to explore the basic differences between the class structures of feudalism and capitalism, then an analysis which revolved entirely around the relationship between capitalists and workers might be adequate. However, for many of the things we want to study with class analysis, we need a more nuanced set of categories. In particular, we need concepts which allow for two kinds of analyses: first, the analysis of the variation across time and place in the class structures of concrete capitalist societies, and second, the analysis of the ways individual lives are affected by their location within the class structure. The first of these is needed if we are to explore macro variations in a fine-grained way; the second is needed if we are to use class effectively in micro-analysis.[9]

Both of these tasks involve elaborating a concept of class structure in capitalist societies that moves beyond the core polarization between capitalists and workers. More specifically, this involves solving two general problems in class structural analysis: first, the problem of locating the "middle class" within the class structure, and second, locating people not in the paid labor force in the class structure.[10]

7.2 The Problem of the "Middle Class" Among Employees

If we limit the analysis of class structure in capitalism to the ownership of, and exclusion from, the means of production, we end up with a class structure in which there are only three locations—the capitalist class, the working class and the petty bourgeoisie (those who own means of production but do not hire workers)—and in which around 85–90% of the population in most developed capitalist countries falls into a single class. While this may in some sense reflect a profound truth about capitalism—that the large majority of the population are separated from the means of production and must sell their labor power on the labor market in order to survive—it does not provide us with an adequate conceptual framework for explaining many of the things we want class to help explain. In particular, if we want class structure to help explain class consciousness, class formation and class conflict, then we need some way of understanding the class-relevant divisions within the employee population.

In ordinary language terms, this is the problem of the "middle class"—people who do not own their own means of production, who sell their labor

power on a labor market, and yet do not seem part of the "working class." The question, then, is on what basis can we differentiate class locations among people who share a common location of nonownership within capitalist property relations? In the analyses in this book, I will divide the class of employees along two dimensions: first, their relationship to authority within production, and second, their possession of skills or expertise.[11]

Authority

There are two rationales for treating authority as a dimension of class relations among employees. The first concerns the role of *domination* within capitalist property relations. In order to insure the performance of adequate effort on the part of workers, capitalist production always involves an apparatus of domination involving surveillance, positive and negative sanctions and varying forms of hierarchy. Capitalists do not simply *own* the means of production and *hire* workers; they also *dominate* workers within production.

In these terms, managers and supervisors can be viewed as exercising delegated capitalist class powers in so far as they engage in the practices of domination within production. In this sense they can be considered *simultaneously* in the capitalist class *and* the working class: they are like capitalists in that they dominate workers; they are like workers in that they are controlled by capitalists and exploited within production. They thus occupy what I have called *contradictory locations within class relations*. The term "contradictory" is used in this expression rather than simply "dual" since the class interests embedded in managerial jobs combine the inherently antagonistic interests of capital and labor. The higher one moves in the authority hierarchy, the greater will be the weight of capitalist interests within this class location. Thus upper managers, and especially Chief Executive Officers in large corporations will be very closely tied to the capitalist class, while the class character of lower level supervisor jobs will be much closer to that of the working class.

The second rationale for treating the authority dimension as a criterion for differentiating class locations among employees centers on the relationship between their earnings and the appropriation of surplus. The strategic position of managers within the organization of production enables them to make significant claims on a portion of the social surplus (defined in the counterfactual manner discussed above) in the form of relatively high earnings.[12] In effect this means that the wages and salaries of managerial labor power are above the costs of producing and reproducing their labor power (including whatever skills they might have).

The specific mechanism through which this appropriation takes place can be referred to as a "loyalty rent." It is important for the profitability of capitalist firms that managers wield their power in an effective and responsible way. The difficulty is that a high level of surveillance and threats is generally not an effective strategy for eliciting this kind of behavior, both because managerial performance is generally rather hard to monitor and because repressive controls tend to undermine initiative rather than stimulate creative behavior. What is needed, then, is a way of generating some level of real commitment on the part of managers to the goals of the organization. This is accomplished by relatively high earnings linked to careers and promotion ladders within authority hierarchies. These higher earnings involve a redistribution of part of the social surplus to managers in order to build their loyalty to the organization. Of course, negative sanctions are still present in the background: managers are sometimes fired, they are disciplined for poor work by failing to get promotions or raises, etc. But these coercive forms of control gain their efficacy from their link to the strong inducements of earnings that, especially for higher level managers, are significantly above the costs of producing the skills of managers.[13] Managers thus not only occupy contradictory locations within class relations by virtue of domination, they occupy what might be termed a *privileged appropriation location within exploitation relations*. Both of these differentiate them from the working class.

Skills and Expertise

The second axis of class differentiation among employees centers on the possession of skills or expertise. Like managers, employees who possess high levels of skills/expertise are potentially in a privileged appropriation location within exploitation relations. There are two primary mechanisms

through which this can happen. First, skills and expertise are frequently scarce in labor markets, not simply because they are in short supply, but also because there are systematic obstacles in the way of increasing the supply of those skills to meet the requirements of employing organizations. One important form of these obstacles is credentials, but rare talents could also constitute the basis for sustained restrictions on the supply of a particular form of labor power.[14] The result of such restrictions on supply is that owners of the scarce skills are able to receive a wage above the costs of producing and reproducing their labor power. This "skill rent" is a way by which employees can appropriate part of the social surplus.

Second, the control over knowledge and skills frequently renders also the labor effort of skilled workers difficult to monitor and control. The effective control over knowledge by such employees means that employers must rely to some extent on loyalty enhancing mechanisms in order to achieve desired levels of cooperation and effort from employees with high levels of skills and expertise, just as they have to do in the case of managers. Employees with high levels of expertise, therefore, are able to appropriate surplus both because of their strategic location within the organization of production (as controllers of knowledge), and because of their strategic location in the organization of labor markets (as controllers of a scarce form of labor power).

Understood in this way, the possession of skills and expertise defines a distinctive location within class relations because of a specific kind of power they confer on employees. It may also be the case that expertise, skills and knowledge are associated with various kinds of "symbolic capital" and distinctive life-styles, as Bourdieu (1984) and others have noted. While these cultural correlates of class may be of considerable explanatory importance for a variety of sociological questions, they do not constitute the essential rationale for treating skills and expertise as a dimension of class location within a materialist class analysis (except in so far as symbolic capital plays a role in acquiring skills and credentials). That rationale rests on the claim that experts, like managers, occupy a privileged appropriation location within exploitation relations that differentiates them from ordinary workers.

Throughout this book I will frequently use "skills and expertise" as a couplet. The term "skill" by itself sometimes is taken to refer simply to manual skills, rather than the more general idea of enhanced or complex labor power, contrasted to "raw" or undeveloped labor power. This enhancement can take many forms, both physical and cognitive. It may provide great flexibility to engage in a variety of work settings, or it may be highly specialized and vulnerable to obsolescence. Enhanced labor power is often legally certified in the form of official credentials, but in some circumstances skills and expertise may function effectively without such certification. The important theoretical idea is that skills and expertise designate an asset embodied in the labor power of people which enhances their power in labor markets and labor processes.

A Map of Middle-Class Class Locations

Adding position within authority hierarchies and possession of scarce skills and expertise to the fundamental dimension of capitalist property relations generates the map of class locations presented in Figure 7.1 With appropriate modifications depending upon our specific empirical objectives, this is the basic schema that underlies the investigations of this book. It is important to

stress that this is a map of class *locations*. The cells in the typology are not "classes" as such; they are locations within class relations. Some of these are contradictory locations within class relations, others are privileged appropriation locations within exploitation relations and still others are polarized locations within capitalist property relations. By convention the polarized locations "capitalists" and "workers" in capitalism—are often called "classes," but the more precise terminology would be to describe these as the fundamental locations within the capitalist class structure. The typology is thus not a proposal for a six-class model of the class structure of capitalism, but rather a model of a class structure which differentiates six locations within class relations.

In some of the empirical analyses we will discuss, we will combine some of the locations in this typology typically to generate a four category typology consisting of capitalists petty bourgeois, "middleclass" locations (contradictory and privileged appropriation locations among employees) and workers. In other analyses we will modify the typology by adding intermediary categories along each of the dimensions. On the relation to means production dimension this involves distinguishing between proper capitalists, small employers who only have a few employees and the petty bourgeois (self-employed people with no employees). On the authority dimension this means differentiating between

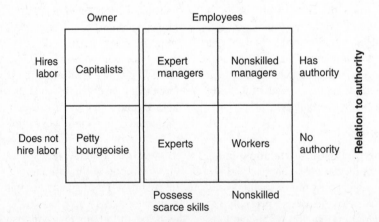

Relation to means of production

	Owner	Employees		
Hires labor	Capitalists	Expert managers	Nonskilled managers	Has authority
Does not hire labor	Petty bourgeoisie	Experts	Workers	No authority
		Possess scarce skills	Nonskilled	

Relation to scarce skills

FIGURE 7.1 Basic class typology.

proper managers—people who are involved in organizational decision making—and mere supervisors, who have power over subordinates but are not involved in policy making decisions. And, on the skill dimension this involves distinguishing between occupations which typically require advanced academic degrees, and other skilled occupations which require lower levels of specialized training. The result will be the twelve-location class-structure matrix presented in Figure 7.2.

This way of specifying the distinctiveness of the class location of managers and experts is similar in certain respects to Goldthorpe's (1982) treatment of the concept of the "service class." Goldthorpe draws a distinction between two kinds of employment relations: one based on a labor contract, characteristic of the working classes; and one based on what he terms a "service relationship," characteristic of managers and experts. In the latter, employees enter a career structure, not simply a job, and their rewards are in significant ways prospective rather than simply payments for labor performed. Such a service relation, Goldthorpe argues, is "likely to be found where it is required of employees that they exercise *delegated authority or specialized knowledge and expertise* in the interests of their employing organization. In the nature of the case . . . their performance will depend upon the degree of moral commitment that they feel toward the organization rather than on the efficacy of external sanctions" (Erikson and Goldthorpe 1993: 42). This characterization is closely related to the idea that, because of their strategic power within organizations the cooperation of middle-class employees is achieved in part through the payment of loyalty rents embodied in their earnings. The main difference between Goldthorpe's conceptual analysis and the one adopted here is, first, that Goldthorpe does not link his analysis of service-class jobs to the problem of exploitation and antagonists interests, and second, that he treats the authority dimension of managerial positions simply in terms of heightened responsibilities, not domination. Nevertheless, Goldthorpe's conceptualization of class structure taps many of the same relational properties of managerial and expert positions as the conceptualization adopted in this book.

7.3   People Not in the Paid Labor Force

Many people in capitalist societies—probably the majority—do not fill jobs in the paid labor force. The most obvious case is children. How should

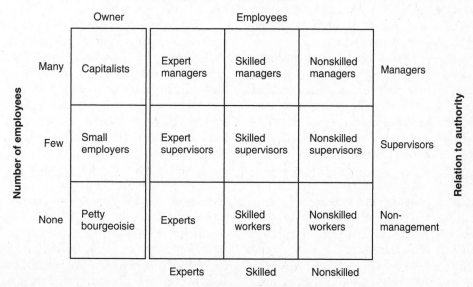

FIGURE 7.2   Elaborated class typology.

babies be located in the class structure? But there are many other categories as well: retirees, permanently disabled people, students, people on welfare, the unemployed and full-time homemakers.[15]

Each of these categories of people poses special problems for class structure analysis.

As a first approximation we can divide this heterogeneous set of situations into two broad categories: people who are tied to the class structure through family relations, and people who are not. To be in a "location" within class structure is to have one's material interests shaped by one's relationship to the process of exploitation. One way such linkages to exploitation are generated by class structures is through *jobs*. This is the kind of class location we have been exploring so far. I will refer to these as *direct class locations*. But there are other mechanisms by which people's lives are linked to the process of exploitation. Of particular importance are the ways in which family structures and kinship relations link an individual's material interests to the process of exploitation. Being born into a wealthy capitalist family links the child to the material interests of the capitalist class via family relations. It makes sense, then, to say that this child is "in" the capitalist class. If that child, as a young adult, works in a factory but stands to inherit millions of dollars of capitalist wealth and can rely on family resources for various needs, then that person would simultaneously be in two class locations: the capitalist class by virtue of family ties and the working class by virtue of the job.

I will refer to these situations as *mediated class locations*. Family ties are probably the most important basis for mediated class locations, but membership in certain kinds of communities or the relationship to the state may also provide such linkages. In each case the question one asks is "how do the social relations in which a person's life is embedded link that person to the various mechanisms of class exploitation and thus shape that person's material interests?" Many people, of course, have both direct and mediated class locations. This is of particular importance in developed capitalist economies for households in which both spouses are in the labor force, for this creates the possibility that husbands and wives will have different direct class locations, and thus each of them will have different direct and mediated locations. . . .

There are, however, people for whom family ties provide at most extremely tenuous linkages to the class structure. Most notably, this is the situation of many people in the so-called "underclass." This expression is used in a variety of ways in contemporary policy discussions. Sometimes it is meant to be a pejorative term rather like the old Marxist concept of "lumpenproletariat"; at other times it is used more descriptively to designate a segment of the poor whose conditions of life are especially desperate and whose prospects for improvement are particularly dismal. In terms of the analysis of (this reading), one way of giving this concept a more precise theoretical status is to link it to the concepts of exploitation and oppression: an "underclass" can be defined as a category of social agents who are economically oppressed but not consistently exploited within a given class system.[16]

Different kinds of class structures will generate different forms of an "underclass." In many parts of the world today and throughout much of human history, the pivotal resource which defines the underclass is land. Landlords, agrarian capitalists, peasants and exploited agrarian producers all have access to land; people who are excluded from such access constitute the underclass of agrarian societies. In these terms, many Native Americans were transformed into an underclass in the nineteenth century when they were pushed off of the land onto the reservations.

In contemporary advanced capitalism, the key resource which defines the predicament of the underclass is labor power itself. This might seem like an odd statement since in capitalism, at least since the abolition of slavery, everyone supposedly owns one "unit" of labor power, him or herself. The point is that some people do not in fact own *productively saleable* labor power. The situation is similar to a capitalist owning outmoded machines. While the capitalist physically controls these pieces of machinery, they cease to be "capital"—a capitalistically productive asset—if they cannot be deployed within a capitalist production process profitably. In the case of labor power, a person can physically control his or her own laboring capacity, but that capacity can cease to have economic value in capitalism if it cannot be deployed productively. This is the essential condition of people in the "underclass." They are oppressed because they are denied access to various kinds of productive resources, above all the necessary means to acquire the skills needed to make their labor power saleable. As a result, they are not consistently exploited.[17]

Understood in this way, the underclass consists of human beings who are largely expendable *from the point of view of the logic of capitalism.* Like Native Americans who became a landless underclass in the nineteenth century, repression rather than incorporation is the central mode of social control directed toward them. Capitalism does not need the labor power of unemployed inner city youth. The material interests of the wealthy and privileged segments of American society would be better served if these people simply disappeared. However, unlike in the nineteenth century, the moral and political forces are such that direct genocide is no longer a viable strategy. The alternative, then, is to build prisons and to cordon off the zones of cities in which the underclass lives.

7.4   Marxist Versus Weberian Class Analysis

As a set of empirical categories, the class structure matrix in Figures 7.1 and 7.2 could be deployed within either a Weberian or Marxist framework. The control over economic resources is central to both Marxist and Weberian class analysis, and both frameworks could be massaged to allow for the array of categories I am using. Indeed, a good argument could be made that the proposed class structure concept incorporates significant Weberian elements, since the explicit inclusion of skills as a criterion for class division and the importance accorded income privileges for both managers and credentialed experts are hallmarks of Weberian class analysis. In a real sense, therefore, the empirical categories . . . can be seen as a hybrid of the categories conventionally found in Marxist and Weberian class analysis.[18] In what sense, therefore, does this class structure analysis remain "Marxist"?

To answer this question we need to compare the theoretical foundations of the concept of class in the Marxist and Weberian traditions.[19] The contrast between Marx and Weber has been one of the grand themes in the history of Sociology as a discipline. Most graduate school programs have a sociological theory course within which Marx versus Weber figures as a central motif. However, in terms of class analysis, posing Marx and Weber as polar opposites is a bit misleading because in many ways Weber is speaking in his most Marxian voice when he talks about class. The concept of class within these two streams of thought share a number of important features:

- Both Marxist and Weberian approaches differ from what might be called simple gradational notions of class in which classes are differentiated strictly on the basis of inequalities in the material conditions of life.[20] This conceptualization of class underwrites the common inventory of classes found in popular discourse and the mass media: upper class, upper middle class, middle class, lower middle class, lower class, underclass. Both Marxist and Weberian class analysis define classes *relationally*, i.e. a given class location is defined by virtue of the social relations which link it to other class locations.

- Both traditions identify the concept of class with the relationship between people and economically relevant assets or resources. Marxists call this relation to the means of production; Weberians refer to "market capacities." But they are both really talking about very similar empirical phenomena.

- Both traditions see the causal relevance of class as operating, at least in part, via the ways in which these relations shape the material interests of actors. Ownership of the means of production and ownership of one's own labor power are explanatory of social action because these property rights shape the strategic alternatives people face in pursuing their material well-being. What people *have* imposes constraints on what they can do to get what they *want.* To be sure, Marxists tend to put more weight on the objective character of these "material interests" by highlighting the fact that these constraints are imposed on individuals, whereas Weberians tend to focus on the subjective conditions, by emphasizing the relative contingency in what people want.

Nevertheless, it is still the case that at their core, both class concepts involve the causal connection between (a) social relations to resources and (b) material interests via (c) the way resources shape strategies for acquiring income.

How then do they differ? The pivotal difference is captured by the contrast between the favorite buzz-words of each theoretical tradition: *life chances* for Weberians, and *exploitation* for Marxists. The reason why production is more central to Marxist than to Weberian class analysis is because of its salience for the problem of exploitation; the reason why Weberians give greater emphasis to the market is because it so directly shapes life chances.

The intuition behind the idea of life chances is straightforward. "In our terminology," Weber (in Gerth and Mills 1958: 181–2) writes:

"classes" are not communities; they merely represent possible, and frequent, bases for communal action. We may speak of a "class" when (1) a number of people have in common a specific causal component of their life chances, in so far as (2) this component is represented exclusively by economic interests in the possession of goods and opportunities for income, and (3) is represented under conditions of the commodity or labor markets. [These points refer to "class situation," which we may express more briefly as the typical chance for a supply of goods, external living conditions and life experiences, in so far as this chance is determined by the amount and kind of power, or lack of such, to dispose of goods or skills for the sake of income in a given economic order. The term "class" refers to any group of people that is found in the same class situation] . . . But always this is the generic connotation of the concept of class: that the kind of chance in the *market* is the decisive moment which presents a common condition for the individual's fate. "Class situation" is, in this sense, ultimately "market situation."

In short, the kind and quantity of resources you own affects your opportunities for income in market exchanges. "Opportunity" is a description of the feasible set individuals face, the trade-offs they encounter in deciding what to do. Owning means of production gives a person different alternatives from owning credentials, and both of these are different from simply owning unskilled labor power. Furthermore, in a market economy, access to market-derived income affects the broader array of life experiences and opportunities for oneself and one's children. The study of the life chances of children based on parents' market capacity is thus an integral part of the Weberian agenda of class analysis.

Within a Weberian perspective, therefore, the salient issue in the linkage of people to different kinds of economic resource is the way this confers on them different kinds of economic opportunities and disadvantages and thereby shapes their material interests. One way of representing this idea in a simple way is by examining the income leisure trade-offs faced by people in different classes as pictured in Figure 7.3. In this figure, everyone faces some trade-off between leisure and income: less leisure yields more income.[21] However, for the propertied class it is

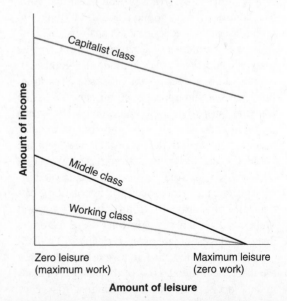

FIGURE 7.3 Leisure vs. consumption trade-offs faced by people in different economic classes.

possible to have high income with no work (thus the expressions "the leisure class" or the "idle rich"), whereas for both the middle class and the working class in this stylized drawing, zero work corresponds to zero income. The middle class has "greater" opportunities (life chances) in the market than workers because the slope they face (i.e. the wage rate) is steeper. Some workers in fact might actually have a higher standard of living than some people in the middle class, but the trade-offs they face are nevertheless less desirable. These common trade-offs, then, are the basis for a potential commonality of interests among members of a class, and thus constitute the basis for potential common action.

Within a Marxist framework, the feature of the relationship of people to economic resources which is at the core of class analysis is "exploitation." Both "exploitation" and "life chances" identify inequalities in material well-being that are generated

by inequalities in access to resources of various sorts. Thus both of these concepts point to conflicts of interest over the *distribution* of the assets themselves. What exploitation adds to this is a claim that conflicts of interest between classes are generated not simply by what people *have,* but also by what people *do* with what they have.[22] The concept of exploitation, therefore, points our attention to conflicts within production, not simply conflicts in the market.

This contrast between the Marxist and Weberian traditions of class analysis is summarized in Figure 7.4. Weberian class analysis revolves around a single causal nexus that works through market exchanges. Marxist class analysis includes the Weberian causal processes, but adds to them a causal structure within production itself as well as an account of the interactions of production and exchange. Part of our analysis of the class location of managers, for example, concerns the

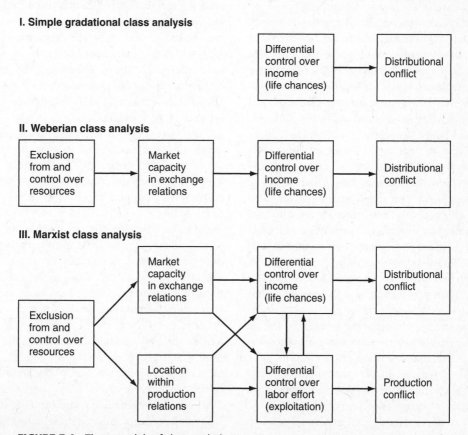

FIGURE 7.4   Three models of class analysis.

"loyalty rent" which managers receive by virtue of their position within the authority structure of production. This reflects the way in which location within the relations of production and not simply within market relations affects the "life chances" of managers. Our analysis of the shmoo—and more broadly, the analysis of such things as the way transfer payments of the welfare state affect the market capacity of workers—illustrates how market capacity has an impact on the extraction of labor effort within production. The Marxist concept of class directs our attention both theoretically and empirically towards these interactions.

A Weberian might reply that there is nothing in the Weberian idea of market-based life chances that would *prevent* the analysis of the extraction of labor effort within production. A good and subtle Weberian class analyst could certainly link the analysis of market capacities within exchange relations to power relations within the labor process, and thus explore the causal structures at the center of Marxist class analysis. In systematically joining production and exchange in this way, however, the Weberian concept would in effect become Marxianized. Frank Parkin (1979: 25), in a famous gibe, said, "Inside every neo-Marxist there seems to be a Weberian struggling to get out." One could just as easily say that inside every left-wing Weberian there is a Marxist struggling to stay hidden.

There are three main reasons why one might want to ground the concept of class explicitly in exploitation rather than simply market-based life chances. First, the exploitation-centered class concept affirms the fact that production and exchange are intrinsically linked, not merely contingently related. The material interests of capitalists and workers are *inherently* shaped by the interaction of these two facets of the social relations that bind them together. This provides us with the way of understanding the class location of managers as determined not simply by their position within the market for managerial labor power, but also by their position within the relations of domination in production. More broadly, the exploitation-based class concept points our attention to the fact that class relations are relations of power, not merely privilege.

Second, theorizing the interests linked to classes as grounded in inherently antagonistic and interdependent practices facilitates the analysis of social conflict. Explanations of conflict always require at least two elements: an account of the opposing *interests* at stake in the conflict and an account of the *capacity* of the actors to pursue those interests. A simple opposition of interests is not enough to explain active conflict between groups. Exploitation is a powerful concept precisely because it brings together an account of opposing interests with an account of the rudimentary capacity for resistance. Exploiters not only have a positive interest in limiting the life chances of the exploited, but also are *dependent* upon the exploited for the realization of their own interests. This dependency of the exploiter on the exploited gives the exploited an inherent capacity to resist. Exploitation, therefore, does not simply predict an opposition of interests, but a tendency for this antagonism of interests to generate manifest conflicts between classes. This understanding of the inherent power of exploited classes is marginalized when class is defined strictly in terms of market relations.

Finally, the exploitation-centered class analysis implies that classes can exist in nonmarket societies, whereas Weberian class analysis explicitly restricts the relevance of class to markets. For Marxist class analysis, the relationship between slave master and slave or lord and serf are instances of class relations because they all involve exploitation linked to property rights in the forces of production.[23] The relationship between bureaucratic exploiters and producers in command economies can also be considered a form of class relations since the capacity of the state bureaucratic elite to appropriate surplus rests on their effective control over the society's productive resources (Wright 1994: ch. 6). For Weberian class analysis these are not class relations, but rather examples of castes or estates or some other form of inequality of power, since the differences in "life chances" of the slave and slave master, the lord and serf, the bureaucratic appropriator and producer, are not the result of their meeting within a market. The Weberian restriction of the concept of class to market societies, therefore, directs our attention away from the underlying commonality of these relations across different kinds of social systems.

There is, of course, no metatheoretical rule of sociology which says that every sociologist must choose between these two ways of grounding class analysis. It certainly might be possible to construct an eclectic hybrid between Marxist and Weberian class analysis by seeing exploitation as defining the central cleavages within a class structure and differential market capacities as defining salient *strata within classes*. Strata within the capitalist class would be defined by differential capacity to appropriate surplus; strata within the working class would be determined by differences in incomes and working conditions generated by different market capacities. In such a hybrid class analysis, what I have been calling the "middle class" might be more appropriately described as privileged strata within the working class.

Nevertheless, throughout this book I will interpret the class-structure matrix we will be using within a neo-Marxist class analysis framework. In the end, the decision to do this rather than adopt a more eclectic stance comes at least in part from political commitments, not simply dispassionate scientific principles. This does not mean that Marxist class analysis is pure ideology or that it is rigidly dictated by radical egalitarian values. My choice of analytical framework is also based on my beliefs in the theoretical coherence of this approach—which I have argued for (in this reading)—and in its capacity to illuminate empirical problems. . . . But this choice remains crucially bound up with commitments to the socialist tradition and its aspirations for an emancipatory, egalitarian alternative to capitalism.

Readers who are highly skeptical of the Marxist tradition for whatever reasons might feel that there is no point in struggling through the masses of numbers, graphs and equations. . . . If the conceptual justifications for the categories are unredeemably flawed, it might be thought, the empirical results generated with those categories will be worthless. This would be, I think, a mistake. The empirical categories themselves can be interpreted in a Weberian or hybrid manner. Indeed, as a practical set of operational categories, the class structure matrix used (in this reading) does not dramatically differ from the class typology used by Goldthorpe (1980) and Erikson and Goldthorpe (1993). As is usually the case in sociology, the empirical categories of analysis are *under* determined by the theoretical frameworks within which they are generated or interpreted. This means that readers who are resolutely unconvinced about the virtues of understanding classes in terms of exploitation can still engage the empirical analyses . . . as investigations of classes differentially situated with respect to life chances in the market. . . .

Notes

1. An example of an exclusion from productive resources which is not backed by force but which, nevertheless, could be the basis for exploitation is the unequal distribution of talents. While one could stretch the notion of "coercive" exclusion to cover talents (since the untalented are coercively prohibited from owning the talented as slaves), in the actual functioning of capitalist societies, the relevant exclusion is not primarily guaranteed by force.

2. The expression "appropriation of the fruits of labor" refers to the appropriation of that which labor produces. It does *not* imply that the value of those products is exclusively determined by labor effort, as claimed in the labor theory of value. All that is being claimed here is that a surplus is appropriated—a surplus beyond what is needed to reproduce all of the inputs of production—and that this surplus is produced through labor effort but not that the appropriate metric for the surplus is labor time. For a discussion of this way of understanding the appropriation of the fruits of labor, see Cohen (1988: 209–238).

3. There are situations in which conditions (a) and (c) are present, but not (b). For example, in what is sometimes called a "tributary mode of production," a centralized, authoritarian state apparatus appropriates surplus from peasants through taxation without directly being involved in production at all. The peasants are surely being exploited in this situation, but the state elite is not a fully-fledged "class" insofar as their social location and power is not determined by their location within the social relations of production. One could, perhaps, stretch the meaning of condition (b) somewhat by treating the direct appropriation of the peasants' product by the state elite as a form of "exclusion" of peasants from productive resources (since the surplus itself is a productive resource). But the core mechanism involved does not center

on the social relations of *production,* but the direct control of violence by the state, and thus the state elite is not a "class" in the standard sense.

4. This is not to deny that in certain specific instances the settlers benefited from the knowledge of Native Americans, but simply to affirm the point that the displacement of the indigenous people from the land was a costly and troublesome process.

5. For an insightful discussion of radical egalitarian values that provides a basis for regarding capitalist appropriations as exploitative, see Cohen (1988: ch. 11).

6. If homeowners exchanged housing in vacant rooms for domestic service, then the property rights in housing might become the basis for a class relation. The sheer fact of homeownership and homelessness, however, does not itself constitute a form of exploitation and thus is not a class division. It is only when this property right is translated into a power relation between actors within which labor is appropriated that it becomes exploitative.

7. As Roemer (1982) argues, it is possible that some petty bourgeois might be exploited or even be exploiters through uneven exchange in the market. A petty bourgeois working with highly capital intensive means of production, for example, may be able to appropriate the fruits of labor of others through exchange.

8. To be somewhat more precise, in order to acquire the means of subsistence, at least some members of a propertyless family (defined as the unit of shared consumption) must sell labor power to employees. In some times and places, this has meant that the male "breadwinner" entered the labor market while the female "housewife" stayed home. In contemporary advanced capitalism, generally all adult members of households sell their labor power.

9. For an extended discussion of the limitations of the overly abstract polarized concept of class structure see Wright (1989: 271–278).

10. There are additional problems in the elaboration of the concept of class structure which will be discussed later in this book. The location of state employees in the class structure will be discussed in chapter 15. The issue of the temporal dimension of class locations—the fact that some jobs are organized within careers that span class boundaries—will be discussed in chapters 5 and 6.

11. The conceptual discussion here differs in a number of ways from the way I approached these questions in my earlier book, *Classes* (Wright 1985). In that book I argued that the rationale for considering authority and skills to be dimensions of the class structure was that the control of organizational assets (i.e. authority) and skill assets were the basis for distinctive forms of exploitation. For reasons which I elaborated in a subsequent essay (Wright 1989: ch. 8) this no longer seems a satisfactory way of specifying the class character of the "middle class." While the formulation presented here lacks the symmetry of the earlier strategy of analysis, I believe it is conceptually sounder.

12. In earlier work I argued that by virtue of this appropriation of surplus by managers they should be seen as exploiters. The problem with this formulation is that managers also contribute to the surplus through their own laboring activity, and thus their surplus income may simply reflect a capacity to appropriate part of the surplus which they contribute to production. Instead of being "exploiters," therefore many managers may simply be less exploited than other employees. Because of this ambiguity, therefore, it is better simply to see managers as occupying a *privileged* position with respect to the process of exploitation which enables them to appropriate part of the social surplus in the form of higher incomes.

13. This rent component of the earnings of managers has been recognized in "efficiency wage" theory which acknowledges that the market-clearing wage may be suboptimal from the point of view of the goals of the employer. Because of the difficulty in enforcing labor contracts, employers have to pay employees more than the wages predicted by theories of competitive equilibria in order to gain compliance. While this mechanism may generate scene small "employment rents" for all employees, it is especially salient for those employees who occupy strategic jobs requiring responsible, diligent performance of duties. For the mainstream economics discussion of efficiency wages, see Akerloff and Yellen (1986). For arguments that extend efficiency wage theory to Marxist arguments about the "extraction" of labor effort from workers, see Bowles and Gintis (1990).

14. Credentials would not constitute a restriction on the supply of a particular kind of skill if there were no obstacles for individuals acquiring the credentials. A variety of such obstacles exist: restrictions on the number of slots in the training programs; restrictions in credit markets to get loans to obtain the training; inequality in the distribution of "cultural capital" (including such things as mariners, accent, appearances etc.) and

"social capital" (especially such things as access to networks and information); and, of course, inequalities in genetic endowments.

15. The claim that the people in these categories do not participate directly in production is simple enough for the unemployed, retirees and children, but it is problematic for housewives, since housewives obviously work and produce things in the home. This has led some theorists (e.g. Delphy, 1984) to argue that the work of housewives should be treated as domestic labor performed within a domestic mode of production in which housewives occupy a distinctive class location, the domestic worker. Others have argued that household production is a subsidiary part of the capitalist mode of production. It has even been argued (Fraad, Resnick and Wolff, 1994) that household production is a special form of feudal production in which housewives are feudally exploited by their husbands since the husbands directly "appropriate" use-values from their wives. All of these views in one way or another attempt to treat the gender and kinship relation within a family as if they were a form of class relations. This amalgamation of class and gender undercuts the explanatory specificity of both class and gender and does not, I believe, enhance our capacity to explain the processes in question. In any case, since the analysis in this book is restricted to people in the paid labor force, we will bracket these issues.

16. Although he does not explicitly elaborate the term "underclass" in terms of a theory of exploitation and economic oppression, the definition proposed here is consistent with the more structural aspects of way the term is used by William Julius Wilson (1982, 1987) in his analysis of the interconnection between race and class in American society. Wilson argues that as legal barriers to racial equality have disappeared and as class differentiation within the black population has increased, the central determining structure of the lives of many African-Americans is no longer race as such, but class. More specifically he argues that there has been a substantial growth of an urban underclass of people without marketable skills and with very weak attachments to the labor force, living in crumbling central cities isolated from the mainstream of American life and institutions.

17. It is perhaps controversial to amalgamate the exclusion of the contemporary urban underclass from human capital and other job resources with the exclusion of Native Americans from the land.

In the latter case there was a zero-sum character to access the resource in question and massive coercion was used to enforce the exclusion, whereas in the case of education, skills and even good jobs, it is not so obvious that the resources in question are a fixed quantity and that access is being denied through force. Thus the factual inequalities of access to these resources may not in fact be instances of coercively enforced exclusions which benefit certain groups of people at the expense of others. The plight of the underclass might still be a matter of serious moral concern, but it would not count as an instance of nonexploitative oppression analogous to the condition of Native Americans.

18. It should not be so surprising to see Marxist and Weberian elements conjoined in class analysis. After all, Weber's class analysis was deeply indebted to the Marxist legacy which was part of the general intellectual discourse of his time. In spite of the fact that Weber constantly distanced himself from Marxism, particularly because of its tendencies toward economic determinism which were especially pronounced in his day, when Weber talks of classes he is speaking in a rather Marxian voice.

19. For discussions of the contrast between Marxist and Weberian class analysis, see for example, Parkin (1979), Burris (1987), Giddens (1973), Wright (1979: ch. 1).

20. The contrast between "gradational" and "relational" concepts of class was first introduced into sociology by Ossowski (1963). For a more extended discussion of gradational concepts of class, see Wright (1979: ch. 1).

21. For simplicity, the leisure–consumption trade-off is pictured here as a linear relation. For the working class and the middle class the slope of the line thus represents a linear wage rate. Of course, in the real world, because of such things as overtime on the one hand, and substandard wages for part-time work on the other the relation would not be linear. The slope of the capitalist class curve in the figure is given as roughly the same as that of the middle class. If we consider all capitalists not simply those with great entrepreneurial talent, there is no reason to assume *a priori* that their imputed hourly wage (i.e. the part of their earnings that is derived from labor time rather than from their property) would be greater than that of the middle class (skilled employees and managers). In any event, for our present purposes the main point about the capitalist curve is that it does not intersect the x-axis.

22. The conceptual distinction between life chances and exploitation being argued for here runs against the arguments of John Roemer (1985), who insists that exploitation is strictly a way of talking about the injustice of the effects of what people have (assets) on what people get (income). In this sense, he collapses the problem of exploitation into the problem of life chances and thus dissolves the distinction between Marxist and Weberian class analysis. The notion of the extraction of labor effort disappears from his analysis of exploitation.

23. The classic Marxist description of feudalism is a society in which the lords appropriate surplus products directly from the serfs through the use of what is generally called "extra-economic coercion." This coercion either takes the form of forcing the peasant to work part of the week on the land of the lord, or exacting some portion of the produce of the peasant. An alternative characterization is to say that in feudalism the lord and the serf are joint owners of the labor power of the serf. This gives the lord property rights in the laboring capacity of serfs. Slavery, in these terms, is simply the limiting case in which the slave has lost all property rights in his or her own labor power. This joint ownership of the serf's labor power is reflected in the laws which tie serfs to the land and which prevent the flight of serfs to the city. Such flight is simply a form of theft the fleeing serf, like the fleeing slave, has stolen property from the lord. The use of extra economic coercion, then, is simply the means of enforcing these property rights, no different from the use of extra-economic coercion to prevent workers from taking over a factory. For an extended discussion of this way of understanding feudalism, see Wright (1985: 77–78).

References

Akerloff, G. A. and J. L. Yellen (eds.). 1986. *Efficiency Wage Models of the Labor Market*. Cambridge: Cambridge University Press.

Bourdieu, Pierre. 1984. *Distinction: A Social Critique of the Judgement of Taste*. Translated by Richard Nice. London and New York: Routledge and Kegan Paul.

Bowels, Samuel and Herb Gintis. 1990. "Contested Exchange: New Microfoundations for the Political Economy of Capitalism," *Politics & Society* 18, 2: 165–222.

Burris, Val. 1987. "The Neo-Marxist Synthesis of Marx and Weber on Class," in N. Wiley (ed.) *The Marx–Weber Debate*. Newbury Park, CA: Saga Publications.

Cohen, G. A. 1988. *History, Labour and Freedom*. Oxford University Press.

Delphy, Christine. 1984. *Close to Home*. London: Hutchinson.

Erikson, Robert and John H. Goldthorpe. 1993. *The Constant Flux*. Oxford: Oxford University Press.

Fraad, Harriet, Stephen Resnick and Richard Wolff. 1994. *Bringing it All Back Home: Class, Gender and Power in the Modern Household*. London: Pluto Press.

Gerth, Hans and C. W. Mills. 1958. *From Max Weber*. New York: Oxford University Press.

Giddens, Anthony. 1973. *The Class Structure of the Advanced Societies*. New York: Harper and Row.

Goldthorpe, John. 1980. *Social Mobility and Class Structure in Modern Britain*. Oxford: Oxford University Press.

Ossowski, Stanislaw. 1963. *Class Structure in the Social Consciousness*. London: Routledge & Kegan Paul.

Parkin, Frank. 1974. "Strategies of Social Closure in Class Formation." In Frank Parkin (ed.). *The Social Analysis of the Class Structure*. London: Tavistock.

——. 1979. *Marxism and Class Theory: A Bourgeois Critique*. New York: Colombia University Press.

Roemer, John. 1983. *A General Theory of Exploitation and Class*. Cambridge, MA: Harvard University Press.

Wilson, William Julius. 1982. *The Declining Significance of Race*. Chicago: University of Chicago Press.

——. 1987. *The Truly Disadvantaged*. Chicago: University of Chicago Press.

Wright, Erik Olin. 1976. "Class Boundaries in Advanced Capitalist Society," *New Left Review* 98 (July–August): 3–41.

——. 1978. *Class, Crisis and the State*. London: New Left Books.

——. 1979. *Class Structure and Income Determination*. New York: Academic Press.

——. 1985. *Classes*. London: New Left Books.

——. 1989. "Rethinking, Once Again, The Concept of Class Structure." Pp. 269–348 in Wright, et al. (1989). *The Debate on Classes*. London: Verso.

——. 1994. *Interrogating Inequality*. London: Verso.

II

Class

INTRODUCTION

As insightful as the analyses of Marx and Weber were about class, scholars have spent considerable energy trying to extend and refine their understanding. One of the most successful efforts has been that of Erik Olin Wright. Beginning with Marx's emphases on production, property, and exploitation, and also taking into account Weber's ideas related to skills, credentials, and domination, Wright develops a theory of how class structure works. As presented in this excerpt from *Class Counts*, class structure includes three dimensions: property, credentialed skills, and managerial authority. That is, depending on a person's property, skills, and authority, he or she occupies a higher or lower class location. Because an individual could have more of one asset and less of another, this combination allows for the interesting concept of "contradictory class locations." Such categories refer to those people in middle-class positions involved in exploiting others while being exploited at the same time as well as those who are not exploitative or exploited.

In addition to the significance of social structure in systemic inequality, various scholars have also recognized that human agency and performance complicate the actual distribution of resources and opportunities. Echoing elements of DuBois, Cooper, as well as Davis and Moore, Annette Lareau documents in this excerpt from *Unequal Childhoods* how the reality of social class involves socialized and learned behaviors.

Just as Lareau reveals how the micro-level factors allow for both change and continuity in social classes, William Wilson shares a broad perspective illustrating the macro-level factors behind the change and continuity of larger structures of inequality. Drawing from Marx, he argues in this excerpt from *The Declining Significance of Race* that the change in the mode of production in the United States from the plantation economy to industrial capitalism has facilitated a shift in emphasis from inequality centered around race to inequality based on class.

One of the results of this history is a stratification system that includes a relatively high level of poverty. As Cliff Brown explains in "Poverty in the United States: An Overview," a legacy of slavery and discrimination has contributed to disproportionate numbers of minorities, especially African Americans, among those living in poverty. However, the majority of poor people are white. He also notes that there is a growing incidence of fully employed people living under or near the poverty line. Another piece contributed by Brown for this reader can be found in the Appendix, which provides more details about current patterns of poverty and inequality.

While the inability of some people to make a decent living under capitalism is an old theme in the study of stratification, new forms of marginalization are still evolving. One of the most important developments of our era is the information revolution, which has led to a "Digital Divide," as documented by Paul DiMaggio and his colleagues. Differential access to hardware, software, training, and skills has led to a new dimension of social inequality.

All of the dynamics related to social inequality explored in this volume are shaped in some way by the broader context of global political economy. A key part of that context is the power of the transnational capitalist class, as described by Joseph E. Stiglitz in "Globalism's Discontents." This essay summarizes a few key findings from the vast literature on global political economy. Among them is the point that a global class system allows affluent countries to benefit through inequitable trade agreements at the expense of poor countries.

8

Excerpts from
Unequal Childhoods
ANNETTE LAREAU

Laughing and yelling, a white fourth-grader named Garrett Ballinger splashes around in the swimming pool in the backyard of his four-bedroom home in the suburbs on a late spring afternoon. As on most evenings, after a quick dinner his father drives him to soccer practice. This is only one of Garrett's many activities. His brother has a baseball game at a different location. There are evenings when the boys' parents relax, sipping a glass of wine. Tonight is not one of them. As they rush to change out of their work clothes and get the children ready for practice, Mr. and Mrs. Ballinger are harried.

Only ten minutes away, a Black fourth-grader, Alexander Williams, is riding home from a school open house.[1] His mother is driving their beige, leather-upholstered Lexus. It is 9:00 P.M. on a Wednesday evening. Ms. Williams is tired from work and has a long Thursday ahead of her. She will get up at 4:45 A.M. to go out of town on business and will not return before 9:00 P.M. On Saturday morning, she will chauffeur Alexander to a private piano lesson at 8:15 A.M., which will be followed by a choir rehearsal and then a soccer game. As they ride in the dark, Alexander's mother, in a quiet voice, talks with her son, asking him questions and eliciting his opinions.

Discussions between parents and children are a hallmark of middle-class child rearing. Like many middle-class parents, Ms. Williams and her husband see themselves as "developing" Alexander to cultivate his talents in a concerted fashion. Organized activities, established and controlled by mothers and fathers, dominate the lives of middle-class children such as Garrett and Alexander. By making certain their children have these and other experiences, middle-class parents engage in a process of *concerted cultivation*. From this, a robust sense of entitlement takes root in the children. This sense of entitlement plays an especially important role in institutional settings, where middle-class children learn to question adults and address them as relative equals.

Only twenty minutes away, in blue-collar neighborhoods, and slightly farther away, in public housing projects, childhood looks different. Mr. Janelle, a white working-class father, picks up his son Little Billy, a fourth-grader, from an after-school program. They come home and Mr. Janelle drinks a beer while Little

Billy first watches television, then rides his bike and plays in the street. Other nights, he and his Dad sit on the sidewalk outside their house and play cards. At about 5:30 P.M. Billy's mother gets home from her job as a house cleaner. She fixes dinner and the entire family sits down to eat together. Extended family are a prominent part of their lives. Ms. Janelle touches base with her "entire family every day" by phone. Many nights Little Billy's uncle stops by, sometimes bringing Little Billy's youngest cousin. In the spring, Little Billy plays baseball on a local team. Unlike for Garrett and Alexander, who have at least four activities a week, for Little Billy, baseball is his only organized activity outside of school during the entire year. Down the road, a white working-class girl, Wendy Driver, also spends the evening with her girl cousins, as they watch a video and eat popcorn, crowded together on the living room floor.

Farther away, a Black fourth-grade boy, Harold McAllister, plays outside on a summer evening in the public housing project in which he lives. His two male cousins are there that night, as they often are. After an afternoon spent unsuccessfully searching for a ball so they could play basketball, the boys had resorted to watching sports on television. Now they head outdoors for a twilight water balloon fight. Harold tries to get his neighbor, Miss Latina, wet. People sit in white plastic lawn chairs outside the row of apartments. Music and television sounds waft through the open windows and doors.

The adults in the lives of Billy, Wendy, and Harold want the best for them. Formidable economic constraints make it a major life task for these parents to put food on the table, arrange for housing, negotiate unsafe neighborhoods, take children to the doctor (often waiting for city buses that do not come), clean children's clothes, and get children to bed and have them ready for school the next morning. But unlike middle-class parents, these adults do not consider the concerted development of children, particularly through organized leisure activities, an essential aspect of good parenting. Unlike the Malingers and Williams's, these mothers and fathers do not

focus on concerted cultivation. For them, the crucial responsibilities of parenthood do not lie in eliciting their children's feelings, opinions, and thoughts. Rather, they see a clear boundary between adults and children. Parents tend to use directives: they tell their children what to do rather than persuading them with reasoning. Unlike their middle-class counterparts, who have a steady diet of adult organized activities, the working-class and poor children have more control over the character of their leisure activities. Most children are free to go out and play with friends and relatives who typically live close by. Their parents and guardians facilitate the *accomplishment of natural growth*.[2] Yet these children and their parents interact with central institutions in the society, such as schools, which firmly and decisively promote strategies of concerted cultivation in child rearing. For working-class and poor families, the cultural logic of child rearing at home is out of synch with the standards of institutions. As a result, while children whose parents adopt strategies of concerted cultivation appear to gain a sense of entitlement, children such as Billy Janelle, Wendy Driver, and Harold McAllister appear to gain an emerging sense of distance, distrust, and constraint in their institutional experiences.

America may be the land of opportunity, but it is also a land of inequality. This book identifies the largely invisible but powerful ways that parents' social class impacts children's life experiences. It shows, using in-depth observations and interviews with middle-class (including members of the upper-middle-class), working-class, and poor families, that inequality permeates the fabric of the culture. . . . I report the results of intensive observational research for a total of twelve families when their children were nine and ten years old. I argue that key elements of family life cohere to form a cultural logic of child rearing.[3] In other words, the differences among families seem to cluster together in meaningful patterns. In this historical moment, middle-class parents tend to adopt a cultural logic of child rearing that stresses the concerted cultivation of children. Working-class and poor parents, by contrast, tend to undertake the accomplishment of natural growth. In the accomplishment of natural growth, children experience long stretches of leisure time, child-initiated play, clear boundaries between adults and children, and daily interactions with kin. Working-class and poor children, despite tremendous economic strain, often have Concerted Cultivation and more "childlike" lives, with autonomy from adults and control over their extended leisure time. Although middle-class children miss out on kin relationships and leisure time, they appear to (at least potentially) gain important institutional advantages. From the experience of concerted cultivation, they acquire skills that could be valuable in the future when they enter the world of work. Middle-class white and Black children in my study did exhibit some key differences; yet the biggest gaps were not within social classes but, as I show, across them. It is these class differences and how they are enacted in family life and child rearing that shape the ways children view themselves in relation to the rest of the world.

Cultural Repertoires

Professionals who work with children, such as teachers, doctors, and counselors, generally agree about how children should be raised. Of course, from time to time they may disagree on the ways standards should be enacted for an individual child or family. For example, teachers may disagree about whether or not parents should stop and correct a child who mispronounces a word while reading. Counselors may disagree over whether a mother is being too protective of her child. Still, there is little dispute among professionals on the broad principles for promoting educational development in children through proper parenting.[4] These standards include the importance of talking with children, developing their educational interests, and playing an active role in their schooling. Similarly, parenting guidelines typically stress the importance of reasoning with children and teaching them to solve problems through negotiation rather than with physical force. Because these guidelines are so generally accepted, and because they focus on a set of practices concerning how parents should raise children, they form a *dominant set of cultural repertoires* about how children should be raised. This widespread agreement among professionals about the broad principles for child rearing permeates our society. A small number of experts thus potentially shape the behavior of a large number of parents.

Professionals' advice regarding the best way to raise children has changed regularly over the last two centuries. From strong opinions about the merits of bottle feeding, being stern with children, and utilizing physical punishment (with dire warnings of problematic outcomes should parents indulge children), there have been shifts to equally strongly worded recommendations about the benefits of breast feeding, displaying emotional warmth toward children, and using reasoning and negotiation as mechanisms of parental control. Middle-class parents appear to shift their behaviors in a variety of spheres more rapidly and more thoroughly than do working-class or poor parents.[5] As professionals have shifted their recommendations from bottle feeding to breast feeding, from stern approaches to warmth and empathy, and from spanking to time-outs, it is middle-class parents who have responded most promptly.[6] Moreover, in recent decades, middle-class children in the United States have had to face the prospect of "declining fortunes."[7] Worried about how their children will get ahead, middle-class parents are increasingly determined to make sure that their children are not excluded from any opportunity that might eventually contribute to their advancement.

Middle-class parents who comply with current professional standards and engage in a pattern of concerted cultivation deliberately try to stimulate their children's development and foster their cognitive and social skills. The commitment among working-class and poor families to provide comfort, food, shelter, and other basic support requires ongoing effort, given economic challenges and the formidable demands of child rearing. But it stops short of the deliberate cultivation of children and their leisure activities that occurs in middle-class families. For working-class and poor families, sustaining children's natural growth is viewed as an accomplishment.[8]

What is the outcome of these different philosophies and approaches to child rearing? Quite simply, they appear to lead to the *transmission of differential advantages* to children. In this study, there was quite a bit more talking in middle-class homes than in working-class and poor homes, leading to the development of greater verbal agility, larger vocabularies, more comfort with authority figures, and more familiarity with abstract concepts. Importantly, children also developed skill differences in interacting with authority figures in institutions and at home. Middle-class children such as Garrett Ballinger and Alexander Williams learn, as young boys, to shake the hands of adults and look them in the eye. In studies of job interviews, investigators have found that potential employees have less than one minute to make a good impression. Researchers stress the importance of eye contact, firm handshakes, and displaying comfort with bosses during the interview. In poor families like Harold McAllister's, however, family members usually do not look each other in the eye when conversing. In addition, as Elijah Anderson points out, they live in neighborhoods where it can be dangerous to look people in the eye too long.[9] The types of social competence transmitted in the McAllister family are valuable, but they are potentially less valuable (in employment interviews, for example) than those learned by Garrett Ballinger and Alexander Williams.

The white and Black middle-class children in this study also exhibited an emergent version of the *sense of entitlement* characteristic of the middle-class. They acted as though they had a right to pursue their own individual preferences and to actively manage interactions in institutional settings. They appeared comfortable in these settings; they were open to sharing information and asking for attention. Although some children were more outgoing than others, it was common practice among middle-class children to shift interactions to suit *their* preferences. Alexander Williams knew how to get the doctor to listen to his concerns (about the bumps under his arm from his new deodorant). His mother explicitly trained and encouraged him to speak up with the doctor. Similarly, a Black middle-class girl, Stacey Marshall, was taught by her mother to expect the gymnastics teacher to accommodate her individual learning style. Thus, middle-class children were trained in "the rules of the game" that govern interactions with institutional representatives. They were not conversant in other important social skills, however, such as organizing their time for hours on end during weekends and summers, spending long periods of time away from adults, or hanging out with adults in a nonobtrusive, subordinate fashion. Middle-class children also learned (by imitation and by direct training) how to make the rules work in their favor. Here, the enormous stress on reasoning and negotiation in the home also has a potential advantage for future institutional negotiations. Additionally, those in authority responded positively to such interactions. Even in fourth grade, middle-class children appeared to be acting on their own behalf to gain advantages. They made special requests of teachers and doctors to adjust procedures to accommodate their desires.

The working-class and poor children, by contrast, showed an emerging *sense of constraint* in their interactions in institutional settings. They were less likely to try to customize interactions to suit their own preferences. Like their parents, the children accepted the actions of persons in authority (although at times they also covertly resisted them). Working-class and poor parents sometimes were not as aware of their children's school situation (as when their children were not doing homework). Other times, they dismissed the school rules as unreasonable. For example, Wendy Driver's mother told her to "punch" a boy who was pestering her in class; Billy Janelle's parents were proud of him when he "beat up" another boy on the playground, even though Billy was then suspended from school. Parents also had trouble getting "the school" to respond to their concerns. When Ms. Janelle complained that she "hates" the school, she gave her son a lesson in powerlessness and frustration in the face of an important institution. Middle-class children such as Stacey Marshall learned to make demands on professionals, and when they succeeded in making the rules work in their favor they augmented their "cultural capital" (i.e., skills individuals inherit that can then be translated into different forms of value as they move through various institutions) for the future.[10] When working-class and poor children confronted institutions, however, they generally were unable to make the rules work in their favor nor did they obtain capital for adulthood. Because of these patterns of legitimization, children raised according to the logic of concerted cultivation can gain advantages, in the form of an emerging sense of entitlement, while children raised according to the logic of natural growth tend to develop an emerging sense of constraint.[11]

Social Stratification and Individualism

Public discourse in America typically presents the life accomplishments of a person as the result of her or his individual qualities. Songs like "I Did It My Way," memoirs, television shows, and magazine articles, celebrate the individual. Typically, individual outcomes are connected to individual effort and talent, such as being a "type A" personality, being a hard worker, or showing leadership. These cultural beliefs provide a framework for Americans' views of inequality.

Indeed, Americans are much more comfortable recognizing the power of individual initiative than recognizing the power of social class. Studies show that Americans generally believe that responsibility for their accomplishments rests on their individual efforts. Less than one-fifth see "race, gender religion, or class as very important for 'getting ahead in life.' "[12] Compared to Europeans, individuals in the United States are much more likely to believe they can improve their standard of living. Put differently, Americans believe in the American dream: "The American dream that we were all raised on is a simple but powerful one—if you work hard and play by the rules, you should be given a chance to go as far as your God-given ability will take you."[13] This American ideology that each individual is responsible for his or her life outcomes is the expressed belief of the vast majority of Americans, rich and poor.

Yet there is no question that society is stratified. . . . highly valued resources such as the possession of wealth; having an interesting,

well-paying, and complex job; having a good education; and owning a home, are not evenly distributed throughout the society. Moreover, these resources are transferred across generations: One of the best predictors of whether a child will one day graduate from college is whether his or her parents are college graduates. Of course, relations of this sort are not absolute: Perhaps two-thirds of the members of society ultimately reproduce their parents' level of educational attainment, while about one-third take a different path. Still, there is no question that we live in a society characterized by considerable gaps in resources or, put differently, by substantial *inequality* . . . however, reasonable people have disagreed about how best to conceptualize such patterns. They also have disagreed about whether families in different economic positions "share distinct, life-defining experiences."[14] Many insist that there is not a clear, coherent, and sustained experiential pattern. In this book, I demonstrate the existence of a cultural logic of child rearing that tends to differ according to families' social class positions. I see these interweaving practices as coming together in a messy but still recognizable way. In contrast to many, I suggest that social class does have a powerful impact in shaping the daily rhythms of family life. . . .

The Value of Cultivating the Child

Educators were quite supportive of parents' efforts to cultivate their children's talents and skills through out-of-school activities. In interviews, teachers at both schools reported viewing children's organized activities as helpful:

> They all need some physical activity. I think the activities are good, because physical activity can stimulate the mind. The music lessons help with the concentration. I think that it is good to have outside activities.
>
> There is an awful lot going on in the world. The wider variety you expose them to—you never know if you have a future playwright in the group or not. It is just something that they can enjoy and participate in, even if it is not their occupation.

They just need to be aware and to talk about the different talents and occupations.

In their interactions with children, teachers also express approval, as in this fourth-grade classroom:

> [The Monday following Thanksgiving, Ms. Nettles asked the children to describe what they did for Thanksgiving.] Garrett Ballinger volunteered, "My soccer team won a tournament." Ms. Nettles says, "Your soccer team won a tournament this weekend?" Garrett nods. Ms. Nettles says, "You must be very proud."

At both schools, children's out-of-school activities routinely spill into classroom life. In Ms. Nettles' classroom, students are required to keep a journal in class. Children's activities are a common theme, as field notes from October II show:

> Five of the five boys talked about soccer games. One said that "after the game I am mad because we lose." Two of the four girls talked about playing soccer.

At Lower Richmond, Wendy Driver proudly describes her dance recital to her third-grade teacher, Ms. Green, as the children are getting ready to line up for recess. She also brought in her trophy to show Ms. Green and her classmates. Adults give organized events such as tournaments and dance recitals more weight than informal play by children, such as playing ball in the yard or watching television. When children volunteer to teachers that they watched particular television shows or that they played an informal game with cousins the previous day, teachers did not express the same level of interest or approval that they do when the children reveal their involvement in an organized activity.

Teachers also promote the concerted cultivation of their own children through a busy schedule of organized activities. Lower Richmond teacher Ms. Stanton had a daughter enrolled in a fourth-grade suburban school relatively close to Swan School. Her daughter's program of activities is similar to that of the other middle-class children in this study: art lessons, dance lessons, music lessons, Sunday school, youth church choir, and horseback riding were regular weekly events. Another third-grade teacher reported that she has all of her children enrolled in Catholic instruction (CCD), Scouts, Little League, piano lessons, and swim team.

Through their actions at home, teachers demonstrate their commitment to the logic of child rearing of concerted cultivation.

Still, teachers complain about children being overscheduled and about concerted cultivation diminishing children's school experience through exhaustion or absence. As a teacher at Swan complained:

> Soccer will take precedence over homework, regularly . . . Sometimes they would go on weekend trips. They would play soccer, would be up late, and they would be tired. I like sports, but when it interferes with what the children need to do for their academics, I think it needs to be looked at again.
>
> You can't fight City Hall. It's their child and they have a right to do it. Tommy Daniels was on three one-week vacations with his family this year. Then she [his mother] is concerned about his progress in math! Hey, keep him in school.

Teachers also support parents' efforts to develop their children's vocabulary. They all encourage parents to read to children, take children to the library, buy children books, and make sure that the children read at home. Ms. Bernstein, a fourth-grade teacher at Lower Richmond, gave her students a homework assignment of at least ten minutes of reading each night. When Ms. Stanton, who also teaches fourth grade, made a list of Christmas gifts that parents might give their children, she included books. At Swan, Ms. Nettles has a bulletin board where she lists the books that her students have read recently outside of class.

Teachers said relatively little to parents directly about the value of reasoning with children (as opposed to giving them directives). Still, there were numerous indications that educators at both Lower Richmond and Swan strongly prefer verbal interactions oriented to reasoning over directives. In their classroom interactions, these educators, like their counterparts nationwide, often use reasoning with the children, particularly in lessons. As teachers answer questions with questions[15] they seek to develop children's reasoning capacities in routine interactions. In addition, educators are generally (although not uniformly) supportive of parents' use of "time outs" as a form of discipline.

Interventions in Institutions

Teachers want parent involvement in schooling, especially parental supervision of homework. At Swan School, children must have their parents sign their homework book daily. Teachers interpret a failure to show up for a parent-teacher conference as a sign that parents do not value schooling—even though at Lower Richmond the conferences were scheduled on relatively short notice and without parents' input regarding their assigned time slot. In emphasizing parental intervention in education, these educators mirror practices common in the profession.[16] Still, educators are selective in the kind of parent involvement they prefer, as this Lower Richmond fourth-grade teacher indicates:

> An unsupportive parent is one who is antagonistic with the teacher. I've had situations like that. And it makes the job virtually impossible. If you have a problem with the child, the parent is not supportive of you or the school's position. And [then] the child is at odds with you and they fight you tooth and nail and they basically say, "I don't have to listen to you; [I] don't have to do what you say."

A third-grade teacher from Swan School uses strikingly similar terms in expressing her concern:

> [Parents have] gotten this attitude now where they question so much. The children see and hear this. Then they come to

your classroom with an attitude. Not many, but you can sure pick it up right away. Some of them are very surly. . . I think a lot of it comes from home.

Although educators want parents to offer them positive and deferential support, they also feel strongly that parents should respond to their requests for educational assistance. Ms. Bernstein is frustrated by how few parents actually read to their children:

> The [parents] want them to do well in school. They all say that they want their kids to do their homework. They always say that, but they don't know how to accomplish it in many situations . . . They want to . . . They want to. But do they ever sit down and read to their child? But they mean well.

Educators at both schools believe parents should take a leadership role in solving their children's educational problems. They complain about parents who do not take children's problems "seriously" enough to initiate contact with educators. In short, educators want contradictory behaviors from parents: deference and support, but also assertive leadership when children had educational problems.

Moreover, by law, educators are required to intervene if a family violates state standards for child rearing. Some child-rearing practices that were commonplace throughout society in earlier historical periods (e.g., vigorously beating children) are now condemned. Regardless of their personal opinion, educators are bound by the law to turn a child over to authorities if, for example, she shows up at school with red welts on her body from being disciplined. As I show in subsequent chapters, this legal requirement put working-class and poor families in the study at risk for intervention by school officials in a way that middle-class families were not.

In sum, there is a paradox in the institutions that children and their families encounter. On the one hand, there are profound differences in the quality of services provided by institutions. On the other hand, institutions accept and promote the same standards regarding cultural repertoires. Thus, teachers placed a shared emphasis on the cultivation of children's talents through organized activities, the importance of parental development of children's vocabulary, and the importance of responsive and positive parental participation in schooling. As we shall see, these standards privileged the cultural practices of middle-class families over those of their working-class and poor counterparts. This pattern made it more comfortable, and easier at times, for middle-class children and their parents to achieve their wishes.

Inequality

The differences in the quality of school life in Lower Richmond and Swan schools are part of a more general pattern of inequality in the broader society. A relatively small number of people, and institutions such as schools, in the population have considerably more assets than others. For example, across families, key resources are unequally distributed. Parents' income and wealth, educational accomplishments, and quality of work life all vary dramatically. If inequality were not a powerful force in the United States, then these coveted resources would be distributed in a much more equitable fashion.

In terms of income and wealth, the richest 10 percent of families in our society own almost 80 percent of all real estate (other than family homes), more than 90 percent of all securities (stocks and bonds) and about 60 percent of all the money in bank accounts.[17] One widely used indicator of inequality in income is the child poverty rate, a rate that is heavily dependent on social policy. (There are many more poor children in the United States than in most Western European countries.)[18] In the United States, one-fifth of all children live below the poverty level, and the figure is approximately twice as high for Black children.[19] The distribution of income and wealth became even more heavily concentrated in the hands of a few during the last decades of the twentieth century.[20] Still, during the study period, one-seventh of Black Americans were making over fifty thousand dollars annually.[21]

Educational accomplishments are also lopsided. In the United States, just under one-quarter of all adults have completed a bachelor's degree; the figure is a bit higher for individuals in their twenties. More than 10 percent of high school students drop out.[22] Even among younger people, for whom college education is becoming increasingly common, a clear majority (from two-thirds to three-quarters) do not graduate.[23] Although some studies show that, after taking into account parents' social position, Black youth are *more* likely to pursue higher education than whites, overall levels of educational attainment are far lower for Black children.[24] Substantial stratification also exists within higher education, ranging from community colleges to elite universities. The more elite the school, the more richly graduates are rewarded.[25]

Moreover there has been a profound shift in the U.S. and world economies, with a decline in "good jobs" with high wages, pensions, health benefits, and stability, and a rise in "bad jobs" with relatively low wages, no benefits, little opportunity for career promotion, and lack of stability.[26] In the lives of most people, these separate threads—their educational attainment, what kind of job they get, and how much money they earn—are all tightly interwoven. Together, these factors constitute parents' social position or social structural location.

Many studies have demonstrated that parents' social structural location has profound implications for their children's life chances. Before kindergarten, for example, children of highly educated parents are much more likely to exhibit 'educational readiness" skills, such as knowing their letters, identifying colors, counting up to twenty, and being able to write their first names.[27] Schooling helps, and during the school year the gap in children's performance narrows quite a bit (but widens again during the summer). Children of highly educated mothers continue to outperform children of less educated mothers throughout their school careers. By the time young people take the SAT examinations for admission to college, the gap is dramatic, averaging 150 points (relative to an average score of 500 points) between children of parents who are high school dropouts and those with parents who have a graduate degree.[28] There are also differences in other aspects of children's school performance according to their parents' social structural location.[29] Many studies demonstrate the crucial role of educational success in determining occupational success. Parents' social class position predicts children's school success and thus their ultimate life chances.[30]

Many people in the United States hold the view that the society is, in fundamental ways, *open*. They believe that individuals carve out their life paths by drawing on their personal stores of hard work, effort, and talent. All children are seen as having approximately equal life chances. Or, if children's life chances appear to differ, this is seen as due to differences in raw talent, initiative, aspirations, and effort. This perspective directly rebuffs the thesis that the social structural location of the family systematically shapes children's life experiences and life outcomes. Rather, the outcomes individuals achieve over the course of their lifetime are seen as their own responsibility.

A second perspective, held by some social scientists, recognizes the existence of important forms of social inequality. Differences in parents' educational levels, occupational experiences, income, and other factors are all duly noted. Yet these social scientists, such as Paul Kingston, in his book *The Classless Society,* argue that inequalities of this sort are best understood as a series of disparate patterns. In other words, these scholars adopt a *gradational* approach. They see it as helpful to focus on differences within the society as a matter of degree. Put strongly, sharply defined categories of social class are useless in understanding "life-defining experiences" within the family. In addition, Kingston and others do not believe that these gradational differences cohere across spheres. Instead, they see haphazard patterns, results here and there, but no clear, definitive, overarching pattern.[31] Kingston is joined in this approach by those who stress the lack of "class consciousness" or "class identification" on the part of those who are similarly situated within the economic domain. Taking a historical perspective,

these authors assert that "the communal aspects of class, class subcultures and milieu, have long since disappeared."[32] These social scientists are simply not persuaded that there are recognizable, categorical differences by social class.

One problem with these claims, however, is that the studies on which they draw have been fragmented and overly specialized, asking precise but small questions. In assessing the common linkages, researchers have drawn on multiple studies that they put together in an ill-fitting, jigsaw-puzzle form of explanation. What is needed is research that is less narrow. Specifically, studies are required that investigate wide swaths of social life in order to determine how social class makes a substantial difference in children's lives *and* also acknowledge those areas of life that may be largely immune to class influence. In short, we need a more holistic picture that accurately reflects both the permeability and impermeability of the home-to-class forces. And, such research needs to be conceptually guided but nonetheless open to the possibility of erring in its expectations.

In this study, the research assistants and I followed a small number of families around in an intensive fashion to get a sense of the rhythms of their everyday lives. On the basis of the data collected, I develop the claim that common economic position in the society, defined in terms of social class membership, is closely tied to differences in the cultural logic of child-rearing. Following a well-established Western European tradition, I provide a categorical analysis, grouping families into the social categories of middle class, working class, and poor. . . .[33] I see this approach as more valuable than the gradational analysis often adopted by American scholars.[34] In addition, I demonstrate that class differences in family life cut across a number of different and distinct spheres, which are usually not analyzed together by social scientists.

In particular, I delineate a pattern of concerted cultivation in middle-class families and a pattern of the accomplishment of natural growth in working-class and poor families. . . . It indicates that concerted cultivation entails an emphasis on children's structured activities, language development, language development and reasoning in the home, and active intervention in schooling. By contrast, the accomplishment of natural growth describes a form of child rearing in which children "hang out" and play, often with relatives, are given clear directives from parents with limited negotiation, and are granted more autonomy to manage their own affairs in institutions outside of the home. These patterns help us unpack the mechanisms through which social class conveys an advantage in daily life. In addressing these important issues, I have been guided heavily by the work of the late Pierre Bourdieu. . . .[35]

Despite these differences in social structural experiences, some important aspects of children's lives are *not* differentiated by class, including watching favorite television shows, having meals at fast food restaurants such as McDonald's, taking an interest in specific dolls and action figures, and eagerly anticipating Halloween and important family holidays. As I show in subsequent chapters, all parents (regardless of social class) face the task of getting children up, dressed, fed, and transported to school, and getting them medical attention when sick. Thus, some experiences are threaded through the lives of all families. Nevertheless, social class differences influence the very pace and rhythm of daily life. The next chapter, which examines the life of Garrett Ballinger, shows how middle-class parents' efforts to develop their children's talents through organized leisure activities can create a frenetic family life.

Notes

1. Choosing words to describe social groups also becomes a source of worry, especially over the possibility of reinforcing negative stereotypes. I found the available terms to describe members of racial and ethnic groups to be problematic in one way or another. The families I visited uniformly described themselves as "Black." Recognizing that some readers have strong views that Black should be capitalized, I have followed that convention, despite the lack of symmetry with the term white. In sum, this book alternates among the terms "Black," "Black American," "African American," and "white," with the understanding that "white" here refers to the subgroup of non-Hispanic whites.

2. Some readers have expressed concern that this phrase, "the accomplishment of natural growth," underemphasizes all the labor that mothers and fathers do to take care of children. They correctly note that working-class and poor parents themselves would be unlikely to use such a term to describe the process of caring for children. These concerns are important. As I stress in the text . . . it does take an enormous amount of work for parents, especially mothers, of all classes to take care of children. But poor and working-class mothers have fewer resources with which to negotiate these demands. Those whose lives the research assistants and I studied approached the task somewhat differently than did middle-class parents. They did not seem to view children's leisure time as their responsibility; nor did they see themselves as responsible for assertively intervening in their children's school experiences. Rather the working-class and poor parents carried out their chores, drew boundaries and restrictions around their children, and then, within these limits, allowed their children to carry out their lives. It is in this sense that I use the term "the accomplishment of natural growth."

3. I define a child-rearing context to include the routines of daily life, the dispositions of daily life, or the "habitués" of daily life. I focus on two contexts: concerted cultivation and the accomplishment of natural growth. In this book, I primarily use the concept of child rearing, but at times I also use the term *socialization*. Many sociologists have vigorously criticized this concept, noting that it suggests (inaccurately) that children are passive rather than active agents and that the relationship between parents and their children is unidirectional rather than reciprocal and dynamic. See, for example, William Corsair, *Sociology of Childhood;* Barrie Thorne, *Gender Play;* and Glen Elder, "The Life Course as Development Theory." Nonetheless, existing terms can, ideally, be revitalized to offer more sophisticated understandings of social processes. Child rearing and socialization have the virtue of being relatively succinct and less jargon laden than other alternatives. As a result, I use them.

4. For discussions of the role of professionals, see Eliot Freedom, *Professional Powers;* Magalia Scarlatti Larson, *The Rise of Professionalism;* and, although quite old, the still valuable collection by Amite Etienne, *The Semi-Professionals and Their Organizations.* Of course, professional standards are always contested and are subject to change over time. I do not mean to suggest there are not pockets of resistance and contestation. At the most general level, however, there is virtually uniform support for the idea that parents should talk to children at length, read to children, and take a proactive, assertive role in medical care.

5. Sharon Hays, in her 1996 book *The Cultural Contradictions of Motherhood,* studies the attitudes of middle-class and working-class mothers toward child rearing. She finds a shared commitment to "intensive mothering," although there are some differences among the women in her study in their views of punishment (with middle-class mothers leaning toward reasoning and working-class women toward physical punishment). My study focused much more on behavior than attitudes. If I looked at attitudes, I saw fewer differences; for example, all exhibited the desire to be a good mother and to have their children grow and thrive. The differences I found, however, were significant in how parents *enacted* their visions of what it meant to be a good parent.

6. See Urie Bronfenbrenner's article, "Socialization and Social Class through Time and Space."

7. Katherine Newman, *Declining Fortunes,* as well as Donald Barlett and James B. Steele, *America: What Went Wrong?* See also Michael Hout and Claude Fischer, "A Century of Inequality."

8. Some readers expressed the concern that the contrast to natural would be "unnatural," but this is not the sense in which the term *natural growth* is used here. Rather, the contrast is with words such as cultivated, artificial, artifice, or manufactured. This contrast in the logic of child rearing is a heuristic device that should not be pushed too far since, as sociologists have shown, all social life is constructed in specific social contexts. Indeed, family life has varied dramatically over time. See Philippe Aries, *Centuries of Childhood,* Herbert Gutman, *The Black Family in Slavery and Freedom, 1750–1925,* and Nancy Scheper-Hughes, *Death without Weeping.*

9. Elijah Anderson, *Code of the Street;* see especially Chapter 2.

10. For a more extensive discussion of the work of Pierre Bourdieu see the theoretical appendix; see also David Swartz's excellent book *Culture and Power.*

11. I did not study the full range of families in American society, including elite families of tremendous wealth, nor at the other end of the spectrum home-less families. In addition, I have a purposively drawn sample. Thus, I cannot state whether there are other forms of child rearing corresponding to other cultural logics. Still, data from quantitative studies based on nationally representative data support the patterns' observed. For differences by parents' social class position and children's time use, see especially Sandra Hofferth and John Sandberg, "Changes in American Children's Time, 1981–1997." Patterns of language use with children are harder to capture in national surveys, but the work of Melvin Kohn and Carmi Schooler, especially *Work and Personality,* shows differences in parents' childrearing values. Duane Alwin's studies of parents' desires are generally consistent with the results reported here. See Duane Alwin, "Trends in Parental Socialization Values." For differences in interventions in institutions, there is extensive work showing social class differences in parent involvement in education. See the U.S. Department of Education, *The Condition of Education, 2001,* p. 175.

12. In this book, unless otherwise noted, the statistics reported are from 1993 to 1995, which was when the data were collected. Similarly, unless otherwise noted, all monetary amounts are given in (unadjusted) dollars from 1994 to 1995. The figure reported here is from Everett Ladd, *Thinking about America,* pp. 21–22.

13. This quote is from President Bill Clinton's 1993 speech to the Democratic Leadership Council. It is cited in Jennifer Hochschild, *Facing Up to the American Dream,* p. 18.

14. Paul Kingston, *The Classless Society,* p. 2.

15. See especially Shirley Brice Heath, *Ways with Words.*

16. See Joyce Epstein and Mavis G. Sanders, "Connecting Home, School, and Community," as well as Annette Lareau, *Home Advantage.*

17. In this book, all statistics, unless otherwise noted, are targeted to 1993–1995 (usually 199), which was the time of data collection. William Kornblum, *Sociology: The Central Questions,* p. 159.

18. Childhood poverty has been demonstrated to predict a host of negative life outcomes,

including lower levels of health, scores on standardized tests, school grades, and emotional well-being. See Greg J. Duncan and Jeanne BrooksGunn, eds., *Consequences of Growing Up Poor.* For a comparative view of poverty rates in the United States and other industrialized countries, see Rainwater and Smeeding, "Doing Poorly."

19. See Greg J. Duncan and Jeanne Brooks-Gunn, eds., *Consequences of Growing Up Poor.* Twenty percent of all children were officially poor, but for white children the figure was 16% and for Black children it was 37%; for Black children under the age of six, 40% were poor. Lawrence Mishel, Jared Bernstein, and John Schmitt, *The State of Working America 1998–1999,* p. 281.

20. For example between 1989 and 1997 the wealth of the top fifth of the country grew by 9% while it declined by 6% for the bottom tenth of the population. Mishel et al., *The State of Working America,* p, 264. See also Michael Hout and Claude S. Fischer, "A Century of Inequality."

21. See Dalton Conley, *Being Black, Living in the Red,* and Melvin Oliver and Thomas Shapiro, *Black Wealth/White Wealth.*

22. The high school dropout rate in 1995 was 9% for whites and 12% for Black youth; by the end of the decade it had dropped slightly for white youth and increased slightly for Black youth. See U. S. Department of Education, *The Condition of Education, 2001,* p. 142.

23. In 1995, 2.8% of young people 25–29 had completed a bachelor's degree; by 2000 it had risen to 33%. There is a significant difference between the proportion of white high school graduates who eventually earn college degrees (31% in 1995, 36% in 2001) and Black high school graduates who eventually earn degrees (18% in 1995, and 21% in 2001). For the adult population as a whole, (ages 25–64) the proportion of college graduates is 2.4%. See U. S. Department of Education, *Condition of Education 1995,* pp. 245–249, and U.S. Department of Education, *Condition of Education 2001,* pp. 142, 150–151.

24. See Dalton Conley, *Being Black, Living in the Red,* as well as U. S. Department of Education, *The Condition of Education,* 2001.

25. See Derek Bok and William G. Bowen, *The Shape of the River.*

26. See Donald Barlett and James B. Steele, *America: What Went Wrong?* and Arne Kalleberg, Barbara F. Reskin, and Ken Hudson, "Bad Jobs in America."

27. For example, only 51% of children of high school dropouts can recognize the colors red, yellow, blue, and green by name, but the figures for high school graduates is 78%, for parents with some college it is 92%, and for college graduates it is 95%. For knowing all of the letters of the alphabet, the respective figures are 9%, 19%, 29%, and 42%. U. S. Department of Education, *Condition of Education 1995,* p. 182.

28. See U. S. Department of Education, *Condition of Education, 1995* and Entwhistle et al., *Children, Schools, and Inequality.* At the same level of parental education, white students generally receive higher scores than do Black students. See also Christopher Jencks and Meredith Phillips, eds., *The Black-White Test Score Gap.*

29. In 1995, 61% of high school graduates enrolled in college; for children of high school dropouts, the rate was 27%, for children of high school graduates 47%, and for children of college graduates, 88%. U. S. Department of Education, *Condition of Education, 2001,* p. 147.

30. As Paul Kingston has noted (personal communication) the relationship between parents' educational level and occupational level is far from automatic. There is a considerable amount of downward mobility. Also, there is variation among brothers and sisters in the same family. Still, parents' social class position remains one of the most powerful predictors of children's educational success life outcomes. See Paul Kingston's book *The Classless Society* for an elaboration of this position as well as Christopher Jencks et al., *Inequality,* and *Who Gets Ahead?*

31. Kingston, therefore, does *not* deny the existence of inequality: "Beyond question, huge inequalities exist and Americans recognize them." Nevertheless, in his book *The Classless Society,* he is particularly adamant in asserting that cultural habits—as manifest in family life or childrearing, for example—are not associated with different economic groups: "My thesis is that groups of people having a common economic position—what are commonly designated as 'classes'—do not significantly share distinct, life-defining experiences" (p. 1).

32. Jan Pakulski and Malcolm Waters, *The Death of Class,* p. 4.

33. For examples within this tradition see Paul Willis, *Learning to Labour,* and Basil Bernstein, *Class, Codes, and Control.*

34. It is true, of course, that people do not generally see themselves as anything but middle class. Nevertheless, I am not asserting that powerful patterns of class-consciousness exist.

35. My debt to Bourdieu is enormous, especially regarding his preoccupation in the transmission of advantage. Although some have critiqued his model of social reproduction for being overly deterministic, a close reading of his theoretical ideas makes clear that Bourdieu sees a great deal of indeterminacy in how life trajectories unfold (see Marlis Buchman's book *The Script of Life* for a particularly lucid description of Bourdieu's model). Still, there is one key way that I have parted company with Bourdieu. As Elliot Weininger has noted in his article "Class and Causation in Bourdieu," Bourdieu has a gradational (rather than categorical) conception of class structure. In addition, Bourdieu is deeply interested in fractions or divisions within a social class, an issue that space (and sample size) does not permit me to develop here.

Excerpts from *The Declining Significance of Race*

WILLIAM J. WILSON

Race relations in America have undergone fundamental changes in recent years, so much so that now the life chances of individual blacks have more to do with their economic class position than with their day-to-day encounters with whites. In earlier years the systematic efforts of whites to suppress blacks were obvious to even the most insensitive observer. Blacks were denied access to valued and scarce resources through various ingenious schemes of racial exploitation, discrimination, and segregation, schemes that were reinforced by elaborate ideologies of racism. But the situation has changed. However determinative such practices were for the previous efforts of the black population to achieve racial equality, and however significant they were in the creation of poverty-stricken ghettoes and a vast underclass of black proletarians—that massive population at the very bottom of the social class ladder plagued by poor education and low-paying, unstable jobs—they do not provide a meaningful explanation of the life chances of black Americans today. The traditional patterns of interaction between blacks and whites, particularly in the labor market, have been fundamentally altered.

In the antebellum period, and in the latter half of the nineteenth century through the first half of the twentieth century, the continuous and explicit efforts of whites to construct racial barriers profoundly affected the lives of black Americans. Racial oppression was deliberate, overt, and is easily documented, ranging from slavery to segregation, from the endeavors of the white economic elite to exploit black labor to the actions of the white masses to eliminate or neutralize black competition, particularly economic competition. As the nation has entered the latter half of the twentieth century, however, many of the traditional barriers have crumbled under the weight of the political, social, and economic changes of the civil rights era. A new set of obstacles has emerged from basic structural shifts in the economy. These obstacles are therefore impersonal but may prove to be even more formidable for certain segments of the black population. Specifically, whereas the previous barriers were usually designed to control and restrict the entire black population, the new barriers create hardships essentially for the black underclass; whereas the old barriers were based explicitly on racial motivations derived from intergroup contact, the new barriers have racial significance only in their consequences, not in their origins. In short, whereas the old barriers bore the pervasive features of racial oppression, the new barriers indicate an important and emerging form of class subordination.

It would be shortsighted to view the traditional forms of racial segregation and discrimination as having essentially disappeared in contemporary America; the presence of blacks is still firmly resisted in various institutions and social arrangements, for example, residential areas and private social clubs. However, in the economic sphere, class has become more important than race in determining black access to privilege and power. It is clearly evident in this connection that many talented and educated blacks are now entering positions of prestige and influence at a rate comparable to or, in some situations, exceeding that of whites with equivalent qualifications. It is equally clear that the black underclass is in a hopeless state of economic stagnation, falling further and further behind the rest of society.

These brief comments only serve to introduce a problem that is explored in greater detail in the rest of this book as I endeavor to interpret and explain the basis of racial change in America from a macro sociological perspective. The outlines of this perspective are presented in the remaining sections of this chapter, and they provide an analytical framework for examining the shifting areas of racial conflict and the changing experiences of American blacks.

Three Stages of American Race Relations

My basic thesis is that American society has experienced three major stages of black-white contact and that each stage embodies a different form of racial stratification structured by the particular arrangement of both the economy and the polity. Stage one coincides with antebellum slavery and the early post–bellum era and may be designated the period of *plantation economy and racial-caste oppression*. Stage two begins in the last quarter of the nineteenth century and ends at roughly the New Deal era and may be identified as the period of *industrial expansion, class conflict, and racial oppression*. Finally, stage three is associated with the modern, industrial, post–World War II era,

which really began to crystallize during the 1960s and 1970s, and may be characterized as the period of *progressive transition from racial inequalities to class inequalities*. For the sake of brevity I shall identify the different periods respectively as the preindustrial, industrial, and modern industrial stages of American race relations.

Although this abbreviated designation of the periods of American race relations seems to relate racial change to fundamental economic changes rather directly, it bears repeating that the different stages of race relations are structured by the unique arrangements and interactions of the economy and the polity. Although I stress the economic basis of structured racial inequality in the preindustrial and industrial periods of race relations, I also attempt to show how the polity more or less interacted with the economy either to reinforce patterns of racial stratification or to mediate various forms of racial conflict. Moreover, for the modern industrial period, I try to show how race relations have been shaped as much by important economic changes as by important political changes. Indeed, it would not be possible to understand fully the subtle and manifest changes in race relations in the modern industrial period without recognizing the dual and often reciprocal influence of structural changes in the economy and political changes in the state. Thus, my central argument is that different systems of production and/or different arrangements of the polity have imposed different constraints on the way in which racial groups have interacted in the United States, constraints that have structured the relations between racial groups and that have produced dissimilar contexts not only for the manifestation of racial antagonisms but also for racial group access to rewards and privileges.

In contrast to the modern industrial period in which fundamental economic and political changes have made economic class affiliation more important than race in determining Negro prospects for occupational advancement, the preindustrial and industrial periods of black-white relations have one central feature in common, namely, overt efforts of whites to solidify economic racial domination (ranging from the manipulation of black labor to the neutralization or elimination of black economic competition) through various forms of juridical, political, and social discrimination. Since racial problems during these two periods were principally related to group struggles over economic resources, they readily lend themselves to the economic class theories of racial antagonisms that associate racial antipathy with class conflict. A brief consideration of these theories, followed by a discussion of their basic weaknesses, will help to raise a number of theoretical issues that will be useful for analyzing the dynamics of racial conflict in the preindustrial and industrial stages of American race relations. However, in a later section of this chapter I shall attempt to explain why these theories are not very relevant to the modern industrial stage of American race relations.

The Influence of the System of Production

The term "system of production" not only refers to the technological basis of economic processes or, in Karl Marx's terms, the "forces of production," but it also implies the "social relations of production," that is, "the interaction (for example, through employment and property arrangement) into which men enter at a given level of the development of the forces of production." As I previously indicated, different systems of production impose constraints on racial group interaction. In the remainder of this section I should like to provide a firmer analytical basis for this distinction as it applies specifically to the three stages of American race relations, incorporating in my discussion relevant theoretical points raised in the foregoing sections of this chapter. . . .

It has repeatedly been the case that a non manufacturing or plantation economy with a simple division of labor and a small aristocracy that dominates the economic and political life of a society has characteristically generated a paternalistic rather than a competitive form of race relations, and the antebellum south was no exception.[1] Paternalistic racial patterns reveal close symbiotic relationships marked by dominance and subservience, great social distance and little physical distance, and clearly symbolized rituals of racial etiquette. The southern white aristocracy created a split labor market along racial lines by enslaving blacks to perform tasks at a cheaper cost than free laborers of the dominant group. This preindustrial form of race relations was not based on the actions of dominant-group laborers, who, as we shall see,

were relatively powerless to effect significant change in race relations during this period, but on the structure of the relations established by the aristocracy. Let me briefly amplify this point.

In the southern plantation economy, public power was overwhelmingly concentrated in the hands of the white aristocracy. This power was not only reflected in the control of economic resources and in the development of a juridical system that expressed the class interests of the aristocracy, but also in the way the aristocracy was able to impose its viewpoint on the larger society.[2] This is not to suggest that these aspects of public power have not been disproportionately controlled by the economic elite in modern industrialized Western societies; rather it indicates that the hegemony of the southern ruling elite was much greater in degree, not in kind, than in these societies. The southern elite's hegemony was embodied in an economy that required little horizontal or vertical mobility. Further, because of the absence of those gradations of labor power associated with complex divisions of labor, white workers in the antebellum and early post bellum south had little opportunity to challenge the control of the aristocracy. Because white laborers lacked power resources in the southern plantation economy, their influence on the form and quality of racial stratification was minimal throughout the antebellum and early postbellum periods. Racial stratification therefore primarily reflected the relationships established between blacks and the white aristocracy, relationships which were not characterized by competition for scarce resources but by the exploitation of black labor.[3] Social distance tended to be clearly symbolized by rituals of racial etiquette: gestures and behavior reflecting dominance and subservience. Consequently, any effort to impose a system of public segregation was superfluous. Furthermore, since the social gap between the aristocracy and black slaves was wide and stable, ideologies of racism played less of a role in the subordination of blacks than they subsequently did in the more competitive systems of race relations following the Civil War. In short, the relationship represented intergroup paternalism because it allowed for "close symbiosis and even intimacy without any threat to status inequalities."[4] This was in sharp contrast to the more competitive forms of race relations that accompanied the development of industrial capitalism in the late nineteenth century and first few decades of the twentieth century (the industrial period of American race relations), wherein the complex division of labor and opportunities for greater mobility not only produced interaction, competition, and labor-market conflict between blacks and the white working class, but also provided the latter with superior resources (relative to those they possessed under the plantation economy) to exert greater influence on the form and content of racial stratification.

The importance of the system of production in understanding race relations is seen in a comparison of Brazil and the southern United States during the postslavery periods. In the United States, the southern economy experienced a fairly rapid rate of expansion during the late nineteenth century, thereby creating various middle level skilled and unskilled positions that working-class whites attempted to monopolize for themselves. The efforts of white workers to eliminate black competition in the south generated an elaborate system of Jim Crow segregation that was reinforced by an ideology of biological racism. The white working class was aided not only by its numerical size, but also by its increasing accumulation of political resources that accompanied changes in its relation to the means of production.

As white workers gradually translated their increasing labor power into political power, blacks experienced greater restrictions in their efforts to achieve a satisfactory economic, political, and social life. In Brazil, on the other hand, the large Negro and mulatto population was not thrust into competition with the much smaller white population over access to higher-status positions because, as Marvin Harris notes, "there was little opportunity for any member of the lower class to move upward in the social hierarchy."[5] No economic-class group or racial group had much to gain by instituting a rigid system of racial segregation or cultivating an ideology of racial inferiority. Racial distinctions were insignificant to the landed aristocracy, who constituted a numerically small upper class in what was basically a sharply differentiated two-class society originally shaped during slavery. The mulattoes, Negroes, and poor whites were all in the same impoverished lower-ranking position. "The general economic stagnation which has been characteristic of lowland Latin America since the abolition of slavery," observes Marvin Harris, "tends to reinforce the pattern of pacific relationships among the various racial groups in the lower ranking levels of the social hierarchy. Not only were the poor whites outnumbered by the mulattoes and Negroes, but there was little of a significant material nature to struggle over in view of the generally static condition of the economy."[6] Accordingly, in Brazil, segregation, discrimination, and racist ideologies failed to crystallize in the first several decades following the end of slavery. More recently, however, industrialization has pushed Brazil toward a competitive type of race relations, particularly the southern region (for example, São Paulo) which has experienced rapid industrialization and has blacks in economic competition with many lower-status white immigrants.[7]

Whereas the racial antagonism in the United States during the period of industrial race relations (such as the Jim Crow segregation movement in the South and the race riots in northern cities) tended to be either directly or indirectly related to labor-market conflicts, racial antagonism in the period of modern industrial relations tends to originate outside the economic order and to have little connection with labor-market strife. Basic changes in the system of production have produced a segmented labor structure in which blacks are either isolated in the relatively nonunionized, low-paying, basically undesirable jobs of the non–corporate sector, or occupy the higher-paying corporate and government industry positions in which job competition is either controlled by powerful unions or is restricted to the highly trained and educated, regardless of race. If there is a basis for labor-market conflict in the modern industrial period, it is most probably related to the affirmative action programs originating from the civil rights legislation of the 1960s. However, since affirmative action programs are designed to improve job opportunities for the talented and educated, their major impact has been in the higher-paying jobs of the expanding government sector and the corporate sector. The sharp increase of the more privileged blacks in these industries has been facilitated by the combination of affirmative action and rapid industry growth. Indeed despite the effectiveness of affirmative action programs the very expansion of these sectors of the economy has kept racial friction over higher-paying corporate and government jobs to a minimum.

Unlike the occupational success achieved by the more talented and educated blacks, those in the black underclass find themselves locked in the low-paying and dead-end jobs of the non-corporate industries, jobs which are not in high demand and which therefore do not generate racial competition or strife among the national black and white labor force. Many of these jobs go unfilled, and employers often have to turn to cheap labor from Mexico and Puerto Rico. As Nathan Glazer has pointed out, "Expectations have changed, and fewer blacks and whites today will accept a life at menial labor with no hope for advancement, as their fathers and older brothers did and as European immigrants did."[8]

Thus in the modern industrial era neither the corporate or government sectors nor the non corporate low-wage sector provide the basis for the kind of interracial competition and conflict that has traditionally plagued the labor market in the United States. This, then, is the basis for my earlier contention that the economic class theories which associate labor-market conflicts with racial antagonism have little application to the present period of modern industrial race relations.

The Polity and American Race Relations

If the patterned ways in which racial groups have interacted historically have been shaped in major measure by different systems of production, they have also been undeniably influenced by the changing policies and laws of the state. For analytical purposes, it would be a mistake to treat the influences of the polity and the economy as if they were separate and unrelated. The legal and political systems in the antebellum South were effectively used as instruments of the slaveholding elite to strengthen and legitimate the institution of slavery. But as industrialization altered the economic class structure in the postbellum South, the organizing power and political consciousness of the white lower class increased and its members were able to gain enough control of the political and juridical

systems to legalize a new system of racial domination, (Jim Crow segregation) that clearly reflected their class interests.

In effect, throughout the preindustrial period of race relations and the greater portion of the industrial period the role of the polity was to legitimate, reinforce, and regulate patterns of racial inequality. However, it would be unwarranted to assume that the relationship between the economic and political aspects of race necessarily implies that the latter is simply a derivative phenomenon based on the more fundamental processes of the former. The increasing intervention, since the mid-twentieth century, of state and federal government agencies in resolving or mediating racial conflicts has convincingly demonstrated the political system's autonomy in handling contemporary racial problems. Instead of merely formalizing existing racial alignments as in previous periods, the political system has, since the initial state and municipal legislation of the 1940s, increasingly created changes leading to the erosion of traditional racial alignments; in other words, instead of reinforcing racial barriers created during the preindustrial and industrial periods, the political system in recent years has tended to promote racial equality.

Thus, in the previous periods the polity was quite clearly an instrument of the white population in suppressing blacks. The government's racial practices varied, as I indicated above, depending on which segment of the white population was able to assert its class interests. However, in the past two decades interests of the black population have been significantly reflected in the racial policies of the government, and this change is one of the clearest indications that the racial balance of power had been significantly altered. Since the early 1940s the black population has steadily gained political resources and, with the help of sympathetic white allies, has shown an increasing tendency to utilize these resources in promoting or protecting its group interests.

By the mid-twentieth century the black vote had proved to be a major vehicle for political pressure. The black vote not only influenced the outcome of national elections but many congressional, state, and municipal elections as well. Fear of the Negro vote produced enactment of public accommodation and fair employment practices laws in northern and western municipalities and states prior to the passage of federal civil rights legislation in 1964. This political resurgence for black Americans increased their sense of power, raised their expectations, and provided the foundation for the proliferation of demands which shaped the black revolt during the 1960s. But there were other factors that helped to buttress Negro demands and contributed to the developing sense of power and rising expectations, namely, a growing, politically active black middle class following World War II and the emergence of the newly independent African states.

The growth of the black middle class was concurrent with the growth of the black urban population. It was in the urban areas, with their expanding occupational opportunities, that a small but significant number of blacks were able to upgrade their occupations, increase their income, and improve their standard of living. The middle-class segment of an oppressed minority is most likely to participate in a drive for social justice that is disciplined and sustained. In the early phases of the civil rights movement, the black middle class channeled its energies through organizations such as the National Association for the Advancement of Colored People, which emphasized developing political resources and successful litigation through the courts. These developments were paralleled by the attack against traditional racial alignments in other parts of the world. The emerging newly independent African states led the assault. In America, the so-called "leader of the free world," the manifestation of racial tension and violence has been a constant source of embarrassment to national government officials. This sensitivity to world opinion made the national government more vulnerable to pressures of black protest at the very time when blacks had the greatest propensity to protest.

The development of black political resources that made the government more sensitive to Negro demands, the motivation and morale of the growing black middle class that resulted in the political drive for racial equality, and the emergence of the newly independent African states that increased the federal government's vulnerability to civil rights pressures all combined to create a new sense of power among black Americans and to raise their expectations as they prepared to enter the explosive decade of the 1960s. The national government

was also aware of this developing sense of power and responded to the pressures of black protest in the 1960s with an unprecedented series of legislative enactments to protect black civil rights.

The problem for blacks today, in terms of government practices, is no longer one of legalized racial inequality. Rather the problem for blacks, especially the black underclass, is that the government is not organized to deal with the new barriers imposed by structural changes in the economy. With the passage of equal employment legislation and the authorization of affirmative action programs the government has helped clear the path for more privileged blacks, who have the requisite education and training, to enter the mainstream of American occupations. However, such government programs do not confront the impersonal economic barriers confronting members of the black underclass, who have been effectively screened out of the corporate and government industries. And the very attempts of the government to eliminate traditional racial barriers through such programs as affirmative action have had the unintentional effect of contributing to the growing economic class divisions within the black community.

Class Stratification and Changing Black Experiences

The problems of black Americans have always been compounded because of their low position in both the economic order (the average economic class position of blacks as a group) and the social order (the social prestige or honor accorded individual blacks because of their ascribed racial status). It is of course true that the low economic position of blacks has helped to shape the categorical social definitions attached to blacks as a racial group, but it is also true that the more blacks become segmented in terms of economic class position, the more their concerns about the social significance of race will vary.

In the preindustrial period of American race relations there was of course very little variation in the economic class position of blacks. The system of racial caste oppression relegated virtually all blacks to the bottom of the economic class hierarchy. Moreover, the social definitions of racial differences were heavily influenced by the ideology of racism and the doctrine of paternalism, both of which clearly assigned a subordinate status for blacks vis-à-vis whites. Occasionally, a few individual free blacks would emerge and accumulate some wealth or property, but they were the overwhelming exception. Thus the uniformly low economic class position of blacks reinforced and, in the eyes of most whites, substantiated the social definitions that asserted Negroes were culturally and biogenetically inferior to whites. The uniformly low economic class position of blacks also removed the basis for any meaningful distinction between race issues and class issues within the black community.

The development of a black middle class accompanied the Change from a preindustrial to an industrial system of production. Still, despite the fact that some blacks were able to upgrade their occupation and increase their education and income, there were severe limits on the areas in which blacks could in fact advance. Throughout most of the industrial period of race relations, the growth of the black middle class occurred because of the expansion of institutions created to serve the needs of a growing urbanized black population. The black doctor, lawyer, teacher, minister, businessman, mortician, excluded from the white community, was able to create a niche in the segregated black community. Although the income levels and life-styles of the black professionals were noticeably and sometimes conspicuously different from those of the black masses, the two groups had one basic thing in common, a racial status contemptuously regarded by most whites in society. If E. Franklin Frazier's analysis of the black *bourgeoisie* is correct, the black professionals throughout the industrial period of American race relations tended to react to their low position in the social order by an ostentatious display of material possessions and a conspicuous effort to disassociate themselves from the black masses.[9]

Still, as long as the members of the black middle class were stigmatized by their racial status; as long as they were denied the social recognition accorded their white counterparts; more concretely, as long as they remained restricted in where they could live, work, socialize, and be educated, race would continue to be a far more salient and important issue in shaping their sense of group position than their economic class position. Indeed, it was the black middle class that provided the leadership and generated the momentum for the civil rights movement during the mid-twentieth century. The influence and interests of this class were clearly reflected in the way the race issues were defined and articulated. Thus, the concept of "freedom" quite clearly implied, in the early stages of the movement, the right to swim in certain swimming pools, to eat in certain restaurants, to attend certain movie theaters, and to have the same voting privileges as whites. These basic concerns were reflected in the 1964 Civil Rights Bill which helped to create the illusion that, when the needs of the black middle class were met, so were the needs of the entire black community.

However, although the civil rights movement initially failed to address the basic needs of the members of the black lower class, it did increase their awareness of racial oppression, heighten their expectations about improving race relations, and increase their impatience with existing racial arrangements. These feelings were dramatically manifested in a series of violent ghetto outbursts that rocked the nation throughout the late 1960s. These outbreaks constituted the most massive and sustained expression of lower-class black dissatisfaction in the nation's history. They also forced the political system to recognize the problems of human survival and de facto segregation in the nation's ghettoes—problems pertaining to unemployment and underemployment, inferior ghetto schools, and deteriorated housing.

However, in the period of modern industrial race relations, it would be difficult indeed to comprehend the plight of inner-city blacks by exclusively focusing on racial discrimination. For in a very real sense, the current problems of lower-class blacks are substantially related to fundamental structural changes in the economy. A history of discrimination and oppression created a huge black underclass, and the technological and economic revolutions have combined to ensure it a permanent status.

As the black middle class rides on the wave of political and social changes, benefiting from the growth of employment opportunities in the growing corporate and government sectors of the economy, the black underclass falls behind the larger society in every conceivable respect. The economic and political systems in the United States have demonstrated remarkable flexibility in allowing talented blacks to fill positions of prestige and influence at the same time that these systems have shown persistent rigidity in handling the problems of lower-class blacks. As a result, for the first time in American history class issues can meaningfully compete with race issues in the way blacks develop or maintain a sense of group position.[10]

Conclusion

I have tried to show that race relations in American society have been historically characterized by three major stages and that each stage is represented by a unique form of racial interaction which is shaped by the particular arrangement of the economy and the polity. My central argument is that different systems of production and/or different policies of the state have imposed different constraints on the way in which racial groups interact—constraints that have structured the relations between racial groups and produced dissimilar contexts not only for the manifestation of racial antagonisms but also for racial-group access to rewards and privileges. I emphasized in this connection that in the preindustrial and industrial periods of American race relations the systems of production primarily shaped the patterns of racial stratification and the role of the polity was to legitimate, reinforce, or regulate these patterns. In the modern industrial period, however, both the system of production and the polity assume major importance in creating new patterns of race relations and in altering the context of racial strife. Whereas the preindustrial and industrial stages were principally related to group struggles over economic resources as different segments of the white population overtly sought to create and solidify economic racial domination (ranging from the exploitation of black labor in the preindustrial period to the elimination of black competition for jobs in the industrial period) through various forms of political, juridical, and social discrimination; in the modern industrial period fundamental economic and political changes have made economic class position more important than race in determining black chances for occupational mobility. Finally, I

have outlined the importance of racial norms or belief systems, especially as they relate to the general problem of race and class conflict in the preindustrial and industrial periods.

My argument that race relations in America have moved from economic racial oppression to a form of class subordination for the less privileged blacks is not meant to suggest that racial conflicts have disappeared or have even been substantially reduced. On the contrary, the basis of such conflicts have shifted from the economic sector to the sociopolitical order and therefore do not play as great a role in determining the life chances of individual black Americans as in the previous periods of overt economic racial oppression. . . .

Notes

1. Pierre L. van den Berghe, *Race and Racism: A Comparative Perspective* (New York: John Wiley and Sons, 1967), p. 26.
2. See, for example, Genovese, *Roll, Jordan, Roll.*
3. An exception to this pattern occurred in the cities of the antebellum South, where nonslaveholding whites played a major role in the development of urban segregation. However, since an overwhelming majority of the population resided in rural areas, race relations in the antebellum southern cities were hardly representative of the region. . . .
4. van den Berghe, *Race and Racism,* p. 27.
5. Marvin Harris, *Patterns of Race in the Americas* (New York: Walker, 1964), p. 96.
6. *Ibid.,* p. 96.
7. van den Berghe, *Race and Racism*, p. 28.
8. Nathan Glazer, "Blacks and Ethnic Groups: The Difference, and the Political Difference It Makes," in *Key Issues in the Afro-American Experience,* ed. Nathan I. Huggins, Martin Kilson, and Daniel M. Fox (New York: Harcourt Brace Jovanovich, 1971), 2: 209.
9. E. Franklin Frazier, *Black Bourgeoisie* (New York: The Free Press, 1957). See also Nathan Hare, Black Anglo-Saxons (New York: Collier, 1965).
10. The theoretical implications of this development for ethnic groups in general are discussed by Milton Gordon under the concept "ethclass." See Milton M. Gordon, *Assimilation in American Life* (New York: Oxford University Press, 1964).

"Poverty in the United States: An Overview"

CLIFF BROWN

Poverty brings the plight of America's economically marginalized into sharp focus: the poor experience myriad disadvantages, including physical and psychological distress, lower educational attainment, tenuous housing situations, discontinuous employment, diminished personal safety, and limited access to childcare (Bianchi 1999: 326–28; Iceland 2003: 2–3). For instance, 17.6 percent of children living in poverty lack any type of private or government-provided health insurance compared to 11 percent of children overall (DeNavas-Walt, Proctor, and Smith 2008: 24). Women in poverty are disproportionately victims of domestic violence; both the frequency and severity of that violence are inversely related to women's economic resources (Kurz 1999: 135–36). Maintaining a healthy diet can be problematic for the poor, and poor mothers have about twice the rate of low-weight and preterm births as non-poor mothers (Federman et al. 1996: 9–10). Those in poverty are less likely to own many of the material possessions that wealthier Americans take for granted, including homes, vehicles, household appliances, and personal computers (Federman et al. 1996; Iceland 2003: 45–47). These deprivations are consequences of poverty, but their combined effects also impede upward mobility. Improving one's life chances through employment or education, for example, is especially difficult for those suffering from abuse, struggling with untreated health problems, or lacking reliable access to transportation, quality education, childcare, or the Internet. Because these disadvantages impinge on one's ability to cast a ballot or stay politically engaged, poverty also presents a threat to full citizenship (American National Election Studies 2005; Kerbo 2003: 238–40; Mink 2002: 11–12). Thus, individuals who fall below the poverty level are among the most vulnerable and distressed in the United States.

In an effort to promote basic sociological literacy on the subject of poverty, this chapter presents some key facts about the nature, extent, and measurement of poverty in the United States. It provides an introduction to the literature and empirical evidence concerning poverty and the poor, and drawing on these sources, it makes two interrelated claims. First, an aggregate measure like the overall poverty rate obscures the fact that the likelihood of experiencing poverty is unequally distributed across social groups. Although most people generally appreciate this, popular conceptualizations of poverty and the poor are not always well-grounded in empirical or conceptual terms. This chapter shows the extent to which a host of factors—including race, ethnicity, family structure, sex, age, and geography—are linked to poverty, and it makes an attempt to dramatize their cumulative impacts on economic well-being. Second, and as an extension of the first point, the fact that the circumstances of one's birth so clearly affect the odds of experiencing poverty contradicts the notion that all Americans have an equal chance to succeed in life. Our beliefs about poverty and the poor help us to manage that contradiction by explaining economic disadvantage as a consequence of individual choices (Kerbo 2003: 263–68, 427–29; Quadagno 1996: 17–19, 194–95; Wilson 1997: 158–64). Core American values that stress the importance of individual freedom shape the social construction of poverty and do the ideological work of reconciling the plight of the poor with cherished egalitarian ideals.

Who Lives in Poverty?

About 12.5 percent of the U.S. population—more than 37 million people—live below the poverty line (DeNavas-Walt, Proctor, and Smith 2008: 12).

This fact simultaneously reveals and obscures much about social stratification. On one hand, it tells us that the vast majority of the population does not live in poverty. Without further reflection, this may imply that opportunities for success are widespread and stratification is fairly limited in American society. To the extent that we are concerned about poverty as a social problem, changes in the poverty rate over time also suggest that the United States has made strides to minimize its impact. Figure 10.1 shows that after dropping from about 22 percent at the beginning of the 1960s, the proportion of individuals living in poverty has fluctuated between 11 and 15 percent since 1973 and has been fairly stable since 2000 (DeNavas-Walt, Proctor, and Smith 2008: 12; Glasmeier 2006: 1–3). Thus, the 1960s witnessed a steep decline in the overall poverty rate that has been more or less sustained to the present.

On the other hand, the proportion of the population living below the poverty level constitutes a sizable share of the U.S. population. Although the distinction between the poor and the non-poor would seem to constitute a major threshold of disadvantage, it also obscures the full range of economic deprivation within the ranks of the

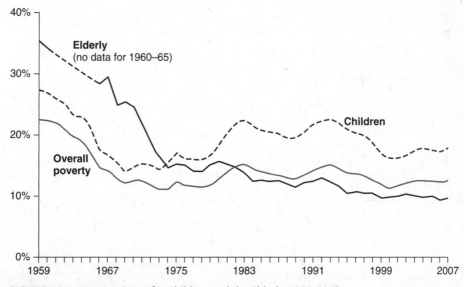

FIGURE 10.1 Poverty Rates for Children and the Elderly, 1959–2007.

Source: Based on DeNavas-Walt, Proctor, and Smith 2008, Tables B-I and B-2.

poor. Toward the bottom of that spectrum are more than 15 million people, or slightly more than 5 percent of the U.S. population, whose incomes are less than one-half their respective poverty levels. For a family of four in 2008, this degree of "deep poverty" would mean surviving on an annual income of less than $11,000 (U.S. Bureau of the Census 2009a). There has long been debate about how to determine who is poor, but because official definitions of poverty affect access to benefits and determine eligibility for social programs, how the federal government establishes poverty thresholds has profound consequences for the well-being of those occupying the lower rungs of the socioeconomic ladder.

The overall poverty rate also conceals significant group-level differences in economic vulnerability: the probability of being poor is much greater for some groups than for others. Which members of society are most vulnerable? In short, poverty tends to be concentrated among children, female-headed families, racial and ethnic minority groups, and regionally, in the southern United States. While overall poverty has declined since the early 1960s, success in combating poverty has

been more dramatic and sustained for adults, and particularly for older adults, than for children. Children under the age of 18 are more likely to live in poverty (18 percent of all children) than adults under the age of 65 (10.9 percent) or elderly adults (9.7 percent), and long-term reductions in child poverty were temporarily offset by significant increases between 1979 and 1993. In contrast, the decline in poverty for the elderly has been striking in terms of its extent and duration: today's poverty rate for elderly adults is approximately one-third the level experienced in the mid-1960s, and as Figure 10.1 shows, children have replaced the elderly as the most vulnerable age group. Nearly 8 percent of all children fall below one-half of their respective poverty thresholds (DeNavas-Walt, Proctor, and Smith 2008: 12–16; Iceland 2003: 43–44; Glasmeier 2006: 2). Because those under 18 cannot be held accountable for their parents' decisions or economic circumstances, it seems particularly unfair that so many children are subjected to the experience of poverty during their formative years.

Family structure is also closely linked to poverty (Figure 10.2). Families headed by females

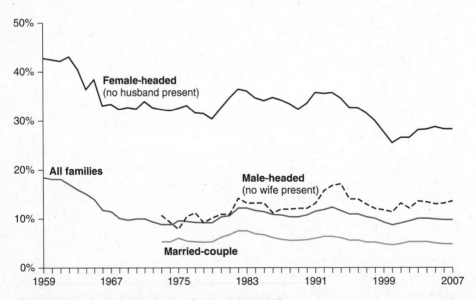

FIGURE 10.2 Poverty Rates by Family Type, 1959–2007.

Source: Based on DeNavas-Walt Proctor, and Smith 2008, Table B-3.

with no husband present are far more likely to experience poverty (28.3 percent) than married-couple families (4.9 percent) or male-headed families (13.2 percent) with no wife present (DeNavas-Walt, Proctor, and Smith 2008: 15). The dramatic growth since 1959 of female-headed families as a proportion of all families helps to explain the plight of poor children and is symptomatic of the tendency for poverty to become concentrated among women, also known as the feminization of poverty (Pearce 1978; also see Bianchi 1999). Single parents face significant challenges in supporting their families on one income, and this may be complicated by lower educational levels and day care costs. For women, these disadvantages may be further exacerbated by earnings discrepancies (discussed below), occupational segregation, and insufficient child support from absent fathers (Iceland 2003: 87–92).

Race and ethnicity are related to poverty and are closely bound to perceptions and stereotypes about the poor (Quadagno 1996). Numerically, non-Hispanic whites constitute the largest group (16 million people) in poverty. As mentioned above, a large share of the poor (nearly 42 percent)

has income that that is less than one-half of their federal poverty thresholds.

Over 4.2 million blacks (more than 10 percent) experience deep poverty by this standard; blacks and Hispanics are more than twice as likely as non-Hispanic whites to fall into this extremely disadvantaged group. Although non-Hispanic whites outnumber other groups among the poor, their poverty rate (8.2 percent) is lower than for blacks (24.5 percent), Hispanics (21.5 percent), or Asians (10.2 percent). Thus, Figure 10.3 shows that the majority of the poor are white, but as Figure 10.4 indicates, members of minority groups are more likely than whites to experience poverty (DeNavas-Walt, Proctor, and Smith 2008: 12–16; Glasmeier 2006: 14; Kerbo 2003: 262).

The reasons for these group-level disparities are complex, but they are linked to public policy outcomes, demographic changes, shifts in the economy, and lingering gaps in education, employment, and wealth that have both historical roots and contemporary causes (Glasmeier 2006; Iceland 2003). For instance, the federal government initiated

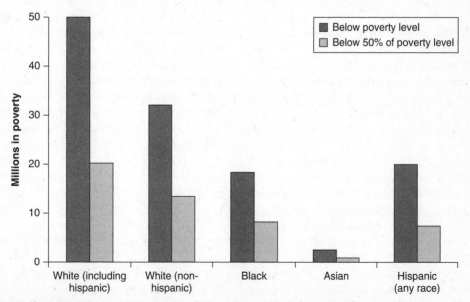

FIGURE 10.3 People in Poverty by Race and Hispanic Origin, 2007. Racial categories are for those reporting a single race.

Source: Based on DeNavas-Walt, Proctor, and Smith 2008, Tables 3 and 4.

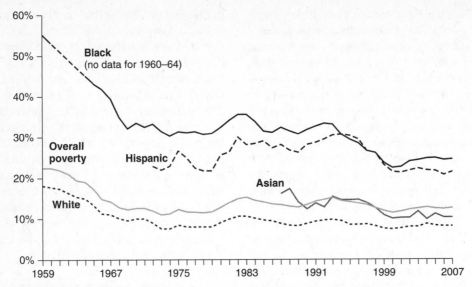

FIGURE 10.4 Poverty Rates by Race and Hispanic Origin, 1959–2007. "White" is for non-Hispanic whites from 1973–2007 but may include Hispanics from 1959–72.

Source: Based on DeNavas-Walt, Proctor, and Smith 2008, Table B-1.

far-reaching efforts to reduce poverty during the Johnson Administration of the 1960s. These efforts included Medicare, Medicaid, and expanded Social Security benefits that dramatically improved welfare of the elderly (Glasmeier 2006: 23; Kerbo 2003: 260; Marger 2008: 149). For non-elderly adults (and by extension, their children), changes in welfare policy in concert with shifting employment patterns have affected individuals' and families' economic prospects. Gender disparities in poverty result in part from a persistent wage gap that makes female-headed families especially vulnerable. Among full-time, year-round workers, women earn about 78 cents for every dollar paid to men (DeNavas-Walt, Proctor, and Smith 2008: 11). Women's earnings are also lower within educational categories. Among full-time employees whose highest educational credential was a bachelor's degree, women's median earnings are $20,000 lower than men's (U.S. Bureau of the Census 2008). Racial and ethnic disparities are a consequence of lingering gaps in education, employment, and wealth that have both historical roots and contemporary causes (Glasmeier 2006: 14–22; Massey and Denton 1994; Oliver and Shapiro 1995; Shapiro 2004; Wilson 1987, 1997).

The distribution of wealth in the United States is particularly unequal, and because levels of familial wealth shape the opportunities that parents can pass along to their children, members of groups that have tended to be poor in the past are prone to poverty in the present. In this regard, it is important to distinguish income—a flow of money derived from salaries, wages, interest, dividends, or government payments—from wealth—a stock of resources derived from the value of property, business assets, or other financial investments (Keister 2005: 5; Oliver and Shapiro 1995: 2). Since the early 1960s, the proportion of all wealth going to the wealthiest 1 percent has ranged from about 33 percent to nearly 40 percent, and the top 20 percent receives over 80 percent of the total wealth. In contrast, the bottom 40 percent receives only about 0.2 to 0.3 percent of all wealth in the United States (Keister 2005: 16–17; Wolff 2007: 11). Wealth inequality has a significant racial dimension that helps to account for the differential poverty rates depicted in Figure 10.4 (Conley 1999; Oliver and Shapiro 1995; Shapiro 2004). At every level of income, blacks and Hispanics have significantly less wealth than whites, and in 2004, whites had ten times the median wealth of blacks and twenty times the median wealth of Hispanics (Wolff

2007: 27–29). As a stock of resources, wealth buffers periods of economic hardship and may enable families to seize emerging opportunities during times of economic growth. Families that are wealth-poor lack the same ability to absorb economic setbacks associated with job loss or health crises, and thus are more likely to become poor, and because limited wealth diminishes their ability to invest in higher education, entrepreneurship, or home ownership, they are more likely to stay poor. Conley (1999: 128–29) finds that among low-income families, parental wealth is a significant predictor of subsequent welfare dependency by children.

The groups that are more likely to experience poverty are not randomly distributed across the United States, and some areas of the country are characterized by low educational attainment, limited employment opportunities, and stagnant local economies. As a result, poverty is deeply inscribed in geography, as shown in Figure 10.5. Poverty is prevalent in the South, particularly in the Mississippi Delta region that spans much of Mississippi, Louisiana, and Arkansas, as well as in the "Black Belt" counties that arc eastward from the Delta through Alabama, Georgia, and into the Carolinas. Deep and persistent poverty is one legacy of the racially oppressive agricultural practices that have shaped the economy and social relations in this part of the United States (Duncan 1999; Glasmeier 2006: 56–61). Nearly one-third of Native Americans on tribal or reservation lands live below the poverty level. The concentration of poverty in parts of Arizona, New Mexico, Utah, the Dakotas, Montana, and other states with significant Native American populations reflects this fact. In the counties along the Mexican border that employ many immigrants in low-wage manufacturing and agricultural work, poverty is often high as well (Glasmeier 2006: 62, 66).

Historically, rural communities have been prone to poverty as a consequence of declining regional economies and steady out-migration, although more recent suburbanization in some parts of the nation has reversed these trends, particularly in the South (Duncan 1999; Glasmeier 2006: 70–71). Poverty remains entrenched in

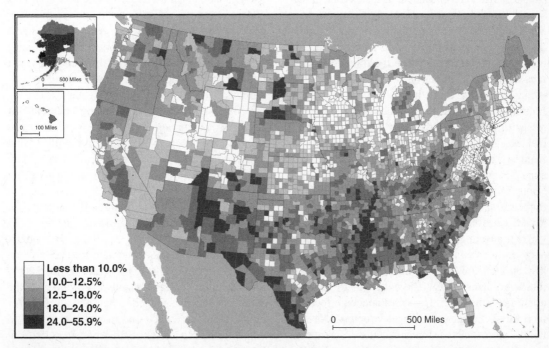

FIGURE 10.5   Percent in Poverty by County, 2007. Map by C. Brown; data from U.S. Census Bureau, Small Areas Estimates Branch (http://www.census.gov//did/www/sajpe/data/statecounty/data/2007.html).

many of the remote Appalachian communities that have relied for generations on coal mining and manufacturing. Appalachian poverty is particularly concentrated in southern Ohio, West Virginia, Kentucky, eastern Virginia, and eastern Tennessee, areas of the country that have been acutely affected by the nation's loss of manufacturing jobs (Duncan 1999; Glasmeier 2006: 52–53).

How Do Americans Think about Poverty?

Since the early 1960s, the federal government has defined poverty based on income (Haveman 2008). The U.S. Census Bureau measures poverty based on family size, age composition, and the cost of necessities such as food and housing. The thresholds are revised annually in accordance with changes in the Consumer Price Index (DeNavas-Walt, Proctor, and Smith 2008: 45; Marger 2008: 144). For instance, in 2008, the poverty level for a single person under age 65 was $11,201 per year. For a two-person family (both under 65 years old) without children, the level is $14,840 annually; for a two-person family with two children, the annual amount rises to $21,834 (U.S. Bureau of the Census 2009). The U.S. Department of Health and Human Services (2009) has developed a similar measure that is used to determine eligibility for certain governmental programs. Because these federal measures shape data gathering and affect access to public welfare programs and other benefits, they play an important role in helping to construct a societal image of poverty and the poor. However, the official income-based measure of poverty has been criticized for a number of reasons. First, it does not consider non-cash benefits (e.g., public housing, Food Stamps, or Medicaid), families' tax liabilities, or their wealth, all of which have a direct bearing on material well-being. Second, the current approach uses an absolute measure that does not take into account how a family's income compares to the average standard of living in a particular region or in society as a whole. The extent of this gap, it could be argued, will have pronounced effects on how families experience poverty: being poor in a middle class society is fundamentally different than being poor in a society of millionaires. Alternate measures of poverty might include factors beyond income, such as wealth, earnings capacity, consumption, or other indicators (see Haveman 2008). Third, the current measure assumes that food costs constitute about one-third of families' expenditures. Over time, the cost of housing, utilities, transportation, child care, and medical care have increased relative to food expenditures, and as a result, critics assert that the current measure grossly underestimates the extent of poverty (Glasmeier 2006: xv; Haveman 2008; Kerbo 2003: 254–55; also see Iceland 2003: 20–32).

Defining the poverty level is more than a statistical exercise. Those living in poverty are also heavily stigmatized, especially when widely shared assumptions concerning equal opportunity meet American cultural ideals emphasizing success, individualism, and personal responsibility (Gans 1996; Kerbo 2003: 263–68). One consequence is that Americans tend to hold the poor responsible for their poverty (Kerbo 2003: 263, 428). This tendency is evident in survey data that tap into Americans' beliefs about poverty, opportunity, and social mobility in the United States. For instance, on the General Social Survey (GSS) respondents are more likely to rate "loose morals and drunkenness" as very important for explaining poverty (39.8 percent) than "not enough jobs" (36.6 percent) or "poor schools" (37.7 percent) (Davis and Smith 2007). The differences are not large, but they do underscore the tendency to emphasize individual failings when explaining poverty. A sizable majority—over 75 percent—of GSS respondents agree that differences in social standing are acceptable because they reflect what people make of their opportunities in life, and an even larger proportion—85 percent—agree that American society is open and that achievement results from abilities and education rather than family background. Nearly 45 percent of GSS respondents disagree that it is the government's responsibility to reduce income differences, while only 32 percent agree (Davis and Smith 2007). The idea that society presents everyone with the same chance to succeed undercuts support for government assistance and makes it tempting to conclude that the plight of the poor results from bad choices, an underdeveloped work ethic, or other innate deficiencies in intellect or ability.

Despite the perception that the poor are largely responsible for their plight, it is increasingly true that the experience of poverty coexists with full-time employment. Full-time, year-round workers have constituted approximately 11 to 12.5 percent of the poor for the last decade, a fact that dramatizes the rise of the working poor and the deterioration of wages for those near the bottom of the employment ladder. In 1978, less than eight percent of the poor were employed full-time (Glasmeier 2006: 26; U.S. Bureau of the Census 2008b). This suggests that poverty cannot be adequately explained without focusing on the economy, which must provide a larger share of better-paying jobs in order to reduce poverty levels. Although individual-level explanations may have relevance in particular cases, applying them comprehensively diverts attention from the structural and institutional features of society that affect the extent of poverty and influence its unequal distribution across social groups.

To underscore the extent to which the cumulative effects of race, geography, and family structure affect individuals' starting points, consider the following contrast. In Mississippi, 16.6 percent of all families live in poverty; Leflore County, one of the poorest counties in the United States, is situated in the heart of the Delta region of Mississippi and has a population that is over 70 percent black. In Leflore, mean household income is approximately $24,500 annually, and just over 37 percent of all families live in poverty. However, family poverty in Leflore climbs to 49.5 percent for families with children and jumps to 68.6 percent for female-headed families with children. In Colorado, 11.5 percent of all families live in poverty; Douglas County, one of the richest counties in the United States, is situated near Denver and has a population that is nearly 93 percent white. In Douglas, mean household income is approximately $94,000 annually, and less than two percent of all families live in poverty. For married-couple families, the rate of poverty is one percent, and for female-headed families with children, the rate of poverty in Douglas is 14.9 percent (U.S. Bureau of the Census 2005–07, 2009b). These contrasting examples underscore two important points: in both cases, family structure is a very powerful predictor of poverty. Even in wealthy Douglas County, a child growing up in a female-headed family is nearly 15 times as likely to experience poverty relative to a child in a married-couple family. Second, geography, race, and family structure have powerful cumulative effects on the probability of experiencing poverty. That a child born to female-headed family in Leflore has roughly 68 times the chance of experiencing poverty (and all the disadvantages that accompany it) compared to a child born to a married-couple family in Douglas demonstrates the overlapping effects of background conditions on individuals' starting points. The idea that all individuals have an equal chance to succeed in life becomes untenable in the face of such disparities. Although Leflore and Douglas present an extreme contrast, they are not unique in terms of their respective levels of wealth and poverty.

There are ample data on poverty and the poor, thus claims about both should be empirically grounded. It is equally critical, however, that explanations for the concentration of poverty among particular groups be informed by the particular histories that produced unequal starting points. Levels of poverty in Leflore County, for instance, cannot be understood independently of the Delta's cotton-based economy and the legacy of racial oppression that plantation and sharecropping agriculture imposed on the region for generations. Focusing only on contemporary inequality severs the explanatory link between current patterns of disadvantage and the histories that are necessary to understand them. Without careful attention to the processes that link past inequality to current disadvantage, it is tempting to explain poverty in terms of individual-level factors that reflect core American values and assume equal opportunity. Sociologically sophisticated explanations of poverty, in contrast, require an appreciation of past discrimination in employment, social welfare policies, and housing that created unequal opportunities to accumulate wealth (Oliver and Shapiro 1995; Shapiro 2004), etched inequality into the spatial configuration of segregated communities (Massey and Denton 1994), and compromised the rights of the poor, especially poor women and minorities (Mink 2002; Quadagno

1996). In that sense, this chapter offers only a starting point, but hopefully it also provides a guidepost to a more sociologically informed point of view.

References

American National Election Studies. 2005. "Voter Turnout 1948–2004" (Table 6A.2.l). Retrieved July 7, 2009 (http://www.electionstudies.org/nesguide/2ndtable/t6a_2_l.htm).

Bianchi, Suzanne M. 1999. "Feminization and Juvenilization of Poverty: Trends, Relative Risks, Causes, and Consequences." *Annual Review of Sociology* 25: 307–333.

Conley, Dalton. 1999. Being Black, Living in the Red: Race, Wealth, ad Social Policy in America. Berkeley, Calif.: University of California Press.

Davis, James Allan and Smith, Tom W. 2007. *General Social Surveys, 1972–2006.* Principal Investigator, James A. Davis; Director and Co-Principal Investigator, Tom W. Smith; Co-Principal Investigator, Peter V. Marsden; Sponsored by National Science Foundation. Chicago: National Opinion Research Center.

DeNavas-Walt, Carmen, Bernadette Proctor, and Jessica C. Smith. 2008. "Income, Poverty, and Health Insurance Coverage in the United States: 2007." U.S. Census Bureau (Current Population Reports, P60-23 5), U.S. Government Printing Office, Washington, D.C. Retrieved July 7, 2009 (http://www.census.gov/prod/2008pubs/p60-235.pdf).

Duncan, Cynthia M. 1999. *Worlds Apart: Why Poverty Persists in Rural America.* Yale University Press: New Haven, Conn.

Federman, Maya, Thesia I. Garner, Kathleen Short, W. Bowman Cutter IV, John Kiely, David Levine, Duane McDough, and Marilyn McMillen. 1996. "What does it mean to be Poor in America?" *Monthly Labor Review* 199(5): 3–17.

Gans, Herbert J. Gans. 1996. *The War Against the Poor: The Underclass and Antipoverty Policy.* New York: Basic Books.

Glasmeier, Amy K. 2006. *An Atlas of Poverty in America: One Nation, Pulling Apart, 1960–2003.* New York: Routledge.

Haveman, Robert. 2008. "What Does It Mean to Be Poor in a Rich Society?" Institute for Research on Poverty Discussion Paper no. 1356-08. Retrieved July 7, 2009 (http://www.irp.wisc.edu/publications/dps/pdfs/dp135608.pdf).

Iceland, John. 2003. *Poverty in America: A Handbook.* Berkeley, C.A.: University of California Press.

Keister, Lisa A. 2005. *Getting Rich: America's New Rich and How They Got that Way.* New York: Cambridge University Press.

Kerbo, Harold R. 2003. *Social Stratification and Inequality: Class Conflict in Historical, Comparative, and Global Perspective* (5th Edition). New York: McGraw-Hill.

Kurz, Demie. 1999. "Women, Welfare, and Domestic Violence." Pp. 132–51 in *Whose Welfare,* edited by Gwendolyn Mink. Ithaca, N.Y.: Cornell University Press.

Marger, Martin M. 2008. *Social Inequality: Patterns and Processes* (4th Edition). New York: McGraw-Hill.

Massey, Douglas S., and Nancy A. Denton. 1994. *American Apartheid: Segregation and the Making of the Underclass.* Cambridge, Mass.: Harvard University Press.

Mink, Gwendolyn. 2002. *Welfare's End.* New York: Cornell University Press.

Oliver, Melvin L. and Thomas M. Shapiro. 1995. *Black Wealth/White Wealth: A New Perspective on Racial Inequality.* New York: Routledge.

Pearce, Diana. 1978. "The Feminization of Poverty: Women, Work, and Welfare." *Urban and Social Change Review* 11: 28–36.

Quadagno, Jill. 1996. *The Color of Welfare: How Racism Undermined the War on Poverty.* New York: Oxford University Press.

Shapiro, Thomas M. 2004. *The Hidden Cost of Being African American: How Wealth Perpetuates Inequality.* New York: Oxford University Press.

U.S. Bureau of the Census. 2009a. "Census Poverty Thresholds for 2008 by Size of Family and Number of Related Children Under 18 Years." Housing and Household Economic Statistics Division. Retrieved July 7, 2009 (http://www.census.gov/hhes/www/poverty/threshld/thresh08.html).

U.S. Bureau of the Census. 2009b. "State and County Quick Facts." Retrieved July 7, 2009 (http://quickfacts.census.gov/qfd/).

U.S. Bureau of the Census. 2008a. "Educational Attainment—People 25 Years Old and Over by Median Income and Sex: 1991 to 2007" (Table P-16). Current Population Survey. Retrieved July 7, 2009 (http://www.census.gov/hhes/www/income/histinc/p16.html).

U.S. Bureau of the Census, 2008b. "Workers as a Proportion of All Poor People, 1978–2007" (Table 18). Historical Poverty Tables. Retrieved July 7, 2009 (http://www.census.gov/hhes/www/poverty/histpov/hstpovl8.xls).

U.S. Bureau of the Census. 2005–07. American Community Survey 3-Year Estimates for Leflore County, Mississippi and Douglas County, Colorado. Retrieved July 7, 2009 (http://www.census.gov/acs/www/).

U.S. Department of Health and Human Services. 2009. "The 2009 HHS Poverty Guidelines." Retrieved July 7, 2009 (http://aspe.hhs.gov/poverty/09 poverty. shtml).

Wilson, William J. 1997. *When Work Disappears: The World of the New Urban Poor.* New York: Vintage Books.

Wilson, William J. 1987. *The Truly Disadvantaged: The Inner City, the Underclass, and Public Policy.* Chicago: University of Chicago Press.

Wolff, Edward N. 2007. "Recent Trends in Household Wealth in the United States: Rising Debt and the Middle-Class Squeeze." Levy Economics Institute Working Paper 502. Retrieved January 27, 2010 (http://www.levy.org/vtype.aspx?doctype= 13).

11

Excerpts from "Digital Inequality: From Unequal Access to Differentiated Use"

PAUL DIMAGGIO, ESZTER HARITTAI, CORAL CELESTE, AND STEVEN SHAFER

The Internet boosts immeasurably our collective capacity to archive information, search through large quantities of it quickly, and retrieve it rapidly. It is said that the Internet will expand access to education, good jobs, and better health and that it will create new deliberative spaces for political discussion and provide citizens with direct access to government. Insofar as such claims are plausible, Internet access is an important resource, and inequality in Internet access is a significant concern for social scientists who study inequality.

This chapter reviews what we know about inequality in access to and use of new digital technologies. Until recently most research has focused on inequality in access (the "digital divide"), measured in a variety of ways. We agree that inequality of access is important, because it is likely to reinforce inequality in opportunities for economic mobility and social participation. At the same time we argue that a more thorough understanding of digital inequality requires placing Internet access in a broader theoretical context and asking a wider range of questions about the impact of information technologies and informational goods on social inequality.

This chapter is structured around five key issues:

1. *The digital divide. Who has access to the Internet, who does not have access, and how has access changed?* This is the topic about which information is currently most abundant.

2. *Is access to and use of the Internet more or less unequal than access to and use of other forms of information technology?* Even if access to and use of the Internet is profoundly unequal, the Internet's spread may represent a net increase in equality over the pre-Web media landscape. The implications of the new digital technologies for inequality in access to information can be

understood only in the context of a comparative analysis of the impact of inequality on access to and use of all the major communication media—not just the Internet but broadcast media, newspapers and magazines, telephones, and even word of mouth. If publishers stopped printing newspapers and put all the news online, would inequality in information about politics and world affairs diminish, become greater, or stay the same?

3. *Among the increasing number of Internet users, how do such factors as gender, race, and socioeconomic status shape inequality in ease, effectiveness, and quality of use? What mechanisms account for links between individual attributes and technological outcomes?* We place great importance on understanding socially structured variation in the ability of persons with formal access to the Internet to use it to enhance their access to valuable information resources. In particular, we are interested in the impact of social inequality on where, how easily, and with how much autonomy people can go online; the quality of the hardware and connection, that users have at their disposal; how skilled users are at finding information; how effectively they can draw on social support in solving problems that they encounter in their efforts to do so; and how productively they use their Internet access to enhance their economic life chances and capacity for social and political participation.

4. *Does access to and use of the Internet affect people's life chances?* From the standpoint of public policy, the digital divide is only a problem insofar as going online shapes Internet users' life chances and capacity for civic engagement. What do we know about the effects of Internet access and use on such things as educational achievement and attainment, labor force participation, earnings, and voting? To what extent, if at all, do returns vary for different types of users? If there are no effects, or if the benefits for

use are restricted to the already advantaged, then the case for government intervention to reduce inequality in access to digital technologies is correspondingly weaker.[1]

5. *How might the changing technology, regulatory environment, and industrial organization of the Internet render obsolete the findings reported here?* Because the Internet is a relatively new technology—browsers have been available for only about a decade and the Web was not fully privatized until the mid-1990s—we cannot assume that the results of research undertaken in past years will be replicated even a few years hence. The Internet is a moving target, with many economic and political interests vying to control its ultimate configuration. How might institutional changes—in economic control, in the codes that drive the technology, or in government regulatory and legislative actions—alter observed patterns of inequality in access and use?

We begin with a brief account of the origins and spread of Internet technology. Next, in order to place this chapter in a broader perspective, we review earlier attempts to address the relationship between technological change and social inequality. Finally, we review the literature on each of the five main questions and, where the research is lacking, develop an agenda for the work that needs to be done.[2]

A Brief History of the Internet

By "Internet" we mean the electronic network of networks that spans homes and workplaces and that people use to exchange e-mail, participate in interactive spaces of various kinds, and visit sites on the World Wide Web. ("Intranets," by contrast, are dedicated to a particular organization or set of organizations.) Because the Internet blazed into public consciousness with blinding rapidity, it is important to recall how briefly it has been a part of our lives: as early as 1994, just 11 percent of U.S. households had online access (NTIA 1995), and that was used almost exclusively for e-mail or for specialized purposes such as financial trading through dedicated connections. At the same time the Internet has deep roots: a computerized network linked scientists by the late 1960s, and the military devised a similar network a few years later. The various forebears were linked into an Internet in 1982. But only since 1993, after graphical interfaces became available and the scope of commercial activity broadened, did use of the medium begin to extend rapidly outside academic and military circles (Abbate 1999; Castells 2001).

From that point on, access to and use of the Internet spread swiftly. The number of Americans online grew from 2.5 million in 1995 (Pew Center for the People and the Press 1995) to 83 million in 1999 (IntelliQuest 1999), with 55 million Americans using the Internet on a typical day by mid-2000 (Pew Internet and American Life Project 2000, 5). Based on the Current Population Survey (CPS), in December 1998 the Internet had penetrated 26.2 percent of U.S. households. Less than two years later the figure stood at 41.5 percent, and almost 45 percent of individuals age three or older were reported to go online at home, school, work, or elsewhere (NTIA 2000). By September 2001 more than half of U.S. households had Internet service, and almost 54 percent of individuals went online (NTIA 2002). (Many more have "access" in the sense of an available connection, whether or not they choose to use it, at home, work, school, a library, or a community center.) Since the autumn of 2001, growth in Internet use has stalled in the United States as fewer new users have come online and some existing users have gone offline (Lenhart et al. 2003).

Compared to other technologies, the Internet diffused rapidly, its trajectory similar to those of television and radio, each of which reached more than 50 percent of households within a few years of commercial introduction (Schement and Forbes 1999). Unlike those media, however, the Internet's adoption rate has slowed well short of full penetration. The gravity of the digital divide depends on whether slowing adoption after 2000 reflected a short-term effect of economic recession or a durable ceiling. Based on the experience of telephone service and cable television, which, like Internet service, entail monthly payments rather than a one-shot purchase, the latter seems more likely.

Technology and Inequality: A Selective Tour of Social-Scientific Perspectives

The Internet is one in a long series of information and communication technologies—from speech to printing, movable type, telegraphy, telephony, radio, and television—that arguably influenced patterns of social inequality by destroying existing competencies and permitting early adopters to interact with more people and acquire more information over greater distances and in a shorter time. Before focusing on the Internet, then, we ask how the work of earlier generations of social analysts might place digital media into a broader context.

The most notable conclusion is that students of social inequality have paid very little attention to changes in communication technology. For the most part, researchers who *have* looked at technology have been more concerned with technologies of production (the factory system and various forms of automation, for example) than with technologies of consumption. Nonetheless, four ways in which technological change may influence social inequality are evident.

1. *Competence destruction increases inequality.* Harry Braverman (1974) argued that capitalist firms seek to develop technologies that "de-skill" workers—that permit firms to substitute unskilled operatives for workers with scarce craft skills in order to reduce wages and exert more effective workplace control. If this were the case, wage inequality would increase as unskilled jobs replace skilled jobs. Research on the de-skilling hypothesis (Spenner 1983) has found substantial support at the occupational level but little for the labor force as a whole. New technologies, it seems, have predictable trajectories, at their inception generating new skilled occupations that are "de-skilled" over time. The continual emergence of new technologies, however, ensures that skill levels in the labor force as a whole are stable or increasing, even as those for specific occupations decline. More recent research finds less support for the de-skilling hypothesis, even at the firm level. Companies vary substantially in the extent to which they implement

versions of technology that locate expertise and control, respectively, in white-collar technicians or shop-floor workers (Kelley 1990). The shift in findings appears to reflect a change in managerial practice, which may reflect the combination of more educated workers, a shift in managerial ideologies, weaker unions, and more capital-intensive labor processes (Fernandez 2001).

2. *New technologies reduce inequality by generating demand for more skilled workers.* In contrast, many students of social change argue that technological advance promotes equality. There are three versions of this argument. First, some claim that technological upgrades that replace workers with machines reduce inequality (at the workplace level) by substituting fewer better-paid and more-skilled workers for larger numbers of unskilled workers. In the short run, whether such a change reduces inequality in the economy at large depends on demographic factors and the speed with which "redundant" workers are retrained. Second, some studies show that management may implement technological change in ways that do not replace operatives but rather make work more complex and workers more autonomous. Indeed, Manuel Castells (1996) argues that the increased use of digital communication technologies to tailor goods and services to smaller markets supports a trend toward more flexible workplaces, more skilled work, and more autonomous workers. Third, some students of inequality believe that, as Peter Blau and Otis Dudley Duncan put it (1967, 428), "technological progress has undoubtedly improved chances of upward mobility and will do so in the future," whether or not it reduces structural inequality. In this view, technological change reshuffles the deck, enabling early movers from modest backgrounds to achieve success in new occupations. Oded Galor and Daniel Tsiddon (1997) contend that technological innovation increases both equality of opportunity and

inequality of income (because employers pay premiums for new workers relative to the existing labor force).

3. *New technologies influence inequality indirectly by altering the structure of political interests and the capacity of groups to mobilize.* In this view, technology alters the occupational structure, which in turn influences the political sphere, leading to changes in policy as an unanticipated result. Despite its Rube Goldberg–esque indirection, this model's history is venerable. Marx argued that the factory system would lead to capitalism's demise by reducing skilled workers to a proletarianized mass and concentrating them in vast workplaces where they would organize revolt (1867/1887). Veblen (in *Engineers and the Price System* [1921/1931]) and others argued that technological advance created a "new class" of intellectual laborers (engineers, scientists, technicians, researchers) with interests and values opposed to those of management. These new workers, so the story goes, are committed to technical rationality, on the one hand, and to cosmopolitan and egalitarian values on the other (Gouldner 1979). Plausible as this formulation is, firm-level research finds little evidence that technical workers view themselves as a collectivity with distinctive interests (Lewin and Orleans 2000). Moreover, in public opinion research, "new class" members, while socially tolerant, are no more egalitarian or economically liberal than other members of the middle class (Brint 1984).

4. *New technologies enhance social equality by democratizing consumption.* Whereas the first three approaches emphasize the results of technological change at the point of production, another tradition has emphasized that new technologies reduce barriers to consumption and, in so doing, level status distinctions and reduce the impact of social honor, conventional manners, dress, deportment, or taste on economic success. According to Max Weber, "every technological repercussion and

economic transformation threatens stratification by Status and pushes the class situation into
the foreground" (1956/1978, 938). In particular,
new information technologies, from movable
type and cheap newsprint to telephone service
and the Internet, may democratize the consumption of information by reducing the cost
of communication. Scholars who believe such
technologies reduce inequality emphasize price
effects, whereas naysayers emphasize the
advantage of the well-off in putting new
information to productive use.

Despite the diversity of views, most students
of technology agree on three conclusions, all of
which apply to the Internet. First, *the specific
forms that new technologies take, and therefore
their social implications are products of human
design that reflect the interests of those who invest
in them.* For example, the military built the
Arpanet as a decentralized network that could
withstand the effects of enemy attack; ironically,
this very decentralization and redundancy made it
attractive to libertarian computer scientists, who
developed the Internet in ways that accentuated
those features. The Internet's architecture is currently changing to better serve the economic interests of commercial enterprises (Lessig 1999;
Castells 2001). Second, *technologies are continually reinvented by their users as well as their
designers.* As the Internet's user base has shifted
from idealistic young technologists to upscale
consumers and government policy has sought to
support emerging e-businesses, sites and technologies that enhance commercial uses and easy access
to information have displaced more complex technologies that emphasized interaction and technical
problem-solving. Third, *it follows from the first
two principles that technologies adapt to ongoing
social practices and concerns rather than "influencing" society as an external force* (Fischer
1992). Rather than exploit all the possibilities
inherent in new technologies, people use them to
do what they are already doing more effectively.
Technology may contribute to change by influencing actors' opportunities constraints, and incentives, but its relationship to the social world is
co-evolutionary, not causal.

The Digital Divide

Social scientists and policymakers began worrying
about inequality in Internet access as early as 1995
(Anderson et al., 1995), when just 3 percent of
Americans had ever used the World Wide Web
(Pew Center for the People and the Press 1995). At
first most believed that the Internet would enhance
equality of access to information by reducing its
cost. As techno-euphoria wore off, however,
observers noted that some kinds of people used the
Internet more than others and that those with
higher Internet access also had greater access to
education, income, and other resources that help
people get ahead (Hoffman and Novak 1998,
1999; Benton Foundation 1998; Strover 1999;
Bucy 2000). Concern that the new technology
might exacerbate inequality rather than ameliorate
it focused on what analysts have called the "digital
divide" between the online and the offline.

Since the mid-1990s researchers have found
persistent differences in Internet use by social category (NTIA 1995, 1998, 1999, 2000, 2002;
Lenhart et al. 2003). Although operational definitions of access vary from study to study, most
make a binary distinction between people who use
the Web and other Internet services (especially
e-mail) and people who do not. At first "access"
was used literally to refer to whether a person had
the means to connect to the Internet *if she or he so
chose* (NTIA 1995). Later "access" became a syn-
onym for use, conflating opportunity and choice.
This is unfortunate, because studies that have
measured both access *and* the extent of Internet
use have found, first, that more people have access
than use it (NTIA 1998 and Lenhart et al. 2003
report that 20 percent of residents of Internet
households never go online), and second, that
whereas resources drive access, demand drives
intensity of use among people who have access.
Thus, young adults are less likely to have home
access than adults between the ages of twenty-five
and fifty-four (NT1A 2000), but in Internet households teenagers spend more time online than
adults (Kraut et al. 1998).

The view of the "digital divide" as a gap
between people with and without Internet access
was natural at the onset of diffusion, because the

Internet was viewed through the lens of a decades-old policy commitment to the principle of universal telephone service. Thus, the federal agency responsible for achieving universal access to telephone service, the National Telecommunications and Information Administration (NTIA), claimed jurisdiction over policies affecting the distribution of access to the Internet. The goal of universal access, enunciated in the Communications Act of 1934, was echoed in the Telecommunication Act of 1996, which mandated that the Federal Communications Commission (FCC) pursue the same objective for new "advanced telecommunications services" that reached high levels of penetration (Neuman, McKnight, and Solomon 1998; Leighton 2001).

The NTIA's research publications echoed this tradition. The universal-service paradigm was profoundly concerned with household access (defined in binary fashion), with special concern for inequality between rural and urban areas (a salient: distinction, owing to both the challenging economics of rural telephone service and the bipartisan appeal of programs that assist rural America) (Hall 1993; Schement and Forbes 1999). The telephone paradigm's influence is evident in the NTIA's (1995, 1) first study of the digital divide, *Falling Through the Net: A Survey of the "Have-nots" in Rural and Urban America.* The report's authors carefully framed their attention to the Internet as continuous with existing policy, noting "At the core of U.S. telecommunications policy is the goal of 'universal service'—the idea that all Americans should have access to affordable telephone service The most commonly used measure of the nation's success in achieving universal service is 'telephone penetration.' "

Consistent with tradition, that report included data only on households, emphasized binary distinction between "haves" and "have-nots," and—most strikingly—presented data separately for rural, urban, and central-city categories. (The latter typology reflected the grafting of Great Society concerns with racial inequality onto traditional concerns with rural America—a union reflected in references to rural "have-nots" and "disadvantaged central-city dwellers.") As the NTIA's research program evolved, new categories

of "have-nots," based on race, income, education, age, and, most recently, disability status (NTIA 2000), were added. Beginning in 1999, data were reported for individuals as well as for households.

Thanks to the NTIA's research program, we have a series of valuable snapshots (based on the Current Population Survey in 1994, 1997, 1998, 2000, and 2001) of intergroup differences in Internet use by:

1. *Region and place of residence:* Rates of Internet use are highest in the Northeast and far West and lowest in the Southeast. Of Americans age three or older (the NTIA reporting base for most purposes), state-level estimates range from 42 percent online in Mississippi to 69 percent in Alaska (NTIA 2002, 78). Suburbanites are most likely to use the Internet (57 percent), followed by rural dwellers (53 percent) and central-city residents (49 percent) (19).

2. *Employment status:* In 2001, 65 percent of employed people age sixteen or older were Internet users, compared to just 37 percent of those who were not working (NTIA 2002, 12).

3. *Income:* Internet use rates rise linearly with family income, from 25 percent for persons with incomes of less than $15,000 to almost 80 percent for those with incomes above $75,000.

4. *Educational attainment:* Among persons age twenty-five or older, educational attainment is strongly associated with rates of Internet use. Proportions online range from fewer than 15 percent of those without a high school diploma to 40 percent of persons with a high school diploma, and more than 80 percent of college graduates (NTIA 2002, 17).

5. *Race-ethnicity:* Rates of Internet use are greater for Asian Americans and non-Hispanic whites (about 60 percent for each) than for non-Hispanic blacks (40 percent) and persons of Hispanic origin (just under 32 percent) (NTIA 2002, 21). Variation among these groups in income and education explains much of the difference, but even among those similar in educational attainment or income

level, fewer African Americans than whites use the Internet (Hoffman, Novak, and Schlosser 2001; Lenhart et al. 2003).

6. *Age:* Rates of Internet use rise rapidly from age three to a peak around age fifteen, when nearly 80 percent of Americans are online; decline to around 65 percent at age twenty-five; then descend gently to just below 60 percent by age fifty-five. At that point rates decline rapidly with age (NTIA 2002, 13).

7. *Gender:* In early surveys men used the Internet at higher rates than women, but by 2001 women and men were equally likely to be online (Losh 2003). From the late teens to the late forties, women are more likely than men to use the Internet; men acquire an increasing edge after age fifty-five (NTIA 2002, 14).

8. *Family structure:* Families with children in the home are more likely to have computers and the Internet than are families without children (NTIA 2002, 14).

These patterns of inequality are similar to those observed in other countries. In Switzerland, for example, in 2000, 69 percent of university graduates but only 19 percent of high school graduates were online, and similar advantages were found for persons with high incomes, the young, and men (with the gender gap notably greater than in the United States) (Bonfadelli 2002, 75; see also De Haan 2003 on the Netherlands; Heil 2002 on the United Kingdom and Germany; and McLaren and Zappala 2002 on Australia). . . .

Dimensions of Inequality Online

We call attention to five broad forms of inequality. The first is variation in the *technical means* (hardware, software, and connections) by which people access the Internet. The second is variation in the extent to which people exercise *autonomy* in using the Web—for example, whether they access it from work or from home, whether their use is monitored or unmonitored, whether they must compete with other users for time online. The third is inequality in the *skill* that people bring to their use of the medium. The fourth is inequality in the *social*

support on which Internet users can draw. The fifth is variation in the *purposes* for which people use the technology. We view each type of inequality as likely to shape significantly the experience that users have online, the uses to which they can put the Internet and the satisfactions they draw from it, and their returns to Internet use in the form of such outcomes as earnings or political efficacy.

Inequality in Technical Apparatus

Rob Kling (1998) distinguishes between technological and social access, calling attention to the importance of "the physical availability of suitable equipment, including computers of adequate speed and equipped with appropriate software for a given activity." How does inequality in the adequacy of hardware, software, and connections limit the ways in which different kinds of users can employ the Internet? As bandwidth increases and more websites require late-model browsers to display Java applications, sophisticated graphics, or streaming video, to what extent can users without access to expensive systems access the full range of Internet content?

Among Internet users, the same factors associated with being online in the first place (income, educational attainment, race, and metropolitan residence) predict having high-speed connections (Horrigan and Rainie 2002, 10; Mossberger, Tolbert, and Stansbury 2003). Research suggests that inferior technical apparatus reduces the benefits that users can gain from the Internet directly and indirectly. First, users with slow connections and obsolete software or hardware are simply unable to access many sites. Second, because their online experience is less gratifying, they go online less often and acquire fewer information retrieval skills. John Horrigan and Lee Rainie (2002) report that, after controlling for experience and demographic variation, broadband users search for information more widely, engage in a broader range of activities, and more often produce their own Web content than users without high-speed connections. Similarly, Elizabeth Davison and Shelia Cotton (2003) report that broadband users spend more time online and are more likely to use online business and consumer services and recreational sites.[3]

Inequality in Autonomy of Use

How much control do people exercise over their Internet use? An important aspect of this dimension is location of access (Bimber 2000)—that is, whether people go online at home or at work, in school, or at a library or community center. If access is outside the home, how much flexibility does the user have in determining the hours at which she or he can go online? How far does the user have to travel? To what extent do regulations, time limits, filtering software, or monitoring arrangement limit use? If access is at work, what uses are permitted (and how does this vary with organizational role), what kinds of filtering or monitoring systems are in place, and how (stringently are rules enforced (O'Mahoney and Barley 1999)? (In 2001, 63 percent of large employers monitored their employees' Internet connections and 47 percent stored and reviewed their e-mail communications [American Management Association 2001].) If access is at home, to what extent is autonomy limited by the actions of other family members or the policies of the Internet service provider (ISP) (Lessig 1999)? Does in-home access have different effects on educational or occupational outcomes than access from other locations? Among people who have access at work, what predicts the degree of autonomy they possess in determining *how* they use the technology?

We have seen that educational attainment, income, and race are all associated with having Internet access at home. We hypothesize that, where individuals have access to the Internet at work, the autonomy with which they can exercise that access is associated with their organizational rank and[4] functional position. Finally, we expect that among people with access to the Internet, the greater the autonomy of use, the greater the benefits the user derives.

Inequality in Skill

Kling (1998) points to the importance of inequality in users' possession of "know-how, a mix of professional knowledge, economic resources, and technical skills, to use technologies in ways that enhance professional practices and social life." Ernest Wilson (2000) refers to inequality in "cognitive access": the extent to which users are trained to find and evaluate the information they seek. Internet users vary in their possession of at least four kinds of relevant knowledge: recipe knowledge about how to log on, conduct searches, and download information; non-domain-specific background knowledge (such as knowledge of Boolean logic for designing search algorithms); integrative knowledge about the way the Web operates that helps them navigate better; and the technical knowledge about software, hardware, and networks necessary for troubleshooting problems or staying up-to-date (for example, by downloading patches and plug-ins). Taken together, these four kinds of knowledge constitute what we might call—after sociolinguists' notion of "communicative competence" (Hymes 1974)—"digital competence": the capacity to respond pragmatically and intuitively to challenges and opportunities in a manner that exploits the Internet's potential and avoids frustration (Hargittai 2002).

We know very little about what explains inequality in the competence needed to find information online. Evolution in website construction and growth in the volume of information has required new skills for the technology's efficient use. Flashy software implemented with little attention to human factors renders many sites accessible only to sophisticated users with state-of-the-art hardware and software and sophisticated navigation skills (Hargittai 2003b). Moreover, limitations in search technology—most search engines index no more than a small percentage of all content online (Lawrence and Giles 1999)—render it difficult for the average user to find many sites.

Despite a growing literature on website usability issues (much of it from library science and social informatics), we know little about how and why skill is related to personal characteristics. A few researchers have examined self-reports of skill and found that users with less formal education are less confident in their abilities (Bonfadelli 2002). We also know that women are less confident in their online skills than men and that self-assessments predict performance poorly (Hargittai 2003a).

Eszter Hargittai's recent study (2003a) is unique in that the author subjected a random sample of residents of a socially heterogeneous New Jersey county to extensive testing, including surveys, open-ended interviews, and, most important, observations while they attempted to locate several kinds of material online, using computers and browsers similar to those they ordinarily employed. Hargittai finds that skill (defined, first, as the ability to complete a task and, second, as the amount of time spent on the task) is only modestly associated with demographic measures (and associated in different ways for different tasks); relatively weakly associated with offline domain familiarity; and more strongly related to autonomy of use and the amount of time subjects spend online in a typical week.

A study of online sessions of a sample of new users (Neuman, O'Donnell, and Schneider 1996) demonstrated that emotional impact—whether users felt frustrated or gratified at the session's end—was a function of their success in attaining their objectives. We infer from this that Internet competence is related to the satisfaction that users derive from the experience, the extent to which they find it stressful or rewarding, and therefore the extent to which they persist in Internet use and acquire additional skills.

Inequality in the Availability of Social Support

Based on these observations, we might expect inequality in competence to deepen inexorably as skillful users find the Internet rewarding and acquire greater skill and less able users grow frustrated and turn away. Yet we know that most new users do gain competence and persist. We suspect that this is the case because novices draw on *social support* from more experienced users when they need help. Such support has become more important as the technology has penetrated new sectors of the population. Anecdotal evidence suggests that early Web users were embedded in dense networks of technically sophisticated peers. By contrast, more recent recruits are often less sophisticated and more isolated (Kiesler et al. 2000) Y. Kim and Joo-Young Jung (2002), in a study of East Asian youth, found strong effects of social support (from both family and friends) on the breadth and extent of online activity.

We hypothesize that three kinds of support increase users' motivation to go online and their digital competence: technical assistance from persons employed to provide it (for example, workplace support staff, customer support staff, librarians, and teachers); technical assistance from friends and family members; and emotional reinforcement from friends and family in the form of commiseration when things go wrong and positive interest when things go right. We further hypothesize that social support influences returns to Internet access, however these are measured.

Variation in Use

How do income, education, and other factors influence *the purposes for which one uses the Internet*? From the standpoint of the contribution of technology use to socioeconomic life chances, not all uses are equal. The Internet prophets who foresaw that the Web would empower citizens, increase social capital, and enhance equality of opportunity probably did not have gambling or pornography sites in mind when they made these predictions. We place high priority on examining determinants of different kinds of use, especially distinguishing among uses that increase economic welfare (for example, skill enhancement, learning about employment opportunities consumer information, or education) or political or social capital (using the Internet to follow the news, gather information relevant to electoral decisionmaking, learn about public issues, engage in civic dialogue, or take part in social movement activities) versus those that are primarily recreational.

The variety of uses to which one puts the Internet is likely to reflect the number of hours one spends online. We have no cumulative data on the latter, but surveys have asked how many hours respondents are online *now* and how many years they have been online, and both measures are associated with variety of use. Moreover, among Internet users, those with more education began to use the Internet earlier and go online more frequently (at least in the early stages of diffusion) than less-educated users (Bonfadelli 2002, 77). In the United States, women with Internet access went online less frequently than otherwise similar men (Bimber 2000).

Evidence that users from more privileged backgrounds are more likely to use the Internet to get ahead and equip themselves to participate in community affairs or politics is beginning to accumulate. DiMaggio and Hargittai (2002) report that among respondents to the 2000 GSS, education, income, and vocabulary test scores have strong effects on "capital-enhancing" uses of the Internet but much weaker (or negative) effects on recreational use. Bonfadelli (2002) finds that, among Swiss Internet users, education is positively associated with using the Web for information and services but negatively associated with using it for entertainment.

DiMaggio and Hargittai (2002) do not find significant effects of race, net controls (see also Alvarez 2003). Tom Spooner and Lee Rainie (2000) find that African American Internet users are more likely than their white counterparts to use the Web for education and job-hunting. The NTIA (1998, 2000) reports that lower-income and less-educated Internet users are more likely than wealthy users to use the Internet to find jobs, a result that may reflect exclusion from the informal social networks through which information about the most desirable jobs is distributed (Lin 2000). Egalitarians should find such results encouraging. Yet relatively early adopters in groups with lower levels of adoption may be atypical in ways that make generalization unwise (see Bourdieu and Passeron 1977 on "overselection").

Note that in distinguishing among uses in this way, we do not suggest that recreational Internet activities are without value—only that both public policy and students of inequality place a higher priority on equality of economic opportunity and civic engagement than on sociability arid the pursuit of happiness. Researchers interested in social inequality and social policy should distinguish between online activities that are likely to cultivate the former and those primarily devoted to the latter. . . .

Notes

1. There may be a case for government action to increase equality in *returns to* Internet use; if such programs succeeded, the case for action to increase equality of access would be strengthened. Even if Internet use does not help people get ahead economically, the case for government intervention would still be very strong if access to the Internet were to become necessary to gain access to government services and sustain a minimal level of social and political participation.

2. Our focus throughout this chapter is on the United States, although we believe that the general framework is applicable to other economically advanced industrial societies.

3. CPS estimates tend to be more conservative than those from other studies. For example, a November—December 2000 survey by the Pew Internet and American Life Project found 58 percent of a national sample online (Horrigan 2000b, 7).

4. Horrigan and Rainie (2002) note that causality is probably reciprocal in that investing in broadband is not attractive to users who use the Internet for a diverse set of purposes, a supposition strengthened by a subsequent report (Horrigan 2003) on users who plan to switch to broadband. Although Davison and Cotton (2002) do not explore the possibility, their findings suggest that broadband adopters may constitute two groups, one business-oriented and one driven by recreational enthusiasms.

References

Abbate, Janet. 1999. *Inventing the Internet.* Cambridge, Mass.: MIT Press.

Access Board. Architectural and Transportation Barriers Compliance Board. 2000. "Electronic and Information Technology Accessibility Standards." *Federal Register* (December 21) Available at: www.access.board.gov/sec508/508standards.htm

Althaus, Scott L., and David Tewksbury. 2000. "Patterns of Internet and Traditional News Media Use in a Networked Community." *Political Communication* 17: 21–45.

Alvarez, Anthony Steven. 2003. "Behavioral and Environmental Correlates of Digital Inequality." *IT and Society* 1(5): 97–140. Available at: www.stanford.edu/group/siqss/itandsociety/v01105/v0li05a06.Pdf.

American Management Association. 2001. "2001 AMA Survey: Workplace Monitoring and Surveillance: Summary of Key Findings." Available at: www.amanet.org/research/summ.htm (last accessed August 8, 2003).

Anderson, Ben, and Karina Tracey. 2001. "Digital Living: The Impact (or Otherwise) of the Internet on Everyday Life." *American Behavioral Scientist* 45: 456–75.

Anderson Robert H., Tora K. Bikson, Sally Ann Law, Bridger M. Mitchell, et al. 1995. *Universal Access to*

E-mail: Feasibility and Societal Implications. Santa Monica, Calif.: Rand Corporation.

Attewell, Paul. 2001. "The First and Second Digital Divides." *Sociology of Education* 74: 252–59.

Attewell, Paul, and Juan Battle. 1999. "Home Computers and School Performance." *The Information Society* 15: 1–10.

Attewell, Paul, Belkis Suzao-Garcia, and Juan Battle. 2003. "Computers and Young Children: Social Benefit or Social Problem?" *Social Forces* 82: 275–94.

Autor, David H., Lawrence F. Katz, and Alan B. Krueger. 1998. "Computing Inequality: Have Computers Changed the Labor Market?" *Quarterly Journal of Economics* 113: 1169–1213.

Barley, Stephen R.1990. "The Alignment of Technology and Structure Through Roles and Networks." *Administrative Science Quarterly* 35: 61–103.

Benton Foundation. 1998. *Losing Ground Bit by Bit: Low-Income Communities in the Information Age.* Washington, D.C.: Benton Foundation and National Urban League.

Bernstein, Basil. 1977. *Class, Codes, and Control,* vol. 3. London: Routledge & Kegan Paul.

Bertot, John Carlo, and Charles R. McClure. 1998. *The 1998 National Survey of U. S. Public Library Outlet Internet Connectivity: Final Report.* Washington, D.C.: American Library Association and National Commission on Libraries and Information Science.

Bikson, Tora K., and Constantijn W A. Panis. 1999. *Citizens, Computers and Connectivity: A Review of Trends.* Santa Monica, Calif.: Rand Corporation. Available at: (last accessed August 26, 2003).

Bimber, Bruce. 2000. "The Gender Gap on the Internet." *Social Science Quarterly* 81: 868–76.

——. 2003. *Information and American Democracy: Technology in the Evolution of Political Power.* New York: Cambridge University Press.

Blau, Peter M. 1977. *Inequality and Heterogeneity: A Primitive Theory of Social Structure.* New York: Free Press.

BIau, Peter M., and Otis Dudley Duncan. 1967. *The American Occupational Structure.* New York: John Wiley.

Bolt, David, and Ray Crawford. 2000. *Digital Divide: Computers and Our Children's Future.* New York: TV Books.

Bonfadelli, Heinz. 2002. "The Internet and Knowledge Gaps: A Theoretical and Empirical Investigation." *European Journal of Communication* 17: 65–84.

Bourdieu, Pierre. 1984. *Distinction.* Cambridge, Mass.: Harvard University Press.

Bourdieu, Pierre, and Jean-Claude Passeron. 1977. *Reproduction in Education, Society, and Culture.* Beverly Hills, Calif.: Sage Publications.

Braverman, Harry. 1974. *Labor and Monopoly Capital.* New York: Monthly Review Press.

Brint, Steven. 1984. "'New·Class' and Cumulative Trend Explanations of Liberal Political Attitudes of Professionals." *American Journal of Sociology* 90: 30–71.

——. 1998. *Schools and Societies.* Thousand Oaks, Calif.: Pine Forge Press.

Bromley, Rebekah V., and Dorothy Bowles. 1995. "Impact of Internet on Use of Traditional News Media." *Newspaper Research Journal* 16.

Brown, Jeffrey R., and Austan Goolsbee. 2002. "Does the Internet Make Markets More Competitive? Evidence from the Life Insurance Industry." *Journal of Political Economy* 110: 481–507.

Bucy, Erik P. 2000. "Social Access to the Internet." *Press/Politics* 5: 50–61.

Card, David, and John E. DiNardo. 2002. "Skill-Biased Technological Change and Rising Wage Inequality: Some Problems and Puzzles."*Journal of Labor Economics* 20: 733–83.

Castells, Manuel. 1996. *The Rise of the Network Society,* vol. 1, *The Information Age: Economy Society and Culture.* Boston: Blackwell.

——. 2001. *Internet Galaxy: Reflections on the Internet, Business, and Society.* New York: Oxford University Press.

Chang, Mariko Lin. 2003. "With a Little Help from My Friends (and My Financial Planner): How Socioeconomic Status and Race Influence the Search for Financial Information." Paper presented to the session on culture and economy at the 2003 annual meeting of the American Sociological Association, Atlanta (August 16–18, 2003).

Chennells, Lucy, and John Van Reenen. 1997. "Technical Change and Earnings in British Establishments" *Economica* 64: 587–604.

Collins, Randall. 1979. *The Credential Society: An Historical Sociology of Education.* New York: Academic Press.

Compaine, Benjamin M. 2000. "Re-examining the Digital Divide." Paper presented to the twenty-eighth Telecommunications Policy Research Conference, Alexandria, Va. (September 23–25).

——. 2001. "Information Gaps: Myth or Reality?" In *The Digital Divide: Facing a Crisis or Creating a Myth?* edited by Benjamin M. Compaine. Cambridge, Mass.: MIT Press.

Cummings, Jonathon N., and Robert Kraut. 2000. "Domesticating Computers and the Internet."

Unpublished paper. Carnegie-Mellon University, Pittsburgh.

Davison, Elizabeth, and Shelia R. Cotton. 2003. "Connection Discrepancies: Unmasking Further Layers of the Digital Divide." *First Monday* 8(3). Available at: firstmonday.org/issues8—3/Davison/index.html (last accessed September 1, 2003).

De Haan, Jos. 2003. "IT and Social inequality in the Netherlands." *IT and Society* 1 (4, Spring): 27–45. Available at: www.stanford.edu/group/siqss/itandsociety/v01i04a04.pdf.

DiMaggio, Paul. 2001. "Social Stratification, Lifestyle, Social Cognition and Social Participation." In *Social Stratification in Sociological Perspective* 2nd ed., edited by David Grusky. Boulder, Colo.: Westview Press.

DiMaggio, Paul, and Eszter Hargittai. 2002. "From the Digital Divide to Digital Inequality." Paper presented to the annual meeting of the American Sociological Association, Chicago (August).

DiNardo, John E., and Jorn-Steffen Pischke. 1997. "The Returns to Computer Use Revisited: Have Pencils Changed the Wage Structure Too?" *Quarterly Journal of Economics* 20: 291–303.

Entorf, Horst, Michel Gollac, and Francis Kramarz. 1999. "New Technologies, Wages, and Worker Selection." *Journal of Labor Economics* 17: 464–91.

Entorf, Horst, and Francis Kramarz. 1997. "Does Unmeasured Ability Explain the Higher Wages of New Technology Workers?" *European Economic Review* 41: 1489–1509.

Ettema, James S., James W Brown, and Russell V. Luepker. 1983. "Knowledge Gap Effects in a Health Information Campaign." *Public Opinion Quarterly* 47: 516–27.

Fernandez, Roberto M. 2001. "Skill-Based Technological Change and Wage Inequality: Evidence from a Plant Retooling." *American Journal of Sociology* 107: 273–320.

Fischer, Claude 5. 1992. *America Calling: A Social History of the Telephone to 1940.* Berkeley: University of California Press.

Fountain, Jane. 2001. *The Virtual State: The Politics of Digital Government.* Washington, D.C.: Brookings Institution.

Freeman, Richard B. 2002. "The Labor Market in the New Information Economy." *Oxford Review of Economic Policy* 18: 288–305.

Gallie, Duncan. 1996. "New Technology and the Class Structure: The Blue-Collar/ White-Collar Divide Revisited." *British Journal of Sociology* 47: 447–73.

Galor, Oded, and Daniel Tsiddon. 1997. "Technological Progress, Mobility, and Economic Growth." *American Economic Review* 87: 363–82.

Gaziano, Cecilie. 1997. "Forecast 2000: Widening Knowledge Gaps." *Journalism and, Mass Communications* 74: 237–64.

Goldfarb, Avi. 2002. "Analyzing Web Site Choice Using Clickstream Data." In *Advances in Applied in Applied Microeconomics.* vol. 11, *The Economics of the Internet and E-Commerce,* edited by Michael R. Baye. London: Elsevier Science.

Goolsbee, Austan, and Jonathan Guryan. 2002. "The impact of Internet Subsidies on Public Schools." Working paper. Cambridge, Mass.: National Bureau of Economic Research.

Goolsbee, Austan, and Peter J. Klenow. 2002. "Evidence on Learning and Network Externalities in the Diffusion of Home Computers." *Journal of Law and Economics* 45: 317–44. Available at: gsb www.uchicago.edu/fac/austan.goolsbee/research/computer.pdf (last accessed August 29, 2003).

Goss, Ernest P., and Joseph M. Phillips. 2002. "How Information Technology Affects Wages: Evidence Using Internet Usage as a Proxy for IT Skills." *Journal of Labor Research* 23:4-63–74.

Gouldner, Alvin. 1979. *The Future of Intellectuals and the Rise of the New Class.* New York: Seabury Press.

Guillén, Mauro, and Sandra Suarez. 2002. "The Political Economy of Internet Development: A Cross-national Time-series Analysis." Working paper. Philadelphia: Wharton School, University of Pennsylvania.

Hall, Peter A. 1993. "Policy Paradigms, Social Learning, and the State: The Case of Economic Policymaking in Britain." *Comparative Politics* 27: 275–96.

Hampton, Keith, and Barry Wellman. 2000. "Examining Community in the Digital Neighborhood: Early Results from Canada's Wired Suburb." In *Digital Cities: Experiences, Technologies, and Future Perspectives,* edited by Toru Ishida and Katherine Isbister. New York: Springer-Verlag.

Hargittai, Eszter. 1999. "Weaving the Western Web: Explaining Differences in Internet Connectivity Among OECD Countries." *Telecommunications Policy* 23: 701–18.

——. 2000. "Open Portals or Closed Gates? Channeling Content on the World Wide Web." *Poetics* 27: 233–53.

——. 2002. "Second-level Digital Divide: Differences in People's Online Skills." *First Monday* 7(4). Available at: www.firstmonday.dk/issues/issue7__4/hargittai (last accessed September 1, 2003).

———. 2003a. "How Wide a Web: inequalities in Access to Information Online." Ph.D. diss., Sociology Department, Princeton University.

———. 2003b. "Serving Citizens' Needs: Minimizing Online Hurdles to Accessing Government Information." *IT and Society* 1: 27–41.

Heil, Alexander. 2002. "The Information Society in the United Kingdom and Germany: Chances, Risks, and Challenges." Master's thesis, University of Leipzig. Available at: www.falling-through-the-net.de/anlysis.pdf (last accessed September 1, 2003).

Hoffman, Donna L., and Thomas P. Novak. 1998. "Bridging the Racial Divide on the Internet." *Science* 280: 390–96.

———. 1999. "Examining the Relationship of Race to Internet Access and Usage over Time." Working paper. Nashville: eLab Manuscripts, Vanderbilt University.

Hoffman, Donna L., Thomas P. Novak, and Ann E. Schlosser. 2001. "The Evolution of the Digital Divide: Examining the Relationship of Race to Internet Access and Usage over Time." In *The Digital Divide: Facing a Crisis or Creating a Myth?*, edited by Benjamin M. Compaine. Cambridge, Mass.: MIT Press.

Horrigan, John. 2000a. *New Internet Users: What They Do Online, What They Don't, and Implications for the Net's Future.* Washington, D.C.: Pew Internet and American Life Project (September 25).

———. 2000b. *The Holidays Online: E-mails and E-greetings Outpace E-commerce.* Washington, D.C.: Pew Internet and American Life Project (December 31).

———. 2003. "Adoption of Broadband to the Home." Pew Internet Project Data Memo. Washington, D.C.: Pew Internet and American Life Project (May).

Horrigan, John, and Lee Rainie. 2002. "The Broadband Difference: How Online Americans' Behavior Changes with High-Speed Internet Connection at Home." Washington D.C.: Pew. Internet and American Life Project (June 23).

Howard, Philip, Lee Rainie, and Steve Jones. 2001. "Days and Nights on the Internet: The Impact of a Diffusing Technology." *American Behavioral Scientist* 45: 383–404.

Hughes, Karen D., and Graham S. Lowe. 2000 "Surveying the 'Post-industrial' Landscape: Information Technologies and Labor Market Polarization in Canada" *Canadian Review of Sociology and Anthropology* 37: 29–53.

Hymes, Dell. 1974. *Foundations in Sociolinguistics: An Ethnographic Approach.* Philadelphia: University of Pennsylvania Press.

IntelliQuest. 1999. "Intelliquest Study Shows 83 Million U.S. Internet Users and 56 Million Online Shoppers." Press release (April 19, 1999). http://www.intelliuquest.com/Press/archive/release.asp. (Last accessed October 21, 2003.)

Introna, Luc, and Helen Nissenbaum. 2000. "Shaping the Web: Why the Politics of Search Engines Matters." *The Information Society* 16: 1–17.

Ishida, Toru, and Katherine Iabister, eds. 2000. *Digital Cities: Experiences. Technologies, and Future Perspectives.* New York: Springer-Verlag.

Karabel, Jerome, and Alexander Astin. 1975. "Social Class, Academic Ability, and College Quality.' " *Social Forces* 53: 381–98.

Katz, James E., and Philip Aspden. 1997. "Motives, Hurdles, and Dropouts." *Communications of the ACM* 40: 97–102.

Katz, James E., and Ronald Rice. 2002. *Social Consequences of Internet Use: Access. Involvement, and Interaction.* Cambridge Mass.: MIT.

Katz, James E., Ronald Rice, and Philip Aspden. 2001. "The Internet, 1995–2000: Access, Civic Involvement, and Social Interaction." *American Behavioral Scientist* 45(3): 405–19.

Kavanaugh, Andrea L., and Scott J. Patterson. 2001. "The Impact of Community Computer Networks on Social Capital and Community Involvement." *American Behavioral Scientist* 45(3): 496–509.

Kelley, Maryellen R. 1990. "New Process Technology, Job Design, and Work Organization: A Contingency Model." *American Sociological Review* 55: 191–208.

Kiesler, Sara, Bozena Adaniuk, Vicki Lundmark, and Robert Kraut. 2001. "Troubles with the Internet: The Dynamics of Help at Home." *Human Computer Interaction* 15: 323–51.

Kiiski, Sampska, and Math Pohjola. 2002. "Cross-country Diffusion of the Internet." *Information Economics and Policy* 14: 297–310.

Kim, Yong-Chan, and Joo-Young Jung. 2002. "Digital Divide in 90 Percent Access: Multidimensional Examination of Adolescents' Internet Connectedness in Seoul, Singapore, and Taipei." In *A Study on the Digital Divide of the Youth*, edited by J. Hwang, J. Yu, and J. Lee. Seoul: Korea Institute for Youth Development.

Kling, Rob. 1998. "Technological and Social Access to Computing, Information, and Communication Technologies." White paper for Presidential Advisory Committee on High-performance Computing and Communications, Information Technology, and the Next Generation Internet. Available at: www.slis.indiana.edu/faculty/kling/pubs/NGI.htm.

Kohn, Melvin L, and Carmi Schooler. 1982. "Job Conditions and Personality: A Longitudinal Assessment of Their Reciprocal Effects." *American Journal of Sociology* 87: 1257–86.

Kraut, Robert, Sara Kiesler, Bonka Boneva, Jonathon Cummings, Vicki Helgeson, and Anne Crawford. 2002. "Internet Paradox Revisited." *Journal of Social Issues* 58: 49–74.

Kraut, Robert, Michael Patterson, Vicki Lundmark, Sara Kiesler, Tridas Mukophadhyay, and William Scherlis. 1998. "Internet Paradox: A Social Technology That Reduces Social Involvement and Psychological Wellbeing?" *American Psychologist* 53: 1011–31.

Krueger, Alan B. 1993. "How Computers Have Changed the Wage Structure: Evidence from Micro Data." *Quarterly Journal of Economics* 108: 33–60.

Lawrence, Steve, and Lee Giles. 1999. "Accessibility of Information on the Web." *Nature* (400): l07–9.

Leigh, Andrew, and Robert Atkinson. 2001. "Clear Thinking on the Digital Divide." Washington, D.C.: Progressive policy Institute (June 26, 1999). Available at: (Last accessed October 21, 2003.)

Leighton, Wayne A. 2001. "Broadband Deployment and the Digital Divide: A Primer." *Policy Analysis* (Cato Institute) 4l0(August 7). Available at: www.cato.org/pubs/Pas/Pa410.pdf (Last accessed August 26, 2003.)

Lenhart, Amanda. 2000. "Who's Not Online: 57 Percent of Those Without Internet Access Say They Do Not Plan to Log On." Washington D.C.: Pew Internet and American Life Project (September 21).

Lenhart, Amanda, John Horrigan, Lee Rainie, Katherine Allen, Angie Boyce, Mary Madden, and Erin O'Grady. 2003. "The Ever-Shifting Internet Population: A New Look at Internet Access and the Digital Divide." Washington, D.C.: Pew Internet and American Life Project (April 16).

Lessig, Lawrence 1999. *Code and Other Laws of Cyberspace.* New York: Basic Books.

Lewin, Clare, and Myron Orleans. 2000. "The Class Situation of Information Specialists: A Case Analysis." *Sociological Research Online* 5. Available at: www.socresonline/org.uk/5/3/lewin.html.

Lin, Nan. 2000. *Social Capital.* New York: Cambridge University Press.

Losh, Susan Carol. 2003. "Gender and Educational Digital Chasms in Computer and Internet Access and Use over Time: 1983–2000." *IT and Society* 1(4, Spring): 73–86. Available at: www.stanford.edu/group/siqss/itandsociety/v0li04/v0li04a06.pdf.

Marsden, Peter V. 1987. "Core Discussion Networks of Americans." *American Sociological Review* 52: 122–31.

Martin, Steven P. 2003. "Is the Digital Divide Really Closing? A Critique of Inequality Measurement in *A Nation Online.*" *IT and Society* 1(4, Spring): 1–13. Available at: www.standford/group/siqss/itandsociety/v01i04/html. (Last accessed June 12, 2003.)

Marx, Karl. 1867/1887. *Capital: A Critical Analysis of Capitalist Production.* Translated by Samuel Moore and Edward Aveling, London: Sonnenschein, Lowrey.

McLaren, Jennifer, and Gianni Zappala. 2002. "The 'Digital Divide' Among Financially Disadvantaged Families in Australia." *First Monday* 7(11). Available at: firstmonday.org/issue7_11/mclaren/index.html. (Last accessed September 1, 2003.)

Mossberger, Karen, Caroline J. Tolbert, and Mary Stansbury. 2003. *Virtual Inequality: Beyond the Digital Divide.* Washington, D.C.: Georgetown University Press.

Mueller, Milton L., and Jorge Reins Schement. 2001. "Universal Service from the Bottom Up: A Study of Telephone Penetration in Camden, New Jersey." In *The Digital Divide: Facing a Crisis or Creating a Myth?,* edited by Benjamin M. Compaine. Cambridge, Mass.: MIT Press.

Nagarajan, Anu, James L. Bander, and Chelsea C. White. 2000. "Trucking." In *U.S. Industry in 2000: Studies in Competitive Performance,* edited by Board on Science, Technology and Economic Policy, National Research Council. Washington, D.C.: National Academy Press.

National Telecommunications and Information Administration (NTIA). 1995. *Falling Through the Net: A Survey of the "Have Nots" in Rural and Urban America.* Washington: U.S. Department of Commerce (July).

——. 1998. *Falling Through the Net II: New Data on the Digital Divide.* Washington: U.S. Department of Commerce (July).

——. 1999. *Falling Through the Net: Defining the Digital Divide.* Washington: U.S. Department of Commerce (November).

——. 2000. *Falling Through the Net: Toward Digital Inclusion.* Washington: U.S. Department of Commerce (October).

——. 2002. *A Nation Online: How Americans Are Expanding Their Use of the Internet.* Washington: U.S. Department of Commerce (February).

Neuman, W Russell, Lee McKnight, and Richard Jay Solomon. 1998. *The Gordian Knot: Political*

Gridlock on the Information Highway. Cambridge, Mass.: MIT Press.

Neuman, W. Russell, Shawn R. O'Donnell, and Steven M. Schneider. 1996. "The Web's Next Wave: A Field Study of Internet Diffusion and Use Patterns." Unpublished paper. MIT Media Laboratory, Cambridge, Mass.

Norris, Pippa. 2001. *Digital Divide? Civic Engagement Information Poverty, and the Internet in Democratic Societies.* New York: Cambridge University Press.

O'Mahoney, Siobban, and Steven R. Barley. 1999. "Do Digital Telecommunications Affect Work and Organization? The State of Our Knowledge." *Research in Organizational Behavior* 21: 125–61.

Ono, Hiroshi, and Madeline Zavodny. 2003. "Gender and the Internet." *Social Science Quarterly* 84: 111–21.

Organization for Economic Cooperation and Development (OECD). 1997. *Webcasting and Convergence: Policy Implications.* Paris: OECD. Available at: www.oecd.org/dsti/sti/it/cm/prod_97-221.htm.

Pandey, Sanjay K., John J. Hart, and Sheela Tiwary. 2002. "Women's Health and the Internet: Understanding Emerging Trends and Implications." *Social Science and Medicine* 56: 179–91.

Pew Center for the People and the Press. 1995. *Technology in the American Household.* Washington, D.C.: Pew Center for the People and the Press.

Pew Internet and American Lift Project. 2000. *Tracking Online Life: How Women Use the Internet to Cultivate Relationships with Family and Friends.* Washington, D.C.: Pew Internet and American Life Project (May 10).

Robinson John P., Meyer Kestnbaum, Alan Neustadtl; and Anthony Alvarez; 2000. "Mass Media Use Anti Social Life Among Internet Users." *Social Science Computer Review* 18: 490–501.

Schement, Jorge Reina. 2003. "Measuring What Jefferson Knew and Tocqueville Saw: Libraries as Bridges Across the Digital Divide." *IT and Society* 1(4, Spring): 118–25, Available at: www.stanford.edu/group/siqss/itandsociety/v0li04/v01i04al.pdf.

Schement, Jorge Reina, and Scott C. Forbes. 1999. "Approaching the Net: Toward Global Principles of Universal Service." Available at: www.benton.org/policy/schement/ptc99/home.html (Last accessed November 16, 2001.)

Scott-Morton, Fiona, Florian Zettehneyer, and Jorge Silva-Risso. 2001. "Internet Car Retailing." *Journal of Industrial Economics* 49: 501–19.

——. 2003. "Consumer Information and Discrimination: Does the Internet Affect the Pricing of New Cars to Women and Minorities?" *Quantitative Marketing Economics* 1: 65–92.

Shah, Dhavan V., Jack M. McLeod, and So-Hyang Yoon. 2001. "Communication, Context, and Community: An Exploration of Print, Broadcast, and Internet Influences." *Communication Research* 28: 464–506.

Silverstein, Craig, Monica Henzinger, Hannea Marais, and Michael Moricz. 1998. "Analysis of a Very Large AltaVista Query Log." *SRC Technical Note* (October 26,1998): 6–12.

Spenner, Kenneth. 1983. "Deciphering Prometheus: Temporal Change in the Skill Level of Work." *American Sociological Review* 48: 824–37.

Spooner, Tom, and Lee Rainie. 2000. *African Americans and the Internet.* Washington, D.C.: Pew Internet and American Life Project (October 22).

Stempel, Guido H., Ill, Thomas Hargrove, and Joseph P. Bernt. 2000. "Relation of Growth of Use of the Internet to Changes in Media Use from 1995 to 1999." *Journalism and Mass Communication Quarterly* 77: 71–79.

Strover, Sharon. 1999. *Rural Internet Connectivity.* Columbia, Mo.: Rural Policy Research Institute.

Tichenor, Phillip, George Donohue, and Clarice Olien. 1970. "Mass Media Flow and Differential Growth of Knowledge." *Public Opinion Quarterly* 34: 159–70.

U.S. Department of Education. 2000. *Internet Access in U.S. Public Schools and Classrooms: 1994–1999: Statistics in Brief.* Washington: U.S. Department of Education, National Center for Educational Statistics (February).

Van Winden, Willem. 2001. "The End of Social Exclusion? On Information Technology Policy as a Key to Social Inclusion in Large European Cities." *Regional Studies* 35: 861–77.

Veblen, Thorstein. 1921/1983. *Engineers and the Price System.* New Brunswick, N.J.: Transaction Books.

Verba, Sidney, Kay Schlozman, and Henry E. Brad. 1995. *Voice and Equality: Civic Voluntarism in American Politics.* Cambridge, Mass. Harvard University Press.

Viswanath, Kasisomayajula, and John Finnegan. 1996. "The Knowledge Gap. Hypothesis: Twenty-five Years Later." In *Communication Yearbook,* vol. 19, edited by Brant R. Burleson. Thousand Oaks, Calif.: Sage Publications.

Viswanath, Kasisomayajula, Gerald M. Kosicki, Eric S. Fredin, and Eunkyung Park. 2000. "Local Community Ties, Community Boundedness, and Local Public Affairs Knowledge Gaps." *Communication Research* 27: 27–50.

Waldfogel, Joel. 2002. "Consumer Substitution Among Media." Working paper. Federal Communications Commission Media Ownership Working Group (September). Available at: hraunfoss.fcc.gov/edocs–Public/attachmatch/DOC-226838A8.pdf. (Last accessed August 29, 2003.)

Waldfogel, Joel, and Lu Chen. 2003. "Does Information Undermine Brand? Information Intermediary Use and Preference for Branded Web Retailers." Working paper. Wharton School, University of Pennsylvania (August 21). Available at: bpp.wharton.upenn.edu/walfogj/pdfs/infoint.pdf (Last accessed August 29, 2003.)

Waxman, Jared. 2000a. *The Old 80/20 Rule Takes One on the Jaw: Internet Trends Report 1999 Review.* San Francisco: Alexa Research.

——. 2000b. *Leading the Pack . . . Internet Trends Report 1999 Review.* San Francisco: Alexa Research.

Weber, Max. 1956/1978. "The Distribution of Power Within the Political Community: Class, Status, and Party." In *Economy and Society.* Edited by Guenther Roth and Claus Wittich: Berkeley: University of California Press. Weliman, Barry. 2001. "Physical Place and Cyber Place: The Rise of Personalized Networking." *International Journal of Urban and Regional Research* 25: 227–52.

Wilson, Ernest J. 2000. *Closing the Digital Divide: In Initial Review: Briefing the President.* Washington, D.C.: Internet Policy Institute (May).

"Globalism's Discontents"

Joseph E. Stiglitz

Few subjects have polarized people throughout the world as much as globalization. Some see it as the way of the future, bringing unprecedented prosperity to everyone, everywhere. Others, symbolized by the Seattle protestors of December 1999, fault globalization as the source of untold problems, from the destruction of native cultures to increasing poverty and immiseration. In this article, I want to sort out the different meanings of globalization. In many countries, globalization has brought huge benefits to a few with few benefits to the many. But in the case of a few countries, it has brought enormous benefit to the many. Why have there been these huge differences in experiences? The answer is that globalization has meant different things in different places.

The countries that have managed globalization on their own, such as those in East Asia, have, by and large, ensured that they reaped huge benefits and that those benefits were equitably shared; they were able substantially to control the terms on which they engaged with the global economy. By contrast, the countries that have, by and large, had globalization managed for them by the International Monetary Fund and other international economic institutions have not done so well. The problem is thus not with globalization but with how it has been managed.

The international financial institutions have pushed a particular ideology—market fundamentalism—that is both bad economics and bad politics; it is based on premises concerning how markets work that do not hold even for developed countries, much less for developing countries. The IMF has pushed these economics policies without a broader vision of society or the role of economics within society. And it has pushed these policies in ways that have undermined emerging democracies.

More generally, globalization itself has been governed in ways that are undemocratic and have been disadvantageous to developing countries, especially the poor within those countries. The Seattle protestors pointed to the absence of democracy and of transparency, the governance of the international economic institutions by and for special corporate and financial interests, and the absence of countervailing democratic checks to ensure that these informal and *public* institutions serve a general interest. In these complaints, there is more than a grain of truth.

Beneficial Globalization

Of the countries of the world, those in East Asia have grown the fastest and done most to reduce poverty. And they have done so, emphatically, via "globalization." Their growth has been based on exports—by taking advantage of the global market for exports and by closing the technology gap. It was not just gaps in capital and other resources that separated the developed from the less-developed countries, but differences in knowledge. East Asian countries took advantage of the "globalization of knowledge" to reduce these disparities. But while some of the countries in the region grew by opening themselves up to multinational companies, others, such as Korea and Taiwan, grew by creating their own enterprises. Here is the key distinction: Each of the most successful globalizing countries determined its own pace of change; each made sure as it grew that the benefits were shared equitably; each rejected the basic tenets of the "Washington Consensus," which argued for a minimalist role for government and rapid privatization and liberalization.

In East Asia, government took an active role in managing the economy. The steel industry that the Korean government created was among the most efficient in the world—performing far better than its private-sector rivals in the United States (which, though private, are constantly turning to the government for protection and for subsidies). Financial markets were highly regulated. My research shows that those regulations promoted growth. It was only when these countries stripped away the regulations, under pressure from the U.S. Treasury and the IMF, that they encountered problems.

During the 1960s, 1970s, and 1980s, the East Asian economies not only grew rapidly but were remarkably stable. Two of the countries most touched by the 1997–1998 economic crises had had in the preceding three decades not a single year of negative growth; two had only one year—a better performance than the United States or the other wealthy nations that make up the Organization for Economic Cooperation and Development (OECD). The single most important factor leading to the troubles that several of the East Asian countries encountered in the late 1990s—the East Asian crisis—was the rapid liberalization of financial and capital markets. In short, the countries of East Asia benefited from globalization because they made globalization work for them; it was when they succumbed to the pressures from the outside that they ran into problems that were beyond their own capacity to manage well.

Globalization can yield immense benefits. Elsewhere in the developing world, globalization of knowledge has brought improved health, with life spans increasing at a rapid pace. How can one put a price on these benefits of globalization? Globalization has brought still other benefits: Today there is the beginning of a globalized civil society that has begun to succeed with such reforms as the Mine Ban Treaty and debt forgiveness for the poorest highly indebted countries (the Jubilee movement). The globalization protest movement itself would not have been possible without globalization.

The Darker Side of Globalization

How then could a trend with the power to have so many benefits have produced such opposition? Simply because it has not only failed to live up to its potential but frequently has had very adverse effects. But this forces us to ask, why has it had such adverse effects? The answer can be seen by looking at each of the economic elements of globalization as pursued by the international financial institutions and especially by the IMF.

The most adverse effects have arisen from the liberalization of financial and capital markets—which has posed risks to developing countries without commensurate rewards. The liberalization has left them prey to hot money pouring into the country, an influx that has fueled speculative real-estate booms; just as suddenly, as investor sentiment changes, the money is pulled out, leaving in its wake economic devastation. Early on, the IMF said that these countries were being rightly punished for pursuing bad economic policies. But as the crisis spread from country to country, even those that the IMF had given high marks found themselves ravaged.

The IMF often speaks about the importance of the discipline provided by capital markets. In doing so, it exhibits certain paternalism, a new form of the old colonial mentality: "We in the establishment, we in the North who run our capital markets, know best. Do what we tell you to do and you will prosper."

The arrogance is offensive, but the objection is more than just to style. The position is highly undemocratic: There is an implied assumption that democracy by itself does not provide sufficient discipline. But if one is to have an external disciplinarian, one should choose a good disciplinarian who knows what is good for growth, who shares one's values. One doesn't want an arbitrary and capricious taskmaster who one moment praises you for your virtues and the next screams at you for being rotten to the core. But capital markets are just such a fickle taskmaster; even ardent advocates talk about their bouts of irrational exuberance followed by equally irrational pessimism.

Lessons of Crisis

Nowhere was the fickleness more evident than in the last global financial crisis. Historically, most of the disturbances in capital flow into and out of a country are not the result of factors inside the country. Major disturbances arise, rather, from influences outside the country. When Argentina suddenly faced high interest rates in 1998, it wasn't because of what Argentina did but because of what happened in Russia. Argentina cannot be blamed for Russia's crisis.

Small developing countries find it virtually impossible to withstand this volatility. I have described capital-market liberalization with a simple metaphor: Small countries are like small boats. Liberalizing capital markets is like setting them loose on a rough sea. Even if the boats are well captained, even if the boats are sound, they are likely to be hit broadside by a big wave and capsize. But the IMF pushed for the boats to set forth into the roughest parts of the sea before they were seaworthy, with untrained captains and crews, and without life vests. No wonder matters turned out so badly!

To see why it is important to choose a disciplinarian who shares ones values, consider a world in which there were free mobility of skilled labor. Skilled labor would then provide discipline. Today, a country that does not treat capital well will find capital quickly withdrawing; in a world of free labor mobility, if a country did not treat skilled labor well, it too would withdraw. Workers would worry about the quality of their children's education and their family's health care, the quality of

their environment and of their own wages and working conditions. They would say to the government: If you fail to provide these essentials, we will move elsewhere. That is a far cry from the kind of discipline that free-flowing capital provides.

The liberalization of capital markets has not brought growth: How can one build factories or create jobs with money that can come in and out of a country overnight? And it gets worse: Prudential behavior requires countries to set aside reserves equal to the amount of short-term lending; so if a firm in a poor country borrows $100 million at, say, 20 percent interest rates short-term from a bank in the United States, the government must set aside a corresponding amount. The reserves are typically held in U.S. Treasury bills—a safe, liquid asset. In effect, the country is borrowing $100 million from the United States and lending $100 million to the United States. But when it borrows, it pays a high interest rate, 20 percent; when it lends, it receives a low interest rate, around 4 percent. This may be great for the United States, but it can hardly help the growth of the poor country. There is also a high *opportunity* cost of the reserves; the money could have been much better spent on building rural roads or constructing schools or health clinics. But instead, the country is, in effect, forced to lend money to the United States.

Thailand illustrates the true ironies of such policies: There, the free market led to investments in empty office buildings, starving other sectors— such as education and transportation—of badly needed resources. Until the IMF and the U.S. Treasury came along, Thailand had restricted bank lending for speculative real estate. The Thais had seen the record: Such lending is an essential part of the boom-bust cycle that has characterized capitalism for 200 years. It wanted to be sure that the scarce capital went to create jobs. But the IMF nixed this intervention in the free market. If the free market said, "Build empty office buildings," so be it! The market knew better than any government bureaucrat who mistakenly might have thought it wiser to build schools or factories.

The Costs of Volatility

Capital-market liberalization is inevitably accompanied by huge volatility, and this volatility impedes growth and increases poverty. It increases the risks of investing in the country, and thus investors demand a risk premium in the form of higher-than-normal profits. Not only is growth not enhanced but poverty is increased through several channels. The high volatility increases the likelihood of recessions—and the poor always bear the brunt of such downturns. Even in developed countries, safety nets are weak or nonexistent among the self-employed and in the rural sector. But these are the dominant sectors in developing countries. Without adequate safety nets, the recessions that follow from capital-market liberalization leads to impoverishment. In the name of imposing budget discipline and reassuring investors, the IMF invariably demands expenditure reductions, which almost inevitably result in cuts in outlays for safety nets that are already threadbare.

But matters are even worse—for under the doctrines of the "discipline of the capital markets," if countries try to tax capital, capital flees. Thus, the IMF doctrines inevitably lead to an increase in tax burdens on the poor and the middle classes. Thus, while IMF bailouts enable the rich to take their money out of the country at more favorable terms (at the overvalued exchange rates), the burden of repaying the loans lies with the workers who remain behind.

The reason that I emphasize capital-market liberalization is that the ease against it—and against the IMF's stance in pushing it—is so compelling. It illustrates what can go wrong with globalization. Even economists like Jagdish Bhagwati, strong advocates of free trade, see the folly in liberalizing capital markets. Belatedly, so too has the IMF—at least in its official rhetoric, though less so in its policy stances—but too late for all those countries that have suffered so much from following the IMF's prescriptions.

But while the case for trade liberalization—when properly done—is quite compelling, the way it has been pushed by the IMF has been far more problematic. The basic logic is simple: Trade liberalization is supposed to result in resources moving from inefficient protected sectors to more efficient export sectors. The problem is not only that job destruction comes before the job creation—so that unemployment and poverty result—but that the IMF's "structural adjustment programs" (designed in ways that allegedly would reassure global investors) make job creation almost impossible. For these programs are often accompanied by high interest rates that are often justified by a single-minded focus on inflation. Sometimes that concern is deserved; often, though, it is carried to an extreme. In the United States, we worry that small increases in the interest rate will discourage investment. The IMF has pushed for far higher interest rates in countries with a far less hospitable investment environment. The high interest rates mean that new jobs and enterprises are not created. What happens is that trade liberalization, rather than moving workers from low-productivity jobs to high-productivity ones, moves them from low-productivity jobs to unemployment. Rather than enhanced growth, the effect is increased poverty. To make matters even worse, the unfair trade-liberalization agenda forces poor countries to compete with highly subsidized American and European agriculture.

The Governance of Globalization

As the market economy has matured within countries, there has been increasing recognition of the importance of having rules to govern it. One hundred fifty years ago, in many parts of the world, there was a domestic process that was in some ways analogous to globalization. In the United States, government promoted the formation of the national economy, the building of the railroads, and the development of the telegraph—all of which reduced transportation and communication costs within the United States. As that process occurred, the democratically elected national government provided oversight: supervising and regulating, balancing interests, tempering crises, and limiting adverse consequences of this very large change in economic structure. So, for instance, in 1863 the U.S. government established the first financial-banking regulatory authority—the Office of the Comptroller of Currency—because it was important to have strong national banks, and that requires strong regulation.

The United States, among the least statist of the industrial democracies, adopted other policies. Agriculture, the central industry of the United States in the mid-nineteenth century, was supported by the 1862 Morrill Act, which established research, extension, and teaching programs. That system worked extremely well and is widely credited with playing a central role in the enormous increases in agricultural productivity over the last century and a half. We established an industrial policy for other fledgling industries, including radio and civil aviation. The beginning of the telecommunications industry, with the first telegraph line between Baltimore and Washington, D.C., was funded by the federal government. And it is a tradition that has continued, with the U.S. government's founding of the Internet.

By contrast, in the current process of globalization we have a system of what I call global governance without global government. International institutions like the World Trade Organization, the IMF, the World Bank, and others provide an ad hoc system of global governance, but it is a far cry from global government and lacks democratic accountability. Although it is perhaps better than not having any system of global governance, the system is structured not to serve general interests or assure equitable results. This not only raises issues of whether broader values are given short shrift; it does not even promote growth as much as an alternative might.

Governance through Ideology

Consider the contrast between how economic decisions are made inside the United States and how they are made in the international economic institutions. In this country, economic decisions within the administration are undertaken largely by the National Economic Council, which includes the secretary of labor, the secretary of commerce, the chairman of the Council of Economic Advisers, the treasury secretary, the assistant attorney general for antitrust, and the U.S. trade representative. The Treasury is only one vote and often gets voted down. All of these officials, of course, are part of an administration that must face Congress and the democratic electorate. But in the international arena, only the voices of the financial community are heard. The IMF reports to the ministers of finance and the governors of the central banks, and one of the important items on its agenda is to make these central banks

more independent—and less democratically accountable. It might make little difference if the IMF dealt only with matters of concern to the financial community, such as the clearance of checks; but in fact, its policies affect every aspect of life. It forces countries to have tight monetary and fiscal policies: It evaluates the trade-off between inflation and unemployment, and in that trade-off it always puts far more weight on inflation than on jobs.

The problem with having the rules of the game dictated by the IMF—and thus by the financial community—is not just a question of values (though that is important) but also a question of ideology. The financial community's view of the world predominates—even when there is little evidence in its support. Indeed, beliefs on key issues are held so strongly that theoretical and empirical support of the positions is viewed as hardly necessary.

Recall again the IMF's position on liberalizing capital markets. As noted, the IMF pushed a set of policies that exposed countries to serious risk. One might have thought, given the evidence of the costs, that the IMF could offer plenty of evidence that the policies also did some good. In fact, there was no such evidence; the evidence that was available suggested that there was little if any positive effect on growth. Ideology enabled IMF officials not only to ignore the absence of benefits but also to overlook the evidence of the huge costs imposed on countries.

An Unfair Trade Agenda

The trade-liberalization agenda has been set by the North, or more accurately, by special interests in the North. Consequently, a disproportionate part of the gains has accrued to the advanced industrial countries, and in some cases the less-developed countries have actually been worse off. After the last round of trade negotiations, the Uruguay Round that ended in 1994, the World Bank calculated the gains and losses to each of the regions of the world. The United States and Europe gained enormously. But sub-Saharan Africa, the poorest region of the world, lost by about 2 percent because of terms-of-trade effects: The trade negotiations opened their markets to manufactured goods produced by the industrialized countries but did not open up the markets of Europe and the United States to the agricultural goods in which poor countries often have a comparative advantage. Nor did the trade agreements eliminate the subsidies to agriculture that make it so hard for the developing countries to compete.

The U.S. negotiations with China over its membership in the WTO displayed a double standard bordering on the surreal. The U.S. trade representative, the chief negotiator for the United States, began by insisting that China was a developed country. Under WTO rules, developing countries are allowed longer transition periods in which state subsidies and other departures from the WTO strictures are permitted. China certainly wishes it were a developed country, with Western-style per capita incomes. And since China has a lot of "capitas," it's possible to multiply a huge number of people by very small average incomes and conclude that the People's Republic is a big economy. But China is not only a developing economy; it is a low-income developing country. Yet the United States insisted that China be treated like a developed country! China went along with the fiction; the negotiations dragged on so long that China got some extra time to adjust. But the true hypocrisy was shown when U.S. negotiators asked, in effect, for developing-country status for the United States to get extra time to shelter the American textile industry.

Trade negotiations in the service industries also illustrate the unlevel nature of the playing field. Which service industries did the United States say were *very* important? Financial services—industries in which Wall Street has a comparative advantage. Construction industries and maritime services were not on the agenda, because the developing countries would have a comparative advantage in these sectors.

Consider also intellectual-property rights, which are important if innovators are to have incentives to innovate (though many of the corporate advocates of intellectual property exaggerate its importance and fail to note that much of the most important research, as in basic science and mathematics, is not patentable). Intellectual-property rights, such as patents and trademarks, need to balance the interests of producers with those of users—not only users in developing countries, but researchers in developed countries. If we underprice the profitability of innovation to the inventor, we deter invention. If we overprice its cost to the research community and the end user, we retard its diffusion and beneficial effects on living standards.

In the final stages of the Uruguay negotiations, both the White House Office of Science and Technology Policy and the Council of Economic Advisers worried that we had not got the balance right—that the agreement put producers' interests over users'. We worried that, with this imbalance, the rate of progress and innovation might actually be impeded. After all, knowledge is the most important input into research, and overly strong intellectual-property rights can, in effect, increase the price of this input. We were also concerned about the consequences of denying lifesaving medicines to the poor. This issue subsequently gained international attention in the context of the provision of AIDS medicines in South Africa. . . . The international outrage forced the drug companies to back down—and it appears that, going forward, the most adverse consequences will be circumscribed. But it is worth noting that initially, even the Democratic U.S. administration supported the pharmaceutical companies.

What we were not fully aware of was another danger—what has come to be called "biopiracy," which involves international drug companies patenting traditional medicines. Not only do they seek to make money from "resources" and knowledge that rightfully belong to the developing countries, but in doing so they squelch domestic firms who long provided these traditional medicines. While it is not clear whether these patents would hold up in court if they were effectively challenged, it is clear that the less-developed countries may not have the legal and financial resources required to mount such a challenge. The issue has become the source of enormous emotional, and potentially economic, concern throughout the developing world. This fall, while I was in Ecuador visiting a village in the high Andes, the Indian mayor railed against how globalization had led to biopiracy.

Globalization and September 11

September 11 brought home a still darker side of globalization—it provided a global arena for terrorists. But the ensuing events and discussions highlighted broader aspects of the globalization debate. It made clear how untenable American unilateralist positions were. President Bush, who had unilaterally rejected the international agreement to address one of the long-term global risks perceived by countries around the world—global warming, in which the United States is the largest culprit—called for a global alliance against terrorism. The administration realized that success would require concerted action by all.

One of the ways to fight terrorists, Washington soon discovered, was to cut off their sources of funding. Ever since the East Asian crisis, global attention had focused on the secretive offshore banking centers. Discussions following that crisis focused on the importance of good information—transparency, or openness—but this was intended for the developing countries. As international discussions turned to the lack of transparency shown by the IMF and the offshore banking centers, the U.S. Treasury changed its tune. It is not because these secretive banking havens provide better services than those provided by banks in New York or London that billions have been put there; the secrecy serves a variety of nefarious purposes—including avoiding taxation and money laundering. These institutions could be shut down overnight—or forced to comply with international norms—if the United States and the other leading countries wanted. They continue to exist because they serve the interests of the financial community and the wealthy. Their continuing existence is no accident. Indeed, the OECD drafted an agreement to limit their scope—and before September 11, the Bush administration unilaterally walked away from this agreement too. How foolish this looks now in retrospect! Had it been embraced, we would have been further along the road to controlling the flow of money into the hands of the terrorists.

There is one more aspect to the aftermath of September 11 worth noting here. The United States was already in recession, but the attack made matters worse. It used to be said that when the United States sneezed, Mexico caught a cold. With globalization, when the United States sneezes, much of the rest of the world risks catching pneumonia. And the United States now has a bad case of the flu. With globalization, mismanaged macroeconomic policy in the United States—the failure to design an effective stimulus package—has global consequences. But around the world, anger at the traditional IMF policies is growing. The developing countries are saying to the industrialized nations: "When you face a slowdown, you follow the precepts that we are all taught in our economic courses: You adopt expansionary monetary and fiscal policies. But when we face a slowdown, you insist on contractionary policies. For you, deficits are okay; for us, they are impermissible—even if we can raise the funds through 'selling forward,' say, some natural resources." A heightened sense of inequity prevails, partly because the consequences of maintaining contractionary policies are so great.

Global Social Justice

Today, in much of the developing world, globalization is being questioned. For instance, in Latin America, after a short burst of growth in the early 1990s, stagnation and recession have set in. The growth was not sustained—some might say, was not sustainable. Indeed, at this juncture, the growth record of the so-called post-reform era looks no better, and in some countries much worse, than in the widely criticized import-substitution period of the 1950s and 1960s when Latin countries tried to industrialize by discouraging imports. Indeed, reform critics point out that the burst of growth in the early 1990s was little more than a "catch-up" that did not even make up for the lost decade of the 1980s.

Throughout the region, people are asking: "Has reform failed or has globalization failed?" The distinction is perhaps artificial, for globalization was at the center of the reforms. Even in those countries that have managed to grow, such as Mexico, the benefits have accrued largely to the upper 30 percent and have been even more concentrated in the top 10 percent. Those at the bottom have gained little; many are even worse off. The reforms have exposed countries to greater risk, and the risks have been borne disproportionately by those least able to cope with them. Just as in many countries where the pacing and sequencing of reforms has resulted in job destruction outmatching job creation, so too has the exposure to risk outmatched the ability to create institutions for coping with risk, including effective safety nets.

In this bleak landscape, there are some positive signs. Those in the North have become more aware of the inequities of the global economic architecture. The agreement at Doha to hold a new round of trade negotiations—the "Development Round"—promises to rectify some of the imbalances of the past. There has been a marked change in the rhetoric of the international economic institutions—at least they talk about poverty. At the World Bank, there have been some real reforms; there has been some progress in translating the rhetoric into reality—in ensuring that the voices of the poor are heard and the concerns of the developing countries are listened to. But elsewhere, there is often a gap between the rhetoric

and the reality. Serious reforms in governance, in who makes decisions and how they are made, are not on the table. If one of the problems at the IMF has been that the ideology, interests, and perspectives of the financial community in the advanced industrialized countries have been given disproportionate weight (in matters whose effects go well beyond finance), then the prospects for success in the current discussions of reform, in which the same parties continue to predominate, are bleak. They are more likely to result in slight changes in the shape of the table, not changes in who is at the table or what is on the agenda.

September 11 has resulted in a global alliance against terrorism. What we now need is not just an alliance *against* evil, but an alliance *for* something positive—a global alliance for reducing poverty and for creating a better environment, an alliance for creating a global society with more social justice.

III

Status

Section A: Race and Ethnicity

INTRODUCTION

As a social force, race matters most when there are two or more relatively discrete racial groups engaged in some kind of struggle over scarce resources and opportunities. Members of different groups make claims about essential characteristics that define their own group versus others. While there is clearly some physiological variation among different groups of human beings, the social circumstances are more important. That is why a woman from Ghana or a man from Ireland will have varying identities and life chances depending on where and when they live. Think of west Africa versus South Carolina in 1700, Dublin or Boston in 1800, or Manhattan in 1900 compared to 2000.

"The Problem of the 20th century is the problem of the color line." While DuBois was looking forward as he wrote these prophetic words, the problem of the color line had been a defining theme since before the country was founded. Indeed, the conquest of lands controlled by Native Americans and the enslavement of Africans made the founding possible. While Weber, DuBois, Cooper, and many others have helped to explain the cultural, historical character of racial identity and how it is entangled in power relations, the concept of race remains elusive. The reason for this, apart from endless debate that gives rise to varied definitions, is that the lived experience of race is extremely complicated.

In "The 'Morphing' Properties of 'Whiteness,'" Troy Duster illuminates this complexity by describing race in terms of the metaphor of H_2O. Like H_2O, racial identity can change from being solid, to fluid, to vaporous. Yet, to extend the metaphor, in American society there is always at least some moisture in the air, as Claude Steele demonstrates in "A Threat in the Air: How Stereotypes Shape Intellectual Identity and Performance." Through a series of experiments, Steele reveals the costs of contemporary "double consciousness" for women and minorities aware that they are being judged both as individuals and as members of subjugated groups.

Edurado Bonilla-Silva argues here in an excerpt from *Racism without Racists* that we do not have to find white supremacists or legal apartheid to encounter the insidious effects of racism that marginalizes whole categories of people. Rosalind S. Chou and Joe R. Feagin contend in *The Myth of the Model Minority: Asian Americans Facing Racism* (excerpted here) that even positive stereotypes can be dehumanizing when they reduce the complexity of the diverse lives of people and obscure forces of oppression. Marta Tienda and other scholars of the National Research Council show how the history of Hispanic peoples from different places channeled through American institutions has made for an intricate story. As this excerpt from *Multiple Origins, Uncertain Destinies*, suggests, the American experience has always been broader and more complicated than the interaction of blacks and whites. Indeed, Latinos themselves encompass a range of varied peoples and stories. As subtle as racial meaning can be, however, social scientists have also identified numerous blatant examples of institutionalized discrimination in very recent research. For all of the efforts in pursuit of

racial integration, Vincent Roscigno and his colleagues document an unyielding pattern in "The Complexities and Processes of Racial Housing Discrimination." The growing concerns about our ecosystem have an important connection to stratification as well, as explained by Robin Saha and Paul Mohai in "Historical Context and Hazard Waste Siting: Understanding Temporal Patterns in Michigan." Sometimes the uneven distribution of resources hurts those who get the most, that is, when the resource in question is toxic. For all the structural stratification systems, it also appears that basic, personal discrimination is alive and well. "Are Emily and Greg More Employable than Lakisha and Jamal?" Marianne Bertrand and Sendhil Mullainathan answer, sadly, yes.

13

"The 'Morphing' Properties of Whiteness"

TROY DUSTER

In discussions of race and the recent rediscovery of the American preoccupation with whiteness, it is possible to isolate two overarching but sharply conflicting frameworks that run at cross-purposes. On the one hand, there are those who portray race and whiteness as fluid, continually reflecting emergent and contingent features of social life, emphasizing the relational and ever-changing character of race. On the other hand, it is not difficult to identify historians, writers, and social analysts who have emphasized the deeply embedded, structural, hard, enduring, solid-state features of race and racism, sustained throughout three centuries even as they have acknowledged the occasional shifting boundaries of who gets included in the category "white."

Race as Arbitrary and Whimsical versus Race as Structural and Enduring

If we take even a casual excursion through the last few centuries of racial classification, there is overwhelming evidence on the side of those who have argued that race is arbitrary, shifting, and often *biologically* and *sociologically* inconsistent, contradictory, and simple-minded. The rule that one drop of black blood makes one black is the easy mark along a full continuum of mind-boggling, ludicrous taxonomies.[1] "Passing" and incoherent "miscegenation laws" and slave-owner/slave offspring do more than simply dot the landscape with the minefields of this topic. This continuum extends well into the present period, in which we find more and more people asserting a mixed-race identity Since the classification of race is arbitrary and often whimsical (for example, one drop of blood), accepting the idea that race is something identifiable with fixed borders that could be crossed and thus "mixed"—while others are "not mixed"—is supplanting one multitiered fiction with another. At the biochemical level of blood types and hematology, at the neurological level of neurotransmission patterns, at the level of cell function–at all these levels, we are all "mixed" by any taxonomy or measure of allele frequency of large population groups.[2] It would seem that we must "score one" for the side that sees the superficiality and artificiality of race.

Other Voices

Yet there is another set of very compelling voices (present in other papers in this volume) emphasizing how race, or in this case whiteness and its attendant privilege, is deeply embedded in the routine structures of economic and political life. From ordinary service at Denny's Restaurants, to far greater access to bank loans to simple peaceful, *police-event–free* driving—all these things have come unreflectively with the territory of being white.[3] One does not give up racial privilege, neither in the United States nor in South Africa, by simply denying that it exists. Whites who have come to a point where they acknowledge their racial privilege are in a difficult circumstance morally because they cannot just shed that privilege with a simple assertion of denial.

So who is right? One side sees race as everchanging. The other side sees enduring race privilege. Oddly, both sides are correct. Or, at least, both sides have an important handle on an elementary truth about race. But *empirically,* one could easily ask, if these two positions are poles apart, how can both be correct about race? How can race be both structural and embedded yet superficial, arbitrary and whimsical—shifting with times and circumstances?

The best way to communicate how this is possible is to employ an analogy—to water or, more precisely, H_2O. While water is a fluid state, at certain contingent moments, under thirty-two degrees, it is transformed into a solid state—ice. This is an easy binary formulation. But things get more complicated, because when H_2O, at still another contingent moment boils, it begins to vaporize or evaporate. And now the coup de grace of the analogy of H_2O to race: H_2O in its vapor state can condense, come back and transform into water, and then freeze and hit you in its solid state as an ice block; what you thought had evaporated into the thin air can return in a form that is decidedly and consequentially real. In short, H_2O is to serve now as more than just my analogy to race—and, in this context, whiteness. Race, like H_2O, can take many forms, but unlike H_2O it can transform itself in a nanosecond. It takes time for ice to boil or for vapor to condense and freeze, but race can be *simultaneously* Janus-faced and

multifac(et)ed—and also produce a singularly dominant social hierarchy. Indeed, if we make the fundamental mistake of reifying any one of those states as more real than another, we will lose basic insights into the nature and character of racial stratification in America. So it depends on when a picture is taken in this sequence and on who takes the picture as to whether race is best understood as fluid or solid or vapor—or has evaporated into a temporally locatable nonexistence, a color-blind fragment in time and space.

If We Are All One Race, How Could There Be "Whiteness" in Its Solid State?

A consortium of leading scientists across the disciplines from biology to physical anthropology issued a "Revised UNESCO Statement on Race" in 1995. This is a definitive declaration that summarizes eleven central issues and concludes that in terms of "scientific" discourse there is no such thing as a "race" that has any scientific utility, at least in the biological sciences: "[T]he same scientific groups that developed the biological concept over the last century have now concluded that its use for characterizing human populations is so flawed that it is no longer a scientifically valid concept. In fact, the statement makes clear that the biological concept of race as applied to humans has no legitimate place in biological science."[4] By the mid-1970s, it had become abundantly clear that there is more genetic variation within the most current common socially used categories of race than between these categories.[5] The consensus is newly formed. For example, in the early part of this century, scientists in several countries tried to link up a study of the major blood groups in the ABO system to racial and ethnic groups.[6] Since researchers knew that blood type B was more common in certain ethnic and racial groups—which they believed to be more inclined to criminality and mental illness—this was often a thinly disguised form of racism.[7] They kept running up against a brick wall.

It is not difficult to understand why they persisted. Humans are symbol-bearing creatures who give meaning to their experiences and to their symbolic worlds. The UNESCO statement of the 1990s is ultimately about the problem of the difference between first-order constructs in science and second-order constructs. Some fifty years ago, Felix Kaufmann made a crucial distinction that throws some light on the controversy.[8] Kaufmann was not addressing whether or not there could be a science of race. Rather, he noted that there are different kinds of issues, methodologies, and theories that are generated by what could be called first-order constructs in the physical and natural sciences versus second-order constructs. For the physical and natural sciences, the naming of objects for investigation and inquiry, for conceptualizing and finding empirical regularities, is in the hands of the scientists and their scientific peers. Thus, for example, the nomenclature for quarks or neurons, genes or chromosomes, nitrogen or sulfides, and so on all reside with the scientist qua scientist in his/her role as the creator of first-order constructs.

This is quite different from the task of the observer, analyst, or scientist of human social behavior. Humans live in a pre-interpreted social world: they grow up, from infancy in a world that has pre-assigned categories and names for those categories, which were in turn provided by fellow commonsense actors, not by "scientists." Persons live in the world that is pre-interpreted for them, and their continual task is to try to navigate, negotiate, and make sense of that world. The task of the social scientist is therefore quite distinct from that of the natural scientist. While the latter can rely on first-order constructs, the former must construct a set of categories based on the pre-interpreted world of commonsense actors. The central problem is that "race" is now, and has been since 1735, both a first- and second-order construct. This was the year that Linnaeus published *Systema Naturae,* in which he revealed a four-part classification scheme of the human races that has residues still today.

We now turn to the matter of whether race can be studied scientifically. If we mean by that, is there a consensus among the natural scientists about race as a first order construct, then the answer since about 1970 is categorically no. The UNESCO Statement summarizes why this is so at every level that is significant to the biological functioning of the organism, with two exceptions. We have already noted that scientific research on first-order constructs

about race as a biological category in science in the last four decades has revealed over and over again that there is greater genetic heterogeneity within rather than between major racial groupings. One of the two exceptions has to do with the fact that the gene frequencies, as demonstrated in the use of specific polymorphic markers, occur more frequently in certain populations than in others.[9] But this distribution of allele frequencies, though occasionally overlapping with racial groupings, is definitely not only a racially defined issue. For example, northern Europeans have greater concentrations of cystic fibrosis than southern Europeans, and both are categorized as "Caucasians." Moreover, southern Europeans have higher rates of beta-thalassemia than northern Europeans—but, even more to the point, sickle-cell anemia is found in greater concentration in Orchomenus, Greece, than among African Americans.[10] While clinical geneticists are quite familiar with these wide patterns of variations between and among persons who appear phenotypically to be of a certain "race," when an African American with cystic fibrosis shows up at a cystic fibrosis clinic, there is as much consternation about this person's possibly being in the wrong place. When a white person with sickle-cell anemia appears in a sickle-cell clinic, there is often explicit speculation that this person is "passing" and is *really* black.[11]

Thus, the "commonsense" question of whether someone is black or white or Asian is frequently difficult to pin down at the margins—but residents of the United States have been acting as if this were self-evident. The allocation of such resources as loans to build houses has been based on such casual visual cues as whether one "appears to be" white or black. Over time, with the patterned distribution of loans, the racialized shape of suburbs and inner cities began to look "quite real"—solidifying into a solid state of racial boundary maintenance—all the while a kind of second-order construct.

Race, Law, and Second-Order Constructs

Three acts were passed by the U.S. Congress in 1934–35 that would seal the accumulation of wealth into white households for the next half-century. There is some new scholarship emerging reexamining the role of race in explaining U.S. domestic policy for the last half century.[12]

The new work is fascinating in that it points out the systematic, integrated character of policies of the federal government that will surprise most Americans who grew up reading high school civics books that trumpeted the race-neutral character of Franklin Roosevelt's New Deal government policies. For example, Jill Quadagno notes that while there is some truth to the claim that the New Deal was designed to provide a "floor of protection for the industrial working class," it was the brokered compromises over the New Deal that simultaneously "reinforced racial segregation through social welfare programs, labor policy, and housing policy" How, and why?

In 1935 Roosevelt had put together a fragile coalition of northern industrial workers and southern whites still engaged in a primarily agrarian economic order. Blacks were a vital part of that agrarian system, but they could not vote in the South. Thus Roosevelt did not need to even try to court what was not there: the black southern vote. During this period, more than three-quarters of the black population still lived in the South. Most of them sharecropped and were tied to the plantation economy at poverty-level wages. Those who were not share-croppers were engaged in day labor— with most of these employed at $2.00 per 100 pounds of cotton. This translated to $2.00 per day for a strong worker.[13]

Black women worked as maids, making $2.00 per week on average. White southerners in control of key positions in Congress explicitly voiced fears that any federal programs that would put money directly into the pockets of blacks would undermine the very infrastructure of this plantation economy. As chairs of the powerful committees of the House and Senate, they blocked any attempt to change the agrarian system that indentured black sharecroppers. Because of this opposition, which is documented in memoranda between Congress and the White House, Roosevelt compromised, and agricultural workers and servants were excluded from the Social Security of 1935. The exclusion of agricultural workers and house servants appears in retrospect to have been race-neutral. At the time, however, *the key actors said they would block all Social Security legislation if it included blacks.*

Similarly the Wagner Act of 1935 labeled in some circles as the Magna Carta of labor, was on closer inspection the Magna Carta of white labor.[14] The original version, which permitted the organization of industrial labor and legalized collective bargaining, *prohibited racial discrimination.* But the American Federation of Labor and the same constellation of white southerners who controlled the key committees of Congress fought it, and the final version permitted racial exclusion. Because the racial exclusion language was applied to closed shops, blacks were blocked by law from challenging the barriers to entry into the newly protected labor unions and securing the right to collective bargaining.[15]

Finally, in 1937 Congress passed the National Housing Act which sealed the fate of America's cities, creating the social policy and economic basis for sustained and exacerbated racial segregation. While many commentators have blamed "white flight" for the creation of ghettos and barrios, it was actually this heavily coded racial policy of the federal government of the United States that created white enclaves in the suburbs. In 1939 the Federal Housing Authority's *Underwriting Manual* guidelines for granting housing loans explicitly used race as the single most important criterion. The following passage is from Section 937 of the FHA manual that covered the period in question: "If a neighborhood is to retain stability, it is necessary that properties shall be continued to be occupied by the same social and racial classes."[16]

On this basis, for the next thirty years, whites were able to get housing loans at 3 to 5 percent, while blacks were routinely denied such loans. For example, of 350,000 new homes built in northern California between 1946 and 1960 with FHA support, *fewer than 100 went to blacks.* That same pattern holds for the whole state, and for the nation as well. Between 1935 and 1950, eleven million homes were built in the United States with federal assistance, and Charles Abrams has documented well his assertion that "discrimination against Negroes was a condition of federal assistance." The official code of ethics of the National Association of Real Estate Boards not only barred its members from selling houses across the racial divide but put teeth behind its code. In a 1943 brochure titled *Fundamentals of Real Estate Practice*, the association outlined grounds for expulsion of realtors who violated race-based sales and then went on to state explicitly what constituted problematic behavior:

> The prospective buyer might be a bootlegger who would cause considerable annoyance to his neighbors, a madame who had a number of Call Girls on her string, a gangster, who wants a screen for his activities by living in a better neighborhood, a colored man of means who was giving his children a college education and thought they were entitled to live among whites. . . No matter what the motive or character of the would-be purchaser, if the deal would instigate a form of blight, then certainly the well-meaning broker must work against its consummation.

The urban redevelopment programs sponsored by the federal government under the National Housing Act of 1949 also served to undermine the financial solidity of the black community. The alignment of corridors in the major cities was chosen so that the freeways almost universally cut through core areas of black settlements, while connecting the white suburbs to the central business districts of the cities. As a direct result of these programs, many urban black areas lost their neighborhood shopping districts of successful small businesses. This was soon followed by empirically demonstrable race-conscious systematic mortgage "redlining," which had a downward-spiraling effect on the economic vitality of scores of black communities.[17]

It should now be clear that the assertion of a fact—that median family net worth of individuals in the United States who are socially designated as "white" is $43,279, while the median family net worth of individuals in the United States who are socially designated as "black" is $4,169—is a matter that can be determined to be true or false by the systematic collection of empirical data, and either replicated or refuted. In other words, it can

be investigated scientifically, without reference to blood groups, the relationship between genotype and phenotype, or the likelihood that one group is more at risk for cystic fibrosis while the other is more at risk for sickle-cell anemia.

To definitively assert that at the blood group level, or at the level of the modulatory environment for neurotransmission in the brain, there are no real racial differences (read biological) is to reify a particular version of the biological sciences as *science*. This would ignore the capacity of scientific inquiry to apprehend the social reality of the ten-to-one economic advantage of corning from a white household in America versus coming from a black household. Although loan allocations based on crude phenotypical versions of racial differences are second-order constructs, the ten-to-one ratio by "race" noted above is subject to scientific investigation as well. It can be challenged or proven false or replicated over and over again. Nonetheless, patterned social behavior associated with "race" leads to a confusion about the role of genetics and the way in which the analyst peers through the prism of heritability at the direction of the causal arrow. Richard Herrnstein and Charles Murray, James Wilson and Richard Herrnstein, Arthur Jensen and a wide band of other claimants with no training in genetics make the common-sense mistake of treating race as a biological construct, then reading back through social patterns (scoring on a test; rate of incarceration) to make inferences about the biological underpinnings of social patterns.[18] For example, *Herrnstein* and Murray posit the dominance of genetics in explaining IQ, concluding that "the genetic component of IQ" is 60 per cent. Then, taking IQ as the independent variable, the authors extend this analysis to the genetic explanation of social achievement or failure, so that unemployment, crime, and social standing are "explained" by IQ.[19] Despite a heavy reliance on the genetic explanation of intelligence as measured by test scores, the basic data from the molecular genetics revolution of the last three decades are completely absent.

Herrnstein and Murry posit that genetics plays an important, even dominant role in IQ, proposing that it is a whopping 60 percent of g, a statistical measure assumed to be related to "general intelligence." Neither Herrnstein (a psychologist) nor Murray (a political scientist) demonstrates sufficient knowledge of contemporary developments in the human biosciences to be aware of a fundamental problem in attributing g to genetics. Even single-gene determined phenotypical expressions such as Huntington's disease, beta-thalassemia, and sickle-cell anemia exhibit a wide range of clinical manifestations. For multifactorial conditions—of which, incontestably, we must include the evolving thought processes of the brain—the interaction between nutrition, cellular development, and neurological sequencing has been firmly established. Developments of the last decade reveal a remarkable feedback loop between the brain and the "experience" of an environment. We now can demonstrate that a single neuron display a variety of activity patterns and will switch between them, depending on the modulatory environment.[20] Anyone aware of current developments in cognitive science knows that a one-way deterministic notion of the firing of the neurotransmitters and subsequent behavior is a deeply reductionist fallacy. Thus to assign to "genetics" a ballpark figure of any kind, without regard to these well-known interaction effects, is to display a profound ignorance of the last three decades of developments in molecular biology and the neurosciences, most especially since Herrnstein and Murray posit genetics (60 percent) as the most powerful explanatory variable.

The inverse of the attempt to get at a biological construct of race is the assertion, by those committed to a class analysis, that class rather than race is ultimately the master stratifying practice in technologically advanced industrial and postindustrial societies. But that is also open to empirical investigation. Both the biological construct and the class construct are attempts at first-order conceptions, and, as such, they appear on the surface to be more scientific. Yet, there is a fundamental error in the logic of inquiry here. As we have seen, when those who make bank loan decisions do so with their own sets of symbolic strategies—*and those practices are routinized*—the stratified outcomes are a compelling site for *scientific* investigation.

The debate about whether race or class is "more real" as a stratifying practice can be better understood by reexamining how the issue is framed. What is it about class that makes it more real than race—save for the empirical fact that more people employ it (or do not) as a way of sorting social, political, and economic relations? The power of apartheid in South Africa and Jim Crow in the United States demonstrates that such facts are as much located in the practices of actors as in the "objective" relations of workers to capital. The answer is that, objectively speaking, class relations are governed by just such an attempt at a first-order construct: the connections to the workplace. But during apartheid (and even after, there is evidence to believe), whites have had greater access to scarce resources than blacks. This is an "objective" reality of a stratifying practice, no less because it is a second-order construct employed by those acting in the world. Rather, during apartheid, it was even definitively a pattern with notable and obvious replicability (i.e., as a stratifying practice).

The trouble with expertise about race is that once we write books and articles about it, we capture some part of it for a particular understanding. We then become committed to that singular version of it, and often become defensive and aggressive in our defense of our "turf" of a particular rendering.[21] But if scholars and researchers have trouble, lay persons have at least as hard a time holding simultaneously conflicting imagery about the multiple realities of race in America. And so I am going to tell a story about my own youth, when I came to understand the contingent character of race and whiteness and how people can make strategic use of it.

Race in Its Fluid State: A Personal Tale

When I attended college many years ago at Northwestern University, I was one of six black undergraduates on a campus of over seven thousand students. Northwestern is just outside Chicago, something of the midwestern equivalent of Stanford in that it draws heavily from the upper middle-class of the Chicago region. And so it follows that it would be very unlikely that my particular phenotype would be expressed at Northwestern.

While I was there, I came to know Jack Doyle, a fellow student who was from an Irish working-class background. Gruff in manner and tough in appearance, Doyle was also something of a standout in that world. He and I became close friends, and we have sustained that friendship long beyond our collegiate careers. After our college days, and over the years, we would often get together whenever I returned to Chicago. A dozen or so years later, after I got my Ph.D. and was teaching at Berkeley I returned to Chicago, visiting my mother for a week. One evening, I gave Jack a call, and he came over on this particular hot August night to join me for a beer. Around eleven o'clock at night, my mother came home from a neighborhood meeting and said she forgot to get food for the next day's breakfast. She asked if I would drive her around to the store on Sixty-third, just off Cottage Grove. So I said, "Of course," and we got in the car and drove around to the store. Jack Doyle joined us, so there we were—the three of us. We parked on Sixty-third Street, and, while Jack and I sat in the car, my mother went in to the store to get the groceries. I noticed that police cars occasionally would circle but that was nothing new to me.

After about the third or fourth time around, however, three big, tough-looking, white police officers jumped out, one with gun drawn, and said to us, "Get out of that car." So we got out. They bent us over the hood of the car and frisked us, and then they said to me, 'What are you doing here?" But before I could answer, they turned to my friend, "And what are you doing here?" Remember this is an all-black area of Chicago.

And he said, "I've come to visit my friend." One of the police officers said, "Your friend from where?" "Northwestern," I replied. He said, "Northwestern? You're college boys?" Then with sardonic disbelief dripping from the question, he asked, "Okay, college boys—what did you study?" We told them. We were not very convincing because one of them said, quite agitatedly, "I asked you, 'What are you doing here on a Saturday night parked in front of a grocery store?'" Sometimes the truth will not set you free. I told the truth: "I'm waiting for my mother." That's when I saw his billy club. He lifted it slowly, deliberately, and I had the experience of all of this happening as if in slow-motion—as in a baseball pitcher's exaggerated wind-up before the delivery. And all the

while he was saying, "You're a real wise ass—" Then, all of a sudden, the voice from the heavens parts the thick hot August night air. It is my mother's voice booming with authority:

"Officer, what's going on here?"

In that one moment, perhaps even a nanosecond, I understood the fluid and Janus-faced character of race. I saw it happen with my own eyes. Within midair, this tough white cop turned officer-of-the-law and literally turned and tipped his hat to my mother and said, "Madam, we're here to serve and protect you." Yes. A remarkable capacity for transmogrification or, perhaps better, *morphing*. He went from solid state to fluid state. He transformed himself from "an occupying force of domination" into someone there "to protect a woman citizen" from a suspicious character—from the sort of person like me who waits out in front of grocery stores casing the joint "round midnight." Back in the 1960s there were two competing versions of the police. One version said, *"The police are a force to serve and protect you."* Bumper stickers with that slogan were pasted on cars all over the country. Contrarily, there was another set of bumper stickers, disproportionately seen in the black communities of the nation, which read, *"The police are an occupation force."* In America, depending more on your race than anything else, you will routinely see this issue of police "occupation" or "service" through one lens or the other.

The concept of race has that complexity. Writers Noel Ignatiev, John Garvey, and David Roediger have discussed "the abolition of whiteness."[22] That is not a bad idea, depending on context and historical circumstances. However, it might not be a good idea either. That is, what would you say if suddenly after forty-eight to fifty years of apartheid, in which whites had begun to collect and accumulate lots of wealth—land—they suddenly turned around and said, "Let's abolish whiteness—now we're all individuals. Apartheid is over, so we'll all start from scratch. Let's have no group designation by color."

To many, this sounds like hollow rhetoric, more like the ideology of privilege in behalf of the accumulation of more privilege of those who take the position that one cannot simply decontextualize or ahistoricize the notion of race.

As the extreme case, let us take the current situation in South Africa. Whites spent the last half century (1947–93) creating and implementing laws that permitted themselves, as whites, to accumulate wealth and land and power, to have access to universities and corporate boardrooms, to have wages five to ten times that of black workers doing the same labor. Blacks had to carry identification cards in order to move out of legally enforced residences in squalid all-black townships and villages, where there was no running water, no sewage drainage, and underfunded and poor schools.[23] Then, in 1993, after forty-five years of official apartheid, white monopoly on access to good jobs and good education suddenly came to a *legal* end—but not before whites had accumulated more than ten times the wealth of blacks.

The new president, a black man imprisoned for twenty-seven of those years because of his opposition to apartheid, issued guidelines for trying to redress some of those past grievances. He and his cabinet would call for a plan of "affirmative action" to redress the following situation: In 1992, when the writing was on the wall and apartheid's days were numbered, the corporate managers at Telkom, South Africa's national telephone company, did a quick review of the racial composition of its corporate structure, an organization with more than 58,000 employees. In late 1993, they found one more black manager than many expected—that is, they found one. By the second half of 1995, Telkom employed eighty-three black managers and since then has embarked on an aggressive affirmative action program to recruit and hire more.

Would it then be imaginable that some groups of whites would step forward and cry foul? They already have. More than 5,000 white workers threatened to strike to protest the new policy.[24] The rhetoric regarding why affirmative action is morally wrong is rich in irony. "It's reverse discrimination," complained A. C. van Wyk, spokesman for the Mine Workers Union of South Africa, a union that still bars blacks from membership!

To illustrate the further abuses of the extraordinary manipulation of power through language, critics of affirmative action programs in South Africa that would place blacks in positions held exclusively by whites for the last half-century are now dubbing affirmative action "neo-apartheid." *The banner under which this all flies is fairness to the individual!*

Now let us imagine an even more unlikely circumstance in which a group with 2,000 years of historic privilege, that has accumulated wealth and power as a consequence of having been part of a group, then suddenly turns around and says, "From now on, we *are* only individuals." This might be the caste system of India. For more than 2,000 years, certain groups had access to literacy—indeed, were required by the caste system to be literate. And, by contrast, other groups were channeled into occupations that required differing skills, training, and education. Finally, some in this system were "outcastes"—literally outside the system and therefore "untouchable." If one inside the system touched one from the wrong category, ritual cleansing had to occur in order to rid oneself of the pollution created by this contact.

Ironically, the apartheid system in South Africa was officially beginning (1948) just one year after the caste system ended officially, formally and legally. But just because the laws ended the caste system, 2,000 years of habit, pattern, ideology, *and privilege* could not be brought to a sudden halt. The caste system prohibited the lowest castes from drawing water from the same wells or from walking down the same paths; and, most relevant to today's debates about individual fairness, the children were forbidden to go to schools—any schools.[25]

The government of India embarked on a program to redress these past exclusionary policies, and much later that policy would be renamed affirmative action. Scheduled castes were to be provided with at least 12.5 percent of vacancies in government positions where there was to be open recruitment across the nation.[26] Not only were places in the workforce set aside for occupancy by members of the scheduled castes; places in universities and in law schools were also set aside for formerly disenfranchised groups. In 1961, after a review of the situation, the figure was raised from 12.5 to 15 percent set-asides.[27] By 1990 the government actually set aside more than twenty percent of jobs that it controls for the scheduled castes and scheduled tribes, It would be difficult to guess what the Brahmans argued. They called the plan "reverse discrimination" and said that it would hurt their chances of finding work after graduation.[28] They argued that to use any group criterion would not be fair to those individual Brahmans who had studied hard and gotten better grades than students from the lower castes. No matter that the Brahmans were the group required to be literate so that they could avail themselves of the sacred books. No matter. After all those centuries of accumulation of cultural capital that came directly from membership in a group category, many of them took to the streets to demonstrate and riot, arguing that the caste system was dead and gone . . . that from now on, they were only individuals . . . that, in short, only individuals without any significant remnants of caste privilege remained in India. Suddenly, after more than 2,000 years of the caste system, and familial access routes to privilege afforded to individuals because of their membership in a group, now nothing remained but *objective* grade-point averages.

Both the Brahmans and the white South Africans who oppose policies to partially redress gross injustices that favored their group can retreat to a comfortable position of personal nonculpability: since "I didn't personally discriminate against anybody, I can't be blamed for apartheid (or caste stratification), and so I should not be penalized for something I didn't do." And with that marvelously simple sleight-of-hand, Brahmans in India and white South Africans can wash their hands of any taint of privilege that they experience for having been born to a position of enormous social and economic advantage. Indeed, since there are only individuals, and individual responsibility and individual entitlement are the only currency in the contemporary discourse about race policies and affirmative action policies—not having had a personal hand in the oppression of others makes one innocent. The mere fact that one is from a group that has accumulated wealth at a ratio of more than ten to one over the capital of another group is rendered irrelevant by the legerdemain of invoking individual fairness. We are all individuals, but we are also simultaneously members of families,

nation-states, racial and/or ethnically designated groups, and sometimes religious groups. "Fairness to the individual" must always have a social and historical context; when that context is ignored, it is a cheap political trick in the service of the ideology of those in power.

In the United States significant wage and salary differences between the races persist, with blacks earning anywhere from about two-thirds to three-quarters of what whites obtain in wages and salaries.[29] Since this gap has narrowed somewhat over the last three decades, analysts who wish to portray the situation as one of a slow improvement inevitably focus on these figures. *However, focusing merely on wages and salary differences obscures a critical measure of wealth: net worth.* Wages and salaries are dependent on employment, and in the current economic situation of the United States there is far less job security than in previous periods. A combination of massive downsizing and layoffs, along with seasonal and part-time employment, characterizes much of the contemporary work setting. Different spheres of work are more likely to employ whites than blacks. For example, blacks are more likely to be employed in the public sector, the focus of systemic and often effective attacks by conservatives for the last decade and a half. All of this means that wages and salaries are not the most secure measures by which to assess the likelihood of sustained socioeconomic improvement and long-term wealth.

At the end of the more than 2,000 years of the official caste system of India, caste law was struck down in the late 1940s, and "all of a sudden" all Indians had equal "formal" legal status. And, of course, what happened was predictable: those groups that had accumulated privilege based on the accumulation of all those years would turn around and say, "We're only individuals." Such a framing of the problem is transparently in the service of the perpetuation of privilege and power. The deck, in short, is stacked when, after systematic accumulation of wealth based on group membership, laws are suddenly passed that have the surface appearance of applying to all. It brings to life Anatole France's famous line, "The law, in its majestic neutrality, forbids both rich and poor from sleeping under bridges at night, begging and stealing bread."

In a society that is racially stratified, the claim that individualistic universalism is the best way to end race or racism—that we should all become color-blind—is itself a not so subtle denial that race has produced deeply consequential structural privilege. But, of course, all whites are not equally privileged. Many do not experience material privilege, and they certainly do not feel it.

Race in Its Solid State

Why study whiteness at this historical moment? What has happened in the last twenty, thirty years in America to generate a remarkable surge of interest in this topic? Several developments help explain it, but one important element is a demographic shift in the urban landscape.

In the last twenty-five years, cities in the United States have under gone the greatest racial transformation of their entire history. In the 1970s almost every major metropolitan area—certainly the top twelve—were primarily white ("Anglo" by those classifications). By 1990, however, the census revealed that of those top twelve, ten now had majority "minority" populations. Indeed, in some jurisdictions, most notably Los Angeles, the ratio had gone from 75 percent white to about 37 percent white. In New York City we witnessed a similar kind of transformation, and that shift was occurring all over the country.

During this period, the white population—especially in urban America—began to experience its "whiteness." It began to feel marked by "race," and, once marked, there's something to observe, to study, and to account for. The need to deny "white flight to the suburbs" and the need to simultaneously deny the accumulation of wealth are reminiscent of the way elites of India and whites in postapartheid South Africa now face their worlds "as individuals." Yet most white Americans find it very hard to swallow that one should even mention these three countries in the same breath. Indeed, they are often offended.

In *Black Wealth/White Wealth*, Melvin L. Oliver and Thomas M. Shapiro show that net worth either entitles or precludes one from getting a loan to buy a home. The median net worth across the racial divides has been relatively stable over time. As noted earlier, the median net worth of white families America is $43,279. For African Americans, median net worth is $4,169. To put it another way, whites in the United States have ten times the median wealth of African Americans. The metaphorical fluidity of race becomes a kind of frozen brick of ice when we understand and acknowledge that net worth is the primary measure of access to bank loans—whether for purchasing a house, starting up a business, purchasing a cat or getting the means to go to college or medical or law school. From this perspective, the bland figure of "net worth" has deeply structural consequences.

Whiteness and the Black-White Model of Race Relations

Another theme in this volume is that the black-white dialogue or paradigm dominates any discussion of race in America—to the near exclusion of a more complex set of relationships that must develop when there are a number of other racial and ethnic groups. We are inclined to rehearse and replay the same old duet—or pas de deux, if one prefers the dance metaphor. But if it is the dance, then it has more often than not been the *danse macabre* in white and black. But when there are only two parties in a "race relationship," then part of how one of the parties knows its own racial identity and boundaries is by knowing that "it" is not "the other"!

Especially in California there is certainly something deeply resonant to the critique that the black-white dialogue misses much of what is important about how "whiteness" plays itself out in different situations. The institution of slavery, which was mainly about white-black relations, frames much of the early part of the country's understandings of race. This occurred alongside the genocidal extermination of Native Americans. Once that was settled (that is, the effective extermination of Native Americans, their confinement to reservations, or their "assimilation"), slavery was the dominant institutional arrangement that shaped our legal structures.

At the Making and Unmaking of Whiteness conference, one of the audience participants said,

"This is 1997. This is California. And California is clearly a place where one can be attentive to this multifaceted feature of race in America. Why not more representation of these issues on the various panels and in the many papers?" It is possible to defend the organizers. It is certainly true that we would have had a fuller portraiture of "whiteness" if we had talked more about the state and federally mandated exclusion of the Chinese at the turn of the last century. Or the discussions might well have incorporated a parallel discussion of the Japanese Gentleman's Agreement during this same period. And finally, in the middle of this century of course, Japanese Americans were forced into concentration camps during World War II. But whenever there is a decision to include a finite number of topics in the short space of two or three days, there are always tough choices of what to emphasize.

There are very strong empirical and theoretical reasons for bringing into this black-white duet more the notion of the third party, the trio, and then the quartet and whatever number there are on the dance floor. Once we change the number, the dance has to change, too. And California has seen a new political alignment based on its peculiar configuration of ethnic and racial groups.[30]

Once we take a closer look at how whiteness gets configured and then reconfigured when there are more than two or three or four groups, the theoretical insights of looking at "whiteness construction as a process" will be more fully illuminated. Remarking on the historically situated, contingent, fluid character of whiteness, Ron Takaki has reported on how Armenians "became white" in the first part of this century in California. This in turn helps explain why Armenians could get housing loans—that is, build equity and gain later leverage to positions of power (like governor of the state). Ian Haney Lopez chronicles the same kind of emergent development of Armenian transformation into whiteness—with case law.[31]

Some of the students who organized this conference have been involved directly in the study of whiteness as a relationship, and that is where the most promising work is likely to develop. We cannot study whiteness in any meaningful way unless or until one sees it as a relational phenomenon. Pamela Perry has completed research in two high schools, taking a look at how white students in a multiethnic environment deal with issues of identity around their whiteness. Because it is California, she describes and analyzes how new Asian immigrants are having to deal creatively with a prefabricated and binary world dominated by notions of whiteness and blackness. Perry chronicles an emergent configuration at the "borderlands," where many of these students are making complex choices—but moving back and forth, navigating "multiple identities," and giving new meaning and substance to the fluidity of ethnicity and race.[32]

Perry reports that some of these Asian American high school students (often second-generation immigrants), chose to adopt a version of the dress style, the language style, and the consumer style of blacks. Others choose the style of suburban whites. In the "borderlands" there will be other developments—not simply this notion that there is a black or white style and the conflict that ensues.[33] Rather, there will be emergent phenomena that will reshape how people think about their whiteness, their Asian-ness, their Latino-ness, their blackness, their American-ness.

Some of our best research is being done, I think, by writers attentive to the borderlands, addressing and analyzing the contingent, fluid character of whiteness: *how the nature and shape of "whiteness" can change nature and shape (morph!) and yet remain structurally privileged.* Here critique is most powerful and most able to inform us about what I call the "fluid and evaporating state" of race.[34] But we should not be fooled into the belief that fluidity substitutes for structure. This is simply a matter of when you take the picture. Recall that vapor can condense; and once back in a fluid state, it can freeze. So it is a fundamental mistake to think that, because we have seen this evaporating condition with our own eyes, it is gone forever and that the use of race will no longer be a powerful stratifying practice in America.

For all the brimming insights of cultural studies around race, a strong caveat is in order. There is a tendency to see only fluidity or at least to so emphasize fluidity that one lacks the capacity to see enduring structure. Well, my story about Jack Doyle and the Chicago police says that under certain conditions, things can change dramatically, in the moment, if only momentarily.

I want to end with another story. I was reminded of it by David Roediger, who has written that blacks have been studying whites for a long time and thus have a particular set of insights about "whiteness" that the current vogue of new studies would do well to mine. Indeed, African Americans have been engaged in white studies for at least three centuries. It is a necessity if one is without formal power, to be attentive and especially alert to power relationships.

I have been a member of the National Advisory Commission for the Human Genome Project's ethical-legal-social issues program. Consequently, I had the occasion to attend meetings at Cold Springs Harbor, New York. As at Northwestern University many years ago, I am often one of a very few African Americans present in a scholarly setting.

The site is in a somewhat remote location—a long distance from New York City—and there is no easy public transportation. One deplanes at JFK Airport, and typically one takes a waiting limousine. I get off the plane, go out to the curb, and find this big, stylish limousine indeed waiting for me. The driver is working-class white male by appearance. He greets me with a kind of heartiness and takes my bags, says, "Cold Spring Harbor, sir?" I say, "Yes," and hop in.

But we can't quite get out onto the main exit because of all the traffic, and the person who is sort of directing traffic and guiding things is not very official-looking. He is wearing street clothes and about thirty-five-years-old. This is an African American male, and his gestures and his movements are, to put it mildly, unorthodox. He gives the strong impression that he is self-appointed to this task. The driver of the limousine is waiting patiently to be told when it is okay to move. (To give the story the proper frame. I would say that this particular person directing traffic was being quite creative and sometimes not very responsible.)

On two occasions, he appears to wave my driver on, then quickly changes his mind and says, "Oops!" Finally, he definitively tells my driver, "Pull out right now!" Then another car seems to come from out of nowhere and nearly bends our fender, and my driver says, "Dumb nigger!"

There are about twelve seconds of silence. I do not break it. Finally, he says, "I'm sorry. I'm terribly sorry" and begins to mumble something. I say, "I understand." And for a moment his shoulders seem to relax, and then I say, "I understand how you must feel in this situation." The rest of the ride was in total silence. Ice. What had evaporated and transformed into choreographed class relations had recondensed into race relations.

Notes

1. The pencil-test is only the latest methodology for precision that I discovered recently on a trip to South Africa. During the apartheid era, only "coloureds" could work in Capetown. So whether one was classified as black or coloured had important consequences for one's livelihood. Thus some "blacks" would apply to have their status changed from black to coloured. The apartheid regime devised a pencil test to make the classification definitive. Applicants were told to place a pencil in their hair. If, when they were told to "shake their head," the pencil fell out, they were classified as "coloured"—but they remained black if the pencil was not easily dislodged by a shaking motion.

2. Alleles are different versions of one gene. For example, while the "generic gene" will instruct the proteins and cells to make an eye, a particular allele variation may produce a blue or brown or grayish-green eye. The same for epicanthic fold (or lack of it) over the eye, hair texture, skin color, and a wide band of human physiognomy. When researchers try to make guesses about which group a person belongs to, they look at variation at several different spots, usually six or seven. What is being assessed is the *frequency* of genetic variation at a particular spot in the DNA in each population. They are not necessarily looking at genes—they may instead be looking at genetic variation in noncoding DNA. Occasionally, these researchers find a locus where one of the populations being observed and measured has, let's call them for example, alleles H, I, and J and another population has alleles H, I, and K. We know that there are alleles that are found primarily among subpopulations of North American Indians. When comparing a group of North American

Indians with a group of Finnish people, one might find a single allele that was present in some Indians but in no Finns (or it's at such a low frequency in the Finns that it is rarely, if ever, seen). However, it is important to note and reiterate again and again that this does not mean that all North American Indians, even in this subpopulation, will have that allele. See Stephen Molnar, *Human Variation: Races, Types, and Ethnic Groups,* 3d ed. (Englewood Cliffs, N.J.: Prentice-Hall, 1992).

3. The perils of "driving while black" have made it into the houses of several state legislatures already. In California, the state assembly considered such a bill in 1998. At the federal level, in March 1999 Attorney General Janet Reno called for an investigation of "profiling" possible suspects by using race.

4. See S. H. Katz, "Is Race a Legitimate Concept for Science?" in *The AAPA Revised Statement on Race: A Brief Analysis and Commentary* (Philadelphia: University of Pennsylvania, 1995).

5. In addition to Molnar, *Human Variation,* see Anthony P. Polednak. *Racial and Ethnic Differences in Disease* (New York: Oxford University Press, 1969); A. H. Bittles and D. F. Roberts, eds., *Minority Populations: Genetics, Demography and Health* (London: Macmillan, 1992); Malcolm Chapman, ed., *Social and Biological Aspects of Ethnicity* (New York: Oxford University Press, 1993); and Pat Shipman, *The Evolution of Racism: Human Differences and the Use and Abuse of Science* (New York: Simon and Schuster, 1994).

6. For the discussion in this paragraph and for the references to the German literature that are cited below, I am indebted to William H. Schneider, a historian at the University of Indiana.

7. For examples, see Max Gundel, "Einige Beobachtungen bei der Rassenbiologischen Durchforschung Schleswig-Holsteins," *Klinische Wochenschrift* 5 (1926): II86, and G. A. Schusterov, "Isohaemoagglutinierende Eigenschaften des Menschlichen Blutes nach den Ergebnissen einer Untersuchung an Straflingen des Reformatoriums (Arbeitshauses) zu Omsk," *Moskovskü Meditsinksii Jurnal* I (1927): 1–6.

8. First published in 1994, Felix Kaufmann's *Methodology of the Social Sciences* (New York: Humanities Press, 1958) was one of the key works that was later developed into a more systematic rendition of the problem of first and second order constructs by Alfred Schutz, "Common Sense and Scientific Interpretation of Human Action," in Maurice Natanson, ed., *Collected Papers I: The Problem of Social Reality* (The Hague: Martinus Nijhoff, 1973), 3–47.

9. Molnar, *Human Variation*, 72–79.

10. Troy Duster, *Backdoor to Eugenics* (New York: Routledge, 1990), 89–92.

11. See Melbourne Tapper, *In the Blood: Sickle Cell Anemia and the Politics of Race* (Philadelphia: University of Pennsylvania Press, 1999).

12. I refer primarily to Jill Quadagno, *The Color of Welfare* (New York: Oxford University Press, 1994); Douglas Massey and Nancy Denton, *American Apartheid: Segregation and the Making of the Underclass* (Cambridge, Mass.: Harvard University Press, 1993); and Kenneth O'Reilly. *Nixon's Piano: Presidents and Racial Politics from Washington to Clinton* (New York: Free Press, 1995). There were, of course, earlier analysts who described parts of the picture. For example, Charles Abrams, writing in the 1950s and 1960s, had documented how the Federal Housing Authority's policies were explicitly racist. See his essay "The Housing Problem and the Negro" in *The Negro American*, ed. T. Parsons and K. Clark (Boston: Houghton Mifflin, 1966), 512–24.

13. Quadagno, *Color of Welfare*, 21.

14. The CIO was far more receptive to blacks than the AFL, but complete racial exclusionary practices in many CIO locals continued well into the 1970s.

15. Quadagno, *Color of Welfare*, 23.

16. Quoted in Abrams, "The Housing Problem and the Negro," 523.

17. Literally, those authorized to make loans at banks would draw on a map a red line around a black community and no one inside that red line could get a loan. Until 1949 the FHA also encouraged the use of restrictive covenants banning African Americans from given neighborhoods and refused to insure mortgages in integrated neighborhoods. Thanks to the FHA, no bank would insure loans in the ghetto, and few African Americans could live outside it. See Quadagno, *Color of Welfare,* 24–25, and Massey and Denton, *American Apartheid.*

18. See Richard J. Herrnstein and Charles Murray, *The Bell Curve: Intelligence and Class Structure in American Life* (New York: Free Press, 1994); James Q. Wilson and Richard Herrnstein, *Crime and Human Nature* (New York: Simon and Schuster, 1985); and Arthur R. Jensen, "How Much Can We Boost IQ and Scholastic Achievement?" *Harvard Educational Review* (winter 1969): 1–123.

19. Herrnstein and Murray, *Bell Curve*, 105.

20. Ronald M. Harris-Warrick and Eve Marder, "Modulation of Neural Networks for Behavior," *Annual Review of Neuroscience* 14 (1991): 41.

21. Many of my colleagues will recognize the phenomenon that I am describing. Over coffee, over dinner, we will hear a textured version of the complexity of what we know about race. But the very next day, from the public stage, we hear (and speak of) a more singular and unidimensional characterization of scholarly work and empirical results of research.

22. Noel Ignatiev and John Garvey, eds., *Race Traitor* (New York: Routledge, 1996), and David R. Roediger, *Towards the Abolition of Whiteness: Essays on Race, Politics, and Working Class History* (New York: Verso, 1994).

23. In fact, black miners in South Africa, during apartheid, worked for one-tenth the wage of white workers. For more on wage differentials, see George M. Fredrickson, *Black Liberation: A Comparative History of Black Ideologies in the United States and South Africa* (New York: Oxford University Press, 1995).

24. Bob Drogin, "South Africa's Hot Issue—Affirmative Action," *San Francisco Chronicle*, 22 August 1995.

25. Frederick G. Bailey, *Tribe, Caste and Nation: A Study of Political Activity and Political Change in Highland Orissa* (Manchester: Manchester University Press, 1960).

26. The term "scheduled caste" was first used by the Simon Commission and then embodied in the Government of India Act of 1935. Until this time, the term "untouchables" was used. Gandhi renamed these groups "Harijans," but many resented and rejected the name. After 1938, the word "Harijan" was officially replaced by the government with the term "scheduled castes," which has been in place as the formal term ever since. Of course, in the population at large, the terms "Harijan" and "untouchables" are in various locations still used. See B. D. Purohit and S. D. Purohit, *Handbook of Reservation for Scheduled Castes and Scheduled Tribes, on the Matters Concerning Employment, Education, and Election* (New Delhi: Jainsons Publications, 1990).

27. There was an exemption for jobs classified as scientific and technical. While this classification has been the source of some contention as to which jobs apply, it is not a matter that bears substantially on the current attack on affirmative action in India. See Purohit and Purohit, *Handbook, and Brochure on Reservation for Scheduled Castes, Scheduled Tribes, and Other Categories of Backward Classes in Services and Posts* (Bangalore, India: Department of Personnel and Administrative Reforms, Government of Karnataka, 1987).

28. "Students in India Riot over Favored-job Plan for Backward Castes," *Oakland Tribune*, 25 August1990.

29. Melvin L Oliver and Thomas M. Shapiro, *Black Wealth/White Wealth: A New Perspective on Racial Inequality* (New York: Routledge, 1995).

30. It has permitted, for example, the manipulation of sentiment around matters of ethnicity and race that one could not even have thought about forty years ago. Asians, after all, are now 10 percent of the population in California; blacks are 7.5 percent; Latinos, upward of 27 or 28 percent. In that kind of mix, where African Americans are number four among the four "groups," the politics changes sharply. In my view, that is why California was selected as the major site of the attack on affirmative action. It was seen by the Republican Party as a wonderfully propitious circumstance. This is a position that is explored more extensively in my article "Individual Fairness, Group Preferences, and the California Strategy," in Robert Post and Michael Rogin, eds., *Race and Representation: Affirmative Action* (New York: Zone Books, 1998); originally published in *Representations* 55 (summer 1996): 41–58.

31. Ronald T. Takaki, *Strangers from a Different Shore: A History of Asian Americans* (Boston: Little, Brown, 1989), and Ian F. Haney Lopez, *White by Law: The Legal Construction of Race* (New York: New York University Press, 1996).

32. Pamela Perry, "Beginning to See the White" (Ph.D. diss., University of California, Berkeley, 1998).

33. Thomas Kochman, *Black and White Styles in Conflict* (Chicago: University of Chicago Press. 1981).

34. See George Lipsitz, *The Possessive Investment in Whiteness: How White People Profit from Identity Politics* (Philadelphia: Temple University Press, 1998).

"A Threat in the Air: How Stereotypes Shape Intellectual Identity and Performance"

CLAUDE M. STEEL

A general theory of domain identification is used to describe achievement barriers still faced by women in advanced quantitative areas and by African Americans in school. The theory assumes that sustained school success requires identification with school and its subdomains; that societal pressures on these groups (e.g., economic disadvantage, gender roles) can frustrate this identification; and that in school domains where these groups are negatively stereotyped, those who have become domain identified face the further barrier of stereotype threat, the threat that others' judgments or their own actions will negatively stereotype them in the domain. Research shows that this threat dramatically depresses the standardized test performance of women and African Americans who are in the academic vanguard of their groups (offering a new interpretation of group differences in standardized test performance), that it causes disidentification with school, and that practices that reduce this threat can reduce these negative effects.

From an observer's standpoint, the situations of a boy and a girl in a math classroom or of a Black student and a White student in any classroom are essentially the same. The teacher is the same; the textbooks are the same; and in better classrooms, these students are treated the same. Is it possible, then, that they could still experience the classroom differently, so differently in fact as to significantly affect their performance and achievement there? This is the central question of this article, and in seeking an answer it has both a practical and a theoretical focus. The practical focus is on the perhaps obvious need to better understand the processes that can hamper a group's school performance and on what can be done to improve that performance. The theoretical focus is on how societal stereotypes about groups can influence the intellectual functioning and identity development of individual group members. To show the generality of these processes and their relevance to important outcomes, this theory is applied to two groups: African Americans, who must contend with negative stereotypes about their abilities in many scholastic domains, and women, who must do so primarily in math and the physical sciences. In trying to understand the schooling outcomes of these two groups, the theory has a distinct perspective, that of viewing people, in Sartre's (1946/1965) words, as "first of all beings in a situation" such that if one wants to understand them, one "must inquire first into the situation surrounding [them]" (p. 60).

The theory begins with an assumption: that to sustain school success one must be identified with school achievement in the sense of its being a part of one's self-definition, a personal identity to which one is self-evaluatively accountable. This accountability—that good self-feelings depend in some part on good achievement—translates into sustained achievement motivation. For such an identification to form, this reasoning continues, one must perceive good prospects in the domain, that is, that one has the interests, skills, resources, and opportunities to prosper there, as well as that one belongs there, in the sense of being accepted and valued in the domain. If this relationship to schooling does not form or gets broken, achievement may suffer. Thus, in trying to understand what imperils achievement among women and African Americans, this logic points to a basic question: What in the experience of these groups might frustrate their identification with all or certain aspects of school achievement?

One must surely turn first to social structure: limits on educational access that have been imposed on these groups by socioeconomic disadvantage, segregating social practices, and restrictive cultural orientations, limits of both historical and ongoing effect. By diminishing one's educational prospects, these limitations (e.g., inadequate resources, few role models, preparational disadvantages) should make it more difficult to identify with academic domains. To continue in math, for example, a woman might have to buck the low expectations of teachers, family, and societal gender roles in which math is seen as unfeminine as well as anticipate spending her entire professional life in a male-dominated world. These realities, imposed on her by societal structure, could

so reduce her sense of good prospects in math as to make identifying with it difficult.

But this article focuses on a further barrier, one that has its effect on the already identified, those members of these groups who, having survived structural obstacles, have achieved identification with the domain (of the present groups, school-identified African Americans and math-identified women). It is the social–psychological threat that arises when one is in a situation or doing something for which a negative stereotype about one's group applies. This predicament threatens one with being negatively stereotyped, with being judged or treated stereotypically, or with the prospect of conforming to the stereotype. Called *stereotype threat,* it is a situational threat—a threat in the air—that, in general form, can affect the members of any group about whom a negative stereotype exists (e.g., skateboarders, older adults, White men, gang members). Where bad stereotypes about these groups apply, members of these groups can fear being reduced to that stereotype. And for those who identify with the domain to which the stereotype is relevant, this predicament can be self-threatening.

Negative stereotypes about women and African Americans bear on important academic abilities. Thus, for members of these groups who are identified with domains in which these stereotypes apply, the threat of these stereotypes can be sharply felt and, in several ways, hampers their achievement.

First, if the threat is experienced in the midst of a domain performance—classroom presentation or test-taking, for example—the emotional reaction it causes could directly interfere with performance. My colleagues and I (Spencer, Steele, & Quinn, 1997; C. M. Steele & Aronson, 1995) have tested this possibility with women taking standardized math tests and African Americans taking standardized verbal tests. Second, when this threat becomes chronic in a situation, as for the woman who spends considerable time in a competitive, male-oriented math environment, it can pressure *disidentification,* a re-conceptualization of the self and of one's values so as to remove the domain as a self-identity, as a basis of self-evaluation. Disidentification offers the retreat of not caring about the domain in relation to the self. But as it protects in this way, it can undermine sustained motivation in the domain, an adaptation that can be costly when the domain is as important as schooling.

Stereotype threat is especially frustrating because, at each level of schooling, it affects the vanguard of these groups, those with the skills and self-confidence to have identified with the domain. Ironically, their susceptibility to this threat derives not from internal doubts about their ability (e.g., their internalization of the stereotype) but from their identification with the domain and the resulting concern they have about being stereotyped in it. (This argument has the hopeful implication that to improve the domain performance of these students, one should focus on the feasible task of lifting this situational threat rather than on altering their internal psychology.) Yet, as schooling progresses and the obstacles of structure and stereotype threat take their cumulative toll, more of this vanguard will likely be pressured into the ranks of the unidentified. These students, by not caring about the domain vis-à-vis the self, are likely to underperform in it regardless of whether they are stereotype threatened there. Thus, although the identified among these groups are likely to underperform only under stereotype threat, the unidentified (casualties of sociocultural disadvantage or prior internalization of stereotype threat) are likely to underperform and not persist in the domain even when stereotype threat has been removed.

In these ways, then, the present analysis sees social structure and stereotypes as shaping the academic identities and performance outcomes of large segments of society. But first, for the two groups under consideration, what are these outcomes?

As is much discussed, these outcomes are in a crisis state for African Americans. Although Black students begin school with standardized test scores that are not too far behind those of their White counterparts, almost immediately a gap begins to appear (e.g., Alexander & Entwistle, 1988; Burton & Jones, 1982; Coleman et al., 1966) that, by the sixth grade in most school districts, is two full grade levels (Gerard, 1983). There have been encouraging increases in the number of African Americans completing high school or its equivalence in recent years: 77% for Black students versus 83% for White students (American Council on Education, 1995–1996). And there have been modest advances in the number of African American high school graduates enrolling in college, although these have not been as substantial as in other groups (American Council on Education, 1995–1996). Perhaps most discouraging has been the high dropout rate for African American college students: Those who do not finish college within six years is 62%, compared with a national dropout rate of 41% (American Council on Education, 1995–1996). And there is evidence of lower grade performance among those who do graduate of, on average, two thirds of a letter grade lower than those of other graduating students (Nettles, 1988). On predominantly White campuses, Black students are also underrepresented in math and the natural sciences. Although historically Black colleges and universities now enroll only 17% of the nation's Black college students, they produce 42% of all Black BS degrees in natural science (Culotta & Gibbons, 1992). At the graduate level, although Black women have recently shown modest gains in PhDs received, the number awarded to Black men has declined over the past decade more than for any other subgroup in society (American Council on Education, 1995–1996).

Women clearly thrive in many areas of schooling. But in math, engineering, and the physical sciences, they often endure lesser outcomes than men. In a meta-analysis involving over 3 million participants, Hyde, Fennema and Lamon (1990), for example, found that through elementary and middle school, there are virtually no differences between boys and girls in performance on standardized math tests but that a trend toward men doing better steadily increases from high school ($SD = .29$) through college ($SD = .41$) and into adulthood ($SD = .59$). And, as their college careers begin, women leave these fields at a rate two and a half times that of men (Hewitt & Seymour, 1991). Although White women constitute 43% of the U.S. population, they earn only 22% of the BS degrees and 13% of the PhDs and occupy only 10% of the jobs in physical science, math, and engineering, where they earn only 75% of the salary paid to men (Hewitt & Seymour, 1991).

These inequities have compelled explanations ranging from the sociocultural to the genetic.

In the case of African Americans, for example, past and ongoing socioeconomic disadvantage, cultural orientations (e.g., Ogbu, 1986), and genetic differences (e.g., Herrnstein & Murray, 1994; Jensen, 1969) have all been proposed as factors that, through singular and accumulated effect, could undermine their performance. In the case of women's performance in math and the physical sciences, there are parallel arguments: structural and cultural gender role constraints that shunt women away from these areas; culturally rooted expectations (e.g., Eccles, 1987; Eccles-Parsons et al., 1983); and, again, genetic limitations (Benbow & Stanley, 1980, 1983). But, like crumbs along the forest floor, several findings lead away from these analyses as fully sufficient.

For one thing, minority student achievement gaps persist even in the middle and upper socioeconomic classes. Using data from the Coleman report (Coleman et al., 1966) and a more recent College Board study of Scholastic Assessment Test (SAT) scores, Miller (1995, 1996) found that the gaps in academic performance (grades as well as standardized test scores) between Whites and non-Asian minorities (e.g., African Americans, Hispanics, and Native Americans) were as large, or larger, in the upper and middle classes (as measured by parental education and occupation) than in the lower classes. Group differences in socioeconomic status (SES), then, cannot fully explain group differences in academic performance.

Another point is that these differences are not even fully explained by group differences in skills. This is shown in the well-known *overprediction* or *underperformance* phenomenon of the test bias literature. Overprediction occurs when, at each level of performance on a test of preparation for some level of schooling (e.g., the SAT), students from one group wind up achieving less—getting lower college grades, for example—than other students with the same beginning scores. In this sense, the test scores of the low-performing group overpredict how well they will actually achieve, or, stated another way, the low-performing group underperforms in relation to the test's prediction. But the point here is that because the students at each test-score level have comparable initial skills, the lower eventual performance of one group must be due to something other than skill deficits they brought with them.

In the case of African Americans, overprediction across the academic spectrum has been so reliably observed as to be almost a lawful phenomenon in American society (e.g., Jensen, 1980; Vars & Bowen, 1997). Perhaps the most extensive single demonstration of it comes from a recent Educational Testing Service study (Ramist, Lewis, & McCamley-Jenkins, 1994) that examined the predictiveness of the SAT on 38 representative college and university campuses. As is typically the case, the study found that the predictive validity to the SAT—its correlation with subsequent grades—was as good for African American, Hispanic, and Native American students as for White and Asian students. But for the three non-Asian minority groups, there was sizable overprediction (underperformance) in virtually all academic areas. That is, at each level of preparation as measured by the SAT, something further depressed the grades of these groups once they arrived on campus.

As important, the same study found evidence of SAT overprediction for female students (i.e., women performing less well than men at comparable SAT levels) in technical and physical science courses such as engineering, economics, and computer science but not in nontechnical areas such as English. It is interesting though that women in this study were not overpredicted in math per se, a seeming exception to this pattern. The overprediction of women's college math performance has generally been unreliable, with some studies showing it (e.g., Benbow & Arjmand, 1990; Levin & Wyckoff, 1988; Lovely, 1987; Ware, Steckler, & Leserman, 1985) and others not (e.g., Adelman, 1991; DeBoer, 1984; Ware & Dill, 1986). However, a recent study (Strenta, Elliott, Adair, Scott, & Matier; 1993) involving over 5,000 students at four prestigious northeastern colleges identified a pattern of effects that suggests why these different results occur: Underperformance reliably occurred among women who were talented in math and science and who, perhaps for that reason, took courses in these areas that were intended for majors, whereas it did not occur among women with less math and science preparation who took courses in these areas intended for nonmajors. Thus, women may be reliably overpredicted in math and the physical sciences, just as Black students are more generally, but only when the curriculum is more advanced and only among women who are more identified with the domain. Among this vanguard, though, something other than skill deficits depresses their performance. What are these further processes?

Social and Stereotype Structure as Obstacles to Achievement Identification

The proposed answer is that at least one of these processes is a set of social psychological phenomena that obstructs these groups' identification with domains of schooling.[1] I turn first to school identification.

Academic Identification

As noted, this analysis assumes that sustained school achievement depends, most centrally, on identifying with school, that is, forming a relationship between oneself and the domains of schooling such that one's self-regard significantly depends on achievement in those domains. Extrinsic rewards such as better career outcomes, personal security, parental exhortation, and so on, can also motivate school achievement. But it is presumed that sustaining motivation through the ebb and flow of these other rewards requires school identification. How, then, is this identification formed?

Not a great deal is known about the process. But several models (e.g., Schlenker & Weigold, 1989; C. M. Steele, 1988; Tesser, 1988) share an implicit reasoning, the first assumption of which is that people need positive self-regard, a self-perception of "adaptive and moral adequacy" (C. M. Steele, 1988, p. 289). Then, the argument goes, identification with a given domain of life depends, in large part, on the self-evaluative prospects it offers. James (1890/1950) described the development of the self as a process of picking from the many, often incompatible, possible selves, those "on which to stake one's salvation" (p. 310). This choice and the assessment of prospects that goes into it are, of course, multifaceted: Are the rewards of the domain attractive or important? Is an adequate opportunity structure available? Do I have the requisite skills, talents, and interests? Have others like me succeeded in the domain? Will I be seen as belonging in the domain? Will I be

prejudiced against in the domain? Can I envision wanting what this domain has to offer? and so on. Some of these assessments undergird a sense of efficacy in the domain (e.g., Bandura, 1977, 1986). Others have to do with the rewards, importance, and attractiveness of the domain itself. And still others have to do with the feasibility and receptiveness of the domain. The point here is that students tacitly assess their prospects in school and its subdomains, and, roughly speaking, their identifications follow these assessments: increasing when they are favorable and decreasing when they are unfavorable. As for the two groups under consideration, then, this analysis suggests that something systematically downgrades their assessments of, and thus their identification with, critical domains of schooling.

Threat to Academic Identification

Structural and Cultural Threats

Both groups have endured and continue to endure sociocultural influences that could have such effects. Among the most replicable facts in the schooling literature is that SES is strongly related to school success and cognitive performance (e.g., Coleman et al., 1966; Miller, 1996). And because African Americans have long been disproportionately represented in lower socioeconomic classes, this factor surely contributes to their achievement patterns in school, both through the material limitations associated with lower SES (poor schools, lack of resources for school persistence, etc.) and through the ability of these limitations, by downgrading school-related prospects, to undermine identification with school. And beyond socioeconomic structure, there are cultural patterns within these groups or in the relation between these groups and the larger society that may also frustrate their identification with school or some part of it, for example, Ogbu's (1986) notion of a lower-class Black culture that is "oppositional" to school achievement or traditional feminine gender roles that eschew math-related fields (e.g., Eccles-Parsons et al., 1983; Linn, 1994).

Stereotype Threat

Beyond these threats, waiting for those in these groups who have identified with school, is yet another threat to their identification, more subtle perhaps but nonetheless profound: that of stereotype threat. I define it as follows: the event of a negative stereotype about a group to which one belongs becoming self-relevant, usually as a plausible interpretation for something one is doing, for an experience one is having, or for a situation one is in that relevance to one's self-definition. It happens when one is in the *field* of the stereotype, what Cross (1991) called a "spotlight anxiety" (p. 195), such that one can be judged or treated in terms of a racial stereotype. Many analysts have referred to this predicament and the pressure it causes (e.g., Allport, 1954; Carter, 1991; Cose, 1993; Goffman, 1963; Howard & Hammond, 1985; E. E. Jones et al., 1984; Sartre, 1946/1965; C.M. Steele, 1975; C. M. Steele & Aronson, 1995; S. Steele, 1990). The present definition stresses that for a negative stereotype to be threatening, it must be self-relevant. Then, the situational contingency it establishes—the possibility of conforming to the stereotype or of being treated and judged in terms of it—becomes self-threatening. It means that one could be limited or diminished in a domain that is self-definitional. For students from groups in which abilities are negatively stereotyped in all or some school domains and yet who remain identified with those domains, this threat may be keenly felt, felt enough, I argue, to become a further barrier to their identification with the domain.

There is, however a more standard explanation of how negative stereotypes affect their targets. Beginning with Freud (as cited in Brill, 1938) in psychology and Cooley (1956) and Mead (1934) in sociology, treatises on the experience of oppression have depicted a fairly standard sequence of events: Through long exposure to negative stereotypes about their group, members of prejudiced-against groups often internalize the stereotypes, and the resulting sense of inadequacy becomes part of their personality (e.g., Allport, 1954; Bettelheim, 1943; Clark, 1965; Grier & Coobs, 1968; Erikson, 1956; Fanon, 1952/1967; Kardiner & Ovesey, 1951; Lewin, 1941).

In recent years, the tone of this argument has constructively lightened, replacing the notion of a broad self-hatred with the idea of an inferiority anxiety or low expectations and suggesting how situational factors contribute to this experience. S. Steele's (1990) essays on *racial vulnerability* (i.e., a vulnerability of both Blacks and Whites that stems, in part, from the situational pressures of reputations about their groups) offered an example. This work depicts the workings of this anxiety among African Americans in an interconnected set of ideas: *integration shock* that, like Goffman (1963), points to settings that integrate Blacks and Whites as particularly anxiety arousing; *objective correlatives* or race-related situational cues that can trigger this anxiety; and the inherent sense of risk, stemming from an internalized *inferiority anxiety* and from a *myth of inferiority* pervading integrated settings, of being judged inferior or of confirming one's own feared inferiority. Howard and Hammond (1985) earlier made this argument specifically in relation to the school achievement of Black students. They argued that once "rumors of inferiority" . . . about Black students' abilities pervade the environment—through, for example, national debates over the genetic basis of racial differences in IQ—they can intimidate Black students; become internalized by them; and, in turn, lead to a low sense of self-efficacy, demotivation, and underperformance in school. Analogous arguments have been applied to women interested in math-related areas (cf. Eccles-Parsons et al., 1983).

These models recognize the situational influence of negative stereotypes (e.g., Allport, 1954; Howard & Hammond, 1985; S. Steele, 1990) but most often describe it as a process in which the stereotype, or more precisely the possibility of being stereotyped, triggers an internalized inferiority doubt or low expectancy. And because this anxiety is born of a socialization presumed to influence all members of the stereotyped group virtually all members of the group are presumed to have this anxiety to one degree or another.

Stereotype threat, in contrast, refers to the strictly situational threat of negative stereotype, the threat that does not depend on cuing an internalized anxiety or expectancy. It is cued by the mere recognition that a negative group stereotype could apply to oneself in a given situation. How threatening this recognition becomes depends on the person's identification with the stereotype-relevant domain. For the domain identified the situational relevance of the stereotype is threatening because it threatens diminishment in a domain that is self-definitional. For the less domain identified, this recognition is less threatening or not threatening at all, because it threatens something that is less self-definitional.

Stereotype threat, then, as a situational pressure "in the air" so to speak, affects only a subportion of the stereotyped group and, in the area of schooling, probably affects confident students more than unconfident ones. Recall that to be identified with schooling in general, or math in particular, one must have confidence in one's domain-related abilities, enough to perceive good prospects in the domain. This means that stereotype threat should have its greatest effect on the better, more confident students in stereotyped groups, those who have not internalized the group stereotype to the point of doubting their own ability and have thus remained identified with the domain—those who are in the academic vanguard of their group.[2]

Several general features of stereotype threat follow:

1. Stereotype threat is a general threat not tied to the psychology of particular stigmatized groups. It affects the members of any group about whom there exists some generally known negative stereotype (e.g., a grandfather who fears that any faltering of memory will confirm or expose him to stereotypes about the aged). Stereotype threat can be thought of as a subtype of the threat posed by negative reputations in general.

2. That which turns stereotype threat on and off, the controlling "mechanism" so to speak, is a particular concurrence: whether a negative stereotype about one's group becomes relevant to interpreting oneself or one's behavior in an identified-with setting. When such a setting integrates stereotyped and nonstereotyped people, it may make the stereotype, as a dimension of difference, more salient and thus more strongly felt (e.g., Frable, Blackstone, & Sherbaum, 1990; Goffman, 1963; Kleck & Strenta, 1980; Sartre, 1946/1965; S. Steele, 1990). But such integration is neither necessary nor *sufficient* for this threat to occur. It can occur even when the person is alone, as for a woman taking an important math test alone in a cubicle but under the threat of confirming a stereotyped limitation of ability. And, in integrated settings, it need not occur. Reducing the interpretive relevance of a stereotype in the setting, say in a classroom or on a standardized test, may reduce this threat and its detrimental effects even when the setting is integrated.[3]

3. This mechanism also explains the variabilities of stereotype threat: the fact that the type and degree of this threat vary from group to group and, for any group, across settings. For example, the type and degree of stereotype threat experienced by White men, Black people, and people who are overweight differ considerably, bearing on sensitivity and fairness in the first group, on school performance in the second, and on self-control in the third. Moreover, for any of these groups, this threat will vary across settings (e.g., Goffman, 1963; S. Steele, 1990). For example, women may reduce their stereotype threat substantially by moving across the hall from math to English class. The explanation of this model is straightforward: Different groups experience different forms and degrees of stereotype threat because the stereotypes about them differ in content, in scope, and in the situations to which they apply.

4. To experience stereotype threat, one need not believe the stereotype nor even be worried that it is true of oneself. The well-know African American social psychologist James M. Jones (1997) wrote,

> When I go to the ATM machine and a woman is making a transaction, I think about whether she will fear I may rob her. Since I have no such intention, how do I put her at ease? Maybe I can't . . . and maybe she has no such expectation. But it goes through my mind. (p. 262)

Jones felt stereotype threat in this situation even though he did not believe that the stereotype characterized him. Of course, this made it no less a life-shaping force. One's daily life can be filled with recurrent situations in which this threat pressures adaptive responses.

5. The effort to overcome stereotype threat by disproving the stereotype—for example, by outperforming it in the case of academic work—can be daunting. Because these stereotypes are widely disseminated throughout society, a personal exemption from them earned in one setting does not generalize to a new setting where either one's reputation is not known or where it has to be renegotiated against a new challenge. Thus, even when the stereotype can be disproven, the need to do so can seem Sisyphean, everlastingly recurrent. And in some critical situations, it may not be disprovable. The stereotypes considered in this work allege group-based limitations of ability that are often reinforced by the structural reality of increasingly small group representations at more advanced levels of the schooling domain. Thus, for group members working at these advanced levels, no amount of success up to that point can disprove the stereotype's relevance to their next, more advanced performance. For the advanced female math student who has been brilliant up to that point, any frustration she has at the frontier of her skills could confirm the gender-based limitation alleged in the stereotype, making this frontier because she is so invested in it, a more threatening place than it is for the nonstereotyped. Thus, the work of dispelling stereotype threat through performance probably increases with the difficulty of work in the domain, and whatever exemption is gained has to be rewon at the next new proving ground.

Empirical Support for a Theory of Stereotype Threat and Disidentification

In testing these ideas, the research of my colleagues and I has had two foci: The first is on intellectual performance in the domain in which negative group stereotypes apply. Here, the analysis has two testable implications. One is that for domain-identified students, stereotype threat may interfere with their domain-related intellectual performance. Analysts have long argued that behaving in a situation in which one is at risk of confirming a negative stereotype about one's group, or of being seen or treated stereotypically, causes emotional distress and pressure (e.g., Cross, 1991; Fanon, 1952/1967; Goffman, 1963; Howard & Hammond, 1985; Sartre, 1946/1965; C. M. Steele & Aronson, 1995; S. Steele, 1990). The argument here is that for those who identify with the domain enough to experience this threat, the pressure it causes may undermine their domain

performance. Disruptive pressures such as evaluation apprehension, test anxiety, choking, and token status have long been shown to disrupt performance through a variety of mediating mechanisms: interfering anxiety, reticence to respond, distracting thoughts, self-consciousness, and so on (Baumeister & Showers, 1984; Geen, 1991; Lord & Saenz, 1985; Sarason, 1980; Wine, 1971). The assumption of this model is that stereotype threat is another such interfering pressure. The other testable implication is that reducing this threat in the performance setting, by reducing its interfering pressure, should improve the performance of otherwise stereotype-threatened students.

The second research focus is the model's implication that stereotype threat, and the anticipation of having to contend with it unceasingly in school or some domain of schooling, should deter members of these groups from identifying with these domains, and, for group members already identified, it should pressure their disidentification.[4]

Stereotype Threat and Intellectual Performance

Steven Spencer, Diane Quinn, and I (Spencer et al., 1997) first tested the effect of stereotype threat on intellectual performance by testing its effect on the standardized math test performance of women who were strong in math.

The Stereotype Threat of Women Performing Math

At base, of course, the stereotype threat that women experience in math-performance settings derives from a negative stereotype about their math ability that is disseminated throughout society. But whether this threat impaired their performance, we reasoned, would depend on two things. First, the performance would have to be construed so that any faltering would imply the limitation of ability alleged in the stereotype. This means that the performance would have to be difficult enough so that faltering at it would imply having reached an ability limit but not so difficult as to be nondiagnostic of ability. And second, as has been much emphasized, the women in question would have to be identified with math, so that faltering and its stereotype-confirming implication would threaten something they care about, their belongingness and acceptance in a domain they identify with. Of course, men too (at least those of equal skill and identification with math) could be threatened in this situation; faltering would reflect on their ability too. But their faltering would not carry the extra threat of confirming a stereotyped limitation in math ability or of causing them to be seen that way. Thus, the threat that women experience, through the interfering pressure it causes, should worsen their performance in comparison to equally qualified men. Interestingly, though, these otherwise confident women should perform equally as well as equally qualified men when this situational threat is lessened.

To explore these questions, Spencer, Quinn, and I (Spencer et al., 1997) designed a basic research paradigm: We recruited female and male students, mostly college sophomores, who were both good at math and strongly identified with it in the sense of seeing themselves as strong math students and seeing math as important to their self-definition. We then gave them a very difficult math test one at a time. The items were taken from the advanced math General Records Examination (GRE) and we assumed would frustrate the skills of these students without totally exceeding them. As expected, and presumably reflecting the impairing effects of stereotype threat, women significantly underperformed in relation to equally qualified men on this difficult math test. But more important, in another condition of this experiment in which the test was an advanced literature test rather than a math test and in which participants had been selected and matched for their strong literature skills and identification women performed just as well as equally qualified men. This happened, we reasoned, because women are not stereotype threatened in this area.

A second experiment replicated women's underperformance on the difficult math test and showed that it did not happen when the test was easier, that is when the items, taken from the regular quantitative section of the GRE, were more within the skills of these strong math students. The lack of performance frustration on this easier test, presumably, reduced women's stereotype threat by making the stereotype less relevant as an interpretation of their performance.

Stereotype Threat Versus Genes

So went our interpretation. But an alternative was possible: The biological limits of women's math ability do not emerge until the material tested is difficult. It is this very pattern of evidence that Benbow and Stanley (1980, 1983) used to suggest a genetic limitation in women's math ability. Thus, the first two experiments reproduced the gender effects on math performance reported in the literature: that women underperform primarily in math and mainly when the material is difficult. But they fall short of establishing our interpretation.

To do this, we would need to give women and men a difficult math test (one capable of producing women's underperformance) but then experimentally vary stereotype threat, that is, vary how much women were at risk of confirming the stereotype while taking the test. A third experiment did this by varying how the test (the same difficult one used in the earlier experiments) was represented. Participants were told either that the test generally showed gender differences, implying that the stereotype of women's limitations in math was relevant to interpreting their own frustration, or that it showed no gender differences, implying that the gender stereotype was not relevant to their performance and thus could not be confirmed by it on this particular test. The no-gender-differences representation did not challenge the validity of the stereotype; it simply eliminated the risk that the stereotype could be fulfilled on this test. In the gender-differences condition, we expected women (still stereotype threatened) to underperform in relation to equally qualified men, but in the no-gender-differences condition, we expected women (with stereotype threat reduced) to perform equal to such men. The genetic interpretation, of course, predicts that women will underperform on this difficult test regardless of how it is represented.

In dramatic support of our reasoning, women performed worse than men when they were told that the test produced gender differences, which replicated women's underperformance observed in the earlier experiments but they performed equal to men when the test was represented as insensitive to gender differences, even though, of course, the same difficult "ability"

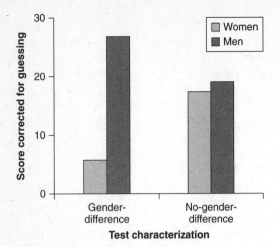

FIGURE 14.1 Mean Performance on a Difficult Math Test as a Function of Gender and Test Characterization.

test was used in both conditions (see Figure 14.1). Genetic limitation did not cap the performance of women in these experiments. A fourth experiment showed that reducing stereotype threat (through the no-gender-differences treatment) raised women's performance to that of equally qualified men, even when participants' specific performance expectancies were set low, that is, when participants were led to expect poor test performance. Also, a fifth experiment (that again replicated the treatment effects of the third experiment) found that participants' posttreatment anxiety, not their expectancies or efficacy, predicted their performance. Thus, the disruptive effect of stereotype threat was mediated more by the self-evaluative anxiety it caused than by its lowering of perform expectations or self-efficacy.

Internal or Situational Threat

These findings make an important theoretical and practical point: The gender-differences conditions (including those in which the possibility of gender differences was left to inference rather than stated directly) did not impair women's performance by triggering doubts they had about their math ability. For one thing, these women had no special doubts of this sort; they were selected for being very good at math and for reporting high confidence in their ability. Nor was this doubt a factor in their test performance. Recall that the math test was represented

as an ability test in all conditions of these experiments. This means that in the no-gender-differences conditions, women were still at risk of showing their own math ability to be weak—the same risk that men had in these conditions. Under this risk (when their own math ability was on the line), they performed just as well as men. Whatever performance-impairing anxiety they had, it was no greater than that of equally qualified men. Thus, the gender-differences conditions (the normal condition under which people take these tests) could not have impaired their performance by triggering some greater internalized anxiety that women have about their own math ability—an anxiety acquired, for example, through prior socialization. Rather, this condition had its effect through situation pressure. It set up an interpretive frame such that any performance frustration signaled the possible gender-based ability limitation alleged in the stereotype. For these women, this signal challenged their belongingness in a domain they cared about and, as a possibly newly met limit to their ability, could not be disproven by their prior achievements, thus its interfering threat.

The Stereotype Threat of African Americans on Standardized Tests

Joshua Aronson and I (C. M. Steele & Aronson, 1995) examined these processes among African American students. In these studies, Black and White Stanford University students took a test composed of the most difficult items on the verbal GRE exam. Because the participants were students admitted to a highly selective university, we assumed that they were identified with the verbal skills represented on standardized tests. The first study varied whether or not the stereotype about Black persons' intellectual ability was relevant to their performance by varying whether the test was present as *ability-diagnostic,* that is, as a test of intellectual ability, or as *ability-diagnostic* that is, as a laboratory problem-solving task unrelated to ability and thus to the stereotype about ability. Analysis of covariance was used to remove the influence of participants' initial skills, measured by their verbal SAT scores, on their test performance. This done, the results showed strong evidence of stereotype threat: Black participants greatly underperformed White

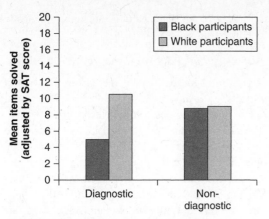

FIGURE 14.2 Mean Performance on a Difficult Verbal Test as a Function of Race and Test Characterization.

Note. SAT = Scholastic Assessment Test.

participants in the diagnostic condition but equaled them in the nondiagnostic condition (see Figure 14.2). A second experiment produced the same pattern of results with an even more slight manipulation of stereotype threat: whether or not participants recorded their race on a demographic questionnaire just before taking the test (described as nondiagnostic in all conditions). Salience of the racial stereotype alone was enough to depress the performance of identified Black students (see Figure 14.3).

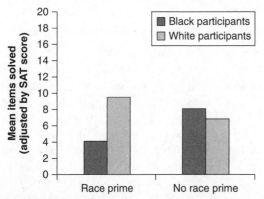

FIGURE 14.3 Mean Performance on a Difficult Verbal Test as a Function of Whether Race Was Primed.

Note. SAT = Scholastic Assessment Test.

The Cognitive Mediation of Stereotype Threat

Stereotype threat, then, can impair the standardized test performance of domain-identified students; this effect generalizes to several ability-stereotyped groups, and its mediation seems to involve anxiety more than expectancies. But do these manipulations cause a specific state of stereotype threat, that is, a sensed threat specifically about being stereotyped or fitting the stereotype? To address this question, Aronson and I (C. M. Steele & Aronson, 1995) tested two things: whether manipulating stereotype threat actually activates the racial stereotype in the thinking and information processing of stereotype-threatened test takers and whether it produces in them a specific motivation to avoid being seen stereotypically. Again, Black and White participants were run in either an ability-diagnostic or ability-nondiagnostic condition, except that just after the condition instructions, and completion of the sample test items (so that participants could see how difficult the items were) and just before participants expected to take the test, they completed measures of stereotype activation and avoidance. The stereotype activation measure asked them to complete 80 word fragments, 10 of which we knew from pretesting could be completed with, among other words, words symbolic of African American stereotypes (e.g.,_ _ce [race], la_ _[lazy], or _ _or [poor]) and 5 of which could be completed with, among other words, words signifying self-doubts (e.g., lo_ _ _ [loser], du_ _ [dumb], or sha_ _ [shame]). The measure of participants' motivation to avoid being seen stereotypically simply asked them how much they preferred various types of music, activities, sports, and personality traits, some of which a pretest sample had rated as stereotypic of African Americans.[5]

If expecting to take a difficult ability-diagnostic test is enough to activate the racial stereotype in the thinking of Black participants and to motivate them to avoid being stereotyped, then these participants, more than those in the other conditions, should show more stereotype and self-doubt word completions and fewer preferences for things that are African American. This is precisely what happened. Black participants in the diagnostic condition completed more word fragments with stereotype- and self-doubt-related words and had fewer preferences for things related to African American experience (e.g., jazz, basketball, hip-hop) than Black participants in the nondiagnostic condition or White participants in either condition, all of whom were essentially the same (see Figure 14.4). Also, as a last item before participants expected to begin the test, they were given the option of recording their race, a measure we thought might further tap into an apprehension about being viewed stereotypically. Interestingly, then, all of the Black participants in the nondiagnostic condition and all of the White participants in both condition listed their race, whereas

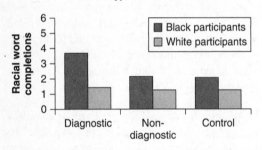

Stereotype activation measure

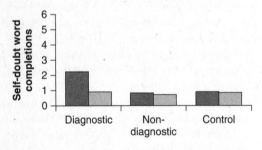

Self-doubt activation measure

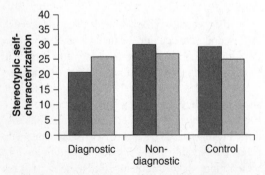

Stereotype avoidance measure

FIGURE 14.4   Indicators of Stereotype Threat.

only 25% of the Black participants in the diagnostic condition did so.

Self-Rejection or Self-Presentation?

A troubling implication of the earlier mentioned models (e.g., Allport, 1954; Bettelheim, 1943; Clark, 1965; Grier & Coobs, 1968; Erikson, 1956; Fanon, 1952/1967; Kardiner & Ovesey, 1951) is that negative stereotypes about one's group eventually become internalized and cause rejection of one's own group, even of oneself—*self-hating* preferences. The famous finding of Clark and Clark (1939) that Black children preferred White dolls over Black dolls has been interpreted this way. The preferences of Black participants in the diagnostic condition fit this pattern; with negative stereotypes about their group cognitively activated, they valued things that were African American less than any other group. But the full set of results suggests a different interpretation. In those conditions in which Black participants did not have to worry about tripping a stereotypic perception of themselves, they valued things that were African American more strongly than did other participants. Thus, rather than reflecting self- or own-group rejection, their devaluing of things that were African American in the diagnostic condition was apparently a strategic self-presentation aimed at cracking the stereotypic lens through which they could be seen. So it could be, then, in the general case, rather than reflecting real self-concepts, behavior that appears group rejecting or self-rejecting may reflect situation-bound, self-presentational strategies.

Stereotype Threat and Domain Identification

Not being identified with a domain, our (C. M. Steele & Aronson, 1995) theory reasons, means that one's experience of stereotype threat in the domain is less self-threatening. Although we have yet to complete a satisfactory test of this prediction, partially completed experiments and pretests show that stereotype threat has very little, if any, effect on participants not identified with the domain of relevance. Most typically, these participants give up and underperform on the difficult test regardless of whether they are under stereotype threat. Although not yet constituting a complete test of this implication of the theory these data do emphasize that the above results generalize only to domain-identified students.

Stereotype Threat and the Interpretation of Group Difference in Standardized Test Performance

Inherent to the science of quantifying human intelligence is the unsavory possibility of ranking societal groups as to their aggregated intelligence. It is from this corner of psychology that the greatest controversy has arisen, a controversy that has lasted throughout this century and that is less about the fact of these group differences than about their interpretation (cf. Herrnstein & Murray, 1994; Kamin, 1974). To the set of possible causes for these group differences, our (C. M. Steele & Aronson, 1995) findings add a new one: the differential impact of stereotype threat on groups in the testing situation itself. Thus, stereotype threat may be a possible source of bias in standardized tests, a bias that arises not from item content but from group differences in the threat that societal stereotypes attach to test performance. Of course, not every member of an ability-stereotyped group is going to be affected by stereotype threat every time they take a test. As our research has shown, the experience of success as one takes the test can dispel the relevance of the stereotype. Nonetheless, among the most identified test takers in the stereotype-threatened group—those in its academic vanguard who have the greatest confidence and skills—this threat can substantially depress performance on more difficult parts of the exam. And this depression could contribute significantly to the group's underperformance in comparison with nonstereo-type-threatened groups.[6]

Reaction of Disidentification

Stereotype threat is assumed to have an abiding effect on school achievement—an effect beyond its impairment of immediate performance—by preventing or breaking a person's identification with school, in particular, those domains of schooling in which stereotype applies. This reasoning has several implications for which empirical evidence can be brought to bear: the resilience of self-esteem to stigmatization; the relationship between stigmatized status and school achievement; and,

among ability-stigmatized people, the relationship between their school performance and self-esteem.

Self-Esteem's Resilience to Stigmatization

In a recent review, Crocker and Major (1989) were able to make a strong case for the lack of something that common sense suggests should exist: a negative effect of stigmatization on self-esteem. Following the logic of the internalization models described above and viewing stigmatization as, among other things, an assault to self-esteem, one might expect that people who are stigmatized would have lower self-esteem than people who are not. Yet, as Crocker and Major reported, when the self-esteem of stigmatized groups (e.g., Blacks, Chicanos, the facially disfigured, obese people, etc.) is actually measured, one finds that their self-esteem is as high as that of the nonstigmatized.

Crocker and Major (1989) offered the intriguing argument that stigma itself offers esteem-protective strategies. For example, the stigmatized can blame their failures on the prejudice of out-group members, they can limit their self-evaluative social comparisons to the in-group of other stigmatized people, and they can devalue the domains in which they feel devalued. Other models have also described esteem-saving adaptations to stigma. For example, models that assume internalization of stereotype-related anxieties often posit compensatory personality traits (e.g., grandiosity) that protect self-esteem but leave one poorly adapted to the mainstream (e.g., Allport, 1954; Clark, 1965; Grier & Coobs, 1968; Kardiner & Ovesey, 1951; S. Steele, 1990). In the present reasoning, stigmatization stems from stereotype threat in specific domains. Thus, it adds to the list of stigma adaptations the possibility of simple domain disidentification, the rescuing of self-esteem by rendering as self-evaluatively irrelevant the domain in which the stereotype applies. Herein may lie a significant source of the self-esteem resilience shown in stigmatized groups. This idea also implies that once domain disidentification is achieved, the pressure for adaptations of attribution and personality may be reduced.

A Universal Connection Between Stigmatization and Poor School Achievement

If disidentification with school, and the resulting underachievement, can be a reaction to ability-stigmatizing stereotypes in society, then it might be expected that ability stigmatization would be associated with poor school performance wherever it occurs in the world. Finding such a relationship would not definitively prove the present theory; the direction of causality could be quarreled with, as could the mediation of such a relationship. Still, it would be suggestive, and, in that respect, Ogbu (1986) reported an interesting fact: Among the caste-like minorities in industrial and nonindustrial nations throughout the world (e.g., the Maoris of New Zealand, the Baraku of Japan, the Harijans of India, the Oriental Jews of Israel, and the West Indians of Great Britain), there exists the same 15-point IQ gap between them and nonstigmatized members of their society as exists between Black and White Americans. These groups also suffer poorer school performance, higher dropout rates, and related behavior problems. Moreover, these gaps appear even when the stigmatized and nonstigmatized are of the same race, as in the case of the Baraku and other Japanese. What these groups share that is capable of explaining their deficits is a caste-like status that, through stereotypes in their societies, stigmatizes their intellectual abilities—sowing the seeds, I suggest, of their school disidentification.

The Disassociation of Self-Esteem and School Achievement

If the poor school achievement of ability-stigmatized groups is mediated by disidentification, then it might be expected that among the ability stigmatized, there would be a disassociation between school outcomes and overall self-esteem. Several kinds of evidence suggest this process among African Americans. First, there is the persistent finding that although Black students underperform in relation to White students on school outcomes from grades to standardized tests (e.g., Demo & Parker, 1987; Simmons, Brown, Bush, & Blyth, 1978; C. M. Steele, 1992), their global self-esteem is as high or higher than that of White students

(e.g., Porter & Washington, 1979; Rosenberg, 1979; Wylie, 1979). For both of these facts to be true, some portion of Black students must have acquired an imperviousness to poor school performance.

Several further studies suggest that this imperviousness is rooted in disidentification. In a study of desegregated schools in Champaign, Illinois, Hare and Costenell (1985) measured students' school achievement; overall self-esteem; and self-esteem in the specific domains of home life, school, and peer-group relations. Like others, they found that although Black students performed less well than White students, they still had comparable levels of overall self-esteem. Their domain-specific measures suggested why: Although Black students were lower than White students in school and home-life self-esteem, Blacks slightly exceeded Whites in peer-group self-esteem. Here then, perhaps, was the source of their overall self-regard: disidentification with domains in which their evaluative prospects were poor (in this case, school and home life) and identification with domains in which their prospects were better (i.e., their peers).

A recent study suggests that this may be a not uncommon phenomenon. Analyzing data available from the National Educational Longitudinal Survey (National Center for Educational Statistics, 1992; a nationally representative longitudinal survey begun in 1988), Osborne (1994) found that from the 8th through 10th grades, Black students had lower achievement and somewhat higher self-esteem than White students, which replicated the general pattern of findings described above. But more than this, he found evidence of increasing Black students' disidentification over this period: The correlation between their school achievement and self-esteem for this period decreased significantly more for Black than for White students. Also, using a scale measure of school disidentification, Major, Spencer, Schmader, Wolfe, and Crocker (in press) found that Black students were more disidentified than White students in several college samples and that for disidentified students of both races, negative feedback about an intellectual task had less effect on their self-esteem than it did for identified students. Major et al. further showed that when racial stereotypes were primed, neither negative nor positive feedback affected Black students' self-esteem, whereas the self-esteem of White students followed the direction of the feedback. Ability stigmatization of the sort experienced by African Americans, then, can be associated with a protective "disconnect" between performance and self-regard, a disconnect of the sort that is consistent with disidentification theory.

Can stereotype threat directly cause this disconnect? To test this question, Kirsten Stoutemeyer and I varied the strength of stereotype threat that female test takers (Stanford students) were under by varying whether societal differences between women and men in math performance were attributed to small but stable differences in innate ability (suggesting an inherent, gender-based limit in math ability) or to social causes such as sex-role prescriptions and discrimination (suggesting no inherent, gender-based limit in math ability). We then measured their identification with math and math-related careers, either before or after they took a difficult math test. Regardless of when identification was measured, women under stronger stereotype threat disidentified with math and math-related careers more than women under weaker stereotype threat. Although domain identification has several determinants, these findings suggest that stereotype threat is an important one of them.

"Wise" Schooling: Practice and Policy

As a different diagnosis, the present analysis comes to a different prescription: The schooling of stereotype-threatened groups may be improved through situational changes (analogous to those manipulated in our experiments) that reduce the stereotype threat these students might otherwise be under. As noted, psychological diagnoses have more typically ascribed the problems of these students to internal processes ranging from genes to internalized stereotypes. On the face of it, at least, internal states are more difficult to modify than situational factors. Thus, the hope of the present analysis, encouraged by our research, is that these problems might be more tractable through the situational design of schooling, in particular, design that secures these students in the belief that they will not be held under the suspicion of negative stereotype about

their group. Schooling that does this, I have called *wise,* a term borrowed from Irving Goffman (1963), who borrowed it from gay men and lesbians of the 1950s. They used it to designate heterosexuals who understood their full humanity despite the stigma attached to their sexual orientation: family and friends, usually, who knew the person beneath the stigma. So it must be, I argue, for the effective schooling of stereotype-threatened groups.

Although "wisdom" may be necessary for the effective schooling of such students, it may not always be sufficient. The chief distinction made in this analysis (between those of these groups who are identified with the relevant school domain and those who are not) raises a caution. As noted, stereotype threat is not keenly felt by those who identify little with the stereotype-threatening domain. Thus, although reducing this threat in the domain may be necessary to encourage their identification, it may not be sufficient to build an identification that is not there. For this to occur, more far-reaching strategies that develop the building blocks of domain identification may be required: better skills, greater domain self-efficacy, feelings of social and cultural comfort in the domain, a lack of social pressure to disidentify, and so on.

But for the identified of these groups, who are quite numerous on college campuses, the news may be better than is typically appreciated. For these students, feasible changes in the conditions of schooling that make threatening stereotypes less applicable to their behavior (i.e., wisdom) may be enough. They are already identified with the relevant domain, they have skills and confidence in the domain, and they have survived other barriers to identification. Their remaining problem is stereotype threat. Reducing that problem, then, may be enough to bring their performance on par with that of nonstereotyped persons in the domain.

This distinction raises an important and often overlooked issue in the design of schooling for stereotype-threatened students, that of *triage,* the issue of rendering onto the right students the right intervention. Mistakes can easily be made. For example, applying a strategy to school-identified students (on the basis of their membership in a stereotype-threatened group) that assumes weak identification, poor skills, and little confidence could backfire. It could increase stereotype threat and underperformance by signaling that their abilities are held under suspicion because of their group membership. But the opposite mistake could be made by applying a strategy that assumes strong identification, skills, and confidence to those who are actually unidentified with the relevant domain. Merely reducing stereotype threat may not accomplish much when the more primary need of these students is to gain the interests, resources, skills, confidences, and values that are needed to identify with the domain.

Some wise strategies, then, may work for both identified and unidentified students from these groups, but others may have to be appropriately targeted to be effective. I offer some examples of both types.

For both domain-identified and domain-unidentified students:

1. Optimistic teacher–student relationships. The prevailing stereotypes make it plausible for ability-stigmatized students to worry that people in their schooling environment will doubt their abilities. Thus, one wise strategy, seemingly suitable for all students, is to discredit this assumption through the authority of potential-affirming adult relationships. The Comer (1988) Schools Project has used this strategy with great success at the elementary school level, and Johnides, von Hippel, Lerner, and Nagda (1992) have used it in designing a mentoring program for incoming minority and other students at the University of Michigan. In analogous laboratory experiments, Geoffrey Cohen, Lee Ross, and I (Cohen, Steele, & Ross, 1997) found that critical feedback to African American students was strongly motivating when it was coupled with optimism about their potential.

2. Challenge over remediation. Giving challenging work to students conveys respect for their potential and thus shows them that they are not regarded through the lens of an ability-demeaning stereotype. Urie Treisman (1985) used this strategy explicitly in designing his successful group-study workshops in math for college-aged women and minorities. Taking students where they are skillwise, all students can be given challenging work at a challenging, not overwhelming, pace, especially

in the context of supportive adult–student relationships. In contrast, remedial work reinforces in these students the possibility that they are being viewed stereotypically. And this, by increasing stereotype threat in the domain, can undermine their performance.

3. Stressing the expandability of intelligence. The threat of negative-ability stereotypes is that one could confirm or be seen as having a fixed limitation inherent to one's group. To the extent that schooling can stress what Carol Dweck (1986) called the *incremental* nature of human intelligence—its expandability in response to experience and training—it should help to deflect this meanest implication of the stereotype. Aronson (1996) recently found, for example, that having African American college students repeatedly advocate the expandability of intelligence to their elementary school tutees significantly improved their own grades.

For domain-identified students:

1. Affirming domain belongingness. Negative-ability stereotypes raise the threat that one does not belong in the domain. They cast doubt on the extent of one's abilities, on how well one will be accepted, on one's social compatibility with the domain, and so on. Thus, for students whose primary barrier to school identification is stereotype threat, direct affirmation of their belongingness in the domain may be effective. But it is important to base this affirmation on the students' intellectual potential. Affirming social belonging alone, for those under the threat of an ability stereotype, could be taken as begging the question.

2. Valuing multiple perspectives. This refers to strategies that explicitly value a variety of approaches to both academic substance and the larger academic culture in which that substance is considered. Making such a value public tells stereotype-threatened students that this is an environment in which the stereotype is less likely to be used.

3. Role models. People from the stereotype-threatened group who have been successful in the domain carry the message that stereotype threat is not an insurmountable barrier there.

For domain-unidentified students:

1. Nonjudgmental responsiveness. Research by Lepper, Woolverton, Mumme, and Gurtner (1993) has identified a distinct strategy that expert tutors use with especially poor students: little direct praise, Socratic direction of students' work, and minimal attention to right and wrong answers. For students weakly identified with the domain, who are threatened by a poor reputation and who probably hold internalized doubts about their ability, this Socratic strategy has the wisdom of securing a safe teacher–student relationship in which there is little cost of failure and the gradual building of domain efficacy from small gains.

2. Building self-efficacy. Based on Bandura's (1977, 1986) theory of self-efficacy, this strategy attempts to build the student's sense of competence and self-efficacy in the schooling domain. Howard and Hammond (1985) have developed a powerful implementation of this strategy for African American and other minority students, especially in inner-city public schools.

Existence Proof: A Wise Schooling Intervention

Providing a definitive test of wise schooling theory will require, of course, an extensive research program. But as a first step, something might be learned from what Uric Treisman (1985) called an existence proof, in this case, a demonstration that an intervention derived from the theory could stop or reverse a tenacious negative trajectory in the school performance of stereotype-threatened students. Such an intervention would of necessity confound things: different wise practices as well as other practices and structures, peculiar to that setting, that could also affect academic outcomes. It could not stand as a test of the psychological theory per se. But if a particular architecture of wise strategies succeeded, it would encourage their applicability to the real-world schooling of these students.

With this rationale, my colleagues and I (Steven Spencer, Richard Nisbett, Mary Hummel, David Schoem, Kent Harber, Ken Carter) implemented a freshman-year program at the University of Michigan aimed at the underachievement and low retention rates of African American students. Each year, the program included approximately 250 freshmen in the ethnic proportions of the larger campus but with an oversampling of approximately 20% Black students and 20% non-Black minority students (i.e., Asian, Hispanic, and Native American students as a single group). Program students were randomly selected from the students admitted to Michigan and then recruited by phone to participate. All program participants lived together in the wing of a large, 1,200-student dormitory throughout their freshman year.

In this context, we implemented several wise strategies. The program was presented as a transition program aimed at helping students maximize the advantages of university life. We also recruited students honorifically; they were told that, as Michigan admittees, they had survived a very competitive selection process and that our program was designed to help them maximize their strong potential. These practices represented the program as nonremediational and represented the university as having acknowledged their intellectual potential and as having high expectation for them—all things that signal the irrelevance of negative group stereotypes. Once the students were in the program these expectations were reinforced by their being offered a "challenge" workshop, modeled on those developed by Treisman (1985) for calculus, in either freshman calculus, chemistry, physics, or writing. These were taken on a voluntary basis in the dormitory. Students also participated in small weekly discussion groups, centered on brief readings that allowed discussion of adjustment-relevant social arid even personal issues. This activity has the wisdom of letting students know that they, or other member of their group, are not the only ones with concerns about adjusting to university life—an insight that can deflect the relevance of negative group stereotypes. These formal program components lasted for the first 10 weeks of the school year, and, as voluntary activities, approximately half of the students regularly participated in either one or both of them.

The first-semester grades averaged over the first two years of this ongoing project give a reliable picture of the program's initial impact. To show the size of the program's effect on students at different levels of preparation, Figure 14.5 graphs first-semester grades, using regression lines, for the different student groups as a function of standardized test scores on entry into the university (they are presented as standard deviation units in this figure to provide a common scale for students who took either the SAT or American College test exam). The first thing to notice is the two essentially parallel lines for White and Black students outside of any program at Michigan. They replicate the standard overprediction–underperformance of Black students alluded to earlier, and it is against this pattern that the effects of the program can be evaluated. Looking first at the line for White students in our program, there is a modest tendency for these students to do better than the White control students (i.e., those outside the program), but given our accumulation of *n* throughout these first two years, this difference is not significant. It is the results for Black students in our program (but who were not also in the campus minority program) that are most promising. Their line is considerably above that for Black control students (i.e., Black students outside any program) and, even with the modest sample size ($n = 27$), is significantly higher than this control line in the top one third of the standardized test distribution, $t = 2.72, p < .05$. It is important that this group of Black students showed almost no underperformance; in the top two thirds of the test distribution, they had essentially

the same grades as White students. We also know from follow-up data that their higher grade performance continued at least through their sophomore year and that as long as four years later only one of them had dropped out.

Theoretically just as important, is the bottom line in Figure 14.5, depicting the results for Black students in a large minority remediation program. Despite getting considerable attention, they performed worse than the other groups at nearly every level of preparation. The difference between Black students in the minority program and Black students not in any program becomes significant at 1.76 standard deviations below the mean for test performance and is significant from that point on, $ps < .05$. Also, by the beginning of their junior year, 25% of these students had failed to register, and among those who entered with test scores in the top one third of the test distribution, this figure was 40%. Some selection factor possibly contributed to this. Despite our having controlled for test scores and high school grade point averages in these analyses, some portion of these students may have been assigned to this program because they evidenced other risk factors. Still, these results suggest that the good intentions of the minority-remediation framework for schooling African American students can backfire by, in our terms, institutionalizing the racial stereotype by which they are already threatened.

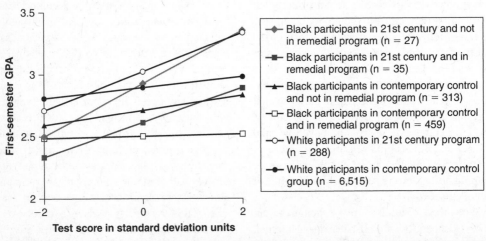

FIGURE 14.5   First-Semester Grade Point Average (GPA) as a Function of Program and Race Controlling for High School GPA.

Although these findings are preliminary and we do not know that they were mediated as our theory claims, they are a step toward an existence proof; they show that wise practices can reduce Black students' underachievement in a real-school context and, as important, that unwise practices seem to worsen it.

Conclusion

In social psychology, we know that as observers looking at a person or group, we tend to stress internal, dispositional causes of their behavior, whereas when we take the perspective of the actor, now facing the circumstances they face, we stress more situational causes (e.g., E. E. Jones & Nisbett, 1972; Ross, 1977). If there is a system to the present research, it is that of taking the actor's perspective in trying to understand the intellectual performance of African American and female students. It is this perspective that brings to light the broadly encompassing condition of having these groups' identification with domains of schooling threatened by societal stereotypes. This is a threat that in the short run can depress their intellectual performance and, over the long run, undermine the identity itself, a predicament of serious consequence. But it is a predicament— something in the interaction between a group's social identity and its social psychological context, rather than something essential to the group itself. Predicaments can be treated, intervened on, and it is in this respect that I hope the perspective taken in this analysis and the early evidence offer encouragement.

Notes

1. Other factors may also contribute. For example, there are persistent reports of women and minorities being treated differently in the classroom and in other aspects of schooling (e.g., Hewitt & Seymour. 1991). This treatment includes both the "chilly-climate" sins of omission—the failure to call on them in class or to recognize and encourage their talents, and so on and, in the case of low-income minorities, sins of commission— disproportionate expulsion from school, assignment to special education classes, and administration or corporal punishment ("National Coalition of Advocates for Students Report," 1988).

2. The point is not that negative stereotypes are never internalized as low self-expectation and self-doubts. It is that in such internalization, disidentification is the more primary adaptation. That is, once the stereotype-relevant domain (e.g., math) is dropped as a self-definition, the negative stereotype (e.g., that women are limited in math) can be accepted as more self-descriptive (i.e., internalized) without it much affecting one's self-regard (as for the woman who, not caring about math, says she is lousy at it). But this internalization is probably resisted (e.g., Crocker & Major, 1989) until disidentification makes it less self-threatening. Once this has happened the person is likely to avoid the domain because of both disinterest and low confidence regardless of whether stereotype threat is present.

3. As a process of social devaluation, stereotype threat is both a subform of stigmatization and something more general. It is that form of stigmatization that is mediated by collectively held, devaluing group stereotypes. This means that it does not include stigmatization that derives from nonstereotyped features such as a facial disfigurement or for example, what Goffman (1963) called abominations of the body. Stereotype threat is a situational predicament. And, in this sense, it is also more general than stigmatization. It is a threat that can befall anyone about whom a negative reputation or group stereotype exists.

4. Moreover, a protective avoidance of identification can become a group norm. In reaction to a shared sense of threat in school, for example, it can become a shared reaction that is transmitted to group members as the normative relation to school. Both research (e.g., Ogbu, 1986; Solomon, 1992) and the media have documented this reaction in minority students from inner-city high schools to Harvard University's campus. Thus, disidentification can be sustained by normative pressure from the in-group as well as by stereotype threat in the setting.

5. Participants did not actually take the test in this experiment, as completing these measures would likely have activated the stereotype in all conditions.

6. Those who are less domain identified in the stereotype-threatened group may also underperform on standardized tests. Because they care less about the domain it represents, they may be undermotivated or they may withdraw effort in the face of frustration. And for all of the reasons I have discussed, the greater portion of the stereotype-threatened group

may be academically unidentified. This fact too, then, may contribute to the group's overall weaker performance on these tests in comparison with nonstereotype-threatened groups.

References

Adelman, C. (1991). *Women at thirty-something: Paradoxes of attainment.* Washington, DC: U.S. Department of Education, Office of Research and Development.

Alexander, K. L., & Entwistle, D. R. (1988). Achievement in the first two years of school: Patterns and processes. *Monographs of the Society for Research in Child Development, 53*(2).

Allport, G. (1954). *The nature of prejudice.* New York: Doubleday.

American Council on Education. (1995–1996). *Minorities in higher education.* Washington, DC: Office of Minority Concerns.

Aronson, J. (1996). *Advocating the malleability of intelligence as an intervention to increase college grade performance.* Unpublished manuscript. University of Texas.

Bandura, A. (1977). Seff-efficacy: Toward a unifying theory of behavior change. *Psychological Review, 84,* 191–215.

Bandura, A. (1986). *Social foundations of action: A social-cognitive theory.* Englewood Cliffs, NJ: Prentice Hall.

Baumeister, R. F., & Showers, C. J. (1984), A review of paradoxical performance effects: Choking under pressure in sports and mental tests. *European Journal of Social Psychology, 16,* 361–383.

Benbow, C. P., & Arjmand O. (1990). Predictions of high academic achievement in mathematics and science by mathematically talented students: A longitudinal study. *Journal of Educational Psychology, 82,* 430–441.

Benbow, C. P., & Stanley, J. C. (1980). Sex differences in mathematical ability: Fact or artifact? *Science, 210,* 1262–1264.

Benbow, C. P., & Stanley, J. C. (1983). Sex differences in mathematical reasoning ability: More facts. *Science, 222,* 1029–1031.

Bettelheim, B. (1943). Individual and mass behavior in extreme situations. *Journal Abnormal and Social Psychology, 38,* 417–452.

Brill, A. A. (Ed.). (1938). *The basic writings of Sigmund Freud.* New York: Random House.

Burton, N. W., & Jones, L. V. (1982). Recent trends in achievement levels of Black and White youth. *Educational Researcher, 11,* 10–17.

Carter, S. (1991). *Reflections of an affirmative action baby.* New York: Basic Books.

Clark, K. B. (1965). *Dark ghetto: Dilemmas of social power.* New York: Harper & Row.

Clark, K. B., & Clark, M. K. (1939). The development of consciousness of self and the emergence of racial identification of Negro school children. *Journal of Social Psychology, 10,* 591–599.

Cohen, G., Steele, C. M., & Ross, L. (1997). *Giving feedback across the racial divide: Overcoming the effects of stereotypes.* Unpublished manuscript, Stanford University.

Coleman, J. S., Campbell, E. Q., Hobson, C. J., McPartland, J., Mood, A. M., Weinfield, F. D., & York, R. L. (1966). *Equality of educational opportunity.* Washington, DC: U.S. Government Printing Office.

Comer, J. (1988, November). Educating poor minority children. *Scientific American, 259,* 42.

Cooley, C. H. (1956). *Human nature and the social order.* New York: Free Press.

Cose, E. (1993). *The rage of a privileged class.* New York: Harper Collins.

Crocker, J., & Major, B. (1989). Social stigma and self-esteem: The self-protective properties of stigma. *Psychological Review, 96,* 608–630.

Cross, W. E., Jr. (1991). *Shades of black: Diversity in African-American identity.* Philadelphia: Temple University Press.

Culotta, E., & Gibbons, A. (Eds.). (1992, November 13). Minorities in science [Special section]. *Science, 258,* 1176–1232.

DeBoer, G. (1984). A study of gender effects in science and mathematics course-taking behavior among students who graduated from college in the late 1970s. *Journal of Research in Science Teaching, 21,* 95–103.

Demo, D. H., & Parker, K. D. (1987). Academic achievement and self-esteem among Black and White college students. *Journal of Social Psychology, 4,* 345–355.

Dweck, C. (1986). Motivational processes affecting learning, *American Psychologist, 41,* 1040–1048.

Eccles, J. S. (1987). Gender roles and women's achievement-related decisions. *Psychology of Women Quarterly, 11,* 135–172.

Eccles-Parsons, J. S., Adler, T. F., Futterman, R., Goff, S. B., Kaczala, C. M., Meece, J. L. & Midgley, C. Expectations, values, and academic behaviors. In J. T. Spence (Ed.) (1983). *Achievements and achievement motivation* (pp. 75–146). New York: Freeman.

Erikson, E. (1956). The problem of ego-identity. *Journal of the American Analytical Association, 4*, 56–121.

Fanon, F. (1967). *Black skins, white masks.* New York: Grow Press (Original work published 1952).

Frable, D., Blackstone, T., & Sherbaum, C. (1990). Marginal and mindful: Deviants in social interaction. *Journal of Personality and Social Behavior, 59*, 140–149.

Geen, R. G. (1991), Social motivation. *Annual Review of Psychology, 42,* 377–399.

Gerard, H. (1983). School desegregation: The social science role. *American Psychologist, 38*, 869–878.

Goffman, E. (1963). *Stigma: Notes on the management of spoiled identity.* New York: Touchstone.

Grier, W. H., & Coobs, P M. (1968). *Black rage.* New York: Basic Books.

Hare, B. R., & Costenell, L. A. (1985). No place to run, no place to hide: Comparative status and future prospects of Black boys. In M. B. Spencer, G. K. Brookins, & W. Allen (Eds.), *Beginnings: The social and affective development of Black children* (pp. 201–214). Hillsdale, NJ: Erlbaum.

Herrnstein, R. A., & Murray, C. (1994). *The bell curve.* New York: Grove Press.

Hewitt, N. M., & Seymour, E. (1991). *Factors contributing to high attrition rates among science and engineering undergraduate majors.* Unpublished report to the Alfred P. Sloan Foundation.

Howard, J., & Hammond, R. (1985, September 9). Rumors of inferiority. *New Republic, 72*, 18–23.

Hyde, J. S., Fennema, E., & Lamon, S. J. (1990). Gender differences in mathematics performance: A meta-analysis. *Psychological Bulletin, 107,* 139–155.

James, W. (1950). *The principles of psychology* (Vol. 1). New York: Dover (Original work published 1890).

Jensen, A. R. (1969). How much can we boost IQ and scholastic achievement? *Harvard Educational Review, 39,* 1–123.

Jensen, A. R. (1980). *Bias in mental testing.* New York: Free Press.

Johnides, J., von Hippel, W., Lerner J. S., & Nagda, B. (1992, August). *Evaluation of minority retention programs: The undergraduate research opportunities program at the University of Michigan.* Paper presented at the 100th Annual Convention of the American Psychological Association, Washington, DC.

Jones, E. E., Farina, A., Hastorf, A. H., Markus, H., Muller O. T, & Scott, R. A. (1984). *Social stigma: The psychology of marked relationships.* New York: Freeman.

Jones, E. E., & Nisbett, R. E. (1972). The actor and the observer: Divergent perceptions of the causes of behavior. In E. E. Jones, D. E. Kanouse, H. H. Kelley, R. E. Nisbett, S. Valins, & B. Weiner (Eds.), *Attribution: Perceiving the causes of behavior* (pp. 79–94). Morristown, NJ: General Learning Press.

Jones, J. M. (1997). *Prejudice and racism (*2nd ed.). New York: McGraw-Hill.

Kamin, L. (1974). *The science and politics of I.Q.* Hillsdale, NJ: Erlbaum.

Kardiner, A., & Ovesey, L. (1951). *The mark of oppression: Explorations in the personality of the American Negro.* New York: Norton.

Kleck, R. E., & Strenta, A. (1980). Perceptions of the impact of negatively valued physical characteristics on social interactions. *Journal of Personality and Social Psychology, 39,* 861–873.

Lepper, M. R., Woolverton, M., Mumme, D. L., & Gurtner, J.-L. (1993). Motivational techniques of expert human tutors: Lessons for the design of computer-based tutors. In S. P. Lajoie & S. J. Derry (Eds.), *Computers as cognitive tools* (pp. 75–104). Hillsdale, NJ: Erlbaum.

Levin, J., & Wyckoff, J. (1988). Effective advising: Identifying students most likely to persist and succeed in engineering. *Engineering Education, 78*, 178–182.

Lewin, K. (1941). *Resolving social conflict.* New York: Harper & Row.

Linn, M. C. (1994). Tyranny of the mean: Gender and expectations. *Notices of the American Mathematical Society, 41,* 766–769.

Lord, C. G., & Saenz, D. S. (1985). Memory deficits and memory surfeits: Differential cognitive consequences of tokenism for tokens and observers. *Journal of Personality and Social Psychology, 49,* 918–926.

Lovely, R. (1987, February). *Selection of undergraduate majors by high ability students: Sex difference and attrition of science majors.* Paper presented at the annual meeting of the Association for the Study of Higher Education, San Diego, CA.

Major, B., Spencer; S., Schrnader, T., Wolfe, C., & Crocker, J. (in press). Coping with negative stereotypes about intellectual performance: The role of psychological disengagement. *Personality and Social Psychology Bulletin.*

Mead, G. H. (1934). *Mind, self, and society.* Chicago: University of Chicago Press.

Miller, L. S. (1995). *An American imperative: Accelerating minority educational advancement.* New Haven, CT: Yale University Press.

Miller, L. S. (1996, March). *Promoting high academic achievement among non-Asian minorities.* Paper presented at the Princeton University Conference on Higher Education, Princeton, NJ.

National Center for Educational Statistics. (1992). *National Educational Longitudinal Study of 1988: First follow-up. Student component data file user's manual.* Washington, DC: U.S. Department of Education, Office of Educational Research and Improvement.

National Coalition of Advocates for Students Report. (1988, December 12). *The Ann Arbor News,* pp. Al, A4.

Nettles, M. T (1988). *Toward undergraduate student equality in American higher education.* New York: Greenwood.

Ogbu, J. (1986). The consequence: of the American caste system. In U. Neisser (Ed.), *The school achievement of minority children. New perspectives* (pp. 19–56). Hillsdale, NJ: Erlbaum.

Osborne, J. (1994). Academics, self-esteem, and race: A look at the underlying assumption of the disidentification hypothesis. *Personality and Social Psychology Bulletin, 21,* 449–455.

Porter, J. R., & Washington. R. E. (1979). Black identity and self-esteem: A review of the studies of Black self-concept, 1968–1978. *Annual Review of Sociology, 5,* 53–74.

Ramist, L., Lewis, C., & McCamley-Jenkins, L. (1994). *Student group differences in predicting college grades: Sex, language, and ethnic groups* (College Board Report No. 93-1, ETS No. 94.27). New York: College Entrance Examination Board.

Rosenberg, M. (1979). *Conceiving self.* New York: Basic Books.

Ross, L. (1977). The intuitive psychologist and his shortcomings: Distortions in the attribution process. In L. Berkowitz (Ed.), *Advances in experimental social psychology* (Vol. 10, pp. 337–384). New York: Academic Press.

Sarason, I. G. (1980). Introduction to the study of test anxiety. In I. G. Sarason (Ed.), *Test anxiety: Theory, research, and applications* (pp. 57–78). Hillsdale, NJ: Erlbaum.

Sartre, J. P. (1965). *Anti-Semite and Jew.* New York: Schocken Books (Original work published 1946).

Schlenker, B. R., & Weigold. M. F. (1989). Goals and the self-identification process: Constructing desired identities. In L. A. Pervin (Ed.), *Goals concepts in personality and social psychology* (pp. 243–290). Hilladale, NJ: Erlbaum.

Simmons, R. G., Brown, L., Bush, D. M., & Blyth. D. A. (1978). Self-esteem and achievement of Black and White adolescents. *Social Problems, 26,* 86–96.

Solomon. R. P. (1992). *Forging a separatist culture.* Albany: State University of New York Press.

Spencer, S., Steele, C. M., & Quinn, D. (1997). *Under suspicion of inability: Stereotype threat and women's math performance.* Manuscript submitted for publication.

Steele, C. M. (1975). Name-calling and compliance. *Journal of Personality and Social Psychology, 31,* 361–369.

Steele, C. M. (1988). The psychology of self-affirmation: Sustaining the integrity of the self. In L. Berkowitz (Ed.), *Advances in experimental social psychology* (Vol. 21, pp. 261–302). New York: Academic Press.

Steele, C. M. (1992, April). Race and the schooling of Black Americans. *The Atlantic Monthly,* pp. 68–78.

Steele, C. M., & Aronson, J. (1995). Stereotype threat and the intellectual test performance of African Americana. *Journal of Personality and Social Psychology, 69,* 797–811.

Steele, S. (1990). *The content of our character.* New York: St. Martin's Press.

Strenta, A. C., Elliott, R., Adair, R., Scott, J., & Matier, M. (1993). *Choosing and leaving science in highly selective institutions.* Unpublished report to the Alfred P. Sloan Foundation.

Tesser, A. (1988). Toward a self-evaluation maintenance model of social behavior. In L. Berkowitz (Ed.), *Advances in experimental social psychology* (Vol. 21, pp.181–227). New York: Academic Press.

Teisman, U. (1985). *A study of mathematics performance of Black students at the University of California, Berkeley.* Unpublished report.

Vars, F. E., & Bowen, W. G. (1997). *SAT scores, race, and academic performance: New evidence from academic successful colleges.* Unpublished manuscript.

Ware, N. C., & Dill, D. (1986, March). *Persistence in science among mathematically able male and female college student with pre college plans for a scientific major.* Paper presented at the annual meeting of the American Educational Research Association, San Francisco.

Ware, N. C., Steckler, N. A., & Leserman, J. (1985). Undergraduate women: Who chooses a science major? *Journal of Higher Education, 56,* 73–84.

Wine, J. (1971). Test anxiety and direction of attention. *Psychological Bulletin, 76,* 92–104.

Wylie, R. (1979). *The self-concept* (Vol. 2). Lincoln: University of Nebraska Press.

15

"The Complexities and Processes of Racial Housing Discrimination"

VINCENT J. ROSCIGNO, DIANA L. KARAFIN, AND GRIFF TESTER

Black-White inequality remains a lingering social problem in the United States, and this is partly reflected in the housing arena (Charles 2003; Massey and Denton 1993). Several explanations for persistent segregation have been posited, ranging from persistent economic disparities to race-specific housing preferences, yet the most convincing analytical evidence points to the prevalence of discrimination in housing markets. Central here are audit analyses—analyses that have effectively delineated minority vulnerability and gatekeeper discretion in enacting housing exclusion (Massey and Lundy 2001; Yinger 1998a, 1998b; Yinger 1995).

In this article, we build on housing audit and racial stratification literatures in two important ways. First, we highlight the wide range of potential exclusionary practices—practices often occurring at various stages of the rental/sales processes—that a singular audit study simply cannot. Secondly, and no less important, our data and analyses shed light on "non-exclusionary" forms of housing discrimination that traditional audit methodology is unable to capture. Here we are referring specifically to forms of discrimination (e.g., racial harassment, differential treatment, and discriminatory terms and conditions having to do with current leases, insurance arrangements, and mortgages terms and refinancing) within already established and existing housing arrangements.

Following background discussion pertaining to racial discrimination in housing and what audit analyses have revealed, we embed our focus on discriminatory processes in classic sociological concerns pertaining to social closure, power and status, and the interactional foundations of inequality (e.g., Parkin 1967; Blau 1967; Tomaskovic-Devey 1993). The aim, both in conception and analyses, is to address the call for "mechanism-oriented" analyses of stratification and its origins (Reskin 2000, 2003) by highlighting the multiple processes of housing discrimination that contribute to inequitable outcomes—a call that has been clearly echoed in recent overviews of the housing inequality literature (e.g., see especially Charles 2003; Ondrich, Ross, & Yinger 2003; Massey 2005).

Drawing on unique quantitative and qualitative data, comprised of over 750 verified housing discrimination cases, we ask how the discrimination revealed in these data aligns with the results of housing audits. Are there particular vulnerabilities among victims in terms of race, gender, and/or familial status, and who are most often the agents of discrimination? And finally, how do processes of exclusionary and non-exclusionary housing discrimination play out in real residential settings, and what are the implications for victims? These questions, particularly those pertaining to victim and perpetrator status and the complexity and diversity of discriminatory forms, are addressed by using conventional quantitative comparative techniques. Insights on process, and how precisely discrimination is carried out, are derived from qualitative immersion and analyses of case materials themselves. We conclude by discussing the implications of our analyses for the housing literature and more general conceptions of social stratification, interaction, and status-based social closure.

Racial Housing Discrimination in the U.S.

The latest U.S. Census reveals that Blacks, compared to Hispanics and Asians, continue to experience relatively high levels of residential segregation. According to Charles (2003), black-white segregation is extreme in 29 of the 50 largest metropolitan areas of the U.S., while remaining areas have seen little to no change over the last two decades. Though Hispanic and Asian segregation rates continue to rise, black segregation remains disproportionately higher (Iceland 2004; Charles 2003).

How does one make sense of high and persistent segregation levels, even forty years after passage of the Fair Housing Act? The most compelling evidence, derived from historical case analyses of residential turnover and contemporary audit designs, points to discrimination. Massey and Denton (1993), credited with bringing racial residential segregation to the forefront of scholarly debates surrounding the plight of the black

urban underclass with their publication *American Apartheid,* certainly concur that discriminatory action is to blame. They describe the maintenance of the black ghetto through purposeful discrimination towards blacks by individuals, organizations, public policy, the real estate industry, and various lending institutions (see also Farley and Frey 1994). Similarly notable is Gotham's (2002) analyses of neighborhood racial transition in the 1950's through 1970's and Orser's (1994) analyses of Baltimore from 1955–1965. In addition, Hirsch's (1998) historical analysis of Chicago's South Side demonstrates the role of political elites, including government agencies and local businesses, in resisting the in-migration of Blacks from the South from 1940–1960. Indeed, organized resistance has often been shaped by home owner's associations, tenants' councils, and parent-teacher groups, as well as city coder enforcement agencies, real estate companies, and public school officials (Seligman 2005).

Consistent with case-specific historical treatments are the results of contemporary housing audits. Housing audit (or racial testing) studies have been used for some time by fair housing groups as a systematic means of uncovering actual discrimination. Characterized by two, racially distinct, though similarly situated, individuals (one minority and one white), testers are sent into similar circumstances in the housing market. With efforts to control for social and human capital characteristics, such tests have served as an effective way to uncover discrimination and, thus, violations of the law. Although the intent is typically to provide a legal foundation for discrimination suits, audits can provide excellent quantitative and qualitative information on discriminatory practices—practices that are, by their nature, difficult to observe (Yinger 1995).

Beginning in 1977, HUD launched the Housing Market Practices Survey (HMPS), which conducted 3,264 tests in 40 metropolitan areas. The study provided evidence of significant discrimination against blacks in sales and rental markets. The results of HMPS played a role in the passage of the 1988 amendment to the Fair Housing Act and demonstrated the need for a second national study (The Housing Discrimination

Study) which was launched in 1989 and covered 25 metropolitan areas. A comparison of the two nation-wide studies demonstrated that discrimination had not decreased between 1977 and 1989 (Yinger 1995). Initial analyses from the most recent nation-wide HUD audit indicate that African Americans and Hispanics continue to face significant discriminatory barriers when searching for a home to rent or buy (Ross and Turner 2005). Rates of overall discrimination may have decreased somewhat between 1989 and 2000, with the exception of racial steering of African Americans and limitations in the financing opportunities and access to rental units for Hispanics (Ross and Turner 2005).[1]

As noted by Massey (2005), interpreting such declines as straightforward "decreases in housing discrimination" is potentially problematic insomuch as such audit testing can only gauge housing *exclusion*. Indeed, audits do not and cannot capture what we refer to as "non-exclusionary" forms of housing discrimination—forms that entail harassment and differential treatment *once an individual is housed*. It may very well be the case that prevailing forms of housing discrimination may simply be shifting over time—and that housing discrimination has consequently become a "moving target"—as realtors, landlords, etc., have become more astute to exclusion and its illegalities. Declines may also be a function of changes in state and federal policy that affect the number of complaints filed and/or processed, changes in the overall political climate of the U.S., or budget and funding cuts that have impacted fair housing enforcing agencies. Our data, discussed momentarily, are not constrained to one particular form of housing discrimination and, thus, help circumvent potential blind spots. And, although our analytic intent lies largely in delineating "processes" rather than predicting precisely how much discrimination occurs in the real world, our over-time data do reveal a subtle shift from exclusion toward non-exclusionary forms.

Audits are a useful method for assessing levels of discrimination faced by potential residents. Indeed, they can capture discrimination in face-to-face interactions, and allow scholars to match testers on similar characteristics relevant to discrimination

in the housing market (Yinger 1986; Yinger 1998a, 1998b; Fischer and Massey 2004). The comparative nature of the audit design itself importantly also reveals discrimination otherwise difficult to detect (as the discrimination is only uncovered by comparing the experiences of each of the testers). It is not surprising, then, that some have extended the methodology to potential discrimination prior to face-to-face interaction, such as telephone audits that capture linguistic profiling (Massey and Lundy 2001; Fischer and Massey 2004).

There are, however, important limitations. Some argue, for instance, that audit testers are predisposed to find discrimination (Fix and Struyk 1992), that testers' characteristics (e.g., work experience, education, etc.) and behavior impact the test itself (Heckman and Seigelman 1993), and that testing samples do not effectively capture the various forms of discrimination that manifest in the housing market (Ross and Yinger 2002). This includes non-exclusionary forms, noted previously, but also less-proximate, institutionalized forms such as lending.[2] Audit studies are also arguably constrained by the sampling frame of the study (i.e., units advertised in major metropolitan newspapers), and may not be as useful for studying complex transactions, transactions involving interaction at later stages, and cases involving adverse impact rather than disparate treatment (Fix and Struyk 1992; Yinger 1998a, 1998b; Ross and Yinger 2002). In fact, some scholars argue that audits do not provide a direct measure of discrimination, but rather provide a measure of discrimination among qualified minorities who actively seek units advertised in the newspaper (Ross and Turner 2005).

No less important that the limitations noted above, social scientists have seldom drawn from the significant body of audits focusing on other forms of discriminatory housing practices, such as federal protections based on family status (e.g., a single mother with children)—an issue that, given complexities of family poverty, single parenthood, and preexistent racial stereotypes, may be especially pronounced for African American women. In this regard, evidence suggests that black and Hispanic couples with children face more discrimination than minorities without children (Yinger

1995; Page 1995), and that white resistance is even more pronounced among white families with children under eighteen (Emerson, Chai, and Yancey 2001). It is for this reason that our own analyses considers victim status, not only in terms of race and gender, but also in terms of familial status and potential vulnerabilities that may be related.

Processes & Dimensions of Housing Discrimination

A focus on both exclusionary and non-exclusionary forms of racial discrimination in housing, and the status-based and interactional processes involved, helps advance our understanding of this particular form of inequality while also informing broader sociological conceptions of the micro-interactional foundations of group disadvantage. By exclusionary, we are referring to *actions and practices that exclude an individual or family from obtaining the housing of their choosing.* Non-exclusionary discrimination, in contrast, refers to *discriminatory actions and practices that occur within an already established housing arrangement, most often entailing racial harassment, differential treatment of tenants, or disparate application of contractual terms and conditions of residency.* Our intent in delineating between the two is not to construct a mutually-exclusive typology. Indeed, periodically they are mutually reinforcing—a point we return to in our conclusion. Rather, empirically disentangling the two offers insight into the heterogeneity of discriminatory processes, actors implicated, and vulnerabilities and consequences for victims.

Our analytic interest in *processes* of discrimination is consistent with classical theory pertaining to "social closure" and the ways in which it may be activated in the course of interaction. Social closure—a term utilized by Weber to denote the process or processes by which collectivities seek to maximize advantage by restricting access and privileges to others—often occurs through institutional exclusion and dominant group positioning. It also comes about, consciously and unconsciously, within the context of everyday interaction—interaction that, through language, symbolic acts, and/or physical control

or force, has as its aim status-hierarchy preservation and the various advantages/disadvantages that hierarchy affords. . . .

As an orienting lens through which to study inequality, social closure directs us toward an in-depth understanding of the processes through which stratification hierarchies, including those pertaining to race and housing, are both defined and maintained. Especially central are status and power and the ways in which they: (1) shape vulnerabilities to inequality and, in our case, discrimination and; (2) are enacted by gatekeepers (i.e., realtors, landlords, banks, etc.) within the course of interaction—gatekeepers who may have *status-based power* derived from their race (and gender) but, perhaps more notably, *position-based power* derived from their location within an institution or organization. In terms of victims or likely victims of racial housing discrimination, all African Americans may be vulnerable owing to their racial status. Yet, it is more than plausible that African American women will be more likely to experience both exclusionary and non-exclusionary discrimination in housing owing to the compounding nature of race, gender, disproportionate single-parenthood, and even economic status. Our analyses empirically examine this question.

Status and power differentials are also arguably central to understanding *who the perpetrators are* and *how the discrimination is enacted.* Mortgage brokers, for instance, with significant institutional (or position-based) power, can shape exclusion in profound ways for minority groups in general, whether or not minority group members are aware of such effects. Residential neighbors, in contrast, who may have status-based power derived from their race, can harass and intimidate black tenants despite a lack of institutionalized exclusionary power. Although such action may not be systematic or aggregate in its consequences, it will nevertheless hold important implications for the day-to-day experiences and social-psychological well-being of minorities in their current residential context. Residential landlords are likely an interesting case in point, with some institutional power to exclude. Yet, they may also attempt to reify the prevailing racial hierarchy and draw from status-based power when engaging in non-exclusionary forms of discrimination (i.e., differential treatment or harassment)—a point on which our analyses concur.

Racially discriminatory action is, of course, officially constrained by both law and organizational mandates. Yet, it would be naïve to assume that there is not significant discretion even in the most formalized, bureaucratic environments, or that informal subcultures do not play a role in shaping either individual behavior or the impact of diversity policies. Indeed, gate keeping actors likely exert flexibility in defining, rather informally, what attributes would make the best client or resident. Moreover, they often have the power to ignore or invoke formal procedures and rules—procedures and rules that are arguably neutral but that may, in fact, be discriminatorily applied or used in targeted, detrimental ways toward a particular group. . . . Our analyses speak to these very possibilities.

Data

Data were obtained from the Ohio Civil Rights Commission (OCRC). We include as the main sampling frame all racial discrimination in housing cases filed in the state for the period of 1988 through 2003. The OCRC is mandated to enforce civil rights laws pertaining to employment, housing, credit and places of public accommodation. The OCRC maintains a data set of basic case information for each instance of housing discrimination filed at any of the six regional offices located throughout Ohio. Ohio's law prohibiting housing discrimination (O.C.R.C. 4112) is "substantially equivalent" to federal laws (Title VIII of the Civil Rights Act of 1968) and, because of this, the OCRC has had, since 1988, a work-share agreement with the U.S. Department of Housing and Urban Development (HUD). As a result of this agreement, and after investigation, OCRC determinations are adopted and enforced by HUD. Thus, these data provides a rich body of discrimination suits from a state that, given the overlap with federal law, the heterogeneity in housing and neighborhood types, degree of urbanicity, and significant minority composition in quite large cities (i.e., Cincinnati, Akron, Cleveland, Toledo, Dayton, Columbus), is a reasonably generalizable case in point.[3]

Such case data, rarely used in research beyond aggregate descriptive patterns of case filings, reflect instances whereby an individual, family, or group had the knowledge that their rights may have been violated and that their grievances might be addressed through a formal political agency. As such, levels of actual discrimination throughout the state during the fifteen year time period, though not our particular focus, are unquestionably underestimated (Galster 1987). Indeed, there are numerous, unreported acts of race discrimination in housing every year—unreported due to lack of knowledge of one's rights, fear of retaliation, or lack of knowledge that certain behaviors are, in fact, discriminatory under the law. Housing audits are particularly useful in uncovering otherwise undetectable exclusionary discrimination by comparing tester experiences in securing housing through random sampling of advertised units (e.g., a black tester told that an apartment is unavailable would have no way of verifying discrimination without comparing their experience with a white tester later told the same apartment is, indeed, available). As such, no population data of all discrimination episodes exists, nor will it ever. While our case data certainly do not capture all discriminatory events and experiences, and potentially miss cases of discrimination uncovered through testing of randomly sampled advertisements of available housing units in audits, the diverse range of discrimination represented expand significantly upon the traditional exclusionary focus of the housing audit literature. At the same time, the data in this study represent a range of discriminatory actors—from landlords and neighbors to lenders and real estate agents—that could not be captured within in a single audit study.

The richness of detail in our case data itself also provides significant qualitative analytic leverage on questions of discriminatory forms, actors and processes. Such qualitative data includes the alleged discriminator's position (e.g., bank, owner, landlord, co-resident, etc.), information about outside actors or representatives (i.e., complainant's and respondent's representatives, if representatives were involved), the OCRC's case activity log (i.e., a record of the activity that occurred during the investigation), witness statements, audit/testing reports provided by fair housing groups, transcripts from depositions of various actors involved (i.e. witnesses, the charging party, the respondent, etc.), and other documents related to the case investigation from the charging party, the respondent, their representatives, and OCRC staff. Despite potential biases,[4] the richness of such data allow us to capture important interactional processes and dynamics between various actors that quantitative data simply cannot.[5]

It would, of course, be erroneous to assume that a discrimination *claim* necessarily implies that discrimination occurred. OCRC's case determination helps distinguish cases with little supporting evidence from those with significant and supporting evidence in favor of the charging party's claim. OCRC acts as a neutral third party whose job it is to collect evidence, eyewitness accounts, and case histories, and to weigh the preponderance of all evidence following HUD and federal civil rights law guidelines. We use this third party evaluation of evidence, and a probable cause finding in particular, to distinguish *verified* cases from those that are either frivolous or lacking corroborating evidence. Along with probable cause findings, we also include among verified cases those settled in the charging party's favor prior to litigation. Settlement prior to litigation is often deemed as supporting evidence from the point of view of legal scholars who both study and testify in discrimination suits. While the analyses of only verified cases certainly underestimates

discrimination by excluding those where there simply was not enough evidence and by including only those where a charge was filed in the first place, it bolsters confidence and the ability to conclude that the processes discussed pertain directly to serious cases of discrimination (rather than alleged or perceived discrimination).[6]

Over the 15 year time period, approximately 2,176 cases of racial discrimination in housing were filed that provided adequate data for research purposes. Of these, and using the criteria noted above, 757 or approximately 35 percent were verified by the Civil Rights Commission. Table 15.1 reports breakdowns of all 2,176 cases alongside the subset of those verified. Given the somewhat limited population of Asians, Hispanics, and other race/ethnic minorities within these cases and in the state of Ohio more generally, these groups are combined into the category of "other."

Notably, the distributional patterns are relatively parallel between all cases and those verified, with African American men and women making up the preponderance of those filing. Also noteworthy is lower overall verification of white cases—an artifact perhaps of the seriousness with which OCRC takes white claims, but much more likely (given neutral investigative criteria) the consequence of limited evidence and frivolous "reverse discrimination" claims.

Recent discussions of discrimination trends, driven by audit findings on exclusion in particular, have pointed out the possibility that discrimination may be a "moving target." The argument here is that old exclusionary practices have

Table 15.1	Cases of Racial Housing Discrimination			
	All Cases Filed		**Verified Cases**	
	N	**%**	**N**	**%**
Black Females	1,110	51%	431	57%
Black Males	631	29%	220	29%
White Females	152	7%	30	4%
White Males	152	7%	8	1%
Other Females	44	2%	38	5%
Other Males	87	4%	30	4%
Total	2,176	100%	757	100%

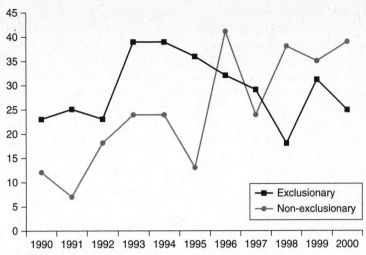

FIGURE 15.1 Verified Exclusionary and Non-Exclusionary Racial Discrimination Cases, 1990–2000.

become too easily recognizable. Potential discriminatory actors correspondingly may adjust behaviors (in this regard, see especially Massey 2005). Since the most systematic analyses to date have only been able to capture exclusionary discrimination via audit tests, however, it remains difficult to assess whether shifts have, in fact, occurred. Our data, with both exclusionary and non-exclusionary types, provides some leverage in this regard. Figure 15.1 provides a plot of the distribution of verified exclusionary and non-exclusionary cases between 1990 and 2000.[7] Notably, whereas exclusion represents the greatest portion of verified cases in the first half of the decade, non-exclusionary cases increase over time and become the more common form. Although these data by no means capture all discrimination occurring in the "real world," this pattern seems to suggest that prevalent discriminatory patterns may indeed by shifting.

Table 15.2 reports race and gender breakdowns of verified exclusionary versus non-exclusionary cases. Notably, verified cases appear to be split quite evenly between exclusionary and non-exclusionary forms. Further analyses, using Chisquare and independent samples mean tests, reveal that patterns by race and gender are nearly identical. The one exception appears to be black women,

who are most highly represented overall, but especially in terms of exclusionary discrimination. This likely indicates the conflated reality of race, gender, and social class disadvantage that black women, especially those with children, face in the housing market. Our qualitative analyses, presented below, confirm this.

Given the distributions reported, and the fact that housing discrimination against African American men, women, and families accounts for between 80 and 90 percent of all verified claims over the fifteen year period, we center attention primarily on the processes, actors, and consequences within these cases in our qualitative analyses. Qualitative case file material for the 757 verified cases was content coded by the authors specifically on the type of discrimination and injury that occurred, and who the perpetrator was. Many forms of housing discrimination are noted in the case material. These include exclusion and efforts toward exclusion, unfair practices in lending and insuring, and various forms of harassment, differential treatment, and intimidation. Key actors include banks, insurance companies, realtors, landlords, building complex owners, and neighbors. Variations in discriminatory actors and processes across exclusionary and non-exclusionary discrimination cases are discussed within our results.

Table 15.2	Cases of Housing Discrimination: Race and Sex of Victims				
	Exclusionary			Non-Exclusionary	
	N	**%**		**N**	**%**
Black Females	197	55%		164	47%*
Black Males	79	22%		77	22%
Black Household	47	13%		42	12%
White Females	4	1%		17	5%
White Males	4	1%		7	2%
White Household	0	0%		3	1%
Other Females	11	3%		17	5%
Other Males	11	3%		14	4%
Other Household	7	2%		7	2%
Total	358	100%		349	100%

*denotes statistically significant within-group difference in distribution of exclusionary versus non-exclusionary forms.

Exclusion and Housing Discrimination

As noted earlier in Table 15.2 African Americans are by far the most impacted by exclusionary forms of discrimination. African American women, men, and households represent 90 percent of these cases. This is particularly noteworthy, given that African Americans constitute only about 18 percent of the entire population of the state. Consistent with Massey and Lundy's (2001) finding, derived from a housing search telephone audit, African-American women appear to be especially vulnerable, representing 55 percent of the total number. African American males constitute 22 percent and other minorities represent 8 percent, while whites represent just 2 percent.

One benefit of having access to case-specific data is that it allows for deeper inspection of the processes involved, including statements from witnesses interviewed and defense statements received from perpetrators during the investigation. Accordingly, Table 15.3 reports the most prevalent and general forms of exclusion noted in the case material. It is clear that the majority of cases of exclusionary discrimination (82 percent) entail various forms of outright exclusion, such as a direct refusal to rent or even negotiate a rental with a prospective tenant (70 percent), refusal to sell or negotiate the sale of a property (6 percent),

Table 15.3 Distribution of Exclusionary Discrimination Cases, by Major Issue and Subcategories of of Charge

Advertising	**1%**
Terms and Conditions	**17%**

Discriminatory financing/making
of loans—6%

Steering/Restriction of choices—1%

Differential **terms/conditions/privileges**
relating to rental requirements—8%

Refuse to provide insurance—2%

Outright Exclusion	**82%**

Refuse to rent and negotiate
for rental—70%

Refuse to sell and negotiate
for sale—6%

False denial/representation
of availability—6%

or the false denial or representation of apartments or homes actually available for rent or sale (6 percent). Outright exclusion is sometimes characterized by the use of overt racial slurs and verbal refusal to rent out an apartment, yet more often consists of subtle actions, such as lying about apartment availability, or relaying differential standards for rental qualification that immediately disqualifies certain individuals.

An additional 17 percent of exclusionary cases are characterized by discriminatory terms and conditions pertaining to the rental or sale of a home, in which the final outcome is a denial of access. Such discrimination, which prevents minority home seekers from obtaining housing, includes: unfair financing or loan qualifications or terms (6 percent), steering or restricting the choices of home seekers (1 percent), differential terms and conditions to qualify to rent a home (8 percent), and refusing to provide insurance which prevents the acquisition of a home (1 percent). Perpetrators typically utilize legitimate appearing processes to exclude minorities from gaining access to housing. Applicants, for instance, may go through several steps of the rental or sales process—steps auditors are often unable to take because of their fictitious role as a potential renter/buyer—and spend significant time and resources with the hopes of gaining housing. Yet, they are participating in a false process, tainted with discriminatory practices and conditions that ultimately result in exclusion. Discriminatory advertising is represented in 1 percent of exclusionary cases. Notable is the fact that most cases of exclusion, approximately 84.5 percent, are in rental compared to housing sales.

We speculated earlier that the principal perpetrators of exclusion would largely be institutional actors—actors with positional power to impede or outright exclude. Figure 15.2 denotes the distribution of perpetrator status. Notably, landlords and owners are most likely to exclude individuals from housing, comprising 84 percent of the cases. Other actors or institutions responsible for exclusion include real estate agents or institutions (6 percent), banking/lending agents or institutions (4 percent), and insurance agents or institutions (4 percent). Whereas owners and landlords tend to exclude outright, banks are largely implicated in exclusion by refusal to provide loans. For their part, insurance agents can reject applications for homeowners insurance, while realtors in our data either steer or refuse service to potential African

American clients. City and Metropolitan Housing Authorities are the perpetrators in only 2 percent of cases. Neighbors, who have no real institutional power to exclude, are predictably absent.

That landlords and complex owners are, by and far, most often implicated in exclusionary discrimination should not come as a surprise. These agents are often the most proximate to potential tenants. Indeed, they may act in a manner that signals to prospective tenants that there may be biases, and that discrimination is occurring. Consistent with this point, research in the sociology of grievance framing and resistance suggests grievance formation that invokes action often requires an understanding and interpretation that puts a malicious face on the inequality that is occurring (Gamson 1995). Such a causal interpretation provides those experiencing inequality with not only a more concrete target, but also an essentially moral justification for acts of contention (identifying reference 2001; Snow and Benford 1992). Such is likely the case here, as denoted by the qualitative data reported momentarily. One important implication, however, is that exclusionary actions undertaken by institutional actors not so proximate to the targets are less-often observed, felt, or challenged. Correspondingly, although much of discriminatory exclusion is likely to be undertaken by landlords and owners, that enacted by other, more distant institutional agents (e.g., banks, insurance companies, etc.) will often be unrealized and, thus, significantly under-reported (see Massey 2005).

Our qualitative immersion reveals that the over-representation of African American women among victims of exclusionary discrimination is, to a considerable extent, a function of the intersections of familial status, race, and sex.[8] Take, for instance, the case of Susan[9], an African American female with children. She entered the office of a small apartment complex to inquire about an available apartment, and was told that she had too many kids and to "get your black ass out." The following is taken from her deposition with the Attorney General.

Q: Tell me about your efforts to look for another place to live?

A: Every time I tried to find a place, they would tell me I had too many children.

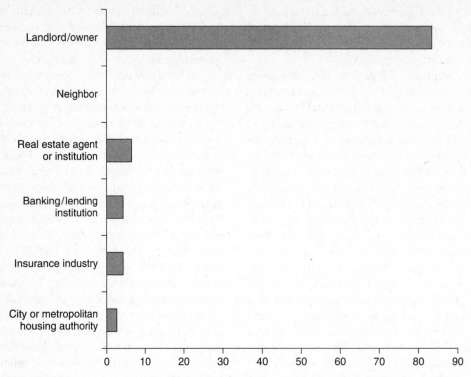

FIGURE 15.2   Perpetrator in Verified Cases of Exclusionary Discrimination in Housing by Race.

Q: Okay

A: And that being a single mother and having all those children I was not accepted anywhere.

Q: What type of place were you looking to move to?

A: A three bedroom home or apartment or whatever, in a decent area for what income I could afford to pay. (After saying she was told by a person on the phone that they would not rent to her.)

Q: Okay, what was your reaction after hearing that news?

A: I got off the phone and I cried to my mom because I couldn't find a home for my children. I was afraid I was going to end up homeless with four children, all because of my husband

beating me up. I'm . . . nobody would take me because I didn't have a husband.

In this case, Susan was repeatedly denied the opportunity to rent an apartment when prospective landlords learned that she had children. She had reasonable hope that she would find a place "in a decent area for what income I could afford to pay," yet was still illegally denied access as a result of her status as an African American mother with "too many children." This was all the more troublesome, given her efforts to escape an abusive situation. The tremendous stress and psychological turmoil she experienced as a result of this process is evident in her stated fear of becoming homeless.

Discriminatory exclusion on the basis of familial status—the presence of children under 18 years of age—is related to stereotypes about single women, especially single African American mothers, and may be impacting the larger patterns we find in these data. Indeed, a significant amount of case materials reveal a similar tendency. For example, in one case, a sales agent asked an African American woman with children if she "was going to operate a day care center from her home," despite the fact that the woman had never operated a day care center before and said nothing to infer she would if the apartment was rented to her. In other cases, the roots of exclusion and its relation to family status are explicit:

> Anna Miller, a black female with children, was told by the landlord that he would not rent to her because "there were too many in my family." When Anna asked if her race had anything to do with his decision the landlord became belligerent . . .

A witness in this particular case, who is also a black female with one child, testified that when she asked the landlord if she could have pets he said no. When she asked the landlord why, he told her that she had "no business taking care of pets when she had her hands full taking care of her child." The case investigator interviewed other residents and found that white tenants with children were permitted to have pets. Margaret Sims, a white female tenant, told the investigator that it was her fault that the landlord did not rent to Anna Miller because she (Sims) had asked him "not to rent the downstairs unit to anymore niggers" because the Black family that lived there previously "were terrible." The landlord told Margaret Sims that he "would do his best to find her a good neighbor." Here, the landlord is certainly the culpable party, although a white neighbor is also partially to blame. Additionally, although Anna appeared to suspect that her race was a factor in the landlord's decision from the initial interaction, it was evidence garnered after this interaction, during the investigation, from residents and the landlord himself that made it clear that race was a factor in the decision. In fact, considering that the landlord initially said he would not rent to Anna because the number of children in her family (which is also illegal) and that there were African Americans living in the rental complex, some

prospective tenants may not have thought that their race was a factor from that initial interaction with the landlord.

Exclusion of African Americans occurs not only in rental markets, but also in sales markets, as is evidenced by 14 percent of the cases. Here, the perpetrator is more often than not an agent within a real estate, insurance, or banking/lending institution. Although such discrimination tends to be characterized by subtle and difficult to detect processes, such as application of differential criteria to qualify for loans or for a low interest rate, more blatant actions are also evident. Take, for instance, the case of Patricia, an African American female attempting to purchase a home. When initially meeting with her realtor to discuss qualifying for an apartment, the realtor "asked me what made me think I could afford a home costing $190,000." When Patricia complained to the company, she was assigned a new agent, who asked her similar questions. Patricia then directly complained to the new agent that such behavior was inappropriate, yet was told "It's you people who get on my nerves." The investigation revealed that white housing seekers were not subject to such rude, blatant questions in their intake meetings.

In a similar case, Terry, an African American male, made a $239,000 offer on a house. That same day, after Terry's offer was received, the white seller accepted a four thousand dollar lower offer from a white family. During the investigation, the seller told the OCRC that she "seriously doubted [Terry's] ability to obtain financing." In addition to dealing with hurtful and rude statements and stereotypes, Patricia's and Terry's housing searches were delayed. Instead of moving forward with her housing search by viewing homes in her price range, Patricia was forced to find a new company. As for Terry, instead of moving into the home he had wanted, he was forced to continue looking.

African American couples are clearly vulnerable to exclusionary treatment as well. Michael and Tyree, for instance, were continually asked to verify their income and the source of their income because the lending agent stated that he had to "make sure that their money was not made illegally or from drugs." Like the prior cases discussed, the lending agent here delayed the application process by subjecting the couple to more stringent screening standards than similarly situated white loan applicants, due to stereotypes about their race. The dearth of qualitative case materials, including but not limited to the examples reported here, demonstrate delays in the loan application process—delays resulting in the lose of loan closing "specials" and lower interest rates. Case material also demonstrates that some lenders target African American borrowers with "teaser rates which allow people on fixed incomes to borrow more money than they can afford to pay back."

A somewhat unexpected dynamic of housing exclusion that emerged is the denial of housing to interracial couples. Indeed, immersion into the case material wherein the charging party is either white or African American revealed that discrimination sometimes centers on disapproval of interracial coupling. Desmond, an African-American male, for instance, suggests that:

> I was approved to rent on Feb. 22, 1996 a two bedroom apartment. However, when management found out that Teresa Landon, Caucasian female, was moving in with me we were both denied occupancy. We were denied occupancy due to being perceived as an interracial couple.

The investigation revealed that Teresa and her children had been living with a different person at the same complex for four months (a Caucasian male), with the landlord's knowledge, without being on the lease. However, when the manager learned Teresa would be moving in with Desmond, the landlord required that her name be placed on the lease and that she apply for rental. After claiming that Teresa did not qualify to rent the apartment, both Desmond and Teresa were denied rental. What is particularly interesting here is that the African American charging party (Desmond) was not excluded until after the initial interaction with management, when he was identified as part of an interracial couple. Also notable is the subtle and legitimate-appearing means by which the discrimination was carried out—i.e., claiming that Teresa did not qualify to rent the apartment. The investigation, however, revealed

that this standard of qualification was not utilized for other white tenants in the complex. Desmond and Teresa were both placed in the uncomfortable position of having to find a new place to live on short notice despite their prior understanding of having secured a place to live. Other cases of exclusionary discrimination, filed by Caucasian males and females, similarly revealed that the foundations of the discriminatory treatment revolved around interracial coupling.

Importantly, and relative to what audits might reveal, other prospective tenants in our case materials were excluded from housing *after* their initial interactions with landlords as well. For example, a few days after Robert and Hazel, an African American couple, were told that they had gotten the apartment they had applied for, the landlord called back to inform them that they could not move in because he found another tenant with a better income. The tenant who actually obtained the apartment was white, and the investigation revealed that Robert and Hazel's income was more than enough to cover the monthly rent. Similarly, after being told she could move into the apartment and paying the rental deposit, Norma, an African American, was told by the landlord that he could not let her move in because a friend of the family wanted the apartment. As Norma stated and the OCRC verified, the "for rent" sign remained in the window of the apartment long after she was informed she could not move in. During the investigation, the landlord told the OCRC investigator that the friend of the family who expressed interest in the apartment changed his mind and that he did not think to contact Norma. The temporal nature of these exclusionary processes might have very well been missed had the victims in these cases been audit testers.

Exclusionary discrimination remains an important part of contemporary stratification, with implications for housing segregation patterns highlighted in much prior work. African American women seem to be especially vulnerable in the arena of housing searches due to their sex and especially their familial status—statuses that may be providing institutional actors, such as landlords, with shorthand information that can be enacted in discriminatory ways. Whether directed toward African American mothers, African Americans generally, or interracial couples, the qualitative material on exclusion also reveals that the costs of exclusion do not revolve solely around housing access. Rather, in much of the qualitative material, including the specific cases reported here, individuals are not only denied access to housing options of choice, but also must spend significantly more time in housing searches.

Nonexclusionary Discrimination

Racial discrimination discourages attempts to garner housing, often resulting in insult and distress for victims. Such distress is perhaps even more evident in instances of non-exclusionary housing discrimination, wherein an individual, couple, or family who are already housed experience ongoing differential treatment, harassment, and intimidation. Such discrimination is especially problematic given that the residential victim is often legally bound to a rental agreement or lease, and is often in direct interactional contact with the perpetrator on an ongoing basis, especially in the case of neighbors and landlords. Given what would arguably be significant implications for minority victims' overall sense of safety and well-being, it is surprising that so little attention has centered explicitly on this type of discrimination.

As with exclusionary forms, African Americans (females, males, and households) are most highly represented, representing 81 percent of the non-exclusionary cases (see Table 15.2). African American women are, again, the most likely to be victimized, as they are the primary victim 47 percent of the time. However, with non-exclusionary discrimination, other minorities (11 percent) and Caucasians (8 percent) make up a slightly higher percentage of the total (19 percent compared to only 10 percent for exclusion). In-depth examination of qualitative material reveals that much of these verified discriminatory actions against whites are triggered by disapproval of interracial coupling (i.e., the Caucasian charging party is harassed or intimidated after the landlord or neighbor discovers that the charging party's boyfriend or girlfriend is Black).

Table 15.4   Distribution of Non-Exclusionary Cases, by Major Issue and Subcategories of Charge

Harassment/Intimidation/Coercion	**16%**
Terms and Conditions	**84%**
Discriminatory financing/loans/appraisals—16%	
Failure to provide insurance—3%	
Unfavorable services/facilities—13%	
Rental Terms/conditions/Privileges—52%	

Table 15.4 reports the distribution of non-exclusionary housing discrimination represented in our data. Whereas exclusionary cases are characterized largely by outright processes of exclusion, nonexclusionary cases entail unfair or differential terms, treatment and conditions. Indeed, 84 percent of non-exclusionary cases involve the application of discriminatory terms and conditions *within the current residential setting of the victim.* The majority of these cases, 52 percent, involve terms, conditions, and privileges relating to a current rental arrangement. Examples include differential enforcement of pet policies within a rental complex, unfairly raising the rent of a select group of tenants, or only allowing certain tenants privileges (e.g., using the pool after hours, having parties, etc.). Thirteen percent of terms and conditions cases involve failure to provide equal access to services and facilities. This is typically characterized by purposeful neglect of service needs, such as refusing to fix a leaking bathtub or broken water heater.

An additional 16 percent of terms and conditions encompass discriminatory financing, loans, and appraisals of one's current property, while 3 percent involve inequitable failure to provide homeowners insurance. In these cases, perpetrators often utilize subtle, financially lucrative, tactics that take advantage of minority home owners in predominantly African American neighborhoods. Finally, and certainly noteworthy, 16 percent of non-exclusionary cases in our data

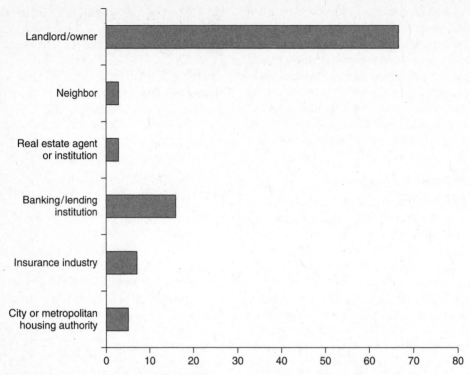

FIGURE 15.3 Perpetrator in Verified Cases of Non-Exclusionary Discrimination by Race.

reflect the direct use of harassment, intimidation, and coercion toward blacks and other minorities. Examples include the continual use of racial slurs toward black residents in an apartment complex, or personal racial threats of violence, rape, or even death. Certainly illegal, this form of discrimination creates a racially tainted environment that victims are forced to navigate, and sometimes on a daily basis.

Who is doing the discriminating? As with exclusionary forms of discrimination, landlords and owners are the largest group of perpetrators represented (Table 15.3). Notably, though, they are responsible for 17 percent less of these discriminatory actions relative to exclusion. Through coercion or intimidation, neighbors represent 3 percent of the perpetrators of non-exclusionary discrimination cases. Interestingly, actors embedded in more formal institutions, such as banks or insurance agencies, also appear in these cases. Banking and insurance institutions are the perpetrators in 16 and 7 percent of the time, respectively.

Qualitative materials suggest that such institutions engage in differential and/or unfavorable terms and conditions in the re-financing of an individual's current home, or the refusal to provide or renew home owner's insurance for individuals living in predominantly African American neighborhoods. Hence, while these victims are not directly excluded from housing, they often suffer financial loss and/or excessive anxiety and stress as a result of illegal actions of the perpetrator. Finally, City or Metropolitan Housing Authorities and real estate companies represent 5 and 3 percent of cases, respectively (Figure 15.3).

Qualitative immersion offers some insight into the patterns identified above, and especially the nature of non-exclusionary discrimination and its social-psychological consequences. Especially revealing are the ways in which landlords, complex owners, and other actors discriminate against African-Americans in the context of their current residential setting. Non-exclusionary housing discrimination takes many forms, ranging from racial slurs to responding differently or more quickly to whites who report maintenance problems. And, as denoted by the example below, the same individual may experience multiple types of such discriminatory treatment. Alvin, an African American male, claimed he had been subject to housing discrimination by the owner of the boarding house in which he lived. Specifically, he notes how the owner of the house raised his rent, but not the rent of white tenants.

> Since my first day at respondent's facility I have been subject to racial slurs and different rules not imposed on other white tenants . . . Gordon said he was raising my rent because I was the only one who cooked, and this was causing the electric bill to go up. I informed Gordon that the electric was going up because other white tenants were using space saver heaters. Gordon said, "You lying nigger." "After I could not use the cooking facility, Gordon gave me permission to cook on a grill. I came home and discovered that Steve (a white manager) threw my grill away. Steve has been known on numerous occasions to refer to me as "nigger."

The evidence collected by the civil rights investigator substantiated the charging party's claim. Indeed, after interviewing the manager, the investigator notes that:

> The manager admits to using derogatory racial slurs while in the complainant's presence, but he claims that he used such words "in fun," and that he did not mean it derogatorily.

In addition, numerous witnesses provided statements stating that Alvin, the only black resident, was treated differently than other residents and that white residents who interacted with Alvin were also sometimes treated differently. One witness commented that the owner told him that, "we get this nigger out of here and we'll be back to an all-white building." Thus, although Alvin successfully acquired housing at a point in the past, the antagonistic racial slurs and differential treatment

he was subject to within this setting resulted in a less than ideal, safe, or secure situation. Undoubtedly, the impact of this experience on the victim's sense of well-being and security is as consequential, if not more, than that which might have been caused had he been excluded from the housing initially.

The breadth of discriminatory processes is no less extensive in non-exclusionary cases. Bertha and Howard, an African American couple renting an apartment in one of the state's largest cities, filed a charge of discrimination based on repeated harassment from their neighbor who also happened to be the complex's rental agent. They describe what occurred, as well as their interpretation of it as being racially motivated.

> Since the time of October 1, 2001 and continuing, we have been subject to ongoing harassment from our next door neighbor, and rental agent Julia Wright. An example of this harassment includes Ms. Wright placing trash on our property. We have complained about this harassment to Brian Anderson, Ms. Wright's supervisor, however, no action has been taken to address our concerns. The neighbor who lives on the other side of Ms. Wright is White and has not been subject to such harassment.

A neutral investigation by the Civil Rights Commission found probable cause that the harassment experienced by Bertha and Howard was racially motivated. Though one might conclude this to be a less severe case of discrimination, the mental anxiety, stress, and compromised aesthetic enjoyment of their property over a long period of time, in this case by a neighbor, was quite consequential for this couple. Bertha and Howard paid their rent on time each month and, as with other tenants, were entitled to the same privileges and standards of treatment.

Many cases of non-exclusionary discrimination do take on an even more severe form, such as intimidation and physical threat. Such was the experience of Alicia, an African American mother renting an apartment in a large complex. After several altercations, the boyfriend of her white neighbor (Betty) made several threats. According to the qualitative material and investigative documents:

> Brian Stanley, who is Betty's boyfriend and who is moving on to the property, has harassed Complainant and has threatened to kill Complainant, Complainant's boyfriend, and their "Nigger" baby because of their allegations against Betty. The property manager, Jason Short, has been aware of the harassment and threats since April, and is still allowing Brian Stanley to move on to the property. Jason Short is good friends with Betty.

Though not all cases are this extreme, the powerlessness and lack of ability to get help from legitimate individuals who hold authority (i.e., the landlord/manager) is common among non-exclusionary discrimination cases. Indeed, in many of the cases, if the harassment does not cease to exist, the victim must either move (exclude themselves) or seek outside assistance (i.e., from the Civil Rights Commission, an Attorney, or a Fair Housing Group). For example, Sandy, a Caucasian female:

> states that she and her children, four white and one bi-racial, have been subjected to harassment, racial slurs and physical confrontations by other, Caucasian, residents. Sandy states that the landlord has failed to take any action to stop the harassment. Evidence indicates that Sandy, her children, and other African American residents and their children were subjected to a racially charged, tainted environment.

Cases, such as these, suggest quite clearly that conceptualization of housing discrimination need to be broadened to include discriminatory acts that occur within residential settings. Indeed, in many cases minorities may gain access to housing, yet their daily experiences are far from comfortable. Neither can we assume that if exclusionary discrimination ended, minorities would no longer be discriminated in the housing market. Clearly, housing discrimination is a multi-dimensional phenomenon characterized by dynamic and interactional processes between multiple actors. Moreover, while certainly a large portion of discriminatory actions are aimed at institutional exclusion altogether, others seem more geared toward preserving status and maintaining racial hierarchy.

To date, the preponderance of the racial stratification and housing literature has been concerned with residential segregation, and to some extent the exclusion that may be driving it. Yet, there may be a connection between the prevalence of non-exclusionary discrimination in the housing arena, in the form of differential treatment, intimidation, and harassment, and persistent patterns of residential segregation or the avoidance of certain neighborhoods, areas, and complexes. It is certainly plausible that non-exclusionary forms of housing discrimination, such as in the cases reported above, either through personal experience or through communication within the broader minority community, may push individuals, families, and interracial couples to seek housing in predominately minority neighborhoods. Indeed, we found several complex cases which provide an initial glimpse of this process. The following case in point revolves around a Jamaican immigrant, who experiences various non-exclusionary forms of discrimination and who is clearly embedded in the broader immigrant community where housing information and experiences are exchanged.

> This new manager does not welcome Jamaican citizens to this property. I am here as a student and I have friends who are Jamaican who were told nothing was available. Other persons not of Jamaican origin called and were told there were units available. Jamaican residents who live here are moving out because of the lack of services. The most recent incident occurred when I reported I had no hot water in my shower. I called both offices and was assured the repair would be made. When I called the main office, I could never speak to the person in charge . . . I spoke to a white resident who told me he is not having a problem with his hot water and he has had no problem with repairs being made.

Such a case—and this is but one among many—demonstrates the complex, and perhaps interconnected, nature of non-exclusionary and exclusionary forms of discrimination. Indeed, to the extent that non-exclusionary discrimination is ongoing at a particular location, impacting several minority residents over time, it may very well lead to information sharing and, correspondingly, avoidance by the minority community generally. In essence, persistent harassment, intimidation, or differential treatment may, by default or design, may very well impact exclusion and segregation levels.

Conclusions

Over the past two decades research using the audit methodology has contributed greatly to our understanding of discrimination in housing and to the role of discrimination in the creation and maintenance of residential segregation of minorities within and across U.S. cities. In this article, we have expanded on this literature by:(1) highlighting exclusionary forms of discrimination that occur at various stages of the rental/sales processes, some of which audits are unable to capture, as well as more complex processes, such as home sales transactions, and; (2) denoting a broad range of non-exclusionary discriminatory processes and consequences that simply cannot be investigated using an audit design. Admittedly, we can not make claims about the magnitude of non-exclusionary and exclusionary discrimination in the U.S. with these data. We nevertheless believe, given the heterogeneity of discriminatory forms evidenced in our data, that future research should take on the methodological challenge of accurately assessing the extent of *both* exclusionary and non-exclusionary housing discrimination in the U.S. Failure to do so may result in biased or skewed perceptions of discrimination and patterns of change in U.S. housing markets.

Our findings highlight aggregate patterns pertaining to both victims and perpetrators, and revealed the sometimes complex, sometimes explicit, and sometimes more subtle forms of racial discrimination that minorities are likely to encounter. African American women are most likely to face both exclusionary and non-exclusionary forms of housing discrimination—a pattern we interpret as a function of several factors, including their gender and class status, as well as their status as mothers. It is no doubt the case that stereotypical notions of the single black mother are playing a part in these relations, shaping landlords' willingness to rent, banks' willingness to provide mortgages, and neighbors' levels of civility. Alongside African American women, African American men, families, and even interracial couples face discrimination that is both exclusive in nature and aimed at differential treatment, harassment, and intimidation.

Findings pertaining to exclusion speak to, and indeed are consistent with, the large body of audit research on housing discrimination. At the same time, however, our findings demonstrate that discriminatory forms uncovered by audit methods are present at *multiple* stages of the rental and sales process. Furthermore, our data highlight the actual experiences of minority tenants as they navigate the sales and rental markets—experiences of discrimination that were investigated and verified by civil rights investigators and often confirmed by witnesses. Findings on exclusion also reveal the ways in which less or more proximate institutional actors play a role. Landlords and owners of housing units are on the front line, accounting for over 80 percent of all exclusionary discrimination cases in our data. We expect that this is actually an overestimate, given that discriminatory actions in lending and insurance are more covert in nature and possibly even unintended. Nevertheless, the institutional power of landlords and owners—power to allow access or not—combined with the face-to-face interactions they have with prospective tenants, sets up the most prevalent situation in which discrimination is both explicit and experienced by minorities. The consequences, as witnessed in some of the exemplary material reported, include exclusion (and the associated costs in resources and delayed time to securing housing), but also stress, anxiety, anger, and despair.

Less often directly studied are forms of discrimination that occur once minorities are actually housed, something we have referred to throughout as non-exclusionary discrimination. Such discrimination entails, most generally, differential treatment, harassment, and intimidation and has as its explicit intent the expression of intolerance, the reification of status on a social-interactional level, and even psychological and physical intimidation. Neighbors play a part, as revealed in our examples of biracial couples and families with biracial children, wherein the victims were harassed, threatened, and in some cases eventually evicted from their dwellings.

Interestingly, and somewhat contrary to what we expected, institutional actors (i.e., again, disproportionately landlords) continue to play a quite obvious role in non-exclusionary forms, most often by denying equal treatment to minority persons who are already residing in housing units. Massey (2005: 149) argues that discrimination is a moving target; as "federal anti-discrimination policies become more effective in overcoming certain forms of racial bias in housing, new forms have emerged to perpetuate residential segregation." While we are not suggesting that non-exclusionary forms of discrimination are necessarily "new," this form of discrimination may become more prevalent as awareness and enforcement increases about, what Massey (2005: 149) calls "the classic discriminatory mechanisms" (i.e., exclusion). Housing providers, out of fear of prosecution, may provide minorities access to housing but that does not necessarily mean that they will be treated fairly, as Alvin's experience discussed earlier illustrated. Furthermore, exposure to harassment and intimidation in and around the home or neighborhood on a daily basis may impact minority preferences over time, as the literature on transitioning neighborhoods and neighborhood preferences highlights (for a helpful discussion and overview of this process, see Yinger 1995). The interaction between experiences with discrimination and minority preferences, and the relationship between the two with aggregate patterns of segregation, may only be fully disentangled if scholars incorporate non-exclusionary forms of discrimination into their conceptualizations and research agendas.

Housing discrimination continues to be a social problem in the U.S. for racial minorities, although the processes of inequality and closure we have highlighted are not merely characteristic of housing. As many of our qualitative materials attest, gatekeeping actors exercise considerable discretion in their decision-making, and invoke a relatively flexible set of filters when determining institutional access. Such discretion is activated not only in the course of allowing or constraining access, but also in day-to-day treatment and monitoring. This is no less true of other institutional arenas, such as employment, where minorities as well as women face numerous inequalities pertaining to both access (e.g., hiring and firing) and mobility and harassment (e.g., Huffman and Cohen 2004; Padavic and Reskin 2002; Pager 2003). It is obvious that discretion, even within bureaucratic or legal bounds, is part and parcel of stratification maintenance, creation, and challenge. As the qualitative materials so poignantly suggest, human beings actively engage in reifying inequality, and victims of inequality are much more than mere recipients of differential treatment. Victims, instead, often go through a series of steps to try to counter the inequality they are experiencing, including negotiation, avoidance, confrontation and, in the case of filing a discrimination suit, politically and legally fighting what is unjust.

Obviously there is an interplay between status, power, discretion and the environments within which they are embedded. And, it is at the crux of this interplay where the most interesting sociological questions lie. How does the structure of neighborhoods, for instance, alter the nature of individual and group interactions in a manner that reifies or mitigates prevailing stratification arrangements and social status hierarchies? Or, how might micro-level interactions reinforce or alter structural arrangements themselves? Whether one builds one's research question from micro to macro or from macro to micro, or defines the question itself in terms of agency to structure or structure to agency, does not really matter. What is more paramount is that theorists and researchers alike make explicit the ways in which human action, conditioned and constrained to some degree by structure, is responsible for the patterns they describe.

Notes

1. Since the original study, numerous other housing market audit studies have been conducted in specific cities (Yinger 1998a, 1998b; Galster 1990a, 1990b). Like national studies, these studies reveal that most Blacks and Hispanics encounter discrimination revolving around housing availability and access to the housing sales and rental markets (Ondrich, Stricker, & Yinger 1999; Yinger 1991, 1995). Similar evidence is reported from analyses of rental inquiries by phone (Massey and Lundy 2001), and interactions with mortgage lenders and homeowner's insurance agents (Squires 2003; Smith & Cloud 1996; Squires & Velez 1988).

2. This is not to suggest, of course, that scholars have completely neglected non-exclusionary forms of housing discrimination. Some important work has been undertaken in this regard, most often case- or survey-centered, dealing with racial harassment and intimidation (Feagin and Sikes 1994), discrimination or violence directed at "pioneer" black residents in predominantly white neighborhoods (Massey and Denton 1993; Orfield and Ashkinaze 1991) and racially motivated crimes associated with "defending" one's neighborhood against racial transition (Buell 1980; Green, Strolovitch and Wong 1998; Suttles 1972). Systematic sociological analyses of verified cases of such discrimination, however, are wanting and cannot be captured using an audit methodology.

3. The use of case materials in sociological analyses of discrimination is not entirely unique. Burstein (1991), for instance, analyzed published case decisions by the federal appellate courts based on Title VII, the Equal Pay Act, and other laws prohibiting discrimination in employment. Citing Zemans (1983), he argues that laws like Title VII are intentionally designed so that individuals who file charges of discrimination, based on their own personal experience, are also effectively acting on behalf of others within the same protected class (age, race, sex, etc.). Like Burstein's (1991) study, our analyses make use of discrimination cases based on laws designed to protect individuals within a protected class, as well as the protected class as a whole.

4. It is likely, for instance, that more cases will be reported in black and integrated neighborhoods than in white neighborhoods given that African Americans are more likely to search in these neighborhoods. And, more easily detected forms of discrimination, such as an inflated rent or security deposit, may be over-represented in the data while forms of discrimination that are harder to detect, such as steering, may be under-represented (Galster 1987).

5. These data are also useful for investigating processes that audit studies are unable to investigate, such as transactions occurring later in the process and negotiations about the final sales price (Yinger 1998a, 1998b).

6. There is undoubtedly some underestimation here as well. Specifically, discrimination may have indeed occurred in cases that do receive a probable cause determination when and if corroborating evidence was simply unavailable (thus shaping the investigator's determinations which are bound by evidentiary criteria). Moreover, charging parties may not have the financial and emotional resources to see cases to completion. Thus, while non-verified cases may be capturing false or frivolous charges, they are much more likely to be a mix of cases, some more serious than others.

7. We limit the time range considered here to the decade of 1990–2000, even though some of our cases fall into the wider time range of 1988–2003. We do this for several reasons, the principal of which is an under-reporting and under-recording of cases at the tail ends. OCRC only entered a work share agreement and thus began processing the preponderance of housing cases around 1988, which explains why less overall cases are reported in these early years. Many cases post-2000 are still being processed, and at multiple investigative and legal levels. As such, they have yet to be recorded in the overall data set and were not made available to the authors.

8. It is also illegal to discriminate against a housing seeker's sex and to discriminate against families with children. In addition, charges can be filed on multiple bases—race and familial status. However, all the cases in our analyses include race as at least one of the bases and the investigative finding was, at least in part, based on race.

9. All names have been changed in our reporting of qualitative materials.

References

Blau, Peter. 1977. *Inequality and Heterogeneity: A Primitive Theory of Social Structure.* New York: Free Press.

Buell, Emmett H., Jr. 1980. Busing and the Defended Neighborhood: South Boston, 1974–1977. *Urban Affairs Review* 16: 161–188.

Burstein, Paul. 1991. "Policy Domains: Organizations, Culture, and Policy Outcomes." *Annual Review of Sociology* 17: 327–350.

Charles, Camille Zubrinsky. 2003. "The Dynamics of Racial Residential Segregation." *Annual Review of Sociology* 29: 167–207.

Emerson, Michael O., Chai, Karen J. and George Yancey. 2001. "Does Race Matter in Residential Segregation? Exploring the Preferences of White Americans." *American Sociological Review* 66: 922–935.

Farley, Reynolds and William H. Frey. 1994. "Changes in the Segregation of Whites from Blacks during the 1980's: Small Steps Toward a More Integrated Society." *American Sociological Review* 66: 922–935.

Feagin, Joe R. and Melvin Sikes. 1994. *Living with Racism: The Black Middle-Class Experience.* Boston: Beacon Press.

Fischer, Mary J. and Douglas S. Massey. 2004. "The Ecology of Racial Discrimination." *City and Community* (3)3: 221–241.

Fix, Michael and Raymond Struyk, eds. 1992. Clear and Convincing Evidence: Measurement of Discrimination in America. Washington, D.C.: Urban Institute Press.

Galster, George C. 1987. "The Ecology of Racial Discrimination in Housing." *Urban Affairs Quarterly* 23: 84–107.

———. 1990a. "Racial Discrimination in Housing Markets during the 1980s: A Review of the Audit Evidence." *Journal of Planning Education and Research* 9(3): 165–175.

———1990b. "Racial Steering by Real Estate Agents: Mechanisms and Motives." *Review of Black Political Economy* 19 (Summer): 39–63.

Gamson, William A. 1995. "Constructing Social Protest." In *Social Movements and Culture,* edited by H. Johnston and B. Klandermans, 85–107. Minneapolis: University of Minnesota Press.

Gotham, Kevin F. 2002. "Beyond Invasion and Succession: School Segregation, Real Estate Blockbusting, and the Political Economy of Neighborhood Transition." *City and Community* 1(1): 83–111.

Green, Donald P., Dara Z. Strolovitch and Janelle S. Wong. 1998. "Defended Neighborhoods, Integration, and Racially Motivated Crime." *American Journal of Sociology* 104: 372–403.

Heckman, James J. and Peter Seigelman. 1993. "The Urban Institute Studies: Their Methods and Findings," in *Clear and Convincing Evidence: Testing for Discrimination in American,* Eds Michael Fix and Raymond Struyk. Washington D.C.: The Urban Institute Press.

Hirsch, Arnold R. 1998. *Making the Second Ghetto: Race and Housing in Chicago 1940–1960.* Chicago: University of Chicago Press.

Huffman, Matthew L. and Philip N. Cohen. 2004. "Race Wage Inequality: Job Segregation and Devaluation Across U.S. Labor Markets." *American Journal of Sociology* 109: 902–936.

Iceland, John. 2004. "Beyond Black and White: Metropolitan Residential Segregation in Multi-Ethnic America." *Social Science Review* 33: 248–271.

Massey, Douglas. 2005. "Racial Discrimination in Housing: A Moving Target" *Social Problems* 52: 148–151.

Massey Douglas, and Garvey Lundy. 2001. "Use of Black English and Racial Discrimination in Urban Housing Markets: New Methods and Findings." *Urban Affairs Review* 36(4): 452–469.

Massey, Douglas S., and Nancy Denton. 1993. *American Apartheid.* Cambridge: Harvard University Press.

Ondrich, Jan, Stephen Ross, and John Yinger. 2003. "Now You See It, Now You Don't: Why Do Real Estate Agents Withhold Available Housing to Black Customers," *The Review of Economics and Statistics* MIT Press, 85: 854–873.

Ondrich, Jan, Stricker, Alex, and John Yinger. 1999. "Do Landlords Discriminate? The Incidence and Causes of Racial Discrimination in Rental Housing Markets." *Journal of Housing Economics* 8: 185–204.

Orfield, Gary and Carole Ashkinaze. 1991. *The Closing Door: Conservative Policy and Black Opportunity.* Chicago: University of Chicago Press.

Orser, W. Edward. 1994. *Blockbusting in Baltimore. The Edmondson Village Story.* Lexington: University of Kentucky Press.

Padavic, Irene and Barbara Reskin. 2002. *Women and Men at Work.* Thousand Oaks, California: Pine Forge Press.

Page, Marianne. 1995. "Racial and Ethnic Discrimination in Urban Housing Markets: Evidence from a Recent Audit Study." *Journal of Urban Economics* 38 (September): 183–206.

Pager, Devah. 2003. "The Mark of a Criminal Record." *American Journal of Sociology* 108: 937–975.

Parkin, Frank. 1979. *Marxism and Class Theory: A Bourgeois Critique.* Cambridge: Tavistock.

Reskin, Barbara F. 2000. "The Proximate Causes of Discrimination." *Contemporary Sociology* 29: 319–329.

———. 2003. "Including Mechanisms in Our Models of Ascriptive Inequality." *American Sociological Review* 68: 1–21.

Ross, Stephen L. and Margery A. Turner. 2005. "Housing Discrimination in Metropolitan America: Explaining Changes Between 1989 and 2000." *Social Problems* 52: 152–180.

Seligman, Amanda I. 2005. *Block by Block. Neighborhoods and Public Policy on Chicago's West Side.* Chicago: University of Chicago Press.

Smith, Shanna L. and Cathy Cloud. 1996. "The Role of Private, Nonprofit Fair Housing Enforcement Organizations in Lending Testing." In *Mortgage Lending, Racial Discrimination, and Federal Policy,* edited by J. Goering and R. Wienk, 589–610. Washington, D.C.: Urban Institute Press.

Snow, David A. and Robert D. Benford. 1992. "Master Frames and Cycles of Protest." Pp. 133–155 in *Frontiers of Social Movement Theory,* edited by Aldon Morris and Carol Mueller. New Haven, CT: Yale.

Squires, Gregory D., and William Velez. 1988. "Insurance Redlining and the Process of Discrimination." *Review of Black Political Economy* 16: 63–75.

Squires, Gregory D. 2003. "Racial Profiling, Insurance Style: Insurance Redlining and the Uneven Development of Metropolitan America." *Journal of Urban Affairs* 24(4): 391–410.

Suttles, G. D. 1972. *The Social Construction of Communities.* Chicago: University of Chicago Press.

Tomaskovic-Devey, Donald. 1993. *Gender and Racial Inequality at Work: The Sources & Consequences of Job Segregation.* Ithaca: Cornell.

Weber, Max. 1978. *Economy and Society. An Outline of Interpretive Sociology,* edited by G. Roth and C. Wittich. Berkeley: University of California Press.

Yinger, John Milton. 1986. "Measuring Discrimination with Fair Housing Audits: Caught in the Act." *American Economic Review* 76: 881–893.

———. 1991. "Acts of Discrimination: Evidence for the 1989 Housing Discrimination Study." *Journal of Housing Economics* 1: 318–346.

———. 1995. *Closed Doors, Opportunities Lost: The Continuing Costs of Housing Discrimination.* New York: Russell Sage Foundation.

———. 1998a. "Evidence on Discrimination in Consumer Markets." *Journal of Economic Perspectives* 12: 23–40.

———. 1998b. "Housing Discrimination Is Still Worth Worrying About." *Housing Policy Debate* 9: 823–927.

Zemans, Frances Kahn. 1983. "Legal Mobilization: The Neglected Role of the Law in the Political System." *American Political Science Review* 77: 690–703.

16

Excerpts from "Historical Context and Hazard Waste Facility Siting: Understanding Temporal Patterns in Michigan"

Robin Saha and Paul Mohai

Historical Context and Siting of Hazardous Waste Facilities

We provide below an historical account of the development of public environmental concern about solid and hazardous wastes and the associated Not-in-My-Backyard (NIMBY) phenomenon. We delineate three distinct periods relevant to understanding public attitudes and anxieties about hazardous waste, social group political participation in siting decisions, and their effects on facility siting outcomes. These periods include: (1) the pre-NIMBY/pre-RCRA era (pre-1970); (2) the early NIMBY era (1970–1980); and 3) the post-Love Canal era (post-1980). We hypothesize that disparate siting patterns did not exist for facilities sited in the pre-NIMBY/ pre-RCRA era, but that such patterns emerged in the early NIMBY era, and increased in severity in the post-Love-Canal era.

Pre-NIMBY/Pre-RCRA Era (Pre-1970)

The unprecedented growth in public awareness and concern during the 1960s and early 1970s about a wide range of environmental issues likely had a primary influence on the siting process. In addition to growing public concern about air and water pollution, population control, and natural resource protection, concern about waste disposal also developed during the 1960s, and would later expand in the 1970s (Dunlap 1992; Kanagy, Humphrey, and Firebaugh 1994). To address concerns about adverse health and environmental impacts of ever-growing amounts of solid waste, Congress passed the Solid Waste Disposal Act of 1965 and the Resource

Recovery Act of 1970, which together created a limited federal role in solid waste management. These laws encouraged states and municipalities to shift from open dumping to sanitary landfills by providing grants, training programs, and technical standards. Prior to 1965, few states participated in waste management activities (Blumberg and Gottlieb 1989).

Although solid waste issues were squarely on the public agenda, hazardous wastes were not, and would not be until the Love Canal story broke in 1979 (see below). Prior to the enactment of RCRA of 1976 and the Hazardous and Solid Waste Amendments of 1984 no national policies regulated the siting of hazardous waste facilities. A similar situation existed at the state level. For example, in Michigan, no specific state policies provided oversight of hazardous waste facility siting until the passage of the state Hazardous Waste Management Act (Act 64) of 1979. The so-called Superfund Act (Comprehensive Environmental Remediation, Compensation, and Liability Act of 1979, or CERCLA) and its list of abandoned, contaminated sites are testimony to prior decades of unregulated handling of hazardous waste.

For waste facilities sited prior to RCRA and Act 64, governmental siting decisions rested with the appropriate local governmental approval bodies (e.g., city building departments and planning offices or zoning boards), which assured that standard building code, zoning requirements, and the like were met. Even in areas where zoning may have precluded siting in certain locations, zoning could be changed or variances issued. For example, Detroit was known for the "flexibility" of its ordinances (Sugrue 1996). There were typically no specific requirements pertaining to design safety, operating conditions, or public participation in siting decisions beyond those required for any other industrial facility. Due to the lack of public awareness of the risks of hazardous waste and a similar lack of development of environmental and health sciences, public and governmental involvement in siting decisions was minimal, and many facilities "functioned with an absolute minimum of technical safeguards or provisions for community input or oversight of facility management" (Rabe 1994:28). Prior to the NIMBY

phenomenon and RCRA, pollution was more generally accepted as a necessary price of economic prosperity, local approvals were routine, public opposition was rare, and the legal or regulatory context allowed little democratic deliberation in siting decisions (Davy 1997).

Early NIMBY Era (1970–1980)

Although sanitary landfills offered a significant improvement over open dumping in protecting public health and the environment, growing concern over the risks of old dump sites (many that were later to be designated Superfund sites) transferred to the new landfills and other disposal facilities, such as incinerators. According to the U.S. Environmental Protection Agency (EPA), community opposition to the siting of waste facilities grew throughout the 1970s and threatened to undermine governmental efforts to improve solid waste management (Bacow and Milkey 1982; U.S. EPA Office of Water and Waste Management 1979). Thus, public concern about waste facilities appears to have contributed to widespread growth of community organizing as environmental concern became expressed through local citizen action. This phenomenon became widely recognized and somewhat pejoratively labeled as the Not-In-My-Backyard (NIMBY) syndrome, fueled by highly visible events such as the Three-Mile Island nuclear accident of 1979.[1]

Despite the early emergence of mass environmental consciousness and growth in concern and citizen activism regarding solid waste facilities, accounts suggest that specific concern related to hazardous waste did not develop until around the time of Love Canal. These concerns centered around potential health risks, the impact on property values, the inability to keep out other undesirable land uses, and overall declines in the quality of life in a host community (Edelstein 1988). Environmental public opinion surveys by the EPA in 1973 and by the Council on Environmental Quality and Resources for the Future in 1980 show a shift in attitudes during the 1970s from disinterest and acceptance to extreme concern and opposition in regard to the local placement of hazardous waste facilities (Lindell and Earle 1983). Thus, in the late 1970s, public environmental concern over hazardous waste appears to have been increasing.

In the late 1970s and early 1980s, public concern about hazardous waste and grassroots organizing against new facility siting was generated by several well-publicized and controversial cases such as those in Love Canal, New York, and in Times Beach, Missouri (Kasperson 1986). Peter M. Sandman (1985) asserts that prior to Love Canal "citizens were not very involved in, nor knowledgeable about, the siting of landfills and other hazardous waste disposal practices" (p. 439). The significance of Love Canal in catapulting public awareness (and fear) about hazardous waste does not mean that concern did not exist beforehand (Morell and Magorian 1982; U.S. EPA Office of Water and Waste Management 1979).[2] However, what distinguishes the early 1970s from the late 1970s and, more so, from the early 1980s is the extent of social embeddedness of hazardous waste concern. Andrew Szasz (1994) explains that

> As recently as 1976, "toxic waste" was not yet a well-formed social issue. There was no clear public opinion concerning it, no crystallized mass perception that it is a serious threat to people's health. Hazardous waste became a true mass issue between 1978 and 1980, when sustained media coverage made *Love Canal* and *toxic waste* household words. By 1980, the American public feared toxic waste as much as it feared nuclear power after Three Mile Island. (p. 5)

Thus, any public opposition to hazardous waste facilities that existed in the early-NIMBY era might have related more to the type of facility. Local opposition to hazardous waste landfills and incinerators might have stemmed from their being similar technologies to familiar solid waste management facilities, rather than the hazardous wastes themselves. But that would soon change.

Post-Love Canal Era (Post-1980)

Love Canal is a town near Niagara Falls where a residential neighborhood had been built on hazardous wastes dumped by a chemical company and covered with a thin layer of soil. Because of growing health concerns among residents, Lois Gibbs, a mother and housewife, led a lengthy campaign that captured the national spotlight. Her efforts eventually led to government action culminating in a federal buy-out of homes, President Carter visiting the site, and Congress enacting the "Superfund Act" (see Gibb 1982; Levine 1982). Love Canal heightened public fears that other communities were also unknowingly at risk of exposure to hazardous wastes and, more importantly, added new fuel to the NIMBY phenomenon.

According to Szasz (1994), public opposition to the siting of hazardous waste facilities was "sporadic and isolated" prior to Love Canal but became widespread and vigorous afterward. Those who share this view note that public opposition grew steadily after the late 1970s and early 1980s (Mazmanian and Morell 1994). Studies of local reactions to hazardous waste sites document the emergence of increasing numbers of community groups organized around hazardous waste issues in the early 1980s (Freudenberg 1984; Quarantelli 1989).

Concern about hazardous wastes paralleled that of pesticides and other forms of toxic contamination (Brown 1981). For example, in Michigan, contamination of cattle feed with a flame retardant (PBB) heightened concerns about toxic chemicals and food safety in the late 1970s and early 1980s (Reich 1991). In 1984 came news coverage of the Union Carbide (now part of Dow Chemical) factory accident in Bhopal, India, which led to community right-to-know provisions of Superfund Amendments and Reauthorization Act of 1986 (i.e., creation of the Toxic Release Inventory [TRI]).

The growth of groups organized around toxics issues was so sudden and dramatic that a popular social movement with a formal infrastructure developed (Cable and Benson 1993). The emergence of an anti-toxics movement in many middle- and working-class neighborhoods reflected a change in societal views regarding the role of citizen involvement in siting decisions (Portney 1991b). The expansion of the movement is evidenced not only by the explosive growth in the number of grassroots groups during the 1980s, but also by national networks and international organizations such as the Citizen's Clearinghouse for

Hazardous Waste (recently renamed the Center for Health, Environment, and Justice), the now-defunct National Toxics Campaign, and Greenpeace (Gottlieb 1993). Dorceta E. Taylor (1998) reports that, although localized opposition existed in the 1970s, throughout the 1980s grassroots organizations increased in number by over three-fold and grew in sophistication (see also Davy 1997).

Various accounts indicate that political mobilization around hazardous waste siting proposals from the 1970s to the 1990s progressively moved from white middle-class, to white working-class, to minority communities (Hurley 1995; Morrison 1986; Taylor 1993, 1997). In fact, surveys of citizens' groups from the early 1980s did not report involvement of minority and low-income populations in opposition campaigns, but noted participation primarily from the white-collar middle class and sometimes the "working class" (Freudenberg 1984; Quarantelli 1989). Nevertheless, mobilization in communities of people of color in the late 1970s and early 1980s has been documented, such as the widely publicized Warren County protests in North Carolina. However, the emergence of a coherent grassroots people of color movement (i.e., the environmental justice movement) does not appear to have occurred until the late 1980s and early 1990s (Taylor 2000), suggesting that minority and poor communities were initially politically vulnerable to waste facility sitings.

The impact of public opposition has been significant, especially regarding the siting of new hazardous waste facilities (Dinkins 1995; Freudenberg and Steinsapir 1991). In the 1980s, some analysts considered public opposition "the single most critical factor in developing new hazardous waste management facilities" (Furuseth 1989:358; see also Daly and Vitaliano 1987). The role of public opposition in unsuccessful siting proposals is well-documented (O'Hare, Bacow, and Sanderson 1983; Rabe 1994). The difficulty of siting new facilities in the face of nearly universal public opposition was cited as evidence of the failure of RCRA (Mazmanian and Morell 1994) and prompted calls for new approaches to siting (NGA 1981; Rabe 1994). Thus, the historic growth of public concern about hazardous waste and resulting growth in grassroots activism has changed

fundamentally the sociocultural context in which facility siting occurs.

There are some important implications regarding (1) the steady and increasing environmental concern in response to increasing recognition of the seriousness of environmental problems, and (2) the explosive growth of citizen opposition to siting of environmental hazards, which appeared to have occurred relatively late in minority and working-class communities. These developments suggest that facility siting increasingly followed the path of least resistance throughout the 1970s and 1980s. As middle-class, upper-class, and (later) working-class communities became involved in citizen opposition groups, new facilities were increasingly likely to be deflected or directed to minority and low-income neighborhoods and communities, which were seen as the paths of least resistance due to their need for jobs and their political vulnerability associated with limited access to resources and allies in government (Bullard and Wright 1987). Because the environmental justice movement did not develop in earnest until the 1990s (see Taylor 2000), siting in minority and low-income communities may have increased throughout the 1970s and 1980s. Although mobilization of people of color has been significant in the 1990s, with the subsequent prominence of "success stories," their ability to resist unwanted facilities appears limited (Cole and Foster 2001; Hurwitz and Sullivan 2001; Moss 2001), suggesting that disparate siting persisted in the 1990s, though perhaps to a lesser degree.

The Legal Context of Siting

Public environmental concern also resulted in RCRA of 1976, the Hazardous and Solid Waste Amendments (HSWA) of 1984, and corresponding state legislation (Davis 1993). These laws fundamentally altered the playing field of siting contestation, particularly in the post-Love Canal era when the laws took effect. We argue below that these changes in the legal and regulatory context of siting, by changing the dynamics of NIMBY-ism, further contributed to racial and socioeconomic siting disparities. We explain how siting laws served as an additional factor to encourage sitings to follow the path of least resistance by shifting authority from the local level to state and federal agencies. By shaping the political opportunity structure for public participation in siting decisions (Tarrow 1996), thereby leading to discriminatory outcomes, these institutional arrangements constitute an indirect form of institutional discrimination.

In enacting RCRA and HSWA, Congress sought for states, rather than the EPA, to administer their own hazardous waste programs. States were encouraged to pass their own legislation modeled after RCRA and to develop programs at least as stringent as the EPA's. Since passage of RCRA and Michigan's corresponding legislation, Act 64, decision-making authority in Michigan shifted from local government to the Michigan Department of Environmental Quality (DEQ).[3] Local government authority under Act 64 is minimal, and merely consists of verifying that siting proposals comply with local zoning. At the same time, Act 64 gives preemptive decision-making authority to the DEQ to override local opposition to siting. This authority also exists in the majority of other states managing RCRA programs (Rabe 1994).

State siting decisions are made through permitting systems prescribed under RCRA. The purpose of permitting programs is to ensure government oversight and protection of human health and the environment in the construction, operation, and closure of facilities. In Michigan, waste facility developers must obtain a permit from the DEQ before construction can begin. Although developers can be denied a permit, the DEQ is obligated to approve a permit if a proposal meets legal and technical requirements (Davy 1997). Prior to issuance of a final permit, the agency issues a draft permit, which starts a 45-day public comment period. In Michigan, if a public hearing is requested (they are not required), a Site Review Board oversees them and subsequently advises the DEQ (Fletcher 2003). The draft permit signals imminent state approval provided that no substantial new questions concerning the permit are raised" (U.S. EPA Office of Solid Waste 1990: III-79). Thus, public participation in siting decisions under RCRA occurs essentially after the decision has been made (Cole and Foster 2001; Kraft and Kraut 1988). Nevertheless, the provisions provide limited access points for the public

to influence final permitting decisions, and these changes and state pre-emption alter the political opportunity structure for collective action in proposed host communities (McAdam 1982).

Public participation rules allow certain communities to delay or curtail the siting process. Administrative and legal challenges at the state and federal levels, and even local zoning disputes, may also stall the process, thereby encouraging facility sponsors to withdraw their applications and to seek more receptive locations (Cerrell Associates, Inc. 1984; Daly and Vitaliano 1987). For facilities such as incinerators that also must obtain Clean Air Act (CAA) permits, citizen groups may file CAA appeals or law suits. However, bringing such challenges or delaying permit approvals by taking advantage of the public participation provisions of Act 64, RCRA, or other environmental laws requires considerable technical, legal, and financial resources that often are available only to affluent, politically well-connected communities. This policy environment, in disadvantaging minority and low-income communities and leading to disparate outcomes, is a form of indirect institutional discrimination (Feagin and Feagin 1986; Lake 1996; Stretesky and Hogan 1998). In fact, Thomas H. Fletcher (2003) documents affluent white communities' effective use of delay strategies to oppose hazardous waste facility siting in Michigan during the 1980s. However, less empowered communities tend to lack the political clout and resources needed to mount effective public opposition campaigns (Hurwitz and Sullivan 2001). In fact, evidence such as a report commissioned by the California Waste Management Board, entitled "Political Difficulties Facing Waste-to-Energy Conversion Plant Siting," indicates that opposition from low-income and minority neighborhoods might be less likely than from other areas (Cerrell Associates 1984; Portney 1991a).

In summary, we posit that a historical convergence of several interacting factors has contributed to disparate siting in recent decades. These developments include the growth of public concern about hazardous waste, laws to manage it, growth in local opposition to the placement of it, as well as concern about the failure to successfully site new facilities. Changes in the historical context of siting in the 1970s and 1980s contributed significantly to sociopolitical conditions in which the siting of new waste facilities followed the path of least resistance that allowed patterns of disparate siting of hazardous waste facilities during the early NIMBY era (in the 1970s). Conversely, facilities sited in the pre-NIMBY/pre-RCRA era (prior to 1970) would not necessarily have been sited disproportionately in areas least able to resist them. Furthermore, the consequences of new siting laws and policies favoring affluent communities, along with the progressive growth of environmental concern and NIMBY behaviors ignited by public fears about hazardous waste in the wake of Love Canal, suggest that disparate siting has been more prevalent and severe in the 1980s than in the 1970s.

Discussion

Models of environmental injustice tend to assume that public opposition, attitudes that drive the NIMBY phenomenon and government and industry responses have been constant over time; therefore, they predict siting disparities regardless of the historical context of siting. However, we found evidence of disparate siting in the early NIMBY and post-Love Canal eras, but not in the pre-NIMBY/pre-RCRA era. This finding is consistent with the proposition that growth of environmental concern, public opposition, and changes in the policy environment—and thus the political opportunity structure—prompted hazardous waste facilities sitings to follow the path of least resistance. Although widespread concern about hazardous waste did not develop until the late 1970s, general public awareness in the late 1960s and early 1970s about waste facilities, pollution, and other environmental issues may have spilled over to siting of hazardous waste facilities. Following Love Canal, specific concern about hazardous waste, hazardous waste facilities, and related NIMBY behaviors expanded greatly, particularly in the 1980s when RCRA provided new opportunities for neighborhoods with high levels of political clout and technical know-how necessary to influence siting decisions. Industry, in turn, altered its site-selection strategy through the permitting process;

as the antitoxic movement emerged and public opposition posed a serious threat to siting, minority and low-income neighborhoods were increasingly attractive locations (Brulle 2000; Cerrell Associates, Inc. 1984; Daly and Vitaliano 1987). Thus, the basic factors driving the sociopolitical and rational choice explanations have changed dramatically over recent decades. While it is less clear how factors underlying racial discrimination explanations have changed over time, institutional discrimination may have been relatively constant in its presence, if not its exact character or causal mechanisms (see discussion below).

The increased magnitude of economic disparities from the 1970s to 1980s supports the hypothesis that the burgeoning NIMBY phenomenon and new opportunities for public participation in siting decisions, coupled with the assertion of pre-emptive state authority, increasingly encouraged disparate siting. Although the magnitude of racial siting disparities did not increase from the 1970s to 1980s, they remained significant. Host neighborhoods of TSDFs sited in the 1980s were predominantly African-American. Sitings in both the 1970s and 1980s exhibited signs of progressively worsening economic and housing conditions, as new commercial hazardous waste facilities were increasingly located in the deteriorating urban core of Detroit. Consequently, host neighborhoods exhibited increasingly lower housing values, lower new home construction rates, and larger and more pervasive losses of population and housing. In fact, in these recent decades, neighborhood demographic and housing changes took place prior to and during the decade of siting.

The Detroit metropolitan area includes a highly segregated central city and smaller African-American enclaves (such as parts of the City of Pontiac), which appear to have been targeted for new TSDFs sited in the 1980s, by a process very similar to that which Laura Pulido, Steve Sidawi, and Robert O. Vos (1996) describe in detail regarding the Mobil refinery and other industry in Torrance, California. The siting of new TSDFs in older residential areas with aging and deteriorating housing occurred at a time when Detroit experienced de-industrialization and white flight, processes that further concentrated people of color and the poor in the central city (Sugrue 1996; Wilson 1992). Host neighborhoods of TSDFs sited in the 1970s underwent dramatic racial transition and economic decline during the 1970s, whereas host neighborhoods of TSDFs sited in the 1980s already had undergone such changes. By reducing neighborhood social cohesion and political capacity, as Pastor and associates (2001) also observed, demographic instability could make such neighborhoods particularly vulnerable to new facility sitings. While this last observation is consistent with sociopolitical models, racial discrimination explanations also apply.

For example, a history of industrial and residential development in the East Los Angeles area similarly notes how housing segregation and disinvestment helped to concentrate minorities in areas with the least desirable types of land uses (Pulido et al. 1996). The limited redevelopment options of blighted areas, the courting of polluting industry, and the establishment of industrial zoning in minority enclaves paved the way for siting of waste and other polluting facilities—a case of siting following the "path of most assistance" rather than the path of least resistance. Christopher Boone and Ali Modarres (1999), Robert Hersh (1995), Hurley (1995), Chad Montrie (2005), David N. Pellow (2002), and Andrew Szasz and Michael Meuser (2000) have documented similar examples of how racial segregation, economic decline, uneven redevelopment, and industrial zoning concentrated low-income populations and segregated minorities where environmental hazards were then located in Commerce, California; Pittsburgh, Pennsylvania; Gary, Indiana; Memphis, Tennessee; Chicago, Illinois; and San Jose, California, respectively. The racial disparities and increasing magnitude of disparities in economic and housing conditions associated with TSDFs sited in Michigan supports a similar conclusion. In fact, nationwide, factors increasing such vulnerability to siting were particularly virulent in the 1970s and 1980s (Jargowsky 1997; Massey and Denton 1993; Wilson 1987). Because the breadth of social forces contributing to these temporal patterns have a decidedly institutional character, disparate siting can be viewed as a form of indirect institutional discrimination.

The slight decrease in the magnitude of racial disparities in the 1980s is consistent with the early emergence of the environmental justice movement and growth in the capacity of minority and low-income communities to oppose new facility siting effectively. However, because no new commercial hazardous waste facilities were sited in Michigan during the 1990s, the decade in which the movement came to the fore, this possibility was not assessed.

Conclusions

Our longitudinal study of disparate siting in Michigan reveals temporal patterns that correspond to historic changes in sociopolitical conditions (i.e., pubic attitudes and actions, institutional arrangements and the policy environment of siting). Pre-NIMBY/Pre-RCRA era facilities were located in economically vibrant neighborhoods with relatively good housing and employment conditions. In contrast, host neighborhoods of TSDFs sited in the early NIMBY and post-Love Canal eras exhibited progressively more depressed economic and housing conditions. Furthermore, host neighborhoods of these TSDFs, sited in the 1970s and 1980s, had increasingly severe income and poverty disparities, low housing demand, and high rates of residential housing decline at the time of siting. These findings are generally consistent with the review of previous studies of disparate siting and facility expansion plans (e.g., Hamilton 1995; Hurley 1997).

However, to firmly establish the role that historical context plays in disparate siting, more longitudinal studies are needed. These studies should examine other states and regions and the nation as a whole, as well as other types of locally unwanted land uses. If possible, they should extend their temporal scopes to before 1970, and assess effects of the environmental justice movement on siting decisions since 1990. We also suggest that future environmental justice studies, both cross-sectional and longitudinal, not assume that sociopolitical conditions and policy environment in the past were the same as they are today or that conditions in previous periods were uniform. Better understanding is also needed of how changes in the types of racial discrimination—overt and subtle, individual and institutional—have influenced siting decisions over time. Finally, we encourage greater exploration than was possible in this study of ways to integrate rational choice, sociopolitical, and racial discrimination models, for example, by further understanding how they may be mutually reinforcing, or interacting, over time (Pulido 1996).

Over the past several decades, siting decisions have occurred in a highly contested political landscape. Our findings support the argument that siting increasingly has followed the path of least resistance as a result of unprecedented growth in public environmental concern and citizen action. Institutional factors also are likely to have contributed to the historical patterns. As state and federal agencies assumed responsibility for approving siting proposals of industry, legislatively mandated permitting processes have provided new political opportunities for public involvement, both administrative and judicial. Distributional politics appear to have prevailed such that those segments of the population with fewer political, organizational, and technical resources have borne a disproportionate share of the society's environmental burdens.

Moreover, the historic patterns found in this study suggest that discriminatory siting is here to stay, given the current sociopolitical and legal terrain. As long as the most polluted and disempowered communities are seen and remain as paths of least resistance, attention to post-siting neighborhood changes that may exacerbate siting disparities might only serve as a diversion from the difficult task of addressing institutional forms of discrimination that pervade industry and governmental siting decisions. Government and industry policies that equalize the playing field and pay attention to the racial and socioeconomic composition and existing pollution burden of proposed host neighborhoods could help. Also helpful would be reform of economic development policies and practices by which local officials court or assist polluting industries in locating in already overburdened areas and overlook such areas for more benign forms of redevelopment.

Notes

1. The apparent parochial nature of NIMBY does not suggest that participants in NIMBY campaigns all view the siting of facilities in other communities besides their own as acceptable. The term NIMBY is used here mainly for convenience to refer to the recent historical period in which vigorous opposition has been prevalent. NIMBY groups have grown in their sophistication and understanding of the broad context of hazardous waste problems (Szasz 1994). Some groups redefine the problem of "where to put it" by advocating, instead, for more comprehensive solutions such as source reduction and recycling (Bryant 1995).

2. The U.S. EPA Office of Waste and Waste Management (1979) report, produced by Centaur Associates, provides examples of successful public opposition from early 1970s, including the IT Corporation facility in Brentwood, California; Padre Juan facility in Ventura County, California; and Resource Recovery Corporation in Pasco, Washington. Other unsuccessful campaigns included Wes-Con in Grandview and Bruneau, Idaho; and Calabasas, in Los Angeles, California. The vast majority of cases (16 of 21) met substantial public opposition in the late 1970s.

3. This state agency was created in 1996 as a result of a reorganization of the Department of Natural Resources (DNR). Functions related to Act 64 that were previously carried out by the DNR are now performed by the DEQ. To avoid confusion, the subsequent discussion refers only to the DEQ.

References

Bacow, Lawrence S. and James R. Milkey. 1982. "Overcoming Local Opposition to Hazardous Waste Facilities: The Massachusetts Approach." *Harvard Environmental Law Review* 6: 265–305.

Blumberg, Louis and Robert Gottlieb. 1989. *War on Waste: Can America Win Its Battle with Garbage*. Covelo, CA: Island Press.

Boone, Christopher G. and Ali Modarres. 1999. "Creating a Toxic Neighborhood in Los Angeles County: A Historical Examination of Environmental Inequality." *Urban Affairs Review* 35: 163–87.

Brown, Michael H. 1981. *Laying Waste: The Poisoning of America by Toxic Chemicals*. New York: Washington Square Press.

Brulle, Robert J. 2000. *Agency, Democracy, and Nature: The U.S. Environmental Movement from a Critical Theory Perspective.* Cambridge, MA: The MIT Press.

Bryant, Bunyan, ed. 1995. *Environmental Justice: Issues, Policies, and Solutions.* Washington, DC: Island Press.

Bullard, Robert D. 1983. "Solid Waste Sites and the Black Houston Community." *Sociological Inquiry* 53: 273–88.

Bullard, Robert D. and Beverly Hendrix Wright. 1987. "Blacks and the Environment." *Humboldt Journal of Social Relations* 14(1/2): 165–84.

Cable, Shari and Michael Benson. 1993. "Acting Locally: Environmental Injustice and the Emergence of Grassroots Environmental Organizations." *Social Problems* 40: 464–77.

Cerrell Associates, Inc. 1984. "Political Difficulties Facing waste-to-energy Conversion Plant Siting." Report prepared for California Waste Management Board, Los Angeles, CA.

Cole, Luke W. and Sheila R. Foster. 2001. *From the Ground Up: Environmental Racism and the Rise of the Environmental Justice Movement.* New York: New York University Press.

Daly, John B. and Eric N. Vitaliano. 1987. *Hazardous Waste Facility Siting: A National Survey.* Albany, NY: Legislative Commission on Toxic Substances and Hazardous Wastes.

Davis, Charles B. 1993. *The Politics of Hazardous Waste.* Englewood Cliffs, NJ: Simon & Schuster.

Davy, Benjamin. 1997. *Essential Justice: When Legal Institutions Cannot Resolve Environmental and Land Use Disputes.* New York: Springer-Verlag Wien.

Dinkins, Carol E. 1995. "Impact of the Environmental Justice Movement on American Industry and Local Government." *Administrative Law Review* 47: 337–53.

Dunlap, Riley B. 1992. "Trends in Public Opinion toward Environmental Issues: 1965–1990." Pp. 89–116 in *American Environmentalism,* edited by Riley E. Dunlap and Angela G. Mertig. Washington, DC: Taylor and Francis New York Inc.

Edelstein, Michael R. 1988. *Contaminated Communities: The Social and Psychological impacts of Residential Toxic Exposure.* Boulder, CO: Westview Press.

Feagin, Joe R. and Clarece B. Feagin 1986. *Discrimination American Style: Institutional Racism and Sexism.* 2d ed. Malabar, FL: Kriege publishing Co.

Fletcher, Thomas H. 2003. *From Love Canal to Environmental Justice: The Politics of Hazardous Waste on the Canada-U.S. Border.* Peterborough, Ontario: Broadview Press.

Freudenberg, Nicholas. 1984. "Citizen Action for Environmental Health: Report on a Survey of Community Organizations." *American Journal of Public Health* 74: 444–48.

Freudenberg, Nicholas and Carol Steinsapir. 1991. "Not in Our Backyards: The Grassroots Environmental Movement." *Society and Natural Resources* 4: 235–45.

Furuseth, Owen J. 1989. "Community Sensitivity to a Hazardous Waste Facility." *Landscape and Urban Planning* 17: 357–70.

Gibb, Lois M. 1982. *Love Canal: My Story.* Albany, NY: State University of New York Press.

Glickman, Theodore S. 1994. "Measuring Environmental Equity with GIS." *Renewable Resources Journal* 12(3): 17–21.

Gottlieb, Robert. 1993. *Forcing the Spring: The Transformation of the American Environmental Movement.* Washington, DC: Island Press.

Hamilton, James, T. 1995. "Testing for Environmental Racism: Prejudice, Profits, Political Power?" *Journal of Policy Analysis and Management* 14(1): 107–32.

Hersh, Robert. 1995. *Race and Industrial Hazards: An Historical Geography of the Pittsburgh Region, 1900–1990.* Discussion Paper 95-18. Washington, DC: Resources for the Future.

Hurley, Andrew. 1995. *Environmental Inequities: Class, Race, and Industrial pollution in Gary, Indiana, 1945–1990.* Chapel Hill: University of North Carolina Press.

——. 1997. "Fiasco at Wagner Electric: Environmental Justice and Urban Geography in St. Louis." *Environmental History* 2: 460–81.

Hurwitz, Julie H. and E. Quita Sullivan. 2001. "Using Civil Rights Law to Challenge Environmental Racism: From Bean to Guardians to Chester to Sandoval." *The Journal of Law in Society* 2: 5–70.

Jargowsky, Paul A. 1997. *Poverty and Place: Ghettos, Barrios, and the American City.* New York: Russell Sage Foundation.

Kanagy, Conrad L., Craig R. Humphrey, and Glenn Firebaugh. 1994. "Surging Environmentalism: Changing Public Opinion of Changing Publics?" *Social Science Quarterly* 75: 804–19.

Kasperson, Roger E. 1986. "Hazardous Waste Facility Siting: Community, Firm, and Governmental Perspectives." Pp. 118–44 in *Hazards: Technology and Fairness.* Washington, DC: National Academy Press.

Kraft, Michael E. and Ruth Kraut. 1988. "Citizen Participation and Hazardous Waste Policy implementation." Pp. 63–80 in *Dimensions of Hazardous Waste* Policy, edited by Charles E. Davis and James P. Lester. New York: Greenwood Press.

Lake, Robert W. 1996. "Volunteers, NIMBY, and Environmental Justice: Dilemmas of Democratic Practice." *Antipode* 28: 160–74.

Levine, Adeline. 1982. *Love Canal: Science, Politics, and People.* Lexington, MA: Lexington Books.

Lindell, M. and T. Earle. 1983. "How Close Is Close Enough: Public Perception of the Risks of Industrial Facilities." *Risk Analysis* 3: 245–53.

Massey, Douglas S. and Nancy A. Denton. 1993. *American Apartheid: Segregation and the Making of the Underclass.* Cambridge, MA: Harvard University Press.

Mazmanian, Daniel A. and David Morell. 1994. "The 'NIMBY' Syndrome: Facility Siting and the Failure of Democratic Discourse." Pp. 233–50 in *Environmental Policy in the 1990s: Toward a New Agenda,* 2d ed., edited by Norman J. Vig and Michael E. Kraft. Washington, DC: Congressional Quarterly Press.

McAdam, Doug. 1982. *Political Process and the Development of Black Insurgency, 1930–1970.* Chicago: University of Chicago Press.

Montrie, Chad. 2005. "From Dairy Farms to Housing Tracts: Environment and Race in the Making of a Memphis Suburb." *Journal of Urban History* 31(2): 219–40.

Morell, David and Christopher Magorian. 1982. *Siting Hazardous Waste Facilities: Local Opposition and the Myth of Preemption.* Cambridge, MA: Ballinger.

Morrison, Denton. 1986. "How and Why Environmental Consciousness Has Trickled Down." Pp. 187–220 in *Distributional Conflicts in Environmental and Resource* Policy, edited by Allan Schnaiberg, Nicholas Watts, and Klaus Zimmerman. Aldershot, UK: Gower Publishing Company Limited.

Moss, Kary L. 2001. "Environmental Justice at the Crossroads." *The Journal of Law in Society* 2: 71–108.

National Governors' Association (NGA). 1981. "Siting Hazardous Waste Facilities." *The Environmental Professional* 3: 133–42.

O'Hare, Michael, Lawrence Bacow, and Debra Sanderson. 1983. *Facility Siting and Public Opposition.* New York: Van Nostrand Reinhold.

Pastor, Manuel, Jr., Jim Sadd, and John Hipp. 2001. "Which Came First? Toxic Facilities, Minority Move-in, and Environmental Justice." *Journal of Urban Affairs* 23: 1–21.

Pellow, David N. 2000. "Environmental inequality Formation: Toward a Theory of Environmental Injustice." *American Behavioral Scientist* 43: 581–601.

——. 2002. *Garbage Wars: The Struggle for Environmental Justice in Chicago.* Cambridge, MA: MIT Press.

Portney, Kent E. 1991a. *Siting Hazardous Waste Treatment Facilities: The NIMBY Syndrome.* New York: Auburn House.

——. 1991b. "Public Environmental Policy Decision Making: Citizen Roles." Pp. 195–215 in *Environmental Decision Making: A Multidisciplinary Perspective,* edited by Richard A. Chechila and Susan Carlisle. New York: Van Nostrand Reinhold.

Pulido, Laura. 1996. "A Critical Review of the Methodology of Environmental Racism Research." *Antipode* 28: 142–59.

Pulido, Laura, Steve Sidawi, and Robert O. Vos. 1996. "An Archaeology of Environmental Racism in Los Angeles." *Urban Geography* 17: 419–39.

Quarantelli, E. L. 1989. "Characteristics of Citizen Groups which Emerge with Respect to Hazardous Waste Sites." Pp. 177–95 in *Psychosocial Effects of Hazardous and Toxic Waste Disposal on Communities,* edited by Dennis L. Peck. Springfield, IL: Charles C. Thomas.

Rabe, Barry G. 1994. *Beyond NIMBY: Hazardous Waste Siting in Canada and the United States.* Washington, DC: The Brookings Institute.

Reich, Michael R. 1991. *Toxic Politics: Responding to Chemical Disasters.* Ithaca, NY: Cornell University Press.

Sandman, Peter M. 1985. "Getting to Maybe: Some Communications Aspects of Siting Hazardous Waste Facilities." *Seton Hall Legislative Journal* 9: 437–65.

Stretesky, Paul and Michael J. Hogan. 1998. "Environmental Justice: An Analysis of Superfund Sites in Florida." *Social Problems* 45: 268–87.

Sugrue, Thomas J. 1996. *The Origins of the Urban Crisis: Race and Inequality in Postwar Detroit.* Princeton, NJ: Princeton University Press.

Szasz, Andrew. 1994. *EcoPopulism Toxic Waste and the Movement for Environmental Justice.* 2d ed. Minneapolis: University of Minnesota Press.

Szasz, Andrew and Michael Meuser. 2000. "Unintended, Inexorable: The Production of Environmental Inequalities in Santa Clara County, California." *American Behavioral Scientist* 43: 602–32.

Tarrow, Sidney 1996. "States and Opportunities: The Political Structuring of Social Movements." Pp. 41–60 in *Comparative Perspectives on Social Movements: Political Opportunities, Mobilizing Structures, and*

Cultural Framing, edited by Doug McAdam, John D. McCarthy, and Mayer N. Zald. Cambridge: Cambridge University Press.

Taylor, Dorceta E. 1993. "Environmentalism and the Politics of Inclusion." Pp. 53–61 in *Confronting Environmental Racism: Voices from the Grassroots,* edited by Robert D. Bullard. Boston: South End Press.

——. 1997. "American Environmentalism: The Role of Race, Class, and Gender in Shaping Activism 1820–1995." *Race, Gender Class* 5: 16–62.

——. 1998. "Mobilizing for Environmental Justice in Communities of Color: An Emerging Profile of People of Color Environmental Groups." Pp. 32–67 in *Ecosystem Management: Adaptive Strategies for Natural Resource Organizations in the 21st Century,* edited by Jennifer Alley, William R. Burch, Beth Canover, and Donald Field. Philadelphia, PA: Taylor & Francis.

——. 2000. "The Rise of the Environmental Justice Paradigm: Injustice Framing and the Social Construction of Environmental Discourse." *American Behavioral Scientist* 43: 508–80.

U.S. EPA Office of Solid Waste. 1990. *RCRA Orientation Manual: 1990 Edition.* EPA 530-SW-90-036. Washington, DC: U.S. Government Printing Office.

U.S. EPA Office of Water and Waste Management. 1979. *Siting of Hazardous Waste Management Facilities and Public Opposition.* EPA SW 809. Washington, DC: Government Printing Office.

Wilson, Carter A. 1992. "Restructuring and the Growth of Concentrated Poverty in Detroit." *Urban Affairs Quarterly* 28: 187–205.

Wilson, William J. 1987. *The Truly Disadvantaged.* Chicago, IL: University of Chicago Press.

17

Excerpts from "Are Emily and Greg More Employable than Lakisha and Jamal? A Field Experiment on Labor Market Discrimination"

MARIANNE BERTRAND AND SENDHIL MULLAINATHAN

Every measure of economic success reveals significant racial inequality in the U.S. labor market. Compared to Whites, African-Americans are twice as likely to be unemployed and earn nearly 25 percent less when they are employed (Council of Economic Advisers, 1998). This inequality has sparked a debate as to whether employers treat members of different races differentially. When faced with observably similar African-American and White applicants, do they favor the White one? Some argue yes, citing either employer prejudice or employer perception that race signals lower productivity. Others argue that differential treatment by race is a relic of the past, eliminated by some combination of employer enlightenment, affirmative action programs and the profit maximization motive. In fact, many in this latter camp even feel that stringent enforcement of affirmative action programs has produced an environment of reverse discrimination. They would argue that faced with identical candidates, employers might favor the African-American one.[1] Data limitations make it difficult to empirically test these views. Since researchers possess far less data than employers do, White and African-American workers that appear similar to researchers may look very different to employers. So any racial difference in labor market outcomes could just as easily be attributed to differences that are observable to employers but unobservable to researchers.

To circumvent this difficulty, we conduct a field experiment that builds on the correspondence testing methodology that has been primarily used in the past to study minority outcomes in the United Kingdom.[2] We send resumes in response to help-wanted ads in Chicago and Boston newspapers and measure callback for interview for each sent resume. We experimentally manipulate perception of race via the name of the fictitious job applicant. We randomly assign very White-sounding names (such as Emily Walsh or Greg Baker) to half the resumes and very African-American-sounding names (such as Lakisha Washington or Jamal Jones) to the other half. Because we are also interested in how credentials affect the racial gap in callback, we experimentally vary the quality of the resumes used in response to a given ad. Higher-quality applicants have on average a little more labor market experience and fewer holes in their employment history; they are also more likely to have an e-mail address, have completed some certification degree, possess foreign language skills, or have been awarded some honors.[3] In practice, we typically send four resumes in response to each ad: two higher-quality and two lower-quality ones. We randomly assign to one of the higher- and one of the lower-quality resumes an African-American-sounding name. In total, we respond to over 1,300 employment ads in the sales, administrative support, clerical, and customer services job categories and send nearly 5,000 resumes. The ads we respond to cover a large spectrum of job quality, from cashier work at retail establishments and clerical work in a mail room, to office and sales management positions.

We find large racial differences in callback rates.[4] Applicants with White names need to send about 10 resumes to get one callback whereas applicants with African-American names need to send about 15 resumes. This 50-percent gap in callback is statistically significant. A White name yields as many more call-backs as an additional eight years of experience on a resume. Since applicants' names are randomly assigned, this gap can only be attributed to the name manipulation.

Race also affects the reward to having a better resume. Whites with higher-quality resumes receive nearly 30-percent more callbacks than Whites with lower-quality resumes. On the other hand, having a higher-quality resume has a smaller effect for African-Americans. In other words, the gap between Whites and African-Americans widens with resume quality. While one may have expected improved credentials to alleviate employers' fear that African-American applicants are deficient in some unobservable skills, this is not the case in our data.[5]

The experiment also reveals several other aspects of the differential treatment by race. First, since we randomly assign applicants' postal addresses to the resumes, we can study the effect of neighborhood of residence on the likelihood of callback. We find that living in a wealthier (or more educated or Whiter) neighborhood increases callback rates. But, interestingly, African-Americans are not helped more than Whites by living in a "better" neighborhood. Second, the racial gap we measure in different industries does not appear correlated to Census-based measures of the racial gap in wages. The same is true for the racial gap we measure in different occupations. In fact, we find that the racial gaps in callback are statistically indistinguishable across all the occupation and industry categories covered in the experiment. Federal contractors, who are thought to be more severely constrained by affirmative action laws, do not treat the African-American resumes more preferentially; neither do larger employers or employers who explicitly state that they are "Equal Opportunity Employers." In Chicago, we find a slightly smaller racial gap when employers are located in more African-American neighborhoods. . . .

Identities of Fictitious Applicants

The next step is to generate identities for the fictitious job applicants: names, telephone numbers, postal addresses, and (possibly) e-mail addresses. The choice of names is crucial to our experiment.[6] To decide on which names are uniquely African-American and which are uniquely White, we use name frequency data calculated from birth certificates of all babies born in Massachusetts between 1974 and 1979. We tabulate these data by race to determine which names are distinctively White and which are distinctively African-American.

Distinctive names are those that have the highest ratio of frequency in one racial group to frequency in the other racial group.

As a check of distinctiveness, we conducted a survey in various public areas in Chicago. Each respondent was asked to assess features of a person with a particular name, one of which is race. For each name, 30 respondents were asked to identify the name as either "White," "African-American," "Other," or "Cannot Tell." In general, the names led respondents to readily attribute the expected race for the person but there were a few exceptions and these names were disregarded.[7]

The final list of first names used for this study is shown in Table 17.2. The table reports the relative likelihood of the names for the Whites and African-Americans in the Massachusetts birth certificates data as well as the recognition rate in the field survey.[8] As Table 17.2 indicates, the African-American first names used in the experiment are quite common in the population. This suggests that by using these names as an indicator of race, we are actually covering a rather large segment of the African-American population.[9]

Applicants in each race/sex/city/resume quality cell are allocated the same phone number. This guarantees that we can precisely track employer callbacks in each of these cells. The phone lines we use are virtual ones with only a voice mailbox attached to them. A similar outgoing message is recorded on each of the voice mailboxes but each message is recorded by someone of the appropriate race and gender. Since we allocate the same phone number for applicants with different names, we cannot use a person name in the outgoing message.

While we do not expect positive feedback from an employer to take place via postal mail, resumes still need postal addresses. We therefore construct fictitious addresses based on real streets in Boston and Chicago using the White Pages. We select up to three addresses in each 5-digit zip code in Boston and Chicago. Within cities, we randomly assign addresses across all resumes. We also create eight e-mail addresses, four for Chicago and four for Boston.[10] These e-mail addresses are neutral with respect to both race and sex. Not all applicants are given an e-mail address. The e-mail addresses are used almost exclusively for the higher-quality resumes. This procedure leaves us with a bank of names, phone numbers, addresses, and e-mail addresses that we can assign to the template resumes when responding to the employment ads.

Responding to Ads

The experiment was carried out between July 2001 and January 2002 in Boston and between July 2001 and May 2002 in Chicago.[11] Over that period, we surveyed all employment ads in the Sunday editions of *The Boston Globe* and *The Chicago Tribune* in the sales, administrative support, and clerical and customer services sections. We eliminate any ad where applicants were asked to call or appear in person. In fact, most of the ads we surveyed in these job categories ask for applicants to fax in or (more rarely) mail in their resume. We log the name (when available) and contact information for each employer, along with any information on the position advertised and specific requirements (such as education, experience, or computer skills). We also record whether or not the ad explicitly states that the employer is an equal opportunity employer.

For each ad, we use the bank of resumes to sample four resumes (two high-quality and two low-quality) that fit the job description and requirements as closely as possible.[12] In some cases, we slightly alter the resumes to improve the quality of the match, such as by adding the knowledge of a specific software program.

One of the high- and one of the low-quality resumes selected are then drawn at random to receive African-American names, the other high- and low-quality resumes receive White names.[13] We use male and female names for sales jobs, whereas we use nearly exclusively female names for administrative and clerical jobs to increase callback rates.[14] Based on sex, race, city, and resume quality, we assign a resume the appropriate phone number. We also select at random a postal address. Finally, email addresses are added to most of the high-quality resumes.[15] The final resumes are formatted, with fonts, layout, and cover letter style chosen at random. The resumes are then faxed (or in a few cases mailed) to the employer. All in all, we respond to more than 1,300 employment ads over the entire sample period and send close to 5,000 resumes.

Measuring Responses

We measure whether a given resume elicits a callback or e-mail back for an interview. For each phone or e-mail response, we use the content of the message left by the employer (name of the applicant, company name, telephone number for contact) to match the response to the corresponding resume-ad pair.[16] Any attempt by employers to contact applicant via postal mail cannot be measured in our experiment since the addresses are fictitious. Several human resource managers confirmed to us that employers rarely, if ever, contact applicants via postal mail to set up interviews.

Weaknesses of the Experiment

We have already highlighted the strengths of this experiment relative to previous audit studies. We now discuss its weaknesses. First, our outcome measure is crude, even relative to the previous audit studies. Ultimately, one cares about whether an applicant gets the job and about the wage offered conditional on getting the job. Our procedure, however, simply measures callbacks for interviews. To the extent that the search process has even moderate frictions, one would expect that reduced interview rates would translate into reduced job offers. However, we are not able to translate our results into gaps in hiring rates or gaps in earnings.

Another weakness is that the resumes do not directly report race but instead suggest race through personal names. This leads to various sources of concern. First, while the names are chosen to make race salient, some employers may simply not notice the names or not recognize their racial content. On a related note, because we are not assigning race but only race-specific names, our results are not representative of the average African-American (who may not have such a racially distinct name).[17] We return to this issue in Section IV, subsection B.

Finally, and this is an issue pervasive in both our study and the Pair-matching audit studies,

newspaper ads represent only one channel for job search. As is well known from previous work, social networks are another common means through which people find jobs and one that clearly cannot be studied here. This omission could qualitatively affect our results if African-Americans use social networks more or if employers who rely more on networks differentiate less by race.[18]

Interpretation

Three main sets of questions arise when interpreting the results above. First, does a higher callback rate for White applicants imply that employers are discriminating against African-Americans? Second, does our design only isolate the effect of race or is the name manipulation conveying some other factors than race? Third, how do our results relate to different models of racial discrimination?

Interpreting Callback Rates

Our results indicate that for two identical individuals engaging in an identical job search, the one with an African-American name would receive fewer interviews. Does differential treatment within our experiment imply that employers are discriminating against African-Americans (whether it is rational, prejudice- based, or other form of discrimination)? In other words, could the lower callback rate we record for African-American resumes *within our experiment* be consistent with a racially neutral review of the *entire pool* of resumes the surveyed employers receive?

In a racially neutral review process, employers would rank order resumes based on their quality and call back all applicants that are above a certain threshold. Because names are randomized, the White and African-American resumes we send should rank similarly on average. So, irrespective of the skill and racial composition of the applicant pool, a race-blind selection rule would generate equal treatment of Whites and African-Americans. So our results must imply that employers use race as a factor when reviewing resumes, which matches the legal definition of discrimination.

But even rules where employers are not trying to interview as few African-American applicants as possible may generate observed differential treatment in our experiment. One such hiring rule would be employers trying to interview a target level of African-American candidates. For example, perhaps the average firm in our experiment aims to produce an interview pool that matches the population base rate. This rule could produce the observed differential treatment if the average firm receives a higher proportion of African-American resumes than the population base rate because African-Americans disproportionately apply to the jobs and industries in our sample.[19]

Some of our other findings may be consistent with such a rule. For example, the fact that "Equal Opportunity Employers" or federal contractor do not appear to discriminate any less may reflect the fact that such employers receive more applications from African-Americans. On the other hand, other key findings run counter to this rule. As we discuss above, we find no systematic difference in the racial gap in call back across occupational or industry categories, despite the large variation in the fraction of African-Americans looking for work in those categories. African-Americans are underrepresented in managerial occupations, for example. If employers matched base rates in the population the few African-Americans who apply to these jobs should receive a higher callback rate than Whites. Yet, we find that the racial gap in managerial occupations is the same as in all the other job categories. This rule also runs counter to our findings on returns to skill. Suppose firms are struggling to find White applicants but overwhelmed with African-American ones. Then they should be less sensitive to the quality of White applicants (as they are trying to fill in their hiring quota for Whites) and much more sensitive to the quality of Black applicants (when they have so many to pick from). Thus, it is unlikely that the differential treatment we observe is generated by hiring rules such as these.

Potential Confounds

While the names we have used in this experiment strongly signal racial origin, they may also signal some other personal trait. More specifically, one might be concerned that employers are inferring social background from the personal name. When employers read a name like "Tyrone" or "Latoya,"

they may assume that the person comes from a disadvantaged background.[20] In the extreme form of this social background interpretation, employers do not care at all about race but are discriminating only against the social background conveyed by the names we have chosen.[21]

While plausible, we feel that some of our earlier results are hard to reconcile with this interpretation. For example, . . . we found that while employers value "better" addresses, African-Americans are not helped more than Whites by living in Whiter or more educated neighborhoods. If the African-American names we have chosen mainly signal negative social background, one might have expected the estimated name gap to be lower for better addresses. Also, if the names mainly signal social background, one might have expected the name gap to be higher for jobs that rely more on soft skills or require more interpersonal interactions. . . .

We, however, directly address this alternative interpretation by examining the average social background of babies born with the names used in the experiment. We were able to obtain birth certificate data on mother's education (less than high school, high school or more) for babies born in Massachusetts between 1970 and 1986.[22] For each first name in our experiment, we compute the fraction of babies with that name and, in that gender-race cell, whose mothers have at least completed a high school degree.

In Table 17.1, we display the average callback rate for each first name along with this proxy for social background. Within each race-gender group, the names are ranked by increasing callback rate. Interestingly, there is significant variation in callback rates by name. Of course, chance alone could produce such variation because of the rather small number of observations in each cell (about 200 for the female names and 70 for the male names).[23]

The row labeled "Average" reports the average fraction of mothers that have at least completed high school for the set of names listed in that gender-race group. The row labeled "Overall" reports the average fraction of mothers that have at least completed high school for the full sample of births in that gender-race group. For example, 83.9 percent of White female babies born between

Table 17.1 Callback Rate and Mother's Education by First Name

White Female			African-American Female		
Name	Percent Callback	Mother Education	Name	Percent Callback	Mother Education
Emily	7.9	96.6	Aisha	2.2	77.2
Anne	8.3	93.1	Keisha	3.8	68.8
Jill	8.4	92.3	Tamika	5.5	61.5
Allison	9.5	95.7	Lakisha	5.5	55.6
Laurie	9.7	93.4	Tanisha	5.8	64.0
Sarah	9.8	97.9	Latoya	8.4	55.5
Meredith	10.2	81.8	Kenya	8.7	70.2
Carrie	13.1	80.7	Latonya	9.1	31.3
Kristen	13.1	93.4	Ebony	9.6	65.6
Average		91.7	Average		61.0
Overall		83.9	Overall		70.2
Correlation	−0.318	($p = 0.404$)	Correlation	−0.383	($p = 0.309$)

White Male			African-American Male		
Name	Percent Callback	Mother Education	Name	Percent Callback	Mother Education
Todd	5,9	87.7	Rasheed	3.0	77.3
Neil	6.6	85.7	Tremayne	4.3	—
Geoffrey	6.8	96.0	Kareem	4.7	67.4
Brett	6.8	93.9	Darnell	4.8	66.1
Brendan	7.7	96.7	Tyrone	5.3	64.0
Greg	7.8	88.3	Hakim	5.5	73.7
Matthew	9.0	93.1	Jamal	6.6	73.9
Jay	13.4	85.4	Leroy	9.4	53.3
Brad	15.9	90.5	Jermaine	9.6	57.5
Average		91.7	Average		66.7
Overall		83.5	Overall		68.9
Correlation	−0.0251	($p = 0.949$)	Correlation	−0.595	($p = 0.120$)

Notes: This table reports, for each first name used in the experiment, callback rate and average mother education. Mother education for a given first name is defined as the percent of babies born with that name in Massachusetts between 1970 and 1986 whose mother had at least completed a high school degree (see text for details). Within each sex/race group, first names are ranked by increasing callback rate. "Average" reports, within each race-gender group, the average mother education for all the babies born with one of the names used in the experiment. "Overall" reports, within each race-gender group, average mother education for all babies born in Massachusetts between 1970 and 1986 in that race-gender group. "Correlation" reports the Spearman rank order correlation between callback rate and mother education within each race-gender group as well as the p-value for the test of independence.

1970 and 1986 have mothers with at least a high school degree; 91.7 percent of the White female babies with one of the names used in the experiment have mothers with at least a high school degree.

Consistent with a social background interpretation, the African-American names we have chosen fall below the African-American average. For African-American male names, however, the gap between the experimental names and the population average is negligible. For White names, both the male and female names are above the population average.

But, more interestingly to us, there is substantial between-name heterogeneity in social background. African-American babies named Kenya or Jamal are affiliated with much higher mothers' education than African-American babies named Latonya or Leroy. Conversely, White babies named Carrie or Neil have lower social background than those named Emily or Geoffrey. This allows for a direct test of the social background hypothesis within our sample: are names associated with a worse social background discriminated against more? In the last row in each gender-race group, we report the rank-order correlation between callback rates and mother's education. The social background hypothesis predicts a positive correlation. Yet, for all four categories, we find the exact opposite. The p-values indicate that we cannot reject independence at standard significance levels except in the case of African-American males where we can almost reject it at the 10-percent level ($p = 0.120$). In summary, this test suggests little evidence that social background drives the measured race gap.

Names might also influence our results through familiarity. One could argue that the African-American names used in the experiment simply appear odd to human resource managers and that any odd name is discriminated against. But as noted earlier, the names we have selected are not particularly uncommon among African-Americans (see Table 17.2). We have also performed a similar exercise to that of Table 17.1 and measured the rank-order correlation between name-specific callback rates and name frequency within each gender-race group. We found no systematic positive correlation.

There is one final potential confound to our results. Perhaps what appears as a bias against African-Americans is actually the result of *reverse discrimination*. If qualified African-Americans are thought to be in high demand, then employers with average quality jobs might feel that an equally talented African-American would never accept an offer from them and thereby never call her or him in for an interview. Such an argument might also explain why African-Americans do not receive as strong a return as Whites to better resumes, since higher qualification only strengthens this argument. But this interpretation would suggest that among the better jobs, we ought to see evidence of reverse discrimination, or at least a smaller racial gap. However, . . . we do not find any such evidence. The racial gap does not vary across jobs with different skill requirements, nor does it vary across occupation categories. Even among the better jobs in our sample, we find that employers significantly favor applicants with White names.[24]

Relation to Existing Theories

What do these results imply for existing models of discrimination? Economic theories of discrimination can be classified into two main categories: taste-based and statistical discrimination models.[25] Both sets of models can obviously "explain" our average racial gap in callbacks. But can these models explain our other findings? More specifically, we discuss the relevance of these models with a focus on two of the facts that have been uncovered in this paper: (i) the lower returns to credentials for African-Americans; (ii) the relative uniformity of the race gap across occupations, job requirements and, to a lesser extent, employer characteristics and industries.

Taste-based models (Gary S. Becker, 1961) differ in whose prejudiced "tastes" they emphasize: customers, coworkers, or employers. Customer and co-worker discrimination models seem at odds with the lack of significant variation of the racial gap by occupation and industry categories, as the amount of customer contact and the fraction of White employees vary quite a lot across these categories. We do not find a larger racial gap among jobs that explicitly require "communication skills" and jobs for which we expect

Table 17.2   First Names Used in Experiment

White Female			African-American Female		
Name	L(W)/L(B)	Perception White	Name	L(B)/L(W)	Perception Black
Allison	∞	0.926	Aisha	209	0.97
Anne	∞	0.962	Ebony	∞	0.9
Carrie	∞	0.923	Keisha	116	0.93
Emily	∞	0.925	Kenya	∞	0.967
Jill	∞	0.889	Lakisha	∞	0.967
Laurie	∞	0.963	Latonya	∞	1
Kristen	∞	0.963	Latoya	∞	1
Meredith	∞	0.926	Tamika	284	1
Sarah	∞	0.852	Tanisha	∞	1
Fraction of all births:			Fraction of all births:		
3.8 percent			7.1 percent		

White Female			African-American Female		
Name	L(W)/L(B)	Perception White	Name	L(B)/L(W)	Perception Black
Brad	∞	1	Darnell	∞	0.967
Brendan	∞	0.667	Hakim		0.933
Geoffrey	∞	0.731	Jamal	257	0.967
Greg	∞	1	Jermaine	90.5	1
Brett	∞	0.923	Kareem	∞	0.967
Jay	∞	0.926	Leroy	44.5	0.933
Matthew	∞	0.888	Rasheed	∞	0.931
Neil	∞	0.654	Tremayne	∞	0.897
Todd	∞	0.926	Tyrone	62.5	0.900
Fraction of all births:			Fraction of all births:		
1.7 percent			3.1 percent		

Notes: This table tabulates the different first names used in the experiment and their identifiability. The first column reports the likelihood that a baby born with that name (in Massachusetts between 1974 and 1979) is White (or African-American) relative to the likelihood that it is African-American (White). The second column reports the probability that the name was picked as White (or African-American) in an independent field survey of people. The last row for each group of names shows the proportion of all births in that race group that these names account for.

either customer or coworker contacts to be higher (retail sales for example).

Because we do not know what drives employer tastes, employer discrimination models could be consistent with the lack of occupation and industry variation. Employer discrimination also matches the finding that employers located in more African-American neighborhoods appear to discriminate somewhat less. However, employer discrimination models would struggle to explain why African-Americans get relatively lower returns to their credentials. Indeed, the cost of indulging the discrimination taste should increase as the minority applicants' credentials increase.[26]

Statistical discrimination models are the prominent alternative to the taste-based models in the economics literature. In one class of statistical discrimination models, employers use (observable) race to proxy for *unobservable* skills (e.g., Edmund S. Phelps, 1972; Kenneth J. Arrow, 1973). This class of models, struggle to explain the credentials effect as well. Indeed, the added credentials should lead to a larger update for African-Americans and hence greater returns to skills for that group.

A second class of statistical discrimination models "emphasize the precision of the information that employers have about individual productivity" (Altonji and Blank, 1999). Specifically, in these models, employers believe that the same observable signal is more precise for Whites than for African-Americans (Dennis J. Aigner and Glenn G. Cain, 1977; Shelly J. Lundberg and Richard Startz, 1983; Bradford Cornell and Ivo Welch, 1996). Under such models, African-Americans receive lower returns to observable skills because employers place less weight on these skills. However, how reasonable is this interpretation for our experiment? First, it is important to note that we are using the same set of resume characteristics for both racial groups. So the lower precision of information for African-Americans cannot be that, for example, an employer does not know what a high school degree from a very African-American neighborhood means (as in Aigner and Cain, 1977). Second, many of the credentials on the resumes are in fact externally and easily verifiable, such as a certification for a specific software.

An alternative version of these models would rely on bias in the observable signal rather than differential variance or noise of these signals by race. Perhaps the skills of African-Americans are discounted because affirmative action makes it easier for African-Americans to get these skills. While this is plausible for credentials such as an employee-of-the-month honor, it is unclear why this would apply to more verifiable and harder skills. It is equally unclear why work experience would be less rewarded since our study suggests that getting a job is more, not less, difficult for African-Americans.

The uniformity of the racial gap across occupations is also troubling for a statistical discrimination interpretation. Numerous factors that should affect the level of statistical discrimination, such as the importance of unobservable skills, the observability of qualifications, the precision of observable skills and the ease of performance measurement, may vary quite a lot across occupations.

This discussion suggests that perhaps other models may do a better job at explaining our findings. One simple alternative model is lexicographic search by employers. Employers receive so many resumes that they may use quick heuristics in reading these resumes. One such heuristic could be to simply read no further when they see an African-American name. Thus they may never see the skills of African-American candidates and this could explain why these skills are not rewarded. This might also to some extent explain the uniformity of the race gap since the screening process (i.e., looking through a large set of resumes) may be quite similar across the variety of jobs we study.[27]

Conclusion

This paper suggests that African-Americans face differential treatment when searching for jobs and this may still be a factor in why they do poorly in the labor market. Job applicants with African-American names get far fewer call-backs for each resume they send out. Equally importantly, applicants with African-American names find it hard to overcome this hurdle in callbacks by improving their observable skills or credentials.

Taken at face value, our results on differential returns to skill have possibly important policy implications. They suggest that training programs alone may not be enough to alleviate the racial gap in labor market outcomes. For training to work, some general-equilibrium force outside the context of our experiment would have to be at play. In fact, if African-Americans recognize how employers reward their skills, they may rationally be less willing than Whites to even participate in these programs.

Notes

1. This camp often explains the poor performance of African-Americans in terms of supply factors. If African-Americans lack many basic skills entering the labor market, then they will perform worse, even with parity or favoritism in hiring.

2. See Roger Jowell and Patricia Prescott-Clarke (1970), Jim Hubbuck and Simon Carter (1980), Colin Brown and Pat Gay (1985), and Peter A. Riach and Judith Rich (1991). One caveat is that some of these studies fail to fully match skills between minority and nonminority resumes. For example some impose differential education background by racial origin. Doris Weichselbaumer (2003, 2004) studies the impact of sex-stereotypes and sexual orientation. Richard E. Nisbett and Dov Cohen (1996) perform a related field experiment to study how employers' response to a criminal past varies between the North and the South in the United States.

3. In creating the higher-quality resumes, we deliberately make small changes in credentials so as to minimize the risk of overqualification.

4. For ease of exposition, we refer to the effects uncovered in this experiment as racial differences. Technically, however, these effects are about the racial soundingness of names. We briefly discuss below the potential confounds between name and race. A more extensive discussion is offered in Section I, subsection B.

5. These results contrast with the view, mostly based on nonexperimental evidence, that African-Americans receive higher returns to skills. For example, estimating earnings regressions on several decades of Census date, James J. Heckman et al. (2001) show that African-Americans experience higher returns to a high school degree than Whites do.

6. We chose name over other potential manipulations of race, such as affiliation with a minority groups, because we felt such affiliations may especially convey more than race.

7. For example, Maurice and Jerome are distinctively African-American names in a frequency sense yet are not perceived as such by many people.

8. So many of names show a likelihood ratio of because there is censoring of the data at five births. If there are fewer than five babies in any race/name cell, it is censored (and we do not know whether a cell has zero or was censored). This is primarily a problem for the computation of how many African-American babies have "White" names.

9. We also tried to use more White-sounding last names for White applicants and more African-American-sounding last names for African-American applicants. The last names used for White applicants are: Baker, Kelly, McCarthy, Murphy, Murray, O'Brien, Ryan, Sullivan, and Walsh. The last names used for African-American applicants are: Jackson, Jones, Robinson, Washington, and Williams.

10. The e-mail addresses are registered on Yahoo.com, Angelflre.com, or Hotmail.com.

11. This period spans tighter and slacker labor markets. In our data, this is apparent as callback rates (and number of new ads) dropped after September 11, 2001. Interestingly, however, the racial gap we measure is the same across these two periods.

12. In some instances, our resume bank does not have four resumes that are appropriate matches for a given ad. In such instances, we send only two resumes.

13. Though the same names are repeatedly used in our experiment we guarantee that no given ad receives multiple resumes with the same name.

14. Male names were used for a few administrative jobs in the first month of the experiment.

15. In the first month of the experiment, a few high-quality resumes were sent without e-mail addresses and a few low-quality resumes were given e-mail addresses. . . .

16. Very few employers used e-mail to contact an applicant back.

17. As Table 17.2 indicates, the American names we use are, however, quite common among African-Americans, making this less of a concern.

18. In fact, there is some evidence that African-Americans may rely less on social networks for their job search (Harry J. Holzer, 1987).

19. Another variant of this argument is that the (up to) two African-American resumes we sent are enough to significantly distort the racial composition of the entire applicant pool. This is unlikely for two reasons. First, anecdotal evidence and the empirically low callback rates we record suggest that firms typically receive many hundreds of resumes in response to each ad they post. Hence, the (up to) four resumes we send out are unlikely to influence the racial composition of the pool. Second, the similar racial gap in callback we observe across the two cities goes counter to this interpretation since the racial composition base rates differ quite a lot across these two cities. Another variant of this argument is that, for some reason, the average firm in our sample receives a lot of high-quality resumes from African-American applicants and much fewer high-quality resumes from White applicants. Hypothetically, this might occur if high-quality African-Americans are much more likely to use

help-wanted ads rather than other job search channels. If employers perform within-race comparisons and again want to target a certain racial mix in their interviewing and hiring, our African-American resumes may naturally receive lower callbacks as they are competing with many more high-quality applicants. This specific argument would be especially relevant in a case where the average sampled employer is "known" to be good to African-Americans. But our selection procedure for the employment ads did not allow for such screening: we simply responded to as many ads as possible in the targeted occupational categories.

20. Roland Fryer and Steven Levitt (2003) provide a recent analysis of social background and naming conventions amongst African-Americans.

21. African-Americans as a whole come from more disadvantaged backgrounds than Whites. For this social class effect to be something of independent interest, one must assert that African-Americans with the African-American names we have selected are from a lower social background than the average African-American and/or that Whites with the White names we have selected are from a higher social background than the average White. We come back to this point below.

22. This longer time span (compared to that used to assess name frequencies) was imposed on us for confidentiality reasons. When fewer than 10 births with education data available are recorded in a particular education-name cell, the exact number of births in that cell is not reported and we impute five births. Our results are not sensitive to this imputation. One African-American female name (Latonya) and two male names (Rasheed and Hakim) were imputed in this way. One African-American male name (Tremayne) had too few births with available education data and was therefore dropped from this analysis. Our results are qualitatively similar when we use a larger data set of California births for the years 1989 to 2000 (kindly provided to us by Steven Levitt).

23. We formally tested whether this variation was significant by estimating a probit regression of the callback dummy on all the personal first names, allowing for clustering of the observations at the employment-ad level. For all but African-American females, we cannot reject the null hypothesis that all the first name effects in the same race- gender group are the same. Of course, a lack of a rejection does not mean there is no underlying pattern in the between-name variation in callbacks that might have been detectable with larger sample sizes.

24. One might argue that employers who reverse-discriminate hire through less formal channels than help-wanted ads. But this would imply that African-Americans are less likely to find jobs through formal channels. The evidence on exit out of unemployment does not paint a clear picture in this direction (Holzer, 1987).

25. Darity and Mason (1998) provide a more thorough review of a variety of economic theories of discrimination.

26. One could, however, assume that employer tastes differ not just by race but also by race and skill, so that employers have greater prejudice against minority workers with better credentials. But the opposite preferences, employers having a particular distaste for low-skilled African Americans, also seem reasonable.

27. Another explanation could be based on employer stereotyping or categorizing. If employers have coarser stereotypes for African-Americans, many of our results would follow. See Melinda Jones (2002) for the relevant psychology and Mullainathan (2003) for a formalization of the categorization concept.

References

Aigner, Dennis J. and Cain. Glenn G. "Statistical Theories of Discrimination in Labor Markets." *Industrial and Labor Relations Review,* January 1977, *30*(1), pp. 175–87.

Altonji, Joseph G. and Blank, Rebecca M. "Race and Gender in the Labor Markey," in Orley Ashenfelter and David Card, eds., *Handbook of labor economics*, Vol. 30. Amsterdam: North-Holland, 1999, pp. 3143–259.

Arrow, Kenneth, J. "The Theory of Discrimination," in Orley Ashenfelter and Albert Rees, eds., *Discrimination in labor markets.* Princeton, NJ: Princeton University Press, 1973, pp. 3–33.

Becker, Gary S. *The economics of discrimination,* 2nd Ed. Chicago: University of Chicago Press, 1961.

Brown, Colin and Gay, Pat. *Racial discrimination 17 years after the act.* London: Policy Studies Institute, 1985.

Cornell, Bradford and Welch, Ivo. "Culture, Information, and Screening Discrimination." *Journal of Political Economy,* June 1996 *104*(3), pp. 542–71.

Council of Economic Advisers. *Changing America: Indicators of social and economic well-being by race and Hispanic origin.* September 1998, http://w3.access.gpo.gov/eop/ca/pdfs/ca.pdf.

Darity, William A., Jr. and Mason, Patrick L. "Evidence on Discrimination in Employment: Codes of Color, Codes of Gender." *Journal of Economic Perspectives,* Spring 1998, *12*(2), pp. 63–90.

Fryer, Roland and Levitt, Steven. "The Causes and Consequences of Distinctively Black Names." Mimeo, University of Chicago, 2003.

Heckman, James J.; Lochner, Lance J., and Todd, Petra E. "Fifty Years of Mincer Earnings Regressions." Mimeo, University of Chicago, 2001.

Holzer, Harry J. "Informal Job Search and Black Youth Unemployment." *American Economic Review,* June 1987, *77*(3), pp. 446–52.

Hubbuck, Jim and Carter, Simon. *Half a chance? A report on job discrimination against young blacks in Nottingham.* London: Commission for Racial Equality, 1980.

Jones, Melinda. *Social psychology of prejudice.* Saddle River, NJ: Pearson Education, 2002.

Jowell, Roger and Prescott-Clark, Patricia. "Racial Discrimination and White-Collar Workers in Britain." *Race,* November 1970, *11*(4), pp. 397–417.

Lundberg, Shelly J. and Starz, Richard. "Private Discrimination and Social Intervention in Competitive Labor Market." *American Economic Review,* June 1983, *73*(3), pp. 340–47.

Mullainathan, Sendhil. "Thinking Through Categories." Mimeo, Massachusetts Institute of Technology, 2003.

Nisbett, Richard E. and Cohen, Dov. *The culture of honor: The psychology of violence in the South.* Boulder, CO: Westview Press, 1996.

Phelps, Edmund S. "The Statistical Theory of Racism and Sexism." *American Economic Review,* September 1972, *62*(4), pp. 659–61.

Riach, Peter A. and Rich, Judity. "Testing for Racial Discrimination in the Labour Market." *Cambridge Journal of Economics,* September 1991, *15*(3), pp. 239–56.

Weichselbaumer, Doris. "Sexual Orientation Discrimination in Hiring." *Labour Economics,* December 2003, *10*(6), pp. 629–42.

———. "Is It Sex or Personality? The Impact of Sex-Stereotypes on Discrimination in Applicant Selection." *Eastern Economic Journal,* Spring 2004, *30*(2), pp. 159–86.

18

Excerpts from
Racism without Racists
EDUARDO BONILLA-SILVA

. . . If Jim Crow's racial structure has been replaced by a "new racism," what happened to Jim Crow racism? What happened to beliefs about blacks' mental, moral, and intellectual inferiority, to the idea that "it is the [black man's] own fault that he is a lower-caste . . . a lower-class man" or the assertion that blacks "lack initiative, are shiftless, have no sense of time, or do not wish to better themselves";[1] in short, what happened to the basic claim that blacks are subhuman?[2] Social analysts of all stripes agree that most whites no longer subscribe to these tenets. However, this does not mean the "end of racism,"[3] as a few conservative commentators have suggested. Instead, a new powerful ideology has emerged to defend the contemporary racial order: the ideology of color-blind racism. Yet, color-blind racism is a curious racial ideology. Although it engages, as all ideologies do, in "blaming the victim," it does so in a very indirect, "now you see it, now you don't" style that matches the character of the new racism. Because of the slipperiness of color-blind racism, in this article I examine its central frames and explain how whites use them in ways that justify racial inequality.

The Frames of Color-Blind Racism

Ideologies are about "meaning in the service of power."[4] They are expressions at the symbolic level of the fact of dominance. As such, the ideologies of the powerful are central in the production and reinforcement of the status quo. They comfort rulers and charm the ruled much like an Indian snake handler. Whereas rulers receive solace by believing they are not involved in the terrible ordeal of creating and maintaining inequality, the ruled are charmed by the almost magic qualities of a hegemonic ideology.[5]

The central component of any dominant racial ideology is its frames or *set paths for interpreting information*. These set paths operate as cul-de-sacs because after people filter issues through them, they explain racial phenomena following a predictable route. Although by definition dominant frames must *mis*represent the world (hide the fact of dominance), this does not mean that they are totally without foundation. (For instance, it is true that people of color in the United States are much better off today than at any other time in history. However, it is also true—facts hidden by color-blind racism—that because people of color still experience *systematic* discrimination and remain appreciably behind whites in many important areas of life, their chances of catching up with whites are very slim.) Dominant racial frames, therefore, provide the intellectual road map used by rulers to navigate the always rocky road of domination and . . . derail the ruled from their track to freedom and equality.

Analysis of the interviews with college students and DAS respondents revealed that color-blind racism has four central frames and that these frames are used by an overwhelming majority of the white respondents. The four frames are *abstract liberalism, naturalization, cultural racism,* and *minimization of racism.* Of the four frames, abstract liberalism is the most important, as it constitutes the foundation of the new racial ideology. It is also the hardest to understand (What is *racial* about opposing busing or affirmative action, policies that clearly interfere with our American individualism?). Thus, I dedicate more space in this article to its discussion and to how it plays out in the color-blind drama.

In order to adequately understand the *abstract liberalism* frame, first we need to know what is liberalism. According to John Gray, liberalism, or "liberal humanism," is at the core of modernity; of the philosophical, economic, cultural, and political challenge to the feudal order. Although he acknowledges that liberalism has no "essence," he points out that it has a "set of distinctive features," namely, individualism, universalism, egalitarianism, and meliorism (the idea that people and institutions can be improved).[6] All these components were endorsed and placed at the core of the constitutions of emerging nation-states by a new set of actors: the bourgeoisies of early modern capitalism. When the bourgeoisie lauded freedom, they meant "free trade, free selling and buying"; when they applauded "individualism," they had in mind "the bourgeois . . . the middle-class owner of property"; "The ideas of religious liberty and freedom of conscience merely gave expression to the sway of free competition within the domain of knowledge."[7]

Hence, classical liberalism was the philosophy of a nascent class that as an aspiring ruling class expressed its needs (political as well as economic) as general societal goals. But the bourgeois goals were not extended to the populace in their own midst until the twentieth century.[8] Moreover, the liberal project was never inclusive of the countries that Spain, Portugal, France, Britain, the Netherlands, Italy, and later on, Germany used as outposts for raw materials and racialized workers (e.g., slaves). Although contemporary commentators debate the merits of liberal humanism as it pertains to current debates about race-based policies, muticulturalism, and "equality of results,"[9] many seem oblivious to the fact that *"European humanism* (and liberalism) *usually meant that only Europeans were human."*[10] Philosophers such as Kant stated that the differences between blacks and whites were "to be as great in regard to mental capacities as in colour." Voltaire, the great French philosopher, said on the same subject that "only a blind man is permitted to doubt that Whites, Blacks, and Albinoes . . . are totally different races." Lastly, even the father of modern liberalism, John Stuart Mill, author of *On Liberty,* justified 19th-century colonialism and supported slavery in antiquity and in certain 19th-century colonial situations.[11] To be clear, my intent here is not to vilify the founders of liberalism, but to point out that modernity, liberalism, and racial exclusion were all part of the same historical movement.

The liberal tradition informed the American Revolution, the U.S. Constitution, and "the leading American liberal thinker of this period, Thomas Jefferson."[12] And in the United States as in Europe, the exclusion of the majority of white men and all white women from the rights of citizenship and the classification of Native Americans and African Americans as subpersons accompanied the development of the new liberal nation-state.[13] Specifically, racially based policies such as slavery, the removal of Native Americans from their lands and their banishment to reservations, the superexploitation and degrading utilization of Mexicans and various Asian groups as contract laborers, Jim Crow, and many other policies were part of the United States' "liberal" history from 1776 until the 1960s.

Nevertheless, I would be remiss if I failed to acknowledge that, in both Europe and the United States, disenfranchised groups and progressive politicians used the liberal rhetoric to advance social and legal reforms (e.g., the Civil Rights Movement, the National Organization of Women, Liberal parties in Europe).[14] Thus liberalism, when extended to its seemingly logical conclusions ("Life, liberty, and the pursuit of happiness for *all*") and connected to social movements, can be progressive. My point, however, is less about social-reform liberalism (although I contend many reform organizations and many white reform-minded individuals[15] have adopted color-blind racism) than about how central elements of liberalism have been *rearticulated* in post–Civil Rights America to rationalize racially unfair situations.

1. The frame of *abstract liberalism* involves using ideas associated with political liberalism (e.g., "equal opportunity," the idea that force should not be used to achieve social policy) and economic liberalism (e.g., choice, individualism) in an *abstract* manner to explain racial matters. By framing race-related issues in the language of liberalism, whites can appear "reasonable" and even "moral," while opposing almost all practical approaches to deal with de facto racial inequality. For instance, the principle of equal opportunity, central to the agenda of the Civil Rights Movement and whose extension to people of color was vehemently opposed by most whites, is invoked by whites today to oppose affirmative-action policies because they supposedly represent the "preferential treatment" of certain groups. This claim necessitates ignoring the fact that people of color are *severely* underrepresented in most good jobs, schools, and universities and, hence, it is an abstract utilization of the idea of "equal opportunity." Another example is regarding each person as an "individual" with "choices" and using this liberal principle as a justification for whites having the right of choosing to live in segregated neighborhoods or sending their children to segregated schools. This claim requires ignoring the multiple institutional and state-sponsored practices behind segregation and being unconcerned about these practices' negative consequences for minorities.

2. *Naturalization* is a frame that allows whites to explain away racial phenomena by suggesting they are natural occurrences. For example, whites can claim "segregation" is natural because people from all backgrounds "gravitate toward likeness." Or that their taste for whiteness in friends and partners is just "the way things are."

Although the above statements can be interpreted as "racist" and as contradicting the colorblind logic, they are actually used to reinforce the myth of nonracialism. How? By suggesting these preferences are almost biologically driven and typical of all groups in society, preferences for primary associations with members of one's race are rationalized as nonracial because "*they* (racial minorities) do it too."

3. *Cultural racism* is a frame that relies on culturally based arguments *J* such as "Mexicans do not put much emphasis on education" or "blacks have too many babies" to explain the standing of minorities in society. This frame has been adequately discussed by many commentators and does not require much discussion.[16] During slavery and Jim Crow a central rationale for excluding racial minorities was their presumed biological inferiority. Even as late as 1940, a white newspaper editor in Durham, North Carolina, could confidently state that:

> A Negro is different from other people in that he's an unfortunate branch of the human family who hasn't been able to make out of himself all he is capable of. He is not capable of being rushed because of the background of the jungle. Part of his human nature can't be rushed; it gets him off his balance. . . . You can't wipe away inbred character in one year or a hundred years. It must be nursed along. We look upon him for his lack of culture, as being less reliable, in business and unsafe socially. His passions are aroused easily.[17]

Today only white supremacist organizations spout things such as this in open forums. Yet, these biological views have been replaced by cultural ones that, as I will show, are as effective in defending the racial status quo.[18] For example, George McDermott, one of the white middle-class residents interviewed by Katherine Newman in her *Declining Fortunes,* stated:

> I believe in morality: I believe in ethics: I believe in hard work: I believe in all the old values. I don't believe in handouts. . . . So that the whole welfare system falls

into that [category]. . . . The idea of fourteen-year-old kids getting pregnant and then having five children by the time they're twenty is absurd! It's ridiculous! And that's what's causing this country to go downhill.

And as Newman poignantly comments, "George does not see himself as racist. Publicly he would subscribe to the principle everyone in this society deserves a fair shake."[19] Color-blind racism is racism without racists!

4. *Minimization of racism* **is a frame that suggests discrimination is no longer a central factor affecting minorities' life chances ("It's better now than in the past" or "There is discrimination, but there are plenty of jobs out there").** This frame allows whites to accept facts such as the racially motivated murder of James Byrd Jr. in Jasper, Texas,[20] the brutal police attack on Rodney King, the Texaco case,[21] the 2005 lawsuit by black workers alleging that Tyson Foods maintained a "Whites Only" bathroom in one of their Alabama plants, the neglect and slow response by government officials toward a mostly black population during Hurricane Katrina, and many other cases and still accuse minorities of being "hypersensitive," of using race as an "excuse," or of "playing the infamous nice card." More significantly, this frame also involves regarding discrimination exclusively as all-out racist behavior, which, given the way "new racism" practices operate in post-Civil Rights America . . . , eliminates the bulk of racially motivated actions by individual whites and institutions by fiat.

Before proceeding to illustrate how whites use these frames, I need to clarify a few points about the data and how I present them. First, whites used these frames in combination rather than in pure form. This is understandable, since informal expressions of ideology are a constructive effort, a process of building arguments in situ. Therefore, the examples of how whites use a particular frame may be mixed with other frames. Second, the frames were verbalized by participants in various emotional tones, ranging from sympathy to absolute disgust and outrage toward

minorities. This suggests whites with differing levels of sympathy toward minorities resort to the *same* frames when constructing their accounts of racial matters. I attempt to represent this range of emotion in the quotes. Third, because the college student and DAS samples represent two different populations, I present quotes from the two studies separately in the text. I do so to better identify differences in style or content among the two populations. Fourth, the quotes in the chapter were selected to embrace the variety of ways in which the frames are used by respondents. This implies that many outrageously racist quotes were left out for the sake of representing the variance in the samples. Fifth, the interviews were transcribed to be as close to what the respondents uttered as possible. Thus the transcripts include nonlexical expressions (umm, ahh, umhmm), pauses (indicated by ellipses when they are short and by a number in seconds in parentheses representing the duration of the pause, when they are longer than five seconds), emphases (indicated by *italics* or, for notations of the respondent tone, by italic letters in brackets), self-corrections (denoted by a short line, —), and other important discursive matters (laughs and changes in tone are indicated with italic letters in brackets). Whenever I have added words they appear in brackets; the interviewers' interventions appear in brackets and in italic letters. However, to improve its readability, I edited the material lightly.

Abstract Liberalism: Unmasking Reasonable Racism[22]

Because of the curious way in which liberalism's principles are used in the post–Civil Rights era, other analysts label modern racial ideology "laissez-fare racism" or "competitive racism" or argue that modern racism is essentially a combination of the "American Creed" with antiblack resentment.[23] The importance of this frame is evident in that whites use it on issues ranging from affirmative action and interracial friendship and marriage to neighborhood and residential segregation. Because of the pivotal role played by this frame in organizing whites' racial views, I provide numerous examples below.

Rationalizing Racial Unfairness in the Name of Equal Opportunity

An archetype of how white students use the notion of equal opportunity in an abstract manner to oppose racial fairness is Sue, a student at SU.

When asked if minority students should be provided unique opportunities to be admitted into universities, Sue stated:

> I don't think that they should be provided with unique opportunities. I think that they should have the same opportunities as everyone else. You know, it's up to them to meet the standards and whatever that's required for entrance into universities or whatever. I don't think that just because they're a minority that they should, you know, not meet the requirements, you know.

Sue, like most whites, ignored the effects of past and contemporary discrimination on the social, economic, and educational status of minorities. Therefore, by supporting equal opportunity for everyone without a concern for the savage inequalities between whites and blacks, Sue's stance safeguards white privilege. Sue even used the notion of equal opportunity to avoid explaining why blacks tend to perform worse than whites academically: "I don't know . . . um, like I said, I don't see it as a group thing. I see it more as an individual [thing] and I don't know why as a whole they don't do better. I mean, as I see it, they have the same opportunity and everything. They *should* be doing equal."

College students are not the only ones who use this abstract notion of equal opportunity to justify their racial views. For example, Eric, a corporate auditor in his forties, and a very affable man who seemed more tolerant than most members of his generation (e.g., he had dated a black woman for three years, recognized that discrimination happens "a lot" and identified multiple examples, and even said that "the system is. . . is white"), erupted in anger when asked if reparations were due to blacks for the injuries caused by slavery and Jim Crow: "Oh tell them to shut up, OK! I had nothing to do with the whole situation. The opportunity is

there, there is no reparation involved and let's not dwell on it. I'm very opinionated about that!" After suggesting that Jews and Japanese are the ones who really deserve reparation, Eric added, "But something that happened three God-damned generations ago, what do you want us to do about it now? Give them opportunity, give them scholarships, but reparations?"

Was Eric just a white with a "principled opposition" to government intervention. . . ? This does not seem to be the case since Eric, like most whites, made a distinction between government spending on behalf of victims of child abuse, the homeless, and battered women (whom whites deem as legitimate candidates for assistance) and government spending on blacks (whom whites deem as unworthy candidates for assistance). This finding was consistent with DAS survey results. For instance, whereas 64.3 percent of whites agreed that "we should expand the services that benefit the poor," only 39.6 percent (as opposed to 84 percent of blacks) agreed with the proposition "The government should make every effort to improve the social and economic position of blacks living in the United States." Furthermore, whereas 75.2 percent of white respondents approved of increasing federal spending for the environment and 59.7 percent for social security, only 31.7 percent approved such increases for programs to assist blacks. And when the question dealt with government programs that were not perceived as "racial" in any way,[24] the proportion of whites supporting the program increased even more.

"The Most Qualified . . . ": A Meritocratic Way of Defending White Privilege

Another tenet of liberalism whites use to explain racial matters is the Jeffersonian idea of "the cream rises to the top," or meritocracy (reward by merit). And whites seem unconcerned that the color of the "cream" that usually "rises" is white. For example, Diane, a student at SU, expressed her dissatisfaction about providing blacks unique opportunities to be admitted into universities: "I don't think you should admit anyone. It's gotta be, you've gotta be on the level to do it. If they were prepared beforehand to handle the college level to succeed in it, then there you go, anyone can." Diane then added, "They've gotta have the motivation to do well before you get there, I mean, I can't imagine being unprepared to go [to college] like just barely getting by in high school and then coming here to take the classes, you just can't go, 'OK, we want to put minorities in here so put anyone in, you know.'" Diane also used the notion of meritocracy to explain her opposition to affirmative action.

> That's so hard. I still believe in merit, you know, I still believe in equality, you know. If you did have two people with the same qualifications, one's minority and one's not, you know, I'd want to interview them and just maybe a personality stands out that works with the job, I don't know. Just find something other than race to base it on, you know? Let that not be a factor if they qualify.

How could Diane maintain these views and remain "reasonable"? Diane could say these things and seem reasonable because she believes discrimination is not the reason why blacks are worse off than whites. Instead, she relied on the cultural racism frame to explain blacks' status. This view can be seen too in her response to a question on why blacks fare worse academically than whites: "I don't know why. Mine was a personal motivation so, you know, I don't know. I don't want to say they weren't personally motivated to get good grades, but that's what it was for me." Diane expanded on this matter and said, "maybe some of them don't have parents to push them or . . . maybe the schools are not equal." She also speculated, "maybe, you know, they've got in their mind that they can't succeed because they're a minority and they don't try, you know, no one there to tell them 'You can do it, it doesn't matter who you are.'"

Whites from the Detroit metro area used the meritocratic frame as extensively as college students. For instance Jim, a thirty-year-old computer software salesperson from a privileged background, explained in the following way his opposition to affirmative action:

> I think it's unfair top to bottom on everybody and the whole process. It often, you know, discrimination itself is a bad word,

right? But you discriminate everyday. You wanna buy a beer at the store and there are six kinda beers you can get, from Natural Light to Sam Adams, right? And you look at the price and you look at the kind of beer, and you . . . *it's a choice.* And a lot of that you have laid out in front of you, which one you get? Now, should the government sponsor Sam Adams and make it cheaper than Natural Light because it's brewed by someone in Boston? That doesn't make much sense, right? Why would we want that or make Sam Adams eight times as expensive because we want people to buy Natural Light? And it's the same thing about getting into school or getting into some place. And universities it's easy, and universities is a hot topic now, and I could bug you, you know, Midwestern University I don't think has a lot of racism in the admissions process. And I think Midwestern University would, would agree with that pretty strongly. So why not just pick people that are going to do well at Midwestern University, pick people by their merit? I think we should stop the whole idea of choosing people based on their color. It's bad to choose someone based on their color; why do we, why do we enforce it in an institutional process?

Since Jim posited hiring decisions are like market choices (choosing between competing brands of beer), he embraced a laissez-faire position on hiring. The problem with Jim's view is that discrimination in the labor market is alive and well (e.g., it affects black and Latino job applicants 30 to 50 percent of the time) and that most jobs (as many as 80 percent) are obtained through informal networks.[25] Jim himself acknowledged that being white is an advantage in America because "there's more people in the world who are white and are racist against people that are black than vice versa." However, Jim also believes that although blacks "perceive or feel" like there is a lot of discrimination, he does not believe there is much discrimination out there. Hence, by upholding a strict laissez-faire view on hiring and, at the same time, ignoring the significant impact of past and contemporary discrimination in the labor market, Jim can safely voice his opposition to affirmative action in an apparently race-neutral way.

"Nothing Should Be Forced upon People": Keeping Things the Way They Are

A central tenet of liberal democracies is that governments should intervene in economic and social matters as little as possible because the "invisible hand of the market" eventually balances states of disequilibrium. A corollary of this tenet, and part of the American mythology, is the idea that social change should be the outcome of a rational and democratic process and not of the government's coercive capacity.[26] During the Jim Crow era, the belief that racial change should happen through a slow, evolutionary process in "peoples' hearts" rather than through governmental actions was expressed in the phrase "you cannot legislate morality." [27] This old standpoint has been curiously reformulated in the modern era to justify keeping racial affairs the way they are. These ideas appeared occasionally in discussions on affirmative action, but most often in discussions about school and residential integration in America.

Sonny, a student at MU, explained in typical fashion her position on whether school segregation is the fault of government, whites, or blacks. As almost all the students, Sonny first stated her belief that school integration is in principle a good thing to have: "In principle, yeah, I think that's a good idea because like with, like with people interacting, they will understand each other better in future generations." But Sonny also, as most students, was not too fond of government attempts to remedy school segregation or, in her words, "I, I don't— I mean, it should be done if people want to do it. If people volunteer for it, and they want that part of their lives, then they should do it, but the government should not force people to bus if they don't want that." When asked to clarify her stance on this matter, she added, "I don't think the government should impose any legislation thinking that it will

change people's hearts because people have to change them on their own. You can't force them to say 'Well, OK, now that I have to bus my kid there, I like it.'"

DAS respondents were as adamant as students in arguing that it is not the government's business to remedy racial problems. For example, Lynn, a human resources manager in her early fifties, explained why there has been so little school integration since the 1954 *Brown v. Board of Education* decision:

> I don't and that's another one. *I do not believe in busing.* The reason I don't believe in busing, you know, I said I don't. I didn't encourage my children to play with the neighborhood kids. I still felt that going to school in your community was the key to developing a child's sense of community and I still believe that. One of the reasons, another reason I moved from where I was [was] that I didn't want my children to be bused. I didn't want to have them got on a bus, especially me working. So I don't think that is an answer. I think the answer is education and helping people learn to make a life for themselves and, you know, any type of social program that interacts, that provides interaction between races I think is excellent. But I'm just not a busing person.

Lynn wants equal opportunity in education as well as community schools, a position that sounds perfectly reasonable. However, one would expect Lynn to support doing something to make sure that communities throughout America are diverse, a policy that other things being equal would guarantee school integration. Yet, Lynn took a very strong laissez-faire, antigovernment intervention stance on this matter. Lynn answered as follows the question, "America has lots of all-white and all-black neighborhoods. What do you think of this situation?"

> I don't have a problem with all-white and all-black neighborhoods if that's the choice of the people, the *individuals.* But, if it's *forced* either way, if I'm a black person and I've come into the neighborhood

and I want to live here and selectively denied that option, that's wrong. But, again, there still has to be some type of social interaction for growth and if the social interaction takes place then, the cross-integration will take place, I think.

When pressed about what she thought could be done specifically to increase the mixing of the races in neighborhoods, Lynn restated that this could only be achieved "through educating (people) and encouraging businesses." Lynn was not alone in having this abstract view on school and neighborhood integration. Only one of the white respondents who opposed busing in the interviews (69.7 percent of whites opposed busing in the survey) provided a specific proposal that if implemented would increase residential as well as school integration.[28]

Individual Choice or an Excuse for Racial Unfairness and Racially Based Choices?

Individualism[29] today has been recast as a justification for opposing policies to ameliorate racial inequality because they are "group based" rather than "case by case." In addition, the idea of individual choice is used to defend whites' right to live and associate primarily with whites (segregation) and for choosing whites exclusively as their mates. The problem with how whites apply the notion of individualism to our present racial conundrum is that a relation of domination-subordination still ordains race relations in the United States (see chapters 1 and 4 in my *White Supremacy and Racism in the Post–Civil Rights Era*). Thus, if minority groups face group-based discrimination and whites have group-based advantages, demanding individual treatment for all can only benefit the advantaged group.[30] And behind the idea of people having the right of making their own "choices" lays the fallacy of racial pluralism—the false assumption that all racial groups have the same power in the American polity. Because whites have more power, their unfettered, so-called individual choices help reproduce a form of white supremacy in neighborhoods, schools, and society in general.

Lynn, a human resources manager, used the notion of individualism in a very curious way. Although Lynn expressed her support for affirmative action because "there's still a lot of discrimination," she thinks that "there isn't as much discrimination as there used to be." Lynn also acknowledged white males have advantages in society and said "the white male is pretty much instilled" and "very much represses . . . um, people and other minorities." Nevertheless, when it came to the possibility of affirmative action affecting her, Lynn said:

> Um, because affirmative action is based on a group as a whole, but when it comes down to the individual, like if affirmative action were against me one time, like it would anger me. I mean, because, you know, *I* as an individual got ripped off and, you know, getting a job.

DAS respondents also used individualism to justify their racial views and race-based preferences. For example, Mandi, a registered nurse in her thirties, said she had no problems with neighborhood segregation. She justified her potentially problematic position by saying that people have the right to choose where and with whom they live.

> Umm, I think that people select a neighborhood to live in that they are similar to and people, you know, whatever similarities they *find* [*louder voice*], you know, it's race, economical level, religion, or, you know, whatever. When you are looking at somebody you don't know what, what denomination they are or what political preference they have, but you can tell right off in race. I think that they choose to live in a neighborhood that is their race.

Naturalization: Decoding the Meaning of "That's the Way It Is"

A frame that has not yet been brought to the fore by social scientists is whites' naturalization of race-related matters. Although the naturalization frame was the least used frame of color-blind racism by respondents in these two projects, about 50 percent of DAS respondents and college students used it, particularly when discussing school or neighborhood matters, to explain the limited contact between whites and minorities, or to rationalize whites' preferences for whites as significant others. The word "natural" or the phrase "that's the way it is" is often interjected to normalize events or actions that could otherwise be interpreted as racially motivated (residential segregation) or racist (preference for whites as friends and partners). But, as social scientists know quite well, few things that happen in the social world are "natural," particularly things pertaining to racial matters. Segregation as well as racial preferences are produced through social processes and that is the delusion/illusion component of this frame.

The importance and usefulness of this frame can be illustrated with Sara, a student at MU who used the frame on three separate occasions. Sara, for example, used the frame to answer the question on black self-segregation.

Hmm, I don't really think it's a segregation. I mean, I think people, you know, spend time with people that they are like, not necessarily in color, but you know, their ideas and values and, you know, maybe their class has something to do with what they're used to. But I don't really think it's a segregation. I don't think I would have trouble, you know, approaching someone of a different race or color. I don't think it's a problem. It's just that the people that I do hang out with are just the people that I'm with all the time. They're in my organizations and stuff like that.

Sara also used the naturalization frame to explain the paltry level of school integration in the United States.

Well, I also think that, you know, where you are in school has to do with the neighborhood that you grow up in and, like, I grew up in mainly all-white communities so that community was who I was going to school with. And if that community had been more black, then that would be, I guess, more integrated and that would be just fine. I don't know if there's any way you can change the places in which people live because

I think there *are* gonna be white communities and there are gonna be black communities and, you know, I don't know how you can get two communities like in the same school system.

The interviewer followed up Sara's answer with the question, "Why do you think there are white communities and black communities?" Sara's answer was: "Maybe like I said before, if people like to be with people that they're similar with and it means, you know—well, I don't think it has anything to do with color. I think it has to do with where they. . . ." Sara did not complete her thought as a light seems to have clicked on in her mind. She then proceeded to change her answer and acknowledged that race has a bearing on how people select neighborhoods: "Well, I guess it does [*laughs*]." The interviewer asked Sara if she thought her parents would move into an almost all-black neighborhood. Sara employed all sorts of rhetorical maneuvers . . . to defend her parents by conveying the idea that racial considerations would have never been a criterion for selecting a neighborhood.

Finally Liz, a student at SU, suggested that self segregation is a universal process or, in her own words: "I do think they segregate themselves, but I don't necessarily think it's on purpose. I think it's that, you know, *we all try to stay with our own kind* so, therefore, you know, *they get along better with their own people* or whatnot [my emphasis]." By universalizing segregation as a natural phenomenon, Liz was able to justify even her own racial preference for white mates. When asked if she had ever been attracted to minority people, Liz said:

Um no, just because I wasn't really attracted to them, you know, I'm more attracted to someone that's like kinda more like me. But, you know, and I wouldn't say that, I mean, I like if he's good looking or not, you know, it's not that, it's just I'm more attracted to someone white, I don't know why [*laughs*].

DAS respondents naturalized racial matters too, but in general did it in a more crude fashion. For instance, Bill, a manager in a manufacturing firm, explained the limited level school integration:

> I don't think it's anybody's fault. Because people tend to group with their own people. Whether it's white or black or upper-middle class or lower class or, you now, upper class, you know, Asians. People tend to group with their own. Doesn't mean if a black person moves into your neighborhood, they shouldn't go to your school. They should and you should mix and welcome them and everything else, but you can't force people together. If people want to be together, they should intermix more. [*Interviewer: OK. So the lack of mixing is really just kind of an individual lack of desire?*] Well, individuals, its just the way it is. You know, people group together for lots of different reasons: social, religious. Just as animals in the wild, you know. Elephants group together, cheetahs group together. You bus a cheetah into an elephant herd because they should mix? You can't force that [*laughs*].

Bill's unflattering and unfitting metaphor comparing racial segregation to the separation of species, however, was not the only crude way of using the naturalization frame. For example, Earl, a small-time contractor in his fifties, explained segregation in a matter-of-fact way.

> I think you're never going to change that! I think it's just kind of, you know, it's going to end up that way. . . Every race sticks together and that's the way it should be, you know. I grew up in a white neighborhood, you know, most of the blacks will live in the black neighborhood. [*interviewer: So you don't think there's anything wrong?*] No. Well, they can move, they still have the freedom to move anywhere they want anyway.

A significant number of DAS respondents naturalized racial matters in a straightforward manner. For example, Jim, a thirty-year-old computer software salesperson for a large company, naturalized school segregation as follows:

> Eh, you know, it's more of the human nature's fault. It's not the government's fault, right? The government doesn't tell people where to live. So as people decide where to live or where to move into or where they wanna feel comfortable, [they] move to where they feel comfortable. We all kinda hang out with people that are like us. I mean, you look at Detroit, we have a Mexican village, why do we have a Mexican village? Why aren't Mexican people spread out all over on metro Detroit? Well, they like being near other Mexican people; that way they could have a store that suited them close by the, you know, those sort of things probably together. So, it's more human nature that I would blame for it.

Despite whites' belief that residential and school segregation, friendship, and attraction are natural and raceless occurrences, social scientists have documented how racial considerations affect all these issues. For example, residential segregation is created by white buyers searching for white neighborhoods and aided by realtors, bankers, and sellers.[31] As white neighborhoods develop, white schools follow—an outcome that further contributes to the process of racial isolation. Socialized in a "white habitus" . . . and influenced by the Eurocentric culture, it is no wonder whites interpret their racialized choices for white significant others as "natural." They are the "natural" consequence of a white socialization process.[32]

"They Don't Have It Altogether": Cultural Racism

Pierre-André Taguieff has argued that modern European racism does not rely on an essentialist interpretation of minorities' endowments.[33] Instead, it presents their presumed cultural practices as fixed features (hence he labels it as the "biologization of racism") and uses that as the rationale for justifying racial inequality. Thus, Europeans may no longer believe Africans, Arabs, Asian Indians, or blacks from the West Indies are biologically inferior, but they assail them for their presumed lack of hygiene, family disorganization, and lack of morality.[34] This cultural racism frame is very well established in the United States. Originally labeled as the "culture of poverty"[35] in the 1960s, this tradition has resurfaced many times since, resurrected by conservative scholars such as Charles Murray and Lawrence Mead, liberals such as William Julius Wilson, and even radicals such as Cornel West.[36] The essence of the American version of this frame is "blaming the victim," arguing that minorities' standing is a product of their lack of effort, loose family organization, and inappropriate values.

Since there is little disagreement among social scientists about the centrality of this frame in the post–Civil Rights era, I focus my attention on highlighting what this frame allows whites to accomplish. I begin my illustration of this frame with two, clear-cut examples of college students who used it. The students agreed with the premise of the question, "Many whites explain the status of blacks in this country as a result of blacks lacking motivation, not having the proper work ethic, or being lazy. What do you think?" The first student is Kara, an MU student.

> I think, to some extent, that's true. Just from, like, looking at the black people that I've met in my classes and the few that I knew before college, not like they're— I don't want to say waiting for a handout, but to some extent, that's kind of what I'm like hinting at. Like, almost like they feel like they were discriminated against hundreds of years ago, now what are you gonna give me? You know, or maybe even it's just their background, that they've never, like maybe they're the first generation to be in college, so they feel like just that is enough for them.

The second quote is from Kim, a student at SU:

> Yeah, I totally agree with that. I don't think, you know, they're all like that, but, I

mean, it's just that if *it* wasn't that way, why would there be so many blacks living in the projects? You know, why would there be so many poor blacks? If they worked hard, they could make it just as high as anyone else could. You know, I just think that's just, you know, they're raised that way and they see what their parents are like so they assume that's the way it should be. And they just follow the roles their parents had for them and don't go anywhere.

When cultural racism is used in combination with the "minimization of racism" frame, the results are ideologically deadly. If people of color say they experience discrimination, whites, such as Kara and Kim, do not believe them and claim they use discrimination as an "excuse" to hide the central reason why they are behind whites in society: their presumed "laziness."

Although Kara and Kim used the cultural racism frame in a crude form, most students did not. They articulated their culture of poverty views in a gentler, at times even "compassionate," way. For example, Ann, a student at WU, inserted the frame in her answer to a question about why blacks as a group fare worse than whites academically.

> Um, I guess I would have to say primarily family structure. Maybe it's not [being] able to support the child and, you know, in school and really encourage. It might be that it's a single-parent family and it's necessary [for them] to get out and get a job, you know, a full-time job and work a part-time job and still try to go to school. Maybe it's not encouraged as much for, like long term, it's mainly survival. I don't know, something, income; if the family is really skimping by it would be really far fetched, well, it wouldn't be probably necessarily the first thing that a child from [such] a family would think of, you know, expensive college rather than paying the rent, you know what I mean [*laughs*]? So, I mean, you know, the priorities are different.

Although Ann's arguments seem "reasonable" (poor people may have a different set of priorities than other people based on their economic situation), her explanation is wanting because it avoids mentioning the institutional effects of discrimination in the labor, housing, and educational markets and the well-documented[37] impact that discrimination has on middle- and upper-middle-class blacks. More significantly, Ann's failure to recognize how old- and new-fashioned discrimination affects blacks' life chances is not an argumentative slip, but the way in which most whites construe the situation of blacks, as evidenced by how respondents in both samples used similar arguments in answering questions about blacks' status.

This kinder and gentler way of using the cultural frame was the preferred choice of students. For example, Jay, a student at WU, explained as follows why blacks have a worse overall standing than whites:

> Hmm, I think it's due to lack of education. I think because if they didn't grow up in a household that afforded them the time to go to school and they had to go out and get jobs right away, I think *it* is just a cycle [that] perpetuates things, you know. I mean, I can't say that blacks can't do it because, obviously, there are many, many of them [that] have succeeded in getting good jobs and all that.

Jay, as most whites, admits to the "exceptional black." However, Jay immediately goes back to the gentle cultural argument:

> So it's possible that the cycle seems to perpetuate itself because—I mean, let's say they go out and get jobs and they settle down much earlier than they would normally if they had gone to school and then they have kids at a young age and they—these kids—have to go and get jobs and so.

How did DAS respondents use this cultural frame? They relied on this frame as often as students did but were significantly more likely to use it in a straightforward and crude manner. The following two cases exemplify how most DAS respondents used this frame. First is Isaac, an

engineer in his fifties. In response to the question comparing blacks' and whites' overall standing, Isaac argued that few blacks have the education to work as engineers. This led to the following exchange between Isaac and the interviewer:

> *Interviewer: So you feel maybe there's a lack of interest in education that black people have?*
>
> *Isaac: They want to get a short cut to make money. There's no urgency to get education. They want to make, to get money faster than whites. They don't want to take the time to get educated. They want to get money fast.*
>
> *Interviewer: So they also don't put the time into developing their educational skills?*
>
> *Isaac: Yeah the way you learn, the way you grow, is the way you become.*
>
> *Interviewer: Some people say that minorities are worse off than whites because they lack motivation, are lazy, or do not have the proper values to succeed in our society. What do you think?*
>
> *Isaac: Right now I think our minorities are lazy. They don't have the patience to keep going.*

Ian, the manager of information security at an automotive company, explained why blacks are worse off than whites as follows:

> The majority of 'em just don't strive to do anything, to make themselves better. Again, I've seen that all the way through. "I do this today, I'm fine, I'm happy with it, I don't need anything better." Never, never, never striving or giving extra to, to make themselves better.

Ian's perception of blacks as lazy emerged from his understanding of blacks as culturally deficient. This view was clearly expressed in his response to the question, "Do you think that the races are naturally different?"

> Well I think that genes have something, some play in this, but I think a lot of it is

past history of the people and the way they're brought up. You look at Chinese, if you're gonna get ahead in China, you've gotta be very intellectual and you've gotta be willing to, uh, to fight for everything that you're gonna get. Ja-Japan is the same way. For a kid just to get into college, they gonna take two years of going through entrance exams to get in. Then you kinda look at the blacks' situation. It's like, "Well, because of slavery, I ought to be given this for nothing, so I don't have to work for it, just give it to me." So culture and their upbringing is the big part of this.

Although Ian came close to the old biological view ("Well, I think genes have something, some play in this"), overall he made use of the cultural frame to explain blacks' status (Asians do well because they "gotta be intellectual," whereas blacks believe that because of slavery they do not have to work).

Minimization of Racism: Whites' Declining Significance of Race Thesis

When William Julius Wilson published *The Declining Significance of Race* in 1978, he made many whites in academia feel good about themselves. Wilson's main claim—that class rather than race was the central obstacle for black mobility—was an argument that had been brewing among whites for quite a while. Yet, whites believe that discrimination exists. For example, when white and black respondents in the DAS survey were given the statement, "Discrimination against blacks is no longer a problem in the United States," a high proportion of *both* groups (82.5 percent of whites and 89.5 percent of blacks) "disagreed" or "strongly disagreed" with that statement. Although whites and blacks believe discrimination is still a problem, they dispute its salience as a factor explaining blacks' collective standing. Thus, in response to the more specific statement, "Blacks are in the position that they are today as a group because of present day discrimination," only 32.9 percent of whites "agreed" or "strongly agreed" (compared to 60.5 percent of blacks). This means that in general whites believe discrimination has all but disappeared, whereas

blacks believe that discrimination—old and new—is alive and well.

College students were more likely than DAS respondents to give lip service to the existence of discrimination. Because students for this study were taking social science courses at the time of the interviews, they may have become sensitized to the significance of discrimination as well as to the new character of contemporary discrimination. However, despite this sensitization, few believed discrimination and institutionalized racism are the reasons minorities lag behind whites in this society. In general, the students articulated their declining significance of race thesis in three ways. A plurality (18 of 41) used an indirect strategy of denial set by one of the following two phrases, "I am not black" or "I don't see discrimination" . . . , others (9 of 41) minimized racism directly, and yet others (7 of 41) argued minorities make things look racial when they are not.

The following example illustrates how students used the indirect strategy of denial. The response of Mary, a student at SU, to the statement, "Many blacks and other minorities claim that they do not get access to good jobs because of discrimination and that when they get the jobs they are not promoted at the same speed as their white peers," was:

> I think before you really start talking about hiring practices and promotion practices, you have to look at credentials. I mean, you know, I've only really had one job. I worked for a general contractor so it was basically me in the office all day with him, my boss. But I, in fact, you have to look at credentials. I mean, I don't know if, you know, a white person gets a job over a minority, I can't sit here and say "Well, that's discrimination" because I don't know what the factors were. This person got a master's degree versus a bachelor's degree, or more in-depth training than this person, you know? I mean, I definitely do not doubt that [discrimination] happens, that minorities get passed over for promotions and that they are not hired based on their race. I have absolutely no doubt that it happens.

I think that before you can sit there and start calling a lot of things discrimination, you need to look into the background, the credentials behind it.

Rather than stating "I don't believe minorities experience discrimination," Mary suggested they may not get jobs or promotions because they lack the credentials. And although Mary, as most whites, recognizes discrimination exists ("I definitely do not doubt that [discrimination] happens"), she clearly believes most claims are bogus ("I think that before you can sit there and start calling a lot of things discrimination, you need to look into the background, the credentials behind it").

The next example is of students who minimized the significance of racism directly. Andy, a student at WU, answered a question on whether discrimination is the central reason why blacks are behind whites today by saying, "I think they do." Yet his answer was wanting, since he could not provide a meaningful explanation of how discrimination affects minorities' life chances. More importantly, Andy's answers to the other questions minimized the salience of racism. For instance, his answer to the question of whether or not discrimination affects the chances of minorities getting jobs and promotions was, "I think that there's probably less than it used to be, but that it still happens. It's just in isolated places or, you know, it happens in different places, but in most jobs, I think it probably does not happen." When asked to elaborate, Andy stated he believes the reason why blacks do not get good jobs is, "if anything, it's probably education" because "you can't apply for certain jobs without a lot of education."

The last example is of students who argued blacks make situations racial that are not. Janet, an SU student, answered all the questions on discrimination by denying that discrimination is a salient factor in minorities' life chances and suggesting alternative interpretations. For instance, Janet's answer to the same question, on whether or not discrimination is the central reason why blacks lag behind whites was: "I would say it depends on the individual. I'm sure there are some . . . that do and others [that] don't, so. . . ." When asked to clarify, she said, "Right. But I would say for the most part, most of them don't unless they make it out to be

the case." When the interviewer asked Janet if she thought most claims of discrimination by minorities were a perception issue, she replied: "If they looked at it as a different way or something, they might see—might not see it as racism, you see what I'm saying? [*Interviewer: You are saying that they are seeing more than is actually out there?*] Right." When asked about discrimination in jobs, Janet answered in a blunt fashion.

I would say that's a bunch of crap [*laughs*]. I mean, if they're qualified, they'll hire you and if you are not qualified, then you don't get the job. It's the same way with, once you get the job, if you are qualified for a promotion, you'll get the promotion. It's the same way with white, blacks, Asians, whatever. If you do the job, you'll get the job.

DAS respondents used similar argumentative strategies to deny the significance of discrimination. The strategy they used the most was direct minimization (18 of 66), followed by outright denial (13 of 66), stating that minorities make things racial (11 of 66), and indirect minimization (3 of 66). The remaining respondents (20 of 66) include a few who sincerely believe discrimination is important . . . and others who denied the centrality of discrimination in their own peculiar way.

The first case exemplifies DAS respondents who minimized the significance of discrimination directly. Joann, a poor white woman in her fifties who works in a large chain store, answered the direct discrimination question by stating, "I don't see any in the store." When asked about discrimination against minorities in general, Joann said:

I don't think it's as bad as it was. It probably needs improvement. What [society] needs is a knowledgeable crew and I think that is the truth there. I think that the work will have to be done up continually until we're all one big happy family. [*Interviewer: Do you foresee that happening?*] It wouldn't surprise me. My great granddaughter might marry a black, I don't know. *I have no idea!*

The next case is an example of respondents who denied discrimination outright. It is worth pointing out that all the DAS respondents who used this strategy were from working- or lower-class backgrounds. Scott, a twenty-three-year-old drafter for a mechanical engineering company, answered the direct question on discrimination as follows:

> I don't—nowadays I don't, I don't really feel that way, I really don't at all. Maybe like when I was younger I would notice it, but right now I don't really feel that there's too much segregation anymore. If it is because of the person, you know, from their past experience. And, I mean, if you got a record, you're not gonna go too far, you know. So then they might feel like "Just being held back just because, you know, Just 'cause I'm black."

The interviewer followed up Scott's answer with the question, "So you don't think that discrimination is a factor in most blacks lives nowadays?" His answer was: "It might be just because of their past and their attitudes toward life. But if you just took it as everyday life and just went with it, no, I don't feel it at all, I don't see it. I don't practice it and my friends, all my friends [don't] practice it."

Next are examples of respondents who argued blacks make things racial that are not. Sandra, a retail salesperson in her early forties, explained her view on discrimination as follows:

> I think if you are looking for discrimination, I think it's there to be *found*. But if you make the best of any situation, and if *you don't use it as an excuse*. I think sometimes it's an excuse because people felt they deserved a job, whatever! I think if things didn't go their way I know a lot of people have tendency to use prejudice or racism as whatever as an *excuse*. I think in some ways, *yes* there is people who are prejudiced. It's not only blacks, it's about Spanish, or women. In a lot of ways there [is] a lot of *reverse* discrimination. It's just what you wanna make of it.

Finally, I provide an example of respondents who used the indirect minimization strategy. Dave, an engineer in his forties who owns a smalltime employment agency, answered the direct question on discrimination by paying: "[*laughs*] I don't know any blacks so I don't know. But, in general, I probably have to say it's true." When asked for clarification, Dave stated:

> Oh that's a hard one to just, well, I guess it comes down to stereotypes though like I said earlier. It just—some people may try to say that some blacks don't work as hard as whites. So, in looking for a job they may feel like they didn't get the job because they have been discriminated against because they were black, that's very possible. That may not really be, but as a person, they make the assumption.

Dave explained blacks' inferior status as compared to whites by suggesting that it "really comes down to individuals" and that he has "especially noted that if you want a job, there's jobs out there." In this reply Dave intimates his belief that racial discrimination is not a factor in the labor market since "there's jobs out there."

The last case is of DAS respondents who did not fit the overall strategies and used sui generis arguments to deny the significance of racial discrimination. Henrietta, a transsexual school teacher in his fifties, said the following in response to the question on discrimination:

> [*9-second pause*] Trying to be an unbiased observer because as a transsexual I am discriminated against. I think if people act responsible they will not be discriminated against. People who are acting irresponsible, in other words, demanding things, ah, "I need this" or "You did this because of my skin color" yeah, then they will be discriminated against. People who are intelligent present themselves in a manner that is appropriate for the situation and will not be discriminated against.

Thus, Henrietta suggests that blacks who experience discrimination deserve so because they act irresponsibly or complain too much.

Conclusion

In this reading I illustrated how whites use the four central frames of color-blind racism, namely, abstract liberalism, naturalization, cultural racism, and minimization of racism. These frames are central to the views of whites, young (college-student sample) and old (DAS respondents), and serve them as an interpretive matrix from where to extract arguments to explain a host of racial issues. More significantly, together these frames form an impregnable yet elastic wall that barricades whites from the United States' racial reality. The trick is in the way the frames bundle with each other, that is, in the wall they form. Whites, for example, would have a tough time using the abstract liberalism frame if they could not resort to the minimization of racism frame as well. Precisely because they use these frames the way children use building blocks, whites can say things such as "I am all for equal opportunity, that's why I oppose affirmative action" and also say "Everyone has almost the same opportunities to succeed in this country because discrimination and racism are all but gone." And if anyone dares to point out that in this land of milk and honey there is a tremendous level of racial inequality—a fact that could deflate the balloon of color blindness—they can argue this is due to minorities' schools, lack of education, family disorganization or lack of proper values and work ethic. In short, whites can blame minorities (blacks in particular) for their own status.

But what if someone pokes holes in whites' color-blind story by pointing out that whites live mostly in white neighborhoods marry and befriend mostly whites, interact mostly with whites in their jobs, and send their children to white schools or, if they attend mixed schools, make sure they take most of their classes with white children. Whites have two discursive options to avoid the potentially devastating effects of these arguments. They can resort to the abstract liberalism frame and say something like "I support integration, but I do not believe in forcing people to do anything that they do not want to do" or "People have the right to make their own individual choices and no one can interfere." Alternatively, they can naturalize the whiteness in which they live ("Blacks like living with blacks, and whites

like living with whites . . . it's a natural thing"). As I documented in this reading, whites mix and match arguments as they see fit. Therefore, someone can say, "Segregation is a natural thing" but also say that "I believe that no one has the right of preventing people from moving into a neighborhood." These frames then form a formidable wall because they provide whites a seemingly nonracial way of stating their racial views without appearing irrational or rabidly racist.

But if the ideological wall of color-blind racism were not pliable, a few hard blows would suffice to bring it down. That is why the flexibility of the frames is so useful. Color-blind racism's frames are pliable because they do not rely on absolutes ("All blacks are . . ." or "Discrimination ended in 1965"). Instead, color-blind racism gives some room for exceptions ("Not all blacks are lazy, but most are") and allows for a variety of ways of holding on to the frames—from crude and straightforward to gentle and indirect. Regarding the former, almost every white respondent in these studies mentioned the exceptional black ("Well, Robert, my black friend, is not like that"), agreed in principle with racially progressive notions ("I believe that school integration is great because we can learn so much from each other" or "Gee, I wish I could see the day when we have the first black president"), or even joined Martin Luther King Jr. in the dream of color blindness ("In two or three generations race will disappear and we will all just be Americans"). Regarding the latter, whites used the color-blind frames in crude ways displaying resentment and anger toward minorities ("Blacks are God-damned lazy") or in compassionate ways ("It is terrible the way they live in those neighborhoods with those schools, without fathers, with crime just around the corner . . . it saddens me whenever I see all that on TV").

The pliability of the color-blind wall is further enhanced by the style of color blindness. For instance, if whites find themselves in a rhetorical bind, such as having disclosed a personal taste for whiteness or a dislike for blackness, they can always utter a disclaimer such as, "I am not prejudiced," or "If I ever fall in love with a black person, the race thing will never be an obstacle for us getting together." They can tiptoe around the most dangerous racial minefields because the stylistic elements of color blindness provide them the necessary tools to get in and out of almost any discussion.

Notes

1. John Dollard, *Caste and Class in a Southern Town,* 2d ed. (New York: Doubleday, 1949).

2. For discussions on the "defensive beliefs" that supported Jim Crow, see Dollard, *Caste and Class;* Gunnar Myrdal, *An American Dilemma: The Negro Problem and Modern Democracy* (New York: Harper Brothers, 1944); Allison Davis et al., *Deep South* (Chicago: University of Chicago Press, 1941); and Charles S. Johnson, *Patterns of Negro Segregation* (New York: Harper Brothers, 1943).

3. This is taken from the title of conservative commentator Dinesh D'Souza's book, *The End of Racism: Principles for a Multiracial Society* (New York: Free Press, 1995). This book is, among other things, a crude example of color-blind racism.

4. J. B. Thompson, *Studies in the Theory of Ideology* (Cambridge, UK: Polity, 1984).

5. All ideologies aspire to be hegemonic, to rule the hearts of rulers and ruled. However, only those that incorporate elements of the "common sense" of the oppressed (albeit in partial and refracted manner) can truly become hegemonic.

6. See John Gray, *Liberalism* (Minneapolis: University of Minnesota Press, 1986).

7. All these quotes are from *The Communist Manifesto.* See David McLellan, ed., *Karl Marx: Selected Writings* (London: Oxford University Press, 1982). For a detailed intellectual assault at the farce of liberalism, see Karl Marx and Frederick Engels, *The German Ideology* (New York: International, 1985).

8. For a marvelous discussion of this point and of "racial capitalism," see Cedric J. Robinson, *Black Marxism: The Making of the Black Radical Tradition* (Chapel Hill: University of North Carolina Press, 2000).

9. Good examples of this trend are Andrea T. Baumeister, *Liberalism and the "Politics of Difference"* (Edinburgh: Edinburgh University Press, 2000), and Patrick Neal, *Liberalism and Its Discontents* (New York: New York University Press, 1997). Although Baumeister skillfully

shows the tensions in traditional liberal discourse that foreshadow some of today's debates and provides a reasonable philosophical resolution based on "value pluralism," she fails to point out the exclusionary character of liberalism and the Enlightenment. Neal's account produces two interesting modifications of liberalism: the idea that liberal states cannot be neutral and the notion of "modus vivendi liberalism," which entails an open liberal approach to social issues. Yet, like Baumeister, Neal is silent about the racism of the founding fathers of liberalism and the meaning of their racial exclusions for today's liberal project.

10. Charles W. Mills, *The Racial Contract* (Ithaca, N.Y.: Cornell University Press, 1997), 27.

11. The quotes by Kant and Voltaire as well as the views of Mill on slavery and colonialism can be found in chapter 2 of David Theo Goldberg, *Racist Culture* (Cambridge, UK: Blackwell, 1993). See also Zygmunt Bauman, *Modernity and Ambivalence* (Ithaca, N.Y.: Cornell University Press, 1991).

12. Richard Bellamy, "Liberalism," in *Contemporary Political Ideologies,* edited by Roger Eatwall and Anthony Wright (Boulder, Cob.: Westview, 1993), 23–49.

13. See Dana D. Nelson, *National Citizenship: Capitalist Citizenship and the Imagined Fraternity of White Men* (Durham, N.C.: Duke University Press, 1998), and chapter 5 in Howard Zinn, *A People's History of the United States* (New York: HarperCollins, 1980).

14. From a social movements perspective, "liberal groups are those that attempt to reform social systems for the purpose of giving all groups equal opportunities." Margaret L. Andersen, *Thinking about Women: Sociological Perspectives on Sex and Gender* (New York: Macmillan, 1988), 299.

15. For a scathing critique of color-blind "radicals" such as Todd Gitlin, Michael Tomasky, Richard Rorty, Jim Sleeper, Barbara Epstein, and Eric Hobsbawm, see chapter 4 in Robin D. G. Kelley, *Yo' Mama's Disfunktional: Fighting the Culture Wars in Urban America* (Boston: Beacon, 1997).

16. The classic statement on the subject still is William Ryan, *Blaming the Victim* (New York: Vintage, 1976).

17. Charles S. Johnson, *Racial Attitudes: Interviews Revealing Attitudes of Northern and Southern White Persons, of a Wide Range of Occupational and Educational Levels, toward Negroes* (Nashville,

Tenn.: Social Science Institute, Fisk University, 1946), 153.

18. It is important to note that cultural racism was part and parcel of European and American racisms. My point is that this theme has supplanted biological racism in importance and effectiveness.

19. Katherine S. Newman, *Declining Fortunes: The Withering of the American Dream* (New York: Basic, 1993), 168.

20. James Byrd was a black man murdered by three white supremacist exconvicts in 1998 in Jasper, Texas.

21. High-level Texaco executives were caught on tape saying some racially insensitive things about blacks and other minorities a few years back, which led them to settle a lawsuit brought by minority employees accusing the company of racial discrimination in pay and promotion.

22. I borrow the phrase "reasonable racism" from Jody David Armour, *Negrophobia and Reasonable Racism* (New York: New York University Press, 1997).

23. The former label is used in the works of Lawrence Bobo and his coauthors . . . and the latter by Philomena Essed, in *Diversity: Gender, Color, and Culture* (Amherst: University of Massachusetts Press, 1996).

24. When the question at hand could be perceived as racial, white support declined significantly. Thus, for example, only 21 percent of whites agreed with the proposition to increase welfare spending.

25. The specific citations for these facts can be found in the introduction, or the reader can consult my chapter, coauthored with Amanda E. Lewis, "The 'New Racism': Toward an Analysis of the U.S. Racial Structure, 1960–1990s," in *Race, Nationality, and Citizenship,* edited by Paul Wong (Boulder, Cob.: Westview, 1999).

26. Bringing about social change in this country has never been a rational, civilized feat, particularly when racial considerations have been involved. Force and resistance have accompanied the most significant changes in America's political and racial order. We used force to achieve our independence from Britain, to keep the Union together, and to end state-sanctioned Jim Crow. An excellent little book on this subject is Irving J. Sloan, *Our Violent Past: An American Chronicle* (New York: Random House, 1970).

27. Southern sociologist Howard W. Odum took William Graham Sumner's idea of "mores" and suggested that racial conflicts must be solved through an evolutionary approach that he labeled "racial adjustments." In a similar vein, northern sociologist Robert E. Park argued that race contacts went through "race cycles" that ended in racial assimilation. See Howard W. Odum, *American Social Problems* (New York: Holt, 1939), and Robert E. Park, *Race and Culture* (Glencoe, Ill.: Free Press, 1950).

28. One respondent suggested a tax incentive policy to stimulate residential integration.

29. Despite its elitist origins in American history (see chapter 5 in Zinn, *A People's History of the United States),* the notion of individualism has been used by social reform movements such as the Jacksonian democracy movement of the nineteenth century, the Civil Rights Movement of the 1950s and 1960s ("one man, one vote"), and the Woman's Suffrage Movement of the early 20th century ("one person, one vote") to advance truly inclusive democratic agendas.

30. David Ingram, *Group Rights: Reconciling Equality and Difference* (Lawrence: University Press of Kansas, 2000).

31. For a review, see chapter 4 in my *White Supremacy and Racism in the Post–Civil Rights Era* (Boulder, Colo.: Rienner, 2001).

32. On all these matters, see Beverly Daniel Tatum, *"Why Are All the Black Kids Sitting Together in the Cafeteria?: And Other Conversations about Race"* (New York: Basic, 1997).

33. Most of the work of this important French scholar has not been published in English. A few of his pieces have appeared in *Telos* and, fortunately, the University of Minnesota Press translated his *La Force du prédjugé: Essai sur lc racisme et ses doubles.* Pierre-André Taguieff, *The Force of Prejudice: Racism and Its Doubles* (Minneapolis: University of Minnesota Press, 2001). See also Pierre-André Taguieff, ed., *Face au racisme, Tome II: Analyse, hypothèses, perspectives* (Paris: La Découverte, 1991).

34. See my " 'This Is a White Country': The Racial Ideology of the Western Nations of the World-System," *Research in Politics and Society* 6, no. 1 (1999): 85–102.

35. The culture of poverty argument was formally developed by anthropologist Oscar Lewis. His claim was that the poor develop a culture based on adaptations to their poverty status, which is then transmitted from generation to generation and becomes an obstacle for moving out of

poverty. Although Lewis formulated his thesis as a class-based one, because the characters in his famous books, *The Children of Sánchez* (1961) and *La Vida* (1965), were Mexican and Puerto Rican, respectively, it was almost impossible not to interpret his argument as especially pertinent for understanding minorities' well-being in America. Lewis's argument was roundly condemned by many of his contemporaries, but it stuck in scholarly policy circles as well as among conservative politicians and a few "liberals" such as Senator Patrick Moynihan.

36. Charles A. Murray, *Losing Ground: American Social Policy, 1950–1980* (New York: Basic, 1984); Lawrence M. Mead, *Beyond Entitlement: The Social Obligations of Citizenship* (New York: Free Press, 1986); William Julius Wilson, *The Truly Disadvantaged: The Inner City, the Underclass, and Public Policy* (Chicago: University of Chicago Press, 1987); Cornel West, *Race Matters* (Boston: Beacon, 1993).

37. See Sharon Collins, *Black Corporate Executives: The Making and Breaking of a Black Middle Class* (Philadelphia: Temple University Press, 1997); Ellis Cose, *The Rage of a Privileged Class* (New York: HarperCollins, 1995); and Joe R. Feagin and Melvin Sikes, *Living with Racism: The Black Middle Class Experience* (Boston: Beacon, 1994).

19

Excerpts from
The Myth of the Model Minority: Asian Americans Facing Racism

RosALIND S. CHOU AND JOE R. FEAGIN

In the fall of 2001, R.W., a young Chinese American, bludgeoned and strangled her mother. While her mother lay dead on the floor, she covered her and called the police, confessing her crime. This school valedictorian is an accomplished musician who had begun her education at a prestigious Ivy League school and graduated with honors from her southern university. Her crime received little local notice. Only one full-length newspaper article was published, and after her indictment she was barely mentioned. This tragic incident hit home for the first author because she is acquainted with the family, which was one of the few Chinese families in her hometown. The incident sent shock waves through the Asian American community of which they were part. R.W.'s failure to stay at her first college program, an elite institution, may well have contributed to her several suicide attempts and eventually to the homicide. She may now live out her years in a mental institution, and family and friends are left stressed and wondering "why?"[1]

On the outside, R.W. appeared to be a model student at her historically white educational institutions. Her demeanor was quiet, which likely suggested to white outsiders only a stereotyped Asian passivity. Thus, even with numerous warning signs of mental illness, she was never seen as a concern. The white-created "successful model minority" stereotype made it difficult for non-Asians around her to see her illness and encouraged silence among the Asian Americans who knew her.

The 2007 shootings of students and staff at Virginia Tech University by Cho Seung-Hui suggest somewhat similar issues. A Korean American student at a historically white institution, Cho was viewed by outsiders as unusually quiet, and although he demonstrated numerous warning signs of mental illness, he was mostly ignored, especially by those with the most authority to take action. Not much has been revealed about his life growing up in a Virginia suburb except that he was an "easy target" at school and endured substantial teasing from white children. When younger, he struggled to learn English, which made it difficult to adapt in his predominantly white environment. Cho seems to have lived as an outcast and in social isolation. Given his parents' success in business and his sister's success as a Princeton graduate, Cho and his family seem to outsiders like a proverbial model family that "lifted themselves up by their bootstraps" and thus are living the American dream.[2] Yet, these stereotyped images and Cho's own struggle to achieve may well have worked against his mental health. As the interviews in this book reveal, this young Asian American's struggle to make it in a predominantly white world was not unique in being both very invisible and excruciatingly tormented.

Our argument here is *not* that Asian Americans are distinctively prone to serious mental illness or violence. Rather, we accent in this book the institutionally racist situations in which Asian Americans find themselves—those highly pressured situations that create much stress and deeply felt pain. One major societal problem is that Asian Americans are typically viewed and labeled as "model minorities" by outsiders, especially by whites with power over them. This highly stereotyped labeling creates great pressure to conform to the white-dominated culture, usually in a one-way direction.

In recent books titled *YELL-Oh Girls! and Asian American X,* several hundred young Asian Americans discuss their often difficult lives. These young people recount recurring experiences with coercive pressures to assimilate into the prestigious white end of the prevailing U.S. racial status continuum—to white ways of dress, speech, goal attainment, thinking, and physical being. Most are torn between the culture of immigrant parents or grandparents, with its substantial respect for Asianness, and the burdensome pressures of a white-controlled society. As one young Korean American who grew up in a white community puts it, the dominance of whites explains the "thoughtless ways white Americans often inhabit a sense of entitlement and egocentric normality."[3] Like other Asian Americans, these young people report racialized mistreatment, ranging from subtle to

covert to overt discrimination. The successful minority image does not protect them from the onslaughts of discriminatory whites.

Our research here attempts to give voice to numerous Asian Americans as they describe and assess their discriminatory and other life experiences. Using in-depth interviews, we collected accounts of Asian American experiences in everyday life, including incidents of racial hostility and discrimination, responses of assimilation and conformity, and ways that individuals, families, and communities cope with and resist white-imposed racism. Our interviews indicate that Asian Americans suffer from much discrimination, ranging from subtle to blatant, at the hands of whites. The interviews show that, even after Herculean efforts to conform to the dominant racial hierarchy and to the white framing of them— efforts seeking to achieve the fabled American dream—Asian Americans frequently feel stressed, embattled, isolated, and inadequate. Many passively accept that they must hide or abandon their home culture, values, and identity to prevent future mistreatment. Significant educational and economic achievements do not effectively shield them. Some analysts have argued that Asian Americans are "lucky" that they do not face the "invisibility" and negative imagery that African Americans experience.[4] This view of Asian Americans is incorrect. The Asian American experience with racial hostility and discrimination is also very negative and largely untold, and such an untold experience is indeed a very *harmful* invisibility.

The Reality of Systemic Racism

Traditional analytical approaches to immigrants and immigration to the United States mostly emphasize various assimilation orientations and processes. Some assimilation analysts have argued that all incoming immigrant groups will eventually be fully integrated into U.S. society, including the more distinctive ethnic and racial groups. Many social science researchers view the adaptation of Asian immigrants and their children to U.S. society since the 1960s through an assimilation lens, one similar to that used for assessing the adaptations of past and present European immigrants. Numerous assimilation analysts have argued that Asian American groups are on their way to full integration into the "core society," by which they mean white middle-class society. For example, Paul Spickard has argued that by the 1980s whites no longer viewed Japanese Americans "as very different from themselves, and that fact is remarkable."[5] To make this case, these analysts usually focus on Asian American progress in areas such as educational and income achievements. However, this limited definition of success in adaptation in the United States is mostly white-generated and ignores other important areas of Asian American lives.

Indeed, the fact that Asian immigrants and their children are heavily pressured to conform to a white-imposed culture, racial frame, and racial hierarchy—and suffer from much racial hostility and discrimination—is usually left out of most assessments of Asian immigrants and their children and grandchildren. Here we go beyond the typical assimilation approach and accent a systemic racism perspective. Since at least the seventeenth century, European Americans have created a complex North American society with a foundation of racial oppression, one whose nooks and crannies are generally pervaded with racial discrimination and inequality. Near their beginning, the new European colonies in North America institutionalized white-on-Indian oppression (land theft and genocide) and white-on-black oppression (centuries of slavery), and by the mid-nineteenth century the Mexicans and the Chinese were incorporated as dispossessed landholders or exploited workers into the racial hierarchy and political-economic institutions of a relatively new United States. Our systemic racism approach views racial oppression as a foundational and persisting underpinning of this society. From the beginning, powerful whites have designed and maintained the country's economic, political, and social institutions to benefit, disproportionately and substantially, their own racial group. For centuries, unjust impoverishment of Americans of color has been linked to unjust enrichment of whites, thereby creating a central racial hierarchy and status continuum in which whites are generally the dominant and privileged group.[6]

Since the earliest period of colonization, moreover, European Americans have buttressed this hierarchical and entrenched system of unjust material enrichment and unjust material impoverishment with legal institutions and a strong white racial *framing* of this society. In the past and in the present, whites have combined within this pervasive white frame a good many racist stereotypes (the cognitive aspect), racist concepts (the deeper cognitive aspect), racist images (the visual aspect), racialized emotions (feelings), and inclinations to take discriminatory action. This white racial frame is old, enduring, and oriented to assessing and relating to Americans of color in everyday situations. Operating with this racial frame firmly in mind, the dominant white group has used its power to place new non-European groups, such as Asian immigrants and their children, somewhere in the racial hierarchy whites firmly control—that is, on a white-to-black continuum of status and privilege with whites at the highly privileged end, blacks at the unprivileged end, and other racial groups typically placed by whites somewhere in between. This white racist framing of society is now a centuries-old rationalizing of the racism systemic in this society.

Our concept of *systemic* racism thus encompasses a broad range of racialized realities in this society: the all-encompassing white racial frame, extensive discriminatory habits and exploitative actions, and numerous racist institutions. This white-generated and white-maintained system entails much more than racial bigotry, for it has been from the beginning a material, structural, and ideological reality.

The Exploitation and Oppression of Asian Immigrants

While some Asian Americans today trace family histories back to nineteenth-century immigrants, most have a more recent immigration background. Older members of the families of R.W. and Cho are relatively recent immigrants, and thus these families are typical. Changes in immigration laws since 1965 have allowed a substantial increase in immigration from Asian and Pacific countries, and thus Asian/Pacific Islander Americans have become the fastest growing U.S. racial group. In 1940, they made up less than 1 percent of the population, but by the late 2000s their numbers had grown to more than 14 million, about 5 percent of the population.

The largest Asian/Pacific Islander group is Chinese American, totaling more than 3.3 million. In numbers, Filipino Americans are not far behind, at 2.8 million. Japanese, Korean, Asian-Indian, and Vietnamese Americans constitute other large Asian-origin groups.

Much scholarship on Asians in North America has addressed Asian experiences with racial hostility and discrimination over a long history of immigration. Scholars have examined more than 150 years of Asian immigration and shown, to take one example, that Asian workers have regularly been pitted against white workers. The first major immigrant group was Chinese. Between the 1850s and 1880s, Chinese contract laborers migrated in large numbers to the West Coast to do low-wage work in construction and other economic sectors. The preference that white employers had for Chinese workers fueled tensions in the racial hierarchy, often pitting white workers against Asian workers. After whites' racist agitation and exclusionary legislation stopped most Chinese immigration, Japanese immigrants were recruited by employers to fill the labor demand on white-run farms and construction projects. (By the late nineteenth century the Chinese were viewed by whites as the stereotyped "yellow peril," a term apparently coined by German Kaiser Wilhelm II.) The racially motivated termination of Japanese immigration in 1907–1908 spurred white employers to recruit other Asians and Pacific Islanders (such as Filipinos) to fill labor needs on the U.S. mainland and in Hawaii. This employers' strategy of using immigrant workers from Asia and the Pacific Islands to replace white and other native-born workers has continued in some U.S. workplaces to the present.[7]

In the nineteenth and early twentieth centuries, Asian and Pacific Islander immigrants and their children—mostly Chinese, Japanese, and Filipino—suffered extremely blatant and institutionalized racism. They were negatively positioned, and imaged, by whites as "black" or "near black" on the dominant socioracial continuum. Powerful whites imposed a strong racial framing on these subordinated immigrants, with its barbed racist stereotypes and images. Reviewing the history, Robert Lee has commented on white constructions of hated "Orientals": "Six images—the pollutant, the coolie, the deviant, the yellow peril, the model minority, and the gook—portray the Oriental as an alien body and a threat to the American national family."[8] For example, from the 1850s onward the first Asian Americans, the Chinese, were stereotyped by white officials and commentators as "alien," "dangerous," "docile," and "dirty." At that time, such negative images were not new to the white racist framing of Americans of color. They had precedents in earlier white views of African Americans and Native Americans.[9]

In 1896, even as he defended some rights for black Americans as the dissenter in the *Plessy v. Ferguson* Supreme Court decision upholding legal racial segregation, Justice John Marshall Harlan included this racial argument: "There is a race so different from our own that we do not permit those belonging to it to become citizens of the United States. Persons belonging to it are, with few exceptions, absolutely excluded from our country. I allude to the Chinese race."[10] In the first decades of the 1900s, this negative view was applied to other Asian Americans as well. U.S. government agencies have played a central role in defining racial groups. Thus, in the important 1922 *Ozaw* case, the U.S. Supreme Court ruled that Asian immigrants were *not white* and thus could not become citizens. The "not white," "alien race," and related racist notions had been generated by elite whites in earlier centuries in stereotyping and naming Native Americans and African Americans as an early part of a white racist framing for a "civilized" Eurocentric society. These ideas have persisted for four centuries, with at least 150 years now of application to Americans of Asian descent.[11]

Racist Framing and Large-Scale Discrimination

New ways of circulating the racist framing of Americans of color were developed by innovative white entrepreneurs in the early decades of the twentieth century. These included a burgeoning advertising industry making use of many magazines and radio stations, as well as the developing movie industry. White advertisers, cartoonists, and movie makers commonly portrayed Chinese, Japanese, and other Asian/Pacific Islanders as outsiders or villains, who were often crudely stereotyped as "inscrutable," poor at English, criminal, and dangerous.

For example, between the early 1900s and the 1940s, hostile visual images and stereotypes of "buck-toothed Japs" were prominent in U.S. media, contributing to anti-Japanese and other anti-Asian hostility in the United States. With extensive media support and facilitation, white commentators and political leaders spoke of an alleged alien character and immorality of Japanese Americans, sometimes using vicious apelike images.[12] These very negative images and other white racist framing of the Japanese and Japanese Americans contributed greatly to the international tensions leading to World War II, especially the recurring conflicts between the growing U.S. empire and the expanding Japanese empire, both in and around the rim of the Pacific Ocean.[13] This white racist framing of the Japanese also contributed to extreme discriminatory actions undertaken by the U.S. government: the imprisonment of Japanese Americans in U.S. concentration camps during World War II. The government's rationale for the camps was openly racist. In 1943, West Coast military commander General John DeWitt articulated what most whites then believed when he argued that "A Jap's a Jap. The Japanese race is an enemy race, and while many second- and third-generation Japanese born on U.S. soil, possessed of U.S. citizenship, have become 'Americanized,' the *racial strains* are undiluted."[14] With no evidence, mainstream commentators and leading politicians, all white, asserted there were enemy agents in this "alien" Asian population. Significantly, one main reason for the existence of this "alien" population was the discriminatory U.S. law prohibiting Asian immigrants from becoming citizens.

Negative framing of Asian Americans during that era can be observed in a 1940s *Time* magazine article on "How to Tell Your Friends from the Japs." Here the white author offered a biologized and racist explanation of supposed differences between the Japanese and the Chinese—a task taken on because China and the United States had become allies against Japan in World War II:

> Virtually all Japanese are short. Japanese are likely to be stockier and broader hipped than short Chinese. Although both

have the typical epicanthic fold on the upper eyelid, Japanese eyes are usually set closer together. The Chinese expression is likely to be more placid, kindly, open; the Japanese more positive, dogmatic, arrogant. Japanese are hesitant, nervous in conversation, laugh loudly at the wrong time. Japanese walk stiffly erect, hard heeled. Chinese, more relaxed, have an easy gait, sometimes shuffle.[15]

The *Time* editors who published this wildly stereotyped statement probably thought they were saying something positive about the Chinese. Yet, this is a clear example of the arrogant power of *group definition* that has long been part of the dominant white group's historical framing of Americans of color.

However, the white view of the Chinese and of Koreans became more negative with the new conflicts that developed after World War II. With the rise of state communism in China in the late 1940s, Cold War stereotyping again positioned the Chinese, and by implication Chinese Americans, as "dangerous Orientals" in many white minds. Moreover, the U.S. intervention in Korea in 1950 was accompanied by emergency congressional legislation that gave the U.S. attorney general the authority to set up new concentration camps for Koreans, Chinese, and other Asians who might be perceived to be a domestic threat. The U.S. intervention in Korea, and later in Vietnam, further perpetuated an intensive racist stereotyping and framing of Asians and Asian Americans in the minds of many white and other non-Asian Americans.[16]

Even in this crude stereotyping we see a certain ambiguity in white views. Over the past century, whites have sometimes positioned Asian Americans at the bottom end of the dominant racial hierarchy, while at other times they have positioned at least some Asian groups in a more intermediate status. From the late 1940s to the end of legal segregation in the 1960s, whites were sometimes perplexed as to where to place Asian Americans in the racial hierarchy, as we observe in this account from a Japanese American speaking about experiences during the legal segregation era:

> I stopped at a McDonald's in Mississippi and there were two lines, one for whites

and the other for blacks, well, "coloreds." I stood there confused about which line to join. I stood there and decided to go in the colored line because there was nobody in it and I could get my food faster. When I got up to the counter the guy told me "hey you can't use this line, get in that other line." The line for whites was long and I had gone about halfway up when this guy says, "Hey, you can't be in this line, get in the other line." I just stood there and thought, "Ah, what am I!?"[17]

This recollection indicates not only the stereotyping and subordination of Asian Americans but also a white confusion about Asian Americans being closer to whiteness or blackness in the dominant racial hierarchy. This placement has become ever more problematic for white Americans with the dramatic growth in the Asian American population since the 1960s.

White Racial Framing: Anti-Asian Imagery Today

Today whites and others still apply numerous elements of an old anti-Asian framing to Asian Americans. As we will see throughout this book, many whites hold inconsistent views of Asian Americans. They commonly view Asian Americans as high achievers and "model minorities," but will often discount the meaning of those achievements as being done by exotic "foreigners," "nerds," or social misfits. For example, some research studies show that Asian American students are often viewed positively by whites, but mainly in regard to educational achievements. A recent summary of research concludes that most stereotypes of Asian American students "are negative, such as non-Asians' notions that Asians 'don't speak English well,' 'have accents,' and are 'submissive,' 'sneaky,' 'stingy,' 'greedy,' etc."[18]

Subtle and blatant stereotyping of Asians and Asian Americans still predominates in many areas of U.S. society. Consider just a few recent examples. Recently, the Adidas company was challenged by civil rights groups for making shoes that had a negative caricature of a buck-toothed, slant-eyed Asian as a logo. In another case, a large pictorial cartoon concerning fund-raising investigations of Democratic Party leaders appeared on the cover of an issue of the prominent magazine *National Review.* The cover showed caricatures of then president Bill Clinton and his wife Hillary Clinton as slant-eyed, buck-toothed Chinese in Mao suits and Chinese hats—images suggesting old stereotyped images of Asian Americans' characteristics. Since the nineteenth century, white cartoonists, political leaders, and media commentators have portrayed Chinese and other Asian Americans in such stereotyped terms, often to express a fear of the "yellow peril." When confronted, the *National Review's* white editor admitted these were Asian caricatures but refused to apologize. Such reactions, and the fact that there was little public protest of the cover other than from Asian American groups, suggest that such crude images and other associated stereotypes remain significant in a dominant racial framing of people of Asian descent.[19]

Recently, a U.S. animation company made a cartoon *(Mr. Wong)* and placed at its center an extreme caricature of a Chinese "hunchbacked, yellow-skinned, squinty-eyed character who spoke with a thick accent and starred in an interactive music video titled *Saturday Night Yellow Fever.*"[20] Again Asian American and other civil rights groups protested this anti-Asian mocking, but many whites and a few Asian Americans inside and outside the entertainment industry defended such racist cartoons as "only good humor." Similarly, the makers of a recent puppet movie, *Team America: World Police,* portrayed a Korean political leader speaking gibberish in a mock Asian accent. One Asian American commentator noted the movie was "an hour and a half of racial mockery with an 'if you are offended, you obviously can't take a joke' tacked on at the end."[21] Moreover, in a recent episode of the popular television series *Desperate Housewives* a main character, played by actor Teri Hatcher, visits a physician for a medical checkup. Shocked that the doctor suggests she may be going through menopause, she replies, "OK, before we go any further, can I check these diplomas? Just to make sure they aren't, like, from some med school in the Philippines." This stereotyping was protested by many in the Asian and Pacific Islander communities.

Although sometimes played out in supposedly humorous presentations, continuing media-reproduced stereotypes of Asians and Pacific Islanders include old white-framed notions of them as odd, foreign, un-American, relatively unassimilated, or culturally inferior. Noteworthy in these accounts is the connection of recent anti-Asian stereotyping, mostly by whites, to the old anti-Asian stereotyping of the nineteenth and early twentieth centuries, For the majority of non-Asian Americans, particularly those who control the media, certain negative images of Asians and of Asian Americans (especially Asian immigrants and their children) blend together in a common anti-Asian racial framing. The strong protests of Asian American civil rights and other organizations to all such racialized stereotyping and mocking underscore this important point.

Anti-Asian stereotypes are still frequently encountered in everyday discourse. Asian Americans, including children, often note that they face mocking language and other racially hostile words, such as these: "Ching chong Chinaman sitting on a rail, along came a white man and snipped off his tail"; "Ah so. No tickee, no washee. So sorry, so sollee"; and "Chinkee, Chink, Jap, Nip, zero, Dothead, Flip, Hindoo."[22] Recently, a disc jockey on a Toledo, Ohio, radio station called Asian restaurants and made mock Asian commentaries, such as "ching, chong, chung" and "me speakee no English." Similarly, a CBS talk show host mocked an Asian Excellence Awards ceremony by playing a fake excerpt with "Asian men" saying things like "Ching chong, ching chong, ching chong." Comedian Rosie O'Donnell also used a repeated "ching chong" to mock Chinese speech on her ABC talk show. One striking reaction to the O'Donnell comment was hundreds of blogger entries on Internet websites that defended her comments and (erroneously) asserted the comments were *not* racist.[23]

To modern ears such language mocking and other Asian mocking may seem novel, but it is actually an old part of the white racist framing of Asian Americans. White English speakers on the West Coast developed this mocking in the mid- to late-nineteenth century as their way of making fun of the English-Chinese speech of Chinese workers, as well as of racializing them. An early 1900s ragtime song goes: "Ching, Chong, Oh Mister Ching Chong, You are the king of Chinatown. Ching Chong, I love your sing-song."[24]

Anthropologist Jane Hill has shown how in the United States such mocking of language links to systemic racism. In particular, Hill has studied the extensive mocking of Spanish, such as the making up of fake Spanish words and phrases. Mock Spanish—common on birthday cards, on items in gift shops, and in commentaries from board rooms to the mass media—is mostly created by college-educated Americans, especially white Americans. Similar language mocking has long been directed at African Americans and Asian Americans. "Through this process, such people are endowed with gross sexual appetites, political corruption, laziness, disorders of language, and mental incapacity."[25] Language mocking is not just light-hearted commentary of no social importance, because such mocking usually is linked to societal discrimination against the racialized "others." While native speakers of languages such as French or German do not face serious discrimination because of their accents when they speak English, Asian Americans and other Americans of color do often face such discrimination. As one scholar has underscored, "It is crucial to remember that it is not all foreign accents, but only accent linked to skin that isn't white, or which signals a third-world homeland, evokes such negative reactions."[26]

Model Minority Imagery: An Apparent Contradiction?

Today, frequent anti-Asian mocking and caricaturing signal the continuing presence of a strong racist framing of Asians and Americans of Asian descent. Some people, especially whites, may play down the significance of such racist framing and instead argue that a strong positive image of Asian Americans has been asserted by whites. They note that whites, especially in the media and politics, regularly broadcast positive reports on achievements of Asian Americans in schools and workplaces. From this point of view, one should note, an Asian American group has "succeeded" in U.S. society when its attainments on a limited number of quantitative indicators of occupation, education, and income are at least comparable to those of white Americans. A superficial reading of these indicators leads many to view virtually all Asian Americans as successful and thus as not facing significant racial barriers in this society. Such analyses may be correct in regard to a certain type of success measured by particular socioeconomic indicators for Asian American groups as a whole, but not in regard to the socioeconomic problems faced by large segments within these groups or in regard to the various forms of racial discrimination that most Asian Americans still face in their daily lives.

Take Japanese Americans, for example. In 2005, Japanese Americans were more likely to hold managerial or professional jobs than their white counterparts, and their unemployment rate was less than that for whites. Median income for their families was substantially more than for white families nationally, and a smaller percentage fell below the federal poverty line than did whites. However, Japanese American workers mostly live in the West, where there is a relatively high cost of living. We should note too that in California the difference in median incomes between Japanese American families and white families is reversed.

Per capita income for Asian American groups is also generally lower than that for whites, who average smaller families. In addition, many Asian immigrants and their children, especially those from Southeast Asia and rural backgrounds, have experienced much poverty and other serious economic difficulties over the past few decades.[27]

Moreover, although Japanese Americans and certain other Asian American groups have achieved significant socioeconomic success, they still face a substantial array of subtle and overt acts of discrimination, as we demonstrate fully in later chapters. Research studies reveal some of this picture. For example, when researchers have examined Japanese and other Asian American workers in comparison with white workers with similar jobs, educational credentials, and years of job experience, the Asian American workers are found to be paid less on average and are less likely to be promoted to managerial positions.[28] In addition, Asian American workers often face exclusion from numerous positions in business, entertainment, political, and civil service areas, regardless of their qualifications and abilities. Japanese and other Asian Americans periodically report a glass ceiling in corporations or exclusion from business networks. About 5 percent of the population, Asian Americans are far less than 1 percent of the members of the boards of Fortune 500 firms; one tabulation revealed that just *one* Asian American headed up a Fortune 500 firm not founded by an Asian American. White executives periodically assert that in their firms Asian Americans are best as technical workers and not as executives. Given this stereotyped view, Asian Americans are often hired as engineers, computer experts, and technicians, but no matter what their qualifications are they are rarely considered for management. Moreover, given this discrimination, many younger Asian Americans have pursued scientific and technical educations and rejected the fine arts, humanities, and social sciences, areas they might have preferred. Career choices are thus influenced by both past and present discrimination. In addition, many business opportunities in corporate America remain limited by persisting anti-Asian sentiment.[29]

In spite of much data contradicting their commonplace view, numerous social scientists and media commentators have regularly cited the educational and economic "success" of a particular Asian American group, one typically described as the "model minority," as an indication that whites no longer create significant racial barriers for them.[30] We can pinpoint when this model myth was likely first constructed. In the mid-1960s, largely in response to African American and Mexican American protests against discrimination, white scholars, political leaders, and journalists developed the model minority myth in order to allege that all Americans of color could achieve the American dream—and not by protesting discrimination in the stores and streets as African Americans and Mexican Americans were doing, but by working as "hard and quietly" as Japanese and Chinese Americans supposedly did. This model image was created not by Asian Americans but by influential whites for their public ideological use.[31] One example is a 1960s U.S. *News & World Report* article entitled "Success Story of One Minority Group in U.S." This major media article praised the hard work and morality of Chinese Americans, and its analysis strongly implied that if black Americans possessed such virtues, it would not be necessary to spend "hundreds of billions to uplift" them.[32]

For decades now, prominent commentators and politicians have cited the educational or economic success of Asian Americans as proof that they are fully melded into the U.S. "melting pot," with many "ascending above exclusion" by "pulling themselves up by their bootstraps."[33] Today, variations of this model stereotype remain pervasive, and leading politicians, judges, journalists, and corporate executives assert them regularly.[34] Even other Americans of color have sometimes been conned by this model minority view and declared it to be so true that governments do not need to be concerned with the discrimination against Asian Americans. For example, black Supreme Court nominee Clarence Thomas, at his Senate confirmation hearings, asserted that Asian Americans have "transcended the ravages caused even by harsh legal and social discrimination" and should not be the beneficiaries of affirmative action because they are "overrepresented in key institutions."[35]

One of the contemporary ironies of such uninformed views is that private and government reports in recent years have shown that today educational success varies among the Asian American groups and, indeed, that many Asian Americans in numerous groups still face significant obstacles to academic success, in some cases more than in the past.[36] For example, one savvy higher education journalist recently noted that numerous articles in college newspapers have used Asian Americans as the point of humor, but their portrayals usually feed the "model minority" myth. Asian American students are seen as an "invasion" and their demeanors as "inscrutable." On these college campuses lies a "continued pattern of Asian American students being (a) the butt of such jokes, basically the punch line; (b) that the jokes are heavily laden with racial stereotypes; and (c) that these . . . essays reveal volumes about racial relationships, tensions, and perceptions of Asian American students as all being, in some way, the same—foreigners, math and science nerds, and all around different from the regular average college student."[37]

Assimilation and the "Model Minority" Imagery

Several researchers—mostly Asian American—have challenged the rosy view of Asian American success in the complex assimilation process forced on them in the United States. These researchers have shown that Asian immigrants and their children have long faced discrimination and other serious difficulties in adapting to U.S. society. Some have also explored how the societal conditions of Asian Americans are racialized.[38]

Several social scientists have focused on Asian American adaptation to the dominant culture and society using traditional assimilation theories. For example, drawing on interviews with young Asian American professionals, Pyong Gap Min and Rose Kim report that they have highly assimilated socially and culturally, with significant friendship ties to middle-class whites and significant assimilation to white folkways. They found that these Asian American professionals are bicultural, with strong assimilation to "American culture," but expressing strong national-origin or pan-Asian identity as well. An earlier study of Korean immigrants by Won Moo Hurh and Kwang Chung Kim reported similar findings, in that their respondents demonstrated what they term "additive" or "adhesive" adaptation—that is, assimilating substantially to the new economy and society, yet maintaining a strong sense of their ethnic and racial identities. While both research studies discuss difficult identity choices of their respondents, like most contemporary researchers looking at immigrant assimilation they do not examine in depth the harsh racial realities surrounding these choices. In this still-racist society, personal or group identity choices by Asian immigrants and their children are severely limited by the racial identity typically *imposed* on them by white outsiders.[39]

In a study of second-generation Chinese and Korean Americans, social scientist Nazli Kibria has also explored the formation of identities. Assessing the adaptation of Asian immigrants and their children, she distinguishes between an "ethnic American" model and a "racial minority" model of assimilation. The old ethnic assimilation model, asserted by scholars and others, has set the framework for Asian assimilation into the core society, yet creates significant problems because it assumes that an ethnic immigrant group is white. In Kibria's view, as Asian immigrants and their children accent a new umbrella identity of "Asian American," they are updating the old ethnic assimilation model to include their racial minority experience. While Kibria recognizes that her respondents are set apart, discriminated against, and stereotyped as foreigners or model minorities, she keeps her analysis of the perpetrators of this stereotyping and discrimination rather vague and provides no in-depth analysis of the systemic racism context in which these Asian Americans are forced to adapt. Her Chinese and Korean respondents report on some "lessons about race," "race socialization," and not being accepted "by others," yet in her analysis Kibria does not assess the central role of white discriminators or the white-imposed framing and hierarchy in forcing such hard lessons.[40]

One of the few analysts of Asian Americans to explicitly name white discriminators as central is sociologist Mia Tuan. Interviewing nearly one hundred third- and later-generation Chinese and Japanese Americans, she found that although most were well assimilated into the dominant culture, most also had a strong sense of a racialized identity because whites constantly imposed the identity of "Asian foreigner" on them. They reported being caught between feeling perpetually outside, as "forever foreigners," and sometimes being given greater privileges by whites than other people of color. They spoke too of the difficulty they had in viewing themselves in terms of their national origin when they were constantly being defined in "generically racial terms" as "Asian Americans" or as "Orientals." Though offering a probing analysis that assesses well racial-ethnic identity struggles and recognizes whites as having a privileged status, Tuan does not in our view provide enough in-depth analysis of the anti-Asian racism that surrounds, and imposes oppressive predicaments on, Asian Americans.[41]

Several researchers have specifically targeted the model minority stereotype. One early analysis was that of the innovative legal scholar Man Matsuda, who suggested that Asian Americans might be positioned as a "racial bourgeoisie," a racial middle status between whites and other people of color. This protects the white position at the top by diffusing hostility toward them and sets up Asian Americans to be a "scapegoat during times of crisis."[42] In a more recent analysis, Vijay Prashad has shown how Asian Americans are termed model minorities and thus come "to be the perpetual solution to what is seen as the crisis of black America." Prashad does not specifically identify and assess the white agents who have created this crisis for black America. He does note a certain "Orientalism" among white Americans—the view that many have of Asia being "static and unfree" in contrast to a "dynamic and free" Western civilization. Holding to this framing, whites frequently stereotype Asian Americans negatively as exotic, barbaric, or primitive. Prashad adds that for Asian Americans "it is easier to be seen as a solution than as a problem. We don't suffer genocidal poverty and incarceration rates in the United States, nor do we walk in fear and a fog of invisibility."[43] Ironically, he here evokes part of the model minority stereotype yet does not note that this stereotype creates an invisibility cloak hiding severe problems of racism faced regularly by Asian Americans.

The pioneering legal scholar Frank Wu has done much to dispel model minority stereotyping. In his work he has explained the benefits that whites enjoy because of that labeling. Reviewing the long history of anti-Asian discrimination, he notes that "non-Asian Americans can discriminate against Asian Americans by turning us into noncitizens, either officially by prohibiting even legal long-term residents from naturalizing or informally by casting doubt on our status. The alien land laws, passed to drive Japanese immigrants out of farming, are the prime example." While he accents well the many decades of anti-Asian discrimination, Wu regularly uses vague terms such as "non-Asian Americans" and thereby skirts around using the word "whites" for those doing such intense discriminating. While in many of his analyses Wu recognizes how anti-Asian racism is institutionalized, at times he seems to play down certain aspects of white racism: "Other than among a few idealists, as a nation we accept discrimination on the basis of citizenship as necessary. But except among a few extremists, as a society we reject discrimination on the basis of race as immoral."[44]

Wu here seems to neglect the societal reality that *many* whites still do find it acceptable to engage in racial discrimination against Americans of color, yet may find it no longer fashionable to discriminate openly or assert racist views publicly.

Clearly, these often-pioneering Asian American scholars have moved social science analysis of the adaptive barriers faced by Asian Americans in very important directions. Still, some of them tend to avoid explicitly naming and analyzing fully the role of whites (especially elite whites) as central protagonists in creating anti-Asian racism today—often preferring instead to name vague social agents such as "non-Asians," "the law," "the government," or "the larger society" as generators of contemporary racism. Such analytical practices can be found as well among many scholars researching the racialized situations of other Americans of color. They too are often reluctant to name whites specifically as the key actors in past or present dramas of U.S. racism.[45]

One of the few researchers to examine in critical detail the contemporary impact of *systemic racism* on Asian American communities is sociologist Claire Jean Kim. Examining periodic conflicts between Korean American merchants and African American patrons in a few cities, Kim shows that these conflicts should be understood in the context of whites' long-term discriminatory actions against both groups. She illustrates how Asian immigrants have come to be positioned, mainly by *white* actions, between white urbanites and black urbanites, and how these Asian Americans are given a negative evaluation by whites on both the axis of superior/inferior racial groups and the axis of insiders/foreigners. Such intergroup conflict involves more than just stereotyping by African Americans or Korean Americans of the other group, but instead reflects the white-imposed racial hierarchy and its effects on both racially subordinated groups. Like other Americans of color, Asian Americans serve as pawns in the racially oppressive system maintained at the top by whites.[46] White Americans may prize Asian Americans relative to African Americans in certain limited ways so as to ensure white dominance over both. Whites may place or consider Asians as "nearer to whites," a relative valorization, because of Asian American achievements in certain educational and economic areas. Yet this middling status is possible only because other Americans of color, such as African Americans or Mexican Americans, have been allowed fewer opportunities by whites. Whites' use of Asian Americans as a measuring stick for other Americans of color is highly divisive, for it pits groups of color against each other, as well as isolates Asian American from white Americans.

Kim underscores well the price paid for becoming the white-proclaimed model of a successful minority: "By lumping all Asian descent groups together and attributing certain distinctively 'Asian' cultural values to them (including, importantly, political passivity or docility), the model minority myth sets Asian Americans apart as a distinct racial-cultural 'other.' Asian Americans are making it, the myth tells us, but they remain exotically different from Whites Beneath the veneer of praise, the model minority myth subtly ostracizes Asian Americans."[47] In this process of exoticizing and of civic ostracism, whites treat Asian Americans as foreigners not fully assimilable to white culture and society. Exoticized and celebrated for docility, Asian Americans have relatively little political clout and as yet are less involved in the U.S. political process. As Kim's data demonstrate, this lack of political involvement at the local level is often not a voluntary choice but results from active discrimination and exclusion in the political realm by whites.

Discrimination persists in many institutional areas. Savvy scholar Gary Okihiro sums up the contemporary Asian American situation this way: Whites have "upheld Asians as 'near-whites' or 'whiter than whites' in the model minority stereotype, and yet Asians have experienced and continue to face white racism 'like blacks' in educational and occupational barriers and ceilings and in anti-Asian abuse and physical violence. This marginalization of Asians, in fact, within a black and white racial formation, 'disciplines' both Africans and Asians and constitutes the essential site of Asian American oppression."[48]

The Many Costs of Anti-Asian Racism

Conforming to the Hierarchy and Racial Frame

The omnipresent racial hierarchy and its rationalizing racial frame directly or indirectly affect most areas of the lives of those who live in U.S. society.

Whites are collectively so powerful that they pressure all immigrant groups, including those of color, to collude in the white racist system by adopting not only many white ways of doing and speaking, but also numerous stereotyped views and notions from the white racial frame. The white frame is all-encompassing and has infiltrated the minds both of native-born Americans and of European and other immigrants. By adopting the perspective of the dominant racial frame, earlier European immigrant groups, such as the Irish and the Italians, eventually secured a high position on the U.S. racial ladder and are now considered "white," but this has not been the case for darker-skinned groups such as those of African, Latin American, and Asian descent. Asian immigrants often have a chance at some socioeconomic mobility, but they, their children, and their grandchildren have not been awarded full acceptance by whites. Most whites expect the intermediate positions offered to many Asian Americans on the old racial status ladder to be valued by them, but, as later chapters will demonstrate, this middling position has typically come at the high price of conformity, stress, and pain—and often of abandoning much of a person's home culture and national-origin identity.

Generally, new immigrants quickly begin to conform to the dominant hierarchy and frame or else face significant emotional or economic punishment. On the one hand, they often try to conform well, which they generally view as a method to prevent discrimination targeting them. On the other, conforming is pressed hard on them as the targets of white-generated racism. The white racial frame ensures that those at the bottom of the racial order are repeatedly denigrated. In this situation fighting for one's dignity will sometimes mean that another individual or group will be pushed down and set up for failure. Vying for position in a preexisting racial order creates volatility and conflict. Groups of color are frequently pitted against each other for the title as "top subordinate," while whites as a group remain at the top.

The dominant white group and its elite stand in a position of such power that they can rate groups of color socially and assign them "grades" on a type of "minority report card." Whites thus give certain Asian American groups a "model minority" rating while other groups of color receive lower marks as "problem minorities." However, the hierarchical positions that whites are willing to give any group of color are always significantly below them on the racial ladder. Today, some media and scholarly discussions suggest that Asian Americans are now viewed as white or "honorary white" by most white Americans, yet this is not likely the case. In one recent research study, we gave 151 white college students a questionnaire asking them to place numerous racial and ethnic groups into "white" or "not white" categories. An overwhelming majority classified all the listed Asian American groups, including Japanese and Chinese Americans, as clearly *not white*. These well-educated, mostly younger whites still operate with the old racial hierarchy and racial status continuum in mind when they place individuals and groups of color into racialized categories.[49]

Impact on Mental Health

The previously cited incidents involving R.W. and Cho raise the issue of Asian American mental health in a dramatic way. Are these just isolated individual suffering from mental illness that involves only unique personal conditions? Cho does the reality of anti-Asian racism generate much everyday suffering for a large group and thereby contribute significantly to these conditions? Few researchers have probed Asian American mental health data in any depth. One mid-2000 study of Korean, Chinese, and Japanese immigrant youth examined acculturation to the core culture, but only briefly noted that some of these youth experience substantial "cultural stress, such as being caught between two cultures, feeling alienated from both cultures, and having interpersonal conflicts with whites."[50] Another study examined only Korean male immigrants and found some negative impact on mental health from early years of adjustment and some mental "stagnation" a decade so after immigration. Yet the researchers offered little explanation for the findings. One recent study of U.S. teenagers found that among various racial groups, Asian American youth had *by far* the highest incidence of teenager depression, yet the report on this research did *not* even assess the important of this striking finding.[51]

In the modest statistical analysis that exists, Asian American statistics of suicide and alcoholism stand out. Elderly Chinese American women have a suicide rate *ten times* that of their elderly white peers. Although Asian American students are only 17 percent of the Cornell University student body, they make up fully *half* of all completed suicides there. A study of Japanese American men who had been interned during World War II found that they suffered high rate of alcoholism and that 40 percent died before reaching the age of fifty-five.[52] Eliza Noh, a researcher who has done much research on suicide and depression issues for Asian American women, recently reported that among females aged fifteen to twenty-four, Asian Americans have the highest suicide rate of all racial groups. Suicide was found to be the second leading cause of death for these Asian American females. Noh concludes from the data that Asian American women live under greater pressures to achieve, including in education, than even their male counterparts, pressures that create the great stress underlying much depression and suicide. In a recent media report Noh has commented that "pressure from within the family doesn't completely explain the shocking suicide statistics for young women" and that "simply being a minority can also lead to depression." Yet she fails to pursue the implications of this last comment—the likely connection between their stress and depression and the racial hostility and discrimination they regularly face because of this white-imposed minority status. She does not put the necessary white face on the perpetrators of much of their everyday stress.[53] Indeed, in the relatively rare situations where such data on depression or suicide are examined, researchers and other commentators usually cite background ("Asian") cultural factors and culturally related pressures to achieve in education and the workplace as the reasons for Asian American mental health problems—and not their problems with the pressures of everyday racism.

Generally speaking, medical and social scientists have seriously neglected the costs of everyday racism for all Americans of color. A growing but modest research literature addresses some of its impact for African Americans. In the 1950s, Abraham Kardiner and Lionel Ovesey addressed the impact of extensive racial discrimination on African Americans in a book aptly titled *The Mark of Oppression.* They argued from their data that legal segregation significantly affected the mental health of African Americans. Self-esteem was constantly battered by everyday racism's onslaughts. In the 1960s, psychiatrists William Grier and Price Cobbs wrote on the impact of recurring discrimination on their African American patients. The discrimination they faced during legal segregation was again linked to their major physical and emotional problems. Recent research by Joe Feagin and Karyn McKinney involving in-depth and focus group interviews with African Americans found a similar array of physical and mental health problems stemming from everyday discrimination.[54] It seems likely that systemic racism today has a similar impact on Asian Americans. They endure racial hostility and discrimination by whites and must use much psychological maneuvering to function successfully in their lives. In later chapters, our respondents speak of the numerous defensive techniques that they use to deal with discriminatory events. Such psychological gymnastics are always burdensome to those who engage in them.

In a pathbreaking 1999 documentary film, *When You're Smiling,* communications scholar and movie maker Janice Tanaka provides a rare documentation of the heavy costs of racism for Asian Americans, specifically Japanese Americans. The documentary covers the racialized internment of Japanese Americans in World War II concentration camps, then focuses on the psychological effects of this internment on those imprisoned and on their children and grandchildren. In the film, third-generation Japanese Americans (the *Sansei*) share personal stories of pervasive white discrimination. Interviews with the Sansei found that most of their parents (the *Nisei*) were interned as youth in the wartime camps. The Nisei faced much overt and extreme racial oppression during and after World War II. They suffered much psychological trauma, and during and after the war they placed great pressure on themselves and their children to conform to white understandings and racial framing, as well as to the dominant racial hierarchy. (Their parents, the *Issei,* had already accented conformity as a strategy for dealing with white racism since the early

1900s.) Fearful of a recurrence of that extreme oppression, the Nisei responded with a conforming and high-pressure achievement orientation that would later get Japanese Americans labeled the first "model minority." In the documentary, one Sansei talks about how obsessed her family and the Japanese American community were with a local newspaper article that was published each spring. The article spotlighted all the academic scholars in local schools and listed where they planned to attend college. One interviewee said, "You always went to the good schools. Either Stanford, U C–Berkeley, or out of state."[55] Here we see the extraordinarily high expectations that the Japanese American community has long had for its children.

Second- and later-generation Japanese Americans have paid a heavy price for their substantial socioeconomic achievements. The effects of aggressive *conformity* have frequently been negative. Tanaka's documentary shows significant drug abuse among them and discusses the relatively high suicide rate for the Nisei and Sansei. Alcohol abuse was more prevalent among the Nisei than other men of the same age group during the postwar period. Many Sansei reported great personal distress, painful self-blame, mental and physical illnesses, and alcoholism or drug abuse. Some friends and relatives have committed suicide because of these intense conformity-to-whiteness pressures. Not surprisingly, the negative reactions of the Sansei have in turn affected their own children. This documentary destroys the Pollyanna image of a happy minority no longer facing racism. The costs of racial oppression do indeed persist over the generations.[56]

In later chapters, we show in detail how anti-Asian racism is a likely reason for many Asian American health problems, just as recent research has shown that antiblack racism is a major factor in the mental and physical health problems of African Americans. For example, the model minority myth creates very unrealistic expectations for many people. This mythology deflects attention from major racial barriers and hardships, including damaged physical and mental health, that Asian Americans face as they try to become socially integrated into a racist society.

In this book we examine how Asian Americans counter and respond to the racial oppression they face. Experiences with racism accumulate over time, and Asian American children start their collection of such experiences early in life. By the time adulthood is reached, the often substantial and accumulating pain can affect their lives in many detrimental ways. Research studies show that different communities react to racism differentially. For example, in many black families and communities the accumulating experience with racism is not just individualized and held internally. An individual's experiences with racial discrimination are often shared, and the burden of those experiences is frequently taken on by the larger family network or community.[57] Yet, as our respondents indicate in their interviews, the situation is often different for Asian Americans, especially those in predominantly white areas with no large Asian American community. Claire Jean Kim suggests that in order to develop a strong Asian American identity not sabotaged by excessive conformity to whiteness, one must at least have access to a strong Asian American community. Many upwardly mobile Asian Americans do not have such easy access and often find themselves—like the families mentioned in the opening of this chapter—in more isolated, predominantly white spaces where asserting a strong Asian American identity becomes very difficult. Kim further suggests that understanding the reality of societal racism can awaken Asian Americans and move them out of a stage of identifying so heavily with white ways. While all our respondents are aware of the anti-Asian racism surrounding them, very few have moved to a heightened consciousness highly critical of that white racism and to a strong Asian American self-concept unvarnished by substantial conformity to whiteness.

According to our respondents, most lessons from discriminatory incidents do not regularly get passed along to family members and friends, and thus their substantial stress and pain are often just individualized and internalized. As the opening accounts suggest, this internalization, frequently undetected until too late, can create serious problems for families, communities, and the larger society. Asian Americans who deal with racist incidents in such a silent and repressing manner not only suffer alone but also do not create the opportunity for their discrimination to be discussed as a part of a larger societal problem needing attention and organized resistance.[58]

In contrast, many African Americans, with nearly four centuries of experience with systemic racism in North America, have developed a stronger collective memory of racism, as well as a stronger resistance culture and counter framing that enables them to better resist the racial hierarchy and its buttressing frame.

By *collective memory* we here refer to how people of color experience their present reality in light of their own, their family's, and their ancestors' past racial experiences. Sociologist Maurice Halbwachs has suggested that one should not view one's important understandings about the society as just "preserved in the brain or in some nook of my mind to which I alone have access." Instead, important understandings and interpretations "are recalled to me externally, and the groups of which I am a part at any time give me the means to reconstruct them."[59] For many African Americans, and some other Americans of color, past discrimination perpetrated by white antagonists, as well as responses to that, are often inscribed in a sustained and powerful group memory. Memories of negative experiences with white Americans, accumulated and communicated by individuals, families, and communities, are joined with memories of *contending with* and *resisting* racial discrimination.[60] In contrast, our data suggest a majority of Asian American families and communities have yet to develop a routine, strong, and effective means of passing from one generation to the next the necessary information about accumulating discrimination, the history of anti-Asian racism, and successful countering strategies. Remembering the discriminatory past is painful, yet recovering key elements of that past can have major therapeutic value for individuals as well as major resistance value for communities. . . .

Conclusion and Overview*

A central goal of this exploratory study was to interview a diverse and reasonably representative group of middle-class Asian Americans about their everyday experiences in the United States. In the following chapters, we examine important questions about these experiences, especially with reference to the subtle, covert, and overt racism that they have encountered in an array of important spaces—from neighborhoods to schools, shopping centers, and workplaces. We are especially concerned with the physical, mental, and emotional toll that racial hostility and discrimination have had on them. We examine the costs that conformity to the racial hierarchy and its supportive racial framing has brought to their lives. In addition, we ask throughout in what subtle, covert, and overt ways they counter and resist racism.

In Chapters 2 and 3, white-generated discrimination in its major forms is clearly and painfully revealed. Not only are Asian Americans faced with overt discrimination and hate crimes but they also must confront an array of discriminatory actions, mostly from white Americans, of a more subtle or covert nature. As we observe, they rarely find places where they are safe from discrimination and its effects. In Chapter 2, we observe that discriminatory acts take place virtually everywhere—in neighborhoods, at movie theaters, in retail shops, and on city sidewalks. In Chapter 3, we see discriminatory acts occurring at all levels of educational institutions and in various workplace settings. Even though most of our respondents are well educated and at least middle class, they all describe instances of significant discrimination at the hands of white males and females of various classes, occupations, and conditions. Their often significant educational and economic resources do not protect them from racial attacks of different kinds.

Chapter 4 probes deeply the many costs of systemic racism for Asian Americans. Materially and psychologically, these men and women, and their families, are taxed daily by the omnipresent threat of racial hostility and discrimination, and they work to defend themselves from this oppression, most often in an internalizing fashion. As we show, they rarely seek significant help from family or friends to deal with serious racist incidents. When dealing with racial burdens they tend to turn inward, frequently trying to block the necessary expression of deep emotions and to repress painful memories. Successive generations

---

*The overview is included here even though its references to chapters not included in this reader because the summary Chou and Feagin provide here is itself useful.

of Asian Americans find themselves struggling with white-imposed racial identities. First-generation Asian Americans feel particularly isolated in this white-dominated society. Later-generation respondents often feel part of both the dominant white culture and an Asian culture, yet they are thereby marginalized in society and sometimes feel they fit in neither sociocultural world. In addition, many appear to be in denial about much of the harsh reality of the surrounding system of racism.

Chapter 5 details how an often unquestioning conformity to the dominant hierarchy and racial frame operates in their lives. Most try to conform well, which they view as a proactive method they hope will prevent white and other discriminators from further targeting them. However understandable, conforming to white folkways, to the dominant hierarchy and framing, is a conservative tactic that has serious personal, family, and community consequences. Even when they assert that they have never experienced an act of discrimination, as many do early in their interviews, the reality of white hostility and discrimination can usually be sensed even then in their coded words or their body language. Moreover, later in their interviews, they usually contradict this initial assertion. Many go to significant lengths to succeed in being the "solution minority" and to "strive for whiteness." As a result of this conformity, they also internalize hostile racial stereotypes, not only about their own group but often about other Americans of color.

Chapter 6 assesses more centrally how these Asian Americans try to resist the racial hierarchy and its supportive racial framing. They do this too in direct, subtle, and covert ways. Most of those we interviewed rarely directly confront the white perpetrators of discrimination. As they see it, there is too much at stake to openly resist whites. When such resistance is undertaken, our respondents usually attempt to produce tangible social and political changes for themselves or their group. When working more subtly or covertly, which is more common, they are often creative in the measures they take. To appeal to other Asian Americans, they may even play into anti-Asian stereotypes in order to have an opportunity to eventually educate them about the broader issue of racial oppression.

In addition, numerous respondents note how they resist racist views in personal ways; they do not resist for a greater good but rather for their own sanity. Much everyday resistance takes the form of rejecting the dominant racist ideology in their own minds, or sometimes in a small group of Asian American friends.

In Chapter 7, we summarize and assess our findings. We briefly compare the life paths of two Asian Americans who have shared similar starting points, whose lives have run parallel to each other in some ways, yet who over time have diverged dramatically in everyday strategies they use in facing white discriminators and a racist society. One chooses to fully conform and continue to "whiten" in hope of eventual acceptance, with a sense of white-imposed racism being unchangeable. The other decides to fight against racist individuals and structures, hopeful that her efforts will change the world positively for all. Briefly examining some history of collective Asian American resistance, we conclude this book with an examination of policy suggestions and theoretical implications arising from the many racialized experiences described by these courageous Asian Americans.

Notes

1. This information is taken from a local newspaper, which is unnamed to protect the family's identity.
2. Ian Shapira and Michael E. Ruane, "Student Wrote About Death and Spoke in Whispers, But No One Imagined What Cho Seung Hui Would Do," *Washington Post,* April 18, 2007, from http://www.washingtonpost.com/wp-dyn/content/article/2007/04/18/AR2007041800162_pf.html (retrieved October 15, 2007).
3. Vickie Nam, "Introduction," *YELL-Oh Girls,* ed. Vickie Nam (New York: Quill, 2001), pp. 111–116; Michael Kim, "Out and About: Coming of Age in a Straight White World," in *Asian American X: An Intersection of Twenty-first Century Asian American Voices,* ed. Arar Han and John Hsu (Ann Arbor: University of Michigan Press, 2004), p. 141.
4. See Vijay Prashad, *The Karma of Brown Folk* (Twin Cities, MN: University of Minnesota Press, 2003).

5. Paul Spickard, *Mixed Blood* (Madison: University of Wisconsin Press, 1988), p. 347. On assimilation perspectives, see Talcott Parsons, "Full Citizenship for the Negro American? A Sociological Problem," in *The Negro American,* ed. Talcott Parsons and Kenneth B. Clark (Boston: Houghton Mifflin, 1966), p. 740; for a critique, see Ruben G. Rumbaut, "Paradoxes (and Orthodoxies) of Assimilation," *Sociological Perspectives* 40 (1997): 483.

6. In this and later sections we draw on Joe K. Feagin, *Systemic Racism: A Theory of Oppression* (New York: Routledge, 2006), pp. 1–45 and 290–299, and on Joe R. Feagin and Clairece B. Feagin, *Racial and Ethnic Relations,* 8th ed. (Upper Saddle River, NJ: Prentice Hall, 2008), chapters 10–11.

7. See Feagin and Feagin, *Racial and Ethnic Relations,* chapters 10–11.

8. Robert C. Lee, *Orientals: Asian Americans in Popular Culture* (Philadelphia: Temple University Press, 1999), p. 8.

9. See Joe Feagin, *Racist American: Roots, Current Realities, and Future Reparations* (New York: Routledge, 2000), pp. 72–73; and Feagin, *Systemic Racism,* pp. 1–99.

10. *Plessy v. Ferguson* 163 U.S. 537, 561 (1896).

11. *Takao Ozawa v. United States*, 260 U.S. 178 (1922). See E. Manchester-Boddy, *Japanese in America* (San Francisco: R & E Research Associates, 1970), pp. 25–30.

12. Jacobus tenBroek, Edward N. Barnhart, and Floyd W. Matson, *Prejudice, War, and the Constitution* (Berkeley: University of California Press, 1968).

13. Frank Furedi, *The Silent War: Imperialism and the Changing Perception of Race* (New Brunswick, NJ: Rutgers University Press, 1998); Roger Daniels, *The Politics of Prejudice* (New York: Atheneum, 1969); Jacobus tenBroek, Edward N. Barnhart, and Floyd W. Matson, *Prejudice, War, and the Constitution* (Berkeley: University of California Press, 1968).

14. Daniels, *The Politics of Prejudice,* pp. 3–6. Italics added.

15. Quoted in Ronald Takaki, *Strangers from a Different Shore*: *A History of Asian Americans* (New York: Penguin, 1989), p. 370.

16. See Robert C. Lee, "The Cold War Construction of the Model Minority Myth," in *Contemporary Asian America: A Multidisciplinary Reader,* 2nd ed., ed. Min Zhou and J. V. Gatewood (New York: New York University Press, 2007), pp. 475–480.

17. Janice Tanaka, *When You're Smiling* (Janice Tanaka Films, 1999).

18. Long Le, "The Dark Side of the Asian American 'Model Student,' " August 2, 2006, http://news.newamericamedia.org/news (retrieved January 5, 2007).

19. "Daphne Kwok, Organization of Chinese Americans, and John O'Sullivan, *National Review,* Discuss Recent Cover Story for That Magazine That Asian Americans Are Saying Is Offensive and Racist," NBC News Transcripts, March 21, 1997; Mae M. Cheng, "Magazine Cover Ripped; Coalition Calls *National Review* Illustration Racist," *Newsday,* April 11, 1997, p. A4.

20. Doris Lin, "The Death of (Icebox.com's) Mr. Wong," US Asians.net, http://us.asians.tripod.com/articles-mrwong.html (retrieved December 14, 2006).

21. Jennifer Fang, "Team America: Racism, Idiocy, and Two Men's Pursuit to Piss off as Many People as Possible," Asian Media Watch, October 28, 2004, http://www.asianmediawatch.net/teamamerica/review.html (retrieved December 17, 2006). We draw here in part on Feagin and Feagin, *Racial and Ethnic Relations*, chapter 11.

22. Helen Zia, *Asian American Dreams: The Emergence of an American People* (New York: Farrar, Straus, and Giroux, 2000), p. 134ff.

23. Steven A. Chin, "KFRC. Deejay Draws Suspension for On-Air Derogatory Remarks," *San Francisco Examiner*, December 6, 1994, p. A2; "Current Affairs," JACL News, http://www.jacl.org/index.php (retrieved December 19, 2006); Media Action Network for Asian Americans, "Latest Headline News," http://www.manaa.org (retrieved December 18, 2006); Jenn Fang, "Racism Abounds Following Rosie," http://www.racialicious.com/2006/12/15/racism-abounds-following-rosie (retrieved September 25, 2007).

24. Fang, "Racism Abounds Following Rosie."

25. Jane H. Hill, "Mock Spanish: A Site for the Indexical Reproduction of Racism in American English," unpublished research paper, University of Arizona, 1995.

26. Rosina Lippi-Green, *English with an Accent* (New York: Routledge, 1997), pp. 238–239.

27. Feagin and Feagin, *Racial and Ethnic Relations,* pp. 292–293.

28. Tim Wise, *Affirmative Action: Racial Preference in Black and White* (New York: Routledge, 2005), pp. 136–137.

29. Feagin and Feagin, *Racial and Ethnic Relations,* pp. 292–293.

30. Sec Ronald Takaki, "Is Race Surmountable? Thomas Sowell's Celebration of Japanese-American Success," in *Ethnicity and the Work Force,* ed. Winston A. Van Horne (Madison: University of Wisconsin Press, 1985), pp. 218–220.

31. William Petersen, "Success Story, Japanese-American Style," *New York Times,* January 9, 1966, p. 21.

32. "Success Story of One Minority Group in the U.S.," *U.S. News & World Report,* December 26, 1966, pp. 73–76.

33. See J. N. Tinker, "Intermarriage and Assimilation in a Plural Society: Japanese Americans in the United States," *Marriage and Family Review* 5 (1982): 61–74; V. Nee and J. Sanders, "The Road to Parity: Determinants of the Socioeconomic Achievements of Asian-Americans," *Ethnic and Racial Studies* 8 (1985): 75–93; and D. A. Bell, "The Triumph of Asian-Americans," *New Republic,* July 15, 1982, pp. 24–31.

34. See, for example, James T. Madore, "Long-Quiet Asian Group Starts to Mobilize," *Christian Science Monitor,* May 20, 1988, p. 7.

35. Senate Judiciary Committee, "Capitol Hill Hearings," September 20, 1991.

36. Kathleen Wyer, "Beyond Myths: The Growth and Diversity of Asian American College Freshmen, 1971–2005," Research Report, Higher Education Research Institute, UCLA, 2007.

37. Sharon S. Lee, "Satire as Racial Backlash against Asian Americans," *Inside Higher Ed,* February 28, 2008, http://insidehighered.com/views/2008/02/28/lee (retrieved March 1, 2008).

38. See, for example, Susan Lee, *Unraveling the "Model Minority" Stereotype: Listening to Asian-American Youth* (New York: Teachers College Press, 1996); S. M. Nishi, "Perceptions and Deceptions: Contemporary Views of Asian-Americans," in *A Look Beyond the Model Minority Image: Critical Issues in Asian America*, ed. Grace Yun (New York: Minority Rights Group, 1989), pp. 3–10; Mia Tuan, *Forever Foreigners or Honorary Whites? The Asian Ethnic Experience* (New Brunswick, NJ: Rutgers University Press, 2003); Frank Wu, *Yellow: Race in America Beyond Black and White* (New Haven, CT: Yale University Press, 2003); and Ronald Takaki, *Iron Cages: Race and Culture in the 19th-Century US.* (New York: Oxford University Press, 1994).

39. Pyong Gap Min and Rose Kim, "Formation of Ethnic and Racial Identities: Narratives by Asian American Professionals," in *Second Generation: Ethnic Identity among Asian Americans*, ed. Pyong Gap Mm (Walnut Creek, CA: Altamira, 2002), pp. 167–175; Won Moo Hurh and Kwang Chung Kim, "Adhesive Sociocultural Adaptation of Korean Immigrants in the U.S.: An Alternative Strategy of Minority Adaptation," *International Migration Review* 18 (1984): 188–216; and Kwang Chung Kim and Won Moo Hurh, "Beyond Assimilation and Pluralism: Syncretic Sociocultural Adaptation of Korean Immigrants in the U.S.," *Ethnic and Racial Studies* 16 (1993): 696–713.

40. Nazli Kibria, *Becoming Asian American: Second Generation Chinese and Korean American Identities* (Baltimore, MD: Johns Hopkins University Press, 2002), pp. 3–41.

41. See, for example, Tuan, *Forever Foreigners or Honorary Whites?* A recent search on Google for the phrase "honorary white" coupled with the word "Asian" found only 1,900 web pages. Most use of the phrase "honorary white" seems to be by scholars and some web commentators, not by ordinary whites. In contrast, a search for the phrase "model minority" and "Asian" found 153,000 web pages.

42. Mari J. Matsuda, "We Will Not Be Used," in *Where Is Your Body and Other Essays on Race, Gender, and the Law* (Boston: Beacon Press, 1996), pp. 148–151.

43. Vijay Prashad, *The Karma of Brown Folk* (Twin Cities: University of Minnesota: Press, 2003), p. 6.

44. Wu, *Yellow,* p. 91.

45. For example, Wu, *Yellow;* and Prashad, *The Karma of Brown Folk.*

46. Claire Jean Kim, "The Racial Triangulation of Asian Americans," *Politics and Society* 27 (March 1999): 105–138; and Claire Jean Kim, *Bitter Fruit: The Politics of Black-Korean Conflict in New York City* (New Haven, CT: Yale University Press, 2003), p. 16.

47. Kim, *Bitter Fruit,* p. 45.

48. Gary Y. Okihiro, "Is Yellow Black or White?" in *Asian Americans: Experiences and Perspectives,* ed. Timothy P. Fong and Larry H. Shinagawa (Upper Saddle River, NJ: Prentice Hall, 2000), p. 75.

49. Joe R. Feagin and Danielle Dirks, "Who Is White? College Students' Assessments of Key U.S. Racial and Ethnic Groups," unpublished manuscript, Texas A&M University, 2004.

50. Christine Yeh, "Age, Acculturation, Cultural Adjustment, and Mental Health Symptoms of Chinese, Korean, and Japanese Immigrant Youths," *Cultural Diversity and Ethnic Minority Psychology 9* (2003): 34–48.

51. Won Moo Hurh, "Adaptation Stages and Mental Health of Korean Male Immigrants in the United States," *International Migration Review 24* (1990): 456–477; Center for Medicaid Services, *Medicaid Managed Care Enrollment Report: Depression Diagnoses for Adolescent Youth* (New York: Medicaid Statistics Publications, 2002). Other studies report similarly high rates for Native American teenagers.

52. See, for example, C. Browne and A. Broderick, "Asian and Pacific Island Elders: Issues for Social Work Practice and Education," *Social Work 39* (1994): 252–259; Laura Harder, "Asian Americans Commit Half of Suicides at Cornell," *Cornell Daily Sun*, March 29, 2005, p. 1; and Tanaka, *When You're Smiling.*

53. The data and quotes are from Elizabeth Cohen, "Push to Achieve Tied to Suicide in Asian-American Women," http://www.cnn.com/2007/HEALTH/05/16/asian.suicides/index.html (retrieved May 16, 2007).

54. Abraham Kardiner and Lionel Ovesey, *The Mark of Oppression: Explorations in the Personality of the American Negro* (Cleveland: World Publishing, 1962); William H. Grier and Price M. Cobbs, *Black Rage* (New York: Bantam Books, 1968); and Joe R. Feagin and Karyn D. McKinney, *The Many Costs of Racism* (Lanham, MD: Rowman and Littlefield, 2003).

55. Tanaka, *When You're Smiling.*

56. See Feagin and Feagin, *Racial and Ethnic Relations,* chap. 10.

57. Feagin and McKinney, *The Many Costs of Racism.*

58. See Debra Van Ausdale and Joe R. Feagin, *The First R: How Children Learn Race and Racism* (Lanham, MD: Rowman and Littlefield, 2001); and Joe R. Feagin and Melvin P. Sikes, *Living with Racism* (Boston: Beacon Press, 1994).

59. Maurice Halbwachs, *On Collective Memory,* ed. and trans. by Lewis Coser (Chicago: University of Chicago Press, 1992), pp. 38, 52.

60. We draw here on Feagin, *Systemic Racism,* and on Yanick St. Jean and Joe R. Feagin, *Double Burden: Black Women and Everyday Racism* (New York: M. E. Sharpe, 1998).

20

Excerpts from *Multiple Origins, Uncertain Destinies*

NATIONAL RESEARCH COUNCIL

This piece examines four aspects of the Hispanic experience—family and living arrangements; schools and education; employment and economic well-being; and health status and access to care. These attributes not only portray current terms of belonging, but also highlight risks and opportunities that will ultimately define the future of the U.S. Hispanic population. A focus on features that set Hispanics apart from other groups—notably language use, youthfulness, and large shares of unskilled immigrants—helps assess whether the identified risks are likely to be enduring.

Family and Living Arrangements[1]

Hispanic families are often extolled as a source of strength and cohesion that derives from their "familism"—a strong commitment to family life that values collective goals over individual well-being. Indicators of familism that differentiate Hispanics from whites include early childbearing and higher average fertility levels, large family households that often extend beyond nuclear members, and a greater overall tendency to live with kin rather than with unrelated individuals or alone. As a source of support for relatives in the extended network of kin relationships, familism can help mitigate economic and social risks in the face of adversity. These sentiments were echoed across the generational spectrum in focus groups conducted for the panel:

> Sometimes families here, white families, are not as united as Hispanic families are. We're always famous for having aunts and uncles and relatives. Americans, it's just mom and dad and kids. (Mexican immigrant, Raleigh)
>
> . . .
>
> Typically, we have close families. Family is a really big part of our culture. (third-generation Hispanic, Houston)

At the same time, consistent with their varied immigration histories and social conditions, Hispanic families are highly diverse. Specific aspects of family behavior, such as intermarriage patterns, cohesion among relatives, and the content of social exchanges differ by nationality and generation. Mexican Americans are considered particularly familistic, possibly because the large numbers of immigrants among them bring cultural traditions into sharper relief.

Most observers agree that the positive aspects of familism are worth keeping, yet there is no consensus on what can be preserved in the face of the rapid Americanization of second-generation youth. Whether ideals of collective support and other positive features of familism will endure and what forms family structure among Hispanics will take in the future are open questions with far-reaching implications for the evolution of group identity and social well-being.

If Hispanics follow the paths of other immigrant groups, their familism would appear to be in jeopardy as they acculturate, experience socioeconomic mobility, and adopt U.S. norms, which includes many behaviors that tend to erode kinship patterns and traditional family behavior. The rise in divorce and nonmarital childbearing among Hispanics, evident in the growth of mother-only families, signals what some scholars term "family decline."[2] In 1980, fathers were absent in 12 percent of white families, 38 percent of both Dominican and Puerto Rican families, and 40 percent of black families. By 2000, approximately 14 percent of white families had a single female head, compared with about 20 percent of Mexican and Cuban families, 25 percent of Central and South American families, 36 percent of Dominican and Puerto Rican families, and 45 percent of black families.[3] Because mother-only families are significantly more likely to be poor, this trend signals new vulnerabilities for the growing numbers of youths reared by single parents.

Generational transitions also dilute familism, although apparently not uniformly among Hispanic subgroups. For example, among Mexicans and Puerto Ricans born in the United States, the percentage of married-couple households is smaller and the percentage of female-headed households larger than among first-generation immigrants. Compared with the immigrant generation, U.S.-born Mexican Americans exhibit higher divorce rates. Only 56 percent of third-generation Mexican children (those who have American-born parents) live with both parents, compared with about 73 percent of children with Mexican-born parents. Another sign of dwindling familism is the shrinking size of extended families, which often results in reduced safety nets for related individuals.[4]

Rising nonmarital childbearing is another sign of eroding Hispanic familism. Between 1980 and 2000, the percentage of births to unmarried women more than doubled for whites (134 percent), Mexicans (101 percent), and Cubans (173 percent), and increased by more than half for Central and South Americans (64 percent) and other Hispanics (97 percent). Out-of-wedlock childbearing among Puerto Ricans rose more slowly because, as with blacks, their share of nonmarital births was already high in 1980. By 2000, the percentage of births to unmarried Hispanic mothers was between that of whites (22 percent) and blacks (69 percent). The rate for Cubans was closer to that for whites at 27 percent, and the Puerto Rican rate was closer to that for blacks, at 59 percent. At 44 percent, the out-of-wedlock birth rate for Central and South Americans lay between the extremes.

Finally, the cultural mergers produced by rising rates of intermarriage—between Hispanics and non-Hispanics and among Hispanic nationalities—can diminish or redefine the content of familism. As a measure of social distance between groups, an indicator of assimilation, and a force that shapes racial and ethnic boundaries, intermarriage can either redefine or erode Hispanic familism over generations. For all Hispanics, the tendency to marry; cohabit, and procreate with members of their own ethnic group declines across generations, though notable differences exist across groups. Mexican Americans not only are considered to be more familistic than other Hispanics, but also, given their large numbers, are far more likely to be paired with a member of the same ethnic group in marriage, cohabitation, or parenthood than are Puerto Ricans, Cubans, Central/South Americans, or other Hispanics.[5] One possible explanation for this is that high levels of immigration, buttressed by residential segregation, help preserve Mexican familism in the face of erosion from other sources.

Whether traditional Hispanic familistic orientations will persist beyond the third generation, whether they will take the same forms, and whether they will serve similar protective functions is unknown. Trends in marriage, cohabitation, and parenthood offer provocative insights. Hispanics are more likely to partner with another Hispanic in marriage than in cohabitation and nonmarital parenthood. Although generally less common, relationships with white partners frequently involve marriage. U.S.-born Hispanics are more likely than Hispanic immigrants to have a white, or other non-Hispanic, spouse.[6] Unions among partners of different Hispanic origins or between Hispanics and blacks are more likely to involve cohabitation and unmarried childbearing. Hispanic-black unions quite frequently produce children out of wedlock.

Hispanics' interethnic unions foreshadow changing ethnic boundaries through childbearing. In particular, children of mixed unions face complex identity issues: Will they retain a mixed identity, adopt the ethnic (or racial) identity of one parent, or perhaps opt for a panethnic identity? Unions between Hispanic women and white partners can facilitate assimilation into mainstream white society, because these mixed marriages are more common among the better educated. Whether and how Hispanics' ethnic mixing will redraw racial and ethnic boundaries in the United States is uncertain because the prevalence of intermarriage depends on even greater uncertainties, such as the effect of geographic dispersal on the incidence of mixed unions, Future levels of immigration, and the way persons of mixed ancestry self-identify ethnically.[7] Because of their sheer numbers and relatively high residential concentration, Mexican Americans are likely to retain a relatively distinct ethnic identity although generational transitions will blur boundaries through unions with whites. Smaller in size, other Hispanic subgroups are less likely to sustain discrete identities over time because of their higher levels of ethnic mixing with other Hispanic groups and with blacks, which creates greater ambiguity about the place of their offspring in the evolving racial spectrum. How settlement patterns recontour marriage markets will also decide the viability of Hispanicity as a panethnic identity.

Schools and Education[8]

The United States houses some of the most outstanding universities in the world, which coexist with countless highly dysfunctional primary and secondary schools. Thousands of young Hispanics must pursue inter- and intragenerational social mobility predominantly via segregated inner-city schools that feature dropout rates well above the national average. The vastly unequal opportunities for academic achievement they confront in the lower grades contribute to widening disparities at higher levels of the education system.

Although most demographic groups have experienced significant increases in educational attainment since the 1960s, Hispanics are distinguished by their historically low levels of completed schooling, currently completing less formal schooling than any other demographic group.[9] In the context of the rising demand for skills in today's economy, this liability is cause for concern.

In 2000, working-age Hispanics averaged nearly 3 years less of formal schooling than U.S.-born whites and blacks. Moreover, there are large disparities in educational attainment among Hispanic groups, mainly between the native and foreign born. On average, foreign-born Hispanics of working age complete 2.5 years less of formal schooling than their U.S.-born compatriots, with negligible differences between men and women. As Figure 20.1 shows, the educational standing of foreign-born Hispanics has eroded since 1980 compared with both whites and blacks. By contrast, U.S.-born Hispanics have closed the school attainment gap with whites by more than half a year—from 2 to 1.3 years over the same period.

Educational disparities between foreign- and native-born Hispanics play out as inequities among national-origin groups of working age because of the changing volume and composition of immigration in recent decades. . . . Not only do foreign-born Mexicans feature the lowest educational levels of any Hispanic subgroup but the gap in completed schooling between the foreign and native born is larger for Mexicans than for Hispanics of other nationalities—rising from 3 years in 1980 to 4.4 years in 2000—owing to substantial educational advances among the

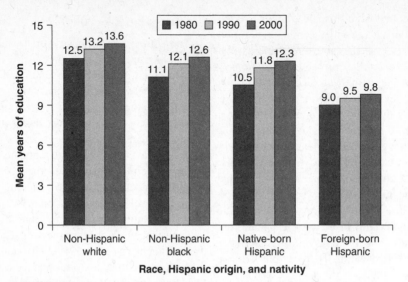

FIGURE 20.1 Mean years of education by race/ethnicity and nativity, 1980–2000.

Note: For ages 25 to 64.

Source: U.S. Bureau of the Census (2000b). Integrated Public Use Microdata Series (IPUMS) 1 percent samples for 1980–2000.

U.S.-born rather than declining attainment of recent immigrants (see Figure 20.2). For other Hispanics the birthplace gap in education rose more modestly during the same period—from 1 to 1.6 years—while for Puerto Ricans it was reduced by half. Cubans are distinguished from other Hispanic ethnicities because their average education level exceeds that of other subgroups, because foreign-born Cubans average more schooling than native-born Hispanics and because the educational attainment of U.S.-born Cubans equals (in the case of men) or surpasses (in the case of women) that of white men and women.[10]

If the schooling deficits of foreign-born Hispanics are imported from Latin America, the disparities among the native born are produced in the United States. Scholastic disadvantages result from a myriad of social and family circumstances mainly low parental education levels—and are compounded by schools that fail to deliver quality education.[11] Fortunately, educational disadvantages can be prevented for Hispanic youths that have not yet begun their school careers and reversed for those already enrolled.

Early Beginnings

Hispanic students' educational disadvantages begin in the early grades for two main reasons—their delayed entry into formal school settings and their limited opportunities to acquire preliteracy skills. Parents of Hispanic preschoolers are less likely than black, white, or Asian parents to be fluent in English and, because many have poor educational levels themselves, to have the resources necessary to promote their children's prescholastic literacy. This is highly significant because reading to preschool children fosters their language acquisition, enhances their early reading performance and social development, and may promote their future academic success.

Participation in home literacy activities such as telling stories of visiting libraries is especially low for children reared in Spanish-dominant homes. In 1999, children of Spanish monolinguals were only half as likely as white children to participate in such activities; if both parents were fluent in English, the gap was just 15 percentage points. The lack of exposure to preschool literacy activities, particularly among children from

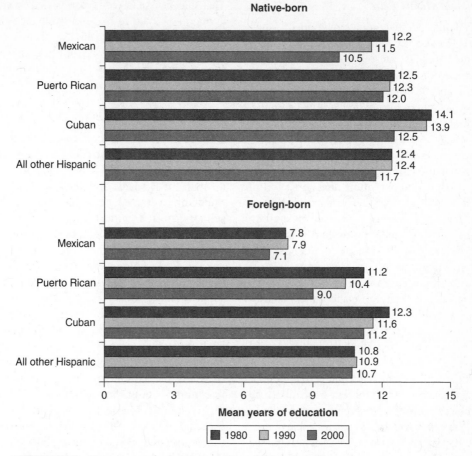

FIGURE 20.2 Mean years of education of Hispanics by ethnicity.

Note: For ages 25 to 64.

Source: U.S. Bureau of the Census (2000b), Integrated Public Use Microdata Series (IPUMS)
1 percent samples for 1980–2000.

Spanish dominant households, often creates literacy disadvantages in the early grades. A 1999 study by the U.S. Department of Education showed that Hispanic kindergarten students trailed their Asian and other non-Hispanic classmates in both reading and math skills.[12] Only Native American students had lower preschool reading literacy rates than Hispanics whose parents spoke Little English (although Hispanic children exhibited Lower math skills).

Household language partly reflects social class divisions and recent immigrant status—two attributes that influence children's exposure to literacy activities before kindergarten. Yet differences in school readiness between Hispanic youth reared in Spanish-dominant homes and English-dominant homes are not an indictment of Spanish-language use per se. Moreover, programs such as Head Start appear to raise Hispanic children's low average preschool literacy rates. Yet quality preschool programs often are either unavailable where the neediest children live or too costly for family budgets. Thus disadvantaged Hispanic children are left to make their way in the public schools, increasing their vulnerability to failure in the years ahead.

Primary and Middle Years

The academic achievement gap evident when Hispanics first enter school continues through the primary grades. During the first two years, teachers' perceptions of their Hispanic students' academic abilities often skew scholastic assessments, regardless of the children's actual aptitude. Results of the Early Childhood Longitudinal Study revealed that kindergarten teachers systematically rated Hispanic students below white students when first enrolled. As Hispanic children performed above their teachers' initial expectations, the gap between test-based abilities and teacher assessments decreased by half to two-thirds during kindergarten and was eliminated by the end of the first grade. Such teacher biases are compounded by a shortage of staff who understand Hispanic children's cultural backgrounds. Nationally, Hispanic students constitute approximately 15 percent of elementary school students—and nearly 20 percent of all school age students—yet only 4 percent of public school teachers are Hispanic.[13]

Although Hispanic elementary school children have made steady progress in reading and math, greater gains by other groups have sustained or in some cases widened Hispanic achievement gaps. A 20-year comparison of test scores reported in the National Assessment of Educational Progress shows that Hispanic students continue to lag behind whites in their scholastic achievement throughout middle and high school.[14] Evident for all Hispanic subgroups, these gaps are decidedly largest for Mexican Americans, the fastest-growing segment of the elementary school population. Carried into future grades, accumulating deficits in literacy and math competencies inhibit the learning of other academic subjects.

Middle school Hispanic students often encounter two circumstances that limit their chances for scholastic success: large, urban schools generally considered suboptimal for learning in the middle grades,[15] and weak ties with their teachers.[16] Weak relations with teachers diminish students' motivation to pursue academic work, and in turn lower teachers' expectations in a self-perpetuating cycle of academic disengagement and underachievement.

That students who become disengaged from school during the middle years cannot well appreciate the practical relevance of what is being taught in the classroom bodes ill for their academic performance in high school and dampens their aspirations for college.

Secondary School and Beyond

Even under optimal circumstances, the transition from middle to high school is a taxing experience for most students. This passage is especially difficult for Hispanic and black adolescents destined for oversized, resource-poor urban high schools staffed with many inexperienced or uncertified teachers.[17] Moreover, students whose parents lack a high school education are most in need of early guidance in course planning and preparation for college. Such guidance is in short supply in the schools these students attend. Given their parents' limited experience with the U.S. educational system and the blind trust many Hispanic parents are willing to place in teachers' authority, Hispanic eighth graders are more likely than any other demographic group to express uncertainty about the classes they will take in high school.[18] Mexican immigrant parents are especially likely to defer to teachers and administrators, rarely questioning their decisions.

High school experiences are vital in shaping students' educational expectations and occupational aspirations. Yet a recent study found that, compared with 25 percent of blacks, 31 percent of whites, and 37 percent of Asian Americans, only 23 percent of Hispanic eighth graders planned to enroll in a college preparatory curriculum.[19] These findings underscore the urgency of effective counseling on course selection in secondary school, particularly for students whose parents may be unfamiliar with the complexities of the U.S. educational system.

Despite modest improvements in recent years, rates of school failure among Hispanics remain unacceptably high. Even counting only those who actually attended U.S. high schools, the share of Hispanic high school students 16 to 19 years old who failed to graduate fell only marginally during the 1990s, from 22 to 21 percent.[20] The numbers involved are sobering because the school-age population in the United States has been growing rapidly as the children of baby boomers and recent immigrants make their way through the education system. That dropout rates for whites and blacks fell even more than for Hispanics—from 10 to 8 percent and from 14 to 12 percent, respectively—widened racial and ethnic disparities in secondary school success. Nor is the General Equivalency Diploma (GED) a viable route for Hispanics to close their high school achievement gap. In 1998, 7.9 percent of white 18- to 29-year-olds achieved high school equivalence by passing the GED test, as compared with 7 percent of Hispanics.[21] Moreover, those with exam-certified high school equivalency fare no better in the labor market than high school dropouts.[22]

Although foreign-born Hispanic youths ages 16 to 19 are significantly more likely than those who are native born to leave high school without a diploma—34 versus 14 percent in 2000—being foreign born is not the main factor explaining their failure to graduate. Many are recent arrivals who were already behind in school before arriving in the U.S.[23] Once here, they are likely to attend urban schools—such as those in Los Angeles, Chicago, and New York—that serve large numbers of low-income minority students and for which low graduation rates are typical. Fully 40 percent of Hispanic students attend high schools that graduate less than 60 percent of entering freshmen.[24]

Popular allegations that Hispanics value education less than do other groups are contradicted by evidence that large numbers of Hispanic high school students aspire to attend college. A study conducted by Public Agenda, a New York-based nonprofit public opinion research organization found that 65 percent of Hispanic parents, compared with 47 percent of black and 33 percent of white parents, believed a college education is the single most important factor for economic success.[25] Yet Hispanics trail all other groups in their ambitions to pursue 4-year college degrees because of their disadvantaged beginnings, limited home educational resources, concentration in scholastically weak high schools, and lack of concrete information about how to prepare for college.[26]

Compared with whites and blacks, more second-generation Hispanic youths are the first in their family to attend college. But college prospects are limited for many because they fail to take courses or exams required for college entrance—another consequence of their poor guidance counseling during high school. Compared with other subjects, achievement in mathematics is the strongest predictor of college enrollment. That Hispanic students are about 20 percent less likely than whites to complete advanced mathematics, as well as less likely than both whites and blacks to take advanced science courses, compromises their post—high school educational options.[27]

Hispanic high school graduates are also less likely than whites, Asians, and blacks to take college entrance examinations or apply to college.[28] Spanish-language use per se does not explain this gap because bilingual Hispanics are more likely than whites to complete Advanced Placement courses and to take College Board exams. And parents who are proficient in both English and Spanish often can advance their children's educational prospects by bridging cultural and language divides.[29]

Despite the above obstacles, college enrollment among Hispanics has been on the rise. There is evidence that Hispanic high school graduates are more likely than white or black students to enroll in some form of college, but Hispanics also are significantly less likely to obtain a 4-year degree because they are more likely to enroll in 2-year colleges, to attend college only part-time, or to work while enrolled full-time.[30] This is especially true for Mexicans. In 2000, Hispanics were 11 percent of high school graduates.[31] They accounted for only 7 percent of students enrolled in 4-year institutions, but 14 percent of enrollees in 2-year colleges. Differences in college attendance between native- and foreign-born Hispanics contribute somewhat to these outcomes, but they are not the driving force.

Major reasons why Hispanics are more likely than whites to enroll in 2-year rather than 4-year colleges are poor academic preparation, weak counseling, and cost. Hispanics from Spanish-speaking families (for whom the risks of dropping out of high school are higher) are nearly as likely as blacks to attend 4-year colleges if they receive adequate academic preparation.[32] Like many students who begin their college careers at community colleges, Hispanics intend to transfer to 4-year institutions, but they are less successful than other groups in making the transition.[33] Furthermore, enrollment in a 4-year institution does not guarantee a degree. Compared with other high-achieving youths who enroll in 4-year institutions, Hispanics are less likely to receive baccalaureate degrees unless they are among the select few who attend a highly selective college.[34]

Economic Well-Being

As in so many other ways, Hispanics are highly diverse with respect to economic well-being. On the one hand, lacking the protections afforded by legal status, millions of undocumented Hispanics fill low-wage jobs; many make ends meet by holding multiple jobs and pooling incomes from several household members. On the other hand, rising rates of home ownership attest that both established immigrants and native-born citizens are increasingly joining the ranks of the middle class.[35] This section reviews two aspects of economic well-being—employment and earnings, and household income—among Hispanics, as well as their experience of the extremes of poverty and wealth.

Employment and Earnings[36]

Hispanics' success in the U.S. labor market depends on their propensity to work, their skills, the kinds of jobs they secure, and, because many U.S. employers discount human capital acquired abroad, where they were born (see Figure 20.3).[37] On average, Hispanic men's employment rate (87 percent) is somewhat lower than that for U.S.-born whites (92 percent), but well above that for U.S.-born blacks (77 percent).[38] Also among men, the average employment rate for both Cubans and Mexicans (both foreign- and U.S.-born) is similar to that for whites, but that for Puerto Rican men is appreciably lower, while that for island-born Puerto Ricans is similar to that for U.S.-born blacks.[39]

Birthplace differences in employment rates are much larger for Hispanic women than men. Overall, some 61 percent of immigrant Hispanic women were employed in 2000, compared with 76 percent of their U.S.-born counterparts. With just over one in two employed, Mexican immigrants have the lowest employment rate of all women, but the rate for island-born Puerto Ricans is only slightly higher at 61 percent. Average employment rates for U.S.-born Mexicans and Puerto Ricans are close to those for blacks (78 percent) and whites (80 percent), while Cubans have the highest rate of all, at 83 percent.

Owing to differences in educational attainment and language skills between native- and foreign-born Hispanics, the types of jobs they hold vary more on this dimension than by nationality. Foreign-born Hispanic men work disproportionately in agriculture (11 percent) and construction (18 percent), while foreign-born Hispanic women are overrepresented in manufacturing (19 percent)—mainly in production of nondurable goods.[40] Consistent with their education and English-language skills, Hispanic men and women born abroad are underrepresented in managerial/professional and technical/sales occupations, and overrepresented in service and operator/laborer occupations.

Hispanics' lower levels of education and English proficiency largely explain their lower employment rates compared with whites.[41] The 6 percentage point employment gap between native-born Mexican and white men would narrow to a mere 2 percentage points if their education and language skills were similar. With education and English proficiency levels comparable to those of whites, the employment rates of foreign-born Mexican immigrants also would be similar.[42] Foreign-born Mexican women provide an even more dramatic example, as their average employment deficit of 25 percentage points would shrink to just 3 with education and English proficiency levels comparable to those of white women. Puerto Ricans and Dominicans are an exception to this pattern because sizable employment gaps persist for them even with human capital endowments comparable to those of whites.[43]

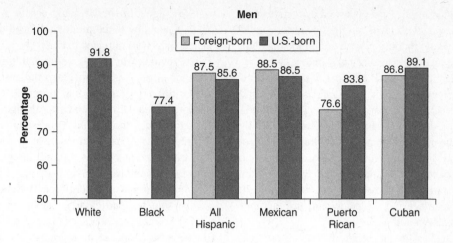

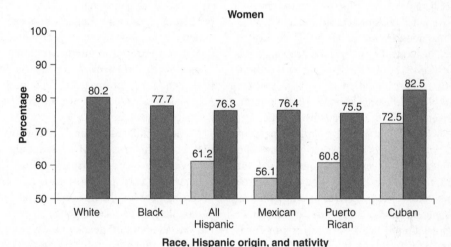

Race, Hispanic origin, and nativity

FIGURE 20.3 Employment rates for white, black, and Hispanic men and women ages 25–59 by nativity.

Source: U.S. Bureau of the Census (2000b), 5 percent samples Integrated Public Use Microdata Series (IPUMS).

On average, native-born Hispanic men earned 31 percent and foreign-born Hispanic men 59 percent less than whites in 1999. With similar human capital endowments, those earnings gaps would shrink to 13 and 5 percent, respectively. By comparison, and despite their higher average education levels and better command of English relative to Hispanics, black men suffer a 44 percent earnings penalty. Foreign-born Hispanic women earn about half as much as white women on average, but this disparity too, would shrink given comparable educational attainment and English fluency.

Hispanics' average earnings also differ by national origin. Native-born Cubans enjoy relatively high earnings: U.S.-born Cuban men earn as much as white men, and native-born Cuban women earn 20 percent *more* than white women. By contrast, both Mexicans and Puerto Ricans—especially those born abroad—exhibit large gaps compared with whites. But if Mexican and Puerto Rican women born abroad—whose average earnings trail those of white women by 63 and 28 percent, respectively—were as fluent in English and as well educated as white women, their earnings gaps would virtually disappear.[44] Legal status also affects wages, with legal immigrants earning substantially more than those who are undocumented, and wage inequality as discussed below.[45]

Thus unlike black men, for whom continuing discrimination in the labor market creates and augments earnings disparities, Hispanics could dramatically reduce their earnings gap with whites by closing the education gap and becoming proficient in English.[46] This does not mean that Hispanics do not experience discrimination in the labor market. There is some evidence of differences in treatment at initial contact and interview and in outcomes based on accent and phenotype.[47]

To understand the origins of earnings differentials and accurately portray Hispanic socioeconomic progress over time, one must consider changes in the birthplace composition of the Hispanic workforce. Since 1980, high rates of immigration have changed the human capital profile of Hispanic workers and widened their earnings disparities with whites. For example, the foreign-born share among Mexican men aged 25 to 59 surged from 37 percent in 1980 to 51 percent in 1990 and 63 percent in 2000. Among Hispanics, Mexicans are the largest ethnic group, average the lowest levels of human capital, and include a sizable share of undocumented workers.[48] With average educational attainment levels of 12 years for the native born and less than 9 years for the foreign born, Mexicans have faced particularly bleak labor market prospects since 1980, as the wage premiums for high skills grew and income inequality widened.

Looking back six decades, in 1940 Mexican men earned just over half (56 percent) of white men's wages. That figure rose to nearly 70 percent in the postwar decade, a period of vigorous economic growth when strong unions protected the wages of laborers. Although the Mexican-white earnings gap remained unchanged during the next two decades, by 1990 Mexican men's wages had deteriorated to 45 percent of those of white men, and this gap persisted through the following decade.[49] By contrast, earnings of black men rose between 1990 and 2000, from 50 to 56 percent of white male earnings. Larger human capital gaps since 1980, especially among the foreign born, are responsible for the stagnation of Hispanic earnings through 2000, especially as the premium placed on work-related skills has continued to rise.[50]

Previous waves of predominantly unskilled immigrants, such as the Irish and Italians, enjoyed substantial intergenerational progress that ultimately enabled their descendants to join the middle class. For most, though, this process required two or three generations to accomplish; moreover, the skill endowments of the immigrant generation were instrumental in the labor market success of their children and grandchildren.[51] Generational comparisons are particularly instructive for envisioning possible economic destinies for Hispanics. But because Hispanic immigrants are so diverse with respect to their length of U.S. residence, and because native-born Hispanics represent multiple generations, comparisons by birthplace are too coarse to portray true intergenerational progress. Snapshots of the Hispanic population taken over time can only approximate such progress, but nonetheless provide rough measures of the direction and pace of change.

Substantial educational gains realized by the U.S.-born offspring of Hispanic immigrants have narrowed the white-Hispanic earnings gap across generations, with the most sizable convergence occurring between the first and second generations. A smaller wage convergence occurs between the second and third generations, which mirror the apparent stagnation of Hispanics' educational progress relative to whites. For example, for the 1998–2000 periods, the earnings gap between Mexican and white men dropped from 66 percent for immigrants to 38 percent for the second generation and 31 percent for the third and subsequent generations combined. Second-generation Mexicans even reaped higher earnings than native-born black men with higher levels of education. Earnings deficits for Puerto Rican men were 46 percent for the first generation, 30 percent for the second generation, and 16 percent for later generations. Reflecting their higher-class origins at arrival, Cuban immigrants' 31 percent initial deficit disappeared by the second generation.[52]

The apparent slowdown in Hispanic socioeconomic progress after the second generation may be more imagined than real because it is impossible to match immigrant parents and grandparents of the first generation with their descendants in later generations.[53] In fact, substantial educational and earnings gains are evident when second-generation Hispanics are compared with their third-generation descendants 25 years later. For example, one study showed that not only is schooling gaps smaller in the second compared with the first generation but they are always lower in the third generation.[54]

Educational gains of younger third-generation relative to older second-generation Hispanics are an encouraging sign of intergenerational progress but they yield conservative estimates of mobility for two reasons. First, the pace of intergenerational progress may be more rapid than available data can accurately portray because of the uncertain volume, pace, and composition of immigrant flows. Decennial censuses can only approximate this highly dynamic process which for Hispanics is further complicated by the presence of a large and growing undocumented population whose integration prospects are highly uncertain. Second, selective opting out of Hispanic ethnicity by third and higher generations would lead to underestimation of intergenerational progress. If the most successful Hispanics are less likely to identify themselves or their children as Hispanic—either because they are more likely to marry non-Hispanics or for other reasons—available estimates of earnings gains achieved between the second and third generations are conservative. Studies focused on documenting the prevalence of such opting out of Hispanic identity are relatively recent, and consensus on this issue has not yet been established.[55]

Recent evidence for Mexicans supports the idea that the most economically assimilated Hispanics—predominantly those from the third and higher generations—may be less likely to self-identify as Hispanic.[56] U.S.-born Mexican Americans who marry non-Mexicans are substantially more educated, on average, than Mexican Americans who marry within their ethnic group (either U.S. or foreign born), as their higher employment levels and earnings attest. Moreover, the children of intermarried Mexican Americans are much less likely to self-identify as Mexican than are the children of two Mexican parents. This implies that children of Mexican origin parents with

low education, employment, and earnings may be more likely to self-identify as Mexican than the offspring of intermarriage, which would bias downward assessments of Mexican Americans' intergenerational progress beyond the second generation. The magnitude of such biases, however, has yet to be systematically assessed.[57]

Given these uncertainties, conclusions about intergenerational changes in the labor market experience of Hispanics remain tentative at best. The evidence is clear as to improvement in educational attainment and earnings growth between first- and second-generation Hispanics, both absolutely and relative to whites. But the evidence regarding progress between the second and third generations, and especially beyond the third, is less clear, because educational gains between the second and third generations are not matched by commensurate progress in earnings, particularly among younger Mexicans.[58] Less debatable is that deficiencies in education and language skills will remain a formidable obstacle to the labor market success of Hispanics, especially for immigrants, and will continue to hamper their economic progress—perhaps even more so in the years ahead than in the past—because of the higher premium placed on skills and because blue-collar jobs that traditionally served as gateways to the middle class have all but vanished. Whether the growing second generation makes sufficient progress in closing these two key obstacles to economic mobility will be decisive in the long-term positioning of the Hispanic population.

Household Income

For obvious reasons, the gaps in employment and earnings experienced by Hispanics are reflected in disparities in household income. On average, incomes of white households are larger than those of Hispanic households, just how much larger depending on the birthplace and ethnicity of the Hispanic householder. Again mirroring employment and earnings disparities, U.S.-born Hispanic householders of all national origins garner higher incomes than blacks, although this pattern does not hold for households headed by immigrants. In 1999, the median income of Hispanic

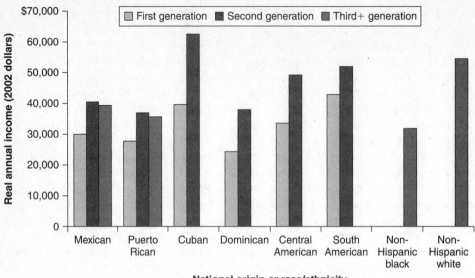

FIGURE 20.4   Median total household incomes by Hispanic national origin or race/ethnicity and generation.

Notes: Includes only households whose head is under age 65. Results for Hispanics are shown only for cells with at least 90 observations.

Source: Pooled March CPS files 998–2002.

households was just about 70 percent that of whites and about 10 percent higher than that of blacks.[59] At the top of the Hispanic household income ladder are South Americans and Cubans who were either born or raised in the United States.[60] Ranking lowest on median household income, as with most other measures of economic well-being, are Puerto Ricans and Dominicans, followed by Mexicans (see Figure 20.4).

As noted, an obvious explanation for the low household incomes of immigrants, and particularly Mexicans, Dominicans, and Central Americans, is their low earnings. In addition, per capita household income depends on household size. Thus, for example, despite having higher average incomes compared with blacks, second-generation Mexicans, Puerto Ricans, and Dominicans have slightly lower median per capita incomes because of their larger households. Central Americans fare somewhat better than Mexicans because of both their higher earnings capacity and smaller average households.

Additionally, Hispanics experienced deterioration in economic well-being over time relative to

whites, whose incomes have risen more when times were good and fallen less during recessions.[61] The median household income of Hispanics averaged 74 percent of that of whites during the early 1970s, but eroded following the 1973 oil crisis-induced recession. On the heels of another economic downturn in the early 1980s, the Hispanic-white income ratio deteriorated further, falling below 70 percent in 1985–1988 and again in 1992–1998, reaching its nadir in 1995 at 61 percent.[62] Although white-Hispanic median household incomes converged during the brisk economic growth of the late 1990s, there are signs that the relative income position of Hispanics is eroding yet again.[63] Median incomes of black households were consistently lower than those of Hispanics throughout the period, but over time their income position improved relative to both whites and Hispanics. In 1972, the median black household income was 77 percent that of whites, compared with 90 percent in 2003.[64] Because these comparisons do not separate out native- and foreign-born house holders, it is difficult to distinguish changes related to increased numbers of low-skill immigrants from

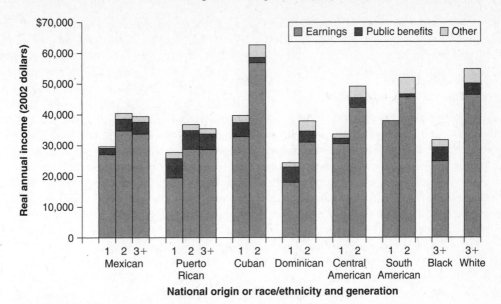

FIGURE 20.5   Sources of median total household income by Hispanic national origin or race/ethnicity and generation.

Notes: Includes only households whose head is under age 65. Means are simple averages across households, using household weights. Households with zero or negative total income or containing persons with negative income from any source are excluded. Results for Hispanics are shown only for cells with at least 90 observations.

Source: Pooled March CPS files, 1998–2002.

those related to business cycle variations. Yet the Survey of Income and Program Participation one of very few surveys that record annual variation in income, poverty and wealth, indicates a convergence of wealth between native- and foreign-born Hispanics between 1996 and 2001.[65]

Hispanics compensate for low household income through two strategies: income pooling based on tended living arrangements and reliance on public benefits (see Figure 20.5). Relative to both whites and blacks, Hispanic households are more likely to include relatives outside the nuclear family, and extended members' average contributions to household income are higher. Extended living arrangements are most common among immigrant generations but decline thereafter. Mexicans, Central Americans, and Dominicans of the immigrant generation are especially reliant on extended-household members for income pooling whereas Hispanics with U.S.-born parents largely resemble blacks in their tendency to rely on other relatives for support.

To what extent complex households reflect Hispanic cultural values (familism) versus economic need is unclear. Clearly, however, reliance on this multiple-source income pooling declines over time as the rising prosperity of second and higher generations reduces the need for such compensatory income strategies.

Among Hispanic subgroups Dominicans and Puerto Ricans under age 65 rely most heavily on public assistance, the second key source of income supplementation. In the case of Puerto Ricans, this largely reflects their high share of single female heads of household; the scarcity of jobs and relatively generous benefit programs in the northeast where many Puerto Ricans live; and the fact that as U.S. citizens, Puerto Ricans (unlike immigrants) are eligible for public benefit programs. Although second-generation Puerto Ricans rely less than the first generation on income from public benefits, even those born on the mainland depend more on this source of household income compared with other Hispanic subgroups—indeed, at rates more similar to those of blacks. Puerto Ricans' high rates of welfare participation reflect their elevated poverty rates.

Poverty and Wealth Among Hispanics

Trends in median household income conceal the poverty of those at the low end and the prosperity of those at the high end of the income Ladder. Indeed, poverty rates dramatize the consequences of poor employment and earnings capacities more effectively than does median household income. Although poverty rates declined during the 1990s—by 3 and 4 percentage points for Hispanics and blacks, respectively—Hispanic poverty held fast at more than 2.5 times the rate among whites.[66] In 1999, more than one in five Hispanics lived below the official poverty line ($16,895 for a family of four or a meager $12 per day per person).[67] Broken out by birthplace, declines in poverty were smallest for Puerto Ricans and greatest for Dominicans, who witnessed the largest drop in absolute poverty during the 1990s.[68] Central American immigrants were less likely to be poor than were Mexicans, Puerto Ricans, and Dominicans of the same generation but their poverty rates were higher than those of South Americans.[69]

The similar overall poverty rates for first-generation Mexicans, Dominicans, and Puerto Ricans have different sources. As the least-educated group, Mexicans have the lowest overall earning capacity a liability that persists beyond the second generation. Predominantly recent immigrants with limited skills, Dominicans are, like Puerto Ricans, further handicapped by a high incidence of female-headed households. Having only one potential earner exacerbates the effects of women's low average earnings in depressing household income. Combined, these conditions produce income shortfalls that are only minimally compensated by benefit programs.[70]

Poverty is especially pernicious for children because it is associated with many deleterious outcomes, such as low scholastic achievement, adolescent parenting, substance abuse, and violence.[71] In 1999, more than one in four Hispanics under the age of 18 were poor, compared with nearly one in ten whites. Child poverty rates among Dominicans and Puerto Ricans—35 and

33 percent, respectively—were comparable to those of blacks. Cuban and South American youths experienced the lowest rates of poverty between 16 and 17 percent. Child poverty rates of Mexicans and Central Americans approached the Hispanic population average—28 and 24 percent, respectively—which is well above the 17 percent overall U.S. poverty rate for those under 18.[72] Elevated Hispanic child poverty rates are particularly disturbing because the relatively young age structure of the population implies large and growing numbers of the youthful poor, and because poverty magnifies the challenges of assimilation and integration for the burgeoning second generation.

Poverty levels are also elevated among elderly Hispanics. The elderly are only a small proportion of the Hispanic population today but their numbers will grow rapidly in the future. Today's elderly provide a glimpse of how current Hispanic workers are likely to fare at advanced ages, depending on whether the present Social Security and Medicare safety nets remain intact. Overall, about one in five elderly Hispanics was poor in 1999, compared with fewer than one in ten whites and one in four blacks. The poverty risk for Hispanic elderly varies according to national origin reflecting incomes and types of jobs held at younger ages as well as Length of time in the U.S. labor market. Mirroring child poverty differentials, elderly poverty rates are highest for Puerto Ricans and Dominicans—24 and 29 percent respectively—and lowest for South Americans, at 16 percent.[73] Poverty rates for other groups are close to the elderly Hispanic population average of 20 percent.

Because Hispanics tend to work for employers that do not offer pensions, elderly Hispanic householders rely more on other sources of income than do either blacks or whites. Moreover, except for Puerto Ricans and Cubans, foreign-born Hispanics rely less on Social Security than do whites and blacks because they are less likely to qualify for the benefits even if they work beyond the required 40 quarters. Until recently, the sectors in which many elderly Hispanics worked, such as agriculture and household service, were not covered by Social Security, which accounts for 42 percent of household income for elderly Central and South

American immigrants, but close to 60 percent for blacks and island-born Puerto Ricans.[74]

Elderly immigrants who have not completed the required 10 years in covered jobs to qualify for Social Security benefits or whose benefits are Low because of a lifetime of low-wage work often qualify for Supplemental Security Income (SSI), which offers less generous benefits than those provided by Social Security.[75] Elderly foreign-born Hispanics (with the exception of South Americans) derive a larger share of their income from SSI than do blacks, signaling their greater vulnerability to poverty, especially during inflationary periods. By qualifying for Social Security at higher rates, U.S.-born elderly Hispanics mitigate this risk to some extent and face better economic prospects relative to blacks.

Less well documented than trends and disparities in Hispanic poverty are changes at the high end of the income distribution—namely wealth. Net worth is a pertinent indicator of economic well-being because it represents assets that can be tapped in times of financial distress. Recent estimates of Hispanic wealth range from 3 to 9 percent of white median wealth.[76] Home equity constitutes the largest component of Hispanic household wealth, about 50 to 60 percent of net worth during the 1996–2002 periods.[77] Less easily converted to cash than other assets in the event of financial crisis, home equity is the source of last resort to offset fluctuations in household income. The reversal of nearly two decades of wage stagnation in the late 1990s also allowed Hispanics to participate in the stock market, albeit to a much lesser extent than whites.[78]

Not only is home equity the largest component of household wealth, but it is also a key marker of middle-class status. Home ownership provides access to myriad social amenities that influence overall well-being, including school quality, neighborhood safety, recreation facilities, and access to health care organizations (see below).[79] Although Hispanic home ownership rates rose from 33 to 44 percent between 1983 and 2001, they have been relatively stagnant since the mid-1990s, even as the rates for white householders have climbed.[80] Consequently, the Hispanic-white ownership ratio, which rose from 48 to 64 percent from the mid-1980s to the mid 1990s, eroded to 60 percent by 2001.[81]

Whether the geographic dispersal of Hispanics from areas with higher to those with lower housing costs will reverse this trend remains unclear. Census data for the largest 100 metro areas indicate that both native- and foreign-born Hispanics participated in rising rates of home ownership during the 1990s owing to favorable interest rates, rising incomes, and the pace of housing construction relative to employment growth.[82] For the foreign born, however, ownership rates increased in the traditional settlement hubs while declining in the new destinations. Because the dispersal of Hispanics to new destinations is a relatively recent phenomenon that involves many recently arrived, low-skill immigrants. . . , it is conceivable that their lower average home ownership rates will improve over time as they acculturate in their new locales.[83]

Health Status and Access to Care

Like other forms of human capital, health status—both physical and psychological—is an asset that requires investments for improvement and maintenance.[84] In addition to nutritious food, regular exercise, and a toxin-free environment, health status depends on a variety of circumstances—some unique to Hispanics and others shared with populations of similar socioeconomic status, some linked to behavior that compromises or promotes health, and others associated with access to care.

Health Status and Behaviors[85]

Like other indicators of integration, Hispanic health status differs according to subgroup, immigrant generation, English proficiency, and degree of acculturation. Puerto Ricans are less healthy, on average, than other Hispanic subgroups while Mexicans, Central Americans, and South Americans often compare favorably with whites on several health indicators, despite their low average socioeconomic status. For example, the age-adjusted mortality of Hispanics is lower than that of blacks or whites; the exception is Puerto Ricans, whose mortality rates are higher than those of other Hispanic subgroups (see Figure 20.6) Dubbed the Hispanic "epidemiological paradox" or "immigrant health paradox" by researchers, the lower mortality rates of

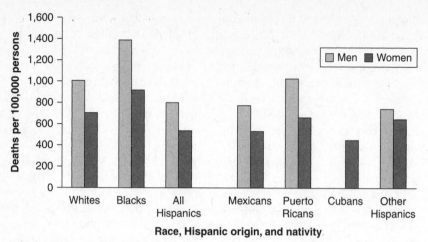

FIGURE 20.6   Age-adjusted mortality for whites, blacks, and Hispanics by sex, 2001.
Source: Arias et al. (2003).

Hispanics relative to those of whites with more favorable socioeconomic status have puzzled social and health scientists since the 1980s. Precise findings differ, but most studies show that foreign-born Mexicans, Central Americans, and South Americans are most likely to experience this advantage. One factor that contributes to their lower mortality is that healthier people are more likely to migrate than the sickly, but it is not a sufficient explanation. Why mortality rates are comparable for U.S.-born Hispanics and whites, however, remains a puzzle.

Hispanics also experience favorable birth outcomes in terms of birth weight and infant mortality, another case in which they fare much better than would be expected given their socioeconomic status. In 2001, Hispanics' infant mortality rate of 5.4 per 1,000 live births compared favorably with those of 5.7 for whites and 13.5 for blacks. Cubans (4.2), Central and South Americans (5.0), and Mexicans (5.2) all had lower infant mortality rates than whites, while Puerto Ricans (8.5) fared better than blacks but worse than whites.[86]

Experts often invoke protective cultural and social behaviors of immigrants to explain their advantage in birth outcomes relative to their U.S.-born counterparts. However, since second-generation Hispanic women also have relatively favorable birth outcomes compared with white women of comparable socioeconomic status,

cultural explanations do not suffice. Other assets in the Hispanic health ledger include a lower incidence of several major cancers and relatively low rates of activity limitation (e.g., climbing stairs, getting dressed) compared with whites, along with mental health profiles that resemble those of whites. In 2000, for example, the age-adjusted death rate from cancer was 134.9 per 100,000 for Hispanics compared with 200.6 per 100,000 for whites. Hispanics also smoke less than whites; the exception is Puerto Ricans, who smoke at similar rates.[87]

Hispanics also experience several health liabilities, diabetes and hypertension being by far the most severe. The rising prevalence of Hispanic adults considered overweight or obese likely contributes to higher rates of both conditions as well as to cardiovascular disease. Although the U.S. epidemic of overweight and obese adults affects all racial and ethnic groups, it is particularly severe for Hispanics. Among Mexicans, 29 percent of men and 40 percent of women are considered obese, compared with 27 percent and 30 percent, respectively of white men and women.[88]

Trends in overweight among Hispanic youths are particularly worrisome. Hispanic children and adolescents—Mexican and Puerto Rican girls in particular—are much more likely than whites to be overweight. Girls of Mexican origin are nearly twice as likely as white girls to be overweight,

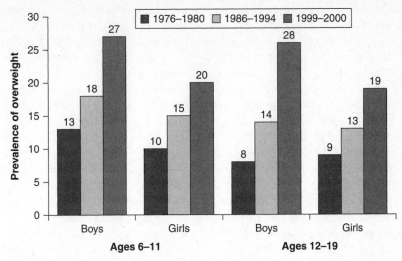

FIGURE 20.7 Time trends in overweight among children and adolescents of Mexican origin 1976–1980 to 1999–2000.

Source: National Center for Health Statistic (2003) (see Escarce et al., 2006).

while Mexican-origin boys are more than twice as likely as white boys to be overweight. Even more troubling, rates of overweight have risen faster for Hispanic than for white youths (see Figure 20.7). Over the last quarter century or so, the prevalence of overweight preadolescent (ages 6–11) Mexican youths doubled—rising from 13 to 27 percent for boys and from 10 to 20 percent for girls. The rate of adolescents (ages 12–19) considered overweight more than trebled for both boys (from 8 to 28 percent) and doubled for girls (from 9 to 19 percent) over the same period.[89]

Those who claim that acculturation contributes to the rise in Hispanic overweight and obesity point to immigrants' diets, which are richer in fruits and vegetables and lower in fats compared with those of native-born youths, who are more prone to consume high-fat processed and fast foods. Generational differences in diet are mirrored in the prevalence of overweight adolescents, as about one in four first-generation adolescent Hispanics is at risk of being overweight, compared with about one in three second- and third-generation youths.[90]

Several other differences in the health circumstances of Hispanic youths are worth noting. With the exception of Puerto Ricans, Hispanic youths have low rates of asthma, the major chronic disease of childhood. This health asset is offset by their worse oral health compared with their white peers. Hispanic youths also register higher blood lead levels than white children, which places them at greater risk for the adverse effects of lead poisoning on cognitive development.[91]

Hispanic adolescents engage in many health-compromising behaviors, such as use of alcohol and illicit drugs and early sex, at rates comparable to those of white teens, although their tobacco use is lower. Cuban-origin youths have the highest levels of tobacco, alcohol, and drug use, followed by those of Mexican and Puerto Rican origin. By comparison youths from other Hispanic subgroups have low rates of drug use— probably because larger shares of these subgroups are a first-generation immigrant, which means they are less acculturated. In general, acculturated youths engage in such health-compromising behaviors more often than the less acculturated. Hispanic young people also experience poor mental health, exhibiting the highest prevalence of depression of any ethnic group. Although Hispanic adolescent girls are as likely as white adolescents to consider suicide, they are twice as likely to attempt it. Their suicide completion rate, however, is lower than that of other ethnic groups.

The significance of these and other health-compromising behaviors among adolescents transcends their own physical well-being. In 2003, Hispanics had the highest teen birthrate, with 82.2 births per 1,000 adolescent females ages 15–19. In comparison, the birthrate for teens of all backgrounds was 41.7, while that for white teens was 27.5 and for black teens were 64.8.[92] Such statistics bode ill for the educational prospects of Hispanic adolescents, who are more likely than either blacks or whites to withdraw from school if they become mothers.[93] Indeed, all health conditions and behaviors that affect scholastic performance—including not only adolescent childbearing, but also drug and alcohol use and exposure to lead and other environmental contaminant especially worrisome because of the lifelong consequences of educational underachievement discussed above.

Access to Quality Care

Hispanics face a variety of financial and nonfinancial obstacles to obtaining appropriate health care. Low rates of insurance coverage are perhaps most notable, but limited access to providers, language barriers,

and uneven quality of care exacerbates inequities in health outcomes between Hispanics and whites and between native- and foreign-born Hispanics.

The lack of insurance coverage is greater among foreign-born compared with U.S.-born Hispanics, Spanish compared with English speakers, recent compared with earlier immigrants, and noncitizens compared with citizens. Undocumented immigrants are least likely to be insured; one estimate of their uninsured rates ranges between 68 and 84 percent.[94] Owing to their large shares of recent immigrants, Mexicans and Central and South Americans have the highest uninsured rates. Puerto Ricans and Cubans have the highest insurance rates, with sources of coverage differing between the two groups. Puerto Rican children and working-age adults are much more likely than their Cuban counterparts to obtain health coverage through public insurance programs such as Medicaid and the State Children's Health Insurance Program (SCHIP), but they are less likely to obtain it through an employer (see Figure 20.8a and 20.8b). For Hispanic seniors, eligibility for the Medicare program keeps insurance coverage rates relatively high.

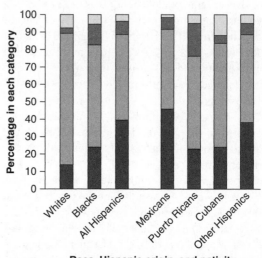

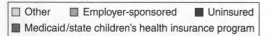

FIGURE 20.8a Health insurance coverage for white, black, and Hispanic children, 1997 to 2001.

Source: 1997 to 2001 Medical Expenditure Panel Survey.

FIGURE 20.8b Health insurance coverage for white, black, and Hispanic working age adults, 1997 to 2001.

Source: 1997 to 2001 Medical Expenditure Panel Survey.

Compared with whites, Hispanics have lower access to employer-provided health insurance because they are more likely than whites to work in small firms, in seasonal occupations and in part-time jobs.[95] Limited eligibility for public insurance programs, such as Medicaid and SCHIP, further accentuates Hispanics' low coverage rates (with the exception of Puerto Ricans). Many Hispanics—especially Mexicans and Cubans—live in states with restrictive eligibility rules for Medicaid and SCHIP. The federal welfare reforms of 1996 placed further limitations on access to public health insurance programs for all recent legal immigrants.[96] General confusion about how the new laws affected immigrants triggered declines in their overall utilization of public insurance programs.

Partly because of low rates of health insurance coverage, Hispanics are less likely than whites to have a usual source of care or regular health care provider, which in turn restricts their access to more specialized forms of care. The relatively low number of Hispanic physicians, especially in Hispanics' new destinations, further hinders access to care because Hispanic physicians are more likely than their non-Hispanic counterparts to care for Hispanic patients. Given their large share of recent immigrants, Mexicans are less likely than Puerto Ricans or Cubans to have a usual source of care, as are Spanish speakers compared with English speakers. Furthermore, language barriers undermine quality health care, even among groups with similar demographic and socioeconomic characteristics, by hindering patient-provider communication; by reducing access to health information; and in the worst case, by decreasing the likelihood that sick patients will seek needed care.[97]

Hispanics' low rates of insurance and reduced likelihood of having a regular health care provider mean less preventive care, fewer ambulatory visits, and higher rates of emergency room use compared with whites, although Hispanics' rates of inpatient care are equivalent to those of whites. The preventive services on which Hispanics trail whites include pneumococcal and influenza vaccinations for seniors; mammography, pap smears, and colon cancer screening; blood pressure and cholesterol measurements and prenatal care for the general population. In 2001, just 75 percent of Mexican and 79 percent of

Puerto Rican women received prenatal care in their first trimester, compared with 92 percent of Cuban and 89 percent of white women. Hispanic-White differences in childhood vaccination rates are trivial.[98]

Evidence on the quality of care received by Hispanics is inconclusive, partly because current assessments are based on populations that are not truly representatives such as low income Medicaid recipients and partly because results from satisfaction surveys are inconsistent. Nonetheless, Hispanics' reported satisfaction with health care delivery reveals large differences, depending on the degree of English proficiency. In general, Hispanics who speak only Spanish report worse experiences with health care than either whites or Hispanics who speak English. Satisfied patients are more likely to seek care when needed, to comply with provider recommendations, and to remain enrolled in health plans and with specific providers. Paradoxically, and for reasons not fully understood, Spanish-speaking Hispanics rate their physicians and health plans higher than do English-proficient Hispanics despite admitting to worse care experiences.

To reduce language barriers to health care, the Department of Health and Human Services issued a directive in August 2000 requiring all federally funded programs and providers to offer interpreter services at no cost.[99] Yet only about half of Hispanic patients who need an interpreter receive one. In most cases, the interpreter is a staff person, relative, or friend rather than a trained medical interpreter; in such cases, reported satisfaction rates remain below those of whites.

Conclusion

Hispanic integration experiences are as diverse as the eclectic subgroups subsumed under the panethnic identity but some general trends are discernible. Hispanic families converge in form and function with those of the white majority and rising intermarriage blurs the boundaries of nationality groups. The rise in divorce and nonmarital childbearing over time and across generations signal family decline. The rise of mother-only families bodes ill for economic prospects of the swelling second generation.

There are dear signs of educational progress at all levels both over time and across generations. That other groups also have improved their educational standing has widened attainment gaps, particularly at the college level. Because the fastest-growing and best-paying jobs now require at least some postsecondary education, Hispanics stand to lose economic ground even as their educational attainment rises. Still, employment and earnings trends show clear evidence of economic assimilation, with the greatest gains between the first and second generation. If the most successful third-generation Hispanics "opt out" of Hispanic identity, as available data suggest, economic progress for the third and later generations may well be understated.

Trends in Hispanic home ownership and median household income signal a growing middle class, although the dollar growth of Hispanic household assets is small compared with that recorded by white households.[100] Variation in financial status by immigrant and citizenship status, by age (favoring middle-aged over young householders) and especially by earnings capacity and educational attainment, largely explains the significant gap in economic well-being between Hispanics and whites. As long as this gap persists however, Hispanics will remain more vulnerable to economic cycles because they have less of a cushion on which to draw during periods of financial distress.

Finally, recent health trends paint the picture of a Hispanic population burdened by the complications of obesity, diabetes, hypertension, and cardiovascular disease, which Americanization appears to worsen rather than improve. The deleterious effects of acculturation are especially evident among second-generation youths and in birth outcomes. Most striking is the high incidence of type 2 diabetes—usually a disease of adults—among young Hispanics and the increased prevalence of multiple risk factors for developing atherosclerosis among children of Mexican origin.[101] These trends foreshadow much higher rates of diabetes and its complications in the future, as large cohorts of Hispanic youths become adults.

The growing number of uninsured Hispanics will place particular stress on the health care safety net—a loosely organized system for delivering care to the uninsured that includes nonprofit organizations, government agencies, and individual providers. By default, some of the responsibility for health care delivery will shift to states and local communities, many of which are already struggling to compensate for shortfalls created by declining federal funding. Experts in both the public and private sectors consider cultural competence—the ability of health systems to provide care to patients with diverse values, beliefs, and behaviors, including tailoring delivery to meet patients social, cultural, and linguistic needs—to be a crucial component of strategies to reduce disparities in care.[102] Compliance with the Federal directive to provide interpreter services at care facilities is especially warranted in new immigrant destinations.

Notes

1. These findings are documented in greater detail in Landale et al., 2006.
2. Popenoe, 1993
3. Landale and Oropesa, 2002.
4. Landale and Drop. The evidence for declines in familism among Central and South American nationalities is less clear than in the case for Mexicans because the generational depth is lower.
5. Landale et al., 2006.
6. Lee and Edmonston, 2005.
7. Edmonston et al., 2002, note that all population projections involve higher rates of intermarriage.
8. These findings are documented in greater detail in Schneider et al., 2006.
9. Mare, 1995.
10. See Duncan et al., 2006: Table 6-1.
11. Crosnoe, 2005; Crosnoe et al., 2004; Valencia, 2000.
12. U.S. Department of Education, National Center For Education Statistics, 1999.
13. U.S. Department of Education, National Center for Education Statistics, 1997.
14. U.S. Department of Education, National Center for Education Statistics, 2003b.
15. Carnegie Council of Adolescent Development.
16. Bryk and Schneider, 2002.
17. U.S. Department of Education, National Center for Education Statistics, 2003b; Valencia, 2002.
18. Bryk and Schneider, 2002.

19. Schneider and Stevenson, 1999.

20. This distinction is important because the Hispanic high school drop-out rate has been inflated by the presence of foreign-born adolescents who withdrew from school before entering the United States.

21. U.S. Department of Education, National Center for Education Statistics, 2003a: Table 106.

22. Cameron and Heckman, 1993.

23. Fry, 2005; Hirschman, 2001.

24. Carnevale, 1999.

25. Tienda and Simonelli, 2001.

26. Kao and Tienda, 1998.

27. U.S. Department of Education, National Center for Education Statistics, 2002.

28. U.S. Department of Education, National Center for Education Statistics, 2003b.

29. Kim and Schneider, 2004 Portes and Rumbaut, 2001.

30. Fry; 2002, 2003.

31. College Enrollment and Work Activity of Year 2000 High School Graduates. Available: ftp://ftp.bls.gov/pub/news.release/History/hsgec.04132001.news [accessed December 23, 2005].

32. Schneider et al., 2006.

33. Velez, 1985.

34. Alon and Tienda, 2005; Fry, 2004.

35. Clark, 2003; Kochhar, 2004; Wolf, 2004.

36. These findings are documented in greater detail in Duncan et al., 2006.

37. Chiswick, 1978; Schoeni, 1997.

38. The annual employment rate is defined as the percentage of individuals who worked at all during the calendar year preceding the census. Similar results are obtained using annual hours of work as a measure of labor supply.

39. Dominican men also have relatively low employment rates, but nativity differentials for them are small.

40. Duncan et al., 2006: Table 6-4.

41. The estimated deficits are for persons ages 25 to 59 who worked during calendar year 1999, based on regressions by Duncan et al., 290 Appendix Table A6-7.

42. This is not the case for black men, however, as their 15 percentage point employment deficit would shrink to only 13 percentage points if their human capital endowments were comparable to those of whites.

43. The employment gaps for Puerto Ricans and Dominicans may be due, in part to their concentration in goods-producing industries in the northeast that have been hurt by deindustrialization, and in part to the fact that their employment patterns are more similar to those of blacks than to those of other Hispanic groups. See DeFreitas, 1991.

44. In contrast to black men, black women's modest earnings disadvantage relative to white women would disappear if they had comparable levels of human capital.

45. Phillips and Massey, 2000; Rivera-Batiz, 1999.

46. See Duncan et al., 2006.

47. Evidence that darker, more Indian-looking Mexican Americans are vulnerable to discrimination based on skin color. See Mien et al., 2000.

48. Lowell and Fry, 2002.

49. Smith, 2001.

50. Duncan et al., 2006: Table 6-7.

51. Borjas, 1994 Chiswick, 1997; Neidert and Farley, 1985; Perlmann and Waldinger, 1997.

52. Duncan et al., 2006: Figure 5-8.

53. Borjas, 1993; Smith, 2003.

54. Smith 2003, reports a 4.-year mean education gap among all first-generation Mexicans (Table 3). This deficit fell to 2.95 years among second-generation Mexicans.

55. Alba and Nee, 1997 Duncan and Trejo, 2005; Idles et al., 2002.

56. Duncan and Trejo, 2005; Duncan et al., 2006; Reimers, 2006.

57. Edmonston et al., 2002; Rutter and Tienda, 2005.

58. Smith, 2003; see Duncan et al., 2006; Reimers, 2006.

59. U.S. Census Bureau; Income 1999. Available: http://www.census.gov/hhes/www/income/income99/99tablea.html [accessed December 27, 2005]

60. Those who were born in the United States have income levels similar to those of whites.

61. U.S. Bureau of the Census, 2004b.

62. U.S. Bureau of the Census, 2004b.

63. Wolff, 2004.

64. The Hispanic-black median income differential exceeded 90 percent between 1995 and 1997, hovering around 94 to 98 percent. See Wolff, 2004: Tables 7 and 8.

65. Kochhar, 2004.

66. Saenz, 2004: Table 11.

67. U.S. Bureau of the Census, 2000c. Poverty thresholds are not adjusted for cost-of-living differences. That large shares of Hispanics live in high-priced cities magnifies the welfare consequences of poverty-level incomes.

68. Saenz, 2004.

69. See Reimers, 2006: Table 7-2.

70. See, Reimers, 2006.
71. McLanahan and Sandefur, 1994.
72. U.S. Bureau of the Census, 2000a.
73. U.S. Bureau of the Census, 2000a.
74. Reimers, 2006.
75. Social Security is an "earned" benefit that automatically increases with the cost of living, but SSI is a minimal, means-tested safety net for those elderly who have no other income. Unlike SSI, Social Security is not viewed as "welfare" by the general public. Persons who qualify for Social Security benefits by working most of their adult years in covered jobs, even at a low wage, receive mote generous Social Security retirement benefits than persons forced to rely on SSI, the benefit rates of which ate below the poverty line.
76. Using the Federal Reserve Board's Survey of Consumer Finances, Wolff 2004, estimates Hispanic median net worth at 3 percent of the white median for 2001, but Kochhar, 2004, estimates the 2002 median gap at 9 percent—$8,000 versus $89,000—based on the Survey of Income and Program Participation. One source of the difference is that Wolff excludes equity in vehicles and other consumer durables from his estimate of wealth. However, both sets of estimates reveal similar trends, if not levels, for their overlapping period, namely mid-1990s to 2001–2002.
77. Kochhar, 2004: Table 9.
78. Wolff 2004: 26. Stock ownership is concentrated among households in the top quintile of the wealth distribution, accounting for 90 percent of all stock holdings.
79. Clark, 2003.
80. Wolff, 2004.
81. This estimate is close to the .62 for 2000 reported by Fischer and Tienda, 2006, on the basis of census data for the largest 100 metro areas.
82. Fischer and Tienda, 2006; Myers et al., 2005.
83. See Kochhar, 2004.
84. Grossman, 1972.
85. Our emphasis on Mexican-white comparisons reflects the paucity of research comparing other Hispanic nationalities in terms of specific health outcomes. This section draws from Escarce et al., 2006.
86. National Center for Health Statistics, 2003.
87. National Center for Health Statistics, 2003.
88. National Center for Health Statistics, 2003. National data are unavailable on the epidemiology of cardiovascular disease for Hispanics. Moreover, experts disagree about a 7 and 8 the differences in death rates from heart disease between Hispanics and whites because regional studies have yielded conflicting findings, Escarce et al., 2006.
89. National Center for Health Statistics, 2003.
90. Escarce et al., 2006.
91. Escarce et al., 2006. The Centers for Disease Control and Prevention is currently lowering the threshold blood lead level for intervention from 10 μg/dL to 5 μg/dL. More than one-fourth of preschool-age children and one-fifth of elementary school children of Mexican origin would meet the revised threshold.
92. Ryan et al., 2005.
93. Ahituv and Tienda, 2000.
94. Berk et al., 1999.
95. See Brown and Yu, 2002; Dushi and Honig, 2005; Schur and Feldman, 2001.
96. The 1996 Personal Responsibility and work Opportunity Reconciliation Act (the federal welfare reform law) barred legal immigrants who entered the United States after August 1996 from receiving federal Medicaid or SCHIP benefits for their first 5 years in the country. Although states can offer coverage for legal immigrants during the 5-year moratorium imposed by the federal regulations, few have elected to do so.
97. Langer, 1999; Ruiz et al., 1922.
98. Escarce and Kapur, 2006. A likely explanation for the shrinking gap in childhood vaccination rates is the Vaccines for Children program, created in 1994, which provides vaccines free of charge to eligible children, including the uninsured.
99. Department of Health and Human Services, 2000.
100. Kochhar 2004: Tables 17 and 19.
101. Te et al., 2006. Other consequences of the overweight epidemic among Hispanic youth include elevated blood pressure and high rates of insulin resistance, hyperinsulinemia, glucose intolerance, and abnormalities in serum lipids. Hispanic youth also have higher triglyceride levels and lower levels of high-density lipoprotein cholesterol than white youth.
102. Betancourt et al., 2002.

References

Ahituv, A., and Tienda, M. (2000). Employment, motherhood, and school continuation decisions of young white, black, and Hispanic women. *Journal of Labor Economics, 22*(1), 115–158.

Alba, R.D., and Nee, V. (1997). Rethinking assimilation theory for a new era of Immigration, *International Migration Review, 31*(Winter), 826–874.

Allen W., Telles, E., and Hunter, M. (2000). Skin color, income and education: A comparison of African Americans and Mexican Americans. *National Journal of Sociology, 12*(1), 129–180.

Alon, S., and Tienda. M. (2005). Assessing the mismatch hypothesis: Differentials in college graduation rates by institutional selectivity. *Sociology of Education, 78,* 294–315.

Berk, M.L., Schur, C.L., Chavez, L.R., and Frankel, M. (2000 July-August). Health care use among undocumented Latino immigrants. *Health Affairs, 19*(4), 51–64.

Betancourt, J.R., Green, A.R., and Carrillo, J.E. (2002, October). *Cultural competence in health care: Emerging frameworks and practical approaches.* New York: The Commonwealth Fund. Available: http://www.cmwf.org [accessed May 12, 2004].

Borjas, G.J. (1993, January). The intergenerational mobility of immigrants. *Journal of Labor Economics, 11*(1), 113–135.

Borjas, G.J. (1994, July). Long-run convergence of ethnic skill differentials: The children and grandchildren of the great migration. *Industrial and Labor Relations Review, 47*(4), 553–573.

Brown, E. R., and Yu, H. (2002). Latinos' access to employment-based health insurance. In M.M. Suarez-Orozco and M.M. Paez (Eds.), *Latinos: Remaking America* (pp. 236–253). Berkeley: University of California Press.

Bryk, A.S., and Schneider, B. (2002). *Trust in schools: A core resource for improvement.* New York: Russell Sage Foundation.

Cameron, S.J., and Heckman, J.J. (1993). The nonequivalence of high school equivalents. *Journal of Labor Economics, 11*(1), 1–47.

Carnegie Council on Adolescent Development (1989). *Turning points: Preparing American youth for the 21st century.* New York: Carnegie Corporation of New York.

Carnevale, A.P. (1999). *Education equals success: Empowering Hispanic youth and adults.* Princeton, NJ: Educational Testing Service for Hispanic Association of Colleges and Universities.

Chiswick, B.R. (1977, February). Sons of immigrants: Are they at an earnings disadvantage? *American Economic Review, 67*(1), 376–380.

Chiswick, B.R. (1978, October). The effect of Americanization on the earnings of foreign-born men. *Journal of Political Economy, 86*(5), 897–921.

Clark, W.A.V. (2003). *Immigrants and the American dream: Remaking the middle class.* New York: Guilford Press.

Crosnoe, R. (2005). Double disadvantage or signs of resilience? The elementary school contexts of children from Mexican immigrant families. *American Educational Research Journal, 42*(2), 269–303.

Crosnoe, R., Kirkpatrick, M., and Elder, G.H., Jr. (2004). School size and the interpersonal side of education: An examination of race/ethnicity and organizational context. *Social Sciences Quarterly, 85*(5), 1259–1274.

DeFreitas, G. (1991. *Inequality at work: Hispanics in the U.S. labor force.* New York: Oxford University Press.

Department of Health and Human Services. (2000, December). *Assuring cultural competence in health care: Recommendations for national standards and an outcomes-focused research agenda.* (The Office of Minority Health, vol. 65, no. 247, pp. 80865–80379.) Available: http://www.omhrc.govlclas/cultucalla.htm [accessed April 22, 2005]. . .

Duncan, B., Hotz, V.J., and Trejo, S.J. (2006). Hispanics in the U.S. labor market. In National Research Council, *Hispanics and the future of America* (Ch. 7). Panel on Hispanics in the United States, Committee on Population Division of Behavioral and Social Sciences and Education. Washington, DC: The National Academies Press.

Duncan, B., and Trejo, S.J. (2005). *Ethnic identification, intermarriage and unmeasured progress by Mexican Americans.* (Report No. 113423. NBER Working Papers National Bureau of Economic Research, Inc.) Orebro University, Sweden.

Dushi, I., and Honig. M. (2005, March). *Offers or take-up: Explaining minorities' lower health insurance coverage.* Available: http://www.umich.edu/~eriu/conferences/vpops_papers.html [accessed April 2005].

Edmonston, B., Lee, S.M., and Passel, J.S. (2002). Recent trends in intermarriage and immigration and their effects on the future racial composition of the U.S. population. In J. Perlmann and M.C. Waters (Eds.), *The new race question: How the census counts multiracial individuals* (pp. 227–255). New York: Russell Sage foundation.

Escarce, J.J., and Kapur, K. (2006). Access to and quality of health care. In National Research Council, *Hispanics and the future of America* (Ch. 10). Panel on Hispanics in the United States, Committee on Population, Division of Behavioral and Social Sciences and Education. Washington. DC: The National Academies Press.

Escarce, J.J., Morales, L.S., and Rumbaut, R.G. (2006). The health status and health behaviors of Hispanics. In National Research Council, *Hispanics and the future of America* (Ch. 9). Panel on Hispanics in the United States, Committee on Population, Division of Behavioral and Social Sciences and Education. Washington, DC: The National Academies Press.

Fischer, M.J., and Tienda, M. (2006). Redrawing spatial color lines: Hispanic metropolitan dispersal, segregation, and economic opportunity. In National Research Council, *Hispanics and the future of America* (Ch. 4). Panel on Hispanics in the United States, Committee on Population, Division of Behavioral and Social Sciences and Education. Washington, DC: The National Academies Press.

Fry, R. (2002). *Latinos in higher education: Many enroll, few graduate.* Washington, DC: Pew Hispanic Center.

Fry, R. (2003). *Hispanic youth dropping out of U.S. schools: Measuring the challenge.* Washington, DC: Pew Hispanic Center.

Fry, R. (2005). *The higher dropout rate of foreign-born teens: The role of schooling abroad.* Washington, DC: Pew Hispanic Center.

Grossman, M. (1972). On the concept of health capital and the demand for health. *Journal of Political Economy, 80,* 223–255.

Hirschman, C. (2001). The educational enrollment of immigrant youth: A text of the segmented-assimilation hypothesis. *Demography, 38,* 317–336.

Kao, G., and Tienda, M. (1998). Educational aspirations of minority youth. *American Journal of Education, 106,* 349–384.

Kim, D., and Schneider, B. (2004). *Social capital in action: Alignment of parental support in adolescents' transition to postsecondary education.* Unpublished paper presented at American sociological Association Annual Meeting, August 16.

Kochhar, R. (2004, October). The wealth of Hispanic households: 1996 to 2002. Washington DC: Pew Hispanic Center.

Landale, N.S., and Oropesa, R.S. (2002). White, black, or Puerto Rican? Racial self-identification among mainland and island Puerto Ricans. *Social Forces, 81,* 231–254.

Landale, N.S., Oropesa R.S., and Bradatan, C. (2006). Hispanic families in the United States: Family structure and process in an era of family change. In National Research Council, *Hispanics and the future of America* (Ch. 5). Panel on Hispanics in the United States, Committee on Population Division of

Behavioral and Social Sciences and Education. Washington, DC: The National Academies Press.

Langer, N. (1999). Culturally competent professional in therapeutic alliances enhance patient compliance. *Journal of Health Care for the Poor and Underserved, 10*(1), 19–26.

Lee, S.M., and Edmonston, B. (2005). *New marriages, new families: U.S. Racial and Hispanic Intermarriage.* (Population Bulletin, 60, No. 2.) Washington, DC: The Population Reference Bureau.

Lowell, LB., and Fry, R. (2002, March). *Estimating the distribution of undocumented workers in the urban labor force: Technical memorandum to how many undocumented (The numbers behind the U.S.-Mexican migration talks,).* Washington, DC: Pew Hispanic Center.

Mare, R. (1995). Changes in educational attainment and school enrollment. In R. Farley (Ed.), *State of the union: America in the 1990s* (pp. 155–214). New York: Russell Sage Foundation.

McLanahan, S., and Sandefur, G. 1994). *Growing up with a single parent: What hurts, what helps?* Cambridge, MA: Harvard University Press.

Myers, D., Pitkin, J., and Park, J. (2005). *California demographic futures: Projections to 2030, by immigrant generations, nativity, and time of arrival in US.* Los Angeles: University of Southern California, School of Policy, Planning, and Development.

National Center for Health Statistics. (2003). *Health, United States, 2003.* (DHHS Publication No. 2003–1232.) Hyattsville, MD: Author.

Neidert, L.J., and Farley, R. (1985). Assimilation in the United States: An analysis of ethnic and generation differences in status and achievement. *American Sociological Review, 50*(6), 840–850.

Perlmann, J., and Waldinger, R. (1997). Second generation decline? Children of immigrants, past and present: A reconsideration. *International Migration Review, 31*(4), 893–922.

Phillips, J.A., and Massey, D.S. (2000). Engines of immigration: Stocks of human and social capital in Mexico. *Social Science Quarterly, 81,* 33–48.

Popenoe, D. (1993). American family decline, 1960-1990: A review and appraisal. *Journal of Marriage and Family, 55,* 527–555.

Portes, A., and Rumbaut, R.G. (2001). *Legacies: The story of the immigrant second generation.* Berkeley and New York: University of California Press and Russell Sage Foundation.

Reimers, C. (2006). Economic well-being. In National Research Council, *Hispanics and the future of America* (Ch. 8). Panel on Hispanics in the United

States, Committee on Population, Division of Behavioral and Social Sciences and Education. Washington, DC: The National Academies Press.

Rivera-Batiz, F.L. (1999). Undocumented workers in the labor market: An analysis of the earnings of legal and illegal Mexican immigrants in the United States. *Journal of Population Economics, 12*(1), 91–116.

Ruiz, M.S., Marks, G., and Richardson, J.L. (1992). Language acculturation and screening practices of elderly Hispanic women: The role of exposure to health-related information from the media. *Journal of Aging and Health, 4*(2), 268–281.

Ryan, S., Franzetta, K., and Manlove, J. (2005, February). *Hispanic teen pregnancy and birth rates: Looking behind the numbers* (Research Brief). Washington, DC: Child Trends.

Saenz, R. (2004). *Latinos and the changing face of America.* New York: Russell Sage Foundation and Population Reference Bureau.

Schneider, B., and Stevenson, D. (1999). *The ambitious generation: America's teenagers, motivated but directionless.* New Haven, CT: Yale University Press.

Schneider, B., Martinez, S., and Owens, A. (2006). Barriers to educational opportunities for Hispanics in the United States. In National Research Council, *Hispanics and the future of America* (Ch. 6). Panel on Hispanics in the United States, Committee on Population, Division of Behavioral and Social Sciences and Education. Washington, DC: The National Academies Press.

Schur, C.L., and Feldman, J. (2001, May). *Running in place: How job characteristics, immigrant status, and family structure keep Hispanics uninsured.* Available: http://www.cmwf.org/pablicationslpublications_show. htm?doc_id=221348 [accessed March 2, 2005].

Smith, J.P. (2001). Race and ethnicity in the labor market: Trends over the short and long term. In N.J. Smelser, W.J. Wilson, and F. Mitchell (Eds.), *America becoming: Racial trends and their consequences* (vol. II, pp. 52–97). Washington, DC: National Academies Press.

Smith, J.P. (2003). Assimilation across the Latino generations. *American Economic Review, 93*(2), 315–319.

Tienda, M., and Simonelli, S. (2001). Unplugging the pipeline: Education and affirmative action. In Institute of Medicine, *The right thing to do, the smart thing to do: Enhancing diversity in health professions. Summary of the Symposium on Diversity in Health Professions in Honor of Herbert W. Nickens, M.D.*

(pp. 117–142). B.D. Smedley, AX. Stith, L. Colburn, and C.H. Evans (Eds.). Nickens Symposium Advisory Committee. Washington, DC: National Academies Press.

U.S. Bureau of the Census. (2000a). *We the people: Hispanics in the United States.* (Special Report CENSR-18). Washington, DC: Author, Ethnic and Hispanic Statistics Branch. Population Division.

U.S. Bureau of the Census. (2000c). *Poverty 1999: Poverty thresholds in 1999.* Available: http://www. Census.gov/hhes/poverty/threshld/thresh99.html [accessed January 26, 2005].

U.S. Bureau of the Census. (2004b). *Historical income tables: Households, Table 5.* Available: http://wwsv. Census.gov/hhes/income/histinc/h05.html [accessed March 11, 2004].

U.S. Department of Education, National Center for teachers: Profile of a profession, 1993–94. (NCES 97-460, R.R. Henke, S.P Choy, X. Chen, S. Geis, and M.N. Alt, eds.) Washington, DC: Author.

U.S. Department of Education, National Center for Education Statistics it (1999). *National household education survey* (Parent Interview Component, public-use data, weighted.) Washington, DC: Author.

U.S. Department of Education, National Center for Education Statistics (2002). *The condition of education.* (Based on 1998 High School Transcripts Study) Washington, DC: Author.

U.S. Department of Education. National Center for Education Statistics (2003a). *Digest of education statistics, 2002.* (NCES 2003-060, T.D. Snyder and C.M. Hoffman, eds.) Washington, DC: U.S. Author.

U.S. Department of Education, National Center for Education Statistics. (2003b). *Status and trends in the education of Hispanics.* (NCES 2003-008.) Washington, DC: Author.

Valencia, R.R. (2000). Inequalities and the schooling of minority students in Texas: Historical and contemporary conditions. *Hispanic Journal of Behavioral Sciences, 22*(4): 445–459.

Valencia. R.R. (2002). *Chicano school failure and success: Past, present and future.* New York: Routledge/Falmer Press.

Velez, W. (1985). Finishing college: The effects of college type. *Sociology of Education, 58*(3), 191–200.

Wolff, E.N. (2004, May). *Changes in household wealth in the 1980s and 1990s in the US.* (Working Paper No. 407.) New York: The Levy Economics Institute of Bard College.

Status

Section B: Gender and Sexuality

INTRODUCTION

Weber never explicitly mentioned gender in "Class, Status, Party." But much of what he wrote regarding status applies to the way gender inequality is maintained. Like class and race, gender is one of the main dimensions of American stratification. As much as the world has changed, and there has certainly been enormous progress, gender has proven very durable as a basis for uneven distribution of resources and opportunities.

Since Marx, the emphasis in the study of inequality has been on how structural circumstances constrain the opportunities individuals have. He tried to explain how people sometimes accommodate or enable their own subordination through "false consciousness" but never really accounted for how power relations are substantively internalized. DuBois recognized how external conditions beyond an individual's control and internal choices one makes become entangled in his portrayal of the "double consciousness" of African Americans.

More recently, Candace West and Don H. Zimmerman offer a fuller description of how individual "choice" is expressed in the construction of certain identities. In an excerpt from "Doing Gender", they explain that gender norms compel us to enact prescribed roles as men and women, which serve to reproduce inequality. Analogous elements of this perspective can be found in relation to arguments about class (see Lareau in Part II) and race (see Duster and Steele in Part III, Section A). That is, we can think of "doing class" or "doing race" as well. Whereas "sex" is often considered the biological differences between the male and female of our species and "gender" is thought to reflect the cultural norms associated with the feminine and masculine extending from sex differences, West and Zimmerman reveal the socially constructed character of both sex and gender.

R. W. Connell complements this perspective by describing the social practices that intertwine different expressions of masculinity with power. Connell suggests in this excerpt from *Masculinities* that gender is enacted, but it is also socially organized into stable forms. The significance of masculinity in a given cultural setting implies much about how femininity works as well, even if Connell does not dwell on it here. In an excerpt from *The Gendered*

Society Michael Kimmel describes the analytical factors underneath the fluidity and continuity of gender identities across cultures.

Also working from a cross-cultural perspective in an excerpt from *Comparative Gender Stratification*, Joan Huber summarizes a large body of anthropological research on gender inequality. She examines robust factors that shape the dynamics of gender relations across numerous cultures.

Physiological differences between males and females, she shows, are not irrelevant. But their significance is powerfully mediated through cultural forces such as technology, social values, and political systems. Walter Williams focuses on one cluster of issues related to gender across cultures in an excerpt from *Benefits of Nonhomophobic Societies: An Anthropological Perspective*. He extols the value of tolerating and affirming sexual diversity in terms of different institutions and constituencies in society and thereby reveals the destructive effects of discrimination beyond the victims directly targeted.

Joan Acker attempts to integrate the conventional analysis of organization so common in sociology with the sensibilities and insights of feminist theory in an excerpt from *Hierarchies, Jobs, Bodies: A Theory of Gendered Organizations*. She examines the linkages between emphases on physical appearance and gender, and the resulting power hierarchy in the workplace. On a related topic, Francine D. Blau and Lawrence M. Kahn summarize recent findings in "The Gender Pay Gap: Have Women Gone as Far as They Can?" Various factors contribute to the gap between what men and women are paid in the workplace. However, some 50 percent of the difference appears to result from discrimination.

Together, these pieces exemplify a diverse range of scholarship on issues related to gender. The influence is sometimes indirect, but we can see here connections to Marx's focus on economic factors, Weber's consideration of status, DuBois's ruminations on the consciousness of subjugated peoples, and Cooper's perspective on overlapping marginalized social categories.

21

Excerpts from "Doing Gender"
Candace West and Don H. Zimmerman

Our purpose in this article is to propose an ethnomethodologically informed, and therefore distinctively sociological, understanding of gender as a routine, methodical, and recurring accomplishment. We contend that the "doing" of gender is undertaken by women and men whose competence as members of society is hostage to its production. Doing gender involves a complex of socially guided perceptual, interactional, and micropolitical activities that cast particular pursuits as expressions of masculine and feminine "natures."

When we view gender as an accomplishment, an achieved property of situated conduct, our attention shifts from matters internal to the individual and focuses on interactional and, ultimately, institutional arenas. In one sense, of course, it is individuals who "do" gender. But it is a situated doing, carried out in the virtual or real presence of others who are presumed to be oriented to its production. Rather than as a property of individuals, we conceive of gender as an emergent feature of social situations: both as an outcome of and a rationale for various social arrangements and as a means of legitimating one of the most fundamental divisions of society. . . .

To elaborate our proposal, we suggest at the outset that important but often overlooked distinctions be observed among *sex, sex category,* and *gender. Sex* is a determination made through the application of socially agreed upon biological criteria for classifying persons as females or males.[1] The criteria for classification can be genitalia at birth or chromosomal typing before birth, and they do not necessarily agree with one another. Placement in a *sex category* is achieved through application of the sex criteria, but in everyday life, categorization is established and sustained by the socially required identificatory displays that proclaim one's membership in one or the other category. In this sense, one's sex category presumes one's sex and stands as proxy for it in many situations, but sex and sex category can vary independently; that is, it is possible to claim membership in a sex category even when the sex criteria are lacking. *Gender,* in contrast, is the activity of managing situated conduct in light of normative conceptions of attitudes and activities appropriate for one's sex category. Gender activities emerge from and bolster claims to membership in a sex category. . . .

Perspectives on Sex and Gender

In Western societies, the accepted cultural perspective on gender views women and men as naturally and unequivocally defined categories of being (Garfinkel 1967, pp. 116–18) with distinctive psychological and behavioral propensities that can be predicted from their reproductive functions. Competent adult members of these societies see differences between the two as fundamental and enduring—differences seemingly supported by the division of labor into women's and men's work and an often elaborate differentiation of feminine and masculine attitudes and behaviors that are prominent features of social organization. Things are the way they are by virtue of the fact that men are men and women are women—a division perceived to be natural and rooted in biology, producing in turn profound psychological, behavioral, and social consequences. The structural arrangements of a society are presumed to be responsive to these differences.

Analyses of sex and gender in the social sciences, though less likely to accept uncritically the naive biological determinism of the view just presented, often retain a conception of sex-linked behaviors and traits as essential properties of individuals (for good reviews, see Hochschild 1973; Tresemer 1975; Thorne 1980; Henley 1985). The "sex differences approach" (Thorne 1980) is more commonly attributed to psychologists than to sociologists, but the survey researcher who determines the "gender" of respondents on the basis of the sound of their voices over the telephone is also making trait-oriented assumptions. Reducing gender to a fixed set of psychological traits or to a unitary "variable" precludes serious consideration of the ways it is used to structure distinct domains of social experience (Stacey and Thorne 1985, pp. 307–8).

Taking a different tack, role theory has attended to the social construction of gender categories, called "sex roles" or, more recently, "gender roles" and has analyzed how these are learned and enacted. Beginning with Linton (1936) and continuing through the works of Parsons (Parsons 1951; Parsons and Bales 1955) and Komarovsky (1946, 1950), role theory has emphasized the social and dynamic aspect of role construction and enactment (Thorne 1980; Connell 1983). But at the level of face-to-face interaction, the application of role theory to gender poses problems of its own (for good reviews and critiques, see Connell 1983, 1985; Kessler, Ashendon, Connell, and Dowsett 1985; Lopata and Thorne 1978; Thorne 1980; Stacey and Thorne 1985). Roles are *situated* identities—assumed and relinquished as the situation demands—rather than *master identities* (Hughes 1945), such as sex category, that cut across situations. Unlike most roles, such as "nurse," "doctor," and "patient" or "professor" and "student," gender has no specific site or organizational context.

Moreover, many roles are already gender marked, so that special qualifiers—such as "female doctor" or "male nurse"—must be added to exceptions to the rule. Thorne (1980) observes that conceptualizing gender as a role makes it difficult to assess its influence on other roles and reduces its explanatory usefulness in discussions of power and inequality. Drawing on Rubin (1975), Thorne calls for a reconceptualization of women and men as distinct social groups, constituted in "concrete, historically changing—and generally unequal—social relationships" (Thorne 1980, p. 11).

We argue that gender is not a set of traits, nor a variable, nor a role, but the product of social doings of some sort. What then is the social doing of gender? It is more than the continuous creation of the meaning of gender through human actions (Gerson and Peiss 1985). We claim that gender itself is constituted through interaction.[2] To develop the implications of our claim, we turn to Goffman's (1976) account of "gender display." Our object here is to explore how gender might be exhibited or portrayed through interaction, and thus be seen as "natural," while it is being produced as a socially organized achievement. . . .

Sex, Sex Category, and Gender

Garfinkel's (1967, pp. 118–40) case study of Agnes, a transsexual raised as a boy who adopted a female identity at age 17 and underwent a sex reassignment operation several years later, demonstrates how gender is created through interaction and at the same time structures interaction. Agnes, whom Garfinkel characterized as a "practical methodologist," developed a number of procedures for passing as a "normal, natural female" both prior to and after her surgery. She had the practical task of managing the fact that she possessed male genitalia and that she lacked the social resources a girl's biography would presumably provide in everyday interaction. In short, she needed to display herself as a woman, simultaneously learning what it was to be a woman. Of necessity, this full-time pursuit took place at a time when most people's gender would be well-accredited and routinized. Agnes had to consciously contrive what the vast majority of women do without thinking. She was not "faking" what "real" women do naturally. She was obliged to analyze and figure out how to act within socially structured circumstances and conceptions of femininity that women born with appropriate biological credentials come to take for granted early on. As in the case of others who must "pass," such as transvestites, Kabuki actors, or Dustin Hoffman's "Tootsie," Agnes's case makes visible what culture has made invisible—the accomplishment of gender.

Garfinkel's (1967) discussion of Agnes does not explicitly separate three analytically distinct, although empirically overlapping, concepts—sex, sex category, and gender.

Sex

Agnes did not possess the socially agreed upon biological criteria for classification as a member of the female *sex*. Still, Agnes regarded herself as a female, albeit a female with a penis, which a woman ought not to possess. The penis, she insisted, was a "mistake" in need of remedy (Garfinkel 1967, pp. 126–27, 131–32). Like other competent members of our culture, Agnes honored the notion that there *are* "essential" biological criteria that unequivocally distinguish females from males. However, if we move away from the commonsense viewpoint, we discover that the reliability of these criteria is not beyond question (Money and Brennan 1968; Money and Erhardt 1972; Money and Ogunro 1974; Money and Tucker 1975). Moreover, other cultures have acknowledged the existence of "cross-genders" (Blackwood 1984; Williams 1986) and the possibility of more than two sexes (Hill 1935; Martin and Voorhies 1975, pp. 84–107; but see also Cucchiari 1981, pp. 32–35).

More central to our argument is Kessler and McKenna's (1978, pp. 1–6) point that genitalia are conventionally hidden from public inspection in everyday life; yet we continue through our social rounds to "observe" a world of two naturally, normally sexed persons. It is the *presumption* that essential criteria exist and would or should be there if looked for, that provides the basis for sex categorization. Drawing on Garfinkel, Kessler and McKenna argue that "female" and "male" are cultural events—products of what they term the "gender attribution process"—rather than some collection of traits, behaviors, or even physical attributes. Illustratively they cite the child who, viewing a picture of someone clad in a suit and a tie, contends, "It's a man, because he has a pee-pee" (Kessler and McKenna 1978, p. 154). Translation: "He must have a pee-pee [an essential characteristic] because I see the *insignia* of a suit and tie." Neither initial sex assignment (pronouncement at birth as a female or male) nor the actual existence of essential criteria for that assignment (possession of a clitoris and vagina or penis and testicles) has much—if anything—to do with the identification of sex category in everyday life. There, Kessler and McKenna note, we operate with a moral certainty of a world of two sexes. We do not think, "Most persons with penises are men, but some may not be" or "Most persons who dress as men have penises." Rather, we take it for granted that sex and sex category are congruent—that knowing the latter, we can deduce the rest.

Sex Categorization

Agnes's claim to the categorical status of female, which she sustained by appropriate identificatory displays and other characteristics, could be *discredited* before her transsexual operation if her possession of a penis became known and after by her surgically constructed genitalia (see Raymond 1979, pp. 37, 138). In this regard, Agnes had to be continually alert to actual or potential threats to the security of her sex category. Her problem was not so much living up to some prototype of essential femininity but preserving her categorization as female. This task was made easy for her by a very powerful resource, namely, the process of commonsense categorization in everyday life.

The categorization of members of society into indigenous categories such as "girl" or "boy," or "woman" or "man," operates in a distinctively social way. The act of categorization does not involve a positive test, in the sense of a well-defined set of criteria that must be explicitly satisfied prior to making an identification. Rather, the application of membership categories relies on an "if-can" test in everyday interaction (Sacks 1972, pp. 332–35). This test stipulates that if people *can be seen* as members of relevant categories, *then categorize them that way*. That is, use the category that seems appropriate, except in the presence of discrepant information or obvious features that would rule out its use. This procedure is quite in keeping with the attitude of everyday life, which has us take appearances at face value unless we have special reason to doubt (Schutz 1943; Garfinkel 1967, pp. 272–77; Bernstein 1986).[3] It should be added that it is precisely when we have special reason to doubt that the issue of applying rigorous criteria arises, but it is rare, outside legal or bureaucratic contexts, to encounter insistence on positive tests (Garfinkel 1967, pp. 262–83; Wilson 1970).

Agnes's initial resource was the predisposition of those she encountered to take her appearance (her figure, clothing, hair style, and so on), as the undoubted appearance of a normal female. Her further resource was our cultural perspective on the properties of "natural, normally sexed persons." Garfinkel (1967, pp. 122–28) notes that in everyday life, we live in a world of two—and only two—sexes. This arrangement has a moral status, in that we include ourselves and others in it as "essentially, originally, in the first place, always have been, always will be, once and for all, in the final analysis, either 'male' or 'female' " (Garfinkel 1967, p. 122).

Consider the following case:

This issue reminds me of a visit I made to a computer store a couple of years ago. The person who answered my questions was truly a *salesperson*. I could not categorize him/her as a woman or a man. What did I look for? (1) Facial hair: She/he was smooth skinned, but some men have little or no facial hair. (This varies by race, Native Americans and Blacks often have none.) (2) Breasts: She/he was wearing a loose shirt that

hung from his/her shoulders. And, as many women who suffered through a 1950s' adolescence know to their shame, women are often flat-chested. (3) Shoulders: His/hers were small and round for a man, broad for a woman. (4) Hands: Long and slender fingers, knuckles a bit large for a woman, small for a man. (5) Voice: Middle range, unexpressive for a woman, not at all the exaggerated tones some gay males affect. (6) His/her treatment of me: Gave off no signs that would let me know if I were of the same or different sex as this person. There were not even any signs that he/she knew his/her sex would be difficult to categorize and I wondered about that even as I did my best to hide these questions so I would not embarrass him/her while we talked of computer paper. I left still not knowing the sex of my salesperson, and was disturbed by that unanswered question (child of my culture that I am). (Diane Margolis, personal communication)

What can this case tell us about situations such as Agnes's (cf. Morris 1974; Richards 1983) or the process of sex categorization in general? First, we infer from this description that the computer salesclerk's identificatory display was ambiguous, since she or he was not dressed or adorned in an unequivocally female or male fashion. It is when such a display *fails* to provide grounds for categorization that factors such as facial hair or tone of voice are assessed to determine membership in a sex category. Second, beyond the fact that this incident could be recalled after "a couple of years," the customer was not only "disturbed" by the ambiguity of the salesclerk's category but also assumed that to acknowledge this ambiguity would be embarrassing to the salesclerk. Not only do we want to know the sex category of those around us (to see it at a glance, perhaps), but we presume that others are displaying it for us, in as decisive a fashion as they can.

Gender

Agnes attempted to be "120 percent female" (Garfinkel 1967, p. 129), that is, unquestionably in all ways and at all times feminine. She thought she could protect herself from disclosure before and after surgical intervention by comporting herself in a feminine manner, but she also could have given herself away by overdoing her performance. Sex categorization and the accomplishment of gender are not the same. Agnes's categorization could be secure or suspect, but did not depend on whether or not she lived up to some ideal conception of femininity. Women can be seen as unfeminine, but that does not make them "unfemale." Agnes faced an ongoing task of *being* a woman—something beyond style of dress (an identificatory display) or allowing men to light her cigarette (a gender display). Her problem was to produce configurations of behavior that would be seen by others as normative gender behavior.

Agnes's strategy of "secret apprenticeship," through which she learned expected feminine decorum by carefully attending to her fiancé's criticisms of other women, was one means of masking incompetencies and simultaneously acquiring the needed skills (Garfinkel 1967, pp. 146–147). It was through her fiancé that Agnes learned that sunbathing on the lawn in front of her apartment was "offensive" (because it put her on display to other men). She also learned from his critiques of other women that she should not insist on having things her way and that she should not offer her opinions or claim equality with men (Garfinkel 1967, pp. 147–148). (Like other women in our society, Agnes learned something about power in the course of her "education.")

Popular culture abounds with books and magazines that compile idealized depictions of relations between women and men. Those focused on the etiquette of dating or prevailing standards of feminine comportment are meant to be of practical help in these matters. However, the use of any such source *as a manual of procedure* requires the assumption that doing gender merely involves making use of discrete, well-defined bundles of behavior that can simply be plugged into interactional situations to produce recognizable enactments of masculinity and femininity. The man "does" being masculine by, for example, taking the woman's arm to guide her across a street, and she "does" being feminine by consenting to be guided and not initiating such behavior with a man.

Agnes could perhaps have used such sources as manuals, but, we contend, doing gender is not so easily regimented (Mithers 1982; Morris 1974). Such sources may list and describe the sorts of behaviors that mark or display gender, but they are necessarily incomplete (Garfinkel 1967, pp. 66–75; Wieder 1974, pp. 183–214; Zimmerman and Wieder 1970, pp. 285–98). And to be successful, marking or displaying gender must be finely fitted to situations and modified or transformed as the occasion demands. Doing gender consists of managing such occasions so that, whatever the particulars, the outcome is seen and seeable in context as gender-appropriate or, as the case may be, gender-inappropriate, that is, *accountable*.

Gender and Accountability

As Heritage (1984, pp. 136–37) notes, members of society regularly engage in "descriptive accountings of states of affairs to one another," and such accounts are both serious and consequential. These descriptions name, characterize, formulate, explain, excuse, excoriate, or merely take notice of some circumstance or activity and thus place it within some social framework (locating it relative to other activities, like and unlike).

Such descriptions are themselves accountable, and societal members orient to the fact that their activities are subject to comment. Actions are often designed with an eye to their accountability, that is, how they might look and how they might be characterized. The notion of accountability also encompasses those actions undertaken so that they are specifically unremarkable and thus not worthy of more than a passing remark, because they are seen to be in accord with culturally approved standards.

Heritage (1984, p. 179) observes that the process of rendering something accountable is interactional in character:

> [This] permits actors to design their actions in relation to their circumstances so as to permit others, by methodically taking account of circumstances, to recognize the action for what it is.

The key word here is *circumstances*. One circumstance that attends virtually all actions is the sex category of the actor. As Garfinkel (1967, p. 118) comments:

> [T]he work and socially structured occasions of sexual passing were obstinately unyielding to [Agnes's] attempts to routinize the grounds of daily activities. This obstinacy points to the *omnirelevance* of sexual status to affairs of daily life as an invariant but unnoticed background in the texture of relevances that compose the changing actual scenes of everyday life. (italics added)

If sex category is omnirelevant (or even approaches being so), then a person engaged in virtually any activity may be held accountable for performance of that activity as a *woman* or a *man,* and their incumbency in one or the other sex category can be used to legitimate or discredit their other activities (Berger, Cohen, and Zelditch 1972; Berger, Conner, and Fisek 1974; Berger, Fisek, Norman, and Zelditch 1977; Humphreys and Berger 1981). Accordingly, virtually any activity can be assessed as to its womanly or manly nature. And note, to "do" gender is not always to live up to normative conceptions of femininity or masculinity; it is to engage in behavior *at the risk of gender assessment.* While it is individuals who do gender, the enterprise is fundamentally interactional and institutional in character, for accountability is a feature of social relationships and its idiom is drawn from the institutional arena in which those relationships are enacted. If this be the case, can we ever *not* do gender? Insofar as a society is partitioned by "essential" differences between women and men and placement in a sex category is both relevant and enforced, doing gender is unavoidable.

Resources for Doing Gender

Doing gender means creating differences between girls and boys and women and men, differences that are not natural, essential, or biological. Once the differences have been constructed, they are used to reinforce the "essentialness" of gender. In a delightful account of the "arrangement between the sexes," Goffman (1977) observes the creation of a variety of institutionalized frameworks through which our "natural, normal sexedness" can be enacted. The physical features of social setting provide one obvious resource for the expression of our "essential" differences. For example, the sex segregation of North American public bathrooms distinguishes "ladies" from "gentlemen" in matters held to be fundamentally biological, even though both "are somewhat similar in the question of waste products and their elimination" (Goffman 1977, p. 315). These settings are furnished with dimorphic equipment (such as urinals for men or elaborate grooming facilities for women), even though both sexes may achieve the same ends through the same means (and apparently do so in the privacy of their own homes). To be stressed here is the fact that:

> The *functioning* of sex-differentiated organs is involved, but there is nothing in this functioning that biologically recommends segregation; *that* arrangement is a totally cultural matter . . . toilet segregation is presented as a natural consequence of the difference between the sex-classes when in fact it is a means of honoring, if not producing, this difference. (Goffman 1977, p. 316)

Standardized social occasions also provide stages for evocations of the "essential female and male natures." Goffman cites organized sports as one such institutionalized framework for the expression of manliness. There, those qualities that ought "properly" to be associated with masculinity, such as endurance, strength, and competitive spirit, are celebrated by all parties concerned—participants, who may be seen to demonstrate such traits, and spectators, who applaud their demonstrations from the safety of the sidelines (1977, p. 322).

Assortative mating practices among heterosexual couples afford still further means to create and maintain differences between women and men. For example, even though size, strength, and age tend to be normally distributed among females and males (with considerable overlap between them), selective pairing ensures couples in which boys and men are visibly bigger, stronger, and older (if not "wiser") than the girls and women with whom they are paired. So, should situations emerge in which greater size, strength, or experience is called for, boys and men will be ever ready to display it and girls and women, to appreciate its display (Goffman 1977, p. 321; West and Iritani 1985).

Gender may be routinely fashioned in a variety of situations that seem conventionally expressive to begin with, such as those that present "helpless" women next to heavy objects or flat tires. But, as Goffman notes, heavy, messy, and precarious concerns can be constructed from *any* social situation, "even though by standards set in other settings, this may involve something that is light, clean, and safe" (Goffman 1977, p. 324). Given these resources, it is clear that *any* interactional situation sets the stage for depictions of "essential" sexual natures. In sum, these situations "do not so much allow for the expression of natural differences as for the production of that difference itself" (Goffman 1977, p. 324).

Many situations are not clearly sex categorized to begin with, nor is what transpires within them obviously gender relevant. Yet any social encounter can be pressed into service in the interests of doing gender. Thus, Fishman's (1978) research on casual conversations found an asymmetrical "division of labor" in talk between heterosexual intimates. Women had to ask more questions, fill more silences, and use more attention-getting beginnings in order to be heard. Her conclusions are particularly pertinent here:

> Since interactional work is related to what constitutes being a woman, with what a woman *is,* the idea that it *is* work is obscured. The work is not seen as what women do, but as part of what they are. (Fishman 1978, p. 405)

We would argue that it is precisely such labor that helps to constitute the essential nature of women *as* women in interactional contexts (West and Zimmerman 1983, pp. 109–11; but see also Kollock, Blumstein, and Schwartz 1985).

Individuals have many social identities that may be donned or shed, muted or made more salient, depending on the situation. One may be a friend, spouse, professional, citizen, and many other things to many different people—or, to the same person at different times. But we are always women or men—unless we shift into another sex category. What this means is that our identificatory displays will provide an ever-available resource for doing gender under an infinitely diverse set of circumstances.

Some occasions are organized to routinely display and celebrate behaviors that are conventionally linked to one or the other sex category. On such occasions, everyone knows his or her place in the interactional scheme of things. If an individual identified as a member of one sex category engages in behavior usually associated with the other category, this routinization is challenged. Hughes (1945, p. 356) provides an illustration of such a dilemma:

> [A] young woman . . . became part of that virile profession, engineering. The designer of an airplane is expected to go up on the maiden flight of the first plane built according to the design. He [sic] then gives a dinner to the engineers and workmen who worked on the new plane. The dinner is naturally a stag party. The young woman in question designed a plane. Her co-workers urged her not to take the risk—for which, presumably, men only are fit—of the maiden voyage. They were, in effect, asking her to be a lady instead of an engineer. She chose to be an engineer. She then gave the party and paid for it like a man. After food and the first round of toasts, she left like a lady.

On this occasion, parties reached an accommodation that allowed a woman to engage in presumptively masculine behaviors. However, we note that in the end, this compromise permitted demonstration of her "essential" femininity, through accountably "ladylike" behavior.

Hughes (1945, p. 357) suggests that such contradictions may be countered by managing interactions on a very narrow basis, for example, "keeping the relationship formal and specific." But the heart of the matter is that even—perhaps, especially—if the relationship is a formal one, gender is still something one is accountable for. Thus a woman physician (notice the special qualifier in her case) may be accorded respect for her skill and even addressed by an appropriate title. Nonetheless, she is subject to evaluation in terms of normative conceptions of appropriate attitudes and activities for her sex category and under pressure to prove that she is an "essentially" feminine being, despite appearances to the contrary (West 1984, pp. 97–101). Her sex category is used to discredit her participation in important clinical activities (Lorber 1984, pp. 52–54), while her involvement in medicine is used to discredit her commitment to her responsibilities as a wife and mother (Bourne and Wikler 1978, pp. 435–37). Simultaneously, her exclusion from the physician colleague community is maintained and her accountability *as a woman* is ensured.

In this context, "role conflict" can be viewed as a dynamic aspect of our current "arrangement between the sexes" (Goffman 1977), an arrangement that provides for occasions on which persons of a particular sex category can "see" quite clearly that they are out of place and that if they were not there, their current troubles would not exist. What is at stake is, from the standpoint of interaction, the management of our "essential" natures, and from the standpoint of the individual, the continuing accomplishment of gender. If, as we have argued, sex category is omnirelevant, then any occasion, conflicted or not, offers the resources for doing gender.

We have sought to show that sex category and gender are managed properties of conduct that are contrived with respect to the fact that others will judge and respond to us in particular ways. We have claimed that a person's gender is not simply an aspect of what one is, but, more fundamentally, it is something that one *does,* and does recurrently, in interaction with others.

What are the consequences of this theoretical formulation? If, for example, individuals strive to achieve gender in encounters with others, how does a culture instill the need to achieve it? What is the relationship between the production of gender at the level of interaction and such institutional arrangements as the division of labor in society? And, perhaps most important, how does doing gender contribute to the subordination of women by men?

Research Agendas

To bring the social production of gender under empirical scrutiny, we might begin at the beginning, with a reconsideration of the process through which societal members acquire the requisite categorical apparatus and other skills to become gendered human beings.

Recruitment to Gender Identities

The conventional approach to the process of becoming girls and boys has been sex-role socialization. In recent years, recurring problems arising from this approach have been linked to inadequacies inherent in role theory *per se*—its emphasis on "consensus, stability and continuity" (Stacey and Thorne 1985, p. 307), its ahistorical and depoliticizing focus (Thorne 1980, p. 9; Stacey and Thorne 1985, p. 307), and the fact that its "social" dimension relies on "a general assumption that people choose to maintain existing customs" (Connell 1985, p. 263).

In contrast, Cahill (1982, 1986a, 1986b) analyzes the experiences of preschool children using a social model of recruitment into normally gendered identities. Cahill argues that categorization practices are fundamental to learning and displaying feminine and masculine behavior. Initially, he observes, children are primarily concerned with distinguishing between themselves and others on the basis of social competence. Categorically, their concern resolves itself into the opposition of "girl/boy" classification versus "baby" classification (the latter designating children whose social behavior is problematic and who must be closely supervised). It is children's concern with being seen as socially competent that evokes their initial claims to gender identities:

> During the exploratory stage of children's socialization . . . they learn that only two social identities are routinely available to them, the identity of "baby," or, depending on the configuration of their external genitalia, either "big boy" or "big girl." Moreover, others subtly inform them that the identity of "baby" is a discrediting one. When, for example, children engage in disapproved behavior, they are often

told "You're a baby" or "Be a big boy." In effect, these typical verbal responses to young children's behavior convey to them that they must behaviorally choose between the discrediting identity of "baby" and their anatomically determined sex identity. (Cahill 1986a, p. 175)

Subsequently, little boys appropriate the gender ideal of "efficaciousness," that is, being able to affect the physical and social environment through the exercise of physical strength or appropriate skills. In contrast, little girls learn to value "appearance," that is, managing themselves as ornamental objects. Both classes of children learn that the recognition and use of sex categorization in interaction are not optional, but mandatory (see also Bern 1983).

Being a "girl" or a "boy" then, is not only being more competent than a "baby," but also being competently female or male, that is, learning to produce behavioral displays of one's "essential" female or male identity. In this respect, the task of four- to five-year-old children is very similar to Agnes's:

For example, the following interaction occurred on a preschool playground. A 55-month-old boy (D) was attempting to unfasten the clasp of a necklace when a preschool aide walked over to him.

A: Do you want to put that on?
D: No. It's for girls.
A: You don't have to be a girl to wear things around your neck. Kings wear things around their necks. You could pretend you're a king.
D: I'm not a king. I'm a boy. (Cahill 1986a, p. 176)

As Cahill notes of this example, although D may have been unclear as to the sex status of a king's identity, he was obviously aware that necklaces are used to announce the identity "girl." Having claimed the identity "boy" and having developed a behavioral commitment to it, he was leery of any display that might furnish grounds for questioning his claim.

In this way, new members of society come to be involved in a *self-regulating process* as they begin to monitor their own and others' conduct with regard to its gender implications. The "recruitment" process involves not only the appropriation of gender ideals (by the valuation of those ideals as proper ways of being and behaving) but also *gender identities* that are important to individuals and that they strive to maintain. Thus gender differences, or the sociocultural shaping of "essential female arid male natures," achieve the status of objective facts. They are rendered normal, natural features of persons and provide the tacit rationale for differing fates of women and men within the social order.

Additional studies of children's play activities as routine occasions for the expression of gender-appropriate behavior can yield new insights into how our "essential natures" are constructed. In particular, the transition from what Cahill (1986a) terms "apprentice participation" in the sex-segregated worlds that are common among elementary school children to "bona fide participation" in the heterosocial world so frightening to adolescents is likely to be a keystone in our understanding of the recruitment process (Thorne 1986; Thorne and Luria 1986).

Gender and the Division of Labor

Whenever people face issues of *allocation*—who is to do what, get what, plan or execute action, direct or be directed, incumbency in significant social categories such as "female" and "male" seems to become pointedly relevant. How such issues are resolved conditions the exhibition, dramatization, or celebration of one's "essential nature" as a woman or man.

Berk (1985) offers elegant demonstration of this point in her investigation of the allocation of household labor and the attitudes of married couples toward the division of household tasks. Berk found little variation in either the actual distribution of tasks or perceptions of equity in regard to that distribution. Wives, even when employed outside the home, do the vast majority of household and childcare tasks. Moreover, both wives and husbands tend to perceive this as a "fair" arrangement. Noting the failure of conventional sociological and economic theories to explain this seeming contradiction, Berk contends that something more complex is involved than rational arrangements for the production of household goods and services:

> Hardly a question simply of who has more time, or whose time is worth more, who has more skill or more power, it is clear that a complicated relationship between the structure of work imperatives and the structure of normative expectations attached to work as *gendered* determines the ultimate allocation of members' time to work and home. (Berk 1985, pp. 195–96)

She notes, for example, that the most important factor influencing wives' contribution of labor is the total amount of work demanded or expected by the household; such demands had no bearing on husbands' contributions. Wives reported various rationales (their own and their husbands') that justified their level of contribution and, as a general matter, underscored the presumption that wives are essentially responsible for household production.

Berk (1985, p. 201) contends that it is difficult to see how people "could rationally establish the arrangements that they do solely for the production of household goods and services"—much less, how people could consider them "fair." She argues that our current arrangements for the domestic division of labor support *two* production processes: household goods and services (meals, clean children, and so on) and, at the same time, gender. As she puts it:

> Simultaneously, members "do" gender, as they "do" housework and child care, and what [has] been called the division of labor provides for the joint production of household labor and gender; it is the mechanism by which both the material and symbolic products of the household are realized. (1985, p. 201)

It is not simply that household labor is designated as "women's work," but that for a woman to engage in it and a man not to engage in it is to draw on and exhibit the "essential nature" of each. What is produced and reproduced is not merely the activity and artifact of domestic life, but the material embodiment of wifely and husbandly roles, and derivatively, of womanly and manly conduct (see Beer 1983, pp. 70–89). What are also frequently produced and reproduced are the dominant and subordinate statuses of the sex categories.

How does gender get done in work settings outside the home, where dominance and subordination are themes of overarching importance? Hochschild's (1983) analysis of the work of flight attendants offers some promising insights. She found that the occupation of flight attendant consisted of something altogether different for women than for men:

> As the company's main shock absorbers against "mishandled" passengers, their own feelings are more frequently subjected to rough treatment. In addition, a day's exposure to people who resist authority in a woman is a different experience than it is for a man. . . . In this respect, it is a disadvantage to be a woman. And in this case, they are not simply women in the biological sense. They are also a highly visible distillation of middle-class American notions of femininity. They symbolize Woman. Insofar as the category "female" is mentally associated with having less status and authority, female flight attendants are more readily classified as "really" females than other females are. (Hochschild 1983, p. 175)

In performing what Hochschild terms the "emotional labor" necessary to maintain airline profits, women flight attendants simultaneously produce enactments of their "essential" femininity.

Sex and Sexuality

What is the relationship between doing gender and a culture's prescription of "obligatory heterosexuality" (Rubin 1975; Rich 1980)? As Frye (1983, p. 22) observes, the monitoring of sexual feelings in relation to other appropriately sexed persons requires the ready recognition of such persons "before one can allow one's heart to beat or one's blood to flow in erotic enjoyment of that person." The appearance of heterosexuality is produced through emphatic and unambiguous indicators of one's sex, layered on in ever more conclusive fashion (Frye 1983, p. 24). Thus, lesbians and gay men concerned with passing as heterosexuals can rely on these indicators for camouflage; in contrast, those who would avoid the assumption of heterosexuality may foster ambiguous indicators of their categorical status through their dress, behaviors, and style. But "ambiguous" sex indicators are sex indicators nonetheless. If one wishes to be recognized as a lesbian (or heterosexual woman), one must first establish a categorical status as female. Even as popular images portray lesbians as "females who are not feminine" (Frye 1983, p. 129), the accountability of persons for their "normal, natural sexedness" is preserved.

Nor is accountability threatened by the existence of "sex-change operations"—presumably, the most radical challenge to our cultural perspective on sex and gender. Although no one coerces transsexuals into hormone therapy, electrolysis, or surgery, the alternatives available to them are undeniably constrained:

> When the transsexual experts maintain that they use transsexual procedures only with people who ask for them, and who prove that they can "pass," they obscure the social reality. Given patriarchy's prescription that one must be *either* masculine or feminine, free choice is conditioned. (Raymond 1979, p. 135, italics added)

The physical reconstruction of sex criteria pays ultimate tribute to the "essentialness" of our sexual natures—as women *or* as men.

Gender, Power, and Social Change

Let us return to the question: Can we avoid doing gender? Earlier, we proposed that insofar as sex category is used as a fundamental criterion for differentiation, doing gender is unavoidable. It is unavoidable because of the social consequences of sex-category membership: the allocation of power and, resources not only in the domestic, economic, and political domains but also in the broad arena of interpersonal relations. In virtually any situation, one's sex category can be relevant, and one's performance as an incumbent of that category (i.e., gender) can be subjected to evaluation. Maintaining such pervasive and faithful assignment of lifetime status requires legitimation.

But doing gender also re... arrangements based on sex category... normal and natural, that is, legitim... organizing social life. Difference... women and men that are created by th... can then be portrayed as fundamental an... ing dispositions. In this light, the instit... arrangements of a society can be seen as respo... to the differences—the social order being merel... accommodation to the natural order. Thus if... doing gender, men are also doing dominance and... women are doing deference (cf. Goffman 1967, pp. 47–95), the resultant social order, which supposedly reflects "natural differences," is a powerful reinforcer and legitimator of hierarchical arrangements. Frye observes:

> For efficient subordination, what's wanted is that the structure not appear to be a cultural artifact kept in place by human decision or custom, but that it appear *natural*—that it appear to be quite a direct consequence of facts about the beast which are beyond the scope of human manipulation. . . . That we are trained to behave so differently as women and men, and to behave so differently toward women and men, itself contributes mightily to the appearance of extreme dimorphism, but also, the *ways* we act as women and men, and the *ways* we act toward women and men, mold our bodies and our minds to the shape of subordination and dominance. We do become what we practice being. (Frye 1983, p. 34)

If we do gender appropriately, we simultaneously sustain, reproduce, and render legitimate the institutional arrangements that are based on sex category. If we fail to do gender appropriately, we as individuals—not the institutional arrangements—may be called to account (for our character, motives, and predispositions).

Social movements such as feminism can provide the ideology and impetus to question existing arrangements, and the social support for individuals explore alternatives to them. Legislative changes... as that proposed by the Equal Rights Amendm... also weaken the accountability of condu...

gory, thereby affording the possibility of more widespread loosening of accountability in general. To be sure, equality under the law does not guarantee equality in other arenas. As Lorber (1986, p. 577) points out, assurance of "scrupulous equality of categories of people considered essentially different needs constant monitoring." What such proposed changes *can* do is provide the warrant for asking why, if we wish to treat women and men as equals, there needs to be two sex categories at all (see Lorber 1986, p. 577).

The sex category/gender relationship links the institutional and interactional levels, a coupling that legitimates social arrangements based on sex category and reproduces their asymmetry in face-to-face interaction. Doing gender furnishes the interactional scaffolding of social structure, along with a built-in mechanism of social control. In appreciating the institutional forces that maintain distinctions between women and men, we must not lose sight of the interactional validation of those distinctions that confers upon them their sense of "naturalness" and "rightness."

Social change, then, must be pursued both at the institutional and cultural level of sex category and at the interactional level of gender. Such a conclusion is hardly novel. Nevertheless, we suggest that it is important to recognize that the analytical distinction between institutional and interactional spheres does not pose an either/or choice when it comes to the question of effecting social change. Reconceptualizing gender not as a simple property of individuals but as an integral dynamic of social orders implies a new perspective on the entire network of gender relations:

> [T]he social subordination of women, and the cultural practices which help sustain it; the politics of sexual object-choice, and particularly the oppression of homosexual people; the sexual division of labor, the formation of character and motive, so far as they are organized as femininity and masculinity; the role of the body in social relations, especially the politics of childbirth; and the nature of strategies of sexual liberation movements. (Connell 1985, p. 261)

Gender is a powerful ideological device, which produces, reproduces, and legitimates the choices and limits that are predicated on sex category. An understanding of how gender is produced in social situations will afford clarification of the interactional scaffolding of social structure and the social control processes that sustain it.

Notes

1. This definition understates many complexities involved in the relationship between biology and culture (Jaggar 1983, pp. 106–13). However, our point is that the determination of an individual's sex classification is a *social* process through and through.
2. This is not to say that gender is a singular "thing," omnipresent in the same form historically or in every situation. Because normative conceptions of appropriate attitudes and activities for sex categories can vary across cultures and historical moments, the management of situated conduct in light of those expectations can take many different forms.
3. Bernstein (1986) reports an unusual case of espionage in which a man passing as a woman convinced a lover that he/she had given birth to "their" child, who, the lover, thought, "looked like" him.

References

Beer, William R. 1983. Househusbands: Men and Housework in American Families. New York: Praeger.

Bern, Sandra L. 1983. "Gender Schema Theory and Its Implications for Child Development: Raising Gender-Aschematic Children in a Gender-Schematic Society." *Signs: Journal of Women in Culture and Society* 8: 598–616.

Berger, Joseph, Bernard P. Cohen, and Morris Zelditch, Jr. 1972. "Status Characteristics and Social Interaction." *American Sociological Review* 37: 241–55.

Berger, Joseph, Thomas L. Conner, and M. Hamit Fisek, eds. 1974. *Expectation States Theory: A Theoretical Research Program*. Cambridge: Winthrop.

Berger, Joseph, M. Hamit Fisek, Robert Z. Norman, and Morris Zelditch, Jr. 1977. *Status Characteristics and Social Interaction: An Expectation States Approach*. New York: Elsevier.

Berk, Sarah F. 1985. *The Gender Factory: The Apportionment of Work in American Households*. New York: Plenum.

Bernstein, Richard. 1986. "France Jails 2 in Odd Case of Espionage." *New York Times* (May 11).

Blackwood, Evelyn. 1984. "Sexuality and Gender in Certain Native American Tribes: The Case of Cross-Gender Females." *Signs: Journal of Women in Culture and Society* 10: 27–42.

Bourne, Patricia G., and Norma J. Wikler. 1978. "Commitment and the Cultural Mandate: Women in Medicine." *Social Problems* 25: 430–40.

Cahill, Spencer E. 1982. "Becoming Boys and Girls." Ph.D. dissertation, Department of Sociology, University of California, Santa Barbara.

———. 1986a. "Childhood Socialization as Recruitment Process: Some Lessons from the Study of Gender Development." Pp. 163–86 in *Sociological Studies of Child Development,* edited by P. Adler and P. Adler. Greenwich, CT: JAI Press.

———. 1986b. "Language Practices and Self-Definition: The Case of Gender Identity Acquisition." *The Sociological Quarterly* 27: 295–311.

Chodorow, Nancy. 1978. *The Reproduction of Mothering: Psychoanalysis and the Sociology of Gender.* Los Angeles: University of California Press.

Connell, R.W. 1983. *Which Way Is Up?* Sydney: Allen & Unwin.

———. 1985. "Theorizing Gender." *Sociology* 19: 260–72.

Cucchiari, Salvatore. 1981. "The Gender Revolution and the Transition from Bisexual Horde to Patrilocal Band: The Origins of Gender Hierarchy." Pp. 31–79 in *Sexual Meanings: The Cultural Construction of Gender and Sexuality,* edited by S. B. Ortner and H. Whitehead. New York: Cambridge.

Firestone, Shulamith. 1970. *The Dialectic of Sex: The Case for Feminist Revolution.* New York: William Morrow.

Fishman, Pamela. 1978. "Interaction: The Work Women Do." *Social Problems* 25: 397–406.

Frye, Marilyn. 1983. *The Politics of Reality: Essays in Feminist Theory.* Trumansburg, NY: The Crossing Press.

Garfinkel, Harold. 1967. *Studies in Ethnomethodology.* Englewood Cliffs, NJ: Prentice-Hall.

Gerson, Judith M., and Kathy Peiss. 1985. "Boundaries Negotiation, Consciousness: Reconceptualizing Gender Relations." *Social Problems* 32: 317–31.

Goffman, Erving. 1967 (1956). "The Nature of Deference and Demeanor." Pp. 47–95 in *Interaction Ritual.* New York: Anchor/Doubleday.

———. 1976. "Gender Display." *Studies in the Anthropology of Visual Communication* 3: 69–77.

———. 1977, "The Arrangement Between the Sexes." *Theory and Society* 4: 301–31.

Henley, Nancy M. 1985. "Psychology and Gender." *Signs: Journal of Women in Culture and Society* 11: 101–19.

Heritage, John. 1984. *Garfinkel and Ethnomethodology.* Cambridge, England: Polity Press.

Hill, W. W. 1935. "The Status of the Hermaphrodite and Transvestite in Navaho Culture." *American Anthropologist* 37: 273–79.

Hochschild, Arlie R. 1973. "A Review of Sex Roles Research." *American Journal of Sociology* 78: 1011–29.

———. 1983. *The Managed Heart: Commercialization of Human Feeling.* Berkeley: University of California Press.

Hughes, Everett C. 1945. "Dilemmas and Contradictions of Status." *American Journal of Sociology* 50: 353–59.

Humphreys, Paul, and Joseph Bergen. 1981. "Theoretical Consequences of the Status Characteristics Formulation." *American Journal of Sociology* 86: 953–83.

Jaggar, Alison M. 1983. *Feminist Politics and Human Nature.* Totowa, NJ: Rowman & Allanheld.

Kessler, S., D. J. Ashendon, R. W. Connell, and G. W. Dowsett. 1985. "Gender Relations in Secondary Schooling." *Sociology of Education* 58: 34–48.

Kessler, Suzanne J., and Wendy McKenna. 1978. *Gender: An Ethnomethodological Approach.* New York: Wiley.

Kollock, Peter, Philip Blumstein, and Pepper Schwartz. 1985. "Sex and Power in Interaction." *American Sociological Review* 50: 34–46.

Komarovsky, Mirra. 1946. "Cultural Contradictions and Sex Roles." *American Journal of Sociology* 52: 184–89.

———. 1950. "Functional Analysis of Sex Roles." *American Sociological Review* 15: 508–16.

Linton, Ralph. 1936. *The Study of Man.* New York: Appleton-Century.

Lopata, Helen Z., and Barrie Thorne. 1978. "On the Term 'Sex Roles,'" *Signs: Journal of Women in Culture and Society* 3: 718–21.

Lorber, Judith. 1984. *Women Physicians: Careers, Status and Power.* New York: Tavistock.

———. 1986. "Dismantling Noah's Ark." *Sex Roles* 14: 567–80.

Martin M. Kay, and Barbara Voorheis. 1975. *Female of the Species.* New York: Columbia University Press.

Mead, Margaret. 1963. *Sex and Temperament.* New York: Dell.

———. 1968. *Male and Female.* New York: Dell.

Mithers, Carol L. 1982. "My Life as a Man." *The Village Voice* 27 (October 5): 1 ff. Money, John. 1968. *Sex Errors of the Body.* Baltimore: Johns Hopkins.

————. 1974. "Prenatal Hormones and Postnatal Sexualization in Gender Identity Differentiation." Pp. 221–95 in *Nebraska Symposium on Motivation,* Vol. 21, edited by J. K. Cole and R. Dienstbier. Lincoln: University of Nebraska Press.

———— and John G. Brennan. 1968. "Sexual Dimorphism in the Psychology of Female Transsexuals." *Journal of Nervous and Mental Disease* 147: 487–99.

———— and Anke, A. Erhardt. 1972. *Man and Woman/Boy and Girl.* Baltimore: John Hopkins.

———— and Charles Ogunro. 1974. "Behavioral Sexology: Ten Cases of Genetic Male Intersexuality with Impaired Prenatal and Pubertal Androgenization." *Archives of Sexual Behavior* 3: 181–206.

———— and Patricia Tucker. 1975. *Sexual Signatures.* Boston: Little, Brown.

Morris, Jan. 1974. *Conundrum.* New York: Harcourt Brace Jovanovich.

Parsons, Talcott, 1951. *The Social System.* New York: Free Press.

———— and Robert F. Bales. 1955. *Family, Socialization and Interaction Process.* New York: Free Press.

Raymond, Janice G. 1979. *The Transsexual Empire.* Boston: Beacon.

Rich, Adrienne. 1980. "Compulsory Heterosexuality and Lesbian Existence." *Signs: Journal of Women in Culture and Society* 5: 631–60.

Richards, Renee (with John Ames). 1983. *Second Serve: The Renee Richards Story.* New York: Stein and Day.

Rossi, Alice. 1984. "Gender and Parenthood." *American Sociological Review* 49: 1–19.

Rubin, Gayle. 1975. "The Traffic in Women: Notes on the 'Political Economy' of Sex." Pp. 157–210 in *Toward an Anthropology of Women,* edited by R. Reiter. New York: Monthly Review Press.

Sacks, Harvey. 1972. "On the Analyzability of Stories by Children." Pp. 325–45 in *Directions in Sociolinguistics,* edited by J. J. Gumperz and D. Hymes. New York: Holt, Rinehart & Winston.

Schutz, Alfred. 1943. "The Problem of Rationality in the Social World." *Economics* 10: 130–49.

Stacey, Judith, and Barrie Thorne. 1985. "The Missing Feminist Revolution in Sociology." *Social Problems* 32: 301–16.

Thorne, Barrie. 1980. "Gender . . . How Is It Best Conceptualized?" Unpublished manuscript.

————. 1986. "Girls and Boys Together . . . But Mostly Apart: Gender Arrangements in Elementary Schools." Pp. 167–82 in *Relationships and Development,* edited by W. Hartup and Z. Rubin. Hillsdale, NJ: Lawrence Erlbaum.

———— and Zella Luria. 1986. "Sexuality and Gender in Children's Daily Worlds." *Social Problems* 33: 176–90.

Tresemer, David. 1975. "Assumptions Made About Gender Roles." Pp. 308–39 in *Another Voice: Feminist Perspectives on Social Life and Social Science,* edited by M. Millman and R. M. Kanter. New York: Anchor/Doubleday.

West, Candace. 1984. "When the Doctor is a 'Lady': Power, Status and Gender in Physician-Patient Encounters." *Symbolic Interaction* 7: 87–106.

———— and Bonita Iritani. 1985. "Gender Politics in Mate Selection: The Male-Older Norm." Paper presented at the Annual Meeting of the American Sociological Association, August, Washington, DC.

———— and Don H. Zimmerman. 1983. "Small Insults: A Study of Interruptions in Conversations Between Unacquainted Persons." Pp.102–17 in *Language, Gender and Society,* edited by B. Thorne, C. Kramarae, and N. Henley. Rowley, MA: Newbury House.

Wieder, D. Lawrence. 1974. *Language and Social Reality: The Case of Telling the Convict Code.* The Hague: Mouton.

Williams, Walter L. 1986. *The Spirit and the Flesh: Sexual Diversity in American Indian Culture.* Boston: Beacon.

Wilson, Thomas P. 1970. "Conceptions of Interaction and Forms of Sociological Explanation." *American Sociological Review* 35: 697–710.

Zimmerman, Don H., and D. Lawrence Wieder. 1970. "Ethnomethodology and the Problem of Order: Comment on Denim." Pp. 287–95 in *Understanding Everyday Life,* edited by J. Denzin. Chicago: Aldine.

Excerpts from *Masculinities*

R.W. CONNELL

All societies have cultural accounts of gender, but not all have the concept 'masculinity'. In its modern usage the term assumes that one's behaviour results from the type of person one is. That is to say, an unmasculine person would behave differently: being peaceable rather than violent, conciliatory rather than dominating, hardly able to kick a football, uninterested in sexual conquest, and so forth.

This conception presupposes a belief in individual difference and personal agency. In that sense it is built on the conception of individuality that developed in early-modern Europe with the growth of colonial empires and capitalist economic relations.

But the concept is also inherently relational. 'Masculinity' does not exist except in contrast with 'femininity'. A culture which does not treat women and men as bearers of polarized character types, at least in principle, does not have a concept of masculinity in the sense of modern European/American culture.

Historical research suggests that this was true of European culture itself before the eighteenth century. Women were certainly regarded as different from men, but different in the sense of being incomplete or inferior examples of the same character (for instance, having less of the faculty of reason). Women and men were not seen as bearers of qualitatively different characters; this conception accompanied the bourgeois ideology of 'separate spheres' in the nineteenth century.[1]

In both respects our concept of masculinity seems to be a fairly recent historical product, a few hundred years old at most. In speaking of masculinity at all, then, we are 'doing gender' in a culturally specific way. This should be borne in mind with any claim to have discovered transhistorical truths about manhood and the masculine.

Definitions of masculinity have mostly taken our cultural standpoint for granted, but have followed different strategies to characterize the type of person who is masculine. Four main strategies have been followed; they are easily distinguished in terms of their logic, though often combined in practice.

Essentialist definitions usually pick a feature that defines the core of the masculine, and hang an account of men's lives on that. Freud flirted with an essentialist definition when he equated masculinity with activity in contrast to feminine passivity—though he came to see that equation as oversimplified. Later authors' attempts to capture an essence of masculinity have been colourfully varied: risk-taking, responsibility, irresponsibility, aggression, Zeus energy . . . Perhaps the finest is the sociobiologist Lionel Tiger's idea that true maleness, underlying male bonding and war, is elicited by 'hard and heavy phenomena'.[2] Many heavy-metal rock fans would agree.

The weakness in the essentialist approach is obvious: the choice of the essence is quite arbitrary. Nothing obliges different essentialist to agree, and in fact they often do not. Claims about a universal basis of masculinity tell us more about the ethos of the claimant than about anything else.

Positivist social science, whose ethos emphasizes finding the facts, yields a simple definition of masculinity: what men actually are. This definition is the logical basis of masculinity/femininity (M/F) scales in psychology, whose items are validated by showing that they discriminate statistically between groups of men and women. It is also the basis of those ethnographic discussions of masculinity which describe the pattern of men's lives in a given culture and, whatever it is, call the pattern masculinity.[3]

There are three difficulties here. First, as modern epistemology recognizes, there is no description without a standpoint. The apparently neutral descriptions on which these definitions rest are themselves underpinned by assumptions about gender. Obviously enough, to start compiling an M/F scale one must have some idea of what to count or list when making up the items.

Second, to list what men and women do requires that people be already sorted into the categories 'men' and 'women'. This, as Suzanne Kessler and Wendy McKenna showed in their classic ethnomethodological study of gender research, is unavoidably a process of social attribution using common-sense typologies of gender. Positivist procedure thus rests on the very typifications that are supposedly under investigation in gender research.

Third, to define masculinity as what-men-empirically-are is to rule out the usage in which we call some women 'masculine' and some men 'feminine', or some actions or attitudes 'masculine' or 'feminine' regardless of who displays them. This is not a trivial use of the terms. It is crucial, for instance, to psychoanalytic thinking about contradictions within personality.

Indeed, this usage is fundamental to gender analysis. If we spoke only of differences between men as a bloc and women as a bloc, we would not need the terms 'masculine' and 'feminine' at all. We could just speak of 'men's' and 'women's', or 'male' and 'female'. The terms 'masculine' and 'feminine' point beyond categorical sex difference to the ways men differ among themselves, and women differ among themselves, in matters of gender.[4]

Normative definitions recognize these differences and offer a standard: masculinity is what men ought to be. This definition is often found in media studies, in discussions of exemplars such as John Wayne or of genres such as the thriller. Strict sex role theory treats masculinity precisely as a social norm for the behaviour of men. In practice, male sex role texts often blend normative with essentialist definitions, as in Robert Brannon's widely quoted account of 'our culture's blueprint of manhood': No Sissy Stuff, The Big Wheel, The Sturdy Oak and Give 'em Hell.[5]

Normative definitions allow that different men approach the standards to different degrees. But this soon produces paradoxes, some of which were recognized in the early Men's Liberation writings. Few men actually match the 'blueprint' or display the toughness and independence acted by Wayne, Bogart or Eastwood. (This point is picked up by film itself, in spoofs such as *Blazing Saddles* and *Play it Again, Sam.*) What is 'normative' about a norm hardly anyone meets? Are we to say the majority of men are unmasculine? How do we assay the toughness needed to resist the norm of toughness, or the heroism needed to come out as gay?

A more subtle difficulty is that a purely normative definition gives no grip on masculinity at the level of personality. Joseph Pleck correctly identified the unwarranted assumption that role and identity correspond. This assumption is, I think, why sex role theorists often drift towards essentialism.

Semiotic approaches abandon the level of personality and define masculinity through a system of symbolic difference in which masculine and feminine places are contrasted. Masculinity is, in effect, defined as not-femininity.

This follows the formulae of structural linguistics, where elements of speech are defined by their differences from each other. The approach has been widely used in feminist and poststructuralist cultural analyses of gender and in Lacanian psychoanalysis and studies of symbolism. It yields more than an abstract contrast of masculinity and femininity, of the kind found in M/F scales. In the semiotic opposition of masculinity and femininity, masculinity is the unmarked term, the place of symbolic authority. The phallus is master-signifier, and femininity is symbolically defined by lack.

This definition of masculinity has been very effective in cultural analysis. It escapes the arbitrariness of essentialism and the paradoxes of positivist and normative definitions. It is, however, limited in its scope—unless one assumes, as some postmodern theorists do, that discourse is all we can talk about in social analysis. To grapple with the full range of issues about masculinity we need ways of talking about relationships of other kinds too: about gendered places in production and consumption, places in institution and in natural environments, places in social and military struggles.[6]

What can be generalized is the principle of connection. The idea that one symbol can only be understood within a connected system of symbols applies equally well in other spheres. No masculinity arises except in a system of gender relations.

Rather than attempting to define masculinity as an object (a natural character type, a behavioural average, a norm), we need to focus on the processes and relationships through which men and women conduct gendered lives. 'Masculinity', to the extent the term can be briefly defined at all, is simultaneously a place in gender relations, the practices through which men and women engage that place in gender, and the effects of these practices in bodily experience, personality and culture.

Gender as a Structure of Social Practice

In this section I will set out, as briefly as possible, the analysis of gender that underpins the argument of the book.

Gender is a way in which social practice is ordered. In gender processes, the everyday conduct of life is organized in relation to a reproductive arena, defined by the bodily structures and processes of human reproduction. This arena includes sexual arousal and intercourse, childbirth and infant care, bodily sex difference and similarity.

I call this a 'reproductive arena' not as a 'biological base' . . . to emphasize the point . . . that we are talking about a historical process involving the body, not a fixed set of biological determinants. Gender is social practice that constantly refers to bodies and what bodies do, it is not social practice reduced to the body. Indeed reductionism presents the exact reverse of the real situation. Gender exists precisely to the extent that biology does *not* determine the social. It marks one of those points of transition where historical process supersedes biological evolution as the form of change. Gender is a scandal, an outrage, from the point of view of essentialism. Sociobiologists are constantly trying to abolish it, by proving that human social arrangements are a reflex of evolutionary imperatives.

Social practice is creative and inventive, but not inchoate. It responds to particular situations and is generated within definite structures of social relations. Gender relations, the relations among people and groups organized through the reproductive arena, form one of the major structures of all documented societies.

Practice that relates to this structure, generated as people and groups grapple with their historical situations, does not consist of isolated acts. Actions are configured in larger units, and when we speak of masculinity and femininity we are naming configurations of gender practice.

'Configuration' is perhaps too static a term. The important thing is the *process* of configuring practice. (Jean-Paul Sartre speaks in *Search for a Method* of the 'unification of the means in action'.) Taking a dynamic view of the organization of practice, we arrive at an understanding of masculinity and femininity as *gender projects*. These are processes of configuring practice through time, which transform their starting-points in gender structures. In the case studies in Part II, I will analyse the lives of several groups of men as gender projects in this sense.[7]

We find the gender configuring of practice however we slice the social world, whatever unit of analysis we choose. The most familiar is the individual life course, the basis of the common-sense notions of masculinity and femininity. The configuration of practice here is what psychologists have traditionally called 'personality' or 'character'.

Such a focus is liable to exaggerate the coherence of practice that can be achieved at any one site. It is thus not surprising that psychoanalysis, originally stressing contradiction, drifted towards the concept of 'identity'. Post-structuralist critics of psychology such as Wendy Hollway have emphasized that gender identities are fractured and shifting, because multiple discourses intersect in any individual life.[8] This argument highlights another site, that of discourse, ideology or culture. Here gender is organized in symbolic practices that may continue much longer than the individual life (for instance: the construction of heroic masculinities in epics; the construction of 'gender dysphorias' or 'perversions' in medical theory).

Previously, I noted how social science. . . . many find it difficult to accept that institutions are substantively, not just metaphorically, gendered. This is, nevertheless, a key point.

The state, for instance, is a masculine institution. To say this is not to imply that the personalities of top male office-holders somehow seep through and stain the institution. It is to say something much stronger: that state organizational practices are structured in relation to the reproductive arena. The overwhelming majority of top office-holders are men because there is a gender configuring of recruitment and promotion, a gender configuring of the internal division of labour and systems of control, a gender configuring of policymaking, practical routines, and ways of mobilizing pleasure and consent.[9]

The gender structuring of practice need have nothing biologically to do with reproduction. The link with the reproductive arena is social. This becomes clear when it is challenged. An example is the recent struggle within the state over 'gays in the military', i.e., the rules excluding soldiers and sailors because of the gender of their sexual object-choice. In the United States, where this struggle was most severe, critics made the case for change in terms of civil liberties and military efficiency, arguing in effect that object-choice has little to do with the capacity to kill. The admirals and generals defended the status quo on a variety of spurious grounds. The unadmitted reason was the cultural importance of a particular definition of masculinity in maintaining the fragile cohesion of modern armed forces.

It has been clear since the work of Juliet Mitchell and Gayle Rubin in the 1970s that gender is an internally complex structure, where a number of different logics are superimposed. This is a fact of great importance for the analysis of masculinities. Any one masculinity, as a configuration of practice, is simultaneously positioned in a number of structures of relationship, which may be following different historical trajectories. Accordingly masculinity, like femininity, is always liable to internal contradiction and historical disruption.

We need at least a three-fold model of the structure of gender, distinguishing relations of (a) power, (b) production and (c) cathexis (emotional attachment). This is a provisional model, but it gives some purchase on issues about masculinity.[10]

a. *Power relations* The main axis of power in the contemporary European/American gender order is the overall subordination of women and dominance of men—the structure Women's Liberation named 'patriarchy'. This general structure exists despite many local reversals (e.g., woman-headed households, female teachers with male students). It persists despite resistance of many kinds, now articulated in feminism. These reversals and resistances mean continuing difficulties for patriarchal power. They define a problem of legitimacy which has great importance for the politics of masculinity.

b. *Production relations* Gender divisions of labour are familiar in the form of the allocation of tasks, sometimes reaching extraordinarily fine detail. (In the English village studied by the sociologist Pauline Hunt, for instance, it was customary for women to wash the inside of windows, men to wash the outside.) Equal attention should be paid to the economic consequences of gender divisions of labour, the dividend accruing to men from unequal shares of the products of social labour. This is most often discussed in terms of unequal wage rates, but the gendered character of capital should also be noted. A capitalist economy working through a gender division of labour is, necessarily, a gendered accumulation process. So it is not a statistical accident, but a part of the social construction of masculinity, that men and not women control the major corporations and the great private fortunes. Implausible as it sounds, the accumulation of wealth has become firmly linked to the reproductive arena, through the social relations of gender.[11]

c. *Cathexis* . . . Sexual desire is so often seen as natural that it is commonly excluded from social theory. Yet when we consider desire in Freudian terms, as emotional energy being attached to an object, its gendered character is clear. This is true both for heterosexual and homosexual desire. (It is striking that in our culture the non-gendered object choice, as 'bisexual' desire, is ill-defined and unstable.) The practices that shape and realize desire are thus an aspect of the gender order. Accordingly we can ask political questions about the relationships involved: whether they are consensual or coercive, whether pleasure is equally given and received. In feminist analyses of sexuality these have become sharp questions about the connection of heterosexuality with men's position of social dominance.[12]

Because gender is a way of structuring social practice in general, not a special type of practice, it is unavoidably involved with other social structures. It is now common to say that gender 'intersects'—better, interacts—with race and class. We might add that it constantly interacts with nationality or position in the world order.

This fact also has strong implications for the analysis of masculinity. White men's masculinities, for instance, are constructed not only in relation to white women but also in relation to black men. Paul Hoch in *White Hero, Black Beast* more than a decade ago pointed to the pervasiveness of racial imagery in Western discourses of masculinity. White fears of black men's violence have a long history in colonial and post-colonial situations. Black fears of white men's terrorism, founded in the history of colonialism, have a continuing basis

in white men's control of police, courts and prisons in metropolitan countries. African-American men are massively over-represented in American prisons, as Aboriginal men are in Australian prisons. This situation is strikingly condensed in the American black expression 'The Man', fusing white masculinity and institutional power. As the black rap singer Ice-T put it,

> It makes no difference whether you're in or out. The ghetto, the Pen, it's all institutionalized. It's being controlled by the Man . . . Ever since 1976, they stop trying to rehabilitate Brothers. Now it's strictly punishment. The Man's answer to the problem is not more education—it's more prisons. They're saying let's not educate them, let's lock them the fuck up. So when you come outta there you're all braindead, so yeah it's a cycle.[13]

Similarly, it is impossible to understand the shaping of working-class masculinities without giving full weight to their class as well as their gender politics. This is vividly shown in historical work such as Sonya Rose's *Limited Livelihoods,* on industrial England in the nineteenth century. An ideal of working-class manliness and self-respect was constructed in response to class deprivation and paternalist strategies of management, at the same time and through the same gestures as it was defined against working-class women. The strategy of the 'family wage', which long depressed women's wages in twentieth-century economies, grew out of this interplay.[14]

To understand gender, then, we must constantly go beyond gender. The same applies in reverse. We cannot understand class, race or global inequality without constantly moving towards gender. Gender relations are a major component of social structure as a whole, and gender politics are among the main determinants of our collective fate.

Relations among Masculinities: Hegemony, Subordination, Complicity, Marginalization

With growing recognition of the interplay between gender, race and class it has become common to recognize multiple masculinities: black as well as white, working-class as well as middle-class. This is welcome, but it risks another kind of oversimplification. It is easy in this framework to think that there is *a* black masculinity or *a* working-class masculinity.

To recognize more than one kind of masculinity is only a first step. We have to examine the relations between them. Further, we have to unpack the milieux of class and race and scrutinize the gender relations operating within them. There are, after all, gay in black men and effeminate factory hands, not to mention middle-class rapists and cross-dressing bourgeois.

A focus on the gender relations among men is necessary to keep the analysis dynamic, to prevent the acknowledgement of multiple masculinities collapsing into a character typology, as power, happened with Fromm and the *Authoritarian Personality* research. 'Hegemonic masculinity' is not a fixed character type, always and everywhere the same. It is, rather, the masculinity that occupies the hegemonic position in a given pattern of gender relations, a position always contestable.

A focus on relations also offers a gain in realism. Recognizing multiple masculinities, especially in an individualist culture such as the United States, risks taking them for alternative lifestyles, a matter of consumer choice. A relational approach makes it easier to recognize the hard compulsions under which gender configurations are formed, the bitterness as well as the pleasure in gendered experience.

With these guidelines, let us consider the practices and relations that construct the main patterns of masculinity in the current Western gender order.

Hegemony

The concept of 'hegemony', deriving from Antonio Gramsci's analysis of class relations, refers to the cultural dynamic by which a group claims and sustains a leading position in social life. At any given time, one form of masculinity rather than others is culturally exalted. Hegemonic masculinity can be defined as the configuration of gender practice which embodies the currently accepted answer to the problem of the legitimacy of patriarchy, which guarantees (or is taken to

guarantee) the dominant position of men and the subordination of women.[15]

This is not to say that the most visible bearers of hegemonic masculinity are always the most powerful people. They may be exemplars, such as film actors, or even fantasy figures, such as film characters. Individual holders of institutional power or great wealth may be far from the hegemonic pattern in their personal lives. (Thus a male member of a prominent business dynasty was a key figure in the gay/transvestite social scene in Sydney in the 1950s, because of his wealth and the protection this gave in the cold-war climate of political and police harassment.)[16]

Nevertheless, hegemony is likely to be established only if there is some correspondence between cultural ideal and institutional power, collective if not individual. So the top levels of business, the military and government provide a fairly convincing *corporate* display of masculinity, still very little shaken by feminist women or dissenting men. It is the successful claim to authority, more than direct violence, that is the mark of hegemony (though violence often underpins or supports authority).

I stress that hegemonic masculinity embodies a 'currently accepted' strategy. When conditions for the defence of patriarchy change, the bases for the dominance of a particular masculinity are eroded. New groups may challenge old solutions and construct a new hegemony. The dominance of *any* group of men may be challenged by women. Hegemony, then, is a historically mobile relation. Its ebb and flow is a key element of the picture of masculinity proposed in this essay. . . .

Subordination

Hegemony relates to cultural dominance in the society as a whole. Within that overall framework there are specific gender relations of dominance and subordination between groups of men.

The most important case in contemporary European/American society is the dominance of heterosexual men and the subordination of homosexual men. This is much more than a cultural stigmatization of homosexuality or gay identity. Gay men are subordinated to straight men by an array of quite material practices.

These practices were listed in early Gay Liberation texts such as Dennis Altman's *Homosexual: Oppression and Liberation*. They have been documented at length in studies such as the NSW Anti-Discrimination Board's 1982 report *Discrimination and Homosexuality*. They are still a matter of everyday experience for homosexual men. They include political and cultural exclusion, cultural abuse (in the United States gay men have now become the main symbolic target of the religious right), legal violence (such as imprisonment under sodomy statutes), street violence (ranging from intimidation to murder), economic discrimination and personal boycotts. It is not surprising that an Australian working-class man, reflecting on his experience of coming out in a homophobic culture, would remark:

> You know, I didn't totally realize what it was to be gay. I mean it's a bastard of a life.[17]

Oppression positions homosexual masculinities at the bottom of a gender hierarchy among men. Gayness in patriarchal ideology, is the repository of whatever is symbolically expelled from hegemonic masculinity, the items ranging from fastidious taste in home decoration to receptive anal pleasure. Hence, from the point of view of hegemonic masculinity, gayness is easily assimilated to femininity. And hence—in the view of some gay theorists—the ferocity of homophobic attacks.

Gay masculinity is the most conspicuous, but it is not the only subordinated masculinity. Some heterosexual men and boys too are expelled from the circle of legitimacy. The process is marked by a rich vocabulary of abuse: wimp, milksop, nerd, turkey, sissy, lily liver, jellyfish, yellowbelly, candy ass, ladyfinger, pushover, cookie pusher, cream puff, motherfucker, pantywaist, mother's boy, four-eyes, ear-'ole, dweeb, geek, Milquetoast, Cedric, and so on. Here too the symbolic blurring with femininity is obvious.

Complicity

Normative definitions of masculinity, as I have noted, face the problem that not many men actually meet the normative standards. This point applies to hegemonic masculinity. The number of men rigorously practising the hegemonic pattern in its entirety may be quite small. Yet the majority of men gain from its hegemony, since they benefit from the patriarchal dividend, the advantage men in general gain from the overall subordination of women.

Accounts of masculinity have generally concerned themselves with syndromes and types, not with numbers. Yet in thinking about the dynamics of society as a whole, numbers matter. Sexual politics is mass politics, and strategic thinking needs to be concerned with where the masses of people are. If a large number of men have some connection with the hegemonic project but do not embody hegemonic masculinity, we need a way of theorizing their specific situation.

This can be done by recognizing another relationship among groups of men, the relationship of complicity with the hegemonic project. Masculinities constructed in ways that realize the patriarchal dividend, without the tensions or risks of being the front-line troops of patriarchy, are complicit in this sense.

It is tempting to treat them simply as slacker versions of hegemonic masculinity—the difference between the men who cheer football matches on TV and those who run out into the mud and the tackles themselves. But there is often something more definite and carefully crafted than that. Marriage, fatherhood and community life often involve extensive compromises with women rather than naked domination or an uncontested display of authority.[18] A great many men who draw the patriarchal dividend also respect their wives and mothers, are never violent towards women, do their accustomed share of the housework, bring home the family wage, and can easily convince themselves that feminists must be bra-burning extremists.

Marginalization

Hegemony, subordination and complicity, as just defined, are relations internal to the gender order. The interplay of gender with other structures such as class and race creates further relationships between masculinities.

Previously, I noted how new information technology became a vehicle for redefining middle-class masculinities at a time when the meaning of labour for working-class men was in contention. This is not a question of a fixed middle-class masculinity confronting a fixed working-class masculinity. Both are being reshaped, by a social dynamic in which class and gender relations are simultaneously in play.

Race relations may also become an integral part of the dynamic between masculinities. In a white-supremacist context, black masculinities play symbolic roles for white gender construction. For instance, black sporting stars become exemplars of masculine toughness, while the fantasy figure of the black rapist plays an important role in sexual politics among whites, a role much exploited by right-wing politics in the United States. Conversely, hegemonic masculinity among whites sustains the institutional oppression and physical terror that have framed the making of masculinities in black communities.

Robert Staples's discussion of internal colonialism in *Black Masculinity* shows the effect of class and race relations at the same time. As he argues, the level of violence among black men in the United States can only be understood through the changing place of the black labour force in American capitalism and the violent means used to control it. Massive unemployment and urban poverty now powerfully interact with institutional racism in the shaping of black masculinity.[19]

Though the term is not ideal, I cannot improve on 'marginalization' to refer to the relations between the masculinities in dominant and subordinated classes or ethnic groups. Marginalization is always relative to the *authorization* of the hegemonic masculinity of the dominant group. Thus, in the United States, particular black athletes may be exemplars for hegemonic masculinity. But the fame and wealth of individual stars has no trickle-down effect; it does not yield social authority to black men generally.

The relation of marginalization and authorization may also exist between subordinated masculinities. A striking example is the arrest and conviction of Oscar Wilde, one of the first men caught in the net of modern anti-homosexual legislation. Wilde was trapped because of his connections with homosexual working-class youths, a practice unchallenged until his legal battle with a wealthy aristocrat, the Marquess of Queensberry, made him vulnerable.[20]

These two types of relationship—hegemony, domination/subordination and complicity on the one hand, marginalization/ authorization on the other—provide a framework in which we can analyse specific masculinities. (This is a sparse framework, but social theory should be hardworking.) I emphasize that terms such as 'hegemonic masculinity' and 'marginalized masculinities' name not fixed character types but configurations of practice generated in particular situations in a changing structure of relationships. Any theory of masculinity worth having must give an account of this process of change.

Historical Dynamics, Violence and Crisis Tendencies

To recognize gender as a social pattern requires us to see it as a product of history, and also as a *producer* of history. I defined gender practice as onto-formative, as constituting reality, and it is a crucial part of this idea that social reality is dynamic in time. We habitually think of the social as less real than the biological, what changes as less real than what stays the same. But there is a colossal reality to history. It is the modality of human life, precisely what defines us as human. No other species produces and lives in history, replacing organic evolution with radically new determinants of change.

To recognize masculinity and femininity as historical, then, is not to suggest they are flimsy or trivial. It is to locate them firmly in the world of social agency. And it raises a string of questions about their historicity.

The structures of gender relations are formed and transformed over time. It has been common in historical writing to see this change as coming from outside gender—from technology or class dynamics, most often. But change is also generated from within gender relations. The dynamic is as old as gender relations. It has, however, become more clearly defined in the last two centuries with the emergence of a public politics of gender and sexuality.

With the women's suffrage movement and the early homophile movement, the conflict of interests embedded in gender relations became visible. Interests are formed in any structure of inequality, which necessarily defines groups that will gain and lose differently by sustaining or by changing the structure. A gender order where men dominate women cannot avoid constituting men as an interest group concerned with defence, and women as an interest group concerned with change. This is a structural fact, independent of whether men as individuals love or hate women, or believe in equality or abjection, and independent of whether women are currently pursuing change.

To speak of a patriarchal dividend is to raise exactly this question of interest. Men gain a dividend from patriarchy in terms of honour, prestige and the right to command. They also gain a material dividend. In the rich capitalist countries, men's average incomes are approximately *double* women's average incomes. (The more familiar comparisons, of wage rates for full-time employment, greatly understate gender differences in actual incomes.) Men are vastly more likely to control a major block of capital as chief executive of a major corporation, or as direct owner. For instance, of 55 US fortunes above $1 billion in 1992, only five were mainly in the hands of women—and all but one of those as a result of inheritance from men.

Men are much more likely to hold state power: for instance, men are ten times more likely than women to hold office as a member of parliament (an average across all countries of the world). Perhaps men do most of the work? No: in the rich countries, time-budget studies show women and men work on average about the same number of hours in the year. (The major difference is in how much of this work gets paid.)[21]

Given these facts, the 'battle of the sexes' is no joke. Social struggle must result from inequalities on such a scale. It follows that the politics of masculinity cannot concern only questions of personal life and identity. It must also concern questions of social justice.

A structure of inequality on this scale, involving a massive dispossession of social resources, is hard to imagine without violence. It is, overwhelmingly, the dominant gender who hold and use the means of violence. Men are armed far more often than women. Indeed under many gender regimes women have been forbidden to bear or use arms (a rule applied, astonishingly, even within armies). Patriarchal definition of femininity (dependence

fearfulness) amount to a cultural disarmament that may be quite as effective as the physical kind. Domestic violence cases often find abused women, physically able to look after themselves, who have accepted the abusers' definitions of themselves as incompetent and helpless.[22]

Two patterns of violence follow from this situation. First, many members of the privileged group use violence to sustain their dominance. Intimidation of women ranges across the spectrum from wolf-whistling in the street, to office harassment, to rape and domestic assault, to murder by a woman's patriarchal 'owner', such as a separated husband. Physical attacks are commonly accompanied by verbal abuse of women (whores and bitches, in recent popular music that recommends beating women). Most men do not attack or harass women; but those who do are unlikely to think themselves deviant. On the contrary they usually feel they are entirely justified, that they are exercising a right. They are authorized by an ideology of supremacy.

Second, violence becomes important in gender politics among men. Most episodes of major violence (counting military combat, homicide and aimed assault) are transactions among men. Terror is used as a means of drawing boundaries and making exclusions, for example, in heterosexual violence against gay men. Violence can become a way of claiming or asserting masculinity in group struggles. This is an explosive process when an oppressed group gains the means of violence—as witnessed in the levels of violence among black men in contemporary South Africa and the United States. The youth gang violence of inner-city streets is a striking example of the assertion of marginalized masculinities against other men, continuous with the assertion of masculinity in sexual violence against women.[23]

Violence can be used to enforce a reactionary gender politics, as in the recent firebombings and murders of abortion service providers in the United States. It must also be said that collective violence among men can open possibilities for progress in gender relations. The two global wars this century produced important transitions in women's employment, shook up gender ideology, and accelerated the making of homosexual communities.

Violence is part of a system of domination, but is at the same time a measure of its imperfection. A thoroughly legitimate hierarchy would have less need to intimidate. The scale of contemporary violence points to crisis tendencies (to borrow a term from Jürgen Habermas) in the modern gender order.

The concept of crisis tendencies needs to be distinguished from the colloquial sense in which people speak of a 'crisis of masculinity'. As a theoretical term 'crisis' presupposes a coherent system of some kind, which is destroyed or restored by the outcome of the crisis. Masculinity, as the argument so far has shown, is not a system in that sense. It is, rather, a configuration of practice *within* a system of gender relations. We cannot logically speak of the crisis of a configuration; rather we might speak of its disruption or its transformation. We can, however, logically speak of the crisis of a gender order as a whole, and of its tendencies towards crisis.[24]

Such crisis tendencies will always implicate masculinities, though not necessarily by disrupting them. Crisis tendencies may, for instance, provoke attempts to restore a dominant masculinity. Michael Kimmel has pointed to this dynamic in turn-of-the-century United States society, where fear of the women's suffrage movement played into the cult of the outdoorsman. Klaus Theweleit in *Male Fantasies* traced the more savage process that produced the sexual politics of fascism in the aftermath of the suffrage movement and German defeat in the Great War. More with recently, Women's Liberation and defeat in Vietnam have stirred new cults of true masculinity in the United States, from violent 'adventure' movies such as the *Rambo* series, to the expansion of the gun cult and what William Gibson in a frightening recent study has called 'paramilitary culture'.[25]

To understand the making of contemporary masculinities, then, we need to map the crisis tendencies of the gender order. This is no light task! But it is possible to make a start, using as a framework the three structures of gender relations defined earlier in this chapter.

Power relations show the most visible evidence of crisis tendencies: a historic collapse of the legitimacy of patriarchal power, and a global movement for the emancipation of women. This is fuelled by an underlying contradiction between the inequality of women and men, on the one hand, and the universalizing logics of modern state structures and market relations, on the other.

The incapacity of the institutions of civil society, notably the family, to resolve this tension provokes broad but incoherent state action (from family law to population policy) which itself becomes the focus of political turbulence. Masculinities are reconfigured around this crisis tendency both through conflict over strategies of legitimation, and through men's divergent responses to feminism. . . . While the tension leads some men to the cults of masculinity just mentioned, it leads others to support feminist reforms.[26]

Production relations have also been the site of massive institutional changes. Most notable are the vast postwar growth in married women's employment in rich countries, and the even vaster incorporation of women's labour into the money economy in poor countries.

There is a basic contradiction between men's and women's equal contribution to production, and the gendered appropriation of the products of social labour. Patriarchal control of wealth is sustained by inheritance mechanisms, which, however, insert some women into the property system as owners. The turbulence of the gendered accumulation process creates a series of tensions and inequalities in men's chances of benefiting from it. Some men, for instance, are excluded from its benefits by unemployment . . .; others are advantaged by their connection with new physical or social technologies. . . .

Relations of cathexis have visibly changed with the stabilization of lesbian and gay sexuality as a public alternative within the heterosexual order. . . . This change was supported by the broad claim by women for sexual pleasure and control of their own bodies, which has affected heterosexual practice as well as homosexual.

The patriarchal order prohibits forms of emotion, attachment and pleasure that patriarchal society itself produces. Tensions develop around sexual inequality and men's rights in marriage, around the prohibition on homosexual affection (given that patriarchy constantly produces homo-social institutions) and around the threat to social order symbolized by sexual freedoms.

This sketch of crisis tendencies is a very brief account of a vast subject, but it is perhaps enough to show changes in masculinities in something like their true perspective. The canvas is much broader than images of a modern male sex role, or renewal of the deep masculine, imply. Economy, state and global relationships are involved as well as households and personal relationships.

The vast changes in gender relations around the globe produce ferociously complex changes in the conditions of practice with which men as well as women have to grapple. No one is an innocent bystander in this arena of change. We are all engaged in constructing a world of gender relations. How it is made, what strategies different groups pursue, and with what effects, are political questions. Men no more than women are chained to the gender patterns they have inherited. Men too can make political choices for a new world of gender relations. Yet those choices are always made in concrete social circumstances, which limit what can be attempted; and the outcomes are not easily controlled.

To understand a historical process of this depth and complexity is not a task for *a priori* theorizing. It requires concrete study; more exactly, a range of studies that can illuminate the larger dynamic. . . .

Notes

1. Bloch 1978 outlines the argument for the Protestant middle classes of England and North America. Laqueur 1990 offers a more sweeping argument on similar lines about views of the body.
2. Tiger 1969: 211. Tiger goes on to suggest that war may be part of 'the masculine aesthetic', like driving a racing car at high speed . . . The passage is still worth reading; like Bly's *Iron John,* a stunning example of the muddled thinking that the question of masculinity seems to provoke, in this case flavoured by what C. Wright Mills once called 'crackpot realism'.
3. The deeply confused logic of M/F scales was laid bare in a classic paper by Constantinople 1973. Ethnographic positivism on masculinity reaches a nadir in Gilmore 1990, who swings between normative theory and positivist practice.
4. Kessler and McKenna 1978 develop the important argument about the 'primacy of gender attribution'. For an illuminating discussion of masculine women, see Devor 1989.
5. Easthope 1986; Brannon 1976.
6. A strictly semiotic approach in the literature on masculinity is not common; this approach is found mostly in more general treatments of gender. However, Saco 1992 offers a very clear defence of the approach, and its potential is shown by the collection in which her paper appears, Craig 1992.
7. Sartre 1968: 159–60.
8. Hollway 1984.
9. Franzway et al. 1989, Grant and Tancred 1992.
10. Mitchell 1971, Rubin 1976. The three-fold model is spelt out in Connell 1987.
11. Hunt 1980. Feminist political economy is, however, under way, and these notes draw on Mies 1986, Waring 1988, Armstrong and Armstrong 1990.
12. Some of the best writing on the politics of heterosexuality comes from Canada: Valverde 1985, Buchbinder et al. 1987. The conceptual approach here is developed in Connell and Dowsett 1992.
13. Interview with Ice-T in *City on a Hilt Press* (Santa Cruz, CA), 21 Jan 1993; Hoch 1979.
14. Rose 1992, ch. 6 especially.
15. I would emphasize the dynamic character of Gramsci's concept of hegemony, which is not the functionalist theory of cultural reproduction often portrayed. Gramsci always had in mind a social struggle for leadership in historical change.
16. Wotherspoon 1991 (chapter 3) describes this climate, and discreetly does not mention individuals.
17. Altman 1972; Anti-Discrimination Board 1982. Quotation from Connell, Davis and Dowsett 1993: 122.
18. See, for instance, the white US families described by Rubin 1976.
19. Staples 1982. The more recent United States literature on black masculinity, e.g., Majors and Gordon 1994, has made a worrying retreat from Staples's structural analysis towards sex role theory; its favoured political strategy, not surprisingly, is counselling programs to resocialize black youth.
20. Ellmann 1987.

21. For patterns of wealth, see the survey of US millionaires by *Forbes* magazine, 19 October 1992. On parliaments, see 1993 survey by Inter-Parliamentary Union reported in *San Francisco Chronicle* 12 September 1993, and United Nations Development Programme 1992: 145. The results of time-budget studies may surprise some readers; see Bittman 1991.

22. The argument here draws on Russell 1982, Connell 1985, Ptacek 1988, Smith 1989.

23. Messerschmidt 1993: 105–17.

24. For the general concept of crisis tendencies, see Habermas 1976, O'Connor 1987; for its relevance to gender, Connell 1987: 158–63.

25. Kimmel 1987; Theweleit 1987; Gibson 1994.

26. A response documented in great detail by Kimmel and Mosmiller 1992.

References

Altman, Dennis. 1972. *Homosexual: Oppression and Liberation*. Sydney: Angus & Robertson.

Anti-Discrimination Board, New South Wales. 1982. *Discrimination and Homosexuality*. Sydney Anti-Discrimination Board.

Armstrong, Pat and Hugh Armstrong. 1990. *Theorizing Women's Work*. Toronto: Garamond Press.

Bittman, Michael. 1991. *Juggling Time: How Australian Families Use Time*. Canberra: Commonwealth of Australia, Office of the Status of Women.

Bloch, Ruth H. 1978. 'Untangling the roots of modern sex roles: a survey of four centuries of change'. *Signs* 4: 237–52.

Brannon, Robert. 1976. 'The male sex role: our culture's blueprint of manhood, and what it's done for us lately'. pp. 1–45 in *The Forty-Nine Percent Majority: The Male Sex Role*, ed. Deborah S. David and Robert Brannon. Reading, MA: Addison-Wesley.

Buchbinder, Howard, Varda Burstyn, Dinah Forbes and Mercedes Steedman.1987. *Who's On Top? The Politics of Heterosexuality*. Toronto: Garamond Press.

Connell, R. W. 1985. 'Masculinity, violence and war', pp. 4–10 in *War/Masculinity,* ed. Paul Patton and Ross Poole. Sydney: Intervention.

——. 1987. *Gender and Power: Society, the Person and Sexual Politics*. Cambridge: Polity press.

Connell, R. W., M. Davis and G. W. Dowsett. 1993 'A bastard of a life: homosexual desire and practice among men in working-class milieux'. *Australian and New Zealand Journal of Sociology* 29: 112–35.

Connell, R.W. and G.W. Dowsett, eds. 1992. *Rethinking Sex: Social Theory and Sexuality Research*. Melbourne: Melbourne University Press.

Constantinople, Anne. 1973. 'Masculinity-femininity: an exception to a famous dictum?' *Psychological Bulletin* 80: 389–407.

Craig, Steve, ed. 1992. *Men, Masculinity and the Media*. Newbury Park, CA: Sage.

Devor, Holly. 1989. *Gender Blending: Confronting the Limits of Duality*. Bloomington and Indianapolis: Indiana University Press.

Easthope, Anthony. 1986. *What a Man's Gotta Do: The Masculine Myth in Popular Culture*. London: Paladin.

Ellmann, Richard. 1987. *Oscar Wilde*. London: Hamish Hamilton.

Franzway, Suzanne, Dianne Court and R.W. Connel. 1989. *Staking a Claim: Feminism, Bureaucracy and the State*. Sydney: Allen & Unwin; Cambridge: Polity Press.

Gibson, James William. 1994. *Warrior Dreams: Paramilitary Culture in Post-Vietnam American*. New York: Hill & Wang.

Gilmore, David D. 1990. *Manhood in the Making: Cultural Concept of Masculinity*. New Haven: Yale University Press.

Grant, Judith and Peta Tancred. 1992. 'A feminist perspective on state bureaucracy'. pp. 112–28 in *Gendering Organizational Analysis*, ed. Albert J. Mills and Peta Tancred. Newbury Park, CA: Sage.

Habermas, Jürgen, 1976. *Legitimation Crisis*. London: Heinemann.

Hoch, Paul.1979. *White Hero, Black Beast: Racism, Sexism and the Mask of Masculinity*. London: Pluto Press.

Hollway, Windy. 1984. 'Gender difference and the production of subjectivity'. pp. 227–63 in *Changing the Subject*, ed. J. Henriques et al. London: Methuen.

Hunt, Pauline. 1980. *Gender and Class Consciousness*. London: Macmillan.

Kessler, Suzanne J. and Wendy McKenna. 1978. *Gender: An Ethnomethodological Approach*. New York: Wiley.

Kimmel, Michael S. 1987. 'Rethinking "masculinity": new directions in research', pp. 9–24 in *Changing Men: New Directions in Search on Men and Masculinity*, ed. Michael S. Kimmel. Newbury Park, CA: Sage.

Kimmel, Michael S. and Thomas E. Mosmiller, eds. 1992. *Against the Tide: Pro-Feminist Men in the United States, 1776–1990, a Documentary History*. Boston: Beacon Press.

Laqueur, Thomas W. 1990. *Making Sex: Body and Gender from the Greeks to Freud*. Cambridge, MA: Harvard University Press.

Majors, Richard G. and Jacob U. Gordon. 1994. *The American Black Male: His Present Status and His Future*. Chicago: Nelson-Hall.

Messerschmidt, James W. 1993. *Masculinities and Crime: Critique and Reconceptualization of Theory*. Lanham, MD: Rowman & Littlefield.

Mies, Maria. 1986. *Patriarchy and Accumulation on a World Scale: Women in the International Division of Labour*. London: Zed Books.

Mitchell, Juliet. 1971. *Women's Estate*. Harmondsworth: Penguin.

——. 1975. *Psychoanalysis and Feminism*. New York: Vintage.

O'Connor, James. 1987. *The Meaning of Crisis: A Theoretical Introduction*. Oxford: Blackwell.

Ptacek, James. 1988. 'Why do men batter their wives?' pp. 133–57 in *Feminist Perspectives on Wife Abuse*, ed. Kersti Yllö and Michele Bograd. Newbury Park, CA: Sage.

Rose, Sonya O. 1992. *Limited Livelihood: Gender and Class in Nineteenth-Century England*. Berkeley: University of California Press.

Rubin, Lillian B. 1976. *Worlds of Pain: Lift in the Working-Class Family*. New York: Basic Books.

Russell, Diana E.H. 1982. *Rape in Marriage*. New York: Macmillan.

Saco, Diana. 1992. 'Masculinity as signs: poststructuralist feminist approaches to study of gender'. pp. 23–39 in *Men, Masculinity and the Media*, ed. Steve Craig. Newbury Park, CA: Sage.

Sartre, Jean Paul. 1968 [1960]. *Search for a Method*. New York: Vintage.

Smith, Joan. 1989. *Misogynies*. London: Faber & Faber.

Staples, Robert. 1982. *Black Masculinity: The Black Male's Role in American Society*. San Francisco: Black Scholar Press.

Theweleit Klaus. 1987. *Male Fantasies*. Cambridge: Polity Press.

Tiger, Lionel. 1969. *Men in Groups*. New York: Random House.

Valverde, Mariana. 1985. *Sex, Power and Pleasure*, Toronto: Women's Press.

Waring, Marilyn. 1988. *Counting for Nothing: What Men Value and What Women are Worth*. Wellington: Allen & Unwin and Port Nicholson Press.

Wotherspoon, Gary. 1991. *City of the Plain: History of a Gay Sub-culture*. Sydney: Hale & Iremonger.

Excerpts from
The Gendered Society
Michael Kimmell

Biological models assume that sex determines gender, that innate biological differences lead to behavioral differences which lead to social arrangements. By this account, social inequalities are encoded into our physiological composition. Biological anomalies alone should account for variation. But the evidence suggests otherwise. When children like the Dominican pseudohermaphrodites are raised as the other *gender* they can easily make the transition to the other sex. And how do we account for the dramatic differences in the definitions of masculinity and femininity around the world? And how come some societies have much wider levels of gender inequality than others? On these questions, the biological record is mute.

What's more, biology is not without its own biases, though these are often hard to detect. Some anthropologists argue that biological models projected contemporary western values onto other cultures. These projections led evolutionists like Steven Goldberg to ignore the role of women and the role of colonialism in establishing gender differences in traditional cultures. Anthropologists like Karen Sacks suggest that biological researchers always assumed that gender *difference* implied gender *inequality*, since western notions of difference do usually lead to and justify inequality. In other words, gender difference is the *result* of gender inequality—not the other way around.[1]

Anthropological research on cultural variations in the development of gender definitions arose, in part, in response to such casual biological determinism. The more we found out about other cultures, the more certain patterns emerged. The evolutionary and ethnographic world offers a fascinating diversity of cultural constructions of gender. Yet, some themes do remain constant. Virtually all societies manifest some amount of difference between women and men, and virtually all exhibit some form of male domination, despite variations in gender definition. So, anthropologists have also tried to explore the link between the near-universals of gender difference and gender inequality. Some search for those few societies in which women hold positions of power; others examined those rituals, beliefs, customs, and practices that tend to increase inequality and those that tend to decrease it.

The Variations in Gender Definitions

When anthropologists began to explore the cultural landscape, they found far more variability in the definitions of masculinity and femininity than any biologist would have predicted. Men possessed relatively similar levels of testosterone, with similar brain structure and lateralization, yet they seemed to exhibit dramatically different levels of aggression, violence, and, especially, aggression toward women. Women, with similar brains, hormones, and ostensibly similar evolutionary imperatives, have widely varying experiences of passivity, PMS, and spatial coordination. One of the most celebrated anthropologists to explore these differences was Margaret Mead, whose research in the South Seas (Samoa, Polynesia, Indonesia) remains, despite some significant criticism, an example of engaged scholarship, clear writing, and important ideas. Mead was clear that sex differences were "not something deeply biological," but rather were learned, and once learned, became part of the ideology that continued to perpetuate them. Here's how she put it:

> I have suggested that certain human traits have been socially specialized as the appropriate attitudes and behavior of only one sex, while other human traits have been specialized for the opposite sex. This social specialization is then rationalized into a theory that the socially decreed behavior is natural for one sex and unnatural for the other, and that the deviant is a deviant because of glandular defect, or developmental accident.[2]

In *Sex and Temperament in Three Primitive Societies* (1935), Mead explored the differences in those definitions, while in several other books, such as *Male and Female* (1949) and *Coming of Age in Samoa* (1928), she explored the processes by which males and females become the men and women their cultures prescribe. No matter what she seemed to be writing about, though, Mead always had one eye trained on the United States. In generating implicit comparisons between our own and other cultures, Mead defied us to maintain the fiction that what we observe in the United States is "natural" and cannot be changed.

In *Sex and Temperament*, Mead directly took on the claims of biological inevitability. By examining three very different cultures in New Guinea, she hoped to show the enormous cultural variation possible in definitions of masculinity and femininity, and, in so doing, enable Americans to better understand both the cultural origins and the malleability of their own ideas. The first two cultures exhibited remarkable similarities between women and men. Masculinity and femininity were not the lines along which personality differences seemed to be organized. Women and men were not "opposite" sexes. For example, all members of the Arapesh culture appeared gentle, passive, and emotionally warm. Males and females were equally "happy, trustful, confident," and individualism was relatively absent. Men and women shared child rearing; both were "maternal," and both discouraged aggressiveness among boys and girls. Both men and women were thought to be relatively equally sexual, though their sexual relationships tended to be "domestic" and not "romantic" nor, apparently what we might call passionate. Although infanticide of female babies and male polygamy were not unknown, marriage was "even and contented." Indeed, Mead pronounced the political arrangements "utopian." Here's how she summed up Arapesh life:

> quiet and uneventful co-operation, singing in the cold dawn, and singing and laughter in the evening, men who sit happily playing to themselves on hand-drums, women holding suckling children to their breasts, young girls walking easily down the centre of the village, with the walk of those who are cherished by all about them.[3]

By contrast, Mead details how the Mundugamor, a tribe of headhunters and cannibals, also viewed women and men as similar, but expected both sexes to be equally aggressive and violent. Women showed little "maternal instinct"; they detested pregnancy and nursing, and could hardly wait to return to the serious business of work and war. "Mundugamor women actively dislike child-bearing, and they dislike children," Mead writes. "Children are carried in harsh opaque baskets that scratch their skins, later, high on their mother's shoulders, well away from the breast."

Among the Mundugamor, there was a violent rivalry between fathers and sons (there was more infanticide of boys than of girls), and everyone experienced a fear that they were being wronged by others. Quite wealthy (partly as a result of their methods of population control), the Mundugamor were, as Mead concludes, "violent, competitive, aggressively sexual, jealous, ready to see and avenge insult, delighting in display, in action, in fighting."[4]

Here, then, were two tribes that saw gender differences as virtually nonexistent—though the two cultures could hardly have been more different. The third culture Mead described was the Tchambuli, where, as in the United States, women and men were seen as extremely different. This was a patrilineal culture in which polygyny was accepted. Here, one sex was composed primarily of nurturing and gossipy consumers who spent their days dressing up and going shopping. They wore curls and lots of jewelry, and Mead describes them as "charming, graceful, coquettish." These, incidentally, were the men, and they liked nothing better than to "go off resplendent in feathers and shell ornaments to spend a delightful few days" shopping. The women were dominant and energetic, the economic providers. It was they who fished, an activity upon which the entire culture depended, and it was they "who have the real positions of power in the society." Completely unadorned, they were efficient, businesslike, controlled all the commerce and diplomacy of the culture, and were the initiators of sexual relations. Mead notes that the Tchambuli were the only culture she had ever seen "where little girls of ten and eleven were more alertly intelligent and more enterprising than little boys." She writes that "[w]hat the women will think, what the women will say, what the women will do lies at the back of each man's mind as he weaves his tenuous and uncertain web of insubstantial relations with other men." By contrast, "the women are a solid group, confused by no rivalries, brisk, patronizing, and jovial."[5]

What Mead found, then, were two cultures in which women and men were seen as similar, and one culture in which they were seen as extremely different from each other, but the reverse of the model familiar to us. Each culture, of course, believed that women and men were the way they were because their biological *sex determined* their

personality. None of them believed that they were the outcome of economic scarcity, military success, or cultural arrangements.

Mead urged her readers to "admit men and women are capable of being molded to a single pattern as easily as a diverse one."[6] She demonstrated that women and men are *capable* of similar or different temperaments, she did not adequately explain *why* women and men turn out to be different or the same. What are the determinants of women's and men's experiences? Nor did she explain why male domination seems to be nearly universal, despite the three exceptions she studied. These questions have been taken up by other anthropologists.

The Centrality of the Gender Division of Labor

In almost every society, labor is divided by gender (as well as by age). Certain tasks are reserved for women, others for men. How do we explain this gender division of labor, if not by some biologically based imperative?

One school of thought, functionalism, maintains that a sex-based division of labor was necessary for the preservation of the society. As society becomes increasingly complex, there arises a need for two kinds of labor: hunting and gathering. Functionalists differ as to whether this division of labor had any *moral* component, whether the work of one sex was more highly valued than the work of the other. But they agree that the sex-based division of labor was functionally necessary for these societies. Such models often assume that because the sex-based division of labor arose to meet certain social needs at one time, its preservation is an evolutionary imperative, or at least an arrangement that is not to be trifled with casually.

On the other hand, since the sex-based division of labor has a history, it is not biologically inevitable; societies have changed and will continue to change. And it's a very recent history at that. "The sexual division of labor as we know it today probably developed quite recently in human evolution," writes anthropologist Adrienne Zihlman.[7] Moreover, this sex-based division of labor is far more varied than we might have assumed. In some cultures, women build the house; in others, they do the cooking. In most cultures women are responsible for child care. But not in all cultures, and they are certainly not doing it all. In some cultures, tasks are dramatically skewed and labor rigidly divided; others, offer far more flexibility and fluidity. Today, a sex-based division of labor is functionally anachronistic, and the biological bases for specific social tasks being assigned to either men or women have long been eroded. In the place of such foundations, though, lie centuries of social customs and traditions that today contribute to our gender ideologies about what is appropriate for one sex and not the other. The gender-based division of labor has become a part of our culture, not a part of our physical constitution.

In fact, our physical constitutions have become less determinative in the assignment of tasks and the choosing of careers. It may even be true that less significance there is to real physical differences, the more emphasis we place on them ideologically. For example, men no longer need to have physical strength to be powerful and dominant. The most highly muscular men, in fact, appear in cultural side-shows of body-building competition, but they do no more physical labor than the average suburban husband mowing the lawn and shoveling snow. As for women, the technologies of family planning and sexual autonomy—birth control technology, legal abortion, and institutional child care—have freed them from performing only child-care duties, and enabled them to participate in the institutions of the public sphere.

Once free, women have entered every area of the public sphere. A century ago, women campaigned to enter the college classroom, the polling place, the professions, the work world. More recently, it's been the military and military colleges that have opened their doors to women, the latter by court order. Today, very few occupations exist for which only women or only men are strictly biologically suited. What occupations do you know of that *biologically* only women or only men could perform? Offhand, I can think of three: for women, wet nurse and surrogate mother; for men, professional sperm donor. None of these is exactly a career of choice for most of us.

If a sex-based division of labor has outlived its social usefulness or its physical imperatives, it must be held in place by something else: the power of one sex over the other. Where did that power come from? How has it developed? How does it vary from culture to culture? What factors exaggerate it; what factors diminish it? These are among the questions that anthropologists have endeavored to answer.

Theories of Gender Differentiation and Male Domination

Several theorists have tried to explain the sexual division of labor and gender inequality by reference to large, structural forces that transform societies' organizing principles. For example, in the late nineteenth century, Frederick Engels applied ideas that he developed with his collaborator, Karl Marx, and assigned to private property the role of central agent in determining the division of labor by sex. In *The Origins of the Family, Private Property and the State*, Engels suggested that the three chief institutions of modern Western society—a capitalist economy, the nation-state, and the nuclear family—emerged at roughly the same historical moment—and all as a result of the development of private property. Before that, Engels asserts, families were organized on a communal basis, with group marriage, male-female equality, and a sexual division of labor without any moral or political rewards going to males or females. The birth of the capitalist economy created wealth that was mobile and transferable—unlike land, which stays in the same place. Capitalism meant private property, which required the establishment of clear lines of inheritance. This requirement led, in turn, to new problems of sexual fidelity. If a man were to pass his property on to his son, he had to be sure that his son was, indeed, *his*. How could he know this in the communal group marriage of precapitalist families?

Out of this need to transmit inheritance across generations of men the traditional nuclear family emerged, with monogamous marriage and the sexual control of women by men. And if inheritance were to be stable, these new patriarchs needed to have clear, binding laws, vigorously enforced, that would enable them to pass their legacies onto their sons without interference from others. This required a centralized political apparatus (the nation-state) to exercise sovereignty over local and regional powers that might challenge them.[8]

Some contemporary anthropologists continue in this tradition. Eleanor Leacock, for example, argues that before the rise of private property and social classes, women and men were regarded as autonomous individuals who held different positions that were held in relatively equal esteem. "When the range of decisions made by women is considered," she writes, "women's autonomous and public role emerges. Their status was not as literal 'equals' of men . . . but as what they were—female persons, with their own rights, duties and responsibilities, which were complementary to and in no way secondary to those of men." In her ethnographic work on the Labrador peninsula, Leacock shows the dramatic transformation of women's former autonomy by the introduction of the fur trade. The introduction of a commercial economy turned powerful women into homebound wives. Here again, gender inequality, introduced by economic shifts, resulted in increasing differences in the meanings of masculinity and femininity.[9]

Karen Sacks examined four African cultures, and found that the introduction of the market economy shifted basically egalitarian roles toward male dominance. As long as the culture was involved in producing goods for their own use, men and women were relatively equal. But the more involved the tribe became in a market exchange economy, the higher the level of gender inequality and the lower the position of women. Conversely, when women and men shared access to the productive elements of the society, the result was a higher level of sexual egalitarianism.[10]

Another school of anthropological thought traces the origins of male domination to the imperatives of warfare in primitive society. How does a culture create warriors who are fierce and strong? Anthropologist Marvin Harris has suggested two possibilities. It can provide different rewards for the warriors, based on their dexterity or skill. But this would limit the solidarity of the fighting force and sow seeds of dissent and enmity among the soldiers. More effective would be to reward virtually all men with the services of women, excluding only the most inadequate or cowardly. Warrior societies tend to practice female infanticide, Harris observes, ensuring that the population of females remains significantly lower than that of males (and thus males will be competing for females). Warrior societies also tend to exclude women from the fighting force, since their presence would reduce the motivation of the soldiers and upset the sexual hierarchy. In this way, warfare leads to female subordination as well as patrilinearity, since the culture will need a resident core of fathers and sons to carry out its military tasks. Males come to control the society's resources, and, as a justification for this, develop patriarchal religion as ideology that legitimates their domination over women.[11]

Two other groups of scholars use different variables to explain the differences, between women and men. Descent theorists like Lionel Tiger and Robin Fox stress the invariance of the mother-child bond. Men, by definition, lack the tie that mothers have with their children. How, then, can they achieve that connection to the next generation, the connection to history and society? They form it with other men in the hunting group. This is why, Tiger and Fox argue, women must be excluded from the hunt. In all societies, men must somehow be bound socially to the next generation to which they are not inextricably, biologically connected. Male solidarity and monogamy are the direct result of men's needs to connect with social life.[12] Alliance theorists like Claude Levi-Strauss are less concerned with the need to connect males to the next generation than they are with the ways that relationships among men come to organize social life. He argues that men turn women into sex objects whose exchange (as wives) cements the alliances among men. Both descent and alliance theorists treat these themes as invariant and natural, rather than as the outcomes of historical relationships that vary dramatically not only over time but also across cultures.[13]

Determinants of Women's Status

Virtually every society of which we have knowledge reveals some differentiation between women and men, and virtually every society exhibits patterns of gendered inequality and male domination. Yet the variety within these universals is still astounding.

Gender differences and gender inequality may be more or less pronounced. It is not simply the case that the higher the degree of gender differentiation, the greater the gender inequality, although this is generally the pattern. One could, conceivably, imagine four such possibilities—high or low levels of gender differentiation coupled with either high or low levels of gender inequality.

What, then are the factors that seem to determine women's status in society? Under what conditions is women's status improved, and under what conditions is it minimized? Economic, political, and social variables tend to produce different cultural configurations. For example, one large-scale survey of different cultures found that the more a society needs physical strength and highly developed motor skills, the larger will be the differences in socialization between males and females. It also seems to be the case that the larger the family group the larger the differences between women and men. In part this is because the isolation of the nuclear family means that males and females will need to take the other's roles on occasion, so that strict separation is rarely enforced.[14]

One of the key determinants of women's status has been the division of labor around child care. Women's role in reproduction has historically limited their social and economic participation. While no society assigns all child-care functions to men, the more that men participate in child care and the more free women are from childrearing responsibility, the higher women's status tends to be. There are many ways to free women from sole responsibility. In non-Western societies, several customs evolved, including child nurses who care for several children at once, sharing child care with husbands or with neighbors, and assigning the role of child care to tribal elders, whose economic activity has been curtailed by age.[15]

Relationships between children and their parents have also been seen as keys to women's status. Sociologist Scott Coltrane found that the closer the relationship between father and son, the higher the status of women is likely to be. Coltrane found that in cultures where fathers are relatively uninvolved, boys define themselves in *opposition* to their mothers and other women, and therefore are prone to exhibit traits of hypermasculinity, to fear and

denigrate women as a way to display masculinity. The more mothers and fathers share child rearing, the less men belittle women. Margaret Mead also emphasized the centrality of fatherhood. Most cultures take women's role in child rearing as a given whereas men must learn to become nurturers. There is much at stake, but nothing inevitable: "every known human society rests firmly on the learned nurturing behavior of men."[16]

That men must learn to be nurturers raises the question of masculinity in general. What it means to be a man varies enormously from one culture to another, and these definitions have a great deal to do with the amount of time and energy fathers spend with their children. Such issues are not simply incidental for women's lives either; it turns out that the more time men spend with their children, the less gender inequality is present in that culture. Conversely, the more free women are from child care—the more that child care is parceled out elsewhere and the more that women control their fertility—the higher will be their status. Coltrane also found that women's status depended upon their control over property, especially after marriage. When she retained control over her property after marriage, a woman's status was invariably higher.

Interestingly, recent research on male bonding, so necessary to those theories that stress warfare or the necessity of attaching males to the social order, also seems to bear this out. Sociologist and geographer Daphne Spain argues that the same cultures in which men developed the most elaborate sex-segregated rituals were those cultures in which women's status was lowest. Spain mapped a number of cultures spatially, and found that the further the distance the men's hut was from the center of the village, the more time the men spent at their hut, and the more culturally important were the men's rituals, the lower was women's status. "Societies with men's huts are those in which women have the least power," she writes. If you spend your time away from your hut, off at the men's hut with the other men, you'll have precious little time, and even less inclination, to spend with your family and sharing in child rearing.[17]

Similarly, anthropologist Thomas Gregor found that all forms of spatial segregation between males and females are associated with gender inequality. The Mehinaku of central Brazil, for example, have well-institutionalized men's huts where the tribal secrets are kept and ritual instruments are played and stored. Women are prohibited from entering. As one tribesman told Gregor, "[t]his house is only for men. Women may not see anything in here. If a woman comes in, then all the men take her into woods and she is raped."[18]

These two variables—the father's involvement in child rearing (often measured by spatial segregation) and women's control of property after marriage—emerge as among the central determinants of women's status and gender inequality. It is no wonder that they are also determinants of violence against women, since the lower women's status in a society, the higher the likelihood of rape and violence against women. In one of the most wide-ranging comparative studies of women's status, Peggy Reeves Sanday found several important correlates of women's status. Contact was one. Sex segregation was highly associated with women's lower status; as if separation were "necessary for the development of sexual inequality and male dominance." (By contrast, a study of a sexually egalitarian society found no ideology of the desirability of sex segregation.) Of course, women's economic power, that crucial determinant, is "the result of a sexual division of labor in which women achieve self-sufficiency and establish an independent control sphere." In addition, in cultures that viewed the environment as relatively friendly, women's status was significantly higher; cultures that saw the environment as hostile were more likely to develop patterns of male domination.[19]

Finally, Sanday found that women had the highest levels of equality, and thus the lowest frequency of rape, when both genders contributed about the same amounts to the food supply. When women contributed equally, men tended to be more involved in child care. Ironically, when women contributed a lot, their status was also low. So, women's status tended to be lower when they contributed either very little or a great deal, and more equal when their contribution was about equal.

Following Tavris and Wade, we can summarize the findings of cross-cultural research on female status and male dominance. First, male dominance is lower when men and women work together, with little sexual division of labor. Sex segregation of work is the strongest predictor of women's status. Second, male dominance is more pronounced when men control political and ideological resources that are necessary to achieve the goals of the culture, and when men control all property. Third, male dominance is "exacerbated under colonization"—both capitalist penetration of the countryside and industrialization generally lower women's status. Male dominance is also associated with demographic imbalances between the sexes: The higher the percentage of marriageable men to marriageable women, the lower is women's status. And, finally, environmental stresses tend to exaggerate male domination.[20]

The Cross-Cultural Explanations of Rape

The quotation above, cited by Gregor, and the research of Peggy Reeves Sanday and others suggest that rape is not the evolutionary reproductive strategy of less successful males, but rather a cultural phenomenon by which relations among men are cemented. Rape may be a strategy to ensure continued male domination or a vehicle by which men can hope to conceal maternal dependence, according to ethnographers, but it is surely not an alternative dating strategy. In her ethnographic study of a gang rape at the University of Pennsylvania, Sanday suggests that gang rape has its origins in both the gender inequality that allows men to see women as pieces of meat and in men's needs to demonstrate their masculinity to one another. Gang rape cements the relations among men. But more than that, gang rape permits a certain homoerotic contact between men. When one participant reported his pleasure at feeling the semen of his friends inside the woman as he raped her, Sanday sensed a distinct erotic component. The woman was the receptacle, the vehicle by which these men could have sex with one another and still claim heterosexuality. Only in a culture that degrades and devalues women could such behaviors take place. Rape, then, is hardly an evolutionary strategy by which less successful males get to pass on their reproductive inheritance. It is an act that occurs only in those societies where there is gender inequality and by men who may be quite "successful" in other forms of mating but believe themselves entitled to violate women. It is about *gender,* not about sex, and it is a way in which gender inequality produces gender difference.[21]

Rituals of Gender

One of the ways that anthropologists have explored the cultural construction of gender is by examining specific gender rituals. Their work suggests that the origins of these rituals lie in nonbiological places. Since questions of reproduction and child rearing loom so large in the determination of gender inequality, it makes sense that a lot of these rituals are concerned with reproduction. And since spatial segregation seems to be highly associated with gender difference and gender inequality, ritual segregation—either in space or in time—may have also been a focus of attention. For example, the initiation of young males has been of particular concern, in part because of the relative disappearance of such formal cultural rituals in the contemporary United States. Initiation rituals provide a sense of identity and group membership to the men who participate in them. Many cultures, especially settled agricultural and pastoral societies, include circumcision, the excision of the foreskin of a boy's penis, in a ritual incorporating a male into the society. The age of this ceremony varies; one survey of twenty-one cultures that practice circumcision found that four perform it in infancy, ten when the boy is about ten years old (before puberty), six perform it at puberty, and one waits until late adolescence.

Why would so many cultures determine that membership in the world of adult men requires genital mutilation? Indeed, circumcision is the most common medical procedure in the United States. Theories, of course, abound. In the Jewish Bible, circumcision is a visible sign of the bond between God and man, a symbol of man's obedience to God's law. (In Gen. 17:10–11, 14, God commands Abraham to circumcise Isaac as a covenant.) But it also seems to have been seen as a trophy. Successful warriors would cut off their foes' foreskins to symbolize their victory, and to permanently disfigure and humiliate the vanquished foe. (In 1 Sam. 18:25, King Saul demands that David slay one hundred enemies and bring back their foreskins as a bride-price. David, a bit overeager, brings back two hundred.)

In other cultures, ethnographers suggest that circumcision creates a visible scar that binds men to one another, and serves as a rite of passage to adult masculinity. Whiting, Kluckhohn, and Anthony argue that it symbolically serves to sever a boy's emotional ties to his mother, and therefore to assure appropriate masculine identification. Other writers point out that cultures that emphasize circumcision of young males tend to be those where both gender differentiation and gender inequality are greatest. Circumcision, which is always a public ceremony, simultaneously cements the bonds between father (and his generation) and son (and his generation), links the males together, and excludes women, visibly and demonstrably. Circumcision, then, tends to be associated with male domination, as do other forms of male genital mutilation.[22] In a very few cultures, for example, the penis is ritually bled by cutting. Such cultures still believe in bleeding as a cure for illness—in this case, illness brought about by sexual contact with women, who are believed to be impure and infectious. And we know of four cultures that practice hemicastration, the removal of one testicle. In one culture, people believe it prevents the birth of twins.[23]

Female "circumcision" is also practiced in several cultures, though far fewer than male circumcision. This consists either of clitoridectomy, in which the clitoris is cut away, or infibulation, in which the labia majora are sewn together with only a very small opening left to allow for urination. It is interesting that female circumcision is often performed by adult women. In other cultures, it is performed by the brother of the girl's father. Clitoridectomy is widespread in Africa, but few other places, and it invariably takes place in societies that also practice male circumcision. Infibulation seems to be most widely practiced in East Africa and Somalia, and its goal is to prevent sexual intercourse, while the goal of clitoridectomy is simply to prevent sexual pleasure and thereby sexual promiscuity. Here is the description of the practice from one who underwent it, a Sudanese woman now working as a teacher in the Middle East:

> I will never forget the day of my circumcision, which took place forty years ago. I was six years old. One morning during my

school summer vacation, my mother told me that I had to go with her to her sisters' house and then to visit a sick relative in Halfayat El Mulook [in the northern part of Khartoum, Sudan]. We did go to my aunt's house, and from there all of us went straight to [a] red brick house [I had never seen].

While my mother was knocking, I tried to pronounce the name that was on the door. Soon enough I realized that it was Haija Alamin's house. She was the midwife who [performed circumcisions] on girls in my neighborhood. I was petrified and tried to break loose. But I was captured and subdued by my mother and two aunts. They began to tell me that the midwife was going to purify me.

The midwife was the cruelest person I had seen . . . [She] ordered her young maid to go buy razors from the Yemeni grocer next door. I still remember her when she came back with the razors, which were enveloped in purple wrappings with a crocodile drawing on it.

The women ordered me to lie down on a bed [made of ropes] that had a little hole in the middle. They held me tight while the midwife started to cut my flesh without anesthetics. I screamed till I lost my voice. The midwife was saying to me "Do you want me to be taken into police custody?" After the job was done I could not eat, drink, or even pass urine for three days. I remember one of my uncles who discovered what they did to me threatened to press charges against his sisters. They were afraid of him and they decided to bring me back to the midwife. In her sternest voice she ordered me to squat on the floor and urinate. It seemed like the most difficult thing to do at that point, but I did it. I urinated for a long time and was shivering with pain.

It took a very long time [before] I was back to normal. I understand the motives of my mother, that she wanted me to be clean, but I suffered a lot.[24]

It is interesting that both cultures that circumcise men and those that circumcise women tend to be those where men's status is highest. The purpose of the ritual reveals some of this difference. For men, it is a marking that simultaneously shows that all men are biologically *and culturally* alike—and that they are different from women. Thus it can be seen as reinforcing male dominance. Historically, there was some evidence that male circumcision was medically beneficial, as it reduced the possibilities of penile infection by removing the foreskin, a place where bacteria could congregate. This is no longer the case; rates of penile infection or urethral cancer show little difference between those who have or have not been circumcised. Among advanced industrial societies, only in the United States are the majority of men circumcised, although that rate has dropped from over 95 percent in the 1960s to about two-thirds today. Australia has the second highest rate, about 10 percent.

For women, circumcision has never been justified by medical benefits; it directly impedes adequate sexual functioning and is designed to curtail sexual pleasure. Female circumcision is nearly always performed when women reach puberty, that is, when they are capable of experiencing sexual pleasure, and seems to be associated with men's control over women's sexuality. Currently, political campaigns are being waged to prohibit female genital mutilation as a violation of women's human rights. However, many of its defenders suggest that such campaigns are motivated by Western values. They insist that afterwards, women are revered and respected as members of the culture. (There are no widespread political campaigns against male circumcision, though some individuals have recently begun to rethink the ritual as a form of genital mutilation, and a few men are even undergoing a surgical procedure designed to replace the lost foreskin.)[25]

One of the more interesting theories about the prevalence of these reproductive and sexual rituals has been offered by Jeffrey and Karen Paige in their book *The Politics of Reproductive Ritual.* Paige and Paige offer a materialist interpretation of these rituals, locating the origins of male circumcision, couvade, and purdah in the culture's relationship with its immediate material environment. Take couvade, for example. This is a ritual that men observe when their wives are having babies. Generally, they observe the same food taboos as their wives, restrict their ordinary activities, and even seclude themselves during their wives' delivery and postpartum period. What could possibly be the point of this? Some might think it is anthropologically "cute," as the men often even imitate the symptoms of pregnancy, in apparent sympathy for their wives. But Paige and Paige see it differently. They argue that couvade is significant in cultures where there are no legal mechanisms to keep the couple together or to assure paternity. Couvade is a way for men to fully claim paternity, to know that the baby is theirs. It is also a vehicle by which the men can control women's sexuality by appropriating control over paternity.[26]

Paige and Paige also examine the politics of purdah, the Islamic requirement that women conceal themselves at all times. Ostensibly, this is to protect women's chastity and men's honor—women must be completely covered because they "are so sexy, so tempting, so incapable of controlling their emotions and sexuality, the men say, that they are a danger to the social order." It is as if by concealing women, they can harness women's sexuality. But this is only half the story. It also suggests that *men* are so susceptible to temptation, so incapable of resistance, such easy prey, that they are likely to fall into temptation at any time. In order to protect women from *men's* sexual rapaciousness, men must control women and take away the source of the temptation.[27]

How Many Genders Are There?

We've explored the relationship between levels of gender difference and levels of inequality. But in some cultures, gender itself doesn't seem to be that important, certainly not the central organizing principle of social life. In fact, it hardly matters at all. What accounts for that difference?

The discussion of gender difference often assumes that differences are based on some biological realities that sort physical creatures into their appropriate categories. Thus we assume that because there are two biological sexes (male and female) there must only be two genders (men and women). But some research challenges such bipolar assumptions. Some societies recognize more

than two genders—sometimes three or four. Research on Native American cultures is particularly fascinating and provocative. The Navaho, for example, appear to have three genders—one for masculine men, one for feminine women, and another, called the *nadle,* for those whose sex was ambiguous at birth. One could decide to become a nadle or be born one; either way, they perform tasks assigned to both women and to men and dress as the gender whose tasks they were performing, though they are typically treated as women, and addressed using feminine kinship terms. But let's not jump to conclusions: Being treated as a woman was a promotion, not a demotion in Navaho society, where women historically had higher status than men and were accorded special rights and privileges, including sexual freedom, control over property, and authority to mediate disputes. Nadles were free to marry either males or females, with no loss of status.[28]

Another custom among some Native American cultures is the *berdache*, which is also found in Southeast Asia and the South Pacific. Berdaches are members of one biological sex who adopt the gender identity of the other sex, although such a practice is far more common for males than for females. In his path-breaking study, *The Spirit and the Flesh,* anthropologist Walter Williams explored the world of the berdache in detail. These were men who dressed, worked, and generally acted as women—though everyone knew that they were biologically males. Among the Crow in North America, the berdache were simply males who did not want to become warriors.[29]

Consider how we treat males who dress and act like women. We treat them like freaks, deviants, or assume they must be homosexual. They are outcasts; acting like a berdache in this culture is not recommended if you value your health and your life. Among the Native American cultures of the Great Plains, though, the berdaches are revered as possessed of special powers, enjoy high social and economic status, and frequently control the tribe's ritual life. The reasoning is straightforward and logical: By being men who act like women, the berdaches are sexually indifferent to women, something that other men are not capable of being.

Surely, they must be possessed of some supernatural power to be able to resist the charms of females! Only the berdache can be counted on to administer fairly without seeking to advance his claim on a specific woman whom he might fancy.

There is one case of what might be called female berdaches. Among the Nahane, a Native American culture, a married couple might decide that they had too many daughters and too few sons to hunt for them when they got old. They would choose one of their daughters to live like a man. When she was about five years old, the dried ovaries of a bear were tied to her belt, and she was treated as if she were a boy from then on. As an adult, she would most likely have lesbian sexual relations.[30]

The Mohave seem to have four genders and permit both women and men to cross genders to carefully demarcated roles. A boy who showed preferences for feminine clothing or toys would undergo a different initiation at puberty and become an *alyha*. He would then adopt a female name, paint his face as a woman, perform female roles, and marry a man. When they married, the alyha would cut his upper thigh every month to signify "his" menstrual period, and he would learn how to simulate pregnancy and childbirth. Martin and Voorhies suggest how this was accomplished:

> Labor pains, induced by drinking a severely constipating drug, culminate in the birth of a fictitious stillborn child. Stillborn Mohave infants are customarily buried by the mother, so that an alyha's failure to return to "her" home with a living infant is explained in a culturally acceptable manner.[31]

If a Mohave female wanted to cross genders, she would undergo an initiation ceremony to become a *hwame*. Hwame lived men's lives—hunting, farming, and the like, and assumed paternal responsibility for children, though they were prohibited from assuming positions of political leadership. Neither hwame nor alyha is considered deviant.

In the Middle East, we find a group of Omani males called *xanith* who are biologically males, but whose social identity is female. They work as skilled domestic servants, dress in men's tunics (but in pastel shades more associated with feminine colors), and

sell themselves in passive homosexual relationships. They are permitted to speak with women on the street (other men are prohibited). At sex-segregated public events, they sit with the women. However, they can change their minds—and their gender experiences. If they want to be seen as males, they are permitted to do so, and they then may engage in heterosexual sex. Others simply grow older and eventually quit homosexual prostitution; they are then permitted to become "social men." Some "become" women, even going as far as marrying men. And still others move back and forth between these positions throughout their lives, suggesting a fluidity of gender identity that would be unthinkable to those who believe in biological determinism.

Sexual Diversity

These studies of gender fluidity are also complemented by studies of sexual variation. Taken together, they provide powerful arguments about the cultural construction of both gender and sexuality. Anthropologists have explored remarkable sexual diversity, and thus have suggested that biological arguments about the naturalness of some activities and arrangements may be dramatically overstated. Take homosexuality, which evolutionary biologists would suggest is a biological "aberration" if ever there were one, because homosexuality is not reproductive, and the goal of all sexual activity is to pass on one's genetic code to the next generation. Not only is homosexual activity ubiquitous in the animal kingdom, but it is also extraordinarily common in human cultures—so common, in fact, that it would appear to be "natural." What varies is not the presence or absence of homosexuality— that's pretty much a constant—but the ways in which homosexuals are treated in those cultures. We've already seen that many cultures honor and respect those who transgress gender definitions and adopt the gender of the other sex. Some of these might be considered "homosexual," if your definition of homosexual has only to do with the biological sex of your sex partner.

Even by that definition, though, we find astonishing variation in the ways in which homosexuals are regarded. In 1948, anthropologist Clyde Kluckohn surveyed North American Indian tribes and found homosexuality accepted by 120 of them and rejected by 54. Some cultures (Lango in east Africa, Koniag in Alaska, and Tanala in Madagascar) all allow homosexual marriages between men. Some cultures have clearly defined homosexual roles for men and women, with clearly defined expectations.[32]

In a remarkable ethnography, Gilbert Herdt described the sexual rituals of the Sambia, a mountain people who live in Papua New Guinea. The Sambia practice ritualized homosexuality as a way to initiate young boys into full adult manhood. Young boys ritually daily fellate the older boys and men so that they (the younger boys) can receive the vital life fluid (semen) from the older men and thus become men. "A boy must be initiated and [orally] inseminated, otherwise the girl betrothed to him will outgrow him and run away to another man," was the way one Sambia elder put it. "If a boy doesn't eat semen, he remains small and weak." When they reach puberty, these boys are then fellated by a new crop of younger boys. Throughout this initiation, the boys scrupulously avoid girls, and have no knowledge of heterosexuality until they are married. Neither the boys nor the older men think of themselves as engaging in homosexual behavior: The older men are married to women, and the younger men fully expect to be. There is no adult homosexuality among the Sambia. But these young boys must become, as Herdt puts it, "reluctant warriors." How else are the boys to receive the vital life force that will enable them to be real men and warriors?[33]

Nearby, also in Melanesia, are the Keraki, who engage in a related practice. There, the boys are sodomized by older men, because the Keraki believe that without the older men's semen, the boys will not grow to be men. This ritual practice occurs until the boys hit puberty and secondary sex characteristics appear—facial hair, dropped voice—at which point the ritual has accomplished its task. When an anthropologist asked Kerki men if they had been sodomized, many responded by saying "Why, yes! Otherwise how should I have grown?" Other ritualized homosexual practices have been reported from other cultures.[34] Interestingly, such ritual practices, as among the Sambia and Keraki, are more evident in cultures in which sex segregation is high and women's status is low. This conforms to other ethnographic evidence that suggests that elaborate rituals of male bonding have the effect of excluding women from ritual life, and thus correlate with women's lower status. Sex segregation is almost always associated with lower status for women—whether among the Sambia or among cadets at The Citadel.[35]

If all this sounds extraordinarily exotic, remember this: In every major city in the United States, there is a group of young men, many of whom are married and virtually all of whom consider themselves to be heterosexual, who have sex with other men for money. These hustlers will perform only certain acts (anal penetration) or will only allow certain acts (they permit their clients to fellate them, but will not reciprocate). By remaining the "insertor" in homosexual acts, these men do not identify as homosexual, but as *men*. Men are insertors, whether with women or with men, so as long as they remain insertors, they believe their masculinity is not compromised. "Objectively," you may argue, they are engaging gay sex. But by their definition, homosexuality equals passivity in sexual contact, having sex like a woman. And by that definition, they are not having gay sex. Whatever you might make of this, though, suddenly the Sambia do not look completely alien; they look more like distant cousins.

Some cultures take permissiveness regarding homosexuality to a remarkable level. Among the Aranda of Australia, Siwans of Northern Africa, and Keraki of New Guinea, every male is homosexual during adolescence and bisexual after marriage. The purpose of this is to divert adolescent sex away from young girls and prevent teenage pregnancy, and therefore to keep the birth rate down in cultures that have very scarce resources. The well-studied Yanomamo have an institutionalized form of male homosexuality as well as female infanticide. This warrior culture feared population explosion and the depletion of resources to females.[36]

The Etero and the Marind-anim, both in New Guinea, prefer homosexuality to heterosexuality, even though they maintain heterosexual marriages. How, you might ask, do they solve the problem of reproduction? The Etero place a taboo on heterosexual sex for most of the year, but prohibit gay sex when the moon is full (and thus when all the women are ovulating). For the Marind-anim, even that much sexual contact with the opposite sex is undesirable. Their birth rate is so low that this warrior culture organizes raids every year, during which it kidnaps the babies of other cultures, raising them to be happy, healthy—and, of course, homosexual—Marind-anim.[37]

One Melanesian society, called "East Bay" in William Davenport's ethnographic study, practices full adult bisexuality. Nearly every male has extensive homosexual sexual contact throughout his life, though all are also heterosexual and married to women. (No one is exclusively homosexual, only a few are exclusively heterosexual.) Women and men are seen as relatively equal in terms of sexual drive, and there are no taboos against contact with women.[38] . . .

Notes

1. See, for example. Karen Sacks, "Engels Revisited: Women, Organization of Production, and Private Property," in *Women, Culture and Society,* M. Rosaldo and L. Lamphere, eds. (Stanford: Stanford University Press, 1974); and *Sisters and Wives: The Past and Future of Sexual Equality* (Westport, Conn.: Greenwood, 1979).
2. Margaret Mead, *Sex and Temperament in Three Primitive Societies* (New York: William Morrow, 1935). Critics such as Derek Freeman have suggested that Mead, like the biologists she was criticizing, simply found what she was looking for, especially in Samoa, where she apparently fabricated some details. Yet challenges to the core insight in her work in New Guinea, that of cultural variation in gender roles, are unsubstantiated and convincing.
3. Mead, *Sex and Temperament.* pp. 29, 35, 57–58, 84, 128, 101.
4. Margaret Mead, *Male and Female* (New York: William Morrow, 1949). p. 69; Mead, *Sex and Temperament,* p. 171.
5. Mend, *Sex and Temperament*, pp. 189, 190, 197; Mead, *Male and Female*, p. 98.
6. Mead, *Sex and Temperament.* p. 228.
7. Adrienne Zihlman, "Woman the Gatherer: The Role of Women in Early Hominid Evolution," in *Gender and Anthropology.* S. Morgen, ed.

8. Frederich Engels, *On the Origin of the Family, Private Property and the State* (New York: International Publishers, 1970).
9. Eleanor Leacock, "Women's Status in Egalitarian Society: Implications for Social Evolution," *Current Anthropology* 19(2): 252 (1978); see also Eleanor Leacock, "Montagnais Women and the Jesuit Program for Colonization." in *Women and Colonization,* M. Etienne and E. Leacock, eds. (New York: Praeger, 1980).
10. Sacks, "Engels Revisited" and *Sisters and Wives.*
11. Marvin Harris. *Cows, Pigs, Wars and Witches: The Riddle of Culture* (New York: Random House. 1974); and *Cannibals and Kings* (New York: Random House, 1977).
12. Lionel Tiger and Robin Fox, *The Imperial Animal* (New York: Holt., 1971).
13. Claude Levi-Strauss, *The Elementary Structures of Kinship* (London: Tavistock, 1969); see Collier and Rosaldo, "Politics and Gender in Simple Societies" in *Sexual Meanings: The Cultural Construction of Gender and Sexuality,* S. B. Ortner and H. Whitehead, eds. (Cambridge: Cambridge University Press, 1981).
14. Bacon, Barry, and Child, "Cross Cultural Survey."
15. Judith Brown, "A Note on the Division of Labor by Sex," *American Anthropologist* 72(5) (1970).
16. Scott Coltrane, "The Micropolitics of Gender in Nonindustrial Societies," *Gender & Society* 6(1) (1992); Margaret Mead, *Male and Female,* pp. 190, 189.
17. Daphne Spain, *Gendered Spaces* (Chapel Hill: University of North Carolina Press, 1992); "The Spatial Foundations of Men's Friendships and Men's Power" in *Men's Friendships,* P. Nardi, ed. (Newbury Park, Calif.: Sage Publications, 1992).
18. Thomas Gregor, "No Girls Allowed," *Science* 82 (December 1982).
19. Peggy Reeves Sanday, *Female Power and Male Dominance* (New York: Cambridge University Press, 1981), pp. 75, 128. See also Maria Lepowsky, "Gender in an Egalitarian Society: A Case Study from the Coral Sea," in *Beyond the Second Sex: New Directions in the Anthropology of Gender,* P. R. Sanday and R. G. Goodenough, eds. (Philadelphia: University of Pennsylvania Press, 1990).
20. See Carol Tavris and Carole Wade, *The Longest War* (New York: Harcourt, Brace, 1984), pp. 330–31.
21. See Peggy Reeves Sanday, *Fraternity Gang Rape* (New York: New York University Press, 1991).

7. (Washington, D.C.: American Anthropological Association, 1989). p. 31.

22. John W. Whiting, Richard Kluckhohn, and Albert Anthony, "The Function of Male Initiation Ceremonies at Puberty," in *Readings in Social Psychology,* E. Maccoby, T. M. Newcomb, and E. L. Hatley, eds. (New York: Henry Holt, 1958).

23. Edgar Gregersen, *Sexual Practices* (New York: Franklin Watts, 1983), p. 104.

24. Cited in "Unmasking Tradition" by Rogaia Mustafa Abusharaf, *The Sciences* (March/April 1998), p. 23.

25. See for example, Joseph Zoske, "Male Circumcision: A Gender Perspective," *Journal of Men's Studies* 6(2) (Winter 1998).

26. Karen Paige and Jeffrey Paige, *The Politics of Reproductive Ritual* (Berkeley: University of California Press, 1981).

27. Tavris and Wade, *The Longest War,* p. 314; see also Paige and Paige, *The Politics of Reproductive Ritual;* Fatima Mernissi, *Beyond the Veil: Male-Female Dynamics in a Modern Muslim Society* (New York: Wiley, 1975).

28. Michael Olien, *The Human Myth* (New York: Harper and Row, 1978); M. K. Martin and B. Voorhies, *Female of the Species* (New York: Columbia University Press, 1975).

29. Walter Williams, *The Spirit and the Flesh* (Boston: Beacon Press, 1986).

30. Gregersen, *Sexual Practices,* p. 270.

31. Martin and Voorhies, *Female of the Species,* p. 97.

32. Clyde Kluckholn (1948) cited in Clyde Kluckholn, *Mirror for Man* (Greenwich, Conn.: Fawcett, 1970).

33. Gilbert Herdt, *Guardians of the Flutes* (Chicago: University of Chicago Press, 1981), pp. 1, 165, 282.

34. F. E. Williams, *Papuans of the Trans-Fly* (Oxford: Oxford University Press, 1936), p. 159; see also E. L. Schiefflin, *The Sorrow of the Lonely and the Burning of the Dancers* (New York: St. Martin's Press, 1976); R. Kelly, *Etero Social Structure* (Ann Arbor: University of Michigan Press, 1977); J. Carrier, "Sex Role Preference as a Explanatory Variable in Homosexual Behavior," *Archives of Sexual Behavior* 6 (1977).

35. William Davenport, "Sex in Cross-Cultural Perspective," in *Human Sexuality in Four Perspectives,* F. Beach and M. Diamond, eds. (Baltimore: Johns Hopkins University Press, 1977); see also Gilbert Herdt, ed., *Ritualized Homosexuality in Melanesia* (Berkeley: University of California Press, 1984), p. 66.

36. Gregersen, *Sexual Practices,* p. 257.

37. Ibid.

38. Davenport, "Sex in Cross-Cultural Perspective."

24

Excerpts from "Comparative Gender Stratification"

JOAN HUBER

1. Introduction

This chapter selectively reviews more than 25 years of research in anthropology to assess the effects of premodern subsistence modes on variation in levels of sex inequality. Inasmuch as hunger is the chief determinant of human relationships (Goody, 1982, p. 15; Messer, 1984, p. 208), no society can be understood without knowing what men and women must do each day in order to eat. I also focus on two societal functions that mesh with a given subsistence technology in complex ways: reproduction and the legitimate use of force. A large interdisciplinary literature on women in development is excluded because it is reviewed elsewhere in this volume.

Most research on gender inequality has appeared since 1970, when anthropologists first began to consider women's work. Earlier, Mead (1973, p. 4) could have been speaking for all social scientists when she said that women anthropologists wanted to do the same work men did and therefore did not study the activities of women and children.

The mode of subsistence refers to the types of energy a society uses to secure food (Friedl, 1975). Subsistence modes tend to respond to population pressure on a given physical environment. The three major theorists of population dynamics—Smith, Marx, and Boserup—agree that humans, like other animal populations, inherently tend to increase toward the environment's short-term carrying capacity (Hammel & Howell, 1987; North & Thomas, 1973). Ensuing population pressure spurs technological innovation and other adaptations for the management of scarce resources (Heider, 1972, p. 211).

Influenced by earlier work in anthropology and by Duncan's (1964) powerful analysis of ecology, Lenski (1970) classified societies by the major tool used in food production to show how the interrelations of population, organization, ecology, and technology affect social stratification, thus making a wide range of data from anthropology accessible to sociologists (Moseley & Wallerstein, 1978, p. 262). Earlier typologies that classified societies by the materials used to make tools (e.g., stone, iron) had been theoretically sterile, yielding no important predictions. A typology based on subsistence modes combines comprehensiveness with minimal ambiguity and maximal reliability (Lenski, 1994, p. 24).

Appearing in rough sequence by order of technological complexity, subsistence modes affected societal size and organization by limiting the number of people who lived long enough to reproduce. I focus on those preindustrial modes whose technologies developed around field and forest resources: hunting and gathering, the hoe, herding, and the plow. I regret any distortions that may result from compressing so many societal types into one chapter.

Lenski's schema went far toward explaining the emergence of caste, class, feudalism, and slavery, but said little about gender stratification. Anthropologist Ernestine Friedl (1975) was first to use a subsistence framework to explain why men tended to be more dominant than women in foraging and hoe cultures. Later, sociologists Rae Blumberg (1978, 1995), Janet Chafetz (1984, 1990), and several anthropologists (see Chafetz, 1984, p. 3) used a typology based on subsistence modes to explain societal variation in gender inequality.

The dependent variable, the level of sex inequality, is an asymmetrical concept. Like a pendulum destined to swing only to the midpoint of a trajectory, women collectively are never more advantaged than men. It is their extent of disadvantage that varies (Chafetz, 1990, p. 117) and justifies attention to causal antecedents (Sen, 1990, p. 124).

Yet the causes of cross-cultural variation in gender disadvantage remain elusive. Sociology texts have nothing to say about the topic (Ferree & Hall, 1996, p. 944). It was much studied in anthropology (under the rubric of women's status), yet reviews in the *Annual Review of Anthropology* (1977 and 1988, respectively) reported that the search for key causes had been unfruitful. What went wrong?

One possibility is that problems encountered in studies based on Murdock's (1967) cross-cultural sample (e.g., Whyte, 1978) dampened enthusiasm for macrolevel theories of women's status (Mason, 1984, p. 5; Mukhopadhyay & Higgins, 1988, p. 462; Quinn, 1977, p. 182).[1] Murdock's sampling was inadequate and the data, of uneven quality, had

not been collected with the Murdock categories in mind (Fedigan, 1986, p. 47). Studies based on such data tend to yield inconclusive findings.

Another reason that causes of variation in sex inequality remain unclear is perhaps more significant. Despite their interest in political affairs, anthropologists gave little attention to a persistent question that puzzled them: men's universal monopoly on politics. They also neglected a related issue, the most puzzling in the literature: women's exclusion from institutionalized competition for prestige (Quinn, 1977, p. 222). Yet a decade later, despite the domination of gender issues in the study of small-scale societies in the 1980s (Flanagan, 1989, p. 253), the reasons for women's lack of attainment in the political or military arenas continued to receive little study (Mukhopadhyay & Higgins, 1988, p. 464; Ross, 1986, p. 844).

A third reason may stem from anthropologists' attempts to avoid nineteenth century errors entailed by grand theorizing by their tendency to concentrate on particularities, leaving theoretical issues implicit and giving little attention to the methods that comparative studies entail (Goody, 1962, p. v). Such practices make their findings hard to generalize.

Despite the problems of focusing on an area that is both underresearched and undertheorized, I proceed on the premise that the key to understanding premodern variation in sex inequality lies in the interrelations of subsistence production, the politico–military arena where rules are made, and patterns of population maintenance. I examine how subsistence modes interact with two activities overwhelmingly the province of one sex: the legitimate use of force and the bearing and rearing of children. Men fight wars. Women bear and suckle children. Are these facts related? If so, how?

2. Reconstructing Human Evolution

I begin by reviewing research on human social evolution for its bearing on the relationship of work, war, and population maintenance. The study of social evolution necessarily involves sociobiology, yet this area has become divisive in anthropology. Only a minority of cultural anthropologists accept the concepts of sociobiological theory, biological anthropology's basic perspective (Lieberman, 1989,

p. 680). Like their counterparts in sociology, feminist anthropologists have been leery of claims that biology affects gender roles, perhaps because biology had long been invoked as the sole explanation. Gender theorists contest the degree to which ecology or evolution links sex differences to the division of labor when the real problem is to assess to what extent and in what ways the differences matter (Worthman, 1995, pp. 594, 602).

It is a mistake to overlook the role of biology in gender stratification, for at least one sex difference matters. The fact that no man can bear a child makes women central to population maintenance in a way that men cannot be, and population maintenance is crucial to species survival. It would be premature to exclude biological factors when the origins of sex stratification are so imperfectly understood. Human software derives from cultural evolution; the hardware is a result of biological evolution (Leach, 1984, p. 20).

Nineteenth century evolutionists held that all human societies progress through technological and social stages to a final civilized state, as in Europe. In the twentieth century, their work was discredited for its ethnocentrism, teleology, methods, data, and conclusions in a reaction that led to the establishment of anthropology as a discipline (Orlove, 1980, p. 236). Classical anthropology then focused on topics such as kinship and symbolism, neglecting the influence of economic factors (Testart, 1988, p. 9)[2] Food production was seen as a dull topic (Netting, 1974, p. 21). The study of social evolution lay dormant until the 1960s, when interest arose on the basis of data produced by twentieth century fieldwork (Fedigan, 1986, p. 32).

Two opposing theories currently explain how the human species evolved. The older one, man the hunter, is the most popular reconstruction of early social behavior (Zihlman, 1981, p. 75). It was drawn from a literature that converged on one distinguishing human trait: the pursuit, killing, and eating of animals with the use of tools. The most influential expression of the older theory, Washburn and Lancaster (1968) argued that hunting demands all those qualities of human behavior that separate man from other primates: male aggressiveness and pleasure in killing, bipedalism, elaborate toolkits, language, appreciation of beauty, the division of labor, the monogamous nuclear family, loss of female estrus, and male bonding (Fedigan, 1986, p. 32). Washburn and Lancaster (1968) argued, further, that the killing of animals with tools had so long dominated human history that it shaped the human psyche for all time (Fedigan, 1986, p. 33). Their argument was repeated in so many articles and texts that it acquired something akin to the status of a received truth.[3] Most of the authors in the two most influential compendiums of the time (Lee, 1968; Washburn, 1961) mentioned only hunting as a way to procure food (Fedigan, 1986, p. 33).

Like Darwin himself, man-the-hunter theorists failed to apply to human females the theory of sexual selection that Darwin developed to explain secondary sex differences: men were selected for intelligence, courage, and technological ability; women, for maternal traits. This view pervades reconstructions based on the primacy of hunting (Fedigan, 1986, p. 62). Tiger and Fox (1971) saw male bonding in hunting as focal; predatory aggression was genetically wired into (male) nature (Zihlman, 1981, p. 82). Wilson (1975), despite his emphasis on parental investment and mate choice as key concepts in sociobiology, failed to apply them to female mammals or primates; nor did he use the concepts of maternal investment, female choice, and mechanisms of sexual selection to incorporate women into human evolution (Zihlman, 1981, p. 84).

Ironically, the article that championed the explanatory power of hunting (Lee & Devore, 1968) provided insights and data that led to its undoing. The data showed gathering as vital to foraging life. One of the editors, Lee (1968), even argued that hunters actually gather for a living. Lee's (1980) continuing analysis of women's contribution to subsistence was a major starting point in a reassessment of women's role in early human society (Fedigan, 1986, p. 34). Subsequent research exposed the male bias that pervaded the ethnographic studies on which the picture of man the hunter was based (Dahlberg, 1981, p. 2).

A newer view of evolution centers on woman the gatherer. Man the hunter came to be seen as a backward projection of sex stereotypes onto humans of more than a million years ago (Zihlman, 1981, p. 76), Themes of male aggression, dominance, and hunting that led to the belief that sex inequality was rooted in biological sex differences were modified to fit a growing body of data on living apes and hunter-gatherers. It is improbable that hominid mothers sat about awaiting the return of the hunters; more likely, they actively sought food while carrying infants. To postulate that early human females were sedentary denies their primate heritage (Zihlman, 1981, p. 89). There were no sedentary females in foraging societies. Available quantitative data show that women were away from camp as long as men and walk the same distances, carrying infants and heavier burdens (Fedigan, 1986, p. 49). Recent data even suggest that our hominid ancestors had no home bases (Potts, 1984), making untenable a house-bound vision of early women (Fedigan, 1986, p. 60).

Moreover, according to sociobiological theory, heavy maternal investment in offspring implies that it was females rather than males who chose mates. Burdened by dependent offspring, females must have chosen sociable males willing to share food and protect them and their babies, turning around the older picture in which dominant males pick females who, in turn, try to remain attractive enough to secure a mate, food, protection, and offspring (Zihlman, 1981, p. 88).

Sociobiology clearly cuts more than one way with regard to theories of sex inequality. If early women were not "house-bound," waiting for their men to supply food for them and their children, how could the domestic responsibilities of women derive from nature? Although its accuracy has never been debated, the assumption that it is natural for women to be found at the hearth still undergirds most theories of human social evolution. Perhaps, as Fedigan (1986, p. 38) suggests, the only division of labor in which sex matters is the one that involves insemination, gestation, and lactation.

In the following paragraph, I discuss human adaptations based on hunting and gathering, the hoe, herding, and the plow. The analysis is based on two principles of stratification. First, a necessary condition for gender equality is that women must be economically interdependent with other producers rather than dependent on male producers (Fedigan, 1986, p. 43; Leacock, 1981). The second, Friedl's (1975) modification of the first, suggests a sufficient

condition: women must not only contribute to subsistence but also exercise control over the distribution of valued goods in order to equal men in power and prestige. In sum, producers have more power and prestige than consumers and in any society those who control the distribution of valued goods beyond the family have the most power and prestige.

3. Hunting and Gathering Societies

Hunting and gathering comprise a way of life that resembles the technological adaptation of all *Homo sapiens* before the domestication of plants and animals about 10,000 years ago (Friedl, 1975, p. 12). Forager groups are small (about 50 persons), mobile, and nonterritorial, which constrains the accrual of a surplus and leads to an egalitarian emphasis on sharing resources (Lee, 1968). The few peoples for whom foraging remains a major source of food today occupy land no one else wants (yet): African and South American rain forest, Arctic tundra, and Australian desert (Spielman & Eder, 1994, p. 311).

Foragers use several methods to obtain most of their food: gathering wild plants and small animals such as mice or clams; hunting large animals such as deer, caribou, whales, or seal; and fishing. Meat is always a favored food (Friedl, 1975, p. 12). Correlated with latitude, the amount in the diet ranges from 10% near the equator to 90% in the Arctic (Testart, 1978, cited in Fedigan, 1986, p. 48).

By consensus, foraging societies exhibit the least social inequality. Whether they are truly or only relatively so has been debated (Flanagan, 1989, p. 254). Feminist scholars tried to document the absence of sex inequality to prove that inequality did not derive from nature (Collier & Yanigasako, 1987); Marxists hoped to show that in the absence of private property, equality prevails (Leacock, 1981; Sacks, 1982). However, most anthropologists see social inequality as universal; all known societies use criteria of sex, age, and personal attributes in allocating power (Sahlins, 1958, p. 1).

Hunter-gatherer subsistence ensures a low level of inequality because foragers, who move when the food supply in a given area is depleted, own only what they can carry. They highly value sharing, which reduces the risks of living in groups that cannot readily buffer a variable environment (Cashden, 1980, p. 117). All foraging societies have rules that order the sharing of meat; the ones that survived were those that found ways to encourage the fulfillment of exchange obligations (Friedl, 1975, p. 20).

On average, women's contribution to foragers' food supply more or less equals men's, which leads to women's being seen as self-sufficient rather than to higher status (Schlegel & Barry, 1986; Sanday, 1973). Gathering produces only enough food for a woman and her family. Hunters earn esteem as generous hosts because hunting enables men to distribute a highly valued food to the entire band (Friedl, 1975).

Both men and women can master the needed skills, so why did women never hunt?[4] Friedl (1975, p. 16) suggests that the answer lies in a complex of interdependent conditions related to childbearing. To offset the effects of high death rates, women foragers are often pregnant or lactating. They are barred from hunting in the later stages of pregnancy by shifts in body balance; after the birth, by the burden of the child, which must remain with its mother while it is breastfed. Although food supplements are added at 1 to 6 months in all preindustrial cultures (Raphael & Davis, 1985, p. 141), lactation occupies 3 to 4 years because shorter periods tend to increase infant mortality (Cronk, 1991, p. 28). Hunting also requires distance running, which may affect ability to ovulate (Graham, 1985).

Although anthropologists traditionally have explained marriage as a male–female bond occasioned by the food needs of a female with dependents (Ember & Ember, 1983, p. 41), it is perhaps better seen as a way to recruit labor, distribute food, and provide for procreation and sexual pleasure (Friedl, 1975, p. 23). Among foragers, monogamy was the most common form. On average, a hunter typically lacked enough meat at any one time to care for more than one set of marital, paternal, and affinal obligations (Friedl, 1975, p. 26).

War is rare among foragers. Population is sparse and land is plentiful. Conflicts within bands are often settled by the departure of one party in a dispute, and women are often involved in the decision (Friedl, 1975, p. 15). Leadership roles are limited to the persuasive influence of skilled hunters, to women skillful enough to attract their married offspring to live with them as adults, and to men and women with shamanistic skills. No leader can coerce others (Friedl, 1975, p. 31). Male dominance is greatest when hunting is the sole source of food; equality is greatest where men and women together perform the major subsistence tasks.

4. Horticulture Societies

Horticulture, plant cultivation with digging stick or hoe in garden-size plots, began in Asia Minor about 10,000 years ago. It marked the beginnings of modern stratification. Boserup (1965), reversing Malthus, suggests that population pressure, driven by the need to feed more individuals, causes rather than follows intensification of cultivation. In the simple form the major subsistence tool is a digging stick. People had to move every few years to replace plots whose fertility was lost.

The advanced form of horticulture appeared about 6000 years ago with the invention of metallurgy. The hoe replaced the digging stick while metal weapons replaced sticks and stones. Because humans can be hurt more easily with metal weapons than with sticks and stones, war for the first time became a profitable way to acquire food produced by someone else (Lenski, 1970). The effect on gender stratification was profound because everywhere war is men's work, associated with the devaluation of women (Hayden, 1995, p. 63).

The use of metal weapons to secure food requires a third principle of gender stratification that concerns the use of force: The more often a Society engages in warfare, the more likely is social control to be vested in politico–military elites that exclude women (see Collins, 1988, pp. 168–173).

Hoe societies, which exemplify the gender role diversity that provided the foundation for the relativist view of human beliefs and behaviors made popular by Boas and his students, vary in patterns of domestic exchange, postmarital residence, and household composition. The crucial variable is the control of economic resources, especially labor. The question is, which sex can command the labor of others and control the distribution of the resulting accumulation (Friedl, 1975, p. 61)?

The gender division of labor takes three forms. Men can prepare land for cultivation (felling trees, cutting and burning underbrush) while both sexes cultivate it, a pattern common to sub-Saharan Africa. Men can clear land and women cultivate it, a pattern among Indians of the eastern United States. Men can both clear and cultivate, a rare pattern found in inland tropical South America (Friedl, 1975, p. 51).

Once the land is cleared, there is no adaptive advantage in having either men or women plant, weed, harvest, and transport crops. Lactating women can carry babies and return with loads of food as women gatherers do. The time and energy women spend on childcare are allocated under the constraints posed by their work, not the other way round. For example, early supplementary feeding of infants is more likely if women do much subsistence work (Nerlove, 1974). Norms concerning family size and systems of childcare typically conform to women's customary work requirements (Blumberg, 1978: Chafetz, 1984; Friedi, 1975; Mukhopadhyay & Higgins, 1988, p. 475; Quinn, 1977, p. 193). According to cross-cultural time allocation studies, women simply add childcare to their other tasks (Zihlman, 1997, p. 194).

In simple hoe societies the sexual division of labor consists of the male monopoly over the initial clearing of new land (Friedl, 1975, pp. 53–60). Once or twice a generation the land to be cleared lies next to land worked by other peoples, leading to warfare. A potential need for defense in the acquisition of new territory probably contributed to making the slash-and-burn process largely men's work, although land-clearing probably fails to confer the advantages that the monopoly on hunting gives forager men.

In both simple and advanced hoe societies, marriage and kinship customs tend to follow the division of labor (Friedl, 1975). Unilateral reckoning of descent is most common in hoe societies, perhaps because women sometimes produce more food than do men. Patrilineality tends to occur when both spouses cultivate. Matrilineality is found in about a quarter of hoe societies, usually when only women cultivate. Matrilineal inheritance tends to occur when women produce more than do men (Goody, 1976).

Patrilocality (postmarital residence with husband's kin) tends to occur when the male contribution to subsistence is high. It disadvantages the wife although she can compensate by bearing sons whose wives she can later dominate. Wives also can become the worms within the apple of a patrilocal domestic group (Collier, 1974, p. 92). Working together separated from kin tends to integrate them as a group and gives them a measure of power (Leis, 1974). Matrilocality typically occurs where female contribution to subsistence is high. The infrequency with which patterns of residence leave related women together and disperse related men, rather than vice versa, helps to explain why the degree of political influence exercised by Iroquois women is found in few societies (Quinn, 1977, p. 214).

The divorce rate should increase as women's share of subsistence tasks rises because couples can more easily part when it affects the food supply of neither of the spouses nor their children. Although data are sketchy, this expectation is upheld: divorce rates among hoe peoples appear high compared to U.S. rates (Friedl, 1975, p. 93).

Because warfare is common and women's subsistence contribution is also high, polygyny occurs more often in advanced hoe societies than in all other types. Warfare enhances male political control because men's service as warriors strengthens their control on rights of citizenship (Grant, 1991, p. 14). War also alters the sex ratio (Ember, 1974)[5]. Under such conditions, polygyny is a way to raise productivity, as economist Ester Boserup (1970) first noted (Lesthaeghe & Surkyn, 1988) and it is widely practiced in a populist form (Huber & Spitze, 1988, p. 488). Nearly everyone marries but women marry early, men late, and a high death rate helps to even the sex ratio. Male incentives to practice polygyny lie not in the desire to collect women but in the need for children's labor (Ember & Ember, 1983, p. 13). Women's incentives likewise derive from their need for children's labor, especially for support in old age.

Warfare affects sex stratification more generally through its close ties with governance (Goldschmidt, 1959, p. 166). The requirements of waging war encourage the establishment of autocratic and hierarchical political organizations and the formation of politico–military elites in which women play no part. Among ordinary men, the presence of an outside enemy, real or imagined, stimulates solidarity and promotes the exclusion of women from political life (Ross, 1986, p. 852). In turn, exclusion from political life leads to lack of control over property. Goheen (1996, p. 137), for example, recounts how Cameroon men's earlier status as hunters and warriors led to the need for women to seek men's permission to cultivate, giving rise to the saying that men own the fields, women own the crops. By contrast, in a rare instance of women's full participation in warfare (among the Fon in Dahomey), women's political activity was also high and they could control property (Ross, 1986, p. 852; see also Collins, 1985, p. 390).

Why do women so rarely take part in organized violence? The male monopoly is often attributed to their relative strength and size within (but not across) populations and to greater aggressiveness, but such explanations pose problems. Larger, stronger males do not generally dominate shorter, weaker ones (Chafetz, 1984, p. 118); adult dominance derives from diverse social talents (flattery, deception, competence, nurturance). Interpersonal aggression may be detrimental to effective leadership (Maccoby & Jacklin, 1974, p. 274).[6]

More than 20 years ago Friedl (1975, p. 57) suggested that the male monopoly on warfare resulted from men's relative expendability in population maintenance, but scholars gave this proposal little attention either before or during the decade 1977–1987 (Mukhopadhyay & Higgins, 1988, p. 470) nor have I located research on this topic conducted after 1987. However, Friedl's conjecture makes sense. In the preindustrial reproductive cycle the most frequent states are pregnancy and lactation (Harrell, 1981). However, pregnancy reduces combat effectiveness; depriving a suckling of nourishment reduces its chances of survival. The real costs of sending pregnant and lactating women off to war are obvious.

5. Herding Societies

Herding and hoe societies appeared in the same time period; animals were domesticated at about the same time as plants. Pastoral economies cover the technological range of hoe and simple plow societies in areas where tillage is hard owing to mountainous terrain, short growing season, or low rainfall as in central Asia, Arabia, North Africa, parts of Europe, and sub-Saharan Africa (Lenski & Lenski, 1978, p. 235). Small-scale use of hoe or plow may occur. As explained in the section on plow societies, the herders' level of living often exceeds that of peasants (Krader, 1968, p. 458). Moreover, owing to historical accident, herding societies uniquely influenced the modern world when the gender norms of ancient Hebrew herders became embedded in law and custom across much of Eurasia and North Africa owing to the political and military victories of Christian and Muslim conquerors.

Ecology matters. Moving livestock to seasonal pastures to convert grass into human food usually requires a nomadic or seminomadic way of life. In turn, the use of spatial mobility as a survival strategy leads to competition with agrarians over territory and disputes over water and stolen animals (Beck, 1978, p. 352). Constant threat of conflict during migration stimulates growth and consolidation of political authority. Men of courage are prized as warfare becomes culturally attractive (Barfield, 1994, p. 161).

Because the open grasslands where most herders live pose few barriers to movement and political consolidation, herding societies may be huge (e.g., the empire of Ghenghis Khan) but their communities are only a little larger than foragers' because effective maintenance of herds is best done in small units and the food supply is limited (Beck, 1978, p. 352). In the ninth century BCE, Asian herders learned to ride their horses, which gave them great advantage over less mobile agrarians in ensuing waves of conquest. Herding groups repeatedly devastated Eurasian agrarian empires over a period of more than 2500 years (Lenski & Lenski, 1978, pp. 237–318).

Generalizing about sex inequality in herding societies is risky because many of them also depend on hoe or plow (which oppositely affect women's economic productivity) and also for lack of data. A careful study of how men and women in any nomadic pastoral society influence decisions on resource allocation has yet to be made. The study of nomads was undoubtedly spurred by romantic stereotypes of fierce and independent peoples but all virtues were defined as male and the role of women was grossly neglected until after 1970 (Dyson-Hudson & Dyson-Hudson, 1980, p. 15ff).

The value placed on a politico–military elite should result in a fairly high level of inequality among men and between men and women. Herding societies are most likely to require patrilocal residence and have hereditary slavery (Lenski & Lenski, 1978, p. 237). Women are excluded from the most important subsistence tasks, a result, according to Evans-Pritchard (1965, p. 50), of their lack of experience in warfare and the diplomacy needed to settle disputes at water holes, their lesser physical strength, and herders' need to be away from home for long periods (Elam, 1973, p. 46).

The practice of polygyny in herding regimes depends on the extent to which ecological conditions permit only herding or also permit use of hoe or plow. Polygyny is rare when the environment (as in central Asia) neither offers men much chance to become rich nor women to become economically active but it may increase when an encounter with a market society gives women an opening such as carpet-making (Barfield, 1981, p. 79). If use of the hoe gives women economic opportunities, as often happens in East Africa, polygyny may be fairly common (Hakansson, 1988), appearing in the populist form common to advanced hoe societies. If the plow is used in conjunction with herding, as in North Africa, some men may become rich enough to marry more than one wife. Women then may be barred from property inheritance, although Islamic law forbids it. For example, Libyan Bedouins know it is against religious law to exclude women from inheritance but they also know that the uncontrolled alienation of property would destroy the basis of corporate life (Peters, 1978, p. 324).

6. Agrarian Societies

Simple agrarian societies appeared in the Middle East about 3000 BCE with the introduction of a wooden plow, probably as a result of population pressure. Techniques to smelt iron, invented about 2000 years later, provided an iron blade and marked the advent of advanced agrarian societies. Warfare became more widespread. Unlike tin and copper, iron is a common metal, which thus permits a great proliferation of weaponry.

Use of the plow spread from the Middle East until agrarian societies covered most of Asia, Europe, and North Africa.[7] Boserup's key insight was that people do not turn the earth, fodder animals, and collect manure unless they must (Netting, 1993, p. 103). With low population density and shifting tillage, women do most of the work with handheld tools; polygyny was a way to increase production. With high population density and settled agriculture, men do most of the work; women become economic liabilities, in need of a dowry as a basis for their support (Boserup, 1970, p. 35).

The most obvious effect of the plow was a vast increase in the food supply. Use of the plow made continuous cultivation possible for the first time by reducing weeds and turning soil deeply enough to restore fertility. It stimulated the domestication of draft animals. Confining them in stalls to prevent their wandering away encouraged the collection of manure to fertilize the fields. The invention of writing soon followed (the better to keep track of a surplus large enough to be stored) as did the beginnings of empire building (Lenski & Lenski, 1978, p. 177).

Eurasian stratification patterns assumed the pyramidal form common to feudalism: a political and economic elite; a sprinkling of merchants, artisans, and craft workers of lesser rank; and swarms of peasants, serfs, and slaves. The plow had a devastating effect on the lives of ordinary people. A food surplus in the countryside coupled with the availability of iron weapons tempted elites to extract as much as possible from impoverished peasants. The flatter and richer the land, the worse off were ordinary people, probably much worse off than were their forager ancestors (Lenski & Lenski, 1978, p. 206). In addition, oral health and skeletal robustness declined as a result of consumption of too many carbohydrates and reduced physical activity (Larsen, 1995).

Yet the plow depressed women's status more than men's. First, because men monopolized it, women's share of food production plummeted.

With oxen, a man could plow in a day an area far larger than a woman could till by hoe (Childe, 1951, p. 100). The plow required the management of heavy draft animals in larger fields further from home, making it hard to arrange a schedule to suit a nursing baby (Blumberg, 1978, p. 50). The less food women produce, the more they are valued only as mothers (Goody, 1976, p. 34).

Second, plow technology makes land the chief form of wealth because a field can be tilled in perpetuity. Coupled with the huge increase in productivity and the specialization that this permits, land becomes a scarce good (Goody, 1976, p. 97). Individual land ownership gives rise to laws and customs that reflect elite men's monopoly on warfare and related political and economic institutions. Women can inherit land (see later) but typically exert little control over it (Agarwal, 1994).

The reason that land ownership so changes law and custom is that land is an impartible inheritance (unlike cattle, for example). A given piece under given technology supports only a given number of persons. Rule and custom come to ensure inheritance patterns that prevent land from being overly subdivided. The scarcer it becomes and the more intensively it is used, the greater the tendency to retain it in the nuclear family, the basic unit of production and reproduction (Goody, 1976, p. 97). Monogamy prevails lest land be dispersed among too many legal heirs, and divorce becomes difficult or impossible. The concern with women's sexual purity stems from their status as transmitters of male property. The larger her endowment, the more her behavior is controlled (Goody, 1976, p. 14). Infibulation and footbinding, for example, began as ways to ensure imperial men's exclusive access to consorts. Both practices elicited a competitive upward flow of women and downward flow of self-enforcing customs that were maintained by interdependent needs on the marriage market. Women needed resources and men needed certain knowledge of paternity (Mackie, 1996).[8]

If land is so valuable, why are women permitted to inherit it? Why does bilateral inheritance prevail in agrarian societies? The answer is that the greater volume of production that the plow affords can support an elaborate division of labor and a variety of lifestyle. If an elite male is to maintain his own and his children's style of life, he must marry a similarly endowed spouse, which is an incentive to establish a bilateral inheritance system (Goody, 1976). The political institutions that permitted elite males to control their wives' property later expand to include a broader segment of the male population.

Different strategies of heirship in sub-Saharan hoe societies and Eurasian plow societies stem from the respective value of land (Goody, 1976, p. 97). In Africa, economic differences among families are minor, land is plentiful, and there is less pressure to provide an heir to an estate (Goody & Tambiah, 1973, p. 22). A daughter's marriage little affects her economic position because women, married or not, grow crops or do craft work. A daughter needs no endowment to maintain her status. In Eurasia, a man provides for his sorts at his death and for his daughters by dowry at marriage lest family status decline in the social hierarchy.

Thus, women's economic contribution to subsistence declines with the introduction of the plow while powerful elites come to control a vastly increased surplus. Both women and men may inherit property but men control that of their wives. Women's sexual behavior is constrained to ensure that only her husband's children inherit his property. In effect, use of the plow puts women under guardianship of husbands or male relatives.

7. The Modern World

Urbanization began relatively late in northern Europe. In technology, Europe was then nearly a millennium behind China, which was probably the main reason why a revolutionary industrial technology could be introduced in so short a time (Boserup, 1981, p. 101),[9] altering patterns of population maintenance, subsistence work, and warfare. Infant mortality and fertility decline; by 1910 safe methods of artificial feeding end a baby's dependence on a lactating woman for survival (Huber, 1990). Education becomes universal, for the modern labor market requires workers whose qualifications are independent of ascribed characteristics (Jackson, 1984; Marwell, 1975). Warfare requires more brains, less brawn. These events spawn social movements that spur the changes in gendered behavior, belief, law, and custom (Chafetz & Dworkin, 1986) that comprise the theme of this handbook.

8. Conclusion

To assess the effects of subsistence technology on sex inequality. I analyze its interrelationships with patterns of population maintenance and politico–military institutions in premodern societies. Three principles of stratification guide the chapter: producers have more power than consumers, those who control the distribution of valued goods beyond the family have the most power, and the more often a society makes war, the more likely is social control to be vested in politico–military elites that include no women. The subsistence modes examined are those of foraging, hoe, herding, and plow. The basic question concerns the relationship of women's monopoly on childbearing to men's monopoly on politico–military affairs. Can women's absence from the arena where rules are made be a result of female centrality in population maintenance?

Both in hunting and gathering and simple hoe cultures, women contribute heavily to subsistence. War is rare, for weapons are inefficient, people are few, land is plentiful. The level of social and gender inequality is low.

Women's economic contribution is also high in advanced hoe cultures but warfare becomes common when the invention of metallurgy improves weaponry, spurring the formation of politico–military elites that include no women because, to offset high death rates, they are so often pregnant or lactating in prime years. It is the invention of metallurgy that makes warriors and political leaders only of men.

Herding limits women's productivity while conflict over water rights and animal theft makes warfare central. Controls on women's behavior tend to moderate if the hoe is also used because women then contribute to subsistence. If the plow is the auxiliary subsistence tool, male elites can acquire many wives, secluding them at little cost for they contribute little to subsistence.

With the plow, women's economic contribution declines sharply from earlier levels while increased productivity and more effective weapons provide incentives for warfare. By making land the chief form of wealth, the plow spurs the emergence of laws and customs that benefit male elites and disadvantage women even more than ordinary men.

This chapter thus suggests (but falls short of proving) that it is the institutionalizing of warfare in advanced hoe cultures that first brings about women's absence from huts or halls of power. After the plow makes land the chief form of wealth, the institution of private property intensifies the effects of men's monopoly on warfare. Even with an ideology of sex equality, the Soviet Union's abolition of private property could not overcome the effects of militarism.

Population maintenance no longer requires serial pregnancy and lactation. Work and warfare require extensive training. Unsurprisingly, women's military participation is rising. The big increase in the number of women in U.S. services came in the 1970s when the draft ended and a volunteer force was created (Holm, 1992, pp. 246–259). The contentious issue today, first made salient by the industrial revolution, is women's service in combat (Goldman, 1982, p. 4). After the 1970s, a majority came to approve some combat roles for women (Peach, 1996, p. 186). Given the potential of biological, chemical, and nuclear warfare, barring women from combat hardly ensures their survival (Segal, 1982, p. 281). Excluding woman from combat simply limits their promotion opportunities and access to job training, education, retirement benefits, medical care, low-cost insurance, bonuses, loans, and state and federal employment preferences (Peach, 1996, p. 175).

The idea that sex inequality results from the interaction of work, war, and childbearing is based on a survey of a literature that would repay further study despite its lack of attention to women as political actors (Ross, 1986, p. 54). Such studies of relatively isolated premodern societies conducted earlier need to be integrated with the current work of anthropologists, economists, and sociologists on regions that harbor a mix of premodern subsistence and modern industrial technologies. How do the interrelations of work, war, and childbearing change when an isolated premodern society is pulled into the vortex of the world political economy? How do the findings speak to theories of sex inequality? Let the work begin.

Notes

1. For a review of studies based on cross-cultural surveys, see Burton and White (1987).
2. For example, Marshall's (1968, p. 13) analysis of marriage in the *International Encyclopedia of the Social Sciences* defines brideprice, dowry, and polygyny without reference to women's economic contributions.
3. Lovejoy's (1981) theory, the best known, sees the central adaptation in human evolution as male provisioning of sedentary, fecund, monogamous females (Fedigan, 1986, p. 62).
4. Well, hardly ever. In Northern Luzon, Agta women always took part in hunting (Estioko-Griffin, 1985).
5. Harris (1984) sees female infanticide as the cause of frequent warfare over women but Ember and Ember (1994, p. 186) note that HRAF data fail to support his claim that this practice actually makes women scarce.
6. Whether men's greater verbal aggressiveness is Western or pancultural has not been studied (Quinn, 1977, p. 190).
7. The plow was rarely used in sub-Saharan Africa until the 1900s. Oxen, the best draft animals, do not thrive in Central Africa's humid tse-tse zones or in West African coastal zones (Shipton, 1994, p. 357).
8. With such powerful incentives as the need to ensure one's subsistence, people come to accept customs that otherwise do them much harm. Thus, Chinese women objected when footbinding was forbidden (Levy, 1966, p. 210), clitoridectomy came to play a part in Kenyan women's authority structure (Robertson, 1996), and the high-heeled shoe remains popular among women in the West.
9. Goody (1996b), unlike Marx and Weber, holds that dominant groups were similarly organized across Eurasia because they faced similar problems in managing resources. The uniqueness of the West requires no explanation. There is nothing to explain.

References

Agarwal, B. (1994). *A field of one's own: Gender and land rights in Asia.* New York: Cambridge University Press.

Barfield, T. (1981). *The Central Asian Arabs in Afghanistan.* Austin: University of Texas Press.

Barfield, T. (1994). The devil's horsemen. In S. Reyna & R. Downs (Eds.), *Studying war* (pp. 157–172), Langhome. PA: Gordon & Breach.

Beck, L. (1978). Women among Qashqa'i nomadic pastoralists in Iran. In L. Beck and N. Keddie (Eds.), *Women in the Middle East* (pp. 351–373). Cambridge: Harvard University Press.

Blumberg, R. L. (1978). *Stratification.* Dubuque, IA: Brown.

Blumberg, R. L. (1995). *Engendering wealth and well-being.* Boulder, CO: Westview.

Boserup, E. (1965). *The conditions of agricultural growth.* Chicago: Aldine.

Boserup, E. (1970). *Women's role in economic development.* London: George Allen & Unwin.

Boserup, E. (1981). *Population and technological change.* Chicago: University of Chicago Press.

Burton, M., & White, D. (1987). Cross cultural surveys today. *Annual Review of Anthropology, 16,* 143–160.

Cashden, E. (1980). Egalitarianism among hunters and gatherers. *American Anthropologist, 82,* 116–120.

Chafetz, J. S. (1984). *Sex and advantage.* Totowa, NJ: Rowman & Allanheld.

Chafetz, J. S. (1990). *Gender equity.* Newbury Park, CA: Sage.

Chafetz, J. S., & Dworkin, G. (1986). *Female revolt.* Totowa, NJ: Rowman & Allanheld.

Childe, V.G. (1951). *Man makes himself.* New York: Mentor.

Collier, J. F. (1974). Women in politics. In M. Rosaldo & L. Lamphere (Eds.), *Woman, culture and society* (pp. 89–96). Stanford: Stanford University Press.

Collier, J., & Yanigasako, S. (Eds.) (1987). *Gender and kinship.* Stanford: Stanford University Press.

Collins, R. (1985). *Sociology of marriage and the family.* Chicago: Nelson-Hall.

Collins, R. (1988). *Theoretical sociology.* San Diego: Harcourt Brace Jovanovich.

Cronk, L. (1991). Human behavioral ecology. *Annual Review of Anthropology, 20,* 25–53.

Dahlberg, F. (1981). In F. Dahlberg (Ed.), *Woman the gatherer* (pp. i–xi). New Haven: Yale University Press.

Duncan, O. D. (1964). Social organization and the ecosystem. In R. Fans (Ed.), *Handbook of modern sociology* (pp. 37–82). Chicago: Rand-McNally.

Dyson-Hudson, R., & Dyson-Hudson, N. (1980). Nomadic pastoralists. *Annual Review of Anthropology, 9,* 15–61.

Elam, Y. (1973). *Social and sexual roles of Hima women.* Manchester: University of Manchester Press.

Ember, M. (1974). Warfare, sex ratio, and polygyny. *Ethnology, 13,* 197–206.

Ember, M., & Ember, D. (1983). *Marriage, family, and kinship.* New Haven: HRAF Press.

Ember, M., & Ember, C. (1994). Cross-cultural studies of war and peace. In S. Reyna & R. Downs (Eds.), *Studying war* (pp. 185–208). Langhorne, PA: Gordon & Breach.

Estioko-Griffin, A. (1985). Women as hunters. In A. Estioko-Griffin & P. Griffin (Eds.), *The Agta of northeastern Luzon* (pp. 18–32). Cebu City: San Carlos.

Evans-Pritchard, E. E. (1965). *The position of women in primitive societies and other essays.* New York: Free Press.

Fedigan, L. M. (1986). The changing role of women in models of human evolution. *Annual Review of Anthropology, 15,* 25–66.

Ferree, M. M., & Hall, H. (1996). Stratification from a feminist perspective. *American Sociological Review, 61,* 929–950.

Flanagan, J. (1989). Hierarchy in simple societies. *Annual Review of Anthropology, 18,* 245–266.

Friedl, H. (1975). *Women and men: An anthropologist's view.* New York: Holt, Rinehart & Winston.

Goheen, M. (1996). *Men own the land, women own the crops.* Madison: University of Wisconsin Press.

Goldman, N. L. (1982). Introduction. In N. L. Goldman (Ed.), *Female soldiers* (pp. 1–17). Westport, CT: Greenwood.

Goldschmidt, W. (1959). *Man's way.* Cleveland, OH: World.

Goody, J. (1962). *Death, property, and the ancestors.* London: Tavistock.

Goody, J. (1976). *Production and reproduction.* New York: Cambridge University Press.

Goody, J. (1982). *Cooking, cuisine, and class.* New York: Cambridge University Press.

Goody, J. (1996b). *The East in the West.* New York: Cambridge University Press.

Goody, J. & Tambiah, S. J. (1973). *Bridewealth and dowry.* Cambridge: Cambridge University Press.

Graham, S. (1985). Running and menstrual dysfunctions. *American Anthropologist, 87,* 878–882.

Grant, R (1991). The sources of gender bias in international relations theory. In R. Grant & K. Newland (Eds.), *Gender and international relations* (pp. 8–26). Bloomingtom, IN: University of Indiana Press.

Hakansson, T. (1988). *Bridewealth, women, and land.* Stockholm: Almqvist and Wiksell.

Hammel, E. A., & Howell, N. (1987). Research in population and culture. *Current Anthropology, 28,* 141–160.

Harrell, B. (1981). Lactation and menstruation in cultural perspective. *American Anthropologist, 83,* 796–823.

Harris, M. (1984). A cultural and materialist theory of band and village warfare. In B. Ferguson (Ed.), *Warfare, Culture, and Environment* (pp. 111–140). Orlando, FL: Academic Press.

Hayden, B. (1995). Pathways to power. In D. Price & G. Feinman (Eds.), *Foundation of social inequality* (pp. 15–86). New York: Plenum.

Heider, K. (1972). Environment, subsistence, and society. *Annual Review of Anthropology, 1,* 207–226.

Holm, J. (1992). *Women in the military.* Novato, CA: Presidio.

Huber, J. (1990). Macro-micro links in gender stratification. *American Sociological Review, 55,* 1–10.

Huber, J. & Spitze, G. (1988). Trends in family sociology. In N. Smelser (Ed.), *Handbook of sociology* (pp. 425–448). Newbury Park, CA: Sage.

Jackson, R. M. (1984). *The formation of craft labor markets.* Orlando, FL: Academic.

Krader, L. (1968). Pastoralism. *International Encyclopedia of the Social Sciences, 11,* 453–461.

Larsen, C. S. (1995). Biological changes in human populations with agriculture. *Annual Review of Anthropology, 24,* 185–213.

Leach, E. (1984). Glimpses of the history of British anthropology. *Annual Review of Anthropology, 13,* 1–23.

Leacock, E. (1981). *Myths of male dominance.* New York: Monthly Review Press.

Lee, R. (1968). What hunters do for a living. In R. Lee & I. Devore (Eds.), *Man the hunter* (pp. 30–48). Chicago: Aldine.

Lee, R. (1980). Lactation, ovulation, and women's work. In M. Cohen, R. Malpass, & H. Klein (Eds.), *Biosocial mechanisms of population regulation* (pp. 321–348), New Haven: Yale University Press.

Leis, N. (1974). Ijaw women's associations. In M. Rosaldo & L. Lamphere (Eds.), *Women, culture and society* (pp. 223–242). Stanford: Stanford University Press.

Lenski, G. (1970). *Human societies.* New York: McGraw-Hill.

Lenski, G. (1994). Social taxonomies. *Annual Review of Sociology, 20,* 1–26.

Lenski, G., & Lenski, J. (1978). *Human societies* (3rd ed.). New York: McGraw-Hill.

Lesthaeghe, R., & Surkyn, J. (1988). *Women in sub-Saharan demographic regimes.* Vrije Universiteit Brussel: Mimeo.

Levy, H. (1966). *Chinese footbinding.* New York: Walton Rawls.

Lieberman, L. (1989). Acceptance of human sociobiological concepts in anthropology. *Current Anthropology, 30,* 676–682.

Lovejoy, C. O. (1981). The origin of man. *Science, 211,* 341–350.

Maccoby, E., & Jacklin, C. (1974). *The psychology of sex differences.* Stanford: Stanford University Press.

Mackie, G. (1996). Ending footbinding and infibulation. *American Sociological Review, 61,* 999–1017.

Marshall, G. (1968). Marriage: Comparative analysis. *International Encyclopedia of the Social Sciences, 11,* 8–19.

Marwell, G. (1975). Why ascription? *American Sociological Review, 40,* 445–455.

Mason, K. (1984). *The status of women, fertility, and mortality.* New York: Rockefeller Foundation.

Mead, M. (1973). Changing styles of anthropological work. *Annual Review of Anthropology, 2,* 1–26.

Messer, E. (1984). Anthropological perspectives on diet. *Annual Review of Anthropology, 13,* 205–249.

Miller, J., & Garrison, H. (1982). Sex roles: The division of labor. *Annual Review of Sociology, 8,* 237–262.

Moseley, K., & Wallerstein, I. (1978). Precapitalist social structures. *Annual Review of Sociology, 4,* 259–290.

Mukhopadhyay, C., & Higgins, P. (1988). Anthropological studies of women's status revisited. *Annual Review of Anthropology, 17,* 461–495.

Murdock, G. P. (1967). Ethnographic atlas: A summary. *Ethnology, 6,* 109–236.

Nerlove, S. (1974). Women's workload and infant feeding practices. *Ethnology, 13,* 207–214.

Netting, R. (1974). Agrarian Ecology. *Annual Review of Anthropology, 3,* 21–56.

Netting, R. (1993). *Smallholders and householders.* Stanford: Stanford University Press.

North, D., & Thomas, R. P. (1973). *The rise of the Western World.* New York: Cambridge University Press.

Orlove, B. (1980). Ecological anthropology. *Annual Review of Anthropology, 9,* 235–273.

Peach, L. (1996). Gender ideology in the ethics of women in combat. In J. Stiehm (Ed.), *It's our military too* (pp. 156–94). Philadelphia: Temple University Press.

Peters, E. (1978). Women in four Middle East Communities. In L. Beck & N. Keddie (Eds.), *Women in the Middle East* (pp. 311–350). Cambridge: Harvard University Press.

Potts, R. (1984). Home bases and early hominids. *American Scientist, 72,* 338–347.

Quinn, N. (1977). Anthropological studies of women's status. *Annual Review of Anthropology, 6,* 181–225.

Raphael, D., & Davis, F. (1985). *Patterns of infant feeding in traditional cultures.* Westport, CT: Greenwood.

Robertson, C. (1996). Women, genital mutilation, and collective action in Kenya, 1920–1990. *Signs, 21,* 615–642.

Ross, M. (1986). Female political participation. *American Anthropologist, 88,* 843–858.

Sacks, K. (1982). *Sisters and wives.* Westport, CT: Greenwood.

Sahlins, M. (1958). *Social stratification in Polynesia.* Seattle: University of Washington Press.

Sanday, P. (1973). Toward a theory of the status of women. *American Anthropologist, 88,* 142–150.

Schlegel, A., & Barry, H. (1986). The cultural consequences of subsistence contribution. *American Anthropologist, 88,* 142–150.

Segal, M. W. (1982). The argument for female combatants. N. L. Goldman (Ed.), *Female soldiers* (pp. 267–290).Westport, CT: Greenwood.

Sen, A. (1990). Gender and cooperative conflicts. In I. Tinker (Ed.), *Persistent inequalities* (pp. 123–149). New York: Oxford University Press.

Shipton, P. (1994). Land and culture in tropical Africa. *Annual Review of Anthropology, 23,* 347–377.

Spielman, K., & Eder, J. (1994). Hunters and farmers: Then and now. *Annual Review of Anthropology, 23,* 303–323.

Testart, A. (1978). Les societies de chasseure-cueilleurs. *Pour la Science, 16,* 99–108.

Testart, A. (1988). Some major problems in the anthropology of hunter gatherers. *Current Anthropology, 29,* 1–31.

Tiger, L., & Fox, R. (1971). *The imperial animal.* New York: Holt, Rinehart & Winston.

Washburn, S. (1961). *Social life of early man.* Chicago: Aldine.

Washburn, S., & Lancaster, C. (1968). The evolution of hunting. In R. Lee & I. Devore (Eds.), *Man the hunter* (pp. 91–103). Chicago: Aldine.

Whyte, M. (1978). *The status of women in preindustrial societies.* Princeton, NJ: Princeton University Press.

Wilson, E. O. (1975). *Sociobiology.* Cambridge, MA: Belknap Press.

Worthman, C. (1995). Hormones, sex, and gender. *Annual Review of Anthropology, 24,* 593–616.

Zihlman, A. (1981). Women as shapers of human adaptation. In F. Dahlberg (Ed.), *Woman the gatherer* (pp. 75–120). New Haven, CT: Yale University Press.

Zihlman, A. (1997). Women's bodies, women's lives. In M. E. Morbeck, A. Galloway, & A. Zihlman (Eds.), *The evolving female* (pp. 185–197). Princeton, NJ: Princeton University Press.

25

Excerpts from "Hierarchies, Jobs, Bodies: A Theory of Gendered Organizations"

Joan Acker

Most of us spend most of our days in work organizations that are almost always dominated by men. The most powerful organizational positions are almost entirely occupied by men, with the exception of the occasional biological female who acts as a social man. Power at the national and world level is located in all-male enclaves at the pinnacle of large state and economic organizations. These facts are not news, although sociologists paid no attention to them until feminism came along to point out the problematic nature of the obvious. Writers on organizations and organizational theory now include some consideration of women and gender, but their treatment is usually cursory and male domination is, on the whole, not analyzed and not explained.

Among feminist social scientists there are some outstanding contributions on women and organizations, such as the work of Kanter (1977), Feldberg and Glenn (1979), MacKinnon (1979), and Ferguson (1984). In addition, there have been theoretical and empirical investigations of particular aspects of organizational structure and process, and women's situations have been studied using traditional organizational ideas. Moreover, the very rich literature, popular and scholarly, on women and work contains much material on work organizations. However, most of this new knowledge has not been brought together in a systematic feminist theory of organizations.

A systematic theory of gender and organizations is needed for a number of reasons. First, the gender segregation of work, including divisions between paid and unpaid work, is partly created through organizational practices. Second, and related to gender segregation, income and status inequality between women and men is also partly created in organizational processes; understanding these processes is necessary for understanding gender inequality. Third, organizations are one arena in which widely disseminated cultural images of gender are invented and reproduced. Knowledge of cultural production is important for understanding gender construction. Fourth, some aspects of individual gender identity perhaps particularly masculinity, are also products of organizational processes and pressures. Fifth, an important feminist project is to make large-scale organizations more democratic and more supportive of humane goals.

In this article, I begin by speculating about why feminist scholars have not debated organizational theory. I then look briefly at how those feminist scholars who have paid attention to organizations have conceptualized them. In the main part of the article, I examine organizations as gendered processes in which both gender and sexuality have been obscured through a gender-neutral, asexual discourse, and suggest some of the ways that gender, the body, and sexuality are part of the processes of control in work organizations. Finally, I point to some directions for feminist theory about this ubiquitous human invention.

Why So Little Feminist Debate on Organizations?

The early radical feminist critique of sexism denounced bureaucracy and hierarchy as male-created and male-dominated structures of control that oppress women. The easiest answer to the "why so little debate" question is that the link between masculinity and organizational power was so obvious that no debate was needed. However, experiences in the feminist movement suggest that the questions are not exhausted by recognizing male power.

Part of the feminist project was to create nonhierarchical, egalitarian organizations that would demonstrate the possibilities of nonpatriarchal ways of working. Although many feminist organizations survived, few retained this radical-democratic form. Others succumbed to the same sorts of pressures that have undermined other utopian experiments with alternative work forms, yet analyses of feminist efforts to create alternative organizations were not followed by

debates about the feasibility of nonpatriarchal, nonhierarchical organization or the relationship of organizations and gender. Perhaps one of the reasons was that the reality was embarrassing; women failing to cooperate with each other, taking power and using it in oppressive ways, creating their own structures of status and reward were at odds with other images of women as nurturing and supportive.

Another reason for feminist theorists' scant attention to conceptualizing organizations probably lies in the nature of the concepts and models at hand. As Dorothy Smith (1979) has argued, the available discourses on organizations, the way that organizational sociology is defined as an area or domain "is grounded in the working worlds and relations of men, whose experience and interests arise in the course of and in relation to participation in the ruling apparatus of this society" (p. 148). Concepts developed to answer managerial questions, such as how to achieve organizational efficiency, were irrelevant to feminist questions, such as why women are always concentrated at the bottom of organizational structures.

Critical perspectives on organizations, with the notable exception of some of the studies of the labor process, although focusing on control, power, exploitation, and how these relations might be changed, have ignored women and have been insensitive to the implications of gender for their own goals. The active debate on work democracy, the area of organizational exploration closest to feminist concerns about oppressive structures, has been almost untouched by feminist insights. For example, Carole Pateman's influential book, *Participation and Democratic Theory* (1970), critical in shaping the discussions on democratic organization in the 1970s, did not consider women or gender. More recently, Pateman (1983a, 1983b, 1988) has examined the fundamental ideas of democracy from a feminist perspective, and other feminist political scientists have criticized theories of democracy, but on the whole, their work is isolated from the main discourse on work organization and democracy.

Empirical research on work democracy has also ignored women and gender. For example, in the 1980s, many male Swedish researchers saw little relation between questions of democracy and gender equality with a few exceptions. Other examples are studies of Mondragon, a community in the Spanish Basque country, which is probably the most famous attempt at democratic ownership, control, and organization. Until Sally Hacker's feminist study (1987), researchers who went to Mondragon to see this model of work democracy failed to note the situation of women and asked no questions about gender. In sum, the absence of women and gender from theoretical and empirical studies about work democracy provided little material for feminist theorizing.

Another impediment to feminist theorizing is that the available discourses conceptualize organizations as gender neutral. Both traditional and critical approaches to organizations originate in the male, abstract intellectual domain and take as reality the world as seen from that standpoint. As a relational phenomenon, gender is difficult to see when only the masculine is present. Since men in organizations take their behavior and perspectives to represent the human, organizational structures and processes are theorized as gender neutral. When it is acknowledged that women and men are affected differently by organizations, it is argued that gendered attitudes and behavior are brought into (and contaminate) essentially gender-neutral structures. This view of organizations separates structures from the people in them.

Current theories of organization also ignore sexuality. Certainly, a gender-neutral structure is also asexual. If sexuality is a core component of the production of gender identity, gender images, and gender inequality, organizational theory that is blind to sexuality does not immediately offer avenues into the comprehension of gender domination. Catharine MacKinnon's (1982) compelling argument that sexual domination of women is embedded within legal organizations has not to date become part of mainstream discussions. Rather, behaviors such as sexual harassment are viewed as deviations of gendered actors, not, as MacKinnon (1979) might argue, as components of organizational structure.

Feminist Analyses of Organizations

The treatment of women and gender most assimilated into the literature on organizations is Rosabeth Moss Kanter's *Men and Women of the Corporation*

(1977). Kanter sets out to show that gender differences in organizational behavior are due to structure rather than to characteristics of women and men as individuals (1977, 291–92). She argues that the problems women have in large organizations are consequences of their structural placement, crowded in dead-end jobs at the bottom and exposed as tokens at the top. Gender enters the picture through organizational roles that "carry characteristic images of the kinds of people that should occupy them" (p. 250). Here, Kanter recognizes the presence of gender in early models of organizations:

> A "masculine ethic" of rationality and reason can be identified in the early image of managers. This "masculine ethic" elevates the traits assumed to belong to men with educational advantages to necessities for effective organizations: a tough-minded approach to problems; analytic abilities to abstract and plan; a capacity to set aside personal, emotional considerations in the interests of task accomplishment; a cognitive superiority in problem-solving and decision making. (1975, 43)

Identifying the central problem of seeming gender neutrality, Kanter observes: "While organizations were being defined as sex-neutral machines, masculine principles were dominating their authority structures" (1977, 46).

In spite of these insights, organizational structure, not gender, is the focus of Kanter's analysis. In posing the argument as structure *or* gender, Kanter also implicitly posits gender as standing outside of structure, and she fails to follow up her own observations about masculinity and organizations (1977, 22). Kanter's analysis of the effects of organizational position applies as well to men in low-status positions. Her analysis of the effect of numbers, or the situation of the "token" worker, applies also to men as minorities in women-predominant organizations, but fails to account for gender differences in the situation of the token. In contrast to the token woman, white men in women-dominated workplaces are likely to be positively evaluated and to be rapidly promoted to positions of greater authority. The specificity of male dominance is absent in Kanter's argument, even though she presents a great deal of material that illuminates gender and male dominance.

Another approach, using Kanter's insights but building on the theoretical work of Hartmann (1976), is the argument that organizations have a dual structure, bureaucracy and patriarchy (Ressner 1987). Ressner argues that bureaucracy has its own dynamic, and gender enters through patriarchy, a more or less autonomous structure, that exists alongside the bureaucratic structure. The analysis of two hierarchies facilitates and clarifies the discussion of women's experiences of discrimination, exclusion, segregation, and low wages. However, this approach has all the problems of two systems theories of women's oppression: the central theory of bureaucratic or organizational structure is unexamined, and patriarchy is added to allow the theorist to deal with women. Like Kanter, Ressner's approach implicitly accepts the assumption of mainstream organizational theory that organizations are gender-neutral social phenomena.

Ferguson, in *The Feminist Case Against Bureaucracy* (1984), develops a radical feminist critique of bureaucracy as an organization of oppressive male power, arguing that it is both mystified and constructed through an abstract discourse on rationality, rules, and procedures. Thus, in contrast to the implicit arguments of Kanter and Ressner, Ferguson views bureaucracy itself as a construction of male domination. In response to this overwhelming organization of power, bureaucrats, workers, and clients are all "feminized," as they develop ways of managing their powerlessness that at the same time perpetuate their dependence. Ferguson argues further that feminist discourse, rooted in women's experiences of caring and nurturing outside bureaucracy's control, provides a ground for opposition to bureaucracy and for the development of alternative ways of organizing society.

However, there are problems with Ferguson's theoretical formulation. Her argument that feminization is a metaphor for bureaucratization not only uses a stereotype of femininity as oppressed, weak, and passive, but also, by equating the experience of male and female clients, women workers, and male bureaucrats, obscures the specificity of women's experiences and the connections between masculinity and power. Ferguson builds on Foucault's (1979) analysis of power as widely diffused and constituted through discourse, and the problems in her analysis have their origin in Foucault, who also fails to place gender in his analysis of power. What results is a disembodied, and consequently gender-neutral, bureaucracy as the oppressor. That is, of course, not a new vision of bureaucracy, but it is one in which gender enters only as analogy, rather than as a complex component of processes of control and domination.

In sum, some of the best feminist attempts to theorize about gender and organizations have been trapped within the constraints of definitions of the theoretical domain that cast organizations as gender neutral and asexual. These theories take us only part of the way to understanding how deeply embedded gender is in organizations. There is ample empirical evidence: We know now that gender segregation is an amazingly persistent pattern and that the gender identity of jobs and occupations is repeatedly reproduced, often in new forms. The reconstruction of gender segregation is an integral part of the dynamic of technological and organizational change. Individual men and particular groups of men do not always win in these processes, but masculinity always seems to symbolize self-respect for men at the bottom and power for men at the top, while confirming for both their gender's superiority. Theories that posit organization and bureaucracy as gender neutral cannot adequately account for this continual gendered structuring. We need different theoretical strategies that examine organizations as gendered processes in which sexuality also plays a part.

Organization as Gendered Processes

The idea that social structure and social processes are gendered has slowly emerged in diverse areas of feminist discourse. Feminists have elaborated gender as a concept to mean more than a socially constructed, binary identity and image. This turn to gender as an analytic category is an attempt to find new avenues into the dense and complicated problem of explaining the extraordinary persistence through history and across societies of the subordination of women. Scott, for example, defines gender as follows: "The core of the definition rests on an integral connection between two propositions; gender is a constitutive element of social relationships based on perceived differences between the sexes, and gender is a primary way of signifying relationships of power" (1986, 1067).

New approaches to the study of waged work, particularly studies of the labor process, see organizations as gendered, not as gender neutral and conceptualize organizations as one of the locations of the inextricably intertwined production of both gender and class relations. Examining class and gender, I have argued that class is constructed through gender and that class relations are always gendered.

The structure of the labor market, relations in the workplace, the control of the work process, and the underlying wage relation are always affected by symbols of gender, processes of gender identity and material inequalities between women and men. These processes are complexly related to and powerfully support the reproduction of the class structure. Here, I will focus on the interface of gender and organizations, assuming the simultaneous presence of class relations.

To say that an organization, or any other analytic unit, is gendered means that advantage and disadvantage, exploitation and control, action and emotion, meaning and identity, are patterned through and in terms of a distinction between male and female, masculine and feminine. Gender is not an addition to ongoing processes, conceived as gender neutral. Rather, it is an integral part of those processes, which cannot be properly understood without an analysis of gender. Gendering occurs in at least five interacting processes that, although analytically distinct, are, in practice, parts of the same reality.

First is the construction of divisions along lines of gender—divisions of labor, of allowed behaviors, of locations in physical space, of power, including the institutionalized means of maintaining the divisions in the structures of labor markets, the family, the state. Such divisions in work organizations are well documented as well as often obvious to casual observers. Although there are great variations in the patterns and extent of gender division, men are almost always in the highest positions of organizational power. Managers' decisions often

initiate gender divisions, and organizational practices maintain them—although they also take on new forms with changes in technology and the labor process. For example, Cynthia Cockburn (1983, 1985) has shown how the introduction of new technology in a number of industries was accompanied by a reorganization, but not abolition, of the gendered division of labor that left the technology in men's control and maintained the definition of skilled work as men's work and unskilled work as women's work.

Second is the construction of symbols and images that explain, express, reinforce, or sometimes oppose those divisions. These have many sources or forms in language, ideology, popular and high culture, dress, the press, television. For example, as Kanter (1975), among others, has noted, the image of the top manager or the business leader is an image of successful, forceful masculinity. In Cockburn's studies, men workers' images of masculinity linked their gender with their technical skills; the possibility that women might also obtain such skills represented a threat to that masculinity.

The third set of processes that produce gendered social structures, including organizations, are interactions between women and men, women and women, men and men, including all those patterns that enact dominance and submission. For example, conversation analysis shows how gender differences in interruptions, turn taking, and setting the topic of discussion recreate gender inequality in the flow of ordinary talk. Although much of this research has used experimental groups, qualitative accounts of organizational life record the same phenomena: Men are the actors, women the emotional support.

Fourth, these processes help to produce gendered components of individual identity, which may include consciousness of the existence of the other three aspects of gender, such as, in organizations, choice of appropriate work, language use, clothing, and presentation of self as a gendered member of an organization.

Finally, gender is implicated in the fundamental, ongoing processes of creating and conceptualizing social structures. Gender is obviously a basic constitutive element in family and kinship, but, less obviously, it helps to frame the underlying relations of other structures, including complex organizations. Gender is a constitutive element in organizational logic, or the underlying assumptions and practices that construct most contemporary work organizations. Organizational logic appears to be gender neutral; gender-neutral theories of bureaucracy and organizations employ and give expression to this logic. However, underlying both academic theories and practical guides for managers is a gendered substructure that is reproduced daily in practical work activities and, somewhat less frequently, in the writings of organizational theorists.

Organizational logic has material forms in written work rules, labor contracts, managerial directives, and other documentary tools for running large organizations, including systems of job evaluation widely used in the comparable-worth strategy of feminists. Job evaluation is accomplished through the use and interpretation of documents that describe jobs and how they are to be evaluated. These documents contain symbolic indicators of structure; the ways that they are interpreted and talked about in the process of job evaluation reveals the underlying organizational logic. I base the following theoretical discussion on my observations of organizational logic in action in the job-evaluation component of a comparable-worth project.

Job evaluation is a management tool used in every industrial country, capitalist and socialist, to rationalize the organizational hierarchy and to help in setting equitable wages. Although there are many different systems of job evaluation, the underlying rationales are similar enough so that the observation of one system can provide a window into a common organizational mode of thinking and practice.

In job evaluation, the content of jobs is described and jobs are compared or criteria of knowledge, skill, complexity, effort, and working conditions. The particular system I observed was built incrementally over many years to reflect the assessment of managers about the job components for which they were willing to pay. Thus today this system can be taken as composed of residues of these judgments, which are a set of decision rules that, when followed, reproduce managerial values. But these rules are also the imagery out of which managers construct and reconstruct their organizations. The rules of job evaluation, which help to determine pay differences between jobs, are not simply a compilation of managers' values or sets of beliefs, but are the underlying logic or organization that provides at least part of the blueprint for its structure. Every time that job evaluation is used, that structure is created or reinforced.

Job evaluation evaluates jobs, not their incumbents. The job is the basic unit in a work organization's hierarchy, a description of a set of tasks, competencies, and responsibilities represented as a position on an organizational chart. A job is separate from people. It is an empty slot, a reification that must continually be reconstructed, for positions exist only as scraps of paper until people fill them. The rationale for evaluating jobs as devoid of actual workers reveals further the organizational logic—the intent is to assess the characteristics of the job, not of their incumbents who may vary in skill, industriousness, and commitment. Human beings are to be motivated, managed, and chosen to fit the job. The job exists as a thing apart.

Every job has a place in the hierarchy, another essential element in organizational logic. Hierarchies, like jobs, are devoid of actual workers and based on abstract differentiations. Hierarchy is taken for granted, only its particular form is at issue. Job evaluation is based on the assumption that workers in general see hierarchy as an acceptable principle, and the final test of the evaluation of any particular job is whether its place in the hierarchy looks reasonable. The ranking of jobs within an organization must make sense to managers, but it is also important that most workers accept the ranking as just if the system of evaluation is to contribute to orderly working relationships.

Organizational logic assumes a congruence between responsibility, job complexity, and hierarchical position. For example, a lower-level position, the level of most jobs filled predominantly by women, must have equally low levels of complexity and responsibility. Complexity and responsibility are defined in terms of managerial and professional tasks. The child-care worker's responsibility for other human beings or the complexity facing the secretary who serves six different, temperamental bosses can only be minimally counted if the congruence between position level, responsibility, and complexity is to be preserved. In addition, the logic holds that two jobs at different hierarchical levels cannot be responsible for the same outcome; as a consequence, for example, tasks delegated to a secretary by a manager will not raise her hierarchical level because such tasks are still his responsibility, even though she has the practical responsibility to see that they are done. Levels of skill, complexity, and responsibility, all used in constructing hierarchy, are conceptualized as existing independently of any concrete worker.

In organizational logic, both jobs and hierarchies are abstract categories that have no occupants, no human bodies, no gender. However, an abstract job can exist, can be transformed into a concrete instance, only if there is a worker. In organizational logic, filling the abstract job is a disembodied worker who exists only for the work. Such a hypothetical worker cannot have other imperatives of existence that impinge upon the job. At the very least, outside imperatives cannot be included within the definition of the job. Too many obligations outside the boundaries of the job would make a worker unsuited for the position. The closest the disembodied worker doing the abstract job comes to a real worker is the male worker whose life centers on his full-time, life-long job, while his wife or another woman takes care of his personal needs and his children. While the realities of life in industrial capitalism never allowed all men to live out this ideal, it was the goal for labor unions and the image of the worker in social and economic theory. The woman worker, assumed to have legitimate obligations other than those required by the job, did not fit with the abstract job.

The concept "a job" is thus implicitly a gendered concept, even though organizational logic presents it as gender neutral. "A job" already contains the gender-based division of labor and the separation between the public and the private sphere. The concept of "a job" assumes a particular gendered organization of domestic life and social production. It is an example of what Dorothy Smith has called "the gender subtext of the rational and impersonal" (1988, 4).

Hierarchies are gendered because they also are constructed on these underlying assumptions: Those who are committed to paid employment are "naturally" more suited to responsibility and authority; those who must divide their commitments are in the lower ranks. In addition, principles of hierarchy, as exemplified in most existing job-evaluation systems, have been derived from already existing gendered structures. The best-known systems were developed by management consultants working with managers to build methods of consistently evaluating jobs and rationalizing pay and job classifications. For example, all managers with similar levels of responsibility in the firm should have similar pay and job-evaluation systems were intended to reflect the values of managers and to produce a believable ranking of jobs based on those values. Such rankings would not deviate substantially from rankings already in place that contain gender typing and gender segregation of jobs and the clustering of women workers in the lowest and the worst-paid jobs. The concrete value judgments that constitute conventional job evaluation are designed to replicate such structures. Replication is achieved in many ways; for example, skills in managing money, more often found in men's than in women's jobs, frequently receive more points than skills in dealing with clients or human relations skills, more often found in women's than in men's jobs.

The gender-neutral status of "a job" and of the organizational theories of which it is a part depend upon the assumption that the worker is abstract, disembodied, although in actuality both the concept of "a job" and real workers are deeply gendered and "bodied." Carole Pateman (1986), in a discussion of women and political theory, similarly points out that the most fundamental abstraction in the concept of liberal individualism is "the abstraction of the 'individual' from the body. In order for the individual to appear in liberal theory as a universal figure who represents anyone and everyone, the individual must be disembodied" (p. 8). If the individual were not abstracted from bodily attributes, it would be clear that the individual represents one sex and one gender, not a universal being. The political fiction of the universal "individual" or "citizen," fundamental to ideas of democracy and contract, excluded women, judging them lacking in the capacities necessary for participation in civil society. Although women now have the rights of citizens in democratic states, they still stand in an ambiguous relationship to the universal individual who is "constructed from a male body so that his identity is always masculine" (Pateman 1988, 223). The worker with "a job" is the same universal "individual" who in actual social reality is a man. The concept of a universal worker excludes and marginalizes women who cannot, almost by definition achieve the qualities of a real worker because to do so is to become like a man.

Organizational Control, Gender, and the Body

The abstract, bodiless worker, who occupies the abstract, gender-neutral job has no sexuality, no emotions, and does not procreate. The absence of sexuality, emotionality, and procreation in organizational logic and organizational theory is an additional element that both obscures and helps to reproduce the underlying gender relations.

New work on sexuality in organizations, often indebted to Foucault (1979), suggests that this silence on sexuality may have historical roots in the development of large, all-male organizations that are the primary locations of societal power. The history of modern organizations includes, among other processes, the suppression of sexuality in the interests of organization and the conceptual exclusion of the body as a concrete living whole.

In a review of historical evidence on sexuality in early modern organizations, Burrell (1984, 98) suggests that "the suppression of sexuality is one of the first tasks the bureaucracy sets itself." Long before the emergence of the very large factory of the nineteenth century, other large organizations, such as armies and monasteries, which had allowed certain kinds of limited participation of women, were more and more excluding women and attempting to banish sexuality in the interests of control of members and the organization's activities. Active sexuality was the enemy of orderly procedures, and excluding women from

certain areas of activity may have been, at least in part, a way to control sexuality. As Burrell (1984) points out, the exclusion of women did not eliminate homosexuality which has always been an element in the life of large all-male organizations, particularly if members spend all of their time in the organization. Insistence on heterosexuality or celibacy were ways to control homosexuality. But heterosexuality had to be practiced outside the organization, whether it was an army or a capitalist workplace. Thus the attempts to banish sexuality from the workplace were part of the wider process that differentiated the home, the location of legitimate sexual activity, from the place of capitalist production. The concept of the disembodied job symbolizes this separation of work and sexuality.

Similarly, there is no place within the disembodied job or the gender-neutral organization for other "bodied" processes, such as human reproduction or the free expression of emotions. Sexuality, procreation, and emotions all intrude upon and disrupt the ideal functioning of the organization, which tries to control such interferences. However, as argued above, the abstract worker is actually a man, and it is the man's body, its sexuality, minimal responsibility in procreation, and conventional control of emotions that pervades work and organizational processes. Women's bodies—female sexuality, their ability to procreate and their pregnancy, breast-feeding, and child care, menstruation, and mythic "emotionality"—are suspect, stigmatized and used as grounds for control and exclusion.

The ranking of women's jobs is often justified on the basis of women's identification with childbearing and domestic life. They are devalued because women are assumed to be unable to conform to the demands of the abstract job. Gender segregation at work is also sometimes openly justified by the necessity to control sexuality, and women may be barred from types of work, such as skilled blue-collar work or top management, where most workers are men, on the grounds that potentially disruptive sexual liaisons should be avoided. On the other hand, the gendered definition of some jobs "includes sexualization of the woman worker as a part of the job" (MacKinnon 1979, 18). These are often jobs that serve men, such as secretaries, or a largely male public.

The maintenance of gendered hierarchy is achieved partly through such often-tacit controls based on arguments about women's reproductions emotionality, and sexuality, helping to legitimate the organizational structures created through abstract, intellectualized techniques. More overt controls, such as sexual harassment, relegating childbearing women to lower-level mobility tracks, and penalizing (or rewarding) their emotion management also conform to and reinforce hierarchy. MacKinnon (1979), on the basis of an extensive analysis of legal cases, argues that the willingness to tolerate sexual harassment is often a condition of the job, both a consequence and a cause of gender hierarchy.

While women's bodies are ruled out of order, or sexualized and objectified, in work organizations men's bodies are not, Indeed, male sexual imagery pervades organizational metaphors and language, helping to give form to work activities. For example, the military and the male world of sports are considered valuable training for organizational success and provide images for teamwork, campaigns, and tough competition. The symbolic expression of male sexuality may be used as a means of control over male workers, too, allowed or even encouraged within the bounds of the work situation to create cohesion or alleviate stress. Management approval of pornographic pictures in the locker room or support for all-male work and play groups where casual talk is about sexual exploits or sports are examples. These symbolic expressions of male dominance also act as significant controls over women in work organizations because they are per se excluded from the informal bonding men produce with the "body talk" of sex and sports.

Symbolically a certain kind of male heterosexual sexuality plays an important part in legitimating organizational power. Connell (1987) calls this hegemonic masculinity, emphasizing that it is formed around dominance over women and in opposition to other masculinities, although its exact content changes as historical conditions change. Currently, hegemonic masculinity is typified by the image of the strong, technically competent, authoritative leader who is sexually potential and attractive, has a family, and has his emotions under control. Images of male sexual function and patriarchal paternalism may also be embedded in notions of what the manager does when he leads his organization. Women's bodies cannot be adapted to hegemonic masculinity; to function at the top of male hierarchies requires that women render irrelevant everything that makes them women.

The image of the masculine organizational leader could be expanded, without altering its basic elements, to include other qualities also needed, according to many management experts, in contemporary organizations such as flexibility and sensitivity to the capacities and needs of subordinates. Such qualities are not necessarily the symbolic monopoly of women. For example, the wise and experienced coach is empathetic and supportive to his individual players and flexibly leads his team against devious opposition tactics to victory.

The connections between organizational power and men's sexuality may be even more deeply embedded in organizational processes. Sally Hacker (1989) argues that eroticism and technology have common roots in human sensual pleasure and that for the engineer or the skilled worker, and probably for many other kinds of workers, there is a powerful erotic element in work processes. The pleasures of technology, Hacker continues, become harnessed to domination, and passion becomes directed toward power over nature, the machine, and other people, particularly women, in the work hierarchy. Hacker believes that men lose a great deal in this transformation of the erotic into domination, but they also win in other ways. For example, many men gain economically from the organizational gender hierarchy. As Crompton and Jones (1984) point out, men's career opportunities in white-collar work depend on the barriers that deny those opportunities to women. If the mass of female clerical workers were able to compete with men in such work, promotion probabilities for men would be drastically reduced.

Class relations as well as gender relations are reproduced in organizations. Critical, but nonfeminist, perspectives on work organizations argue that rational-technical systems for organizing work, such as job classification and evaluation systems and detailed specification of how work is to be done, are parts of pervasive systems of control that help to maintain class relations. The abstract "job," devoid of a human body, is a basic unit in such systems of control. The positing of a job as an abstract category, separate from the worker, is an essential move in creating jobs as mechanisms of compulsion and control over work processes. Rational-technical, ostensibly gender-neutral, control systems are built upon and conceal a gendered substructure (Smith 1988) in which men's bodies fill the abstract jobs. Use of such abstract systems continually reproduces the underlying gender assumptions and the subordinated or excluded place of women. Gender processes, including the manipulation and management of women's and men's sexuality, procreation, and emotion, are part of the control processes of organizations, maintaining not only gender stratification but contributing also to maintaining class and, possibly, race and ethnic relations. Is the abstract worker white as well as male? Are white-male-dominated organizations also built on underlying assumptions about the proper place of people with different skin colors? Are racial differences produced by organizational practices as gender differences are?

Conclusion

Feminists wanting to theorize about organizations face a difficult task because of the deeply embedded gendering of both organizational processes and theory. Commonsense notions, such as jobs and positions, which constitute the units managers use in making organizations and some theorists use in making theory, are posited upon the prior exclusion of women. This underlying construction of a way of thinking is not simply an error, but part of processes of organization. This exclusion in turn creates fundamental inadequacies in theorizing about gender neutral systems of positions to be filled. Creating more adequate theory may come only as organizations are transformed in ways that dissolve the concept of the abstract job and restore the absent female body.

Such a transformation would be radical in practice because it would probably require the end of organizations as they exist today, along with a redefinition of work and work relations. The rhythm and timing of work would be adapted to the rhythms of life outside of work. Caring work would be just as important and well rewarded as any

other; having a baby or taking care of a sick mother would be as valued as making an automobile or designing computer software. Hierarchy would be abolished, and workers would run things themselves. Of course, women and men would share equally in different kinds of work. Perhaps there would be some communal or collective form of organization where work and intimate relations are closely related, children learn in places close to working adults and workmates, lovers, and friends are all part of the same group. Utopian writers and experimenters have left us many possible models (Hacker 1989). But this brief listing begs many questions, perhaps the most important of which is how, give the present organization of economy and technology and the pervasive and powerful, impersonal textually mediated relations of ruling (Smith 1988), so radical change could come about.

Feminist research and theorizing, by continuing to puzzle out how gender provides the subtext for arrangements of subordination, can make some contributions to a future in which collective action to do what needs doing—producing goods, caring for people, disposing of the garbage—is organized so that dominance, control, and subordination, particularly the subordination of women, are eradicated, or at least minimized, in our organization life.

References

Burrell, Gibson. 1984. Sex and organizational analysis. *Organization Studios* 5:97–118.

Cockburn, Cynthia. 1983. *Brothers: Male dominance and technological change.* London: Pluto Press.

——. 1985. *Machinery of dominance.* London: Pluto Press.

Connell, R. W. 1987. *Gender and power.* Stanford, CA: Stanford University Press.

Crompton, Rosemary, and Gareth Jones. 1984. *White-collar proletariat: Deskilling and gender in clerical work.* Philadelphia: Temple University Press.

Feldberg, Roslyn, and Evelyn Nakano Glenn. 1979. Male and female: Job versus gender models in the sociology of work. *Social Problems* 26:524–38.

Ferguson Kathy, F. 1984. *The feminist case against bureaucracy.* Philadelphia Temple University Press.

Foucault, Michel. 1979. *The history of sexuality,* Vol. 1. London: Allen Lane.

Hacker, Sally. 1987. Women workers in the Mondragon system of industrial cooperatives. *Gender & Society* 1:358–79.

——. 1989. *Pleasure, power and technology.* Boston: Unwin Hyman.

Hartmann, Heidi. 1976. Capitalism patriarchy and job segregation by sex. *Signs* 1:137–70.

Kanter, Rosabeth Moss. 1975. Women and the structure of organizations: Explorations theory and behavior. In *Another voice,* edited by Rosabeth Kanter and Marcia Miliman. New York: Doubleday.

——. 1977. *Men and women of the corporation.* New York: Basic Books.

MacKinnon, Catharine, A. 1979. *Sexual harassment of working women.* New Haven, CT: Yale University Press.

——.1982. Feminism, Marxism, method and the state: An agenda for theory. *Signs* 7:515–44.

Pateman, Carole. 1970. *Participation and democratic theory.* Cambridge: Cambridge University Press.

——. 1983a. Feminist critiques of the public private dichotomy. In *Public and private in social life,* edited by S. I. Benn and G. F. Gaus. Beckenham, Kent: Croom Helm.

——. 1983b. Feminism and democracy. In *Democratic theory and practice,* edited by Graeme Duncan. Cambridge: Cambridge University Press.

——. 1986. Introduction The theoretical subversive ness of feminism. In *Feminist challenges* edited by Carole Pateman and Elizabeth Gross. Winchester, MA: Allen & Unwin.

——. 1988. *The sexual contract.* Cambridge, MA: Polity.

——. 1987. The hidden hierarchy. Aldershot: Gower.

Scott, Joan. 1986. Gender: A useful category of historical analysis. *American Historical Review* 91:1053–75.

Smith, Dorothy E. 1979. A sociology for women. In *The prism of sex: Essays in the sociology of knowledge,* edited by Julia A. Sherman and Evelyn Torten Beck. Madison: University of Wisconsin Press.

——. 1988. *The everyday world as problematic.* Boston: Northeastern University Press.

26

Excerpts from "Benefits for Nonhomophobic Societies: An Anthropological Perspective"

WALTER L. WILLIAMS

In a recent publication of the Coalition for Traditional Values, the Reverend Lou Sheldon commits himself to "open warfare with the gay and lesbian community. . . . [This is] a battle with one of the most pernicious evils in our society: homosexuality."[1] What does the Christian Right think is so bad about homosexuality? We are all familiar with the litany: homosexuals are seen as evil because they are said to be a threat to children, the family, religion, and society in general.

In sharp contrast to the heterosexist views of some people in Western society, the majority of other cultures that have been studied by anthropologists condone at least some forms of same sex eroticism as socially acceptable behavior.[2] Beyond that, quite a number of societies provide honored and respected places for people who are roughly comparable to what we in Western culture would call gay men and lesbians. One example is the Navajo people of Arizona and New Mexico, the largest American Indian group in North America. *Nadle,* a Navajo word meaning "one who is transformed," is applied to androgynous male or female individuals who combine elements of both masculinity and feminity in their personalities. The rare case of a person who is born hermaphroditic, with ambiguous genitalia or with the sexual organs of both the male and the female, is also considered to be a *nadle,* but most *nadle* are individuals whom Western society would characterize as effeminate men or masculine women. While each society of course constructs its own categories of sexuality in different ways, Navajo people traditionally accepted the fact that such androgynous people almost always have inclinations to be sexually active with people of the same biological sex.

Today's Navajos, like other Native Americans, have been significantly affected by Christian attitudes condemning homosexuality, but among those who value their traditions, there still continues a strong respect for *nadle*. We can see traditional Navajo attitudes more clearly by reading the testimony of an anthropologist who lived among the Navajos in the 1930s, before they had been so affected by Western values. This anthropologist documented the extremely reverential attitudes toward *nadle*. He wrote that traditional Navajo families who had a child who behaved androgynously were "considered by themselves and everyone else as very fortunate. The success and wealth of such a family was believed to be assured. Special care was taken in the raising of such children and they were afforded favoritism not shown to other children of the family. As they grew older and assumed the character of *nadle,* this solicitude and respect increased. . . . This respect verges almost on reverence in many cases."[3]

To illustrate these attitudes, this anthropologist quoted what the Navajo people told him about *nadle:*

They know everything. They can do both the work of a man and a woman. I think when all the nadle are gone, that will be the end of the Navajo.

If there were no nadle, the country would change. They are responsible for all the wealth in the country. If there were no more left, the horses, the sheep, and Navajo would all go. They are leaders, just like President Roosevelt. A nadle around the hogan will bring good luck and riches. They have charge of all the riches. It does a great deal for the country if you have a nadle around.

You must respect a nadle. They are, somehow, sacred and holy.[4]

On reading such quotations, the insight that immediately springs to mind is how attitudes toward similar phenomenon may differ widely from one culture to another. Presented above are opposing views of homosexually oriented people, condemned by Christian fundamentalist as "one of the most pernicious evils in society," but seen by the Navajo as something "sacred and holy." Why the difference?

My research in societies that do not discriminate against homosexuals suggests that the main reason for nonprejudicial attitudes is that those societies have figured out specific ways that homosexuality can contribute positively to the good of society as a whole. In other words, acceptance of sexual diversity is due not so much to "toleration" on the part of the heterosexual majority as it is to distinct advantages perceived by the general populace in having a certain proportion of the population homosexually inclined.

In Western culture, where only heterosexuality is valued, it occurs to few people that homosexuality might enrich society. From over a decade of research on this topic, I have come to have a different perspective than most Americans. The knowledge that I have gained has come primarily from fieldwork with native people of North American, Pacific, and Southeast Asian cultures. After three years of documentary research in many libraries, I lived among the American Indians of the Great Plains and the Southwest (1982), the Mayas of Yucatan (1983), and Native Alaskans (1989). I also did field research among the peoples of Hawaii (1984, 1985, 1990), Thailand (1987), and Indonesia (1987–88).[5] This essay will refer to the results of my fieldwork among these indigenous peoples. Much more ethnographic fieldwork certainly needs to be conducted in these and other societies before we can draw firm conclusions, but I have formulated some tentative points that I outline below.

Benefits to Religion

In Western writings about homosexuality, the emphasis has usually been on its "cause," with the implication that homosexuality is an "abnormality" that must be prevented. In contrast, among American Indians the reaction is usually acceptance, based on the notion that all things are "caused" by the spirits and therefore have some spiritual purpose. It is left to them only to discover each individual's spiritual purpose.

Traditional American Indians seem more interested in finding a useful social role for those who are different than in trying to force people to change character. One's basic character is a reflection of one's spirit, and to interfere with that is dangerously to disrupt the instructions from the spirit world. Many native North American religions are of a type called "animistic"; they emphasize not one creator god but a multiplicity of spirits in the universe. Everything that exists has a spirit; all things that exist are due equal respect because they are part of the spiritual order of the universe. The world cannot be complete without them.

In this religious view, there is no hierarchy among the beings—the humans, animals, and plants—that populate the earth. Humans are not considered to be any more spiritual or any more important than the other beings. Neither is the spirit of man more important than the spirit of woman. Each spirit may be different, but all are of equal value. However, American Indian religions see an androgynous individual as evidence that that person has been blessed by being bestowed with *two* spirits. Because both women and men are respected for their equal but distinct qualities, a person who combines attributes of both is considered as higher, as above the regular person—who only has one spirit.

In contrast to Western sexist views, where a male who acts like a woman is considered to be "lowering himself" to the subordinate female status, in the egalitarian American Indian religions feminine roles are accorded equal respect with men's roles. Therefore, a male who acts like a woman is not "lowering himself"; rather, he is indicating that he has been favored with an extra gift of spirituality. He is respected as a "double person." Such an individual is considered to be not entirely man and not entirely woman but a mixture of both masculine and feminine elements with additional unique characteristics. Such a distinctive personality is respected as a different gender, distinct from either man or woman.

This concept of respect for gender nonconformity is quite foreign to mainstream American society today. Despite the gains made in recent decades by the women's movement, our culture still does not respect the social contributions of anyone other than masculine men. Perhaps the best way to see this is to look at attitudes toward androgynous males. On American schoolyards today, the worst insult that can be thrown at a boy is to call him a *sissy*. What does it say about a society's gender values when the worst insult that can be directed toward a man is to say that he is like a woman?

While androgyny among males is seldom defended in mainstream American culture, it can be argued that many men need social permission to express those aspects of their personalities that in our society are more commonly associated with women. American men in particular are under constant pressure to conform, to maximize their masculine side—to "be tough," not to show emotion. Seldom verbalized are the dangers to society of excessive masculinity, even though the evidence appears daily in newspaper headlines. Violence is preponderantly a characteristic of masculine personalities: physical and sexual violence by men against women, children, and other men is a major social problem. Not only are men's tempers not conducive to cooperation in the workplace, but they also lead to stress-related health problems for hot-headed men themselves.

In contrast, American Indian cultures that are not prejudiced against androgynous persons allow more flexibility among personality types. A major reason for this flexibility is the basic respect that their religions accord human diversity. According to these religions, since everything that exists comes from the spirit world, people who are different have been made that way by the spirits and therefore maintain an especially close connection to the spirit world. Accordingly, androgynous people are often seen as sacred, as spiritually gifted individuals who can minister to the spiritual needs of others. In many tribes, such androgynous men—called *berdache* by the early explorers and by modern anthropologists—were often shamans or sacred people who work closely with shamans. Females who were inclined to take the traditional masculine role of hunter and warrior were called *amazons* by the early explorers, after the ancient Greek legend of warrior women.

Nonprejudiced Native American societies recognized that the berdache and the amazon were almost always homosexual, but an androgynous personality, not sexual behavior, was the defining characteristic. Many tribes had special career roles for berdache and amazons. Many Indian tribes, believing that sickness can be cured by the intervention of the spirits, will turn to the spiritually powerful as healers. While conducting my field-work on a Lakota reservation in South Dakota, I often observed people who were ill calling on *winkte* (the word in the Lakota language meaning "half man/half woman") to perform healing ceremonies for them. *Winktes* spend much of their time helping others, visiting the ill and infirm, comforting those in distress, and drawing on their spiritual connections to help people get well.

With a spiritual justification provided by the culture, berdache and amazons are not seen as a threat to religion. Instead, they are often considered sacred. Sexuality—indeed bodily pleasure—is seen not as sinful but as a gift from the spirit world. Both the spirit and the flesh are sacred. The homosexual inclinations of such berdache and amazons are accepted as a reflection of their spiritual nature. The American Indian example shows that it is not enough for a religion to "tolerate" sexual diversity; it must also provide a specific religious explanation for such diversity.

Some worldviews see reality as pairs of opposites: everything is viewed as good versus evil, black versus white, the spiritual versus the physical. The latter derides the needs and desires of the physical body as "temptations of the flesh," in contrast to the devotions of the spirit. The American Indian religions take a different view, seeing both the body and the spirit as good, as reflections of each other. As a consequence, sexual behavior—the epitome of the physical body—may be seen as something positively good, as something spiritual in and of itself, at the same time as it is physical.

The conceptualization by Native American societies of the berdache and the amazons as sacred has its practical applications. Those male berdache whom I have met and read about are uniformly gentle, peaceful people who would simply not fill the traditional Indian man's role of hunter and warrior effectively. By recognizing that they are special and encouraging them to become religious leaders and healers. Indian cultures give such people a means by which to contribute constructively to society. Rather than wasting time and energy trying to suppress their true nature or assuming an unsuitable role, they are encouraged to see their uniqueness as a special spiritual gift and to maximize their capabilities to help others. A Crow elder told me, "We don't waste people, the way White society does. Every person has their gift, every person has their contributions to make."[6]

Benefits to the Family

This emphasis on the social usefulness of the person who is different can be seen especially clearly in the contributions of such people to their families. Because most pre-Columbian Native Americans lived in extended families, with wide networks of kin who depended on one other, it was not necessary for everyone to have children. In contrast to a society with only nuclear families (father-mother-children), where all must reproduce to have someone take care of them in old age, an extended family offers some adults the opportunity not to reproduce. Childless people have nephews and nieces care for them. It is actually economically advantageous to the extended family for one or two adults *not* to reproduce because then there is a higher ratio of food-producing adults to food-consuming children. Also, by assuming gender roles that mix both the masculine and the feminine, the berdache and the amazon can do both women's and men's work. Not being burdened with their own childcare responsibilities, they can care for others' children or for their aged parents and grandparents.

The same pattern occurs in Polynesian culture, where an androgynous role similar to that of the berdache exists. Called *mahu* in Hawaii and Tahiti and *fa' afafine* among Samoans, such alternatively gendered people were traditionally those who took care of elderly relatives while their heterosexual siblings were busy raising their own children. With this kind of gender flexibility, and with their families holding high expectations for them (since they are spiritual people), berdache and amazons are often renowned for being hard workers, productive, and intelligent.

Since they are nor stigmatized or alienated, berdache and amazons are free to make positive contributions to family life. Today, they often allow adolescent nieces and nephews to move in with them when the parents' home gets overcrowded and also help them finance schooling.

A Navajo woman whose cousin is a respected *nadle* healer told me,

> They are seen as very compassionate people, who care for their family a lot and help people. That's why they are healers. Nadles are also seen as being great with children, real Pied Pipers. Children love nadles, so parents are pleased if a nadle takes an interest in their child. One that I know is now a principal of a school on the reservation. . . . Nadles are not seen as an abstract group, like "gay people," but as a specific person, like "my relative so-and-so." People who help their family a lot are considered valuable members of the community.[7]

It is thus in the context of individual family relations that much of the high status of the berdache and amazon must be evaluated. When such people play a positive and valued role in their societies and when no outside interference disrupts the normal workings of those societies, unprejudiced family love can exert itself.

In most Western cultures, such people are often considered misfits, an embarrassment to the family. They often leave the family in shame or are thrown out by homophobic relatives, the family thereby losing the benefit of their productive labor. In contrast, traditional Native American families will often make such people central to the family. Since other relatives do not feel threatened by them, family disunity and conflict are avoided. The male berdache is not pressured to suppress his feminine behavior, nor is the female amazon pressured to suppress her masculine inclinations. Neither are they expected to deny their same-sex erotic feelings. Berdache and amazons thereby avoid the tendency of those considered deviant in Western culture to harbor a low self-esteem and to engage in self-destructive behavior. Because they are valued by their families, few become alcoholic or suicidal, even in tribes where such problems are common.

Male berdache are often highly productive at women's work. Unlike biological females, who must take time away from farming or foraging when they are menstruating, pregnant, or nursing children, the berdache is always available to gather or prepare food. Anthropologists have often commented on the way in which berdache willingly take on the hardest work. Many berdache are also renowned for the high quality of their craftswork, whether pottery, beadwork, weaving, or tanning. In many tribes, berdache are known as the best cooks in the community and are often called on to prepare feasts for ceremonies and funerals. Women in particular seem to appreciate the help provided by berdache. An elderly Papago woman for example, spoke fondly of a berdache she had known in her youth (referring to him as *she*): "The man-woman was very pleasant, always laughing and talking, and a good worker. She was so strong! She did not get tired grinding corn. . . . I found the man-woman very convenient."[8]

The female amazon is often appreciated for her prowess at hunting and fighting. In the Crow tribe of the Great Plains, one of the most famous warriors of the nineteenth century was an amazon called "Woman Chief." Edward Denig, a white frontier trader who lived with the Crows for over twelve years, wrote that Woman Chief 'was equal if not superior to any of the men in hunting, both on horseback and foot." After single-handedly warding off an attack by an enemy tribe, she developed a reputation as a brave fighter: She easily attracted male warriors to follow her in battle, where she always distinguished herself by her bravery. According to Denig, the Crows believed that she had "a charmed life which, with her daring feats, elevated her to a point of honor and respect not often reached by male Warriors." Crow singers composed special songs to commemorate her gallantry, and she eventually became the third highest ranked chief in the entire tribe. Her status was so high, in fact, that she easily attracted women to marry her. By 1850, she had four wives, which also gave her additional status in the tribe. Denig concluded his biography of Woman Chief by saying in amazement, "Strange country this, where [berdache] males assume the dress and perform the duties of females, while women turn [like] men and mate with their own sex!"[9]

Whether attaining status as a warrior, a hunter, a healer, or an artist or simply by being hard working and generous, most amazons and berdache share an urge for success and prestige. They might not be good at doing the kinds of things that are typically expected of their sex, but instead of feeling deviant, they merely redirect their efforts into other kinds of prestigious activities. Moreover, berdache and amazons can gain notable material prosperity by selling their craftwork. Since they are considered sacred, their work is highly valued for its magical power as well as for its beauty.

The economic opportunities open to berdache and amazons are especially evident among the Navajo. Whereas average men and women are restricted to certain economic activities, *nadle* know no such constraints. Goods produced by them are much in demand. Also, because they are believed to be lucky, they usually act as the head of the family and make decisions about family property. They supervise the family's farming, sheepherding, and selling or trading. With such opportunities, talented *nadle* are valued and respected for their contributions to the family's prosperity.

More than economic success is involved in such people's striving for excellence, however. Atypical children soon recognize their difference from other people. Psychological theory suggests that if a family does not love and support such children, they will quickly internalize a negative self-image. Severe damage can result from feelings of deviance or inferiority. The way out of such self-hatred is either to deny any meaningful difference or to appreciate uniqueness. Difference is transformed—from *deviant* to *exceptional*—becoming a basis for respect rather than stigma. American Indian cultures deal with such atypical children by offering them prestige and rewards beyond what is available to the average person.

Masculine females and effeminate males in Western culture are often equally productive and successful, but they are so in the face of overwhelming odds. They may eventually come to appreciate their difference, but such self-acceptance comes more easily when one is considered "special" rather than "deviant." Few Western families show such youths more than grudging tolerance. If American families would adopt an appreciative attitude when faced with difference, much conflict and strife could be avoided when a family member turns out to be gay, lesbian, or bisexual. Such children could be nurtured and

supported, and such nonprejudiced treatment would ultimately rebound to the family's great benefit.

Benefits for Children

From the Native American and Polynesian viewpoints, then, homosexuality and gender nonconformity do not threaten the family. An unusual phenomenon is instead incorporated into the kinship system in a productive and nondisruptive manner. Similarly berdache and amazons are not seen as a threat to children. In fact, because they often have the reputation for intelligence, they are encouraged in some tribes to become teachers. In my fieldwork on Indian reservations and in the Yucatan, Alaska, Hawaii, and Thailand, I met a number of gender nonconformists who are highly respected teachers. Many of the venerated teachers of the sacred traditional hula ceremony among native Hawaiians are *mahus*.

Native American amazons also have the opportunity to become fathers. Among the Mohave, for example, the last person to have sex with the mother before she gives birth is considered to be the true father of the child. This allows an amazon to choose a male to impregnate her wife yet still claim paternity. The child is thus socially recognized as having an amazon father, who is thus able to fulfill all social roles that any other father would do.

Berdache have the opportunity to become parents through adoption. In fact, since they have a reputation for intelligence and generosity, they are often the first choice to become adoptive parents when there is a homeless child. For example, a Lakota berdache with whom I lived while conducting my 1982 fieldwork had adopted and raised four boys and three girls in his lifetime. The youngest boy was still living with him at the time, a typical teenager who was doing well in school. The household consisted of the berdache, his adopted son, the berdache's widowed mother, a number of nephews and nieces, and an elderly aunt.

Such an extended family contrasts sharply with contemporary American society where gays, lesbians, and bisexuals are often alienated from their families have trouble becoming adoptive or foster parents, and are often denied custody of their own children. Whereas American Indian communities can remedy the tragedy of a homeless child quickly and easily, foster and adoptive families are not so easy to come by in mainstream American society. As a result, the costs that Americans pay are high—in terms of both tax dollars and crimes committed by homeless youths.

Of course, the main reason for preventing gays and lesbians from becoming adoptive or foster parents—or even Big Brothers or Big Sisters—is the often expressed fear that the youths will be sexually molested. Since recent statistics show that well over 90 percent of child molesters are heterosexual men and their victims young girls, sexual orientation by itself is not a valid criterion on which to base adoption decisions. If it were, heterosexual men would not be allowed to adopt. The fact that homophobic leaders continue to oppose gay and lesbian adoptions when they know the statistics suggests that this issue is merely a rhetorical ploy. The real issue emerges most clearly in custody cases. Children are taken away from lesbian mothers or gay fathers, not because of molestation, but because they will provide "bad role models."

To consider an adult lesbian, gay man, or bisexual a bad role model is simple heterosexism. Children growing up in America today, no matter who their parents are, will see plenty of heterosexual role models—on television, at school, among neighbors and the parents of friends. Why not have a few gay and lesbian role models as an alternative? The answer is simple: American culture still regards it as a tragedy if a youth turns out to be lesbian, gay, or bisexual.

Non heterosexist cultures, by contrast, emphasize an individual's freedom to decide his or her own fate. Paradoxically, those cultures often see sexual variance or gender nonconformity not as matters of choice but as inborn or as determined by the spirit world. Ironically, while the professed American ideal is "freedom of choice," in reality every child is subjected to extreme social pressures to conform. Despite the omnipresent American rhetoric of freedom, mainstream American culture continues to deny lesbian, gay, and bisexual youths the freedom to choose their own lifestyles. Ever since Freud, however, research has made it abundantly clear that many psychological problems arise when childhood sexual desires are repressed. In fact, a greater incidence and severity of mental illness has been documented among more repressive cultures.[10]

Benefits for Friendship

In America today, many men are prevented from expressing their feelings or developing close friendships with other men by the fear that others will think them homosexual. Men can be coworkers, sports buddies, even social companions, but nothing more personal. Consequently, many American men are left with only one legitimate, socially sanctioned intimate relationship in their lives—that with their wives. Is it therefore surprising that most men equate intimacy with sex or that, starved for intimacy, many elect to keep a mistress? To expect marriage to meet all a person's needs—to expect a spouse or significant other to be sexual playmate, economic partner, and best friend—places too heavy a burden on what today is an infirm institution.

During my fieldwork in Indonesia, by contrast, I was struck by the intensity of friendships between men (friendships that reminded me of the intense "blood brother" relationships between Native American men). In Indonesia, the highly structured mixed-sex marriage and kinship system is balanced and strengthened by unstructured same-sex friendship networks. The one complements the other, and both provide men with the support that they need to get through their lives.

Once gay men, lesbians, and bisexuals have transcended the fear of being thought homosexual, they open themselves to whole new possibilities for more satisfying same-sex friendships. In non homophobic societies, heterosexual men are free to develop same-sex friendships and nurture their same-sex friends. Because no stigma is attached to same-sex friendship, no pressure exists to choose between an exclusively homosexual or heterosexual orientation. In contemporary America, by contrast, where men are socialized to equate intimacy with a sexual relationship, some may feel forced to abandon an exclusively heterosexual identity for an exclusively homosexual one. Homophobia creates two distinct classes of men, self-identified heterosexuals and self-iden-tified "homosexuals." More flexible notions of same-sex friendship in societies mean less of a need to compartmentalize people on the basis of sexual behavior and less social consternation should the relationship between same-sex friends become erotic.

Benefits for Society at Large

A culture that does not try to suppress the same-sex desires of its people can focus instead on the contri-butions that can be made by those who are different. We have already seen that American Indian berdache and amazons are honored for their spirituality, their artistic skills, and their hard work, all of which ben-efit the entire community. They are also often called on to mediate disputes between men and women. Married couples in particular turn to them since, as "half men/half women," they can see things from the perspective of both sexes. Their roles as go-betweens is integral to the smooth functioning of Native American communities.

Although there is not as much information on the social roles of amazons, the historical docu-ments suggest that berdache performed their go-between function in traditional Indian cultures for males and females on joyous occasions as well. A number of tribes were noted to have employed berdache to facilitate budding romances between young women and men, a role that reached its high-est development among the Cheyenne tribe of the Great Plains. One Cheyenne informant reported that berdache "were very popular and special favorites of young peoples whether married or not, for they were noted matchmakers. They were fine love talkers. . . . When a young man wanted to send gifts for a young woman, one of these halfmen-halfwomen was sent to the girl's relatives to do the talking in making the marriage."[11] Because of their spiritual connection, berdache were believed to possess the most potent love medicines. A Cheyenne bachelor who gained the assistance of a berdache was believed to be fortunate indeed since the berdache could often persuade the young woman and her family to accept the gift-laden horses that a man offered when he made a mar-riage proposal.

Whereas American Indian societies recog-nize and incorporate sexual diversity, others simply ignore it. When I was in Southeast Asia in 1987 and 1988, I learned that it was commonly known in both Thailand and Indonesia that some major gov-ernment figures were homosexual. Although those men did not publicly broadcast their homosexual-ity, neither did they make any attempt to hide their same-sex lovers from public view. Such tolerance benefits both the individuals, who are allowed to live their lives as they choose, and the nation, which utilized their leadership skills.

In my research, I have found that those societies with accepted homosexual roles ironically do not emphasize the sexual activities of homo-sexuals. Everyone knows their sexual preferences, but those preferences are considered matters for pri-vate, not public, concern. Homosexuality is therefore not politicized. In America, however, the homopho-bic Right has made such an issue of what it considers to be deviant sexuality that it has stimulated the development of a politically active gay community.

The suppression of sexual diversity *inevitably* results in social turmoil. Families and communities are divided by the issue. Suicides are occasioned by the discovery, or the fear of discovery, of secret sex lives. When the individuals whose secrets are uncovered are public figures, the ensuing media scandal can bring a community to the point of hysteria—witness Boise, Idaho, in the 1950s and schoolteacher firings in countless communities.

The persecution of gays, lesbians, and bisex-uals also endangers the freedom of other groups—indeed, any group. For persecution rarely confines itself to one group. For example, Adolf Hitler tried to rid Germany of Jews, but also extended his cam-paign to include homosexuals. The Ayatollah Khomeini similarly exterminated infidels and beheaded homosexuals. The point here is that no one group is safe until all groups are safe.

By continuing to discriminate against lesbians, gay men, and bisexuals, the United States is losing the respect of many in the world community—the Dutch and other progressive governments have already made formal diplomatic protests against discrimina-tory U.S. policies. Sodomy laws remain on the books and are enforced in many states, homosexuals are excluded from the military, sexual minorities are denied equal protection under the law—all this in a nation devoted to "life, liberty, and the pursuit of happiness." The situation today is similar to that in the early 1960s, when progressive governments in Europe, Asia, and especially the newly independent African nations voiced their support for African-American civil rights protestors. Such diplomatic action helped pressure the Kennedy administration to take action against racial segregation. For how could America champion its ideals of freedom and expect to maintain its position as the leader of the "free" world when people of color were treated so unequally?

Acceptance of people's right to be different is the certain hallmark of democracy and freedom. This is why the New Right's attempt to suppress homosexuality is so dangerous for the larger society. The dominant message propounded by the New Right in the 1980s has been that everyone should be the same. That desire for sameness has a strong attraction for people living in a diverse and changing society. Instead, we should be thankful that we are *not* all the same. If we were, society would lose the creativity and vitality that comes from difference. Faced with the new global competitiveness of the 1990s, we as Americans are hardly in a position *not* to promote independent thinking and creativity. Mindless conformity is an economic and emotional and intellectual dead end.

An appreciation of diversity, not just a tolerance of minorities, is what will promote future American progress. As the American Indian example illustrates so well, far from being a threat to religion, to the family, to children, and to society in general, homosexuality can benefit both men and women as well as bring freedom to all.

Notes

1. Quoted in *Project 10 Newsletter* (March 1989), 1.
2. Clellan Ford and Frank Beach, *Patterns of Sexual Behavior* (New York: Harper, 1951).
3. W. W. Hill, "The Status of the Hermaphrodite and Transvestite in Navaho Culture," *American Anthropologist* 37 (1935) 274.
4. Ibid.
5. The results of my 1979–84 fieldwork are reported in Walter L. Williams, *The Spirit and the Flesh: Sexual Diversity in American Indian Culture* (Boston: Beacon, 1986). Part of my Indonesian research is contained in Walter L. Williams, *Javanese Lives: Women and Men in Modern Indonesian Society* (New Brunswick, NJ.: Rutgers University Press, 1991). My research among Polynesians and Native Alaskans has not yet been written up. I express my gratitude to the Council for the International Exchange of Scholars, for a Fulbright research grant to Indonesia with a side trip to Thailand and Malaysia, to the University of Southern California faculty research fund for trips to conduct research in Hawaii, and to the Institute for the Study of Women and Men for a travel grant to go to Alaska. My main work there was among Aleuts and Yupik Eskimos.
6. Quoted in Williams, *Spirit and Flesh,* 57.
7. Ibid., 54.
8. Ibid., 58–59.
9. Ibid., 245–46.
10. George Devereux, Mohave Ethnopsychiatry (Washington, D.C.: Smithsonian Institution, 1969), viii–ix, xii–xiii, and "Institutionalized Homosexuality of the Mohave Indians," *Human Biology* 9 (1937): 498–499, 518. For examples of other sexually free societies, see Williams, *Spirit and Flesh,* chap. 12.
11. Quoted in Williams, *Spirit and Flesh,* 70–71.

27

"The Gender Pay Gap: Have Women Gone as Far as They Can?"

FRANCINE D. BLAU AND LAWRENCE M. KAHN

After a half a century of stability in the earnings of women relative to men, there has been a substantial increase in women's relative earnings since the late 1970s.[1] One of the things that make this development especially dramatic and significant is that the recent changes contrast markedly with the relative stability of earlier years.

These post-1980 earnings changes are also interesting because, when you compare women with their male counterparts, gains have been prevalent across a wide spectrum. So, for example, at first much of the female gains were centered on younger women, but now, while the gains may be a bit larger for younger women, women of all ages have narrowed the pay gap with men. The same broad progress is visible when we look at the trends in the gender pay gap by education. Less-educated women have narrowed the pay gap with less-educated men and highly educated women have narrowed the pay gap with highly educated men.

The earnings gains of women are particularly remarkable because they have occurred during a period when overall wage inequality was rising. That is, the difference in pay between workers with high wages and workers with low wages has widened considerably over the past 25 years or so. And yet, women, a low paid group, have nonetheless been able to narrow the pay gap with a relatively higher paid group, men.

The foregoing supports our initial observation that there has been important, significant progress for women. On the other hand, however, there is still a gender pay gap. Women continue to earn considerably less than men on average. It is also true that convergence slowed noticeably in the 1990s after women had especially gained relative to men in the 1980s. Although there were some larger gains for women in the early 2000s, the long-run significance of this recent experience is unclear. With the evidence suggesting that convergence has slowed in recent years, the possibility arises that the narrowing of the gender pay gap will not continue into the future. Moreover, there is evidence that although discrimination against women in the labor market has declined, some discrimination does still continue to exist.

This paper is organized as follows. We review the trends in detail, examining the female gains and also pointing to the slowing that occurred in the 1990s. Following that, we consider explanations for the pay gap in general, and explanations for the convergence that we have seen so far, paying some attention to the differential experience of the 1980s and 1990s. Finally we attempt to gaze into our crystal ball and consider the future. However, it is important to realize that when social scientists or economists consider the future, they are probably wrong as often as they are right. And the mixed picture we have described here for trends in the gender pay gap makes the future especially difficult to predict. Thus it is difficult to say whether and when robust convergence in the gender pay gap will resume.

Trends in the Gender Pay Gap

In this section we look in more detail at the trends in the relative wages of women. Figure 27.1 presents data drawn from published government statistics on female-to-male earnings ratios of full-time workers. We focus on full-time workers to adjust for gender differences in hours worked. This is important because women are more likely than men to work part-time. Ideally we would like a measure of wages or an hourly rate of pay. Unfortunately, we do not have a similar long data series for hourly wages. Thus, we focus here on the earnings of full-time workers.

The figure gives the gender earnings ratio for two data series available from published government statistics. Again, both pertain to the relative earnings of female and male full-time workers. The first, the annual earnings series, is based on annual earnings data on workers who are employed year round as well as full time. The second, the weekly earnings series, is based on the earnings of full-time workers over the survey week, regardless of how many weeks per year the individual works. The annual earnings series has been available for the longest time period, 1955 to 2003; the weekly earnings series has been available for a somewhat shorter period, 1967 to 2003.

While the exact figure for the gender earnings ratio differs a bit for the two series, they both tell the same story in terms of the trends. Until the late 1970s or early 1980s there was a remarkable constancy in the ratio, at around 60%. There were some year-to-year fluctuations, but the ratio hovered around the 60% level, indeed, if there was any discernible trend, it was a decrease in the ratio between 1955 and 1960. Then, over the 1980s, we see a period of strong, sustained increase in the ratio. This rising trend prevailed through perhaps

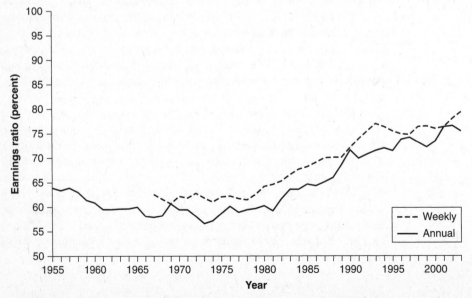

FIGURE 27.1 Female-to-male earnings ratios of full-time workers 1955–2003.

1990 or 1993, depending on the series. However, during the 1990s, the pace of convergence in both the annual and the weekly earnings series slowed and both series behaved more erratically. The pace of change picked up again in the early 2000s.[2] However, as noted above, the long-run significance of this recent experience is unclear. It may signal a resumption of a strong, long-run trend towards convergence in male-female earnings or may prove to be of only short duration.[3]

Abstracting from the differential trends over the various sub periods and focusing on the period since the late 1970s as a whole, the gains have been quite remarkable, especially viewed in terms of the long constancy in the gender ratio that preceded this time. So, for example, based on the weekly earnings series, the gender ratio rose from 61.3% in 1978 to 79.4% in 2003. Again, much of this increase was accomplished in a relatively short period of time, with the ratio reaching 76.8% by 1993. Of course, the 77–79% figure remains below earnings parity. Thus, clearly all sources of the pay differential between men and women have not been eradicated.

How do we explain these earnings gains for women? To address this question as well as to understand why women continue to earn less than men, we need to first consider the basic factors that explain the gender pay gap to begin with.

Economists' Explanations for the Gender Pay Gap

The Role of Qualifications and Discrimination

Economists point to a number of factors that could be important in explaining the lower earnings of women compared to men, but traditionally have focused on two primary factors. Following Juhn, Murphy, and Pierce (1991), we call these "gender-specific" factors in that they relate specifically to differences between women and men, either in their qualifications or how they are treated. With regard to qualifications, the human capital model has been especially important in pointing out the potential role played by education and experience.

The gender gap in educational attainment was never particularly large in the United States. The biggest difference historically was that, although women were more likely to graduate from high school than men, they were less likely to go on to college and graduate education. Moreover, men tended to concentrate in career-oriented fields of study such as engineering, law, medicine and business that led to relatively high earnings. These educational differences have decreased quite a bit in recent years, especially at the college level where women are actually now over half of college students; women have also greatly increased their representation in traditionally-male professional fields. Thus gender differences in education levels have never explained a large portion of the overall gender pay gap; most recently, in some samples gender differences in years of schooling favor women.

The qualification that has proven to be quite important is work experience because traditionally women moved in and out of the labor market based on family considerations. Before World War II, most women left the labor market permanently when they got married and had children. In the immediate postwar period, a pattern arose whereby older married women returned to the labor market after their children were in school or grown. An even bigger change has occurred in the past 20 to 30 years as increasing numbers of women, including married women, started staying in the labor force fairly continuously even when they had small children at home.[4] Today, even the majority of women with children a year or less in age are participating in the labor force. Nonetheless, on average, women have less work experience than men and that difference in qualifications is quantitatively important in explaining the gender pay gap.

Jacob Mincer and Solomon Polachek (1974) have done especially important work in highlighting the role of labor market experience in explaining the gender pay gap. Given the traditional division of labor by gender in the family, women tend to accumulate less labor market experience than men. Further, because women anticipate shorter and more discontinuous work lives, they have lower incentives to invest in market-oriented formal education and on-the-job training. Their resulting smaller human capital investments lower their earnings relative to those of men. An additional way in which the traditional division of labor may disadvantage women is that the longer hours women spend on housework may also decrease the effort they put into their market jobs compared to men, controlling for hours worked, and hence also reduce their productivity and wages (Becker, 1985).[5]

To the extent that women choose occupations for which on-the-job training is less important, gender differences in occupations are also expected. Women may especially avoid jobs requiring large investments in skills that are unique to a particular enterprise, because the returns to such investments are reaped only as long as one remains with that employer. At the same time, employers may be reluctant to hire women for such jobs because the firm bears some of the costs of such firm-specific training, and fears not getting a full return on that investment.[6]

However, even controlling for experience and whatever other qualifications can readily be measured, there tends to be a pay difference between men and women that is not explained and is potentially due to discrimination. Gary Becker (1971; 1st ed., 1957) has been especially instrumental in developing analyses of labor market discrimination. Although he was looking at differences between blacks and whites, the idea of prejudice and its negative consequences are readily transferable to women versus men. Becker conceptualized discriminatory preferences as the desire to maintain social distance from the discriminated group. It may at first seem odd to hypothesize that men would not like to associate with women on the job when they generally live together with women in families. However, the issue here may be more one of socially appropriate roles than of the desire to maintain social distance, as Becker postulated was the case with race.[7]

Standard models in economics suggest discrimination can arise in a variety of ways. In Becker's model, discrimination is due to the discriminatory tastes of employers, co-workers, or customers. Alternatively, in models of "statistical discrimination," differences in the treatment of men and women arise from average differences between the two groups in the expected value of productivity (or in the reliability with which productivity may be predicted), which may lead employers to discriminate on the basis of that average (see for example, Aigner & Cain, 1977).

Finally, discriminatory exclusion of women from "male" jobs can result in an excess supply of labor in "female" occupations, depressing wages there for otherwise equally productive workers, as in Bergmann's (1974) "overcrowding" model.

The typical approach to analyzing the sources of the gender pay gap is to estimate wage regressions specifying the relationship between wages and productivity-related characteristics for men and women. The gender pay gap may then be statistically decomposed into two components: one due to gender differences in measured characteristics, and the other "unexplained" and potentially due to discrimination. Such empirical studies provide evidence consistent with both human capital differences and labor market discrimination in explaining the gender pay gap.

However, any approach that relies on a statistical residual will be open to question as to whether all the necessary explanatory variables were included in the regression. For example, even if measured human capital characteristics can explain only a portion of the wage gap between men and women, it is possible that unmeasured group differences in qualifications may explain part of the residual. If men are more highly endowed with respect to these omitted variables then we would overestimate discrimination. Alternatively, if some of the factors controlled for in such regressions—like occupation and tenure with the employer—themselves reflect the impact of discrimination, then discrimination will be underestimated. Moreover, if women face barriers to entry into certain occupations, they may have higher unmeasured productivity than men in the same jobs. This factor would also suggest an underestimate of discrimination if we controlled for occupation.[8]

Using the residual from a regression to estimate the effects of discrimination will also run into trouble if feedback effects are important. Even small initial discriminatory differences in wages may cumulate to large ones as men and women make decisions about human capital investments and time allocation in the market and the home on the basis of these wage differentials.

Results of statistical studies of the gender pay gap may nonetheless be instructive. Representative findings from analyses of this type may be illustrated by results from a recent paper of ours (Blau & Kahn, 2006). Using data from the Panel Study of Income Dynamics (PSID), which contains information on actual labor market experience for a large, nationally representative sample, we found a wage differential between male and female full-time workers in 1998 of 20%. The restriction to full-time workers is designed to focus on male and female workers who are as similar as possible.[9]

The impact of gender differences in characteristics on the male–female wage differential is shown in Table 27.1, The variables considered include indicators of "human capital," that is, those relating to education and experience, as well as measures of occupation, industry and union status. (Race is also included as a control variable, but its effect is small since the proportion of each race group in the full-time sample is about the same for men and women.)

As would be expected, women's lesser amount of labor market experience is found to be a significant determinant of the gender wage differential, explaining 11% of the gender gap in wages. This reflects a 3.5 year difference in full-time experience between men and women, which, though smaller than in previous years, is still a substantial factor

Table 27.1 Contribution to the Wage Differential Between Men and Women of Differences in Measured Characteristics, 1998

Characteristics	Percent Explained
Educational attainment	–6.7
Labor force experience	10.5
Race	2.4
Occupational category	27.4
Industry category	21.9
Union status	3.5
Unexplained	41.1
Total	100.0
Wage differential (%)	20.3

Source: Calculated from data presented in Blau and Kahn (2006).

explaining the wage gap. Interestingly, women in this sub-sample are found to have higher educational attainment than men, which (as indicated by the negative sign in the table) works to *lower* the gender wage gap by 7%. Putting this somewhat differently, gender differences in educational attainment do not help to explain the gender wage gap, but rather work slightly in the opposite direction. While in the population as a whole, men's educational attainment is still somewhat higher than women's, when we focus on a sub-sample of the population which is not only employed, but employed full time, women have a slight edge.

Finally, gender differences in occupation and industry are substantial and help to explain a considerable portion of the gender wage gap. Men are more likely to be in blue-collar jobs and to work in mining, construction, or durable manufacturing; they are also more likely to be in unionized employment. Women are more likely to be in clerical or professional jobs and to work in the service industry. Taken together, these variables explain 53% of the gender wage gap—27% for occupation, 22% for industry, and an additional 4% for union status.[10]

Although these findings suggest that gender differences in work-related characteristics are important, they also indicate that qualifications are only part of the story. The proportion of the wage differential that is *not* explained by these types of productivity-related characteristics includes the impact of labor market discrimination, although as mentioned above, the residual may also include the effects of gender differences in unmeasured productivity levels or non-wage aspects of jobs. In this case, 41% of the gender gap cannot be explained even when gender differences in education, experience, industries, occupations, and union status are taken into account. We can consider the results of this study somewhat differently by focusing on the gender wage ratio. The actual ("unadjusted") gender wage ratio is 80%; that is, women's wages are, on average, 80% of men's wages. If women had the same human capital characteristics (that is, education and experience), racial composition, industry and occupational distribution, and union coverage as men, the "adjusted" ratio would rise to 91% of men's wages. Thus, while measured characteristics are important, women still earn less than similar men even when all measured characteristics are taken into account. And, as we suggested above, including controls for occupation, industry, and union status may be questionable to the extent that they may be influenced by discrimination.

Nonetheless, the residual gap, however measured, may well reflect factors apart from discrimination. One that has received particular attention recently is the impact of children on women's wages, since evidence of a negative effect of children on wages has been obtained, even in analyses which control for labor market experience (Waldfogel, 1998). The reason may be that, in the past, having a child often meant that a woman withdrew from the labor force for a substantial period, breaking her tie to her employer and forgoing the returns to any firm-specific training she might have acquired, as well as any rewards for having made an especially good job match. Given the sharp increase in the labor force participation of women with young children that has occurred since the 1960s,[11] this factor may have been of growing importance in influencing the aggregate gender gap. However, the greater availability of parental leave, legally mandated in the United States since 1993, may well mitigate the effect of this factor on more recent cohorts. Indeed, Waldfogel finds that the negative effect of children on wages is substantially reduced for mothers who have maternity leave coverage.

Some studies of discrimination have taken different approaches to the question, thus avoiding some of the problems of traditional analyses. First, two studies have applied traditional econometric techniques to especially homogeneous groups and employed extensive controls for qualifications, thus minimizing the effect of gender differences in unmeasured productivity characteristics. Wood, Corcoran, and Courant (1993) studied graduates of the University of Michigan Law School classes of 1972–1975, 15 years after graduation. The gap in pay between women and men was relatively small at the outset of their careers, but 15 years later, women graduates earned only 60% as much as men. Some of this difference reflected choices that workers had made, including the propensity of women lawyers to work shorter hours. But,

even controlling for current hours worked, as well as an extensive list of worker qualifications and other covariates, including family status, race, location, grades while in law school, and detailed work history data, such as years practiced law, months of part-time work, and type and size of employer, a male advantage of 13% remained. In a similar vein, Weinberger (1998) examined wage differences among recent college graduates in 1985. Her controls included narrowly defined college major, college grade point average, and specific educational institution attended. She found an unexplained pay gap of 10 to 15% between men and women.

A second set of studies used an experimental approach. Neumark (1996) analyzed the results of a hiring "audit" in which male and female pseudo-job seekers were given similar résumés and sent to apply for jobs waiting on tables at the same set of Philadelphia restaurants. In high-priced restaurants, a female applicant's probability of getting an interview was 40 percentage points lower than a male's and her probability of getting an offer was 50 percentage points lower. A second study examined the impact of the adoption of "blind" auditions by symphony orchestras in which a screen is used to conceal the identity of the candidate (Goldin & Rouse, 2000). The screen substantially increased the probability that a woman would advance out of preliminary rounds and be the winner in the final round. The switch to blind auditions was found to explain 25% of the increase in the percentage female in the top five symphony orchestras in the United States, from less than 5% of all musicians in 1970 to 25% in 1996.

Third, several recent studies have examined predictions of Becker's (1971) discrimination model. Becker and others have pointed out that competitive forces should reduce or eliminate discrimination in the long run because the least discriminatory firms, which hire more lower-priced female labor, would have lower costs of production and should drive the more discriminatory firms out of business. For this reason, Becker suggested that discrimination would be more severe in firms or sectors that are shielded to some extent from competitive pressures. Consistent with this reasoning, Hellerstein, Neumark, and Troske (2002) found that, among plants with high levels of product market power, those employing relatively more women were more profitable. In a similar vein, Black and Strahan (2001) report that, with the deregulation of the banking industry beginning in the mid-1970s, the gender pay gap in banking declined as men's wages fell by considerably more than women's (12% vs. 3%). This suggests that during the period of regulation, banks shared the rents fostered by regulation primarily with men. It was thus men who lost the most in the shift to deregulation. And, Black and Brainerd (2004) find that increasing vulnerability to international trade reduced apparent gender wage discrimination in concentrated industries, again as predicted by Becker's (1971) model.

Finally, additional evidence on discrimination comes from court cases. A number of employment practices which explicitly discriminated against women used to be quite prevalent; including marriage bars restricting the employment of married women (Goldin, 1990), and the intentional segregation of men and women into separate job categories with associated separate and lower pay scales for women (e.g., Bowe v. Colgate-Palmolive Co., 416 F.2d 711 {7th Cir. 1969}); IUE v. Westinghouse Electric Co., 631 F.2d 1094 {3rd Cir. 1980}). While many such overt practices have receded, recent court cases suggest that employment practices still exist which produce discriminatory outcomes for women.

For example, in 1994, Lucky Stores, a major grocery chain, agreed to a settlement of $107 million after Judge Marilyn Hall Patel found that "sex discrimination was the standard operating procedure at Lucky with respect to placement, promotion, movement to full-time positions, and the allocation of additional hours" (Stender v. Lucky Stores, Inc. 803 F. Supp. 259; {N.D. Cal. 1992}; King 1997). And, in 2000, the U.S. Information Agency agreed to pay $508 million to settle a case in which the Voice of America rejected women who applied for high-paying positions in the communications field. A lawyer representing the plaintiffs said that the women were told things like, "These jobs are only for men," or "We're looking for a male voice" (FEDHR, 2000). A final example is the 1990 case against Price Waterhouse, a major accounting firm, in which the only woman considered for a partnership was denied, even though, of the 88 candidates for partner, she had brought in the most business. Her colleagues criticized her for being "Overbearing, 'macho' and abrasive and said she would have a better chance of making partner if she would wear makeup and jewelry, and walk, talk and dress 'more femininely.' " The Court found that Price Waterhouse maintained a partnership evaluation system that "permitted negative sexually stereotyped comments to influence partnership selection" (BNA, 1990; Lewin, 1990).

Oftentimes, economists serve as expert witnesses in court cases alleging discrimination. Their analyses, when publicly available, provide a window into discriminatory practices that still exist to some extent in the labor market, although there is of course likely to be disagreement between experts employed by each side in the type of evidence that is relevant or in the interpretation of the evidence. For example, the Lucky Stores case cited above generated an interesting exchange summarized in Taylor (2001).[12]

Labor economist John Pencavel testified for the plaintiffs, the women who brought the suit. He found that women at Lucky earned between 76 percent and 82 percent as much as Lucky's male workers earned. Pencavel found that women were regularly placed in jobs that paid less than jobs given male coworkers, although there was no significant difference between the education and experience of the worker. There was little difference in the wages of the male and female workers within each type of job; but some jobs paid more than others and women happened to be assigned to the lower-paying jobs.

Joan Haworth, another labor economist, was an expert witness for the defendant, Lucky Stores. She reported survey evidence showing that Lucky's assignment of women and men to different jobs reflected differences in the work preferences of men and women. Thus, Lucky justified its job assignments by arguing that there was a gender difference in attitudes toward work. Lucky argued that its employment policies were based on observed differences in the career aspirations of male and female employees. For example, one manager at Lucky testified that women were more interested in cash register work and men were more interested in floor work.

As we noted above, Judge Marilyn Hall Patel decided the case in favor of the plaintiffs. With respect to the evidence cited above, she wrote: "The court finds the defendant's explanation that the statistical disparities between men and women at Lucky are caused by differences in the work interests of men and women to be unpersuasive." An interesting aspect of this case is that both sides agreed that male and female employees received equal pay for equal work and that the pay differential was associated with pay differences across occupations. They differed, however, over the source of the occupational differences: the choices of women vs. discrimination. This disagreement mirrors the alternative explanations economists offer in general for wage and occupational difference between men and women: differences in qualifications based on the choices men and women make versus discrimination which limits the opportunities and pay of women compared to men.

Some additional evidence supporting discrimination as a source of the type of occupational differences cited above is provided by a recent study of eight years of data from an unidentified regional grocery chain on gender differences in job titles and wage rates (Ransom & Oaxaca, 2005). As in the case of the Pencavel analysis summarized above, Ransom and Oaxaca find a pattern of gender differences in initial job assignment and upward mobility within the firm that "generally penalized women, even when the analysis account[ed] for individuals' characteristics" (p. 219). While one might again dispute the reason for these differences, the authors found that job segregation of women and men was dramatically lower in the period after the company lost a discrimination suit (1984) and reached a settlement (1986) in which it initiated affirmative action policies. This implies that it was possible to find women interested in higher-level jobs, leading one to doubt that such segregation was entirely voluntary.

These cases emphasize the role of occupational segregation by sex within firms in producing pay differences between men and women. Pencavel explicitly notes that there was little difference in pay between men and women in the same job. It is worth noting that economists and sociologists who have examined this issue across a wider range of firms have tended to come to a similar conclusion: pay differences between men and women in the same narrowly defined occupational categories within the same firm tend to be small (Blau, 1977; Groshen, 1991; Petersen & Morgan, 1995; and Bayard, Hellerstein, Neumark, & Troske, 1999).[13] However, even when men and women are in the same occupation, they tend to be segregated by firm, and such establishment segregation contributes substantially to the gender pay gap.

The Role of Wage Structure

In earlier work, building on a framework suggested by Chinhui Juhn, Kevin Murphy, and Brooks Pierce (1991), we point out that there is another factor that needs to be considered when analyzing gender differences in pay, and that is what we call wage structure (Blau & Kahn, 1996 and 1997). We define wage structure as being the market returns to skills and the rewards for employment in particular sectors of the economy. Market returns to skills denote the premiums the market determines for being a more experienced worker or a more highly educated worker, etc. Rewards for employment in particular sectors of the economy refer to the fact that, for example, unionized workers tend to earn more than comparable non-unionized workers or workers in some industries—durable goods, manufacturing for example—may earn more than similarly-qualified workers in other industries, say services. In addition, considerable research suggests that predominantly female occupations pay less, even controlling for measured personal characteristics of workers and a variety of characteristics of occupations, although the interpretation of such results remains in some dispute.[14]

We distinguish wage structure from gender-specific factors because the idea is that these are the returns to skills or the rewards for working in a particular industry or occupation regardless of whether you are male or female. Why should wage structure affect the gender pay gap? To see how, let's think a bit more about the two factors we discussed earlier—gender differences in qualifications and labor market discrimination. Suppose women do have less experience, on average, than men do. Then, the higher the return to experience the larger the gender pay gap will be. Or, suppose that jobs staffed primarily by women do pay less than jobs staffed primarily by men. Then, the higher the premium for being in a male occupation the larger the gender pay gap will be.

This is interesting because these market returns have in fact varied over time. In the last 25 years or so, the market returns to skills, like those acquired with work experience, have increased. So this is a factor that, taken alone, would have worked to increase the gender pay gap. The rewards to being in male occupations and industries have increased as well, and that factor, taken alone, would have increased the pay gap as well. So, one question that we have raised in our research is: How have women been able to successfully swim against the tide of rising returns to skills and rising rewards to being in particular industries and occupations? That is, how have they managed to narrow the pay differential with men in the face of the adverse trends in wage structure that have worked against them?

Before looking at the results of our research addressing these questions, let's consider the issue of why the returns to skills have been increasing.[15] There is a fairly broad consensus among economists (though not complete unanimity) that within countries like the United States, one of the main reasons that the returns to skills have been rising is that the demand by employers for skilled workers has been rising relative to the demand for unskilled workers. Why has this occurred? There are at least two reasons. The one that that we would put the most weight on is technological change. The information and telecommunications revolution has worked to put more of a premium on skill, at least thus far. There are other scenarios possible, but thus far it has increased the demand for skilled workers compared to less skilled workers. The other reason—we would put less weight on it

although has also played a role—is international trade. Today, less skilled workers in the United States are to some extent competing against less skilled workers from around the world; many of them are available at much lower wages. Factors in addition to demand shifts that appear to have also played a role are—a decline in the union movement since unions tend to push for more egalitarian pay structures, the falling real value the minimum wage (adjusted for inflation, the minimum wage is actually lower today than it was in the 1970s), an influx of unskilled immigrants, and a decrease in the rate of growth of college-educated workers.

While rising returns to skills may be hypothesized to widen the gender pay gap, all else equal, it is possible that the demand shifts discussed above may have favored women relative to men in certain ways, and thus contributed to a decrease in the unexplained gender pay gap (Blau & Kahn, 1997; Welch, 2000). Technological change is believed to have caused within-industry demand shifts that favored white collar workers in general (Berman, Bound, & Griliches, 1994). Given the traditional male predominance in blue-collar jobs, this shift might be expected to benefit women relative to men. Similarly, to the extent that the spread of computer technology is an important source of recent technological change, the observation that women are more likely than men to use computers at work suggests that women as a group may have benefited from shifts in demand associated with computerization (Autor, Katz, & Krueger, 1998; Weinberg, 2000). Diffusion of computers likely also benefits women because computers restructure work in ways that de-emphasize physical strength (Weinberg, 2000).

Explaining the Trends: The 1980s

Returning to the trends in the gender pay gap—how do we explain them? To answer this question, we summarize results from Blau and Kahn (1997 and 2006).[16] Using data from the PSID (we reported on some of our results above), we analyzed women's wage gains over the 1980s (1979–1989), which, as we saw in Figure 27.1, was a period of exceptionally rapid closing of the gender wage gap. We found that higher rewards to skills did indeed retard wage convergence during this period but this was more than offset by improvements in gender-specific factors.

Of particular importance was the decline in the experience difference between men and women: the gender gap in full-time experience fell from 7.5 to 4.6 years over this period. Shifts in major occupations played a significant role too, as the employment of women as professionals and managers rose relative to men's, while their relative employment in clerical and service jobs fell. Women's wages also increased relative to men's because of deunionization (the decline of unions). Deunionization had a larger negative impact on male than female workers because men, who have traditionally been more likely than women to be unionized, experienced a larger decrease in unionization than women. Another factor that worked to increase the gender pay ratio substantially was a decrease in the "unexplained" portion of the gender differential—that is, a decline in the pay difference between men and women with the same measured characteristics (i.e., experience, education, occupation, industry, and union status).

Taken together, changes in qualifications and in the unexplained gap worked to increase the gender wage ratio substantially. Working in the opposite direction, however, were changes in wage structure (or returns to characteristics) that favored men over women during this period. Of particular importance were a rise in the return to experience (since women have less of it) and increases in returns to employment in industries where men are more highly represented. These shifts in labor market returns by themselves would have reduced the gender ratio substantially. Thus, in order for the wage gap to decline, the factors favorably affecting women's wages had to be large enough to more than offset the impact of unfavorable shifts in returns. This was indeed the case, so that the gender pay gap did decline over the 1980s.

Can we say anything about the reasons for the decline in the unexplained gender wage gap that occurred over the 1980s? Such a shift may reflect a decline in labor market discrimination against women, but also an upgrading of women's *unmeasured* labor market skills, a shift in labor market demand favoring women over men, or changes in the composition of the labor force due to the pattern of labor force entries or exits. Indeed all of these factors may well have played a role, and all appear credible during this period.

First, since women improved their relative level of measured skills, as shown by the narrowing of the gap in full-time job experience and in occupational differences between men and women, it is plausible that they also enhanced their relative level of unmeasured skills. For example, women's increasing labor force attachment may have encouraged them to acquire more on-the-job training or encouraged their employers to offer them more training. Evidence also indicates that gender differences in college major, which have been strongly related to the gender wage gap among college graduates (Brown & Corcoran, 1997), decreased over the 1970s and 1980s; the marketability of women's education has probably improved. The male-female difference in SAT math scores has also been declining, falling from 46 points in 1977 to 35 points in 1996, which could be another sign of improved quality of women's education.

Second, the argument that discrimination against women declined in the 1980s may seem less credible than that their unmeasured human capital characteristics improved, since the federal government scaled back its antidiscrimination enforcement effort during the 1980s (Leonard, 1989). However, as women increased their commitment to the labor force and improved their job skills, the rationale for statistical discrimination against them diminished; thus it is plausible that this type of discrimination decreased. Further, in the presence of feedback effects, employers' revised views can generate additional increases in women's wages by raising women's returns to investments in job qualifications and skills. To the extent that such qualifications are not fully controlled for in the statistical analysis used to explain the change in the gender wage gap, this may also help to account for the decline in the "unexplained" gap. Another possible reason for a decline in discrimination against women is that changes in social attitudes have made such discriminatory tastes increasingly less acceptable.

Third, the underlying labor market demand shifts that widened wage inequality over the 1980s may have favored women relative to men in certain ways, and thus may have also contributed to a decrease in the unexplained gender gap. Overall, manufacturing employment declined. In addition, there is some evidence that technological change produced within-industry demand shifts that favored white-collar relative to blue-collar workers in general. As noted above, given the traditional male predominance in blue-collar jobs, this shift might be expected to benefit women relative to men, as would increased computer use.

Finally, another factor contributing to the considerable narrowing of the "unexplained" gender wage gap in the 1980s appears to be favorable shifts in the composition of the female labor force. Specifically, we found that, controlling for the measured characteristics mentioned earlier, the women who entered the labor force over this period tended to be those with relatively high (unmeasured) skills. This improved the quality of the female labor force and thus contributed to the narrowing the gender wage gap.[17]

So far, in considering the effects of changes in wage structure and rising wage inequality on the gender pay gap, we have assumed that estimates of changing labor market returns are a useful indicator of the market rewards facing both men and women. Consistent with this assumption is evidence that widening wage inequality in the 1980s and 1990s was importantly affected by the economy-wide forces discussed above, including technological change, international trade, the decline in unionism, and the falling real value of the minimum wage (see, e.g., Katz & Autor, 1999). Moreover, increases in wage inequality during this period were similar for men and women, suggesting that both groups were fairly similarly affected by these trends. However, it should be pointed out that under some circumstances, the gender pay gap could influence male inequality. For example, suppose there is a fixed overall hierarchy of jobs and that jobs determine wages. In this case, as women succeed in increasing the gender pay ratio by moving up in the overall distribution of jobs (and wages), men who are displaced move down, resulting in widening male

inequality. It has been argued that recent trends in the gender pay gap and male wage inequality are consistent with such a model (Fortin & Lemieux, 2000). In this view, women's gains have to some extent come at the expense of men's losses.

Explaining the Trends: The 1990s

Why did convergence in female and male wages slow over the 1990s? Again, drawing on our previous work (Blau & Kahn, 2006) we may suggest some tentative answers.[18] We found that human capital trends cannot account for the slowdown: women improved their relative human capital by about the same amount in both the 1980s and the 1990s. In the 1980s this upgrading consisted of rising relative experience while in the 1990s it consisted to lesser extent of rising relative experience and to a greater extent of increasing educational attainment of women relative to men. Nor did changes in wage structure in the 1990s have a more adverse effect on women than changes in the previous decade—in fact the impact of changing wage structure was actually more negative for women in the 1980s. Slowing convergence in men's and women's occupations and degree of unionization in the 1990s was found to account for some of the slowdown, but only a small portion.

We found that the major reason for the slowdown in wage convergence in the 1990s was the considerably smaller narrowing of the "unexplained" gender pay gap in the 1990s compared to the 1980s. Our reasoning above suggests that this could be due to slower improvement in women's unmeasured qualifications relative to men's in the 1990s than in the 1980s; a smaller decline in discrimination against women in the 1990s than in the 1980s; or less favorable demand shifts for women in the 1990s than in the 1980s. Each of these factors appears to have played a role in explaining the observed trends. In addition, controlling for measured characteristics, female labor force entrants were less skilled during the 1990s, perhaps as a result of the entry of many relatively low-skilled, female single-family heads. Indeed, differences between the two decades in such shifts in labor force composition were found to explain as much as 25% of the apparent slowdown in

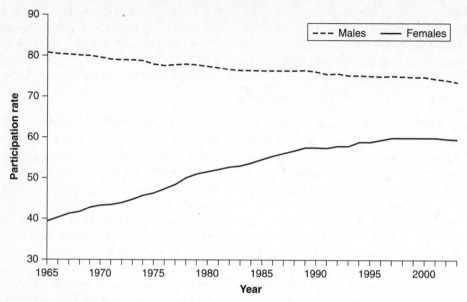

FIGURE 27.2 Trends in female and male labor force participation rates, 1965–2003.

convergence in the unexplained gender pay gap in the 1990s.[19]

As we noted above, women narrowed the experience gap at a slower pace in the 90s than they did in the 80s. Figure 27.2 shows the trends in male and female labor force participation that underlie this development. The most striking trend shown in the figure is that the *difference* in the participation rates of men and women has narrowed considerably since the starting year, 1965. This is due to a slow steady decrease in male labor force participation combined with a much sharper and dramatic increase in female labor force participation. The decrease in male participation does not appear to be due very much to changes in gender roles. Rather it primarily reflects the fact that men are retiring at earlier ages and are staying in school longer. Another factor has been the weakening job market for less skilled men (Juhn, 1992).

While the data in the figure begin in the mid-1960s, the large increases in female participation in fact date back to the 1940s. Interestingly, the trend towards rising female labor force participation was strong and consistent until about 1990. After that the line becomes noticeably flatter. Women's participation increased a bit through 1997, with no further increases thereafter.

How do these participation trends relate to the average experience levels of women workers? Unfortunately, it is not possible to figure this out just by looking at participation rates. This is because the labor force participation rate of women can increase for either of two reasons or a combination of both. On the one hand, participation may rise because a lot of new groups of women come into the labor market. This tends to lower the average experience of women workers because there are a lot of new entrants. On the other hand, participation can increase because women stay in the labor force more consistently over a period of time, rather than moving in and out. This works to raise average experience levels of women workers.

Research has shown that during the 1970s the average experience of women did not increase because those two factors counter balanced each other. There were a lot of new entrants and a lot of women staying in more continuously, thus average experience remained about the same (Goldin, 1990). In the 1980s, though, the increase in the labor force participation of women was due to more of them remaining in the labor force more consistently. And, as we have seen, the average experience of women workers rose accordingly. This suggests that the flattening of the trend in female labor force participation shown in the chart caused the gender gap in experience to decline more slowly in the 1990s than in the 1980s.

Before leaving the subject of the participation trends, it is interesting to consider their larger significance. Viewed more broadly, what the trends show is an enormous change in gender roles and a movement away from the traditional family of breadwinner husband and homemaker wife to a family where both husband and wife work outside the home, although not necessarily giving equal weight to each of their careers. Ralph Smith (1979) called this process a "subtle revolution." The trends suggest that this subtle revolution, having accomplished a great deal, may be slowing down now. Is it stopping? Not necessarily. But we have reached a situation where, looking at women in the prime working ages (that is, 25 to 55), over three quarters of them are in the labor force. This means that female labor force participation rates in the United States are very high, although still below the male rates of around 90% in this age group. So it may not be surprising that, of necessity, future participation trends will be less dramatic than past trends.

Prospects for the Future

Although we readily acknowledge that predicting the future is a tricky business, we cautiously offer some thoughts on the prospects for the future. What will happen to the gender pay gap in the coming years? Recent developments make the answer to this question particularly uncertain. As we have seen, after a period of consistent and sustained narrowing of the gender pay gap over the 1980s, convergence became more fitful in the 1990s. Perhaps what we saw in the 1990s was a mere pause; perhaps we were consolidating the really massive changes that had occurred over the preceding 10 to 20 years—not just in the gender pay gap but also in women's labor force participation and in the occupations in which they work; perhaps the next 20 years will show similar renewed gains on all these fronts. That could very well be. Or we may have reached a point that we are going to stay at for quite a while, a big change from the past but not so much change in the future. It is even possible that under certain circumstances the gender pay gap

could begin to widen, returning to levels of an earlier period. While we cannot choose among these options with certainty, it may be instructive to consider each of the factors that we have identified as influencing the gender pay gap and consider the possible future course of each and its likely impact on the pay gap.

One of the factors influencing the trends in the gender pay gap is overall trends in wage inequality. Rising wage inequality, to the extent that it results from increasing returns to skills like work experience that women have less of than men, on average, is expected to widen the gender pay gap, all else equal. In this respect, it has been noted that wage inequality increased less during the 1990s than during the 1980s (Katz & Autor, 1999). If this tapering off in the trend towards rising inequality should continue into the future, the negative effect of this factor on the pace of convergence in the gender pay gap will be small.

On the other hand, to the extent that rising wage inequality was due to demand shifts that favored women relative to men, it may be hypothesized that such shifts, and the relative advantage they may have given women relative to men, have also tapered off and are likely to be dampened in the future as well. This is suggested by the fact that the shedding of blue collar, manufacturing jobs was particularly pronounced in the 1980s. A closely related development, deunionization, which also disadvantaged men to a greater extent than women, is likely to occur at a slower pace in the future as unionization rates in the private sector have reached single digits, giving little scope for substantial future declines, and public sector unionization remains relatively stable. While demand shifts favoring women may have slowed, so too has the growth in the supply of women to the labor market. If this slower growth in supply continues into the future, it may mean that demand- and supply-side shifts offset each other and thus, taken together, do not have much effect on convergence in the gender pay gap.

Although overall female labor force participation increased modestly in the 1990s, welfare reforms and other government policies spurred an increase in employment among single mothers (see, for example, Meyer & Rosenbaum, 2001). The growth in participation among single heads, who tend on average to be less well educated than other women, could also have slowed wage convergence by shifting the composition of the female labor force toward low-wage women. We did indeed find some evidence consistent with this in our earlier work (Blau & Kahn, 2006), though this factor does not appear to be the main reason for the slowing convergence in the gender wage gap in the 1990s. Thus it seems unlikely that a further entry of single mothers into the labor force in the future will have a large impact on the *aggregate* gender pay gap.

Moving toward the more traditional factors of women's relative qualifications and the possibility of labor market discrimination against them, there is little reason to expect large changes here either. The flattening of the growth in women's labor force participation rates, if it continues, suggests that large increase in women's work experience and labor force commitment are unlikely, although this statement must be qualified somewhat since, as we have explained, trends in the average experience of women cannot be inferred directly from changes in participation rates. Similarly, now that women comprise the majority of college students, further large gains in the relative educational attainment of women appear unlikely, though there is room for continued reductions in the gender differences in college major and at the graduate level in professional schools and Ph.D. programs in many fields.

Turning to labor market discrimination, now that the most open and egregious forms of sex discrimination have been greatly reduced or eliminated and discrimination increasingly becomes more subtle and possibly even unconscious, future large declines in discrimination in the labor market may become more difficult to attain. In addition, the decreases in statistical discrimination that we hypothesized as occurring in response to women's increasing labor force attachment can be expected to slow as increases in women's attachment also slow. However, there seems room for some further decrease in statistical discrimination as the profound changes in gender roles that have already occurred continue to percolate through the labor market and the larger society and as additional changes continue to occur, albeit at a slower pace than in the past. And it is likely that even subtle barriers do change as women increasingly enter new areas and achieve success at higher levels. Putting this somewhat differently, while the glass ceiling may not have broken completely, it is showing a lot of cracks and is likely to show more and more cracks as time goes on.

Taking all these factors into account, our best guess is that we are going to have further changes in the direction of convergence, but most probably at a slower pace. Our own view is that one development that is extremely unlikely is that we will see a reversal of the gains in relative wages and labor force participation women have experienced over the past 25 to 30 years. We do not expect a substantial widening of the male/female pay gap or labor force participation gap to occur. On the other hand, while precisely how much narrowing we will see in the future is an open question, the gender pay gap seems unlikely to vanish in the near term.

For one thing, women continue to confront discrimination in the labor market, and, although its extent seems to be decreasing, it seems unlikely to be completely eliminated soon. In addition, at least some of the remaining pay gap is surely tied to the gender division of labor in the home, both directly through its effect on women's labor force attachment and indirectly through its impact on the strength of statistical discrimination against women. Women still retain primary responsibility for housework and child care in most American families. However, this pattern has been changing as families respond to rising labor market opportunities for women that increase the opportunity cost of such arrangements. Further, policies that facilitate the integration of work and family responsibilities, both voluntary and government mandated, have become increasingly prevalent in recent years. Employers are likely to continue to expand such policies as they respond to the shifting composition of the work force and a desire to retain employees in whom they have made substantial investments. In the longer run, the increasing availability of such policies will make it easier for women to combine work and family, and also for men to take on a greater share of household tasks.

Finally, while our principal concern has been with the pay of women relative to men, trends in inequality among women show a deterioration in the relative economic status of less educated

Table 27.2 Mean Earnings of Education Groups Relative to High School Graduates, 1974 and 2003 (%)

Education	1974		2003	
	Men	**Women**	**Men**	**Women**
High school:				
1–3 years	88.9	85.3	75.9	76.6
4 years	100.0	100.0	100.0	100.0
College:				
1–3 years	113.6	112.6	122.8	119.5
4 or more years	155.0	147.2	211.3	190.4

Notes: Data refer to year-round, full-time workers 18 years of age and older. In 2003, median income for 1–3 years of college is computed as a weighted average of the medians for "some college, no degree" and "associate degree."

Sources: 2003: PINC04 Tables of the U.S. Census Bureau Current Population Survey, 2004 Annual Social and Economic Supplement, from http://ferrets. census.gov/macro/032004/perinc/ new04_000.htm; 1974: U.S. Census Bureau Historical Income Tables—People, Table P-35, from www.census.gov/hhes/ income/histinc/p35.htm.

women that is strikingly parallel to similar trends in the labor market for men (see Table 27.2). These developments for less educated women serve to underscore the widening gap between more and less skilled Americans of both sexes, as well as to emphasize its broad dimensions.

Notes

1. Goldin (1990) and Table 27.1 below. Goldin's work indicates that there were earlier periods of substantial narrowing of the gender pay gap (see pp. 58–63). She presents economy-wide data, available only since 1890, that show a rise in the ratio of female to male earnings from 46% in 1890 to 56% in 1930. Goldin attributes these gains to an increase in the returns to schooling, an increase in the labor market experience of women, and a decrease in the labor market returns to physical strength. She also provides evidence of an increase in the relative pay of women in the manufacturing sector from 1815 to the turn of the 20th century.

2. Between 1980 and 1990, the average annual increase in the ratio was 1.14 percentage points for annual earnings and .74 percentage points for weekly earnings, while, between 1990 and 2000, it was only .16 percentage points for annual earnings

and .42 percentage points for weekly earnings. Relative earnings growth in the early 2000s was more robust: between 2000 and 2003, the average annual increase in the ratio was .75 percentage points for annual earnings and 1.14 percentage points for weekly earnings.

3. One short-term factor could be the recession of 2001 and the relatively high unemployment rates that lingered in its aftermath. The demand for male workers tends to be more cyclically sensitive than that for female workers due to their greater concentration in blue-collar jobs and durable manufacturing industries.

4. For a summary of the trends in female labor force participation, see Blau, Ferber and Winkler (2006), Ch. 4.

5. A number of studies have found that additional hours spent in housework by workers are associated with lower wages, all else equal (e.g., Hersch & Stratton 1997), although, using self-reports of effort levels, Bielby and Bielby (1988) do not find that women put in less effort.

6. While firms may perceive that women are more likely to quit than men, the preponderance of the economic evidence on this question finds that, controlling for qualifications and pay, women are no more likely to quit their jobs than men (Viscusi 1980; Blau & Kahn 1981; Ransom & Oaxaca 2005).

7. The notion of socially appropriate roles may also be a factor in racial discrimination, as when

blacks have little difficulty in gaining access to menial jobs but encounter discrimination in obtaining higher-level positions.

8. If, as is likely, one is unable to completely control for nonwage job characteristics such as fringe benefits, safety, or job security, then the residual may again not give an accurate estimate of the extent of discrimination against women. We cannot say a priori what the effect of such omissions is. On the one hand, to the extent that men are likely to work in less safe or less secure jobs than women, such analyses may overestimate discrimination. On the other hand, to the extent that men have higher fringe benefit levels, an analysis of wage residuals will understate discrimination. To some degree, these nonwage characteristics can be accounted for by controlling for industry and occupation, although as mentioned, these controls may also reflect exclusionary hiring practices.

9. In addition to gender differences in qualifications and the extent of discrimination, the gender earnings differential may also be affected by, the self-selection of women and men into full-time employment, and, more generally, into the labor force. In other words, those choosing to participate—or to work full-time—may differ from those outside the labor force or part-time workers in terms of both their measured and unmeasured characteristics. One possibility, for example, is that labor force participants are a positively selected group of those who have received higher wage offers. Similarly, full-time workers may be more highly qualified and more committed to market work. We in fact find that, at a point in time, the gender pay gap is smaller if only full-time workers are considered than if part-timers and non participants are included; we examine the impact of changes in female and male selection into the labor force for trends in the gender pay gap (see below). Other research that has examined the earnings differential for white and black women has found that, if self-selection is not accounted for, the race differential is underestimated; see Neal (2004).

10. The study controls for 19 occupations and 25 industries.

11. For example only 19% of married women with children less than six years old worked outside the home in 1960, compared to 61% in 1999.

12. This quotation is from the Textbook Site for *Principles of Microeconomics*, 3rd ed., *Additional Topics*, "Using Economics to Explain Gender Pay Gaps," at http://college.hmco.com/economics/taylor/econ/3e/micro/students/add_topics/ch02_genderpay.html, accessed June 28, 2002. The summary is based on materials presented in West's Federal Supplement (1993).

13. Bayard, Hellerstein, Neumark, and Troske (1999) report larger within firm pay differences than the other studies, however, the occupational categories employed in their work are wider than those used in the other studies.

14. See, for example Sorensen (1990) Kilbourne, England, Farkas, Beron, and Weir (1994), and Macpherson and Hirsch (1995).

15. An excellent review and assessment of this literature is provided in Katz and Autor (1999).

16. See also O'Neill and Polachek (1993); Welch (2000); Fortin and Lemieux (2000); and Mulligan and Rubinstein (2005).

17. Blau and Kahn (2006); see also Mulligan and Rubinstein (2005).

18. See also Blau and Kahn (2000) and references cited above in our discussion of the 1980s.

19. See also, Mulligan and Rubinstein (2005), who give a larger role to selection—shifts in labor force composition due to labor force entry—in explaining the trends.

References

Aigner, D., & Cain, G. (1977). Statistical theories of discrimination in labor markets. *Industrial and Labor Relations Review*, 30, 175–187.

Autor, D.H., Katz, L.F., & Krueger, A.B. (1998). Computing inequality: Have computers changed the labor market? *Quarterly Journal of Economics*, 113, 1169–1214.

Bayard, K., Hellerstein, J., Neumark, D., & Troske, K. (1999). New evidence on sex segregation and sex difference in wages from matched employee-employer data. NBER Working Paper No. 7003, March.

Becker, G.S. *The economics of discrimination,* 2nd ed. Chicago: University of Chicago Press, 1971; 1st ed.

Becker, G.S. (1985). Human capital, effort, and the sexual division of labor. *Journal of Labor Economics*, 3, S33–S58.

Bergmann, B. (1974). Occupational segregation, wages, and profits when employers discriminate by race or sex. *Eastern Economic Journal*, 1, 1–2, 103–110.

Berman, E., Bound, J. & Griliches, Z. (1994). Changes in the demand of skilled labor within U.S. manufacturing industries: Evidence from the annual survey of manufacturing. *Quarterly Journal of Economics*, 109, 367–397.

Bielby, D.D., & Bielby, W.T (1988). She works hard for the money: Household responsibilities and the allocation of work effort. *American Journal of Sociology*, 93, 1031–1059.

Black, S.E., & Brainerd, E. (2004). The impact of globalization on gender discrimination. *Industrial & Labor Relation Review*, 57, 540–559.

Black, S.E., & Strahan, P.E. (2001). The division of spoils: Rent-sharing and discrimination in a regulated industry. *American Economic Review*, 91, 814–831.

Blau, F.D. (1977). *Equal Pay in the office.* Lexington, MA: Lexington Books.

Blau, F.D., Ferber, M.A., & Winkler, A.E. (2006). *The economics of women, men, and work*, 5th ed. Upper Saddle River, NJ: Prentice-Hall.

Blau, F.D., & Kahn, L.M. (1981). Race and sex differences in quits by young workers. *Industrial & Labor Relations Review*, 34, 563–577.

Blau, F.D., & Kahn, L.M. (1996). Wage structure and gender earnings differentials: An international comparison. *Economica*, 63, S29–S62.

Blau, F.D., & Kahn, L.M. (1997). Swimming upstream: Trends in the gender wage differential in the 1980s. *Journal of Labor Economics*, 15, 1–42.

Blau, F.D., & Kahn, L.M. (2000). Gender differences in pay. *Journal of Economic Perspectives*, 14, 75–99.

Blau, F.D., & Kahn, L.M. (2006). The US gender pay gap in the 1990s: Slowing convergence. *Industrial & Labor Relations Review*, 60, 45–66.

Brown, C., & Corcoran, M. (1997). Sex-based differences in school content and the male/female wage gap. *Journal of Labor Economics*, 15, 431–65.

Bureau of National Affairs (BNA). (1990). *Daily Labor Report*, no. 235, December 6, pp. A11–A13 and F1–F10.

Federal Human Resources Week (FEDHR). (2000, April 5). Government to pay $508 million for sex discrimination at U.S. Information Agency. Vol.6, p. 47.

Fortin, N.M., & Lemieux, T. (2000). Are women's wage gains men's losses? A distributional test. *American Economic Review*, 90, 456–460.

Goldin, C. (1990). *Understanding the gender gap.* New York: Oxford University Press.

Goldin, C., & Rouse, C. (2000). Orchestrating impartiality: The impact of 'blind' auditions on female musicians. *American Economic Review*, 90, 715–741.

Groshen, E.L. (1991). The structure of the female/male wage differential: Is it who you are, what you do, or where you work? *Journal of Human Resources*, 26, 457–472.

Hellerstein, J.K., Neumark, D., & Troske, K. (2002). Market forces and sex discrimination. *Journal of Human Resources*, 37, 353–380.

Hersch, J., & Stratton, L. (1997). Housework, fixed effects and wages of married workers. *Journal of Human Resources*, 32, 285–307.

Juhn, C. (1992). Decline of male labor market participation: The role of declining market opportunities. *Quarterly Journal of Economics*, 107, 79–121.

Juhn, C., Murphy, K.M., & Pierce, B. (1991). Accounting for the slowdown in black-white wage convergence. In M. Kosters (Ed.), Workers and their wages (pp. 107–143). Washington, D.C.: AEI Press.

Katz, L.F., & Autor, D.H (1999). Changes in the wage structure and earnings inequality. In C.O. Ashenfelter & D. Card (Eds.), *Handbook of labor economics* (Vol. 3A, pp. 1463–1555). Amsterdam: Elsevier.

Kilbourne, B.S., England, P., Farkas, G., Beron, K., & Weir, D. (1994). Returns to skill, compensating differentials, and gender bias: Effects of occupational characteristics on the wages of white women and men. *American Journal of Sociology*, 100, 689–719.

King, R. (1997, April 27). Women taking action against many companies. *The Times-Picayune.*

Lewin, T. (1990, May 16). Partnership awarded to woman in sex bias case. *The New York Times*, pp. A1, A12.

Leonard, J. (1989). Women and affirmative action. *Journal of Economic Perspective*, 3, 61–75.

MacPherson, D.A., & Hirsch, B.T. (1995). Wages and gender composition: Why do women's jobs pay less? *Journal of Labor Economics*, 13, 426–471.

Meyer, B.D., & Rosenbaum, D.T. (2001). Welfare, the earned income tax credit, and the labor supply of single mothers. *Quarterly Journal of Economics*, 116, 1063–1114.

Mincer, J., & Polachek, S. (1974). Family investments in human capital: Earnings of women. *Journal of Political Economy*, 82, S76–S108.

Mulligan, C.B., & Rubinstein, Y. (2005). Selection, investment and women's relative wages since 1975. National Bureau of Economic Research Working Paper 11159, February.

Neal, D. (2004). The measured black-white wage gap among women is too small. *Journal of political Economy*, 112, S1–S28.

Neumark, D.M. (1996). Sex discrimination in restaurant hiring: An audit study. *Quarterly Journal of Economics*, 111, 915–941.

O'Neill, J., & Polachek, S. (1993). Why the gender gap in wages narrowed in the 1980s. *Journal of Labor*

Economics, 11(1), 205–228. Working Paper, Stanford University December.

Petersen, T., & Morgan, L.A. (1995). Separate and unequal: Occupation-establishment sex segregation and the gender wage gap. *American Journal of Sociology* 10, 329–361.

Ransom, M., & Oaxaca, R.L. (2005). Intrafirm mobility and sex differences in pay. *Industrial and Labor Relations Review*, 58, 219–237.

Smith, R.E. (1979). The movement of women into the labor force. In R. E. Smith (Ed.), *The subtle revolution. Women at work* (pp. 1–29). Washington, D.C.: Urban Institute.

Sorensen, E. (1990). The crowding hypothesis and comparable worth issue. *Journal of Human Resources,* 25, 55–89.

Taylor, J.B. (2001). *Principles of economics*, 3rd ed. Boston, MA: Houghton Mifflin.

Viscusi, W.K. (1980). Sex differences in worker quitting. *The Review of Economics and Statistics*, 62, 388–398.

Waldfogel, J. (1998). The family gap for young women in the United States and Britain: Can maternity leave make a difference? *Journal of Labor Economics*, 16, 505–545.

Welch, F. (2000). Growth in women's relative wages and in inequality among men: One phenomenon or two? *American Economic Review*, 90, 444–449.

West's Federal Supplement, (1993). Vol. 803, pp. 259–337. St. Paul, MN: West Publishing Company.

Weinberg, B. (2000). Computer use and the demand for female workers. *Industrial and Labor Relations Review*, 53, 290–308.

Weinberger C.J. (1998). Race and gender wage gaps in the market for recent college graduates. *Industrial Relations*, 37, 67–84.

Wood, R.G., Corcoran, M.E., & Courant, P. (1993). Pay differences among the highly paid: The male-female earnings gap in lawyers' salaries. *Journal of Labor Economics*, 11, 417–441.

IV

Party

INTRODUCTION

The next section focuses on Weber's third category of "party," or those whose "action is oriented toward the acquisition of social power, that is to say, toward influencing social action no matter what its content may be." There is a rich tradition of scholarship related to such issues in other subfields such as political sociology and the sociology of social movements and collective behavior (not to mention other disciplines in general, such as political science) which overlaps a good deal with research in stratification.

In his essay included here (excerpts from "The Structure of Power in American Society") C. Wright Mills introduces the argument from his famous book, *The Power Elite*. He asserts that an American "triangle of power" is composed of the most influential players in economic, political, and military institutions, whose overlapping agendas are formed through common backgrounds, institutional connections, and overt cooperation.

Given the burden of being subject to someone else's power, one question scholars have wrestled with is why subjugated people do not more often rebel or protest. In an excerpt from *Power and Powerlessness: Quiescence and Rebellion in an Appalachian Valley*, John Gaventa contends that part of the answer involves ideology. That is, the most effective way to control marginalized people is to rationalize the status quo so they cannot even imagine alternative arrangements. Those in dominant positions, Gaventa shows, have a stake in promoting ideas that justify current arrangements.

Protecting current power relations may also involve allowing some access to special resources and opportunities to previously excluded groups. In a follow up to Mills's analysis, G. William Domhoff suggests in *Who Rules America?* that those in the top positions of corporations and government are especially influential. More recently Richard L. Zweigenhaft and G. William Domhoff have documented an important shift among members of the power elite from being almost exclusively white, Christian men to a more diverse group that includes minorities and women. In the excerpt included here from *Diversity in the Power Elite*, however, they suggest that an affluent background, significant educational achievement, and light skin persist as prerequisites for access into the highest levels of power.

Pursuing this line of research in *Who's Running America?* Thomas R. Dye focuses on more specific individuals and institutions during recent years, including specific parts of the government. In the excerpt included here, Dye shows how the institutional concentration of power translates into personal influence in the lives of Ted Kennedy, Hillary Clinton, Clarence Thomas, Sandra Day O'Connor, Colin Powell, and others.

Excerpts from "The Structure of Power in American Society"

C. WRIGHT MILLS

I

Power has to do with whatever decisions men make about the arrangements under which they live, and about the events which make up the history of their times. Events that are beyond human decision do happen; social arrangements do change without benefit of explicit decision. But in so far as such decisions are made, the problem of who is involved in making them is the basic problem of power. In so far as they could be made but are not, the problem becomes who fails to make them?

We cannot today merely assume that in the last resort men must always be governed by their own consent. For among the means of power which now prevail is the power to manage and to manipulate the consent of men. That we do not know the limits of such power, and that we hope it does have limits, does not remove the fact that much power today is successfully employed without the sanction of the reason or the conscience of the obedient.

Surely nowadays we need not argue that, in the last resort, coercion is the "final" form of power. But then, we are by no means constantly at the last resort. Authority (power that is justified by the beliefs of the voluntarily obedient) and manipulation (power that is wielded unbeknown to the powerless)—must also be considered, along with coercion. In fact, the three types must be sorted out whenever we think about power.

In the modern world, we must bear in mind, power is often not so authoritative as it seemed to be in the medieval epoch: ideas which justify rulers no longer seem so necessary to their exercise of power. At least for many of the great decisions of our time—especially those of an international sort—mass "persuasion" has not been "necessary"; the fact is simply accomplished. Furthermore, such ideas as are available to the powerful are often neither taken up nor used by them. Such ideologies usually arise as a response to an effective debunking of power; in the United States such opposition has not been effective enough recently to create the felt need for new ideologies of rule.

There has, in fact, come about a situation in which many who have lost faith in prevailing loyalties have not acquired new ones, and so pay no attention to politics of any kind. They are not radical, not liberal, not conservative, not reactionary. They are inactionary. They are out of it. If we accept the Greek's definition of the idiot as an altogether private man, then we must conclude that many American citizens are now idiots. And I should not be surprised, although I do not know, if there were not some such idiots even in Germany. This—and I use the word with care—this spiritual condition seems to me the key to many modern troubles of political intellectuals, as well as the key to much political bewilderment in modern society. Intellectual "conviction" and moral "belief" are not necessary, in either the rulers or the ruled, for a ruling power to persist and even to flourish. So far as the role of ideologies is concerned, their frequent absences and the prevalence of mass indifference are surely two of the major political facts about the western societies today.

How large a role any explicit decisions do play in the making of history is itself an historical problem. For how large that role may be depends very much upon the means of power that are available at any given time in any given society. In some societies, the innumerable actions of innumerable men modify their milieux, and so gradually modify the structure itself. These modifications—the course of history—go on behind the backs of men. History is drift, although in total "men make it." Thus, innumerable entrepreneurs and innumerable consumers by ten-thousand decisions per minute may shape and re-shape the free-market economy. Perhaps this was the chief kind of limitation Marx had in mind when he wrote, in *The 18th Brumaire:* that "Men make their own history, but they do not make it just as they please; they do not make it under circumstances chosen by themselves. . . ."

But in other societies—certainly in the United States and in the Soviet Union today—a few men may be so placed within the structure that by their decisions they modify the milieux of many other men, and in fact nowadays the structural conditions under which most men live. Such elites of power also make history under circumstances not chosen altogether by themselves, yet compared with other men, and compared with other periods of world history, these circumstances do indeed seem less limiting.

I should contend that "men are free to make history," but that some men are indeed much freer than others. For such freedom requires access to the means of decision and of power by which history can now be made. It has not always been so made; but in the later phases of the modern epoch it is. It is with reference to this epoch that I am contending that if men do not make history, they tend increasingly to become the utensils of history-makers as well as the mere objects of indeed seem less limiting.

The history of modern society may readily be understood as the story of the enlargement and the centralization of the means of power—in economic, in political, and in military institutions. The rise of industrial society has involved these developments in the means of economic production. The rise of the nation-state has involved similar developments in the means of violence and in those of political administration.

In the western societies, such transformations have generally occurred gradually, and many cultural traditions have restrained and shaped them. In most of the Soviet societies, they are happening very rapidly indeed and without the great discourse of western civilization, without the Renaissance and without the Reformation, which so greatly strengthened and gave political focus to the idea of freedom. In those societies, the enlargement and the coordination of all the means of power has occurred more brutally, and from the beginning under tightly centralized authority. But in both types, the means of power have now become international in scope and similar in form. To be sure, each of them has its own ups and downs; neither is as yet absolute; how they are run differs quite sharply.

Yet so great is the reach of the means of violence, and so great the economy required to produce and support them, that we have in the immediate past witnessed the consolidation of these two world centres, either of which dwarfs the power of Ancient Rome. As we pay attention to the awesome means of power now available to quite small groups of men we come to realize that Caesar could do less with Rome than Napoleon with France; Napoleon less with France than Lenin with Russia. But what was Caesar's power at its height compared with the power of the changing inner circles of Soviet Russia and the temporary administrations of the United States? We come to realize—indeed they continually remind us—how a few men have access to the means by which in a few days continents can be turned into thermonuclear wastelands. That the facilities of power are so enormously enlarged and so decisively centralized surely means that the powers of quite small groups of men, which we may call elites, are now of literally inhuman consequence.

My concern here is not with the international scene but with the United States in the middle of the twentieth century. I must emphasize "in the middle of the twentieth century" because in our attempt to understand any society we come upon images which have been drawn from its past and which often confuse our attempt to confront its present reality. That is one minor reason why history is the shank of any social science: we must study it if only to rid ourselves of it. In the United States, there are indeed many such images and usually they have to do with the first half of the nineteenth century. At that time the economic facilities of the United States were very widely dispersed and subject to little or to no central authority.

The state watched in the night but was without decisive voice in the day.

One man meant one rifle and the militia were without centralized orders.

Any American as old-fashioned as I can only agree with R. H. Tawney that "Whatever the future may contain, the past has shown no more excellent social order than that in which the mass of the people were the masters of the holdings which they ploughed and the tools with which they worked, and could boast . . . 'It is a quietness to a man's mind to live upon his own and to know his heir certain.' "

But then we must immediately add: all that is of the past and of little relevance to our understanding of the United States today. Within this society three broad levels of power may now be distinguished. I shall begin at the top and move downward.

II

The power to make decisions of national and international consequence is now so clearly seated in political, military, and economic institutions that other areas of society seem off to the side and, on occasion, readily subordinated to these. The scattered institutions of religion, education and family are increasingly shaped by the big three, in which history-making decisions now regularly occur. Behind this fact there is all the push and drive of a fabulous technology; for these three institutional orders have incorporated this technology and now guide it, even as it shapes and paces their development.

As each has assumed its modern shape, its effects upon the other two have become greater, and the traffic between the three has increased. There is no longer, on the one hand, an economy, and, on the other, a political order, containing a military establishment unimportant to politics and to money-making. There is a political economy numerously linked with military order and decision. This triangle of power is now a structural fact, and it is the key to any understanding of the higher circles in America today.

For as each of these domains has coincided with the others, as decisions in each have become broader, the leading men of each—the high military, the corporation executives, the political directorate—have tended to come together to form the power elite of America.

The political order, once composed of several dozen states with a weak federal-centre, has become an executive apparatus which has taken up into itself many powers previously scattered, legislative as well as administrative, and which now reaches into all parts of the social structure. The long-time tendency of business and government to become more closely connected has since World War II reached a new point of explicitness. Neither can now be seen clearly as a distinct world. The growth of executive government does not mean merely the "enlargement of government" as some kind of autonomous bureaucracy: under American conditions, it has meant the ascendency of the corporation man into political eminence. Already during the New Deal, such men had joined the political directorate; as of

World War II they came to dominate it. Long involved with government, now they have moved into quite full direction of the economy of the war effort and of the post-war era.

The economy, once a great scatter of small productive units in somewhat automatic balance, has become internally dominated by a few hundred corporations, administratively and politically interrelated, which together hold the keys to economic decision. This economy is at once a permanent-war economy and a private-corporation economy. The most important relations of the corporation to the state now rest on the coincidence between military and corporate interests, as defined by the military and the corporate rich, and accepted by politicians and public. Within the elite as a whole, this coincidence of military domain and corporate realm strengthens both of them and further subordinates the merely political man. Not the party politician, but the corporation executive, is now more likely to sit with the military to answer the question: what is to be done?

The military order, once a slim establishment in a context of civilian distrust, has become the largest and most expensive feature of government; behind smiling public relations, it has all the grim and clumsy efficiency of a great and sprawling bureaucracy. The high military have gained decisive political and economic relevance. The seemingly permanent military threat places a premium upon them and virtually all political and economic actions are now judged in terms of military definitions of reality: the higher military have ascended to a firm position within the power elite of our time.

In part at least this is a result of an historical fact, pivotal for the years since 1939: the attention of the elite has shifted from domestic problems—centered in the 'thirties around slump—to international problems—centered in the 'forties and 'fifties around war. By long historical usage, the government of the United States has been shaped by domestic clash and balance; it does not have suitable agencies and traditions for the democratic handling of international affairs. In considerable part, it is in this vacuum that the power elite has grown.

(i) To understand the unity of this power elite, we must pay attention to the psychology of its several members in their respective milieux. In so far as the power elite is composed of men of similar origin and education, of similar career and style of life, their unity may be said to rest upon the fact that they are of similar social type, and to lead to the fact of their easy intermingling. This kind of unity reaches its frothier apex in the sharing of that prestige which is to be had in the world of the celebrity. It achieves a more solid culmination in the fact of the interchangeability of positions between the three dominant institutional orders. It is revealed by considerable traffic of personnel within and between these three, as well as by the rise of specialized go-betweens as in the new style high-level lobbying.

(ii) Behind such psychological and social unity are the structure and the mechanics of those institutional hierarchies over which the political directorate, the corporate rich, and the high military now preside. How each of these hierarchies is shaped and what relations it has with the others determine in large part the relations of their rulers. Were these hierarchies scattered and disjointed, then their respective elites might tend to be scattered and disjointed; but if they have many interconnections and points of coinciding interest, then their elites tend to form a coherent kind of grouping. The unity of the elite is not a simple reflection of the unity of institutions, but men and institutions are always related; that is why we must understand the elite today in connection with such institutional trends as the development of a permanent-war establishment, alongside a privately incorporated economy, inside a virtual political vacuum. For the men at the top have been selected and formed by such institutional trends.

(iii) Their unity, however, does not rest solely upon psychological similarity and social intermingling, nor entirely upon the structural blending of commanding positions and common interests. At times it is the unity of a more explicit coordination.

To say that these higher circles are increasingly coordinated, that this is *one* basis of their unity, and that at times—as during open war—such coordination is quite wilful, is not to say that the coordination is total or continuous, or even that it is very surefooted. Much less is it to say that the power elite has emerged as the realization of a plot. Its rise cannot be adequately explained in any psychological terms.

Yet we must remember that institutional trends may be defined as opportunities by those who occupy the command posts. Once such opportunities are recognized, men may avail themselves of them. Certain types of men from each of these three areas, more far-sighted than others, have actively promoted the liaison even before it took its truly modern shape. Now more have come to see that their several interests can more easily be realized if they work together, in informal as well as in formal ways, and accordingly they have done so.

The idea of the power elite is of course an interpretation. It rests upon and it enables us to make sense of major institutional trends, the social similarities and psychological affinities of the men at the top. But the idea is also based upon what has been happening on the middle and lower levels of power, to which I now turn.

III

There are of course other interpretations of the American system of power. The most usual is that it is a moving balance of many competing interests. The image of balance, at least in America, is derived from the idea of the economic market: in the nineteenth century, the balance was thought to occur between a great scatter of individuals and enterprises; in the twentieth century, it is thought to occur between great interest blocs. In both views, the politician is the key man of power because he is the broker of many conflicting powers.

I believe that the balance and the compromise in American society—the "countervailing powers" and the "veto groups," of parties and associations, of strata and unions—must now be seen as having mainly to do with the middle levels of power. It is these middle levels that the political journalist and the scholar of politics are most likely to understand and to write about—if only because, being mainly middle class themselves, they are closer to them. Moreover these levels provide the noisy content of most "political" news and gossip; the images of these levels are more or less in accord with the folklore of how democracy works; and, if the master-image of balance is

accepted, many intellectuals, especially in their current patrioteering, are readily able to satisfy such political optimism as they wish to feel. Accordingly, liberal interpretations of what is happening in the United States are now virtually the only interpretations that are widely distributed.

But to believe that the power system reflects a balancing society is, I think, to confuse the present era with earlier times, and to confuse its top and bottom with its middle levels.

By the top levels, as distinguished from the middle, I intend to refer, first of all, to the scope of the decisions that are made. At the top today, these decisions have to do with all the issues of war and peace. They have also to do with slump and poverty which are now so very much problems of international scope. I intend also to refer to whether or not the groups that struggle politically have a chance to gain the positions from which such top decisions are made, and indeed whether their members do usually hope for such top national command. Most of the competing interests which make up the clang and clash of American politics are strictly concerned with their slice of the existing pie. Labour unions, for example, certainly have no policies of an international sort other than those which given unions adopt for the strict economic protection of their members. Neither do farm organizations. The actions of such middle-level powers may indeed have consequence for top-level policy; certainly at times they hamper these policies. But they are not truly concerned with them, which means of course that their influence tends to be quite irresponsible.

The facts of the middle levels may in part be understood in terms of the rise of the power elite. The expanded and centralized and interlocked hierarchies over which the power elite preside have encroached upon the old balance and relegated it to the middle level. But there are also independent developments of the middle levels. These, it seems to me, are better understood as an affair of intrenched and provincial demands than as a centre of national decision. As such, the middle level often seems much more of a stalemate than a moving balance.

(i) The middle level of politics is not a forum in which there are debated the big decisions of national and international life. Such debate is not carried on by nationally responsible parties representing and clarifying alternative policies. There are no such parties in the United States. More and more, fundamental issues never come to any point or decision before the Congress, much less before the electorate in party campaigns. In the case of Formosa, in the spring of 1955, the Congress abdicated all debate concerning events and decisions which surely bordered on war. The same is largely true of the 1957 crisis in the Middle East. Such decisions now regularly by-pass the Congress, and are never clearly focused issues for public decision.

The American political campaign distracts attention from national and international issues, but that is not to say that there are no issues in these campaigns. In each district and state, issues are set up and watched by organized interests of sovereign local importance. The professional politician is of course a party politician, and the two parties are semi-feudal organizations: they trade patronage and other favours for votes and for protection. The differences between them, so far as national issues are concerned, are very narrow and very mixed up. Often each seems to be forty-eight parties, one to each state; and accordingly, the politician as campaigner and as Congressman is not concerned with national party lines, if any are discernible. Often he is not subject to any effective national party discipline. He speaks for the interests of his own constituency, and he is concerned with national issues only in so far as they affect the interests effectively organized there, and hence his chances of re-election. That is why, when he does speak of national matters, the result is so often such an empty rhetoric. Seated in his sovereign locality, the politician is not at the national summit. He is on and of the middle levels of power.

(ii) Politics is not an arena in which free and independent organizations truly connect the lower and middle levels of society with the top levels of decision. Such organizations are not an effective and major part of American life today. As more people are drawn into the political arena, their associations become mass in scale, and the power of the individual becomes dependent upon them; to the extent that they are effective, they have become

larger, and to that extent they have become less accessible to the influence of the individual. This is a central fact about associations in any mass society: it is of most consequence for political parties and for trade unions.

In the 'thirties, it often seemed that labour would become an insurgent power independent of corporation and state. Organized labour was then emerging for the first time on an American scale, and the only political sense of direction it needed was the slogan, "organize the unorganized." Now without the mandate of the slump, labour remains without political direction. Instead of economic and political struggles it has become deeply entangled in administrative routines with both corporation and state. One of its major functions, as a vested interest of the new society, is the regulation of such irregular tendencies as may occur among the rank and file.

There is nothing, it seems to me, in the makeup of the current labour leadership to allow us to expect that it can or that it will lead, rather than merely react. In so far as it fights at all it fights over a share of the goods of a single way of life and not over that way of life itself. The typical labour leader in the U.S.A. today is better understood as an adaptive creature of the main business drift than as an independent actor in a truly national context.

(iii) The idea that this society is a balance of powers requires us to assume that the units in balance are of more or less equal power and that they are truly independent of one another. These assumptions have rested, it seems clear, upon the historical importance of a large and independent middle class. In the latter nineteenth century and during the Progressive Era, such a class of farmers and small businessmen fought politically—and lost—their last struggle for a paramount role in national decision. Even then, their aspirations seemed bound to their own imagined past.

This old, independent middle class has of course declined. On the most generous count, it is now 40 per cent of the total middle class (at most 20 per cent of the total labour force). Moreover, it has become politically as well as economically dependent upon the state, most notably in the case of the subsidized farmer.

The *new* middle class of white-collar employees is certainly not the political pivot of any balancing society. It is in no way politically unified. Its unions, such as they are, often serve merely to incorporate it as hanger-on of the labour interest. For a considerable period, the old middle class *was* an independent base of power; the new middle class cannot be. Political freedom and economic security *were* anchored in small and independent properties; they are not anchored in the worlds of the white-collar job. Scattered property holders were economically united by more or less free markets; the jobs of the new middle class are integrated by corporate authority. Economically, the white-collar classes are in the same condition as wage workers; politically, they are in a worse condition, for they are not organized. They are no vanguard of historic change; they are at best a rearguard of the welfare state.

The agrarian revolt of the 'nineties, the small-business revolt that has been more or less continuous since the 'eighties, the labour revolt of the 'thirties—each of these has failed as an independent movement which could countervail against the powers that be; they have failed as politically autonomous third parties. But they have succeeded, in varying degree, as interests vested in the expanded corporation and state; they have succeeded as parochial interests seated in particular districts, in local divisions of the two parties, and in the Congress. What they would become, in short, are well-established features of the *middle* levels of balancing powers on which we may now observe all those strata and interests which in the course of American history have been defeated in their bids for top power or which have never made such bids.

Fifty years ago many observers thought of the American state as a mask behind which an invisible government operated. But nowadays, much of what was called the old lobby, visible or invisible, is part of the quite visible government. The "governmentalization of the lobby" has proceeded in both the legislative and the executive domain, as well as between them. The executive bureaucracy becomes not only the centre of decision but also the arena within which major conflicts of power are resolved or denied resolution. "Administration" replaces electoral politics; the manoeuvring of cliques (which include leading Senators as well as civil servants) replaces the open clash of parties.

The shift of corporation men into the political directorate has accelerated the decline of the politicians in the Congress to the middle levels of power; the formation of the power elite rests in part upon this relegation. It rests also upon the semi-organized stalemate of the interests of sovereign localities, into which the legislative function has so largely fallen; upon the virtually complete absence of a civil service that is a politically neutral but politically relevant, depository of brain-power and executive skill; and it rests upon the increased official secrecy behind which great decisions are made without benefit of public or even of Congressional debate.

IV

There is one last belief upon which liberal observers everywhere base their interpretations and rest their hopes. That is the idea of the public and the associated idea of public opinion. Conservative thinkers, since the French Revolution, have of course viewed with alarm the rise of the public, which they have usually called the masses, or something to that effect. "The populace is sovereign," wrote Gustave Le Bon, "and the tide of barbarism mounts." But surely those who have supposed the masses to be well on their way to triumph are mistaken. In our time, the influence of publics or of masses within political life is in fact decreasing, and such influence as on occasion they do have tends, to an unknown but increasing degree, to be guided by the means of mass communication.

In a society of publics, discussion is the ascendant means of communication, and the mass media, if they exist, simply enlarge and animate this discussion, linking one face-to-face public with the discussions of another. In a mass society, the dominant type of communication is the formal media, and publics become mere markets for these media: the "public" of a radio programme consists of all those exposed to it. When we try to look upon the United States today as a society of publics, we realize that it has moved a considerable distance along the road to the mass society.

In official circles, the very term, "the publics" has come to have a phantom meaning, which dramatically reveals its eclipse. The deciding elite can identify some of those who clamour publicly as "Labour," others as "Business," still others as "Farmer." But these are not the public. "The public" consists of the unidentified and the non-partisan in a world of defined and partisan interests. In this faint echo of the classic notion, the public is composed of these remnants of the old and new middle classes whose interests are not explicitly defined, organized, or clamorous. In a curious adaptation, "the public" often becomes, in administrative fact, "the disengaged expert" who, although ever so well informed, has never taken a clear-cut and public stand on controversial issues. He is the "public" member of the board, the commission, the committee. What "the public" stands for, accordingly is often a vagueness of policy (called "open-mindedness"), a lack of involvement in public affairs (known as "reasonableness"), and a professional disinterest (known as "tolerance").

All this is indeed far removed from the eighteenth-century idea of the public of public opinion. That idea parallels the economic idea of the magical market. Here is the market composed of freely competing entrepreneurs; there is the public composed of circles of people in discussion. As price is the result of anonymous, equally weighted, bargaining individuals, so public opinion is the result of each man's having thought things out for himself and then contributing his voice to the great chorus. To be sure, some may have more influence on the state of opinion than others, but no one group monopolizes the discussion, or by itself determines the opinions that prevail.

In this classic image, the people are presented with problems. They discuss them. They formulate viewpoints. These viewpoints are organized, and they compete. One viewpoint "wins out." Then the people act on this view, or their representatives are instructed to act it out, and this they promptly do.

Such are the images of democracy which are still used as working justifications of power in America. We must now recognize this description as more a fairy tale than a useful approximation. The issues that now shape man's fate are neither raised nor decided by any public at large. The idea of a society that is at bottom composed of publics is not a matter of fact; it is the proclamation of an ideal, and as well the assertion of a legitimation masquerading as fact.

I cannot here describe the several great forces within American society as well as elsewhere which have been at work in the debilitation of the public. I want only to remind you that publics, like free associations, can be deliberately and suddenly smashed, or they can more slowly wither away. But whether smashed in a week or withered in a generation, the demise of the public must be seen in connection with the rise of centralized organizations, with all their new means of power, including those of the mass media of distraction. These, we now know, often seem to expropriate the rationality and the will of the terrorized or—as the case may be—the voluntarily indifferent society of masses. In the more democratic process of indifference the remnants of such publics as remain may only occasionally be intimidated by fanatics in search of "disloyalty." But regardless of that, they lose their will for decision because they do not possess the instruments for decision; they lose their sense of political belonging because they do not belong; they lose their political will because they see no way to realize it.

The political structure of a modern democratic state requires that such a public as is projected by democratic theorists not only exist but that it be the very forum within which a politics of real issues is enacted.

It requires a civil service that is firmly linked with the world of knowledge and sensibility, and which is composed of skilled men who, in their careers and in their aspirations, are truly independent of any private, which is to say, corporation, interests.

It requires nationally responsible parties which debate openly and clearly the issues which the nation, and indeed the world, now so rigidly confronts.

It requires an intelligentsia, inside as well as outside the universities, who carry on the big discourse of the western world, and whose work is relevant to and influential among parties and movements and publics.

And it certainly requires, as a fact of power, that there be free associations standing between families and smaller communities and publics, on the one hand, and the state, the military, the corporation, on the other. For unless these do exist, there are no vehicles for reasoned opinion, no instruments for the rational exertion of public will.

Such democratic formations are not now ascendant in the power structure of the United States, and accordingly the men of decision are not men selected and formed by careers within such associations and by their performance before such publics. The top of modern American society is increasingly unified, and often seems wilfully coordinated: at the top there has emerged an elite whose power probably exceeds that of any small group of men in world history. The middle levels are often a drifting set of stalemated forces: the middle does not link the bottom with the top. The bottom of this society is politically fragmented, and even as a passive fact, increasingly powerless: at the bottom there is emerging a mass society.

These developments, I believe, can be correctly understood neither in terms of the liberal nor the Marxian interpretation of politics and history. Both these ways of thought arose as guidelines to reflection about a type of society which does not now exist in the United States. We confront there a new kind of social structure, which embodies elements and tendencies of all modern society, but in which they have assumed a more naked and flamboyant prominence.

That does not mean that we must give up the ideals of these classic political expectations. I believe that both have been concerned with the problem of rationality and of freedom: liberalism, with freedom and rationality as supreme facts about the individual; Marxism, as supreme facts about man's role in the political making of history. What I have said here, I suppose, may be taken as an attempt to make evident why the ideas of freedom and of rationality now so often seem so ambiguous in the new society of the United States of America.

Excerpts from *Diversity in the Power Elite*

RICHARD L. ZWEIGENHAFT AND
G. WILLIAM DOMHOFF

The power elite and Congress are more diverse than they were before the civil rights movement and the social movements that followed in its train brought pressure to bear on corporations, politicians, and government. Although the power elite is still composed primarily of Christian, white men, there are now Jews, women, blacks, Latinos, and Asian Americans on the boards of the country's largest corporations; presidential cabinets are far more diverse than was the case fifty years ago; and the highest ranks of the military are no longer filled solely by white men. In the case of elected officials in Congress, the trend toward diversity is even greater for women and the other previously excluded groups that we have studied. At the same time, we have shown that the incorporation of members of the different groups has been uneven.

Here we look at the patterns that emerge from our specific findings to see if they help explain the gradual inclusion of some groups and the continuing exclusion of others. We also discuss the impact of diversity on the power elite and the rest of American society. We argue that most of the effects were unexpected and are ironic. The most important of these ironies relates to the ongoing tension between the American dream of individual advancement and fulfillment ("liberal individualism") and the class structure: we conclude that the racial, ethnic, and gender diversity celebrated by the power elite and the media actually reinforces the unchanging nature of the class structure and increases the tendency to ignore class inequalities.

Why Are Some Included?

The social movements and pressures for greater openness at the higher levels of American society have led to some representation for all previously excluded groups, but some have been more successful than others. Four main factors explain why some people come to be included: higher class origins, elite educations, a lighter skin color, and the ability to make oneself acceptable to established members of the power elite, which we call "identity management."

The Importance of Class

Those who have brought diversity to the power elite have tended to come from business and professional backgrounds, like the white, Christian males C. Wright Mills studied more than fifty years ago. Fully one-third of the women who have become corporate directors are from the upper class, and many others are from the middle and upper-middle classes. Most of the Cuban Americans and Chinese Americans who have risen to the top have come from displaced ruling classes, a far cry from the conventional image of immigrants who start with nothing. The Jews and Japanese Americans in high positions have mostly been the products of two- and three-generational climbs up the social ladder. The first African American members of the corporate elite and the cabinet tended to come from the small black middle class that predated the civil rights movement. Although there is no systematic information on the social backgrounds of gay and lesbian leaders, who are treated in most studies as if they have no class origins, our anecdotal information suggests that many visible activists and professionals come from business and professional families as well.

A high-level social background, of course, makes it easier to acquire the values, attitudes, and styles that are necessary to hire, fire, and manage the work lives of employees with blue, white, and pink collars. This point can be extended to include even those from more modest circumstances, like Lauro Cavazos, whose father was a ranch foreman, or Katherine Ortega, Sue Ling Gin, and David Geffen, whose families owned small businesses, or David Mixner, whose father was in charge of minority farmhands on a farm he did not own. Most of those we studied, in other words, learned firsthand that a few people boss the majority or have independent professions based on academic credentials and that they were expected to be part of this managerial and professional stratum.

When we compare the newly arrived members of the power elite with their counterparts in Congress, however, two further generalizations emerge. First, members of the power elite tend to come from more privileged social backgrounds than elected officials. Second, the elected officials are more likely to be Democrats than Republicans. These two findings suggest that there are class and political dimensions to our findings on the differences between the power elite and Congress that cut across gender and ethnic lines. Now that the power elite is housed almost exclusively in the Republican Party and the liberal-labor coalition has become more important within the Democratic Party, the country's traditional regional, racial, and ethnic politics is being replaced by a more clear-cut class-and-race politics, with both the Republicans and Democrats now able to say that they are diverse in terms of leaders and candidates from all previously excluded groups. (Even the Republican Party can claim gay and lesbian members thanks to the Log Cabin Republicans, although many conservative Republicans would prefer not to.) And as everyone knows, the number of African Americans who are Republicans is very small, but they are important to the success of the party with centrist white voters because they "prove" that the party is trying to be inclusive of everyone.[1]

The Importance of Education

Class by no means explains all of our findings, however. Education also matters a great deal. The members of underrepresented groups who make it to the power elite are typically better educated than the white males who are already a part of it. This was seen with the European American women and African Americans on corporate boards and in presidential cabinets, as well as the successful Asian American immigrants. Education seems to have given them the edge needed to make their way into the power elite. In the case of many of the African Americans, new educational programs in elite private high schools, created in response to the disruptions of the 1960s, were more than an edge. They were essential. In effect, these scholarship programs in part compensated for the wealth they did not have.[2]

Moreover, it is not merely having academic degrees that matters but also where those degrees are from. Again and again, we saw that a significant number were from the same few schools that educate Christian, white, male leaders, such as Harvard, Yale, Princeton, and MIT on the East Coast, the

University of Chicago in the Midwest, and Stanford on the West Coast. Whether it is Bill Clinton or George W. Bush in the White House, Hillary Clinton in the Senate from New York or Joseph Lieberman in the Senate from Connecticut, or Clarence Thomas on the Supreme Court, they all went to Yale in the 1960s.

These elite schools not only confer status on their graduates but also provide contacts with white male elites that are renewed throughout life at alumni gatherings and on other special occasions. School connections, in turn, lead to invitations to attend exclusive social events and join expensive social clubs, which extend the newcomers' social networks even further. With success in business or a profession comes invitations to serve on boards of trustees of elite foundations and universities, and the circle is completed.

In short, they have acquired the full complement of what is now called "social capital," the network of friends and contacts that provides access to jobs, financial capital, and marriage partners of high social standing. The newcomers thereby become part of the ongoing institutional framework that defines and shapes the power elite in the United States, even though only a few of them are likely to reach the very top. The individuals in the power elite may come and go, and they may diversify in gender, race, ethnicity, and sexual orientation, but there is stability and continuity in terms of the types of people who are fed into the set of institutions that define the power elite and dominate the American social structure.

As was true of social class origins, there is a difference in educational attainment between those in the power elite and those in Congress: the men and women elected to Congress are not as likely as those in the power elite to have attended elite colleges and universities or to have earned postgraduate degrees.

The Importance of Color

Just as class alone cannot explain all of our findings, neither can the combination of class and education: color also matters. African Americans and darker-skinned Latinos find it more difficult than others to use their educational credentials and social capital as passports to occupational success. This can be seen poignantly in our skin-color comparisons of successful blacks and Latinos. Even among those who had achieved some level of prominence (measured by inclusion in *Ebony*'s fiftieth anniversary issue or the *Hispanic Business* listing of "Hispanic influentials"), those who had made it into the power elite were lighter skinned than those who had not. On this score, our data simply reinforce earlier work by others. As the Glass Ceiling Commission reported, "Our society has developed an extremely sophisticated, and often denied, acceptability index based on gradations in skin color."[3]

Julia Alvarez, a writer whose novels have captured the difficulties of leaving one's Latin American home and coming, with far fewer material resources, to the United States to start anew, understands well the importance of one's class background in the old country and of light skin in the new country. In an essay about leaving the Dominican Republic and coming to the United States as a young girl, Alvarez acknowledges the advantages her family had over other immigrant families because they were well educated, had access to money, and (as she says, "most especially") were light skinned: "My family had not been among the waves of economic immigrants that left their island in the seventies, a generally darker-skinned, working-class group, who might have been the maids or workers in my mother's family house. We had come in 1960, political refugees, with no money but with "prospects": Papi had a friend who was a doctor at the Waldorf Astoria and who helped him get a job; Mami's family had money in the Chase Manhattan Bank they could lend us. We had changed class in America—from Mami's elite family to middle-class spics—but our background and education and most especially our pale skin had made mobility easier for us here."[4]

Alvarez's perceptive and honest assessment of the advantages she had (so different from the public relations stories put out by many corporate chieftains), coupled with the findings we have described on color discrimination, may help to explain why so few people of color have made it into the power elite. The failure of American society to accept darker-skinned citizens, especially African Americans, is the most difficult issue that needs to be understood by social scientists. We return to this issue in the next section, "Why Are Some Still Excluded?"

Identity Management

Finally, we have seen that the newcomers who join the power elite have found ways to demonstrate their loyalty to those who dominate American institutions—straight, white, Christian males. They know how to act and interact using the manners, style, and conversational repertoire of the already established elite, and they can hold their own in discussing the fine points of literature and the arts; that is, they have the "cultural capital" that comes from high-class origins or an elite education. When William T. Coleman recited great poetry with his fellow law clerk, Boston Brahmin Elliot Richardson, he was not only sharing a mutual love of poetry with a colleague and friend, he was demonstrating his elite educational background. Reading between the lines of traditional stereotypes, we can imagine Jewish and black executives being properly reserved, Asian American executives acting properly assertive, gay executives behaving in traditionally masculine ways, and lesbian executives acting in traditionally feminine ways. Within this context of identity management, we also can see why Cecily Cannan Selby decided to reduce tension at a dinner meeting with the previously all-male Avon Products board by lighting up a cigar and why Hazel O'Leary decided she had to learn to play golf if she wanted to advance in her corporate career. In all these ways, the newcomers are able to meet the challenge of moving into a "comfort zone" with those who decide who is and who is not acceptable for inclusion.

Previously, we drew on research on the sociology . . . it is, instead, the need for trust and smooth working relationships within complex organizations that leads to the marked preference for women and people of color who think and act like the straight, Christian males running those organizations. Such demonstrations may be especially important when there are suspicions that the newcomers might have lingering loyalties to those they have left behind. The social movements that arose in the 1960s were able to rock the boat enough to open up some space for nontraditional leaders, but not enough to change the way in which work is structured and institutions are managed. Unless, and until, changes are made in work structure and institutional cultures, underrepresented groups will be at a disadvantage in climbing the managerial hierarchy, even though they are now able to enter the competition.

In summary, class origins, an excellent education, and the proper appearance, especially in terms of lighter skin tone, are the building blocks for entry into the power elite, but identity management is the final step, the icing on the cake.

Why Are Some Still Excluded?

How is the continuing exclusion of African Americans and Latinos who are darker skinned to be explained? From the power-structure perspective that we favor, the answer is to be found in the economic and political domination of darker-skinned people that began when European settlers took North and South America from the Native Americans and imported an estimated ten to twelve million slaves from Africa in order to make the southern United States, the West Indies, and parts of Latin America even more profitable to them. This economically driven subjugation, which unfolded in brutal fashion shortly after 1492 in ways that are all too familiar, created the "racial hierarchy" that persists to this day based on a jumble of prejudices, cultural stereotypes, strategies of exclusion, and feelings of superiority on the part of those who are white.

The fact that both indigenous Indians and African slaves were conquered and subjugated in the United States is less visible today because there are so few Native Americans left. They are now often regarded positively as brave and heroic warriors, but until fairly recently, they were treated as less than human due to the first (and most successful, along with that in Australia) large scale ethnic cleansing by a modern democracy. Their numbers dropped from an estimated 4 to 9 million in the pre-Columbian era in what is now the United States to 237,000 in 1900, when they were no longer a threat to the land hunger of the white settlers. Today, most of the approximately 1.5 million self-identified Native Americans not living on reservations are of mixed white and Indian heritage, and 59 percent of those who are married are married to whites.[5]

In the United States, then, and unlike many Latin American countries, where both Indians and former African slaves mostly occupy the bottom rungs of society or are complete outcasts, the brunt of the persistent sense of group superiority on the part of Euro Americans is on the significant percentage of the population—12 percent, as we noted earlier—who are descendants of slaves (and slave masters in some cases). In this country, being "black" means being stigmatized because the dishonored status of being a slave became identified with the racial features of "blackness."[6] In particular, skin color became the major means by which enslaved and conquered groups could be identified and stigmatized for purposes of keeping them subordinated. Hair texture and facial features were also part of the subordinating racial stereotyping, but "color" came to stand for the ensemble of identifying markers. (By contrast, the Slavic peoples enslaved by the Greeks and Romans, from whose language the word "slave" is derived, were able to blend in when their masters released them from bondage.)

In addition to carrying the legacy of slavery, which stripped people of any group or personal identity, rendered them subject to constant surveillance and violence, and regularly broke up roughly one-third of all nuclear families as a way to destroy feelings of kinship, African Americans also continued to endure subordination to white Americans in the postslavery era. In the South, that subordination began with the exploitative system called "tenant farming," which left African Americans with little more than their freedom, a mule, and a few farm implements.[7] In the North, African Americans were kept out of the best-paying construction jobs, often with the use of violence by white workers, despite their having the necessary skills. They also encountered cross burnings, race riots, and racial covenants in deeds of trust when they tried to live in white neighborhoods, which meant they were excluded from predominantly white public schools and forced to pay higher prices for housing that depreciated in value because whites would not live nearby.[8]

Under these circumstances, and until the 1960s, it was rare that any but a small number of African Americans could accumulate any wealth at all. Although the civil rights movement brought formal equality and voting power to African Americans, which in turn led to improved treatment in many social spheres and better jobs, especially with the government the fact remains that it has been impossible for African Americans to close the socioeconomic gap with whites. According to detailed work on wealth accumulation by sociologist Thomas Shapiro, based on his own interviews in several cities, along with national surveys and government statistics, the typical African American family has only one-tenth the wealth of the average white family (a net worth of $8,000 versus $81,000 for whites). This is because whites were able gradually to accumulate wealth throughout the twentieth century with the help of government-backed mortgages, large tax deductions on home mortgages, the GI Bill, and other programs that were available to very few, if any, African Americans at the time. Moreover, whites were able to pass down this wealth to their children through inheritance, not only at the time of death, but also in the form of what Shapiro calls "transformative assets," which include help with college tuition, down payments on new homes (which then appreciate in value), and gifts or loans to survive unexpected crises that cause a temporary drop in income.[9]

On the other hand, the historic legacy of income and wealth discrimination means that African Americans lack similar transformative assets. In addition, more black wealth goes to helping relatives and friends in need and to taking care of aging parents, so the little wealth African Americans do accumulate is less likely to be given to young adult children as transformative assets or eventually inherited by them. Even when blacks and whites are at the same level in terms of earnings, they are at different starting points in terms of wealth, making it impossible to close the gap through earnings. Both black and white families increased their financial wealth between 1988 and 1999, but there was nonetheless a $20,000 increase in the asset gap. Racial inequality is growing worse, not better, because of both the initial advantages enjoyed by whites and their greater capacity to pass on these advantages as transformative assets. As Shapiro concludes, "it is virtually impossible for people of color to earn their way to wealth through wages."[10]

This huge wealth differential is further compounded by continuing discrimination and exclusion on the part of whites, especially in the area of employment, where many whites wrongly think there is now color-blind fairness.[11] Although the official racist ideology of the past is now gone, or at least not verbalized in public, there is strong evidence that more covert forms of racism still persist that make many blacks feel uncomfortable or unwanted in white settings. In covert racism, which also has been called free-market and color-blind racism, traditional American values, especially those concerning the fairness of markets, including labor markets, are blended with antiblack attitudes in a way that allows whites to express antagonism toward blacks' demands ("Blacks are getting too demanding in their push for civil rights") or resentment over alleged special favors for blacks ("The government should not help blacks and other racial minorities—they should help themselves") without thinking of themselves as racists. White Americans say they simply want everyone to be treated the same, even though most of them know that African Americans are not treated equally.[12]

Then, too, more subtle forms of racial discrimination are uncovered in various kinds of social psychology experiments that have revealed "aversive racism," in which whites express egalitarian beliefs but also hold unacknowledged negative feelings about blacks. The resulting ambivalence means that they avoid blacks, especially when the norms are conflicting or ambiguous. The evidence for aversive and other subtle forms of racism is important because it reveals the persistence of cultural stereotypes about blacks and demonstrates that these stereotypes affect behavior, often at an unconscious level. These stereotypes, in turn, convey to African Americans that they continue to be seen as "different." They come to feel they are not respected, which naturally breeds resentment and hostility, which is then sensed by whites and said to be groundless in this day and age.[13]

This cycle of discrimination, exclusion, resentment, and mutual recrimination is very different from what happens to most of the groups who come to the United States as immigrants from Europe, Asia, or Latin America. They arrive with a sense of hope, often as families or in extended kin networks, and with an intact culture; these combine to enable them to endure the discrimination and exclusion they often face at the outset. As they persist in their efforts, the dominant majority grudgingly accepts some of them. The difference can be seen in the two most revealing indicators of acceptance by the dominant group, residential patterns and rates of intermarriage.

The most comprehensive study on residential patterns demonstrates that African Americans continue to live in predominantly black neighborhoods, but this is not the case for Latinos or Asian Americans. In *American Apartheid: Segregation and the Making of the Underclass,* sociologists Douglas Massey and Nancy Denton reveal just how persistent residential segregation has been in the United States. Using computerized data from the U.S. Censuses of 1970 and 1980, they looked at the thirty metropolitan areas with the largest black populations. Based on two different measures ("black-white segregation" and "spatial isolation"), they conclude that the 1970s showed virtually no increase in integration, "despite what whites said on opinion polls and despite the provisions of the Fair Housing Act."[14] Moreover, they did not find that degree of segregation for Hispanics and Asian Americans. "In fact," Massey and Denton conclude, "within most metropolitan areas, Hispanics and Asians are more likely to share a neighborhood with whites than with another member of their own group." In the final chapter of their book, Massey and Denton update their work to include 1990 Census data. They conclude that "there is little in recent data to suggest that processes of racial segregation have moderated much since 1980. . . . Racial segregation still constitutes a fundamental cleavage in American society."[15] This conclusion still holds based on data from the 2000 Census, which shows only a slight decline in residential segregation for African Americans, along with increasing segregation for everyone along class lines.[16]

There have been dozens of studies focusing on the recent marriage patterns of underrepresented groups. All of them point to increasing intermarriage occurring between the large white population and each previously excluded group except African Americans. The exact percentage of "outmarriage" varies with a number of factors, including country

| Table 29.1 | Intermarriage by (U.S.-Born Members of Ethnic and Racial Minorities |

Group	Percentage Married to Non-Hispanic Whites	
	Male (N)	Female (N)
Filipino Americans	61 (106)	66 (103)
Native Americans	57 (1,212)	58 (1,234)
Cuban Americans	61 (92)	47 (137)
Chinese Americans	47 (140)	52 (152)
Japanese Americans	44 (216)	54 (266)
Puerto Rican Americans	42 (528)	35 (602)
Mexican Americans	31 (4,793)	28 (5,261)
African Americans	5 (9,804)	2 (9,581)

Source: Adapted from Jacobs and Labov 'Asian Brides, Anglo Grooms,' 23, table 4.

Note: The table includes only individuals under age forty and excludes war brides and grooms.

of birth, years of residency in the United States, region of residence, educational level, and income. For our emphasis on intermarriage as a sensitive indicator of integration and acceptance, research by sociologists Jerry Jacobs and Teresa Labov, using a 1 percent sample from the 1990 Census (539,279 marriages), provides an ideal test case. Table 29.1 summarizes the findings of their analysis of marriages to non-Hispanic white partners by American-born minorities under the age of forty.[17]

There are many dramatic findings in this table, including the very high percentage of native-born Asian Americans marrying non-Hispanic whites, but none is more germane to our point than the continuing low levels of intermarriage by African Americans to non-Hispanic whites. In a sample that focuses only on married couples, thereby excluding any distortion by the high percentage of unmarried males and females in the African American community, only 5 percent of married African American males and 2 percent of married African American females under age forty were married to non-Hispanic whites. This is less than one-sixth the percentage for the next-lowest group, Mexican Americans, and far below the 44 to 66 percent figures for various groups of Asian Americans.

Even among African American college graduates, only 11 percent of the males and 3 percent of the females had married whites, whereas the

percentages for all married Asian American college graduates as a group were 51 percent for males and 59 percent for females.[18]

As might be deduced from the higher percentage of Asian American college graduates marrying whites, there is a strong tendency for affluent immigrant minorities to marry affluent whites and for less affluent groups, like Mexican Americans and Puerto Ricans, to marry less affluent whites. The same pattern holds for marriages between African Americans and whites: the partners usually have similar education and occupation levels.[19]

To make matters more complex, most recent immigrant groups bring similar negative attitudes toward African Americans from their home countries, as in the case of nonblack Latinos, or soon adopt them once they are in the United States, as seen in the case of some Asian American groups. They often claim that African Americans do not see the "opportunities" that lie before them and do not work hard. Thus, most immigrants come to share the stereotypes and prejudices of the dominant white majority.

This point is demonstrated for Mexican Americans in an analysis of information in the 1990 Latino Political Survey, where 60 percent of all Mexican Americans felt "warmly" toward whites on a "feeling thermometer scale," compared to only 36 percent who felt that way toward African Americans; those with lighter skin or born outside the United States expressed even less warmth toward African Americans.[20] Similar findings are reported in a study of attitudes toward African Americans on the part of both Latinos and Asian Americans in Los Angeles.[21] This distancing from African Americans is also seen in a study that asked Latinos and Asian Americans to construct their "ideal" neighborhood, which included no African Americans for 33 percent of Latinos and 40 percent of Asian Americans.[22]

The power of this comparison between African Americans and immigrant groups is demonstrated in studies of the different course of events for most dark-skinned immigrants of African heritage, as studied most carefully in the case of West Indians. Based on their experience of their home countries, where there are few blacks at the top and few whites at the bottom, they expect to encounter obstacles in occupational advancement due to what is called "structural racism" by sociologist Mary Waters,[23] who conducted revealing interviews with West Indians, African Americans, and their white supervisors at a food service company in New York. Despite their expectations about structural racism, however, West Indian immigrants arrive hopeful and with positive attitudes towards whites as individuals, leading to pleasant interactions with most of the whites they encounter. But their initial hopeful attitudes are gradually shaken by the unexpected "interpersonal racism" they encounter in some of their interaction with Whites. They are also made wary by the degree which everything is "racialized" in the United States. Although most of them still retain a hopeful stance they develop greater sympathy for what they see as the more defensive stance towards whites taken by African Americans.

As black immigrants come to realize the depth of the problem they face, they strive to preserve their accents and try to retain their "foreign" identities in an attempt to avoid the stigmatization applied to African Americans. They also attempt to socialize their children so that white Americans do not see them as African Americans. Earlier generations of West Indian immigrants, for example, sent their children back to the Caribbean to be educated. More recently, West Indians in New York who arrive from middle-class backgrounds have founded private schools that are based on the educational system "back home" in the islands. These schools often emphasize that their teachers have been trained in the West Indies, the curricula are rigorous, the students wear British-style school uniforms, and there is strict discipline.[24]

But these strategies are not always successful. Although some children of middle-class West Indians are able to resist racialization and end up among the blacks of African descent at the most selective universities in the United States (where as many as 25 percent of the black students have at least one parent who is foreign born), many others, as well as the Children of other black immigrants begin to View American Society the same way working class African Americans do because they face the same situation: high rates of unemployment, lack of good jobs, and not-so-subtle racism.[25] Treated like African Americans, many black West Indians, black Puerto Ricans, black Dominicans, and black Cubans come to see themselves subjectively as African Americans. As Waters concludes, "It is in the second generation that this process of rapid cultural change is most evident. The children of these immigrants do grow up exhibiting the racialism their parents are concerned with preventing. Indeed, the rapidity of the change in attitudes about race between parents and children is quite dramatic."[26]

Those white Americans who say that racism is a thing of the past and blame African Americans for creating problems for themselves by dwelling on it often point to their good interpersonal relations with immigrant groups, including West Indians, as evidence for their claim. However, as Waters demonstrates, the persisting racial discrimination practiced (and denied) by whites is in fact the root of the problem, generating the tensions that whites attribute to African Americans:

> It is the continuing discrimination and prejudice of whites, and ongoing structural and interpersonal racism, that create an inability among American, and ultimately West Indian, blacks to ever forget about race. The behavior and beliefs about race among whites, and the culture of racist behaviors among whites, create the very expectations of discomfort that whites complain about in their

dealing with their black neighbors, coworkers, and friends. That expectation is not some inexplicable holdover from the long-ago days of slavery, but rather a constantly re-created expectation of trouble, nourished by every taxi that does not stop and every casual or calculated white use of the word "nigger."[27]

Based on the findings on how differently black and nonblack immigrants are treated, it seems likely to us that, over time, the overwhelming majority of the children and grandchildren of non-black immigrants to the United States will blend together with non-Hispanic whites into a common cultural pool and then sort themselves out along class and educational lines, using ethnic and racial identities for mostly symbolic and strategic purposes. On the other hand, Americans of African descent, whether African Americans or immigrants, will find themselves struggling to hold on to whatever class standing they are able attain. Race, as well as class, will continue to determine their life chances.[28] We therefore agree with those who argue that people of African descent have been treated very differently from all other previously excluded groups. In making this point, we are fully aware that other groups have suffered many forms of discrimination and exclusion, and we do not want to diminish the depth of personal anguish that such mistreatment has caused, but the fact remains that people of African heritage are the only ones to experience the combined effects of race, slavery, and segregation.[29] This confluence is unique because the "dishonored" or "stigmatized" status attached to slavery everywhere it has been practiced cannot easily be overcome or forgotten when there is the constant reminder of skin color.

Based on this analysis, we can see why the gains made by African Americans since the civil rights movement are in constant peril in a context where they have not been able to accumulate sufficient wealth to help their children or provide support in times of crisis. Given the ongoing discrimination and accumulated disadvantages, it may be that even the current rate of entry into the power elite will be difficult to maintain. Upwardly mobile black Americans could continue to be the

exception rather than the rule without the strong support of affirmative action laws and programs at the federal level.[30] But such laws and programs have been trimmed back since the new conservative era began in the 1980s, making further progress problematic.

However, in a clear demonstration of the concerns members of the power elite have on this score a small part of the decline in government support for equal opportunity has been offset by a set of corporate-sponsored programs for identifying and educating academically talented African American youngsters who can be groomed for elite universities and possible incorporation into the power elite. These programs begin in elementary school in some areas of the country, then carry through to private high schools, Ivy League universities, and corporate internships. They are financed by donations from the large charitable foundations that the corporate rich in turn influence through financial donations and directorship positions. Since we have written about these programs elsewhere, with a special emphasis on the first and largest of them, A Better Chance, founded in the early 1960s by a handful of New England boarding school headmasters with help from the Rockefeller Foundation, we will provide only three examples here.[31]

The Black Student Fund in Washington, D.C., places students in 42 private schools in Maryland, Virginia, and the District of Columbia with the help of foundation grants and personal gifts. Since its founding in 1964, it has served over two thousand students, 84 percent of whom have earned at least a BA. The Steppingstone Foundation in Boston and Philadelphia has a program for children in the fourth and fifth grades, who are prepared through two six-week summer sessions, Saturday classes, and after-school classes once a week for acceptance into both private and elite public schools that will see them through their high school years with the help of scholarship support. Between 1997 and 2005, 125 graduates of the Steppingstone program had enrolled in college. About one-third had attended prestigious schools (five went to Columbia or Barnard, four to Yale and Penn, three to Tufts, two to Harvard, Wellesley, Bowdoin, Bates, Georgetown and Williams, and one to Brown, Dartmouth, Duke, Hamilton, Johns Hopkins,

Mt. Holyoke, and Wesleyan), and about 10 percent had attended traditionally black colleges and universities (including four who went to Spelman, three to Hampton, and two to Morehouse). The others had attended a wide range of public and private institutions (five went to the University of Massachusetts, three to George Washington, and two to Temple, Boston College, Boston University, Ford-ham, and Pine Manor).

Prep for Prep in New York City may currently be the largest and most comprehensive of these programs. Created in 1978 as a pilot project under the auspices of Columbia University's Teachers College just as the full-scale attack on affirmative action was beginning, it takes in about 150 fifth graders and 60 seventh graders in New York City each year for a fourteen-month program to prepare them for placement in 36 private day schools and 10 boarding schools. Like the Steppingstone program, it includes two intensive, seven-week, summer programs, as well as after-school classes one day a week and Saturday classes during the school year. It sponsors a leadership institute and offers counseling services. Its program of summer job placements is meant to introduce students to the business and professional worlds. Alumni participate in a summer advisory program to help create what is called the "Prep Community," a support group and sense of group identification, and 75 percent of the children complete the program and go to college.

As of 2003, Prep for Prep had worked with more than 2,500 students, and 951 had graduated from college. Fully 84 percent of those college graduates had attended schools characterized as "most selective" on the annual list published by *U.S. News & World Report,* and 40 percent had attended Ivy League schools. Among the schools with the most Prep for Prep alumni (as of 2005) are Wesleyan (58), the University of Pennsylvania (36), Harvard (32), Columbia (30), Brown (27), Princeton (22), and Dartmouth (18).

Wall Street lawyers and financiers direct the program. For example, its chairman, John L. Vogelstein, is the vice chair of the board of directors of the investment bank E. M. Warburg, Pincus, & Company and sits on the board of directors of three other corporations. The program received $2.8 million from 29 foundations in 2002–2003, starting with $1.5 million from the Goldman Sachs Foundation.

Once African American students are in college, there are programs that encourage any interest they may have in going to law school or business school. A joint program between major corporations and the Harvard Business School is one good example of how African Americans are recruited for the business community. For almost twenty years, the Harvard Business School has sponsored the Summer Venture in Management Program, a weeklong program designed to expose talented minority students to management in the business world. The participants are "underrepresented minority U.S. citizens" who have completed their junior year of college, been hired as interns during the summer by sponsoring companies (generally *Fortune*-level companies), and been nominated by those companies to spend a week at the Harvard Business School learning what a high-powered business school is like. Participation in the program does not guarantee subsequent acceptance into the Harvard Business School, but it does allow the school to identify and encourage applications from highly qualified individuals.

Taken as a whole, this elementary to graduate school pipeline may produce several thousand potential members of the corporate community each year, if successful graduates of public high schools who receive business and law degrees are added to the prep school graduates. However, these programs are not large enough to provide opportunities for more than a tiny fraction of all African Americans without much more help from the government at the national, state, and local levels. They are primarily a way to provide a few highly educated Americans of African descent with the educational credentials to rise in the corporate community. For example, despite all these programs, the percentage of master's degrees awarded to blacks has been flat at about 6.5 percent since 1977, which demonstrates a significant underrepresentation. A shorter time series available from the government for master's degrees in business reveals a slight but steady increase between the 1994–1995 and 1999–2000 school years. During these six years, the percentages of black students receiving business degrees rose from 5.2 to 7.1 percent. We therefore believe that the potential pool of African Americans who can make their way into the power elite is growing at a much slower rate than for the other previously underrepresented groups.

The Many Ironic Impacts of Diversity

The impetus for greater diversity, as we have stressed, did not come from within the power elite but was the result of external pressures brought to bear by the civil rights movement. The fact that the American power elite was in competition with the Soviet Union for access and influence in previously colonized Third World countries also played a role, but that factor can easily be exaggerated in historical hindsight. Faced with the possibility of continuing massive disruption and rioting in the inner cities of major urban areas, most members of the power elite reluctantly accepted integration, and later diversity, as a goal only because they had little choice.

This point is best demonstrated in the case of the affirmative action programs originally designed to create more job opportunities for African Americans. Despite hesitations about breaking the taboo on quotas and preferences, affirmative action policies were adopted by political and business elites very hurriedly in the face of the estimated 329 major disturbances in 257 cities between 1964 and 1968, which resulted in 220 deaths, 8,371 injuries, and 52,629 arrests.[32] At the urging of first President Kennedy and then President Johnson at off-the-record meetings with the Business Council, at the time the most central organization in the power elite, corporate CEOs took the lead in calling on all businesses to provide more jobs for African Americans as quickly as possible. They thereby helped legitimize what they knew was preferential hiring because job programs were seen not only as the fastest and surest way to restore domestic tranquility but also as a means of avoiding larger government programs and expanded welfare benefits as well. Moreover, it was the corporate-backed Nixon administration in 1969 that created the stringent guidelines for hiring by government contractors (under the guise of "good faith" efforts at meeting numerical "targets"), which were soon attacked as a "quota" system.[33]

Once the concern with urban unrest subsided, however, the elite origins of the plan were soon ignored. It was at this point, too, that Nixon abandoned his guidelines, and ultraconservative Republicans began to attack affirmative action as unfair to whites and unconstitutional, a mere experiment by liberals and professors. The fear of disruption was gone, so now the rewriting of history could begin, along with attempts to capitalize on the increasing backlash among white workers. In the first of the many ironies arising from the saga of diversity, African Americans and white liberals, who had been very hesitant about preferential hiring in the beginning, ended up defending a program created and endorsed by white male elites in a time of crisis.[34] In a related irony, the successful Republican campaign to place the "blame" for the affirmative action program on African Americans and white liberals helped to dislodge angry whites from the Democratic Party.

Although it was African Americans and their white allies who created the disruption and pressures that led to government programs, including affirmative action, other previously excluded groups soon became eligible for consideration and benefited greatly, perhaps even more so than African Americans in terms of higher-level jobs.[35] This change, which was gracefully accepted by most African American leaders and even seen by some of them as a way to expand their coalition, not only ended up marginalizing African Americans within the programs they created, but it added to the opposition by middle-American white males, who deeply resented the increased competition they had to face for good blue-collar and government jobs.

In response to this growing resentment, defenders of the program in and around the corporate world began to talk about the need for "diversity" in management circles and to emphasize its importance for business reasons rather than social-justice goals. At this point, the focus shifted to such business advantages as having managers who could interact with an increasingly heterogeneous set of lower-level wage earners. Proponents of diversity also emphasized that a "multicultural" management team would be essential for competing in the many non-European countries that were part of the rapidly expanding global economy. But for all the changes in rationale and the emphasis on bottom-line business objectives, the actual practices of the corporations (and universities and large nonprofit organizations) remained about the same, based on the procedures and programs initially established by social movements and government laws.[36]

Although African American management consultants were part of this effort to redefine the affirmative action programs as diversity programs and thereby fend off the right wing of the Republican Party, a further irony developed: diversity no longer needed to include African Americans. The new goal was to have a high percentage of non-whites and women. And it was not long before foreign-born executives and professionals even those who came to the United States as young educated adults from foreign universities, were included in the statistics, driving the numbers even higher.[37]

In what may be the greatest and most important irony of them all, the diversity forced upon the power elite may have helped to strengthen it. Diversity has given the power elite buffers, ambassadors, tokens, and legitimacy. This is an unintended consequence that few insurgents or social scientists foresaw. As recent social psychology experiments show and experience confirms, it often takes only a small number of upwardly mobile members of previously excluded groups, perhaps as few as 2 percent, to undermine an excluded group's definition of who is "us" and who is "them," which contributes to a decline in collective protest and disruption and increases striving for individual mobility. That is, those who make it are not only "role models" for individuals, but they are safety valves against collective action by aggrieved groups.[38]

Tokens at the top create ambiguity and internal doubt for members of the subordinated group. Maybe "the system" is not as unfair to their group as they thought it was. Maybe there is something about them personally that keeps them from advancing. Once people begin to ponder such possibilities, the likelihood of any sustained group action declines greatly. Because a few people have made it, the general human tendency to think of the world as just and fair reasserts itself: since the world is fair, and some members of my group are advancing, then it may be my fault that I have been left behind. As liberal and left-wing activists have long known, it is hard to sustain a social movement in the face of

"reforms," which has led to long-standing debates about how activists should proceed.[39]

Do Members of Previously Excluded Groups Act Differently?

Perhaps it is not surprising that when we look at the business practices of the members of previously excluded groups who have risen to the top of the corporate world, we find that their perspectives and values do not differ markedly from those of their white male counterparts. When Linda Wachner, one of the first women to become CEO of a *Fortune*-level company, the Warnaco Group, concluded that one of Warnaco's many holdings, the Hathaway Shirt Company, was unprofitable, she decided to stop making Hathaway shirts and to sell or close down the factory. It did not matter to Wachner that Hathaway, which started making shirts in 1837, was one of the oldest companies in Maine, that almost all of the five hundred employees at the factory were working-class women, or even that the workers had given up a pay raise to hire consultants to teach them to work more effectively and, as a result, had doubled their productivity. The bottom-line issue was that the company was considered unprofitable, and the average wage of the Hathaway workers, $7.50 an hour, was thought to be too high. (In 1995, Wachner was paid $10 million in salary and stock, and Warnaco had a net income of $46.5 million.) "We did need to do the right thing for the company and the stockholders," explained Wachner.[40]

Nor did ethnic background matter to Thomas Fuentes, a senior vice president at a consulting firm in Orange County, California, a director of Fleetwood Enterprises, and chairman of the Orange County Republican Party. Fuentes targeted fellow Latinos who happened to be Democrats when he sent uniformed security guards to twenty polling places in 1988 "carrying signs in Spanish and English warning people not to vote if they were not U.S. citizens." The security firm ended up paying $60,000 in damages when it lost a lawsuit stemming from this intimidation.[41] We also can recall that the Fanjuls, the Cuban American sugar barons, have no problem ignoring labor laws in dealing with their migrant labor force, and that Sue Ling Gin, one of the Asian Americans on our list of corporate directors, explained to an interviewer that, at one point in her career, she had hired an all-female staff, not out of feminist principles but "because women would work for lower wages." Linda Wachner, Thomas Fuentes, the Fanjuls, and Sue Ling Gin acted as employers, not as members of disadvantaged groups. That is, members of the power elite of both genders and of all ethnicities practice class politics.

Conclusion

The black and white liberals and progressives who challenged Christian, white, male homogeneity in the power structure starting in the 1950s and 1960s sought to do more than create civil rights and new job opportunities for men and women who had previously been mistreated and excluded, important though these goals were. They also hoped that new perspectives in the boardrooms and the halls of government would spread greater openness throughout the society. The idea was both to diversify the power elite and to shift some of its power to underrepresented groups and social classes. The social movements of the 1960s were strikingly successful in increasing the individual rights and freedoms available to all Americans, especially African Americans. As we have shown, they also created pressures that led to openings at the top for individuals from groups that had previously been ignored.

But as some individuals made it, and as the concerns of social movements, political leaders, and the courts gradually came to focus more and more on individual rights and individual advancement, the focus on "distributive justice:" general racial exclusion, and social class was lost. The age-old American commitment to individualism, reinforced by tokenism and reassurances from members of the power elite, won out over the commitment to greater equality of income and wealth that had been one strand of New Deal liberalism and a major emphasis of left-wing activism in the 1960s.

We therefore conclude that the increased diversity in the power elite has not generated any changes in an underlying class system in which the top 1 percent of households (the upper class) own 33.4 percent of all marketable wealth, and the next 19 percent (the managerial, professional, and small business stratum)

have 51 percent, which means that just 20 percent of the people own a remarkable 84 percent of the privately owned wealth in the United States, leaving a mere 16 percent of the wealth for the bottom 80 percent (wage and salary workers).[42] In fact, the wealth and income distributions became even more skewed starting in the 1970s as the majority of whites, especially in the South and Great Plains, switched their allegiance to the Republican Party and thereby paved the way for a conservative resurgence that is as antiunion, antitax, and antigovernment as it is determined to impose ultraconservative social values on all Americans.

The values of liberal individualism embedded in the Declaration of Independence, the Bill of Rights, and American civic culture were renewed by vigorous and courageous activists in the years between 1955 and 1975, but the class structure remains a major obstacle to individual fulfillment for the overwhelming majority of Americans. The conservative backlash that claims to speak for individual rights has strengthened this class structure, one that thwarts advancement for most individuals from families in the bottom 80 percent of the wealth distribution. This solidification of class divisions in the name of individualism is more than an irony. It is a dilemma.

Furthermore, this dilemma combines with the dilemma of race to obscure further the impact of class and to limit individual mobility, simply because the majority of middle-American whites cannot bring themselves to make common cause with African Americans in the name of greater individual opportunity and economic equality through a progressive income tax and the kind of government programs that lifted past generations out of poverty. These intertwined dilemmas of class and race lead to a nation that celebrates individualism, equal opportunity, and diversity but is, in reality, a bastion of class privilege, African American exclusion, and conservatism.

Notes

1. On the continuing importance of class voting in the United States, contrary to recent claims based on weak methods, see Jeff Manza and Clem Brooks, *Social Cleavages and Political*

Change: Voter Alignments and U.S. Party Coalitions (New York: Oxford University Press, 1999). On class voting by Latinos, see Barry Kosmin and Ariela Keysar, "Party Political Preferences of U.S. Hispanics: The Varying Impact of Religion, Social Class and Demographic Factors," *Ethnic and Racial Studies* 18, no. 2 (1995): 336–47. In surveys of the CEOs of the largest Hispanic-owned businesses in 1989 and 1996, *Hispanic Business* found that 78 percent of them voted Republican in 1988 and that 67 percent said they were Republicans in 1996. See "CEOs and the Entrepreneurial 80s," *Hispanic Business*, April 1989, 30; "HB 500 CEOs Opt for Dole," *Hispanic Business*, June 1996, 34. On class voting by Chinese Americans, see Wendy Tam, "Asians—a Monolithic Voting Bloc?" *Political Behavior* 17, no. 2 (1995): 223–49.

2. Richard L. Zweigenhaft and G. William Domhoff, *Blacks in the White Elite* (Lanham, MD: Rowman & Littlefield, 2003), 158–60.

3. Glass Ceiling Commission, *Good for Business: Making Full Use of the Nation's Human Capital, a Fact-Finding Report of the Federal Glass Ceiling Commission* (Washington, D.C.: U.S. Government Printing Office, 1995), 95.

4. Julia Alvarez, "A White Woman of Color," in *Half and Half: Writers on Growing Up Biracial and Bicultural,* ed. Claudine Chiawei O'Hearn, 139–49 (New York: Pantheon, 1998). Alvarez's novels include *How the Garcia Girls Lost Their Accents* (New York: Plume, 1992) and *In the Time of the Butterflies* (New York: Plume, 1994).

5. Michael Mann, *The Dark Side of Democracy: Explaining Ethnic Cleansing* (New York: Cambridge University Press, 2005); Karl Eschbach, "The Enduring and Vanishing American Indian: American Indian Population Growth and Intermarriage in 1990," *Ethnic and Racial Studies,* 18, no. 1(1995): 89–108.

6. Glenn Loury, *The Anatomy of Racial Inequality* (Cambridge: Harvard University Press, 2002), 69.

7. Michael Schwartz, *Radical Protest and Social Structure: The Southern Farmers' Alliance and Cotton Tenancy,* 1880–1890 (New York: Academic Press, 1976).

8. Kevin Fox Gotham, *Race, Real Estate, and Uneven Development* (Albany: State University of New York Press, 2002); Michael K. Brown, Martin Carnoy, Elliott Currie, Troy Duster, David B. Oppenheimer Marjorie M. Shultz, and David Wellman, *Whitewashing Race: The Myth of a Color-Blind Society* (Berkeley: University of California Press, 2003).

9. Thomas M. Shapiro, *The Hidden Cost of Being African American: How Wealth Perpetuates Inequality* (New York: Oxford University Press, 2004).

10. Shapiro, *Hidden Cost,* 2.

11. Devah Pager and Bruce Western, "Discrimination in Low-Wage Labor Markets: Results from an Experimental Audit Study in New York City" (paper presented at the annual meeting of the American Sociological Association, Philadelphia, Pennsylvania, 2005); Deirdre A. Royster, *Race and the Invisible Hand: How White Networks Exclude Black Men from Blue-Collar Jobs* (Berkeley: University of California Press, 2003).

12. Lawrence Bobo and Ryan Smith, "From Jim Crow to Laissez-faire Racism: The Transformation of Racial Attitudes," in *Beyond Pluralism: The Conception of Groups and Group Identities in America,* ed. Wendy Katkin, Ned Landsman, and Andrea Tyree, 182–220 (Urbana: University of Illinois Press, 1998); Eduardo Bonilla-Silva, *Racism without Racists: Color-Blind Racism and the Persistence of Racial Inequality in the United States* (Lanham, MD: Rowman & Littlefield, 2003).

13. James M. Jones, *Prejudice and Racism,* 2nd ed. (New York: McGraw-Hill, 1997); John F. Dovidio, "On the Nature of Contemporary Prejudice: The Third Wave," *Journal of Social Issues* 57, no. 4 (2001): 829–49.

14. Douglas S. Massey and Nancy A. Denton, *American Apartheid: Segregation and the Making of the Underclass* (Cambridge: Harvard University Press, 1993), 61.

15. Massey and Denton, *American Apartheid,* 67, 223.

16. William Clark and Sarah Blue, "Race, Class, and Segregation Patterns in U.S. Immigrant Gateway Cities," *Urban Affairs Review* 39 (2004): 667–88; John Iceland, Cicely Sharpe, and Erika Steinmetz, "Class Differences in African American Residential Patterns in US Metropolitan Areas: 1990–2000," *Social Science Research* 34 (2005): 252–66.

17. Jerry A. Jacobs and Teresa Labov, "Asian Brides, Anglo Grooms: Asian Exceptionalism in Inter-marriage," Department of Sociology, University of Pennsylvania, October 1995; Jerry A. Jacobs and Teresa Labov, "Sex Differences in Inter-marriage: Exchange Theory Reconsidered,"

Department of Sociology, University of Pennsylvania, September 1995. For similar findings, based on 1990 survey data with native-born Latinos, that are slightly lower due to a wider age range, see Rodolfo de la Garza, Louis DeSipio, F. Chris Garcia, John Garcia, and Angelo Falcon, *Latino Voices: Mexican, Puerto Rican, and Cuban Perspectives on American Politics* (Boulder, CO: Westview, 1992), 25, table 2.6. Jacobs and Labov find low rates of intermarriage among subgroups of Latinos, and de la Garza and colleagues report similarly low rates among Latino groups in the table cited. There is, however, evidence for a growing number of intermarriages among Asian Americans in California, with the rate being higher than intermarriage with whites when the size of the population is taken into account. See Larry Hajima Shinagawa and Gin Yong Pang, "Intraethnic, Interethnic, and Interracial Marriages among Asian Americans in California, 1980," *Berkeley Journal of Sociology* 13 (1988): 95–114. Inter-Asian marriages are also high in Hawaii; see Morrison G. Wong, "A Look at Intermarriage among the Chinese in the U.S. in 1980," *Sociological Perspectives* 32, no. 1(1989): 87–107.

18. Jacobs and Labov, "Sex Differences in Intermarriage," 11.

19. Jerry A. Jacobs and Teresa Labov, "Gender Differentials in Intermarriage among Sixteen Race and Ethnic Groups," *Sociological Forum* 17 (2002): 621–46. On black-white marriages and socioeconomic similarities, see also James H. Gadberry and Richard A. Dodder, "Educational Homogamy in Interracial Marriages: An Update," *Journal of Social Behavior and Personality* 8, no. 6 (1993): 155–63; Matthijs Kalmijn, "Trends in Black/White Intermarriage," *Social Forces* 72, no. 1 (1993): 119–46; Kristyan M. Kouri and Marcia Lasswell, "Black-White Marriages: Social Change and Intergenerational Mobility," *Marriage and Family Review* 19, no. 3–4 (1993): 241–55.

20. Edward Murguia and Tyrone Foreman, "Shades of Whiteness: The Mexican-American Experience in Relation to Anglos and Blacks," in *White Out: The Continuing Significance of Race,* ed. Ashley Doane and Eduardo Bonilla-Silva, 63–79 (New York: Routledge, 2003).

21. Lawrence Bobo and Devon Johnson, "Racial Attitudes in a Prismatic Metropolis: Mapping Identity, Stereotypes, Competition, and Views on Affirmative Action," in *Prismatic Metropolis,*

ed. Lawrence Bobo, Melvin L. Oliver, James H. Johnson, Jr., and Abel Valenzuela, 81–166 (New York: Russell Sage Foundation, 2000).

22. Camille Zubrinsky Charles, "Neighborhood Racial-Composition Preferences: Evidence from a Multiethnic Metropolis," *Social Problems* 47 (2000): 379–407.

23. Mary C. Waters, "Explaining the Comfort Factor: West Indian immigrants Confront American Race Relations," in *The Cultural Territories of Race: Black and White Boundaries,* ed. Michelle Lamont, 63–96 (Chicago: University of Chicago Press, 1999); Mary C. Waters, *Black Identities: West Indian Immigrant Dreams and American Realities* (Cambridge: Harvard University Press, 1999).

24. Philip Kasinitz, *Caribbean New York: Black Immigrants and the Politics of Race* (Ithaca, NY: Cornell University Press, 1992), 76, 220–21.

25. For information on the children of foreign-born blacks at twenty-eight highly selective colleges and universities, see Douglas S. Massey, Camille Z. Charles, Garvey F. Lundy, and Mary J. Fischer, *The Source of the River: The Social Origins of Freshmen at America's Selective Colleges and Universities* (Princeton, NJ: Princeton University Press, 2003), 40. At a forum during a 2004 reunion of black Harvard alumni, law professor Lani Guinier and Henry Louis Gates Jr., the chairman of the African and African American Studies Department, reported that at least a majority, and perhaps as many as two-thirds, of the then current undergraduates at Harvard were either West Indian and African immigrants, their children, or the children of biracial couples. See Sara Rimer and Karen W. Arenson, "Top Colleges Take More Blacks, but Which Ones?" *New York Times,* June 24, 2004, A1.

26. Waters, "Explaining the Comfort Factor."

27. Waters, "Explaining the Comfort Factor," 82.

28. Eduardo Bonilla-Silva, "'New Racism,' Color-Blind Racism, and the Future of Whiteness in America," in Doane and Bonilla-Silva, *White Out,* 271–84; Herbert Gans, "The Possibility of a New Racial Hierarchy in the Twenty-First Century United States," in Lamont, *The Cultural Territories of Race.*

29. Thomas F. Pettigrew, "Integration and Pluralism," in *Modern Racism: Profiles in Controversy,* ed. Phyllis A. Katz and Dalmas A. Taylor, 19–30 (New York: Plenum, 1988), 24–26. For detailed evidence

on the difficulties black Americans, including members of the middle class, still face, see Lois Benjamin, *The Black Elite* (Chicago: Nelson Hall, 1991), and Joe R. Feagin and Melvin P. Sikes, *Living with Racism* (Boston: Beacon, 1994).

30. See Sharon Collins, *Black Corporate Executives: The Making and Breaking of a Black Middle Class* (Philadelphia: Temple University Press, 1997). For a systematic empirical demonstration of the importance of such government policies using time series data, see Martin Carnoy, *Faded Dreams: The Politics and Economics of Race in America* (New York: Cambridge University Press, 1994).

31. Zweigenhaft and Domhoff, *Blacks in the White Elite,* 2003.

32. Brian T. Downes, "A Critical Re-examination of the Social and Political Characteristics of Riot Cities," *Social Science Quarterly* 51(1970): 349–60.

33. John D. Skrentny, *The Ironies of Affirmative Action: Politics, Culture, and Justice in America* (Chicago: University of Chicago Press, 1996), ch. 4 and 7.

34. Skrentny, *The Ironies of Affirmative Action,* 78–91.

35. John D. Skrentny, *The Minority Rights Revolution* (Cambridge: Harvard University Press, 2002).

36. Erin Kelly and Frank Dobbin, "How Affirmative Action Became Diversity Management: Employer Responses to Antidiscrimination Law, 1961–1996," in *Color Lines: Affirmative Action, Immigration, and Civil Rights Options for America,* ed. John D. Skrentny, 87–117 (Chicago: University of Chicago Press, 2001).

37. Skrentny, *The Minority Rights Revolution,* ch. 10.

38. Stephen C. Wright, "Restricted Intergroup Boundaries: Tokenism, Ambiguity, and the Tolerance of Injustice," in *The Psychology of Legitimacy: Emerging Perspectives on Ideology, Justice, and Intergroup Relations,* ed. John Jost and Brenda Major, 223–54 (New York: Cambridge University Press, 2001); Stephen C. Wright, "Strategic Collective Action: Social Psychology and Social Change," in *Blackwell Handbook of Social Psychology: Intergroup Processes,* ed. Rupert Brown and Samuel Gaertner, vol. 4, 409–30 (Malden, MA: Blackwell, 2001).

39. Jost and Major, *The Psychology of Legitimacy.*

40. Sara Rimer, "Fall of a Shirtmaking Legend Shakes Its Maine Hometown," *New York Times,* May 15, 1996. See, also, Floyd Norris, "Market Place," *New York Times,* June 7, 1996; Stephanie Strom, "Double Trouble at Linda Wachner's Twin Companies," *New York Times,* August 4, 1996. Strom's article reveals that Hathaway Shirts "got a reprieve" when an investor group stepped in to save it.

41. Claudia Luther and Steven Churm, "GOP Official Says He OK'd Observers at Polls," *Los Angeles Times,* November 12, 1988; Jeffrey Penman, "Firm Will Pay $60,000 in Suit over Guards at Polls," *Los Angeles Times,* May 31, 1989.

42. Edward N. Wolff, "Changes in Household Wealth in the 1980s and 1990s in the U.S." (working paper 407, Levy Economics Institute, Bard College, 2004), at www.levy.org.

30

Excerpts from *Who's Running America? The Bush Restoration*

Thomas R. Dye

If there ever was a time when the powers of government were limited—when government did no more than secure law and order, protect individual liberty and property, enforce contracts, and defend against foreign invasion—that time has long passed. Today it is commonplace to observe that governmental institutions intervene in every aspect of our lives—from the "cradle to the grave." Government in America has the primary responsibility for providing insurance against old age, death, dependency, disability, and unemployment; for organizing the nation's health-care system; for providing education at the elementary, secondary, collegiate, and postgraduate levels; for providing public highways and regulating water, rail, and air transportation; for providing police and fire protection; for providing sanitation services and sewage disposal; for financing research in medicine, science, and technology; for delivering the mail; for exploring outer space; for maintaining parks and recreation; for providing housing and adequate food for the poor; for providing job training and manpower programs; for cleaning the air and water; for rebuilding central cities; for maintaining full employment and a stable money supply; for regulating business practices and labor relations; for eliminating racial and sexual discrimination. Indeed, the list of government responsibilities seems endless, yet each year we manage to find additional tasks for government to do.

The Concentration of Governmental Power

Government in the United States grew enormously throughout most of the twentieth century, both in absolute terms and in relation to the size of the national economy. The size of the economy is usually measured by the gross domestic product (GDP), the dollar sum of all the goods and services produced in the United States in a year. Governments accounted for only about 8 percent of the GDP at the beginning of the century, and most governmental activities were carried out by state and local governments. Two world wars, the New Deal programs devised during the Great Depression of the 1930s, and the growth of the Great Society programs of the 1960s and 1970s all greatly expanded the size of government, particularly the federal

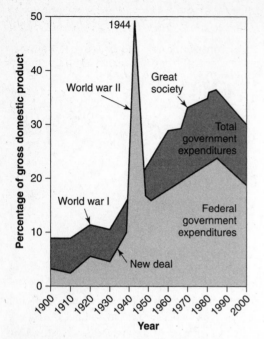

FIGURE 30.1 The Growth of government.

Source: Budget of the United States Government, 2000.

government. The rise in government growth relative to the economy leveled off during the Reagan presidency (1981–89), and no large new programs were undertaken in the Bush and Clinton years. An economic boom in the 1990s caused the GDP to grow rapidly, while government spending grew only moderately. The result was a modest *decline* in governmental size in relation to the economy. Today, federal expenditures amount to about 20 percent of GDP, and total governmental expenditures are about 30 percent of GDP (see Figure 30.1).

Not everything that government does is reflected in governmental expenditures. *Regulatory activity*, for example, especially environmental regulations, imposes significant costs on individuals and businesses; these costs are not shown in government budgets.

We have defined our governmental elite as the top executive, congressional, and judicial officers of the *federal* government; the President and Vice-President; secretaries, undersecretaries, and assistant secretaries of executive departments; senior White House presidential advisers; congressional committee chairpersons and ranking minority members; congressional majority and minority party leaders in the House and Senate; Supreme Court Justices; and members of the Federal Reserve Board and the Council of Economic Advisers. And we add to this definition of political elites the "fat cat" contributors who keep them in power.

The Fat Cat Contributors

More money was spent on political campaigning in 2000 than in any election year in American history. An estimated $3 *billion* was spent by all presidential and congressional candidates, Democratic and Republican parties, political action committees sponsored by interest groups, and independent political organizations in federal, state, and local elections combined. The costs of elections rises in each election cycle (see Figure 30.2). The largest increases in campaign finance came not from regulated "hard money" contributions to candidates, but rather from large unregulated "soft money" contributions to the parties.

Virtually all of the top "fat cat" campaign contributors from the *corporate, banking, and investment* worlds have been previously listed among the nation's largest corporate and monied institutions. AT&T, Philip Morris, Citigroup, and Goldman Sachs regularly appear each election cycle among contributors of $2 to $3 million or more (see Table 30.1). One notable newcomer among top corporate "fat cat" contributors in 2000

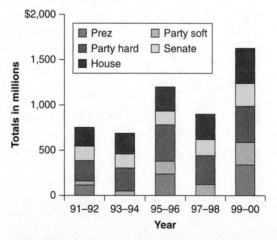

FIGURE 30.2 Campaign fund raising, president and congress.

Table 30.1   Fat Cat Campaign Contributors, 2000

Rank	Contributor	Total Contributions	To Dems.	To Repubs.
1	American Fedn. of St./Cnty./Munic. Employees	$6,935,989	98%	2%
2	Service Employees International Union	$4,961 010	95%	5%
3	AT&T	$4,667,844	38%	61%
4	Microsoft Corp	$4,309,856	46%	54%
5	Communications Workers of America	$3,871,185	99%	0%
6	National Assn. of Realtors	$3,834,600	41%	59%
7	Goldman Sachs Group	$3,646,382	68%	32%
8	United Food & Commercial Workers Union	$3,578,452	99%	1%
9	Intl. Brotherhood of Electrical Workers	$3,561,860	97%	3%
10	Citigroup Inc.	$3,559,566	53%	47%
11	Philip Morris	$3,460,200	18%	81%
12	SBC Communications	$3,418,466	46%	54%
13	Verizon Communications	$3,357,420	36%	64%
14	Carpenters & Joiners Union	$3,183,383	92%	8%
15	United Parcel Service	$3,133,119	26%	73%
16	American Federation of Teachers	$3,110,055	99%	1%
17	Assn. of Trial Lawyers of America	$3,030,750	88%	12%
18	Laborers Union	$2,929,275	93%	7%
19	National Rifle Assn.	$2,885,377	8%	92%
20	MBNA America Bank	$2,733,000	17%	83%
21	National Education Assn.	$2,584,478	92%	7%
22	Sheet Metal Workers Union	$2,551,584	99%	1%
23	Machinists/Aerospace Workers Union	$2,546,138	99%	1%
24	Teamsters Union	$2,517,240	93%	7%
25	Ernst & Young	$2,497,761	42%	58%
26	National Auto Dealers Assn.	$2,410,200	32%	68%
27	Federal Express Corp.	$2,388,428	34%	66%
28	Enron Corp.	$2,365,458	28%	72%
29	National Assn. of Home Builders	$2,336,799	37%	63%
30	Lockheed Martin	$2,333,794	39%	61%
31	Emily's List	$2,328,840	100%	0%
32	Credit Suisse First Boston	$2,325,705	29%	70%
33	Bristol-Myers Squibb	$2,300,792	14%	86%
34	United Auto Workers	$2,248,755	99%	0%
35	Morgan Stanley, Dean Witter & Co.	$2,225,823	39%	60%
36	BellSouth Corp.	$2,219,752	41%	59%
37	Freddie Mac	$2,198,839	48%	52%
38	AFL-CIO	$2,173,638	96%	4%
39	Global Crossing	$2,142,386	50%	50%
40	Pfizer Inc.	$2,136,647	14%	86%

(continued)

Table 30.1   Fat Cat Campaign Contributors, 2000 (*Continued*)

Rank	Contributor	Total Contributions	To Dems.	To Repubs.
41	Blue Cross/Blue Shield	$2,125,552	27%	73%
42	American Medical Assn.	$2,077,644	47%	52%
43	National beer Wholesalers Assn.	$2,059,061	19%	80%
44	Bank of America	$1,889,318	59%	40%
45	Time Warner	$1,860,237	73%	27%
46	National Assn. of Letter Carriers	$1,830,700	86%	13%
47	Union Pacific Corp	$1,805,144	16%	84%
48	General Electric	$1,793,879	39%	61%
49	Joseph E Seagram & Sons	$1,791,060	62%	38%
50	Andersen Worldwide	$1,781,412	29%	70%
51	Marine Engineers Union	$1,776,082	60%	40%
52	Deloitte & Touche	$1,761,826	29%	71%
53	American Online	$1,724,286	50%	50%
54	AFLAC Inc.	$1,716,010	45%	55%
55	Merrill Lynch	$1,713, 377	34%	65%
56	American Bankers Assn.	$1,677,707	35%	65%
57	Pricewaterhouse Coopers	$1,677,281	26%	74%
58	Anheuser-Busch	$1,656,525	49%	51%
59	Credit Union National Assn.	$1,649,439	47%	53%
60	Boeing Co.	$1,624,958	43%	57%
61	WorldCom Inc.	$1,607,681	32%	68%
62	American Hospital Assn.	$1,601,769	50%	49%
63	Prudential Insurance	$1,576,150	45%	54%
64	Fannie Mae	$1,558,357	54%	46%
65	Walt Disney Co.	$1,547,189	59%	41%
66	Eli Lilly & Co.	$1,539,285	19%	81%
67	Plumbers/Pipefitters Union	$1,520,107	96%	3%
68	International Assn. of Fire Fighters	$1,516,150	86%	14%
69	Lehman Brothers	$1,512,700	30%	70%
70	Painters & Allied Trades Union	$1,502,650	99%	1%
71	American International Group	$1,491,662	47%	53%
72	Williams & Bailey	$1,468,300	100%	0%
73	Glaxo Wellcome Inc.	$1,461,758	12%	88%
74	UST Inc.	$1,456,096	10%	89%
75	American Financial Group	$1,442,105	33%	67%
76	Slim-Fast Foods	$1,435,700	99%	1%
77	United Transportation Union	$1,430,800	86%	14%
78	Paine Webber	$1,418,900	33%	67%
79	Loral Spacecom	$1,386,150	98%	2%
80	Mirage Resorts	$1,377,656	44%	56%
81	Exxon Mobil Corp.	$1,373,310	10%	89%

Rank	Contributor	Total Contributions	To Dems.	To Repubs.
82	American Airlines	$1,373,047	37%	62%
83	Ironworkers Union	$1,351,915	91%	8%
84	American Dental Assn.	$1,341,617	45%	55%
85	BP Amoco Corp.	$1,341,264	30%	70%
86	Southern Co.	$1,318,925	27%	73%
87	Saban Entertainment	$1,318,400	100%	0%
88	United Steelworkers	$1,285,050	98%	1%
89	US West Inc.	$1,277,295	34%	66%
90	Bank One Corp.	$1,249,158	34%	66%
91	Northwest Airlines	$1,243,055	48%	51%
92	Chase Manhattan	$1,239,519	47%	52%
93	KPMG LLP	$1,211,464	30%	70%
94	Schering-Plough Corp.	$1,192,576	24%	76%
95	Buttenwieser & ASSOC.	$1,186,500	100%	0%
96	Verner, Liipfert et al.	$1,185,289	56%	43%
97	General Dynamics	$1,184,705	40%	60%
98	Angelos Law Office/Baltimore Orioles	$1,168,440	100%	0%
99	Limited Inc.	$1,140,719	34%	66%
100	National Ass. of Convenience Stores	$1,135,334	13%	87%

Table 30.1   Fat Cat Campaign Contributors, 2000 (*Continued*)

Source: Based on data released by the FEC, January 2, 2001.

is Bill Gates's Microsoft Corporation. In the past, Gates tried to avoid politics altogether; Microsoft was notably absent from previous lists of top campaign contributors. But Gates learned a hard lesson when Clinton's Justice Department under Attorney General Janet Reno launched its costly antitrust suit against Microsoft.

While contributions from the corporate, banking, and investment institutions are usually divided between the parties (albeit weighted toward Republicans), contributions from *unions* are almost exclusively directed toward Democrats. Indeed, union contributions are the single largest source of campaign money for the Democratic Party, followed by contributions from Hollywood's entertainment industry.

Contributions from wealthy individuals failed to match institutional contributions. While more than 100 institutions contributed $1 million or more in 2000, only two individuals contributed over this amount. (Peter Buttenwieser of Buttenwieser & Associates of Philadelphia and S. Daniel Abraham of Slim-Fast Foods both contributed over $1 million to Democrats.)

Expenditures for congressional campaigns also reached a new high. The U.S. Senate race in New York, featuring former First Lady Hillary Clinton against relative newcomer Republican Rick Lazio, set a new combined spending record for congressional elections at more than $85 million. A new individual congressional spending record of $65 million was set by multibillionaire investment banker (Goldman Sachs) Democrat Jon Corzine, who dug into his own fortune to win a U.S. Senate seat from New Jersey.

The *average* candidate for a U.S. Senate seat raised and spent over $5 million. And the *average* candidate for a U.S. House seat raised and spent about $800,000. This means that the average incumbent member of Congress must raise about $8,000 *per week*, every week of their term in office.

The Politicians: Ambition and Office Seeking

Ambition is the driving force in politics. Politics attracts people for whom power and celebrity are more rewarding than money, leisure, or privacy. "Political office today flows to those who want it enough to spend the time and energy mastering its pursuit. It flows in the direction of ambition—and talent."[1]

Political ambition is the most distinguishing characteristic of elected officeholders. The people who run for and win public office are not necessarily the most intelligent, best informed, wealthiest, or most successful business or professional people. At all levels of the political system, from presidential candidates, members of Congress, governors and state legislators, to city councils and school board members, it is the most politically ambitious people who are willing to sacrifice time, family and private life, and energy and effort for the power and celebrity that comes with public office.

Politics is becoming increasingly professionalized. "Citizen-statesmen"—people with business or professional careers who get into politics part-time or for short periods of time—are being driven out of political life by career politicians—people who enter politics early in life as a full-time occupation and expect to make it their career. Politically ambitious young people seek out internships and staff positions with members of Congress, with congressional committees, in state legislators' or governors' offices, or mayors' or council chambers. Others volunteer to work in political campaigns. Many find political mentors, as they learn how to organize campaigns, contact financial contributors, and deal with the media. By their early thirties, they are ready to run for local office or the state legislature. Rather than challenge a strong incumbent, they may wait for an open seat to be created by retirement, reapportionment, or its holder seeking another office. Or they may make an initial attempt against a strong incumbent of the opposition party in order to gain experience and win the appreciation of their own party's supporters for a good effort. Over time, running for and holding elective

office becomes their career. They work harder at it than anyone else, in part because they have no real private sector career to return to in case of defeat.

The prevalence of lawyers in politics is an American tradition. Among the nation's Founders—the fifty-five delegates to the Constitutional Convention in 1787—some twenty-five were lawyers. The political dominance of lawyers is even greater today, with lawyers filling nearly two thirds of U.S. Senate seats and nearly half of the seats in the U.S. House of Representatives.

It is sometimes argued that lawyers dominate in politics because of the parallel skills required in law and politics. Lawyering is the representation of clients; a lawyer employs similar skills whether representing clients in private practice or representing constituents in Congress. Lawyers are trained to deal with statutory law, so they may at least know how to find United States Code (the codified laws of the United States government) in a law library when they arrive in Congress to make or amend these laws.

But it is more likely that the people attracted to politics decide to go to law school, fully aware of the tradition of lawyers in American politics. Moreover, political officeholding, at the state and local level as well as in the national government, can help a struggling lawyer's private practice through free public advertising and opportunities to make contacts with potential clients. Finally, there are many special opportunities for lawyers to acquire public office in "lawyers only" posts in federal, state, and local government as judges and prosecuting attorneys. The lawyer-politician is not usually a top professional lawyer. Instead, the typical lawyer-politician uses his or her law career as a means of support—one that is compatible with political office seeking and officeholding.

A significant number of top politicians have inherited great wealth. The Roosevelts, Rockefellers, Kennedys, Bushes, and others have used their wealth and family connections to support their political careers. However, it is important to note that *a majority of the nation's top politicians have climbed the ladder from relative obscurity to political success.* Many have acquired some wealth in the process, but most political leaders started their climb from very middle-class circumstances. Thus, as in the corporate world, we find more "climbers" than "inheritors" at the top in the world of politics. . . .

Executive Decision-Makers: The Serious People

The politician is a professional office-seeker. The politician knows how to run for office—but not necessarily how to run the government. After victory at the polls, the prudent politician turns to "serious" people to run the government.[2] The corporate and governmental experience and educational credentials of these "serious" decision-makers greatly exceed those of most members of Congress or other elected officials. When presidents turn from the task of *running for office* to the task of *running a government,* they are obliged to recruit higher quality leadership than is typically found among political officeholders.

The responsibility for the initiation of national programs and policies falls primarily upon the top White House staff and the heads of executive departments. Generally, Congress merely responds to policy proposals initiated by the executive branch. The President and his key advisers and administrators have a strong incentive to fulfill their responsibility for decision-making. In the eyes of the American public, they are responsible for everything that happens in the nation, regardless of whether they have the authority or capacity to do anything about it. There is a general expectation that every administration, even one committed to a "caretaker" role, will put forth some sort of policy program.

The President and Vice-President, White House presidential advisers and ambassador-at-large, Cabinet secretaries, undersecretaries, and assistant secretaries constitute our executive elite. Let us take a brief look at the careers of some of the people who have served in key Cabinet positions in recent presidential administrations.

Secretaries of State

John Foster Dulles. (1953–60). Senior partner of Sullivan & Cromwell, and member of the board of directors of the Bank of New York, Fifth Avenue Bank, American Bank Note Co., International Nickel Co. of Canada, Babcock and Wilson Corp., Shenandoah Corp., United Cigar Stores, American Cotton Oil Co., United Railroad of St. Louis, and European Textile Corp. He was a trustee of the New York Public Library, Union Theological Seminary, the Rockefeller Foundation, and the Carnegie Endowment for International Peace; also a delegate to the World Council of Churches.

Dean Rusk. (1961–68). President of the Rockefeller Foundation.

William P. Rogers. (1969–73). U.S. attorney general during Eisenhower administration; senior partner in Royall, Koegal, Rogers and Wells (one of the twenty largest Wall Street law firms).

Henry Kissinger. (1973–77). Special assistant to the president for national security affairs; former Harvard professor of international affairs, and project director for Rockefeller Brothers Fund and for the Council on Foreign Relations.

Cyrus Vance. (1977–80). Senior partner in the New York law firm of Simpson, Thacher & Bartlett. A member of the board of directors of IBM and Pan American World Airways; a trustee of Yale University, the Rockefeller Foundation, and the Council on Foreign Relations; former secretary of the army under President Lyndon Johnson.

Alexander M. Haig, Jr. (1981–82). President of United Technologies Corporation, and former four-star general, U.S. Army. He was former Supreme Allied Commander, NATO forces in Europe; former assistant to the President under Richard Nixon; former deputy assistant to the President for national security under Henry Kissinger; former deputy commandant, U.S. Military Academy at West Point; former deputy secretary of defense.

George P. Shultz. (1982–89). President of the Bechtel Corporation. Former secretary of the treasury, former secretary of labor, and former director of Office of Management and Budget under President Richard Nixon.

Earned Ph.D. in economics from M.I.T. Former dean of the school of business, University of Chicago. Former director of General Motors, Borg-Warner, and Dillon, Read & Co.

James A. Baker III. (1989–92). Houston attorney and oil man who previously served as secretary of the treasury and White House chief of staff in the Reagan administration.

Warren Christopher. (1993–1997). California attorney (former law clerk for U.S. Supreme Court Justice William Douglas); partner, O'Melvany & Meyers; Deputy Secretary of State under President Carter; a director of California Edison, First Interstate Bancorp. Lockheed, and chairman of the Board of Trustees of the Carnegie Corp.

Madeleine Albright. (1997–2001). Georgetown University professor; U.S. Ambassador to the United Nations; member of the Council on Foreign Relations.

Secretaries of Treasury

George M. Humphrey. (1953–57). Former chairman of the board of directors of the M.A. Hanna Co.; member of board of directors of National Steel Corp., Consolidated Coal Co. of Canada, and Dominion Sugar Co.; trustee of M.I.T.

Robert B. Anderson. (1957–61). Secretary of the navy, 1953–54; deputy secretary of defense, 1945–55; member of board of directors of Goodyear Tire and Rubber Co. and Pan American World Airways; member of the executive board of the Boy Scouts of America.

Douglas Dillon. (1961–63). Chairman of the board of Dillon, Read & Co. (one of Wall Street's largest investment firms); member of New York Stock Exchange; director of U.S. and Foreign Securities Corp. and U.S. International Securities Corp.; member of board of governors of New York Hospital and the Metropolitan Museum of Art.

David Kennedy. (1969–71). President and chairman of the board of Continental Illinois Bank and Trust Co.; director of International Harvester Co., Commonwealth Edison, Pullman Co., Abbott Laboratories. Swift and Co., U.S. Gypsum, and Communications Satellite Corp.; trustee of the University of Chicago, the Brookings Institution, the Committee for Economic Development, and George Washington University.

John B. Connally. (1971–72). Secretary of the navy, governor of Texas, administrative assistant to Lyndon B. Johnson; attorney for Murcheson Brothers Investment (Dallas); former director of New York Central Railroad.

George P. Shultz. (1972–74). Secretary of labor and director of the Office of Management and Budget; former dean of the University of Chicago Graduate School of Business; former director of Borg-Warner Corp., General American Transportation Co., and Stein. Roe & Farnham (investments).

William E. Simon. (1974–77). Director of Federal Energy Office, and former deputy secretary of the treasury; formerly a senior partner of Salomon Brothers (one of Wall Street's largest investment firms specializing in municipal bond trading).

Warner Michael Blumenthal. (1977–79). President of the Bendix Corporation; former vice-president of Crown Cork Co.; trustee of Princeton University and the Council on Foreign Relations.

G. William Miller. (1979–81). Chairman and chief executive officer of Textron Corporation. Former partner in Cravath, Swaine & Moore (one of the nation's twenty-five largest and most prestigious law firms); a former director of Allied Chemical and Federated Department Stores; former chairman of the Federal Reserve Board.

Donald T. Regan. (1981–85). Chairman of the board and chief executive officer of Merrill Lynch & Co. Inc. (the nation's largest investment firm); former vice-chairman of the New York Stock Exchange; trustee of the University of Pennsylvania and the Committee for Economic Development; member of the policy committee of the Business Roundtable.

James A. Baker III. (1985–89). Wealthy Houston attorney whose father owned Texas Commerce Bank. Former undersecretary of commerce in the Ford administration and campaign chairman for George Bush's unsuccessful presidential race in 1980. President Reagan's White House chief of staff in his first term.

Nicholas Brady. (1989–93). Former chairman of Dillon, Read & Co.; a director of Purolator, NCR, Georgia International, ASA, and Media General.

Robert E. Rubin. (1995–2001). Chairman of the Wall Street investment firm Goldman Sachs. Trustee, Carnegie Corp.

Secretaries of Defense

Charles B. Wilson. (1953–57). President and chairman of the board of directors of General Motors.

Neil H. McElroy. (1957–59). President and chairman of the board of directors of Procter & Gamble; member of the board of directors of General Electric, Chrysler Corp., and Equitable Life Assurance Co.; member of the board of trustees of Harvard University, the National Safety Council, and the National Industrial Conference.

Thomas S. Gates. (1959–60). Secretary of the navy, 1957–59; chairman of the board and chief executive officer, Morgan Guaranty Trust Co.; member of the board of directors of General Electric, Bethlehem Steel, Scott Paper Co., Campbell Soup Co., Insurance Co. of North America, Cities Service, SmithKline and French (pharmaceuticals) and the University of Pennsylvania.

Roberts. McNamara. (1961–67). President and chairman of the board of directors of the Ford Motor Co.; member of the board of directors of Scott Paper Co.; president of the World Bank, 1967–81.

Clark Clifford. (1967–69). Senior partner of Clifford & Miller (Washington law firm); member of board of directors of the National Bank of Washington and the Sheridan Hotel Corp.; special counsel to the President, 1949–50; member of the board of trustees of Washington University in St. Louis.

Melvin Laird. (1969–73). Wisconsin Republican congressman, and former chairman of Republican conference in the House of Representatives.

James A. Schlesinger. (1973–77). Director, Central Intelligence Agency; former chairman of Atomic Energy Commission; formerly assistant director of the Office of Management and Budget, economics professor; and research associate of the RAND Corp.

Harold Brown. (1977–81). President of the California Institute of Technology. A member of the board of directors of International Business Machines (IBM) and the Times-Mirror Corp. Former secretary of the air force under President Lyndon Johnson, and U.S. representative to the SALT I talks under President Richard Nixon.

Caspar W. Weinberger. (1981–89). Vice-president and director of the Bechtel Corporation, the world's largest privately owned corporation. A member of the board of directors of Pepsico and Quaker Oats Co. Former secretary of Health, Education, and Welfare under President Richard Nixon; former director of the Office of Management and Budget; former chairman of the Federal Trade Commission. A former San Francisco attorney and California state legislator.

Richard B. Cheney. (1989–93). Congressman and chairman of the House Republican Conference; assistant to the President, Gerald Ford; chairman of the Cost of Living Council; director of Office of Economic Opportunity under President Richard Nixon. Attorney.

Les Aspin. (1993–94). Ph.D. Economics. U.S. Army 1966–68; House of Representatives, 1970–92; chairman of the House Armed Forces Committee, 1985–92.

William J. Perry. (1994–1997). Ph.D. Mathematics. Former director of Electronic

Defense Laboratories of GTE; former director of Stanford University Center for International Security; former Deputy Secretary of Defense.

William S. Cohen. (1997–2001). Attorney. U.S. Senator from Maine. . . .

The Judges

Nine people—none of whom is elected and all of whom serve for life—possess ultimate authority over all the other institutions of government. The Supreme Court of the United States has the authority to void the acts of popularly elected Presidents and Congresses. There is no appeal from their decision about what is the "supreme law of the land," except perhaps to undertake the difficult task of amending the Constitution itself. Only the good judgment of the Justices—their sense of "judicial self-restraint"—limits their power. It was the Supreme Court, rather than the President or Congress, that took the lead in important issues such as eliminating segregation from public life, ensuring voter equality in representation, limiting the powers of police, and declaring abortion to be a fundamental right of women.

Social scientists have commented frequently on the class bias of Supreme Court Justices: "White; generally Protestant . . . ; fifty to fifty-five years of age at the time of his appointment; Anglo-Saxon ethnic stock . . . ; high social status; reared in an urban environment; member of a civic-minded, politically active, economically comfortable family; legal training; some type of public office; generally well educated."[3] No blacks had served on the Supreme Court until the appointment of Associate Justice Thurgood Marshall in 1967. No women had served until the appointment of Sandra Day O'Connor in 1981. (See Table 30.2) Of course, social background does not necessarily determine judicial philosophy. But as John R. Schmidhauser observes, "If . . . the Supreme Court is the keeper of the American conscience, it is essentially the conscience of the American upper-middle class sharpened by the imperative of individual social responsibility and political activism, and conditioned by the conservative impact of legal training and professional attitudes and associations."[4]

Clarence Thomas: Up from Pinpoint

Not all Justices, however, conform to the upper-class portrait. No member of the nation's governing elite has ever had a steeper climb to the top than Justice Clarence Thomas. Born to a teenage mother who earned $10 a week as a maid, Clarence Thomas and his brother lived in a dirt-floor shack in Pinpoint, Georgia, where they were raised by strict, hard-working grandparents who taught young Clarence the value of education and sacrificed to send him to a Catholic school. He excelled academically and went on to mostly white Immaculate Conception Seminary College in Missouri to study for the Catholic priesthood. But when he overheard a fellow seminarian express satisfaction at the assassination of Dr. Martin Luther King, Jr., Thomas left the seminary in anger and enrolled at Holy Cross College, where he helped found the college's Black Student Union, and went on to graduate with honors and win admission to Yale Law School.

Upon graduating from Yale, Thomas took a job as assistant attorney general working in Missouri and, after a brief stint as an attorney for the Monsanto Corporation, returned to government as a congressional aide to Republican Missouri Senator John Danforth. Despite misgivings about accepting a "black" post in government, in 1981 Thomas accepted the post as head of the Office of Civil Rights in the Department of Education, using the position to speak out on self-reliance, self-discipline, and the value of education. In 1982, he was named chairman of the Equal Employment Opportunity Commission (EEOC), where he successfully eliminated much of that agency's financial mismanagement and aggressively pursued individual cases of discrimination. At the same time, he spoke out against racial "quotas" and imposed minority hiring goals only on employers with proven records of discrimination. In 1989, President Bush nominated him to the U.S. Court of Appeals and he was easily confirmed by the Senate.

In tapping Thomas for the Supreme Court, the Bush White House reasoned that the liberal groups who had blocked the earlier nomination of conservative Robert Bork would be reluctant to launch personal attacks on an African American. But

Table 30.2 Backgrounds of Supreme Court Justices	
All U.S. Supreme Court Justices, 1789 to Present	**Number of Justices (Total = 109)**
Occupation before Appointment	
Private legal practice	25
State judgeship	22
Federal judgeship	27
U.S. attorney general	7
Deputy or assistant U.S. attorney general	2
U.S. solicitor general	2
U.S. senator	6
U.S. representative	2
State governor	3
Federal executive posts	10
Other	3
Religious Background	
Protestant	85
Roman Catholic	9
Jewish	7
Unitarian	7
No religious affiliation	1
Age on Appointment	
Under 40	4
41–50	30
51–60	59
61–70	15
Political Party Affiliation	
Federalist (to 1835)	13
Democrat-Republican (to 1828)	7
Whig (to 1861)	2
Democrat	45
Republican	42
Sex	
Male	107
Female	2
Race	
Caucasian	107
Other	2

Sources: Congressional Quarterly. *Congressional Quarterly's Guide to the U.S. Supreme Court* (Washington, D.C.: Congressional Quarterly, 1979)*;* and *Congressional Quarterly's Guide to Government,* Spring 1983 (Washington, D.C., 1982). Updated to 2001 by author.

during nationally televised hearings of the Senate Judiciary Committee, University of Oklahoma law professor Anita Hill, a former legal assistant to Thomas both at the Department of Education and later at the Equal Employment Opportunity Commission, contacted the staff of the Judiciary Committee with charges that Thomas had sexually harassed her in both jobs. Initially, Hill declined to make her charges public, but when Senator Joseph Biden, the committee chairman, refused to circulate anonymous charges, she agreed to be interviewed by the F.B.I. and went on to give a nationally televised press conference, elaborating on her charges against Thomas. Her bombshell became a media extravaganza and sent the Senate into an uproar.

The Judiciary Committee reopened its hearings, with televised emotional testimony from both Anita Hill and Clarence Thomas. Indeed, the confirmation process exploded into a sleazy soap opera, with lurid stories about pubic hairs, penis sizes, and pornographic films of women with animals. The only restraint was Chairman Biden's rule that no questions would be asked about either Clarence Thomas's or Anita Hill's sex life. But the damage was done anyway, not only to Clarence Thomas and Anita Hill, but to the Senate confirmation process and the Senate as an institution.

In the end, there was no objective way to determine who was telling the truth. Too often the truth in Washington is determined by opinion polls. An astonishing 86 percent of the general public said they had watched the televised hearings. A majority of blacks as well as whites, and a majority of women as well as men, sided with Clarence Thomas.[5] The final Senate confirmation vote was 52 to 48, the closest vote in the history of Supreme Court confirmations.

Sandra Day O'Connor: In the Center of the Court

For nearly 200 years the U.S. Supreme Court was America's most exclusive male club. After 101 male justices, Sandra Day O'Connor was named to the Supreme Court by President Reagan in 1981. At the time of her appointment, O'Connor was a fifty-one-year-old state appellate court judge in Arizona. Justice O'Connor had no previous experience as a federal court judge, but she had the active support of Arizona's senior U.S. senator and Republican warhorse, Barry Goldwater. More important, she was a "she." Reagan was anxious to deflect attacks on his opposition to the Equal Rights Amendment and his failure to appoint many women in his own administration. As one Reagan aide put it: "This is worth twenty-five assistant secretaries, maybe more!" Feminist groups were forced to support the appointments even though O'Connor's record in Arizona was moderately conservative.

Sandra Day grew up on her family's large Arizona ranch, graduated from Stanford with honors, and then went on to Stanford Law School. She finished near the top of her class, along with Chief justice of the Supreme Court William Rehnquist (who was first in the class). She married John Jay O'Connor, a Phoenix attorney, and raised three sons. She entered Arizona politics about the time her youngest son entered school. She was appointed to the Arizona State Senate in 1969 and was later elected twice to that body. She rose to majority leader in 1973. She left the Arizona legislature in 1975 to become a Phoenix trial judge. In 1979, she was appointed by a Democratic governor to the Arizona Court of Appeals. Work on this state intermediate court, however, does not involve major constitutional questions.

O'Connor had some business experience; she was formerly a director of the First National Bank of Arizona and Blue Cross/Blue Shield of Arizona. But until her appointment to the U.S. Supreme Court, she was an obscure state court judge. Her service as a Republican leader in the Arizona State Senate qualified her as a moderately conservative party loyalist. However, it appears that her professional and political friendships had more to do with bringing her to President Reagan's attention than her record as a jurist. She had known Justice William Rehnquist since her law school days. She had known former Chief Justice Warren Burger for a long time. And Barry Goldwater had been her mentor in Arizona Republican politics. When Reagan's political advisers told him during the presidential campaign that he was not doing well among women voters, the candidate responded by pledging to appoint a woman to the Supreme Court. Reagan's fulfillment of his campaign pledge was a politically popular decision.

In recent years Sandra Day O'Connor has emerged as the leader of a middle bloc of votes on the High Court, mediating between the liberal and conservative blocs. O'Connor has taken the lead in shaping Supreme Court policy on women's issues—including abortion. O'Connor strongly reaffirmed a woman's fundamental right to abortion, yet recognized a state's interest in protecting a "viable" fetus (a late-term fetus capable of surviving outside of the womb).[6] She has also taken the lead in deciding Supreme Court policy in the controversial area of affirmative action, arguing that laws that distinguish between individuals based on their race must be narrowly tailored to remedy specific injustices. "Racial classifications of any sort pose the risk of lasting harm to our society. They reinforce the belief, held by too many for too much of our history, that individuals should be judged by the color of their skin."[7]

The Military Establishment

In his farewell address to the nation in 1961, President Dwight D. Eisenhower warned of "an immense military establishment and a large arms industry." He observed: "In the councils of government, we must guard against the acquisition of unwarranted influence, whether sought or unsought, by the military-industrial complex."

The phrase *the military-industrial complex* caught on with many commentators over the years. It implied that a giant network of defense contractors for example, Lockheed Aircraft, General Dynamics, Rockwell, McDonnell Douglas, Boeing, Litton, Hughes Tool, Grumman Aircraft—together with members of Congress in whose districts their plants were located, conspired with the generals in the Pentagon to create a powerful force in governmental and corporate circles. Indeed, radical social commentators held the military-industrial complex responsible for war and "imperialism."

But whatever the power of defense contractors and the military at the height of the Cold War, their influence today in governing circles is miniscule. Indeed, their goal today is to avoid complete dismantlement. Spending for national defense has declined precipitously from 10 percent of the GNP in the Eisenhower and Kennedy years to less than 3 percent today. Spending on Social Security, Medicare, and welfare, including Medicaid, exceeds 58 percent of the federal budget, compared to 16 percent for national defense.[8] There are 2 million civilian employees of the federal government compared to only 1.4 million people in the armed forces. The long-term decline of U.S. defense spending suggests that the American military-industrial complex was *not* a very powerful conspiracy.

It seems clear in retrospect that C. Wright Mills placed too much importance on the military in his work, *The Power Elite.*[9] Mills was writing in the early 1950s when military prestige was high following victory in World War II. After the war, a few high-level military men were recruited to top corporate positions to add prestige to corporate boards. But this practice ended in the 1960s. The contrast between the political prestige of the military in the post–World War II years and in the post–Vietnam years is striking: The Supreme Allied Commander in Europe in World War II, Dwight D. Eisenhower, was elected President of the United States; the U.S. Commander in Vietnam, William Westmoreland, was defeated in his bid to become governor of South Carolina! Moreover, in contrast with corporate and governmental elites, military officers do *not* come from the upper or upper-middle class of society. Military officers are more likely to be recruited from lower- and lower-middle-class backgrounds, and more likely to have rural and southern roots than are corporate or governmental elites.[10]

Colin Powell: Soldier-Statesman

When General Colin Powell was named chairman of the Joint Chiefs of Staff by President George Bush in 1989, he became the first African American and the youngest man in history to hold that post. During the Gulf War General Powell oversaw the largest military deployment of American troops since the Vietnam War. He is credited with developing and implementing a doctrine of maximum force that kept U.S. casualties to a minimum while Saddam Hussein's army was routed from Kuwait and destroyed. Powell had previously served as national security adviser to President Ronald

Reagan, making him a principal military adviser to three Presidents.

Born in Harlem to Jamaican immigrant parents, Powell recounts his youth as proof that "it is possible to rise above conditions." After his graduation from Morris High School in the South Bronx, Powell's parents encouraged him to attend college, and he enrolled at City College of New York on an ROTC scholarship. He graduated with a degree in geology in 1958 at the top of his ROTC class and was commissioned a second lieutenant in the U.S. Army. Powell went to South Vietnam as a military adviser in 1962 and returned for a second tour in 1968. In Vietnam he was awarded two Purple Hearts for wounds suffered in combat, and a Bronze Star and the Legion of Merit for valor under fire.

Powell returned to the classroom in 1972 and earned a master's degree in business administration from George Washington University. In 1972 he was appointed to the prestigious White House Fellows Program and was assigned to the Office of Management and Budget, where he worked under Caspar Weinberger, who later became secretary of defense in the Reagan administration. Powell's career was on a fast track after this early White House duty. He served as a battalion commander in Korea, graduated from the National War College, served as military assistant to the deputy secretary of defense, and won promotion to general and command of the Second Brigade of the 101st Airborne Division.

In 1983 Powell was recalled to Washington by Defense Secretary Weinberger to become his senior military adviser. During the invasion of Grenada in October 1983, Powell was assigned the task of running interference for the military against meddling White House and National Security Council staff. Later Powell supported Secretary Weinberger in opposing arms sales to Iran; he was overruled by President Reagan, but his memo urging that Congress be notified of the arms transfers would later stand him in good stead with the Congress after the Iran-Contra scandal became public. In 1986 Powell eagerly accepted command of the U.S. Fifth Corps in Germany, declining offers to stay on in Washington. But when President Reagan himself called and urged him to accept the post as national security adviser and reform the operations of the NSC staff, he agreed. Powell lent credibility to Reagan's promises to implement the recommendations of the Tower Commission, which had investigated the Iran-Contra affair.

President Bush chose General Powell in 1989 to be Chairman of the Joint Chiefs of Staff—the nation's highest military position. It was General Powell who helped convince the President that if military force were to be used to oust Saddam Hussein from Kuwait, it should be overwhelming and decisive force, not gradual limited escalation, as in Vietnam. Powell "ran interference" in Washington for the field commander, General Norman Schwarzkopf. Powell's televised briefings during the course of the war, together with those of General Schwarzkopf, assured the American people of the competence and effectiveness of the U.S. military. He summed up U.S. military strategy toward the Iraqi Army in Kuwait: "First we're going to cut it off. Then we're going to kill it." Under Powell's leadership, the U.S. military achieved a brilliant victory in the Gulf War with precious few casualties.

Powell retired from the Army in 1993, inspiring speculation that the popular general might enter the political arena. Throughout his military career, Powell avoided partisan affiliation. Registered as a political independent, Powell always considered himself a soldier first. Powell credits his success to those who "suffered and sacrificed to create the conditions and set the stage for me."

Early in 1996, public opinion polls showed Powell leading all other candidates for president, including incumbent Bill Clinton. But Powell steadfastly refused to become a candidate. Rather, he founded an organization, Alliance for Youth, dedicated to helping disadvantaged youngsters. In the 2000 presidential election he endorsed George W. Bush, the son of his old Boss. He declined to join the Republican ticket as vice-president, but he accepted the position of Secretary of State.

Notes

1. Alan Ehrenhalt, *The United States of Ambition: Politicians' Power and Pursuit of Office* (New York: Random House, 1991), p. 22.

2. Pulitzer Prize–winning writer David Halberstam reports a revealing conversation between newly elected President John F. Kennedy and Robert A. Lovett in December 1960, a month before Kennedy was to take office: "On the threshold of great power and great office, the young man seemed to have everything. He was handsome, rich, charming, candid . . . [But] he had spent the last five years, he said ruefully, running for office, and he did not know any real public officials, people to run a government, *serious men*. The only ones he knew, he admitted, were politicians. . . . Politicians *did* need men to serve, to run the government." Robert Lovett was "the very embodiment of the Establishment." His father had been chairman of the board of Union Pacific Railroad and a partner of the great railroad tycoon, E. H. Harriman. Lovett urged Kennedy to listen to the advice of Lovett's partner and former governor of New York and ambassador to the Soviet Union, Averell Harriman; to see "Jack McCloy at Chase" (then chairman of the board of Chase Manhattan), and "Doug Dillon too" (to become Kennedy's secretary of the treasury); to look up a "young fellow over at Rockefeller, Dean Rusk" (to become Kennedy's secretary of state); and to get "this young man at Ford, Robert McNamara" (to become Kennedy's secretary of defense). Kennedy gratefully accepted the advice: he turned to these "serious men" to run the government. David Halberstam, *The Best and Brightest* (New York: Random House. 1969). pp. 3–4.

3. Henry Abraham, *The Judicial Process* (New York: Oxford University Press, 1962), p. 58.

4. John R. Schmidhauser, *The Supreme Court* (New York: Holt Rinehart and Winston, 1960), p. 59.

5. Gallup Opinion Reports, October 15, 1991, p. 209.

6. *Planned Parenthood v. Casey* (1992).

7. *Shaw v. Reno* (1993).

8. *Budget of the United States Government 2001* gives this breakdown by function: Social Security: 23.2%; Medicare: 12.0%; Income Security: 14.2%; Medicaid: 9.1%.

9. C. Wright Mills, *The Power Elite* (New York: Oxford, 1956).

10. Morris Janowitz, *The Professional Soldier* (New York: Free Press, 1960), p. 378.

31

Excerpts from *Power and Powerlessness: Quiescence and Rebellion in an Appalachian Valley*

JOHN GAVENTA

This is a study about quiescence and rebellion in a situation of glaring inequality. Why, in a social relationship involving the domination of a non-élite by an élite, does challenge to that domination not occur? What is there in certain situations of social deprivation that prevents issues from arising, grievances from being voiced, or interests from being recognized? Why, in an oppressed community where one might intuitively expect upheaval, does one instead find, or appear to find, quiescence? Under what conditions and against what obstacles does rebellion begin to emerge?

The problem is significant to classical democratic and Marxist theories alike, for, in a broad sense, both share the notion that the action of the dispossessed will serve to counter social inequities. Yet, as these views move from political theory to political sociology, so, too, do they appear to move—particularly with reference to the United States—from discussing the necessities of widespread participation and challenge to considering the reasons for their non-occurrence.[1] In their wake, other more conservative theories of democracy present the appearance of quiescence in the midst of inequality as evidence of the legitimacy of an existing order, or as an argument for decision making by the few, or at least as a phenomenon functional to social stability.[2] More recently, these 'neo-élitists' have in turn been challenged by others who, with C. Wright Mills, argue that the appearance of quiescence need neither suggest consent nor refute the classical ideals.[3] Rather, it may reflect the use or misuse of modern-day power.

While the theories of democracy turn, at least to a degree, upon disputes as to the significance of quiescence, the sociological literature of industrial societies offers an array of explanations for its roots: embourgeoisement, hegemony, no real inequality, low rank on a socio-economic status scale, cultural deficiencies of the deprived, or simply the innate apathy of the human race—to name but a few. Rather than deal with these directly, this study will explore another explanation: in situations of inequality, the political response of the deprived group or class may be seen as a function of power relationships, such that power serves for the development and maintenance of the quiescence of the non-élite. The emergence of rebellion, as a corollary, may be understood as the process by which the relationships of power are altered.

The argument itself immediately introduces a further set of questions to be explored: what is the nature of power? How do power and powerlessness affect the political actions and conceptions of a non-élite?

In his recent book, *Power: A Radical View,* Lukes has summarized what has been an extended debate since C. Wright Mills, especially in American political science, about the concept and appropriate methods for its study.[4] Power, he suggests, may be understood as having three dimensions, the first of which is based upon the traditional pluralists' approach, the second of which is essentially that put forward by Bachrach and Baratz in their consideration of power's second face,[5] and the third of which Lukes develops. In this chapter, I shall examine the dimensions briefly, arguing that each carries with it, implicitly or explicitly, differing assumptions about the nature and roots of participation and non-participation. I shall argue further that together the dimensions of power (and powerlessness) may be developed into a tentative model for more usefully understanding the generation of quiescence, as well as the process by which challenge may emerge. Finally, I shall sketch in general terms a methodology by which the notions may be considered empirically. . . .

1. The Nature of Power and Roots of Quiescence

The One-Dimensional Approach

The one-dimensional approach to power is essentially that of the pluralists, developed in American political science most particularly by Robert Dahl

and Nelson Polsby. 'My intuitive idea of power', Dahl wrote in an early essay, 'is something like this: A has power over B to the extent that he can get B to do something that B would not otherwise do'.[6] In the politics of a community, Polsby later added, power may be studied by examining 'who participates, who gains and loses, and who prevails in decision-making'.[7]

The key to the definition is a focus on behaviour—doing, participating—about which several assumptions are made, to be questioned later in this book. First, grievances are assumed to be recognized and acted upon. Polsby writes, for instance, that 'presumably people participate in those areas they care about the most. Their values, eloquently expressed by their participation, cannot, it seems to me, be more effectively objectified'.[8] Secondly, participation is assumed to occur within decision-making arenas, which are in turn assumed to be open to virtually any organized group. Again, Polsby writes, 'in the decision-making of fragmented government—and American national, state and local government are nothing if not fragmented—the claims of small intense minorities are usually attended to'.[9] In his study of New Haven Dahl takes a similar view:

> In the United States the political system does not constitute a homogenous class with well-defined class interests. In New Haven, in fact, the political system is easily penetrated by anyone whose interests and concerns attract him to the distinctive political culture of the stratum . . . The independence, penetrability and heterogeneity of the various segments of the political stratum all but guarantee that any dissatisfied group will find a spokesman. . . .[10]

Thirdly, because of the openness of the decision-making process, leaders may be studied, not as élites, but as representative spokesmen for a mass. Polsby writes, 'the pluralists want to find about leadership's role, presumed to be diverse and fluid'.[11] Indeed, it is the conflict amongst various leaders that ensures the essential responsiveness of the political game to all groups or classes. As Dahl puts it, 'to a remarkable degree, the existence of democratic ceremonials that give rise to the rules of combat has insured that few social elements have been neglected for long by one party or the other'.[12]

Within the one-dimensional approach, because a) people act upon recognized grievances, b) in an open system, c) for themselves or through leaders, then *non-participation* or *inaction* is not a political problem. For Polsby it may be explained away with 'the fundamental presumption that human behaviour is governed in large part by inertia'.[13] Dahl distinguishes between the activist, *homo politicus,* and the non-activist, *homo civicus,* for whom 'political action will seem considerably less efficient than working at his job, earning more money, taking out insurance, joining a club, planning a vacation, moving to another neighbourhood or city, or coping with an uncertain future in manifold other ways. . .'.[14] The pluralists argue that by assuming political action rather than inaction to be the problem to be explained, their methodology avoids the 'inappropriate and arbitrary assignment of upper and middle class values to all actors in the community'[15]—i.e. the value of participation. Yet, the assumption itself allows class-bound conclusions. Dahl's characterization of *homo civicus* is certainly one of a citizen for whom there are comfortable alternatives to participation and relatively low costs to inaction. And for Polsby, the assumption of inertia combines with the assumption of an open system to allow the conclusion, without further proof, that class consciousness has not developed in America because it would be 'inefficient' or 'unnecessary'.[16]

The biases of these assumptions might appear all the more readily were this approach strictly applied to the quiescence of obviously deprived groups. Political silence, or inaction, would have to be taken to reflect 'consensus', despite the extent of the deprivation. Yet, rarely is the methodology thus applied, even by the pluralists themselves. To make plausible inaction among those for whom the status quo is not comfortable, other explanations are provided for what appears 'irrational' or 'inefficient' behaviour. And, because the study of non-participation in this approach is sequestered by definition from the study of power, the explanations must generally be placed within the circumstance or culture of the non-participants themselves. The empirical relationship of low socio-economic status to low participation gets explained away as the apathy, political inefficacy, cynicism or alienation of the impoverished.[17] Or other factors—often thought of as deficiencies—are put forward in the non-political culture of the deprived group, such as in the 'amoral familism' argument of Banfield in reference to Southern Italy.[18] Rather than examining the possibility that power may be involved, this approach 'blames the victim' for his non-participation.[19] And it also follows that by changing the victim—e.g. through remedial education or cultural integration—patterns of nonparticipation will also be changed. Increased participation, it is assumed, will not meet power constraints.

Even within its own assumptions, of course, this understanding of the political behaviour of deprived groups is inadequate. What is there inherent in low income, education or status, or in rural or traditional cultures that itself explains quiescence? If these are sufficient components of explanation, how are variations in behaviour amongst such groups to be explained? Why, for instance, do welfare action groups spring up in some cities but not in others? Why are the peasantry of southern Italy quiescent (if they are), while the *ujamaa* villagers of Tanzania are not? Why do rural farmers of Saskatchewan form a socialist party while those in the rural areas of the southern United States remain 'backward'?[20] If most blacks are of a relatively low socio-economic status, why did a highly organized civil rights movement develop, and itself alter patterns of political participation?

In short, as operationalized within this view, the power of A is thought to affect the action of B, but it is not considered a factor relevant to why B does not act in a manner that B otherwise might, were he not powerless relative to A. That point, among others, is well made by those who put forward the two-dimensional view of power.

The Two-Dimensional Approach

'It is profoundly characteristic', wrote Schattschneider, that 'responsibility for widespread nonparticipation is attributed wholly to the ignorance, indifference and shiftlessness of the people'. But, he continued:

> There is a better explanation: absenteeism reflects the suppression of the options and alternatives that reflect the needs of the nonparticipants. It is not necessarily true that people with the greatest needs participate in politics most actively—whoever decides what the game is about also decides who gets in the game.[21]

In so writing, Schattschneider introduced a concept later to be developed by Bachrach and Baratz as power's 'second face', by which power is exercised not just upon participants within the decision-making process but also towards the exclusion of certain participants and issues altogether.[22] Political organizations, like all organizations, develop a 'mobilization of bias . . . in favour of the exploitation of certain kinds of conflict and the suppression of others . . . Some issues are organized into politics while others are organized out'.[23] And, if issues are prevented from arising, so too may actors be prevented from acting. The study of politics must focus 'both on who gets what, when and how and who gets left out and how'[24]—and how the two are interrelated.

When this view has been applied (explicitly or implicitly) to the political behaviour of deprived groups, explanations for quiescence in the face of inequalities have emerged, which are quite different from those of the one-dimensional view. For instance, Matthew Crenson, in his extended empirical application of the 'non-issues' approach, *The Un-Politics of Air Pollution,* states that 'while very few investigators have found it worthwhile to inquire about the political origins of inaction . . . ', in Gary, Indiana, 'the reputation for power may have been more important than its exercise. It could have enabled U.S. Steel to prevent political action without taking action itself, and may have been responsible for the political retardation of Gary's air pollution issue'.[25] Or, Parenti, in his study of urban blacks in Newark, found that in city hall the 'plurality of actors and interests . . . displayed remarkable capacity to move against some rather modest lower-class

claims'. 'One of the most important aspects of power', he adds, is 'not to prevail in a struggle but to predetermine the agenda of struggle—to determine whether certain questions ever reach the competition stage'.[26] Salamon and Van Evera, in their work on voting in Mississippi, found patterns of participation and non-participation not to be related to apathy amongst low status blacks as much as to 'fear' and 'vulnerability' of these blacks to local power élites.[27] Similarly, in his extensive study, *Peasant Wars,* Wolf found acquiescence or rebellion not to be inherent in the traditional values or isolation of the peasantry, but to vary 'in the relation of the peasantry to the field of power which surrounds it'.[28]

In this view, then, apparent inaction within the political process by deprived groups may be related to power, which in turn is revealed in participation and non-participation, upon issues and non-issues, which arise or are prevented from arising in decision-making arenas. But though the second view goes beyond the first, it still leaves much undone.

Empirically, while the major application of the approach, that by Crenson, recognizes that 'perceived industrial influence, industrial inaction, and the neglect of the dirty air issue go together', it still adds 'though it is difficult to say how'.[29]

Even conceptually, though, this second approach stops short of considering the full range of the possibilities by which power may intervene in the issue-raising process. While Bachrach and Baratz insist that the study of power must include consideration of the barriers to action upon grievances, they equally maintain that it does not go so far as to include how power may affect conceptions of grievances themselves. If 'the observer can uncover no grievances', if 'in other words, there appears to be universal acquiescence in the status quo', then, they argue, it is not 'possible, in such circumstances, to determine empirically whether the consensus is genuine or instead has been enforced'.[30]

However difficult the empirical task, though, their assumption must be faulted on two counts. First, as Lukes points out, 'to assume the absence of grievance equals genuine consensus is simply to rule out the possibility of false or manipulated consensus by definitional fiat'.[31] Secondly, though, the position presents an inconsistency even within their own work. They write further:

> For the purposes of analysis, a power struggle exists, overtly or covertly, either when both sets of contestants are aware of its existence *or when only the less powerful party is aware* of it. The latter case is relevant where the domination of status quo defenders is so secure and pervasive that they are oblivious of any persons or groups desirous of challenging their preeminence.[32]

But, if the power of the 'defenders of the *status quo*' serves to affect their awareness that they are being challenged, why cannot the powerlessness of potential challengers similarly serve to affect their awareness of interests and conflict within a power situation? That is, just as the dominant may become so 'secure' with their position as to become 'oblivious', so, too, may such things as routines, internalization of roles or false consensus lead to acceptance of the *status quo* by the dominated. In short, I shall agree with Lukes that the emphasis of this approach upon observable conflict may lead it to neglect what may be the 'crucial point': 'the most effective and insidious use of power is to prevent such conflict from arising in the first place'.[33]

The Three-Dimensional Approach

In putting forward a further conception of power, Lukes argues that 'A exercises power over B when A affects B in a manner contrary to B's interests'.[34] The means by which A may do so go significantly beyond those allowed within the first two approaches.

First, 'A may exercise power over B by getting him to do what he does not want to do, but *he also exercises power over him by influencing, shaping or determining his very wants*'.[35] Not only might A exercise power over B by prevailing in the resolution of key issues or by preventing B from effectively raising those issues, but also through affecting B's conceptions of the issues altogether. Secondly, 'this may happen in the absence of observable conflict, which may have been successfully averted', though there must be

latent conflict, which consists, Lukes argues, 'in a contradiction between the interests of those exercising power and the *real interests* of those they exclude'.[36] Thirdly, the analysis of power must avoid the individualistic, behavioural confines of the one- and to some extent the two-dimensional approaches. It must allow 'for consideration of the many ways in which *potential issues* are kept out of politics, whether through the operation of social forces and institutional practices or through individuals' decisions'.[37] In so extending the concept of power, Lukes suggests, 'the three-dimensional view . . . offers the prospect of a serious sociological and not merely personalized explanation of how political systems prevent demands from becoming political issues or even from being made'.[38]

Though the prospect has been offered, the task has yet to have been carried out. To do so, though, might bring together usefully approaches often considered separately of the relationship of political conceptions to the social order. For instance, following in a line of American political scientists (beginning perhaps with Lasswell), the emphasis upon consciousness allows consideration of the subjective effects of power, including Edelman's notion that 'political actions chiefly arouse or satisfy people not by granting or withholding their stable, substantive demands but rather by changing their demands and expectations'.[39] At the same time, by not restricting power to individuals' actions, the three-dimensional definition allows consideration of the social forces and historical patterns involved in Gramsci's concept of hegemony, or what Milliband develops as the use of ideological predominance for the 'engineering of consent' amongst the subordinate classes.[40]

Perhaps more significant, however, are the implications of this three-dimensional approach for an understanding of how power shapes participation patterns of the relatively powerless. In a sense, the separation by the pluralists of the notion of power from the phenomenon of quiescence has indicated the need for such a theory, while in the second and third approaches are its beginnings. In the two-dimensional approach is the suggestion of barriers that prevent issues from emerging into political arenas—i.e. that constrain conflict. In the three-dimensional approach is the suggestion of the use of power to pre-empt manifest conflict at all, through the shaping of patterns or conceptions of non-conflict. Yet, the two-dimensional approach may still need development and the three-dimensional prospect has yet to be put to empirical test.

This book therefore will pick up the challenge of attempting to relate the three dimensions of power to an understanding of quiescence and rebellion of a relatively powerless group in a social situation of high inequality. Through the empirical application further refinements of the notion of power may develop, but, of equal importance, more insights may be gleaned as to why non-élites in such situations act and believe as they do.

2. The Mechanisms of Power

What are the mechanisms of power? How might its components be wielded in the shaping or containment of conflict?

First Dimension

In the first-dimensional approach to power, with its emphasis on observable conflict in decision-making arenas, power may be understood primarily by looking at who prevails in bargaining over the resolution of key issues. The mechanisms of power are important, but relatively straightforward and widely understood: they involve the political resources—votes, jobs, influence—that can be brought by political actors to the bargaining game and how well those resources can be wielded in each particular play—through personal efficacy, political experience, organizational strength, and so on.

Second Dimension

The second-dimensional approach adds to these resources those of a 'mobilization of bias',

> A set of predominant values, beliefs, rituals, and institutional procedures ('rules of the game') that operate systematically and consistently to the benefit of certain persons and groups at the expense of others.

Those who benefit are placed in a preferred position to defend and promote their vested interests.[41]

Bachrach and Baratz argue in *Power and Poverty* that the mobilization of bias not only may be wielded upon decision-making in political arenas, but it in turn is sustained primarily through 'non-decisions', defined as:

> A decision that results in suppression or thwarting of a latent or manifest challenge to the values or interests of the decision maker. To be more nearly explicit, nondecision-making is a means by which demands for change in the existing allocation of benefits and privileges in the community can be suffocated before they are voiced, or kept covert; or killed before they gain access to the relevant decision-making arena; or, failing all of these things, maimed or destroyed in the decision-implementing stage of the policy process.[42]

One form of non-decision-making, they suggest, may be force. A second may be the threat of sanctions, 'negative or positive', 'ranging from intimidation . . . to co-optation'. A third may be the 'invocation of an existing bias of the political system—a norm, precedent, rule or procedure—to squelch a threatening demand or incipient issue'. This may include the manipulation of symbols, such as, in certain political cultures, 'communist' or 'troublemaker'. A fourth process which they cite 'involves reshaping or strengthening the mobilization of bias' through the establishment of new barriers or new symbols 'against the challengers' efforts to widen the scope of conflict'.

While the above mechanisms of power involve identifiable actions which prevent issues from entering the decision-making arenas, there may be other processes of non-decision-making power which are not so explicitly observable. The first of these, 'decisionless decisions', grows from institutional inaction, or the unforeseen sum effect of incremental decisions. A second process has to do with the 'rule of anticipated reactions', 'situations where B, confronted by A who has greater power resources decides not to make a demand upon A, for fear that the latter will invoke sanctions against him'.[43] In both cases, the power process involves a non-event rather than an observable non-decision.

Third Dimension

By far the least developed and least understood mechanisms of power—at least within the field of political science—are those of the third dimension. Their identification, one suspects, involves specifying the means through which power influences, shapes or determines conceptions of the necessities, possibilities, and strategies of challenge in situations of latent conflict. This may include the study of social myths, language, and symbols, and how they are shaped or manipulated in power processes.[44] It may involve the study of communication of information—both of what is communicated and how it is done.[45] It may involve a focus upon the means by which social legitimations are developed around the dominant, and instilled as beliefs or roles in the dominated.[46] It may involve, in short, locating the power processes behind the social construction of meanings and patterns[47] that serve to get B to act and believe in a manner in which B otherwise might not, to A's benefit and B's detriment.

Such processes may take direct observable forms, as Lukes suggests. 'One does not have to go to the lengths of talking about Brave New World, or the world of B. F. Skinner to see this: thought control takes many less total and more mundane forms, through the control of information, through the mass media, and through the process of socialization'.[48] His assertions are supported in various branches of contemporary social science. For instance, Deutsch and Rieselbach, in writing of new developments in the field, say that communications theory 'permits us to conceive of such elusive notions as consciousness and the political will as observable processes'.[49] Similarly, the study of socialization, enlightened by learning theory, may help to uncover the means by which dominance is maintained or legitimacy instilled, as Mann or Frey, among others, argue.[50]

In addition to these processes of information control or socialization, there may be other more indirect means by which power alters political conceptions. They involve psychological adaptations

to the state of being without power. They may be viewed as third-dimensional effects of power, growing from the powerlessness experienced in the first two dimensions. Especially for highly deprived or vulnerable groups, three examples might be given of what shall be called the *indirect* mechanisms of power's third dimension.

In the first instance, the conceptions of the powerless may alter as an adaptive response to continual defeat. If the victories of A over B in the first dimension of power lead to non-challenge of B due to the anticipation of the reactions of A, as in the second-dimensional case, then, over time, the calculated withdrawal by B may lead to an unconscious pattern of withdrawal, maintained not by fear of power of A but by a sense of powerlessness within B, regardless of A's condition. A sense of powerlessness may manifest itself as extensive fatalism, self-deprecation, or undue apathy about one's situation. Katznelson has argued, for instance, in *Black Men, White Cities* that 'given the onus of choice, the powerless internalize their impossible situation and internalize their guilt . . . The slave often identified with his master and accepted society's estimate of himself as being without worth . . . The less complete but nonetheless pervasive powerlessness of blacks in America's northern ghettos has had similar effects'.[51] Or, the powerless may act, but owing to the sense of their powerlessness, they may alter the level of their demands.[52] The sense of powerlessness may also lead to a greater susceptibility to the internalization of the values, beliefs, or rules of the game of the powerful as a further adaptive response—i.e. as a means of escaping the subjective sense of powerlessness, if not its objective condition.[53]

The sense of powerlessness may often be found with, though it is conceptually distinct from, a second example of the indirect mechanisms of power's third dimension. It has to do with the inter-relationship of participation and consciousness. As has been seen in the pluralists' literature, it is sometimes argued that participation is a consequence of a high level of political awareness or knowledge, most often associated with those of a favourable socio-economic status. However, it might also be the case, as is argued by the classical democratic theorists, that it is participation itself which increases political consciousness—a reverse argument from the one given above.[54] Social psychology studies, for instance, have found that political learning is dependent at least to some degree of political participation within and mastery upon one's environment.[55] And, as Pizzorno points out, there is a 'singular relationship, well known by all organizers of parties and political movements: class consciousness promotes political participation, and in its turn, political participation increases class consciousness'.[56] If this second understanding of the relationship to participation and consciousness is the case, then it should also be the case that those denied participation—unable to engage actively with others in the determination of their own affairs—also might not develop political consciousness of their own situation or of broader political inequalities.

This relationship of non-participation to non-consciousness of deprived groups is developed by Paulo Freire, one of the few writers to have considered the topic in depth. 'Consciousness', he writes, 'is constituted in the dialectic of man's *objectification* and *action* upon the world'.[57] In situations of highly unequal power relationships, which he terms 'closed societies', the powerless are highly dependent. They are prevented from either self-determined action or reflection upon their actions. Denied this dialectic process, and denied the democratic experience out of which the 'critical consciousness' grows, they develop a 'culture of silence'. 'The dependent society is by definition a silent society'. The culture of silence may preclude the development of consciousness amongst the powerless thus lending to the dominant order an air of legitimacy. As in the sense of powerlessness, it may also encourage a susceptibility among the dependent society to internalization of the values of the dominant themselves. 'Its voice is not an authentic voice, but merely an echo of the metropolis. In every way the metropolis speaks, the dependent society listens'.[58] Mueller similarly writes about groups which 'cannot articulate their interests or perceive social conflict. Since they have been socialized into compliance, so to speak, they accept the definitions of political

reality as offered by dominant groups, classes or government institutions'.[59]

Even as the 'silence' is broken, the initial demands of the dominated may be vague, ambiguous, partially developed. This might help to explain the phenomenon of the 'multiple' or 'split' consciousness[60] often cited in the literature for poor or working-class groups. As long as elements of the sense of powerlessness or the assuming consciousness that grow from non-participation can be maintained, then although there may be a multitude of grievances, the 'unified' or 'critical' consciousness will likely remain precluded. And, in turn, the inconsistencies themselves may re-enforce the pattern of non-challenge. In Gramsci's terms, 'it can reach the point where the contradiction of conscience will not permit any decision, any choice, and produce a state of moral and political passivity.'[61]

This understanding gives rise to a final indirect means through which power's third dimension may work. Garson has described the 'multiple consciousness' as being characterized by 'ambiguity and overlays of consciousness; different and seemingly contradictory orientations will be evoked *depending upon the context*'.[62] If such is the case, then the consciousness of the relatively powerless, even as it emerges, may be malleable, i.e. especially vulnerable to the manipulation of the power field around it. Through the invocation of myths or symbols, the use of threat or rumours, or other mechanisms of power, the powerful may be able to ensure that certain beliefs and actions emerge in one context while apparently contradictory grievances may be expressed in others. From this perspective, a consistently expressed consensus is not required for the maintenance of dominant interests, only a consistency that certain potentially key issues remain latent issues and that certain interests remain unrecognized—at certain times more than at others.

These direct and indirect mechanisms of power's third dimension combine to suggest numerous possibilities of the means through which power may serve to shape conceptions of the necessities, possibilities, or strategies of conflict. Not only, as in the two-dimensional approach, might grievances be excluded from entering the political process, but they might be precluded from consideration altogether. Or, B, the relatively powerless, may recognize grievances against A, the relatively powerful, but desist from challenge because B's conceptions of self, group, or class may be such as to make actions against A seem inappropriate. Or, B may recognize grievances, be willing to act upon them, but not recognize A as the responsible agent towards which action should be directed—e.g. because of the mystifications or legitimations which surround A. Or, B may recognize grievances against A and be willing to act, but may not through viewing the order as immutable or through lacking conceptions of possible alternatives. Or, B may act, but do so on the basis of misconceived grievances, against the wrong target, or through an ineffective strategy. Any or all of these possibilities may serve the same purpose of protecting A's interests owing to B's shaped conceptions of potential conflict, to B's detriment.

But the indirect mechanisms of power's third dimension, seen as a consequence of the powerlessness experienced in the first two, have suggested yet a further consideration: the dimensions of power, each with its sundry mechanisms, must be seen as interrelated in the totality of their impact. In that simple idea lies the basis for developing a more coherent theory about the effects of power and powerlessness upon quiescence and rebellion in situations of great inequality.

3. Power and Powerlessness: Quiescence and Rebellion—A Tentative Relationship

Power, it has been suggested, involves the capacity of A to prevail over B both in resolution of manifest conflict and through affecting B's actions and conceptions about conflict or potential conflict. Intuitively, if the interests of A and B are contrary, and if A (individual, group, class) exercises power for the protection of its interests, then it will also be to A's advantage if the power can be used to generate and maintain quiescence of B (individual, group, class) upon B's interests. In that process, the dimensions of power and powerlessness may be viewed as interrelated and accumulative in nature, such that each dimension serves to reenforce the strength of the other. The relationships may be schematized, as in Figure 31.1 and described as follows:[63]

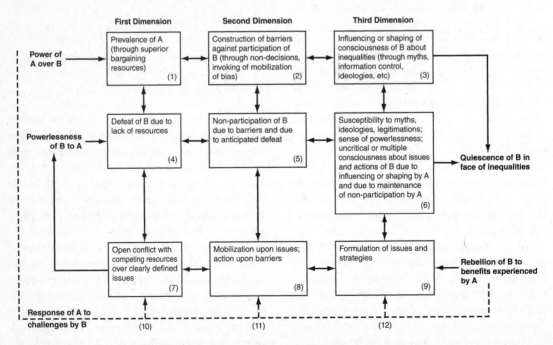

FIGURE 31.1   Power and powerlessness: Quiescence and rebellion—A tentative scheme.

As A develops power, A prevails over B in decision-making arenas in the allocation of resources and values within the political system [1]. If A prevails consistently, then A may accumulate surplus resources and values which may be allocated towards the construction of barriers around the decision-making arenas—i.e. towards the development of a mobilization of bias, as in the second dimension of power [2]. The consistent prevalence of A in the decision-making arenas plus the thwarting of challenges to that prevalence may allow A further power to invest in the development of dominant images, legitimations, or beliefs about A's power through control, for instance, of the media or other socialization institutions [3]. The power of A to prevail in the first dimension increases the power to affect B's actions in the second dimension, and increases the power to affect B's conceptions in the third.

The power of A is also strengthened by the fact that the powerlessness of B is similarly accumulative, and that power and powerlessness may each re-enforce the other towards the generation of B's quiescence. In the decision-making arena, B suffers continual defeat at the hands of A [4]. Over time, B may cease to challenge A owing to the anticipation that A will prevail [5]. But B's non-challenge allows A more opportunity to devote power to creating barriers to exclude participation in the future [2, 5]. The inaction of B in the second-dimensional sense becomes a sum of the anticipation by B of defeat and the barriers maintained by A over B's entering the decision-making arena anyway, and the re-enforcing effect of one upon the other.

In turn, the second-dimensional relationship may re-enforce the sense of powerlessness, the maintained non-participation, the ambiguous consciousness, or other factors which comprise the indirect mechanisms of power's third dimension [5, 6]. Further withdrawal of B though, in turn, allows more security for A to develop further legitimations or ideologies which may be used indirectly to affect the conceptions of B [3, 6]. And, as has been seen, the powerlessness of B may also increase the susceptibility of B to introjection of A's values. In the third-dimensional sense, then, B's response becomes understood as the sum, of B's powerlessness and A's power, and the re-enforcing effects of the one upon the other.

Once such power relationships are developed, their maintenance is self-propelled and attempts at their alteration are inevitably difficult. In order to remedy the inequalities, B must act, but to do so B must overcome A's power, and the accumulating effects of B's powerlessness. In order to benefit from the inequalities, A need not act, or if acting, may devote energies to strengthening the power relationships. Indeed, to the extent that A can maintain conflict within the second- or third-dimensional arenas, then A will continue to prevail simply through the inertia of the situation. Pocock describes what may have been such a relationship with reference to the maintenance of power by Ancient Chinese rulers:

> Where A has the power and B has not, it is a sign of weakness for either to take initiative, but B must take it and A need not . . . Once acquired, it (power) is maintained not by exertion but by inaction; not by imposing norms, but by being prequisite to their imposition; not by the display of virtue, but by the characterless force of its own necessity. The ruler rules not by solving other's problems, but by having none of his own; others have problems—i.e. they desire the power he has—and by keeping these unsolved he retains the power over them.[64]

In such a situation, power relationships can be understood only with reference to their prior development and their impact comprehended only in the light of their own momentum.

Challenge, or rebellion, may develop if there is a shift in the power relationships—either owing to loss in the power of A or gain in the power of B. (The two need not be the same owing to the possibility of intervention by other actors, technological changes, external structural factors, etc.) But even as challenge emerges, several steps in overcoming powerlessness by B must occur before the conflict is on competitive ground.[65] B must go through a process of *issue and action formulation* by which B develops consciousness of the needs, possibilities, and strategies of challenge. That is, B must counter both the direct and indirect effects of power's third dimension [9]. And, B must carry out the process of *mobilization of action upon issues* to overcome the mobilization of bias of A against B's actions. B must develop its own resources—real and symbolic—to wage the conflict [8]. Only as the obstacles to challenge by B in the second and third dimensions are overcome can the conflict which emerges in the first dimension be said to reflect B's genuine participation—i.e. self-determined action with others similarly affected upon clearly conceived and articulated grievances [7].

This formulation of the steps in the emergence of effective challenge provides further understanding of the means by which A may prevail over the outcome of any latent or manifest conflict. In the first instance, A may simply remain aloof from B, for to intervene in a situation of potential conflict may be to introduce the notion of conflict itself. But, if conceptions or actions of challenge do arise on the part of B, A may respond at any point along the process of issue-emergence. That is, the powerless may face barriers to effective challenge in the processes of the formulation of issues, of the mobilization of action upon issues, or in the decision-making about issues—any or all of which may affect the outcome of the conflict [10, 11, 12 . . .]. What are for B barriers to change are for A options for the maintenance of the status quo.

But, by the same token, as the barriers are overcome, so, too, do A's options for control lessen. And, just as the dimensions of power are accumulative and re-enforcing for the maintenance of quiescence, so, too, does the emergence of challenge in one area of a power relationship weaken the power of the total to withstand further challenges by more than the loss of a single component. For example, the development of consciousness of an issue re-enforces the likelihood of attempted action upon it, in turn re-enforcing consciousness.

A single victory helps to alter inaction owing to the anticipation of defeat, leading to more action, and so on. Once patterns of quiescence are broken upon one set of grievances, the accumulating resources of challenge—e.g. organization, momentum, consciousness—may become transferable to other issues and other targets.

For this reason, the development and maintenance of a generalized pattern of quiescence of B by A in situations of latent conflict will always be in A's interests. A will act to thwart challenges by B regardless of whether they appear, in the immediate sense, to be directed against A; for once the patterns are broken, the likelihood of further action by B increases and the options for control wielded by A decrease. For this reason, too, A will support A' on matters of common interest *vis-à-vis* the behaviour and conceptions of B; and B must ally with B' for the emergence of effective challenge against A—giving rise over time to social grouping and social classes of the relatively powerful and the relatively powerless.

4.   Methodological Considerations

What may appear conceptually useful may not correspond to actual circumstance. That which is analytically distinct may in fact occur simultaneously. Thus, a primary task of this study is to consider whether this model of power and participation can be applied to an empirical situation and whether that process in turn can lend further understanding to the relationships so far put forward. That there are methodological difficulties to the task is recognized from the outset. The suggestion of Bachrach and Baratz of even a 'second face' of power met vocal challenge on procedural grounds: how can one find the 'hidden' aspects of power? How can a non-decision be observed? Which non-events are relevant?[66] The presentation of a 'third face' of power poses yet further problems: how can one study what does not happen? What about the problem of imputing interests and values? This book argues that these problems are surmountable. Broad guidelines used for the empirical study are presented here. Then, the telling test for the method, as for the model, will be the extent to which it helps to illuminate the empirical case itself.

In the first instance, the methodology assumes Frey's suggestion that 'we can expect non-issues when: 1) glaring inequalities occur in the distribution of things avowedly valued by actors in the system, and 2) those inequalities do not seem to occasion ameliorative influence attempts by those getting less of those values'.[67] Secondly, rather than assuming the inaction or inertia to be 'natural' in the mass and activism as the phenomenon to be explained (as is done in the pluralist methodology), this approach initially assumes that remedial action upon inequalities by those affected would occur were it not for power relationships. The study of quiescence in a situation of potential conflict becomes the task, rather than the study of manifest conflict in a situation otherwise assumed to be conflict-free.

It is not adequate, however, merely to observe that inequalities exist and that such inequalities are met only by quiescence, to conclude that non-challenge is a product of power. As Lukes questions, 'Can we always assume that the victims of injustice and inequality would, but for the exercise of power, strive for justice and equality?'[68] On the contrary, he writes, 'we need to justify our expectation that B would have thought and acted differently, and we need to specify the means or mechanisms by which A has prevented, or else acted (or abstained from acting) in a manner sufficient to prevent B from doing so.'[69] From the model put forward, I suggest there are several means in an empirical study through which mechanisms can be identified and through which 'relevant counterfactuals' can be demonstrated to substantiate the expectation that B would have thought and acted differently, were it not for A's power.

In general, to do so requires going outside the decision-making arenas and carrying on extensive, time-consuming research in the community in question. There, non-actors and non-leaders become important, not as objects of scrutiny in themselves but to discover through their experiences lives, conditions, and attitudes, whether and by what means power processes may serve to maintain non-conflict.

In pursuing the answer to the question more specifically, it may be necessary, first, to look at the historical development of an apparent 'consensus'. In so doing, it may be possible to determine whether that situation has been arrived at by 'choice' or whether it has been shaped by power relations. And, the background study may help to identify certain key symbols, cues, or routines that affect the maintenance of quiescence in a given situation but which may not be identifiable as part of the 'language of power' without knowledge of their antecedents.

Secondly, within a given situation of apparent non-challenge, processes of communication, socialization, acculturation, etc., can be studied to determine whether there is a specific relationship between the actions or ideologies of the power holder and the action, inaction or beliefs of the powerless. In addition, it might be possible to determine whether the conditions do exist under which the actions and consciousness of B could develop, or whether identifiable power barriers serve to preclude their development, as in the indirect mechanisms of power.

Thirdly, it might be possible in a given or changing situation to posit or participate in ideas or actions which speculate about or attempt to develop challenges. The response of the quiescent population to such possibilities and the response of the powerholders to the beginning formulation or raising of issues may help to show whether power mechanisms are at work to preclude challenge from emerging.

Even if the identification of specific processes of power is successful, it still does not satisfy the requirement of justifying the 'expectation that B would have thought and acted differently'. Several more types of evidence must be gathered. First, as Lukes suggests, it may be possible to observe what occurs on the part of B when the power of A over B weakens, i.e. in 'abnormal times . . . when the apparatus of power is removed or relaxed'.[70] Secondly, it may be possible to observe what occurs when alternative opportunities for action develop within B's field—through the intervention of third parties or new resources. If action or conceptions of action emerge upon previously existing conditions—whether due to alteration in the power of A or the powerlessness of B—then it may be possible to argue that the prior inaction or apparent consensus did not reflect real consensus. Finally, it may be possible to develop a comparative approach to the study of the problem: if similarly deprived groups are faced with observably differing degrees of power, and if one rebels while the other does not, then it should be possible to argue that the differing responses are related to differences in the power relationships.

If, after following such guidelines, no mechanisms of power can be identified and no relevant counterfactuals can be found, then the researcher must conclude that the quiescence of a given deprived group is, in fact, based upon consensus of that group to their condition, owing for instance, to differing values from those initially posited by the observer. In this sense, this approach allows the falsifiability of the hypothetical relationships being explored.[71] Moreover, the 'third-dimensional methodology' provides the possibility of reaching conclusions that power in a given situation is either three- or two- or one-dimensional in nature—a possibility not provided for in the other two approaches. Thus, the conclusions of this approach are less dependent upon the methodological assumptions than they might be in the approach of the pluralists' or of Bachrach and Baratz.

However, assumptions must be made in this, as in all studies of power, about the definitions of three key concepts: interests, consciousness and consensus.

For the observer to posit that B would act towards the attainment of a value X or would want X were it not for the power processes of A may involve avowing that X is in B's interest. However, to do so—unlike it is often alleged[72]— is not necessarily to avow that X is in B's real interest, nor to give the observer the right to impose his interpretation of what is B's interest upon B. Rather, the observer's interpretation of what appears in a given context to be in B's interest may be used as a methodological tool for discovering whether power relationships are such as to have precluded the active and conscious choice by B about such interests, regardless of what the outcome of that choice actually would be. What B would choose (were B free from the power of A to do so) would be B's real interests— but they do not require identification for the study of power. That B is prevented from acting upon or conceiving certain posited interests is sufficient to show that the interests that are expressed by B are probably not B's real ones.[73]

The stance has ramifications for the consideration of consciousness. The unfortunate term 'false consciousness' must be avoided, for it is analytically confusing. Consciousness refers to a *state,* as in a state of being, and thus can only be falsified through negation of the state itself. If consciousness exists, it is real to its holders, and thus to the power situation. To discount it as 'false' may be to discount too simply the complexities or realities of the situation. What is far more accurate (and useful) is to describe the content, source, or nature of the consciousness—whether it reflects awareness of certain interests and not of others, whether it is critical or assuming, whether it has been developed through undue influence of A, and so on.

To argue that existing consciousness cannot be 'false' is not to argue the same for consensus. 'Real' consensus implies a prior process of agreement or choice, which in a situation of apparent consensus may or may not have been the case. The process may not have occurred; it could have been shaped or manipulated; the 'consensus' could be maintained by power processes, etc. In any event, what may appear consensus may not be what would appear were the real process to take place. The investigation of the possibility that power processes have given rise to a 'false' consensus must be carried on to establish more accurately the nature of the first appearance.

Examples: The Closed and Colonial Societies

Even with the help of these methodological guidelines, the identification of power processes may be easier in some situations than in others. For instance, in his pluralist critique of Bachrach and Baratz, Wolfinger readily accepts that power relationships may affect consciousness and action in closed societies, such as the plantation South. He writes, 'Some examples of false consciousness are indisputable, e.g. the long period of feeble protest by southern Negroes. Their reticence was due in part to repression, but much of it was based on myths and procedures'. Moreover, in making such conclusions, Wolfinger attributes to the Negro certain interests (as goals) assumed to be common: 'Almost any social scientist would agree that the blacks have been manipulated, because almost any social scientists' views of rational behaviour, irrespective of their specific character, would attribute certain goals to southern Negroes'.[74] What appears to be in question in this and other pluralists' critiques, then, is not whether the hidden faces of power exist, nor whether methodological assumptions can be made in certain situations for their identification, but whether such methods can be applied to consideration of the concepts in other situations—especially those of the more 'open' industrial democracies. There, the assumption is made in the pluralists' methodology that non-conflict represents social cohesion or integration, not, as others have argued, social control or hegemony.

It may be possible to develop an explanatory theory further, though, by looking not just at the example of the closed society but at situations where penetration (or integration) have not fully occurred and in which power processes, if they are at work, may be more readily self-evident. One example of such a case might be found in the colonial or neocolonial relationship, involving, as it does, the power of a metropolis or developed industrial society over a less developed, more traditional society.

In the first instance, the development of domination, or *the colonizing process,* involves the prevailing of the colonizer over the allocation of resources in the colony owing to superior resources of the former, such as capital, technology, or force. Secondly, however, the maintenance of that power involves the establishment of certain institutions and organizational forms. As Emerson describes:

> Imperialism spread to the world at large the ideas, techniques, and institutions which had emerged from many centuries of European history. By its direct impact . . . it established many of the forms and methods of the West abroad, inevitably disrupting in greater or lesser degree the native societies on which it encroached in the process.[75]

The establishment of dominance includes the development of an administrative relationship by the dominant society over the dominated, either through the direct control of the representatives of the former, or through the development of collaborators or mediating elites amongst the latter.

It includes a prevailing ideology through which the values of the metropolis are legitimated as superior and those of the colony as inferior. In short, the colonization process involves the development of a mobilization of bias—a set of predominant values, beliefs and institutional procedures that operate systematically to the benefit of the colonizer at the expense of the colonized. It is the development of a second-dimensional power relationship.

However, writers of and about the Third World insist that there is a further form of power that grows out of the effective colonizing process—one which serves to shape the legitimacy of the colonizers' dominance. Referring to the internalization of alien norms amongst dependent societies, Balandier wrote in 1951 of the *colonial situation* which 'not only conditioned the reaction of dependent peoples but is still responsible for certain reactions of people recently emancipated'.[76] Others, such as Freire, Fanon, and Memmi have since described further the means by which the consciousness of the colonized is affected by the values of the colonizer, as well as the extent to which the shaping is strengthened because of the sense of inadequacy or submissiveness amongst the dominated. Memmi, for instance, writes that as power develops its justifying ideology, so, too, must powerlessness:

> There undoubtedly exists—at some point in its evolution—a certain adherence of the colonized to colonization. However, this adherence is the result of colonization not its cause. It arises after and not before colonial occupation. In order for the colonizer to be complete master, it is not enough for him to be so in actual fact, but he must believe in its legitimacy. In order for the legitimacy to be complete, it is not enough for the colonized to be a slave, he must also accept this role.[77]

In short, the development of the colonial situation involves the shaping of wants, values, roles, and beliefs of the colonized. It is a third-dimensional power relationship.

Do similar processes exist within developed societies? How can one tell? Admittedly, it may be more difficult to observe whether the second and third faces of power are behind apparent quiescence amongst inequalities in more open or homogenous societies. But the difficulties in observation should not alone refute the possibilities of the occurrence. Rather than avoid the problem, it might be preferable to attempt further to develop a theory of power relationships as well as a method for their study through an intermediary step: a focus upon the perhaps more visible processes that affect a dominated but relatively non-integrated sector within industrial democracy itself. The possibility for such an exploration lies in the study of the impact of power and powerlessness upon the actions and conceptions of the people of an underdeveloped region of the United States known as Central Appalachia.

Notes

1. See for instance, Sidney Verba and Norman H. Nie, *Participation in America: Political Democracy and Social Equality* (Harper and Row, New York, 1972); Anthony Giddens, *The Class Structure of the Advanced Societies* (Hutchinson University Library, London, 1973).
2. i.e. the so-called 'neo-élitists' such as Schumpeter (*Capitalism, Socialism and Democracy,* 1942), Berelson (*Voting,* 1954), Dahl (*A Preface to Democratic Theory,* 1956). The views are neatly summarized and contrasted with classical theories of participation in Carole Pateman, *Participation and Democratic Theory* (Cambridge University Press, 1970).
3. See, for example, Peter Bachrach, *The Theory of Democratic Elitism: A Critique* (University of London Press, 1969); Jack E. Walker, 'A Critique of the Elitist Theory of Democracy', *American Political Science Review,* 60 (1966), 285–95.
4. Steven Lukes, *Power: A Radical View* (Macmillan, London, 1974).
5. Peter Bachrach and Morton S. Baratz, 'The Two Faces of Power', *American Political Science Review,* 56 (1962), 947–52; and Bachrach and Baratz, *Power and Poverty: Theory and Practice* (Oxford University Press, New York, 1970).
6. Robert A. Dahl, 'The Concept of Power', in Roderick Bell, David M. Edwards, R. Harrison Wagner, eds., *Political Power: A Reader in Theory and Research* (Free Press, New York, 1969), p. 80, reprinted from *Behavioural Science,* 2 (1957), 201–5.
7. Nelson W. Polsby, *Community Power and Political Theory* (Yale University Press, New Haven, 1963), p. 55.
8. Nelson W. Polsby, 'The Sociology of Community Power: A Reassessment', *Social Forces,* 37 (1959), 235.
9. Polsby (1963), op. cit., p. 118.
10. Robert A. Dahl, *Who Governs? Democracy and Power in an American City* (Yale University Press, New Haven, 1961), pp. 91, 93.
11. Polsby (1963), op. cit., p. 119.
12. Dahl (1961), op. cit., p. 114.
13. Polsby (1963), op. cit., p. 116.
14. Dahl (1961) op. cit., p. 221.
15. Polsby (1963), op. cit., p. 116.
16. ibid., p. 118.
17. For examples of this approach see Gabriel Almond and Sidney Verba, *The Civic Culture* (Princeton University Press, 1963), especially chaps. 7–8; Lester W. Milbraith, *Political Participation* (Rand, McNally and Co., Chicago, 1965); Stein Rokkan, *Approaches to the Study of Political Participation* (The Christian Michelson Institute for Science and Intellectual Freedom, Bergen, 1962); Peter H. Rossi and Zahava D. Blum, 'Class, Status and Poverty', in Daniel P. Moynihan, ed., *On Understanding Poverty* (Basic Books, New York, 1968), pp. 36–63. For more general discussions of this literature see S.M. Lipset, *Political Man* (William Heinemann, London, 1959), especially pp. 170–219; or, more recently, Verba and Nie, op. cit.
18. Edward C. Banfield, *The Moral Basis of Backward Society* (Free Press, Glencoc, Illinois, 1958).
19. See William Ryan, *Blaming the Victim* (Pantheon Books, New York, 1971).
20. Contrast Lipset's earlier work, *Agrarian Socialism* (University of California Press, Berkeley, 1950), with his later work, *Political Man,* op. cit., pp. 258–9.
21. E.E. Schattschneider, *The Semi-Sovereign People: A Realist's View of Democracy in America* (Holt, Rinehart and Winston, New York, 1960), p. 105.
22. Bachrach and Baratz (1962) and (1970), op. cit. See, too, the same authors', 'Decisions and Nondecisions: An Analytical Framework', *American Political Science Review,* 57 (1963), 641–51.
23. ibid., p. 8, quoting Schattschneider, op. cit., p. 71.
24. ibid., p. 105.

25. Matthew A. Crenson, *The Un-Politics of Air Pollution: A Study of Non-Decision-Making in the Cities* (John Hopkins Press, Baltimore, 1971), pp. 130, 80.

26. Michael Parenti, 'Power and Pluralism: A View from the Bottom', *Journal of Politics,* 32 (1970), 501–30.

27. Lester Salamon and Stephen Van Evera, 'Fear, Apathy and Discrimination: A Test of Three Explanations of Political Participation', *American Political Science Review,* 67 (1973), 1288–306.

28. Eric Wolf, *Peasant Wars of the Twentieth Century* (Faber and Faber, London, 1969), pp. 276–302 generally, and especially p. 290.

29. Crenson, op. cit., p. 124. Also, Crenson's study is more one of inaction amongst decision-makers on a single issue rather than of passivity amongst non-élites who may be outside the decision-making process altogether. See critique by Edward Greer, 'Air Pollution and Corporate Power: Municipal Reform Limits in a Black Community', *Politics and Society,* 4 (1974), 483–510.

30. Bachrach and Baratz (1970), op. cit., pp. 49–50.

31. Lukes, op. cit., p. 24.

32. Bachrach and Baratz (1970), op. cit., p. 50 (emphasis supplied).

33. Lukes, op. cit., pp. 20, 23.

34. ibid., p. 34.

35. ibid., p. 23 (emphasis supplied).

36. ibid., pp. 24–5.

37. ibid., p. 24.

38. ibid., p. 38.

39. Murray Edelman, *Politics as Symbolic Action: Mass Arousal and Quiescence* (Markham Publishing Co., Chicago, 1971), p. 8.

40. Antonio Gramsci, *Selections from the Prison Notebooks of* . . . ed. and trans., by Quinton Hare and Geoffrey Nowell-Smith (Lawrence and Wishart, London, 1971), see especially selections of 'State and Civil Society', in pp. 206–78. Ralph Milliband, *The State in Capitalist Society: An Analysis of the Western Systems of Power* (Weidenfeld and Nicolson, London, 1969), pp. 180–2.

41. Bachrach and Baratz (1970), op. cit., p. 43.

42. ibid., p. 44.

43. ibid., pp. 42–6.

44. See, for instance, Edelman, op. cit.; Edelman, *The Symbolic Uses of Politics* (University of Illinois Press, Urbana, 1967); and Edelman, 'Symbols and Political Quiescence', *American Political Science Review,* 54 (1960), 695–704.

45. For example, as developed by Claus Mueller, *The Politics of Communication: A Study in the Political Sociology of Language, Socialization and Legitimation* (Oxford University Press, New York, 1973).

46. ibid.; see, too, Milliband, op. cit., pp. 179–264; and C. Wright Mills, *The Sociological Imagination* (Oxford University Press, New York, 1956), pp. 36–40.

47. This is to suggest that processes may be similar to those suggested by Berger and Luckmann but that the processes are not random. They occur in a power field and to the advantage of power interests. See Peter L. Berger and Thomas Luckmann, *The Social Construction of Reality* (Doubleday and Co., New York, 1966); and critique by Richard Lichtmann, 'Symbolic Interaction and Social Reality: Some Marxist Queries', *Berkeley Journal of Sociology,* 15 (1970) 75–94.

48. Lukes, op. cit., p. 23.

49. Karl W. Deutsch and Leroy Rieselbach, 'Recent Trends in Political Theory and Political Philosophy', *The Annals of the American Political and Social Science,* 360 (1965), 151.

50. Michael Mann, 'The Social Cohesion of Liberal Democracy', *American Sociological Review,* 35 (1970). Frederick W. Frey, 'Comment: On Issues and Non-Issues in the Study of Power', *American Political Science Review,* 65 (1971), 1081–101.

51. Ira Katznelson, *Black Men, White Cities* (Oxford University Press, 1973), p. 198.

52. Walter Korpi, 'Conflict, Power and Relative Deprivation', *American Political Science Review,* 68 (1974). Korpi writes, 'in the long run the weaker actor will, through internal psychological processes, tend to adjust his aspiration level towards the going rates of exchange in the relationship' (p. 1571).

53. See discussion by Paulo Freire, *The Pedagogy of the Oppressed* (Penguin Rooks. Harmondsworth, Middx, 1972), pp. 1–39.

54. e.g. Rousseau, John Stuart Mill, G.D.H. Cole. See discussion of this theme in Pateman, op. cit., Chap. 3.

55. Melvin Seeman, 'Alienation, Membership, and Political Knowledge: A Comparative Study', *Public Opinion Quarterly,* 30 (1966), 353–67.

56. Allesandro Pizzorno, 'An Introduction to the Theory of Political Participation', *Social Science Information,* 9 (1970), 45.

57. Paulo Freire, *Cultural Action for Freedom* (Penguin Books, Harmondsworth, Middx, 1972), p. 52.

58. ibid., pp. 58–9.

59. Mueller, op. cit., p. 9.

60. David Garson, 'Automobile Workers and the American Dream', *Politics and Society,* 3 (1973), 163–79; Antonio Gramsci, trans., by Lewis Marks, *The Modern Prince and Other Writings* (International Publishers, New York, 1957), p. 66.

61. Gramsci (1957), op. cit., p. 67.

62. Garson, op. cit., p. 163.

63. This is not meant to imply that in an empirical situation the relationships develop in this sequence, or in a linear fashion at all. However, it is analytically useful to describe them in this manner.

64. J.G.A. Pocock, 'Ritual, Language and Power', in *Pocock, Politics, Language, and Time: Essays on Political Thought and History* (Methuen, London, 1970), p. 69.

65. Parenti, op. cit., calls this the problem of political capital accumulation: 'just as one needs capital to make capital, in one needs power to use power' (p. 527).

66. For example, Raymond E. Wolfinger, 'Nondecisions and the Study of Local Politics', *American Political Science Review,* 65 (1971), 1063–80; also, 'Rejoinder to Frey's Comment', *American Political Science Review,* 65 (1971), 1102–4; Richard M. Merelman, 'On the Neo-Elitist Critiques of Community Power', *American Political Science Review,* 62 (1968), 451–60; Polsby (1968), op. cit.

67. Frey, op. cit., p. 1097. This is essentially the approach used by Crenson, who objectively identifies varying levels in air pollution, assumes that people generally do not want to be poisoned, and asks why action upon pollution does not occur.

68. Lukes, op. cit., p. 46.

69. ibid., pp. 41–2.

70. ibid., p. 47.

71. See, for instance, critique by Merelman, op. cit.

72. See, for instance, Polsby (1963), op. cit., p. 96; Wolfinger 'Nondecisions and the Study of Local Politics', op. cit., p. 1066.

73. See discussion by William E. Connolly, 'On "Interests" in Politics', *Politics and Society,* 2 (1972), 459–77. This definition is similar to Connolly's that: 'Policy X is more in A's interest than policy Y if A, were he to *experience* the results of both X and Y, would *choose* X as the result he would rather have for himself' (p. 472). However, less emphasis is put on the ability to experience the unforeseen consequences of a given choice; more on the process of making the choice itself.

74. Wolfinger, 'Nondecisions and the Study of Local Politics', op. cit., p. 1077.

75. Rupert Emerson, *From Empire to Nation: The Rise to Self-Assertion of African and Asian Peoples* (Harvard University Press, Cambridge, Mass., 1960), p. 6.

76. G. Balandier, 'The Colonial Situation: A Theoretical Approach', in Immanuel Wallerstein, ed., *Social Change: The Colonial Situation* (John Wiley and Sons, New York, 1966), pp. 34–61.

77. Albert Memmi, *The Colonizer and the Colonized* (Beacon Press, Boston, 1967), pp. 88–9.

32

Excerpts from "Sex, Race, and Ethnic Inequality in the United States Workplaces"

Barbara F. Reskin and Irene Padavic

The last third of twentieth century witnessed revolutionary reductions in sex and race inequality in the workplace. At the beginning of the 1960s, employers legally could refuse to hire people, assign them to jobs, and set their pay on the basis of their sex and race. The first signs of change were already present: married women had begun to catch up with their single sisters in their participation in the labor force, and African-Americans with their migration North were also pursuing different kinds of work from when they were in the South, especially women who were abandoning domestic work as other opportunities opened to them. But it took the Civil Rights Movement of the early 1960s, the Women's Liberation Movement of the late 1960s, and a series of federal and state laws to challenge the race and sex discrimination that were customary in the United States.

As we will see in this reading, sex, race, and ethnic inequality persist in the kinds of paid work that people do, their advancement opportunities, and their earnings. We shall also see, however, indications of the erosion of these forms of inequality since 1970. We focus on two forms of employment inequality: the differential distribution of workers across occupations and jobs based on their sex, race, and ethnicity, and pay disparities associated with these characteristics. In a departure from most research, we consider three important bases of inequality: sex, race, and ethnicity. Although workers' sex, race, and ethnicity jointly affect their work experiences, few quantitative studies have simultaneously considered both sex and race, and only a handful of studies have examined the joint effects of sex, race, and ethnicity (see Reskin & Charles, 1997).[1] Within the constraints of the available research, we discuss the extent and causes of sex, race, and ethnic inequality in the workplace.

1. Job Segregation by Sex, Race, and Ethnicity

Workers are not distributed across jobs based solely on their qualifications and interests; their sex, race, and ethnicity exert strong effects on the industries and occupations in which they work and thus the jobs they hold.[2] Job segregation is the linchpin in workplace inequality because the relegation of different groups to different kinds of work both facilitates and legitimates unequal treatment. Segregation facilitates unequal treatment in part because the jobs to which women and people of color are assigned are inherently less desirable than those open to white Anglo men. In addition, jobs that are filled predominantly by women and perhaps by minorities are devalued because society devalues women and minorities. Segregation legitimates unequal treatment because both U.S. values and the law permit unequal pay for different work. For these reasons, segregation generates pay and status disparities between persons of different sexes and races.

At the beginning of the twentieth century, Asians, African-Americans, and white women were confined to a limited number of occupations.

A straightforward indicator of the degree to which workers are segregated based on some characteristic is the index of segregation (Duncan & Duncan, 1955). The value of this index, which ranges from 0 to 100, indicates the proportion of one of two groups that would have to change to an occupation in which that group is underrepresented for the two groups to be identically distributed across occupations. As Fig. 32.1 shows between 1900 and 1970, the index of occupational segregation hovered around 70 for women and men (Gross, 1968). In fact, the sexes and races were so segregated that until 1940 the U.S. Census Bureau treated census returns with atypical worker–occupation combinations, such as female train engineer, as errors (Conk, 1981, p. 69).[3] Sex and race discrimination gave white men a semimonopoly over most technical, managerial, and professional jobs until the middle 1960s.[4] Race discrimination confined most blacks to menial agricultural and service jobs, and custom and law closed all but a handful of occupations to women.[5]

After 1940, however, the occupational race segregation index declined among both sexes, from 44 to 24 for men and from 65 to 22 for women. Race

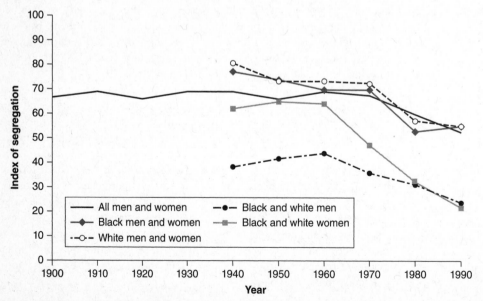

FIGURE 32.1   Indicies of occupational sex and race segregation, 1900 to 1990.

(*Sources:* Data from Gross, 1968, Table 2; Jacobs, 1989a, Table 2; Jacobsen, 1997; King, 1992, Chart 1; Reskin & Cassierer, 1996.)

segregation began declining at this time because the labor shortage brought on by World War II forced factories to hire blacks. The effect of these new opportunities was revolutionary for black women who formerly had few options apart from working in white people's homes.[6] In the 1970s, sex segregation also began declining. About one quarter of the drop in the segregation index was due to the shrinking proportion of the labor force working in occupations that were heavily sex segregated, such as heavy manufacturing, and the increasing proportion in occupations that were moderately integrated; the other three quarters resulted as women began integrating customarily male occupations, such as manager (Spain & Bianchi, 1996, Table 4.6). As a result, between 1970 and 1990 the index of occupational sex segregation fell from 67 to 53 (50.5 for blacks, 53.6 for whites, and 52.7 for Hispanics; Jacobs, 1989a; Reskin, 1994; additional computations from U.S. Bureau of the Census, 1992a). In 1990, to fully sex-integrate occupations would have required that 53% of all female workers—more than 32 million persons—shift to mostly male occupation. Eliminating segregation among whites would have required that 25% of Asians (29% of men and 21% of women), 26.5% of African-Americans (28% of men and 25% of women), and 27% of Hispanics (29% of men and 24% of women) change occupations (Reskin, 1994; additional computations from U.S. Bureau of the Census, 1992a). To eliminate both sex and race segregation across occupations in 1990 would have required 60% of black women, 58% of Hispanic women, 53% of white women, and 30% of black and Hispanic men to shift to occupations in which white men predominated. Asians tend to be less segregated from same-sex whites than are blacks (Reskin, 1994).

Interpreting segregation indices as the proportion of members of a sex/race group that would have to change occupations is a convenient way of summarizing the extent of occupational segregation, but in reality such shifts would take generations under the best of conditions. In 1990, for example, almost 14 million black and white women—about one fifth of these women—held administrative-support occupations (in other words, they did clerical work) compared to 8% of black men and 5% of white men, while almost

19% of white men and 14% of black men held skilled blue-collar jobs, compared to 2% of both white and black women (U.S. Bureau of Labor Statistics, 1997, Table 10). To bring women's representation in administrative-support and skilled blue-collar occupations in line with that of white men would have meant the transfer of more than 10 million female clerical workers to skilled blue-collar occupations.

Regardless of their race, most women work in predominantly female occupations. Of the 57 million women in the labor force in 1990, one third worked in just 10 of the 503 detailed occupations (U.S. Bureau of Labor Statistics, 1996a),[7] and only one woman in nine pursued an occupation that was at least 75% male (Kraut & Luna, 1992, p. 3). Men likewise remain concentrated in predominately male occupations: one quarter of the 69 million men in the labor force worked in just 10 occupations in 1990. Only two occupations appeared on both sex's top 10 list: "manager or administrator, not elsewhere classified" and "sales supervisor or proprietor" (U.S. Bureau of Labor Statistics, 1996a), and these two heterogeneous categories conceal substantial job-level sex segregation. The large number of women working as managers, administrators, sales supervisors, and proprietors are disproportionately white. Neither manager or administrator (not elsewhere classified), nor sales supervisor or proprietor was among the five largest occupations for black women or Latinas (or Latinos) in 1995 (see Table 32.1). Except for black female nurses, none of the occupations that employed large numbers of Hispanic or black women or men were professional or managerial.[8] Black women were overrepresented in just a few professional occupations—dietitian, educational or vocational counselor, and social worker in 1995 (computed from U.S. Bureau of Labor Statistics, 1996a). Hispanic men and women were underrepresented in all professions (U.S. Bureau of the Census, 1996b, Table 637). Most of the top five occupations for black and Hispanic women and men involved cleaning or personal service (maid, private household servant, janitor, cook, gardener, nursing aide); a few involved unskilled labor (farm worker, laborer; see Table 32.1).

Table 32.1   Top Occupations for Black, Hispanic, and White Women and Men, 1995

White Women	Number	%	White Men	Number	%
Secretary	2942	6.1	Manager, n.e.c.*	4503	7.7
Manager, n.e.c.*	1741	3.6	Sales, supervisor, proprietor	2483	4.3
Cashier	1709	3.5	Truck driver	2301	4.0
Registered nurse	1600	3.3	Engineer	1593	2.7
Sales, supervisor, proprietor	1566	3.2	Vehicle mechanic	1516	26
Total labor force	48,344	100.0	Total labor force	58,146	100.0

Black Women	Number	%	Black Men	Number	%
Nursing aide, orderly	482	7.0	Truck driver	352	5.5
Cashier	349	5.1	Janitor	267	4.2
Cook	166	2.4	Manager, n.e.c.*	198	3.1
Maid	151	2.2	Cook	187	2.9
Registered nurse	150	2.2	Laborer, except construction	159	2.5
Total labor force	6857	100.0	Total labor force	6422	100.0

Hispanic Women	Number	%	Hispanic Men	Number	%
Secretary	210	4.8	Truck driver	285	4.2
Cashier	205	4.7	Farm worker	279	4.1
Private household servant	130	3.0	Janitor	267	4.0
Janitor	128	2.9	Cook	263	3.9
Nursing aid, orderly	126	2.9	Gardener	196	2.9
Total labor force	4403	100.0	Total labor force	6725	100.0

*The abbreviation "n.e.c." refers to occupations that are not elsewhere classified.

Note: Blacks and whites include people of Hispanic origin.

Source: Unpublished tabulations of 1995 Current Population Survey data by the U.S. Bureau of Labor Statistics (1997).

Ethnicity also affects workers' occupational outcomes. For example, Filipina, American Indian, and Puerto Rican women resembled black women in that nursing aide was among their top three occupations in 1995. Among the top three occupations for Central American, Chinese, Cuban, Korean, and Southeast Asian women was textile operative. The top three occupations for Mexican and Central American women and for Puerto Rican, Mexican, and Southeast Asian men included janitor (the second largest occupation for black men). Cook was among the top three occupations for Japanese, Chinese, Filipino, Southeast Asian, and Central American men, as it was for black women (computed from the U.S. Bureau of

Labor Statistics, 1996a).[9] All recent data on race and sex workplace segregation are for occupations—a category that combines jobs involving similar activities in the same and in different establishments (Bielby & Baron, 1986, p. 764). Thus, most nominally sex or racially integrated occupations include predominantly female and male specialties (Bielby & Baron, 1984). For example, although the occupation of real estate sales has become sex integrated, women are concentrated in residential sales, while men dominate the more lucrative commercial sales (Reskin & Roos, 1990). Occupational specialties may be differentiated as well by workers' race and ethnicity. For example, black workers tend to hold jobs in which they are more intensely supervised than are white workers in the same occupation (Tomaskovic-Devey, 1993, p. 148). Often members of different race/sex groups perform the same occupation in different establishments or even different parts of the country (Reskin, 1997c). Although declining occupational sex and race segregation signals some job-level integration, the extent of job segregation far exceeds measured levels of occupational segregation (Peterson & Morgan, 1995). In general, women and people of color—regardless of their sex—are underrepresented in desirable and lucrative jobs and disproportionately concentrated in low-status, low-paying service jobs.

1.1. Hierarchical Segregation

Because the desirability of the jobs in which group members are concentrated is positively correlated with the social status of the race/sex group, job segregation is often expressed hierarchically, with women and people of color concentrated in the lower ranks within occupations and organizations and white men dominating the top positions. Hierarchical segregation—by which we mean the segregation of workers across different ranks in the same job (e.g., assistant manager versus manager)—consigns members of favored groups to jobs that are higher in occupational or organizational hierarchies and hence confer more status, authority, and pay. Thus, hierarchical segregation further exacerbates the earnings and authority gaps (McGuire & Reskin, 1993; Reskin & Ross, 1992).[10] Hierarchical segregation—as expressed in the differential distribution of the races and sexes across vertical levels within organizations or occupations—includes both "glass ceilings" that exclude minorities and women from the top jobs in organizations and "sticky floors" that confine women and minorities—especially women of color—to low-ranking jobs (Berheide, 1992). A mere handful of minorities and women have reached the top of corporate hierarchies. In 1990, only five of the 1000 CEOs listed in the *Business Week* 1000 were nonwhite, and only 2.6% of senior managers in nine Fortune 500 companies that the U.S. Department of Labor studied were not white (Bell & Nkomo, 1994). In 1995, only 57 (2.4%) of the 2430 top officers

in Fortune 500 companies were women (Catalyst, 1996). Other work settings show variations on this theme. In 1990, one in 11 partners in large law firms was female, compared to one in three associates (Epstein, 1993). Although corporate sales offer a fast track to management, only one in seven saleswomen get beyond the level of district manager (Catalyst, 1996). While women held half of all federal government jobs in 1992, only one quarter of supervisors and only 10% of senior executives were women, and fewer than 2% of senior executives were minority women (U.S. Merit Systems Protection Board, 1992, p. 33). Even in traditionally female occupations such as librarian or social worker, men advance more rapidly than women (Williams, 1995).

Minorities' and women's representation in managerial jobs offers a summary indicator of hierarchical segregation. Women and people of color remain underrepresented in management compared to white men, although the disparities have been shrinking since 1970. In 1990, almost 13.1% of non-Hispanic white workers held managerial jobs (14.1% of men, 11:8% of women), compared to 12.3% of Asians and Pacific Islanders (13.4% of men, 11.1% of women), 7.9% of Native American groups (7.2% of men, 8.7% of women), 7.3% of African-American workers (6.6% of men, 7,4% of women), and 6.5% of Hispanics (6.2% of men, 7.0% of women; U.S. Bureau of the Census, 1992b, Table 2). Although the representation of African Americans has been increasing, as Fig. 32.2 shows, African-American men's progress stalled during the 1980s, and by 1990 African-American women were more likely to work in managerial occupations than African-American men.

While the trends depicted in Fig. 32.2 show marked progress, we must remember that women and minorities tend to be low- rather than high-level managers. It is white male managers who usually have the final say in important decisions such as hiring, firing, promotions raises, and issues that affect other units. A study comparing the sexes' roles in decision-making found that female mangers' input was more often to provide information or make recommendations while male managers more often made final decisions (Reskin & Ross, 1992). Indeed, other evidence indicates that women and minorities

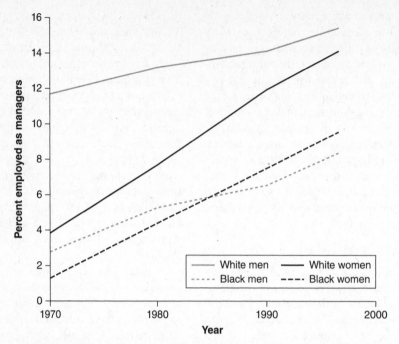

FIGURE 32.2   Percent in managerial employment, by sex and race, 1970 to 1997.
(*Sources:* Data from U.S. Bureau of the Census, 1972, Table 2; 1982; U.S.
Bureau of Labor Statistics, 1998.)

are ghettoized into less desirable managerial jobs that white men eschew (Collins, 1989, p. 329; Reskin & McBrier, 1998). In addition, these and other findings suggest that some of women's and minorities' gains in managerial occupations represent "job-title inflation"—managerial titles without managerial authority—in response to increased federal scrutiny (Smith & Welch, 1984).

The patterns by sex and race in Fig. 32.2 depart from the tendency for the effect of sex to exceed that of race that holds for occupational segregation and therefore for earnings. This departure probably reflects employers' practice of selecting managers of the same or a more highly esteemed sex and race than the workers who will be their subordinates.

Group differences in promotion rates also indicate hierarchical segregation. In the early 1990s, whites were twice as likely as blacks to have been promoted and men were almost twice as likely as women to have been promoted, after taking into account education, training, experience, and type of firm (Baldi & McBrier, 1997; see also

Kalleberg & Reskin, 1995). In eight New York law firms, male associates were three times as likely as female associates to be promoted to partner (American Bar Association, 1996). In 1995, minority women were less likely to be promoted than white women with equivalent experience, although minority men in the federal government were promoted at the same rate as white men (U.S. Merit Systems Protection Board, 1996).

1.2.   Explaining Sex and Race Segregation

Workers' sex and race are linked to the kinds of jobs they do because of employers' and workers' characteristics, preferences, and actions. However, some explanations for the relationship between workers' ascriptive characteristics and their jobs differ for race and sex. Explanations for segregation in general, and hierarchical segregation in particular, emphasize workers characteristics and preferences—"supply-side" explanations—by assuming a two-step process: (1) people decide the kind of work they want to do and (2) they obtain the necessary credentials. These explanations treat getting a job in one's preferred line of work as nonproblematic. Supply-side explanations for sex segregation tend to stress the first step in this process—work preferences, whereas supply-side explanations for race segregation emphasize the second step—obtaining qualifications. We review supply-side explanations first for sex segregation and then for race segregation. We then review explanations that emphasize employers' characteristics, preferences, and actions.

1.2.1. Workers' Characteristics and Preferences

The sexes are concentrated in different kinds of work, according to supply-side approaches, because women and men prefer different kinds of jobs. Social scientists have proposed two reasons the sexes' preferences differ. According to a socialization perspective, men and women pursue different kinds of jobs because gender-role socialization induces in them different life goals; instills in them different values regarding the importance of occupational success, autonomy, or high earnings; teaches them different skills; fosters different personality traits; and induces a distaste for sex-atypical activities and for working with members of the other sex (Marini & Brinton, 1984). To the extent that gender-role socialization has these effects, the kinds of jobs that attract men should disinterest women and vice versa.

Although gender-role socialization may incline young people toward jobs that society labels as appropriate for their sex (Subich, Barrett, Doverspike, & Alexander, 1989), young people's occupational aspirations are both quite unstable and unrelated to the occupations they hold as adults (Jacobs, 1989b). Moreover, adults—especially women—move between predominantly female and predominantly male occupations (Jacobs, 1989b).

Despite gender-role socialization—and readers must bear in mind that no systematic data compare the socialization of contemporary women and men—the sexes tend to value the same job rewards: good pay, autonomy, and prestige (Jencks, Perman, & Rainwater, 1988; Marini, Fan, Finley, & Beutel, 1996). With respect to vertical segregation, women are as likely as men to value promotions (Markham, Harlan, & Hackett, 1987, p. 227). These and other findings suggest that early gender-role socialization is not an important cause of job segregation. Far more influential are the opportunities, social pressures, and social rewards workers face as adults (Reskin & Hartmann, 1986).

The neoclassical economic perspective, another supply-side approach, assumes that occupational preferences are sex differentiated as a result of women's and men's conscious decisions to maximize household well-being. Hypothetically, in response to their different roles in the sexual division of labor, men and women pursue different employment strategies, Men's role as primary breadwinner induces them to maximize their earnings by pursuing jobs that pay well and reward experience and by maximizing the amount of time they spend doing paid work. Women's primary responsibility for homemaking and child-rearing and their recognition that their husbands will earn enough to adequately support the family hypothetically lead women to select jobs that are compatible with domestic duties, both in scheduling and ease of reentry after time out of the labor force (see, e.g., Polachek, 1981). If women can rely on economic support by their husbands, they can eschew lucrative jobs that require overtime, continuous labor force participation, and the exertion of considerable effort, thereby reducing conflict between paid and family work. In anticipation of their differential involvement in labor-market and family work, this approach also assumes that men invest in more education and training than women, making them more qualified for jobs that require skills.

Most research evidence is inconsistent with the neoclassical explanation of sex segregation. First, researchers have found that single women are as likely as married women to work in predominantly female occupations (Reskin & Hartmann, 1986, pp. 71–72). In any event, women who plan to leave the labor force to have children earn more in customarily male than female jobs. Second, predominantly male and female occupations require similar levels of education and skills (England, Chassie, & McCormack, 1982), and most workers acquire their skills on the job. Contrary to the neoclassical theory, women are more likely than men to obtain training before employment (Amirault, 1992). Thus, there is little evidence that men's and women's concentration in different jobs results from their responses to their anticipated or actual family roles. The human-capital account of occupational sex segregation is problematic on other counts as well. If women place family responsibilities ahead of their careers, they should evidence less job commitment than men; yet women's commitment does not differ from men's (Marsden, Kalleberg, & Cook, 1993). Women also expend as much energy on their jobs as men do (in fact, net of family responsibilities, women expend more effort on the job than men; Bielby & Bielby, 1988). Both sexes aspire to advance at work and will work hard for a promotion (Markham et al., 1987; Reskin & Cassirer, 1996). Compared to 74% of male federal employees, 78% of women (and 86% of minority women) were willing to devote as much time as necessary to advance in their career (U.S. Merit Systems Protection Board, 1992).[11] Finally, the characteristics of predominantly female jobs are not especially compatible with stereotypical female domestic roles: jobs in predominantly female occupations are no more flexible, easier, or cleaner than those in predominantly male occupations (Glass, 1990, p. 791; Jacobs & Steinberg, 1990). Two types of evidence are consistent with the neoclassical explanation of sex segregation. First, women are more likely than men to work part-time (in 1990, 22.4% of women and 7.6% of men worked part-time: computed from U.S. Bureau of the Census, 1992a), and part-time employment is associated with higher levels of occupational sex segregation. Second, sex differences in college majors are consistent with the neoclassical explanation (Jacobs, 1995). For example, women earned 47% of the bachelor's degrees in business administration in 1992, but only 34% of the master's degrees. Also, the greater workers' education, the less segregated the sexes are. In 1990, the index of sex segregation was considerably lower for college graduates than for high school graduates: 16.5 points lower for blacks and 18.5 points lower for whites (computed from U.S. Bureau of the Census, 1992a; see also Jacobsen, 1997, p. 235). Nonetheless, we must be careful not to overstate the effect of education on sex segregation. Even among college graduates, the sex segregation index is 38 for blacks and 44 for whites.

The occupational preferences of men and women might differ for a reason unrelated to their domestic roles: people pursue jobs that they believe are available to them (Reskin & Hartmann, 1986; Schultz, 1991, p. 141). Prospective workers do not apply for jobs unless they have reason to expect that they might be hired. Just as the sex-segregated help-wanted ads, common before the enactment of Title VII of the 1964 Civil Rights Act, steered workers into sex-typical lines of work, the sex and race composition of jobs signal would-be employees whether they have a reasonable chance of being hired and being accepted by co-workers. Minorities and women who are pioneers in occupations typically reserved for white men often encounter resistance—heckling, sabotage, and worse—by supervisors co-workers, or customers (Bergmann & Darity, 1981; Padavic, 1991a; Schroedel, 1985; Swerdlow, 1989; U.S. Department of Labor, 1996), contributing to the "revolving door" that returns women to sex-typical occupations (Jacobs, 1989b). When employers make customarily male jobs genuinely accessible to women and mostly white occupations accessible to minorities, the attractiveness of these jobs draws plenty of women and minorities (Reskin & Hartmann, 1986; Reskin & Roos, 1990).

The neoclassical approach to race segregation emphasizes workers' qualifications rather than their preferences. Blacks and Latinos/as have less education and job experience than whites (England, Christopher, & Reid, 1997; Kilbourne, England, & Beron, 1994a, Table 1). Increasing parity in educational quality and quantity appear to have contributed to the occupational integration of black and white women between 1940 and 1990 (King, 1992). For example, in 1990 the segregation index for black and white women was 10 points lower for college graduates than for high school graduates (King, 1992; additional computations from U.S. Bureau of the Census, 1992a). However, men's educational attainment had little effect on the extent of race segregation—the index of race segregation for male high school graduates was 28.2; for college graduates it was 25.4 (computed from U.S. Bureau of the Census, 1992a). Also, 1990 census data indicate that race and ethnic differences in educational attainment—as well as nativity and English fluency—played only minor roles in occupational segregation by race and ethnicity (Reskin, 1997a).

In sum, the neoclassical approach is consistent with white males' concentration in customarily male occupations and their underrepresentation in predominantly female occupations: white men—whose options are not limited by discrimination—pursue the most desirable jobs and eschew predominantly female jobs because they pay less and offer fewer opportunities for advancement. However, the value of neoclassical approach for explaining women's and minorities' concentration in some occupations and underrepresentation in others is limited and largely inconsistent with our understanding of how workers get jobs.[12]

1.2.2. Employers' Preferences and Practices

A major reason women and minorities are concentrated in different jobs than white men is because employers prefer persons of different sexes and races for different jobs. They do so because of their stereotypes and biases and out of deference to their customers' or employees' biases. Employers also segregate workers as a result of superficially neutral employment practices.

One reason employers consider sex and race in filling jobs is out of loyalty to their own group—usually white men. Although little research has focused explicitly on the segregative effects of in-group preference, several studies suggest its importance for the degree of segregation in organizations. First, the sex and race of decision-makers affect their responses to members of their own group and other groups. For example, having a female agency head was associated with progress toward sex integration in California state agencies (Baron, Mittman, & Newman, 1991). In addition, a review of more than 70 studies found that evaluators rated same-race persons higher than other-race persons (Kraiger & Ford, 1985). Second, the nepotism characteristic of small firms and some industries such as construction is, of course, for one's own group (Waldinger & Bailey, 1991), and its effect is segregative. Third, a shortage of white male workers is a major reason firms employ female and minority workers in customarily white-male occupations (Padavic & Reskin, 1990; Reskin & Roos, 1990). Fourth, by restricting cronyism—that is, in-group favoritism—formalized personnel practices appear

to have reduced job segregation (Dobbin, Sutton, Meyer, & Scott, 1993).

According to several recent studies, race and sex stereotyping and bias contribute to sex segregation. For example, comparisons of the job-search outcomes of white-minority pairs in "audit" studies in four cities revealed that white men were substantially more likely to receive job offers than their minority matches (Fix & Struyk, 1992).[13] Qualitative studies in several cities reveal the reasons for the patterns from the audit studies. Employers, most of whom are white men, frankly admit their reluctance to hire black workers based on their stereotypes of blacks as lazy, unintelligent, insubordinate, and prone to criminal acts (Bobo, 1996; Holzer, 1996; Kasinitz & Rosenberg, 1996; Moss & Tilly, 1996: Neckerman & Kirschenman, 1991; Smith, 1990; Wilson, 1996, Chapter 5). The refusal of some employers to hire minorities or their willingness to hire them for only menial jobs inevitably segregates the races. Stereotypes also restrict women's employment opportunities. Stereotyped as unable to do physically demanding jobs, lacking career commitment, and disinterested in advancement (Bielby & Baron, 1986; Fiske, Bersoff, Bogida, Deaux, & Heilman, 1991; Reskin & Padavic, 1988; Segura, 1992, p. 173: Williams & Best, 1986), women are excluded from rewarding white-collar and blue-collar jobs.

Sex and race stereotypes affect hiring and promotion decisions through statistical discrimination, a process in which employers impute to individuals stereotyped or actual attributes of the group to which the individual belongs to avoid the cost of screening applicants' qualifications (Bielby & Baron, 1986; Braddock & McPartland, 1987; Holzer, 1996, pp. 83, 103; Messick & Mackie, 1989; Williams & Best, 1986). Employers' and supervisors' stereotypes also bias their evaluations of women and minorities, thus reducing their chances for promotion (Baron & Bielby, 1985, p. 243; Eagly, Makhijani, & Klonsky, 1992, p. 14; Fiske et al., 1991, p. 1050). Evaluation bias leads supervisors to evaluate whites and men more positively than equally qualified blacks and women (Greenhaus & Parasuraman, 1993; Greenhaus, Parasuraman, & Wormley, 1990, Table 1; Pulakos, White, Oppler,

& Borman, 1989; Sackett, Dubois, & Noe, 1991, p. 265), in part because they hold the latter groups to higher standards (Cox & Nkomo, 1986).[14] Hiring and promotion practices that rely on informal networks are highly subjective, and the more subjective the evaluation, the greater the risk of bias (Braddock & McPartland, 1987, p. 22; Deaux, 1984; Deaux, 1985; Eagly & Wood, 1982; Pettigrew & Martin 1987, pp. 55–58). Queuing models provide a theoretical approach to the effect of employers' race and sex preferences for workers—as expressed in their ordering of the labor queue (Lieberson, 1980, p. 296; Reskin & Roos, 1990; Thurow, 1969, p. 48). According to a queuing approach to occupational segregation, the higher workers stand in labor queues, the greater their access to jobs near the top of job queues. As low-ranked groups, women and minorities obtain access to jobs usually filled with white men when those jobs become less attractive to white men compared to their alternatives. This approach makes sense of the different distributions of the sexes and races across different industries and occupations. For example, white men are overrepresented in the private sector, the highest-paying sector, leaving public-sector and government jobs for women and minorities (historically the only place outside the black community where African-Americans could find work as managers and professionals; Higginbotham, 1987; U.S. Merit Systems Protection Board, 1996).

Regardless of their source—in-group preference, out-group antipathy, stereotypes, or biases—race and sex discrimination significantly restrict workers' options. The large number of formal complaints to antidiscrimination agencies, in combination with employers' candid reports of their stereotypes, suggest that discrimination is widespread: The federal government received more than 91,000 such complaints in 1994 (Leonard, 1994, p. 24; U.S. Department of Labor, 1996).[15] When enforced, antidiscrimination laws, such as Title VII of the 1964 Civil Rights Act (which banned employment discrimination based on race, national origin, or sex) and affirmative action requirements for federal contractors, opened thousands of semiskilled and skilled blue- and white-collar jobs to black men and women (Burstein, 1979, 1985; Donohue & Heckman, 1991; Heckman & Payner,

1989; for a review, see Badgett & Hartmann, 1995). Federal scrutiny helps to reduce sex and race segregation. The requirement by the Equal Employment Opportunity Commission (EEOC; the agency charged with enforcing Title VII) that firms with at least 50 employees annually report employees' distribution across broad occupational categories by race and sex has been an incentive for employers to place more women and minorities in managerial and administrative jobs. Thus, in 1960, 2% of black women, 4% of black men, and 5.5% of white women worked in the broad occupation of managers; by 1996, 9.6% of black women, 8.3% of black men, and 14% of white women were managers (U.S. Bureau of Labor Statistics, 1961, 1997, Table 10).

Recent history shows that when the government enforces antidiscrimination and affirmative-action regulations, minorities' and women's representation in sex- and race- atypical occupations increases (Ashenfelter & Heckman, 1976; Leonard, 1984a, b). More generally, sanctioning discriminating employers reduces job segregation (Badgett & Hartmann, 1995; Martin, 1991; Leonard, 1994, p. 21; Reskin & Roos, 1990). The uneven enforcement of the affirmative action required of federal contractors by Presidential Executive Order 11246 (11374) provided a natural experiment. During the 1980s, when there was no presidential mandate to enforce the executive order, minorities were more poorly represented at federal contractors than at noncontractors (Leonard, 1994), suggesting that federal contractors had reverted to the discriminatory practices that had prompted President Nixon to issue the executive order in the first place. Without the threat of governmental intervention, most employers do business as usual, which means making hiring and promotion decisions that are influenced by sex and race biases (Kern, 1996; Leonard, 1994).

1.2.3. Structural Discrimination

Employers' personnel practices—even those that seem to be race and gender neutral—nonetheless affect race and sex segregation in firms. The clearest example is filling jobs through referrals by current workers. This common recruiting practice perpetuates segregation because workers' social networks tend to be sex and race segregated

(Marsden, 1994, p. 983). In contrast, open-recruitment techniques, such as posting all job openings, can reduce segregation by allowing everyone to learn of sex- and race-atypical jobs.

Requiring credentials that are more common among white men than women and minorities also contributes to segregation. Sometimes segregation itself prevents women and minorities from acquiring qualifications. For example, the military's past exclusion of women from combat positions has blocked their advancement in military careers (Williams, 1989, p. 51). Analogously, blacks' exclusion from apprenticeship programs has kept them out of well-paying unionized craft jobs. Required credentials also can disproportionately affect women and minorities because employers more frequently exempt white men than others from formal requirements (Baron & Bielby, 1985, p. 243).

Pervasive sex segregation has prompted employers to organize work schedules and the labor process on the assumption that men will do some jobs and women will do others. The result can be barriers to women performing some customarily male jobs. For example, most machinery is designed to accommodate white, Anglo men. As a result, people who are shorter than the average white, Anglo man—including many women and some Latino and Asian men—cannot operate it safely or efficiently. Some companies design plant jobs so that workers rotate across different shifts—day, evening, and graveyard—which can discourage women from these jobs by making childcare arrangements difficult (Padavic, 1991b).

Segregated entry-level jobs maintain hierarchical segregation by disproportionately concentrating women and minorities in jobs with limited opportunity for mobility because they are on short ladders, restrict workers' opportunity to acquire skills, and lack visibility (Marsden, 1994, p. 983).[16] Firms tend to employ female and minority managers in staff positions, such as personnel or public relations, while male managers are concentrated in organizationally central line positions, such as sales, finance, and production, from which senior managers are selected. Employers often assign African-Americans to positions that deal with other minorities, such as community relations or affirmative action, regardless of their areas of expertise (Collins, 1989, p. 329, 1997). While staff positions provide few opportunities for workers to display their abilities, complex and challenging line jobs give incumbents a chance to develop and display their skills, such as exercising authority, supervising subordinates, or dealing with difficult situations (Bell & Nkomo, 1994, p. 39; Tomaskovic-Devey, 1994). Thus the segregation of minorities and women into nonchallenging jobs reduces their chances of being promoted by restricting their chances to acquire or demonstrate skills (Erdreich, Slavet, & Amador, 1996, p. xiii).

Minorities' and women's relegation to dead-end or short-ladder jobs is critical for hierarchical segregation (Bell & Nkomo, 1994, pp. 32, 39; Collins, 1989, 1997). To improve advancement opportunities for clerical and service workers, some companies have created "bridge" positions that help workers to switch job ladders—for example, move from a clerical job ladder to a production or administrative one—without risk or penalty (Kanter, 1976; Northrup & Larson, 1979; Roos & Reskin, 1984). Seniority systems can also affect the amount of hierarchical segregation in an organization (Kelley, 1984). For instance, USX (formerly U.S. Steel) helped to integrate customarily male production jobs by altering its seniority rules to allow workers to transfer to plant jobs without losing their seniority (Reskin & Hartmann, 1986, p. 93; Ullman & Deaux, 1981). Other case studies also demonstrate that organizations can eliminate structural barriers that exclude women and minorities from jobs (Badgett, 1995; Deaux & Ullman, 1983; DiTomaso, 1993; Northrup & Larson, 1979).

The segregation of women and men into different kinds of establishments also contributes to hierarchical segregation. The sheer size of large organizations lets them create more opportunities to promote workers, and they are more likely to have job ladders (Kalleberg, Marsden, Knoke, & Spaeth, 1996). Therefore, women's concentration in small, entrepreneurial firms and nonprofit organizations and men's concentration in large corporations and for-profit companies reduce women's odds of promotion relative to men (Kalleberg & Reskin, 1995). Some industries are better than others in promoting women. In female-intensive industries such as apparel, banking, retail trade, and insurance, women are more likely to be high-level managers (Shaeffer & Lynton, 1979). For instance, in 1990 women were only 2.2% of the officers in the chemicals industry, but 10% of the officers in the apparel industry. Although only 5% of the directors in the electronics industry were women in the late 1980s, almost 17% of the directors in the cosmetics and soap industries were women (Von Glinow, 1988). Why do women have greater access to high-level jobs in female-dominated industries? Jobs in female-intensive industries pay less and are thus less desirable to men. Furthermore, firms' experience with female workers makes them less likely to stereotype women.

In sum, workplace segregation is largely due to employers' use of workers' sex, race, and ethnicity in assigning workers to jobs because of stereotypes and outright bias. Pressure from regulatory agencies, internal constituencies, and the public has prompted some employers to reduce stereotyping and bias by replacing informal personnel practices, such as word-of-mouth hiring, with formal ones, such as advertising and posting all openings, reassessing the qualifications jobs require, and using objective criteria for hiring and promotion (Roos & Reskin, 1984; Szafran, 1982).

2. Sex, Race, and Earnings

White men outearn men of color and women from all racial and ethnic groups. In 1995, for example, Hispanic women employed full-time year round earned just 53% of what white men earned, Hispanic men earned 61%, black women earned 63%, white women earned 72%, and black men earned 74%. These disparities translate into a $14,994 pay gap with white men for the average Hispanic woman and a $7744 gap for the average black man (Institute for Women's Policy Research [IWPR], 1996, Table 3). In general, the disparities between the earnings of white men and those of other groups have closed since 1970, as Fig. 32.3 shows. Black women show the most progress relative to white men. However, some reversals of some slopes from positive to negative indicate that gains are not necessarily permanent. Closest to earnings parity with white men were Asian men employed full-time year

round; their median earnings were almost 98% of white men's in 1970 and 1990 (computed from Harrison & Bennett, 1995, Table 4A.1). No other group achieved even three quarters of white men's 1990 earnings.

The trends in racial differences in earnings summarized above are disconcerting. Although the black–white earnings gap shrank between 1965 and 1975, black men's earnings relative to white men deteriorated between 1975 and the late 1980s (Bound & Freeman, 1992), and by 1995 black men still had not regained their 1975 earnings relative to whites (see Fig. 32.3). Figure 32.3 also displays the substantial shortfall of female and male Hispanics' earnings relative to white men. The pay difference between Hispanic and white men widened by 15 percentage points between 1970 and 1995. Young black women's position relative to white women has been deteriorating since the early 1970s, especially among college graduates (Bound & Dresser, 1997, Fig. 1). Although Hispanic women narrowed the gap with white men between 1975 and 1990, they have not continued to do so at the same rate. American Indian women, who earned a little more than half of what men made in 1990, have closed their earnings gap with white men by less than one percentage point per decade since 1970, and American Indian men, who earned three quarters of what white men made in 1990, were relatively worse off in 1990 than in 1970.

Sex differences dominate earnings inequality. In every racial group, men outearn women. The pay gap between women and men who worked full-time, year round did not start to close until 1975 when women earned 58.8% of what men made, the largest disparity since 1920. Although the gap in the median earnings of men and women who worked full-time year round narrowed by more than 11 percentage points between 1975 and 1995, in 1995 men who worked full-time year round still earned $1.40 for every dollar a woman earned (computed from IWPR, 1996, Table 1). Within broad race categories, the sex difference in annual earnings is greatest for whites ($9261) and Asians ($8740: computation based on median income from Table 4A.1 in Harrison & Bennett, 1995), reflecting white and Asian men's high median earnings, and smallest for Hispanics

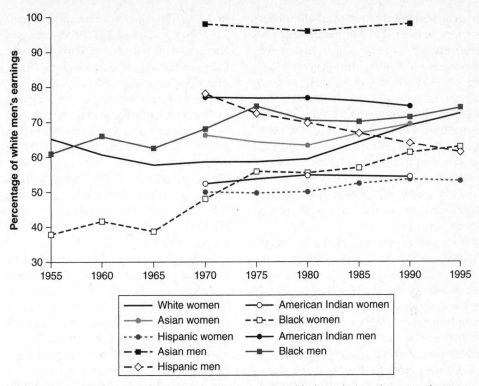

FIGURE 32.3 Median earnings of Asian, American Indian, black, and Hispanic men and women and white women as a percentage of white men's earnings for full-time, year-round employed workers, 1955 to 1995.

(*Sources:* Data from Farley, 1984, Fig. 3.2; U.S. Bureau of the Census, 1981, Table 6; U.S. Bureau of the Census, 1983, Tables 37 and 39; U.S. Bureau of the Census, 1988, Tables 27 and 29; U.S. Bureau of the Census, 1991, Table 24; U.S. Bureau of the Census, 1995, Table 7; data for American Indians, Asians, and 1970 data for Hispanics from Harrison & Bennett, 1995, Table 4A.1.)

($3201) and blacks ($3763), reflecting the low average earnings of Hispanic and black men (computed from U.S. Bureau of the Census, 1996a). American Indian women's shortfall relative to same-ethnicity men was intermediate: $5400 (computation based on median income from Table 4A. 1 in Harrison & Bennett, 1995).

2.1. Explaining Sex and Race Differences in Earnings

Explanations for sex and race disparities in earnings emphasize group differences in workers' education, experience, and jobs, as well as the earnings payoff for these factors. They include differences in (1) group characteristics that hypothetically affect workers' productivity; (2) group rewards for productivity-enhancing characteristics; (3) group distributions across occupations. industries, firms, and jobs; and (4) group payoffs for the same kind of work. A fifth explanation attributes part of the sex gap to sex differences in orientations toward monetary versus nonmonetary rewards. In the following sections we review the evidence for each of these explanations.

2.1.1. Productivity Differences

To the extent that employers reward productivity differences by race and sex in productivity will give rise to pay differences across groups. The difficulty of measuring productivity has led researchers to use as proxies for productivity the amount of time and effort workers spend at work and characteristics that hypothetically increase workers' productivity, such as education and experience.

In general, men are employed more hours per year than women, because they work more hours per week and more weeks per year.[17] Even among workers employed full-time year round, men averaged 3 hours more per week than women in the same broad racial group (computed from U.S. Bureau of the Census, 1992a). Whites tend to work more hours per week than people of color, although this does not hold for Asian compared to white women and is a reversal from the past for African-American compared to white women (Farley, 1984, Table A.2).[18] Whites work more weeks per year than same-sex Asians, Hispanics, or African-Americans (computed from U.S. Bureau of the Census, 1992a).[19] Although the proportion of women employed full-time year round has been increasing since 1970 (Spain & Bianchi, 1996, Table 84) and has helped to reduce the pay gap between the sexes, men's greater average number of hours of paid work per week explains a little of the sex gap in pay: the sexes' earnings ratio tends to be 2 to 4 percentage points closer to equity for hourly earnings than weekly earnings (Bianchi, 1995, p. 129; IWPR, 1996, Table 1; Mishel & Bernstein, 1994, p. 125). As Fig. 32.4 shows, in 1995 the sex gap among full-time workers was smallest for hourly pay, slightly larger for weekly earnings, and slightly larger for annual earnings. The pattern in Fig. 32.4 for all workers varies by race. Although the sex gap in median earnings in 1995 was 12.6% larger for annual earnings than weekly earnings, the difference in weekly and annual earnings explained just 2.4% of the gap between Hispanic women and white men and 9% of the gap between white women and men. Black women's, black men's, and Hispanic men's gaps in weekly pay compared to white men are larger than their annual earnings gaps because white men average more hours (IWPR, 1996, Table 3; U.S. Bureau of Labor Statistics, 1996b, Table 37).

Differences in the extent of employment across groups are not solely a consequence of workers' preferences. Although some people deliberately limit their paid work in response to other demands on their time, such as education and family, others cannot obtain as many hours of paid work as they want or need (Carnoy, 1994, p. 82).

In 1995, for example, one in five part-timers (17.5% of women and 27.7% of men) could not find a full-time job (computed from U.S. Bureau of Labor Statistics, 1996a). Thus, variation in the earnings gaps explained by group differences in extent of employment may not reflect group differences in preference for paid work time.

Although group differences in effort could give rise to unequal pay, there is no evidence that differences in work effort explain white men's higher pay. In fact, the few studies that compared the sexes suggest that women work at least as hard as do men (Bielby & Bielby, 1988; Major, McFarlin, & Gagnon, 1984); we found no similar studies by race.

Neoclassical economists assume that workers' education, training, and experience affect—and are thus proxies for—their productivity. If so, then sex and race differences in education or experience could explain part of the earnings gaps. Overall, women workers have one month less schooling than men, although the difference varies by race, with whites averaging the same number of years of schooling (13.3), Asian men averaging about a half a year more than Asian women (14.0 compared to 13.4), and African-American and Hispanic women averaging slightly more years schooling than their male counterparts (black women average 12.7 years, black men 12.2, Hispanic women 11.3, and Hispanic men 10.5). On average, men are less likely than women to have completed high school and more likely than women to have postgraduate education (Bianchi, 1995). The sexes and races also tend to major in different subjects, but over the past 20 years, college majors have become more similar across sex and race categories (Jacobs, 1995), and women have been catching up with men in the likelihood of postgraduate education. According to O'Neill and Polachek (1993, p. 221), 17% of the declining sex gap in pay between 1976 and 1989 resulted from the convergence in women's and men's years of schooling. However, by 1990, educational differences played a minor role at most in the earnings gap between young-to-middle-aged women and men (England, Reid, & Kilbourne, 1996: England et al., 1997, Table 7).

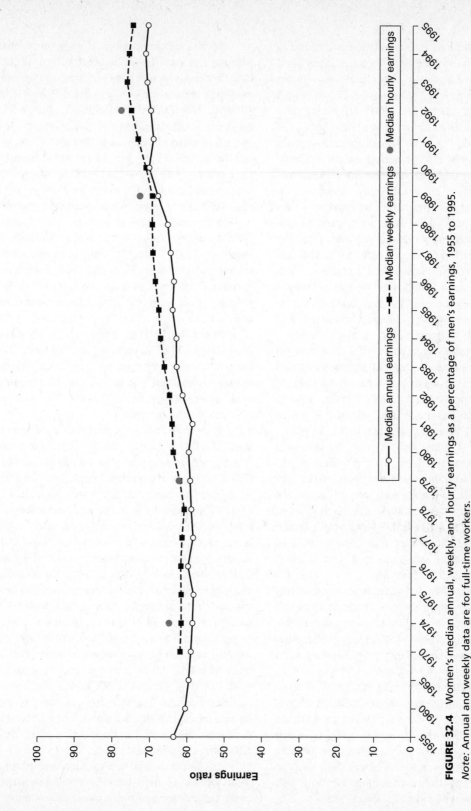

FIGURE 32.4 Women's median annual, weekly, and hourly earnings as a percentage of men's earnings, 1955 to 1995.

Note: Annual and weekly data are for full-time workers.

(*Sources:* Data from Institute for Women's Policy Research, 1996, Table 1; Mishel & Bernstein, 1994, Table 3.9.)

435

Race differences in education contribute to racial disparities in earnings, because blacks and Hispanics average less schooling than whites (Mare, 1995, p. 158).[20] During the 1980s, whites pulled further ahead of blacks, Hispanics, and American Indians in college graduation (Harrison & Bennett, 1995, Fig. 4.5). This difference—a consequence of past discrimination and an indicator of ongoing residential and economic disadvantages of people of color—may contribute to whites' higher earnings, either by making whites more productive or because employers require degree completion for well-paying jobs. One way to assess the importance of race and sex differences in education on the earnings gap is to compare how much minorities' earnings would increase if they averaged the same amount of education as white men. (Equalizing education with white men would not reduce the gap between white women and men because white female workers had as many years of education as white males in 1989.) Having white men's years of schooling would have raised black females' 1989 earnings by 7 percentage points, black males' by 9 points, Latinas' by 13 points, and Latinos' by 19 points (Carnoy, 1994, Table 4.6). Among workers who were 28 to 35 years old in 1993, schooling differences explained about one sixth of the race gap between black and white men, one eighth to one fifth of the gap between black and white women, three eighths to two thirds of the gap between white men and Latinos, and four fifths to 100% of the gap between white women and Latinas (England et al., 1997, Table 3).

Because college graduation strongly affects earnings, the growing black–white disparity in college completion works against reducing race differences in earnings. Discrimination in apprenticeship programs further inhibits minorities' representation in high-paying jobs (Waldinger & Bailey, 1991). Minorities also tend to be underrepresented in occupations that allow them to acquire skills on the job. For example, people of color in contingent work are disproportionately concentrated in occupations that involve tasks that are less complex than those in which white men work; such jobs are less likely to provide the opportunity to acquire job skills that could lead to regular jobs (Reskin, 1997b).

Men average more job experience than women, although the difference has been declining. This convergence has contributed to the narrowing of the sex gap in pay (Mishel & Bernstein, 1994, p. 119; O'Neill & Polachek, 1993). The declining sex difference in work experience produces a positive association between workers' age and the size of the pay gap. In 1995, for example, the median weekly earnings of 25- to 29-year-old women employed full-time were 80% of what same-age men earned, while 40- to 44-year-old women earned just 62% of male age peers' wages (IWPR, 1996, Table 6; see also O'Neill & Polachek, 1993, Table 2).[21] Among mature workers surveyed between 1966 and 1988, experience accounted for one fourth to one third of the sex gap in earnings among African-Americans and one third to one half of the sex gap for whites (Kilbourne et al., 1994a). In contrast, among workers who were 14 to 22 years old in 1979, sex differences in experience explained just 1% of the gap among whites and 9% among blacks (England et al., 1996; see also England et al., 1997, Table 4, for race-specific results).

Race differences in experience—although small (Farley, 1984, Table A2)—contribute to the earnings gap among men. Among mature workers, race differences in experience explained two fifths of the gap between black and white men (England et al., 1996, Table 1). In the past, black women had more job experience on average, than white women, but young white women are now more experienced than young black women (England et al., 1996, Table 1). Black women's declining years of experience relative to white women contributed to the increasing earnings gap with white women during the 1980s (Blau & Beller, 1992). Experience differences explain 6% to 30% of the pay gap between young Latinas and white women, and 13% to 17% of the gap between young Latinos and white men (England et al., 1997, Table 7). Experience explains between 7% and 20% of the pay gap between black and white women and men (Anderson & Shapiro, 1996, p. 277; England et al., 1997, Table 7; Kilbourne et al., 1994a).

In sum, race and sex groups have become more similar in their education and experience (with the exception of black men's falling rates of college participation in the early 1990s), and these changes have contributed to shrinking earnings disparities between groups. Importantly, the extent to which these differences affect workers' productivity depends in part on employers' decisions regarding the organization of work and the use of technology, as well as race and sex segregation in job assignments. The disappearance of educational and experience differences across groups cannot produce earnings equality unless employers assign workers to jobs without regard to their race and sex and compensate workers at the same rate for their education and experience. In the following section, we assess the importance of the last factor for race-and sex-based earnings disparities.

2.1.2. Unequal Rates of Return to Education and Experience

Pay disparities between groups stem partly from employers rewarding workers from different race-sex groups unequally for the same credentials. Schooling, for example, has a smaller payoff for women than men and for nonwhites than whites (Farley, 1984, p. 68). In 1995, white female college graduates who worked full-time year round earned $500 less, on average, than white male high school graduates who worked full-time year round, and white male college graduates out-earned white women with postgraduate degrees by almost $12,000 (computed from IWPR, 1996, Table 4). Black and Hispanic women with high school and college diplomas earned 70% to 75% of what same-race men with the same education earned, and Hispanic and black women with post-graduate degrees earned around 85% of what similar men earned (IWPR, 1996, Table 4).

Blacks have been falling behind whites in returns to education—especially for college graduates—offsetting their increasing parity in schooling. The earnings of young blacks have been lagging behind whites with the same amount of education (Carnoy, 1994, pp. 121, 123). For example, in 1985, young black male college graduates earned 89% of the earnings of white male college graduates, but by 1991 the ratio had fallen to 76%. Young black female college graduates slightly out-earned white female graduates in 1976, but earned

13% less in 1991. During this period, Latinos/as also lost ground relative to Anglos with equal years of schooling, although the amount varies across Hispanic groups (Carnoy & Rothstein, 1996; Corcoran, Heflin, & Reyes, 1997).

Young Asians with at least some college were the only racial group who enjoyed higher returns to education than comparably educated, same-sex whites (Mare, 1995). At the other extreme are American Indian women, who were furthest from parity, followed by African-American and Hispanic women. American Indian college graduates who were 16 to 34 years old, for example, earned 86% of the earnings similar to white women, black women earned 92%, Hispanic women earned 99%, and Asian American women earned 105% (see Carnoy, 1994, Table 6.2). Among men, blacks received the lowest rewards for their education relative to whites, followed by American Indians, and then Hispanics (Mare, 1995, p. 207; see also Harrison & Bennett, 1995, pp. 174–176). In 1995, men of color earned two thirds to three quarters of what white men with the same degrees earned, while women of color earned between 90% and 100% of what white women earned (computed from IWPR, 1996, Table 4). White male high school graduates without any additional schooling were particularly over-rewarded for their schooling compared to minority men (Harrison & Bennett, 1995, pp. 174–175). The same patterns hold after controlling for experience and region: in 1973 blacks at all educational levels earned 10.3% less than whites with the same education, experience, and region, compared to 16% less in 1989 (Mishel & Bernstein, 1994, Table 3.9). These trends mean that additional education will not be sufficient for minorities to catch up with whites in earnings (Harrison & Bennett, 1995, p. 175).

Group differences in payoff for hours worked and years of work experience also contribute to the pay disparities that we have been examining. Net of other factors that affect earnings, men received higher returns to both hours and weeks worked in 1990 than did women (Harrison & Bennett, 1995, Table 4.5), and a year's experience was worth considerably more to men than women (Farley, 1984, Table A.3). Men's greater returns to experience mean that the sex-linked pay disparity increases as workers age. Workers' payoff for experience also differs by race. Although this difference shrank during the 1960s and 1970s—contributing to the declining earnings gap between blacks and whites—in 1980 whites still received about twice the payoff to experience that blacks did (Farley, 1984, pp. 68, 78, Table A.3), and this difference held for young to middle-aged workers (England et al., 1996, Table 2).

These race and sex differences in how employers reward workers' education and experience almost certainly result partly from discrimination, Of course, unequal rewards for the same levels of schooling or experience may reflect unmeasured differences in the quality of education or experience, but sex differences in the returns to experience probably derive largely from job segregation. Whether discrimination stems from segregated jobs that do not provide incumbents with equally valuable experience or from employers' failure to reward education and experience equally for persons regardless of their race or sex, actions by employers perpetuate earnings disparities.

2.1.3. Job Segregation by Sex and Race

The sex and race composition of jobs is associated with incumbents' average pay for two reasons. First, segregation disproportionately relegates women and minorities to the kinds of jobs that employers compensate poorly. Second, employers devalue workers' achievements in jobs filled primarily by women and minorities. Although each of these mechanisms reduces the pay of women and minorities relative to white men, each affects the earnings of white men as well.

Employers' allocation of workers into higher- and lower-paying jobs based on their sex or race guarantees unequal pay across sex/race groups (England, 1992; Hirsch & Schumacher, 1992; Sorensen, 1989).[22] For example, if a retail store employs minority women as janitors, minority men as stock clerks, white women as cashiers, and white men as managers, white men will outearn the other three groups and minority women will earn the least. The relationship between the proportion of women in an occupation and its earnings particularly disadvantages women for two reasons. First, women are more likely than men to work in heavily female

occupations, and second, the penalty for holding a mostly female job is stronger for women—especially women of color—than for men (England et al., 1996, Table 3; Kilbourne et al., 1994a). If young women had been distributed across more and less female occupations in the same way as young men in the 1980s, the disparity in the sexes' starting pay on a job would have been at least one fifth smaller among both blacks and whites (England et al., 1996, p. 519).

Comparing the median weekly earnings of female and male workers employed full-time all year in the same occupations illustrates the more negative effect of a female-dominated job on women than men. For example, in the mid-1990s, the median weekly pay of female sewing-machine operators was about 86% of men's earnings of $280, and female cashiers averaged 87% of men's $265 (computed from U.S. Bureau of Labor Statistics, 1995, 1996b, 1997, Table 39). The larger penalty of working in a female occupation for women than men can have two sources: (1) employers pay men more than women who do identical tasks, and (2) employers segregate men and women in the same occupation into different jobs. The first alternative is illegal under the 1963 Equal Pay Act. In the second instance, although taking into account sex and race in assigning jobs is illegal under Title VII of the 1964 Civil Rights Act, it is legal under the Equal Pay Act, and high levels of segregation are common. The more workers earn, the larger the sex pay gap tends to be. According to a 1993 survey of corporate executives, women at the vice presidential level and higher earned 70% of what their male counterparts earned (Brooks, 1993). Women who sold securities and financial services, for example, earned 55% of men's $951, and female financial managers averaged two thirds of men's earnings of $937 (computed from U.S. Bureau of Labor Statistics, 1995, 1996b, 1997, Table 39).

Women's concentration in low-paying service jobs has insulated them from the big pay cuts that some men experienced as the United States lost well-paying manufacturing jobs. Almost three fourths of the decline in the wage gap between the sexes between 1979 and 1993 resulted from the decline in men's wages stemming from the loss of traditionally male blue-collar jobs and from falling pay in surviving male blue-collar jobs (Mishel

& Bernstein, 1994, pp. 124–125). In response, many men entered service work that was overwhelmingly female. Therefore, although women's likelihood of employment in a job with poverty-level wages is 10 percentage points higher than men's, their likelihood of holding such a job has been declining since 1973, while men's likelihood has been growing since 1979 (Mishel & Bernstein, 1994, p. 127).

Racial segregation increases racial differences in earnings: the more black workers in a job, the lower the pay for black and white women and men. Given the size of estimated effects, working in all-black jobs would lower the pay of white women by 15%, that of black women by 24%, that of black men by 39%, and that of white men by 52% (Hirsch & Schumacher, 1992). Moreover, the narrowing of the earnings gap between black and white women between 1940 and 1980 was due largely to declining race segregation by occupation and industry (Cunningham & Zalokar, 1992, p. 548). Minority workers' concentration in unskilled labor and service occupations and in low-paying specialties within more skilled occupations lowers their pay. For example, more than half of black, American Indian, and Hispanic male college-educated professionals worked as elementary or secondary teachers, social or religious workers, writers, artists, or entertainers—all low-paying professions (Harrison & Bennett, 1995, p. 181). Blacks'—and presumably Hispanics'—concentration in low-paying, nonunionized industries and in occupations and cities with low wage growth has exacerbated the black–white wage disparity (Mishel & Bernstein, 1994, pp. 188–189). The loss of manufacturing jobs that reduced men's average earnings in the late 1980s and early 1990s also adversely affected women of color, who were disproportionately concentrated in these industries (Bound & Dresser, 1997; Mishel & Bernstein, 1994, pp. 124–125).

2.1.4. The Devaluation of Female- and Minority-Dominated Jobs

Given the societal devaluation of women and minorities, employers may devalue and hence underpay jobs that are performed primarily by women or minorities. Sociologists have argued that predominantly female jobs are underpaid relative to the skills and responsibilities they involve because the devaluation of women leads to the undervaluation of stereotypically female work (Acker, 1989, 1990; England, 1992; Reskin, 1988). Although the same logic holds for people of color, their small numbers may prevent occupations from being labeled minority and hence devalued. In sum, although all workers in a devalued job earn less than their job warrants as reflected in its qualifications and duties, the predominance of women or minority men in devalued jobs means that the effect of any devaluation will fall disproportionately on women and minorities and hence contribute to earnings disparities. This tendency to underpay jobs solely because of their sex or race composition has been termed "comparable-worth discrimination."

Comparable-worth discrimination is apparent when an occupation's sex composition affects incumbents' pay, net of measures of workers' education, experience, and job complexity (England, 1992; England et al., 1996; Kilbourne et al., 1994a; Kilbourne, England, Farkas, Beron & Weir, 1994b; Treiman & Hartmann, 1981). For example, among middle-aged workers, performing nurturing tasks customarily sex-typed as female—such as nursing or childcare—is associated with pay losses for all workers, but especially women (Kilbourne et al., 1994b). In other segments of the population, occupations' sex composition explains up to 30% of the pay gap between the sexes (England, 1992, p. 181; Sorensen, 1989). Among workers in their late 20s and early 30s in 1993, sex composition explained between 10% and 42% of the sex difference in hourly wages among whites, 45% to 73% among blacks, and 3% to 21% among Latinas/os (England et al., 1997, Table 6).[23] Whether the race composition of occupations or jobs contributes to the racial gap in earnings because predominantly minority jobs are devalued has not been established, because the few studies of the earnings effect of race composition have not controlled for occupational skills. Controlled studies have found no effect of minority composition on earnings, net of job characteristics (England, 1992), presumably because minorities make up too small a proportion of the labor force to comprise a majority in any occupation. (Even in occupations in which minorities are concentrated, such as nursing aide, janitor, or cook, the majority of workers are white.) According to appellate and Supreme Court decisions, the 1963 Equal Pay Act does not prohibit employers from paying workers in predominantly female jobs less than workers in equally demanding but different jobs dominated by men. For instance, the U.S. Court of Appeals allowed the city of Denver to pay nurses, 97% of whom were female, less than tree trimmers and sign painters, male-dominated jobs (Lemons v. City and County of Denver, 1978). These rulings have led to pressure for laws that require employers to provide equal pay to workers in different jobs that involve similar amounts of skill, effort, and responsibility. Such laws could reduce the pay gap between the sexes by one third (IWPR, 1993, p. 1). Indeed, a Minnesota pay-equity law for state workers reduced a 28-point pay gap to 18% in 4 years (IWPR, 1993). However, bureaucratic inertia and political resistance have set limits on the effectiveness of pay equity as a widespread solution to the pay gap (Bridges & Nelson, 1989; Steinberg, 1987).

2.1.5. Compensating Differentials

Some neoclassical economists suggest that the pay gap between the sexes may stem partly from different job values held by male and female workers. They argue that men seek jobs that will maximize their earnings, even when they involve physically difficult, dirty, or dangerous work; women, in contrast, trade off pay for job characteristics that facilitate combining work and family or for desirable working conditions. There is almost no support for this explanation of the pay gap, however (but see Filer, 1989). Researchers have found that female occupations pay less, net of working conditions (England et al., 1996; Glass & Camarigg, 1992), and that undesirable working conditions are associated with lower, not higher wages (Jacobs & Steinberg, 1990).

3. Conclusions

Workplace inequality by sex, race, and ethnicity is linked to inequality in all social institutions because people's jobs distribute so many social and economic rewards. Jobs are mechanisms that govern workers' access to earnings, authority,

status, and mobility opportunities as well as their exposure to pleasant or unpleasant working conditions. Job segregation is a key mechanism in workplace inequality. Although few data exist on the extent of job segregation, occupations—which aggregate similar jobs—are substantially segregated by workers' sex and somewhat less so by their race and ethnicity. A variety of factors affect the extent of segregation. Workers' education and experience play a limited role in sex segregation and a slightly larger one in race/ethnic segregation. Although workers' preferences matter, most workers "choose" between options that are constrained by employers' preferences and employment practices. Indeed, employers' personnel practices shape workers' preferences (Schultz, 1991, p. 141), as do antidiscrimination and affirmative action regulations that open sex- and race-atypical jobs to minorities and women.

The importance of segregation is seen in its effect on earnings disparities between sex, race, and ethnic groups. The concentration of men and women of different races in different occupations, industries, and jobs is the foremost cause of the earnings gap between the sexes and races. Race segregation contributes to the earnings gap between whites and minorities by disproportionately relegating people of color to lower-paying jobs that prevent incumbents from acquiring and using skills that employers compensate. Sex segregation contributes to the pay gap between the sexes both by concentrating women in jobs that do not reward or enhance their productive capacity and because of the devaluation of predominantly female jobs. Anything that fosters job integration helps to reduce the pay gap between the sexes and races. Thus, the enforcement of antidiscrimination and affirmative action regulations has induced employers to integrate jobs, thereby making a dent in the pay gaps between sex/race groups. Eliminating all of the barriers to women's and minorities' employment in the full range of jobs would go far toward reducing the pay gap. However, job segregation by sex is still the rule, and race segregation—while less extensive—is prevalent. Job segregation means that equalizing human capital will not remedy the earnings disparities across race/sex groups. Pay-equity laws that cover public employees in some states have had a modest effect in reducing the sex gap in earnings.

Sex and race differences in productivity play a minor role in the pay disparities across race/sex groups. Although white men outperform other groups on one or another measure of productivity, the differences are small and have minor effects on earnings differences. However, women and minority men receive lower payoffs than white men for some of the factors that researchers treat as proxies for productivity, and these differences contribute to earnings disparities.

Discrimination is an important source of the earnings disparities between race-sex groups (Anderson & Shapiro, 1996, p. 286; Cunningham & Zalokar, 1992, p. 554; Farley, 1984, p. 68; Gill, 1994; Mishel & Bernstein, 1994, p. 189). First, some group differences in indicators of productivity, such as job experience, result from earlier discrimination by employers, and their contribution to earnings disparities between groups must be chalked up to discrimination. Discrimination also occurs when women and minorities are compensated at a lower rate than white men for the same inputs.[24] Sex- and race-segregated job assignments also contribute to pay discrimination by denying female and minority workers access to well-paying jobs or jobs in which they can acquire skills that will enhance their future earnings. These discriminatory effects are seen in the association between occupations' sex and race composition and incumbents' pay. When the sex composition of a job is associated with incumbents' pay, net of job demands, discrimination results from the devaluation of female-dominated tasks. Legal prohibitions against most of these forms of discrimination have contributed to the declining rate of wage inequality, but the effectiveness of laws depends on good faith efforts by enforcing agencies and the ability of victims to detect their discriminatory treatment (which is impaired by social psychological processes; Clayton & Crosby, 1992, pp. 72–79) and to challenge it.

In the 35 years since the 1963 Equal Pay Act outlawed unequal pay for equal work, women have been catching up with men in earnings at a rate of one third of a percent a year, and the pay gap between the sexes has declined by about 13 cents on the dollar. If this rate of progress continues (and it appears to have slowed in the early 1990s), the sexes would not achieve earnings parity until almost the end of the twenty-first century. Achieving earnings equality more quickly will require women to accumulate work experience more in line with that of men, employers to integrate customarily male jobs, and the spread of pay-equity principles that compensate workers for the worth of their job and not the sex of their co-workers. Racial disparities in earnings also declined in the 1970s and early 1980s. Although minorities are closer to earnings parity with same-sex whites than women are to same-race men, the trend toward declining inequality changed direction in the late 1980s, making it impossible to predict when racial equality in earnings might cease to exist.

Finally, we believe that progress depends in part on the evidence that researchers bring to bear on the extent of inequality in work opportunities and rewards by sex, race, and ethnicity. As we noted at the outset, little research examines the joint effects of race, sex, and ethnicity. Race is typically treated as black/white or minority/white. Available data indicate that the economic situation of groups that are neither white nor black differs from the situations of both blacks and whites. Variation exists, too, among different Asian and different Latin national groups. We encourage researchers to compare the situations of as many groups as their data allow. Such comparisons are essential for identifying the greatest needs for policy intervention and for recommending policies that can reduce workplace inequality.

Notes

1. Space limitations and limitations in available research preclude our considering other factors that influence workplace outcomes, such as social class, sexual orientation, or disability.

2. An occupation is a collection of jobs involving similar activities within or across establishments (Bielby & Baron, 1986, p. 764). The 1990 census distinguished 503 detailed occupations. In contrast, a job is a specified position in an establishment in which workers perform particular activities (Bielby & Baron, 1986, p. 764). *The Dictionary of Occupational Titles* (U.S. Department of Labor, 1977) distinguishes more than 20,000 jobs.

3. The Census Bureau instructed U.S. coders in 1930, for example, to "look up any occupations which involve responsibility and high standing in the community, if the person is colored, Chinese, Japanese, or other" (quoted in Conk, 1981, p. 68).

4. Exceptions were teaching, nursing, and social work for white women, and professional jobs serving black clientele for blacks.

5. Among the occupations that some state laws closed to women were bartending and street car conductor.

6. Despite the existence of better opportunities, some southern white women were able to hold on to their black cleaning women through the passage of local Work or Fight ordinances (Rollins, 1995, p. 163).

7. The most common lines of work for women in 1990 are all but identical to those that employed the most women in 1940. The only recent addition to women's top 10 occupations is the census category "miscellaneous salaried managers."

8. African-American female professionals were concentrated in two customarily female professions—nursing and elementary school teaching (computed from U.S. Bureau of Labor Statistics, 1995). Asian-American women were concentrated in only one profession—accounting.

9. It was the fourth largest occupation for black and Hispanic men.

10. Even women in high-level positions seldom have as much authority as men at the same level (Reskin & Ross, 1992). For example, McGuire and Reskin (1993) found that if black and female workers had received the same authority returns to their experience and other credentials as white men, the authority gap with white men would have shrunk by 62% for white women, 71% for black women, and 93% for black men.

11. The publication did not report the proportion of minority men who were willing to work hard for a promotion.

12. Few job seekers have their choice of jobs; most receive only one or two offers and accept the first offer that meets their minimum acceptable pay (Gera & Hasan, 1982; Kahn, 1978).

13. An audit of sex discrimination found that more expensive restaurants favored males as server, whereas cheaper ones favored women (Neumark, Bank, & Van Non, 1995).

14. Employers in the suburbs, who hire mostly white workers, have lower standards than those in the central city, who draw more heavily on minorities (Holzer, 1996).

15. Approximately 3% charged "reverse discrimination" (Bendick, 1996; Blumrosen, 1995).

16. Many employers adhere to what Bergmann (1986, pp. 114–116) called an "informal segregation code" that prohibits women from supervising men and reserves the training slots leading to higher-level jobs for men. Men rule over women and junior men, women rule over women, but women rarely if ever rule over men. This code applies to minorities as well: minorities may give orders to other minorities, but not to whites.

17. In 1990, all employed men averaged 6 hours more per week than all women (42.3 compared to 36.3 hours), and they worked on average 2 more weeks per year (46.4 compared to 44.5), according to unpublished analyses of the 1990 census data (U.S. Bureau of the Census, 1992a). The sex differences in hours was smallest among African-Americans (2.8 hours per week) and largest among whites (6.6 hours). Hispanic and Asian men averaged 3.5 to 4 more hours per week than did same-race women. In terms of weeks per year, black men worked only .4 more weeks than black women, Hispanic and Asian men worked about 1.5 weeks more than same-race women, and white men averaged 2.1 more weeks than white women.

18. According to unpublished analyses of the 1990 census data (U.S. Bureau of the Census, 1992a), white men employed in 1990 worked an average of 42.7 hours per week, compared to 41.6 hours for Asian men, 41.3 hours for Hispanic men, 39.9 hours for black men, 37.9 hours for Asian women, 37.1 hours for black women, 37.0 hours for Hispanic women, and 36.1 hours for white women.

19. Employed white men averaged 46.9 weeks per year compared to 45.7 for Asian men, 44.8 for white women, 44.2 for Asian women, 44.1 for Hispanic men, 43.9 for black men, 43.5 for black women, and 42.5 for Hispanic women.

20. In 1990, blacks averaged 12.5 years of education and Hispanics averaged 10.8 years, compared to 13.3 years for whites and 13.7 years for Asians (unpublished analysis, U.S. Bureau of the Census, 1992a).

21. The low pay that young workers of both sexes command necessarily restricts the size of the pay gap among younger workers. The larger gap among older workers also reflects the positive association between the extent of sex segregation

and workers' age and men's greater returns to experience (reported below).

22. Although neoclassical economists and sociologists disagree regarding the causes of occupational sex segregation, they agree that it is an important mechanism in the pay gap between the sexes.

23. The racial disparities in earnings in this sample did not stem from comparable-worth discrimination (England et al., 1997, Table 5).

24. To the extent that different returns to productivity reflect unmeasured differences in productivity, treating these differences as indicative of discrimination will overestimate the amount of discrimination.

References

Acker, J. (1989). *Doing comparable worth: Gender, class, and pay equity.* Philadelphia: Temple University Press.

Acker, J. (1990). Hierarchies, jobs, and bodies: A theory of gendered organizations. *Gender & Society, 4,* 139–158.

American Bar Association Commission on Opportunities for Women in the Profession. (1996). *Unfinished business,* Chicago: The American Bar Association.

Amirault, T. (1992). Training to qualify for jobs and improve skills, 1991. *Monthly Labor Review, 115,* 31–36.

Anderson, D., & Shapiro, D. (1996). Racial differences in access to high-paying jobs and the wage gap between black and white women. *Industrial and Labor Relations Review, 49,* 273–286.

Ashenfelter, O., & Heckman, J. (1976). Measuring the effect of an anti-discrimination program. In O. Ashenfelter & J. Blum (Eds.), *Evaluating the labor market effects of social programs* (pp. 46–84). Princeton, NJ: Princeton University Press.

Badgett, M. V. L. (1995). Affirmative action in a changing legal and economic environment. *Industrial Labor Relations, 34,* 489–506.

Badgett, M. V. L., & Hartmann, H. I. (1995). The effectiveness of equal employment opportunity policies. In M. C. Simms (Ed.), *Economic perspectives on affirmative action* (pp. 55–97). Washington: Joint Center for Political and Economic Studies.

Baldi, S., & McBrier, D. B. (1997). Do the determinants of promotion differ for blacks and whites? Evidence from the U.S. labor market. *Work and Occupations, 24,* 470–497.

Baron, J. N., & Bielby, W. T. (1985). Organizational barriers to gender equality: Sex segregation of jobs and opportunities. In A. S. Rossi (Ed.), *Gender and the life course* (pp. 233–251). New York: Aldine.

Baron, J. N., Mittman, B. S., & Newman, A. E. (1991). Targets of opportunity: Organizational and environmental determinants of gender integration within the California Civil Service, 1979–1985. *American Journal of Sociology, 96,* 1362–1401.

Bell, E. L. J., & Nkomo, S. (1994). Barriers to workplace advancement experienced by African-Americans. *Report to the Glass Ceiling Commission.* U.S. Department of Labor, April.

Bendick, M., Jr. (1996). *Declaration.* (Brief challenging California Civil Rights Initiative.) Submitted to the California State Court of Appeals.

Bergmann, B. R. (1986). *The economic emergence of women.* New York: Basic Books.

Bergmann, B. R., & Darity, W., Jr. (1981). Social relations, productivity, and employer discrimination. *Monthly Labor Review, 104,* 47–49.

Berheide, C. W. (1992). Women still 'stuck' in low-level jobs. *Women in public services: A bulletin for the Center for Women in Government* 3 (Fall).

Bianchi, S. (1995). Changing economic roles of women and men. In R. Farley (Ed.), *State of the union: America in the 1990s.* Vol. 1: *Economic trends* (pp. 107–155). New York: Russell Sage Foundation.

Bielby, W. T., & Baron, J. N. (1984). A woman's place is with other women: Sex segregation within organizations. In B. F. Reskin (Ed.), *Sex segregation in the workplace* (pp. 27–55). Washington, D.C.: National Academy Press.

Bielby, W. T., & Baron, J. N. (1986). Men and women at work: Sex segregation and statistical discrimination. *American Journal of Sociology, 91,* 759–799.

Bielby, D. D., & Bielby, W. T. (1988). She works hard for the money: Household responsibilities and the allocation of work effort. *American Journal of Sociology, 93,* 1031–1059.

Blau, F., & Beller, A. (1992). Black-white earnings over the 1970s and 1980s: Gender differences in trends. *Review of Economics and Statistics, 74,* 276–286.

Blumrosen, A. W. (1995). Draft report on reverse discrimination, commissioned by U.S. Department of Labor: How courts are handling reverse discrimination cases. *Daily Labor Report,* March 23. Washington, D.C.: The Bureau of National Affairs.

Bobo, L. (1996). *Declaration.* Submitted to the California State Court of Appeals. November 1.

Bound, J., & Dresser, L. (1997). The erosion of the relative earnings of young African American women during the 1980s. In I. Browne (Ed.), *Race, gender, and economic inequality: African American and*

Latina women in the labor market. New York: Russell Sage Foundation.

Bound, J., & Freeman, R. B. (1992). What went wrong? The erosion of relative earnings among young black men in the 1980s. *Quarterly Journal of Economics, 107,* 201–232.

Braddock, J. H., & McPartland, J. M. (1987). How minorities continue to be excluded from equal employment opportunities: Research on labor market and institutional barriers. *Journal of Social Issues, 43,* 5–39.

Bridges, W. P., & Nelson, R. L. (1989). Markets in hierarchies: Organizational and market influences on gender inequality in a state pay system. *American Journal of Sociology, 95,* 616–658.

Brooks, N. R. (1993). Gender pay gap found among top executives. *Los Angeles Times,* June 30, Dl, D3.

Burstein, P. (1979). Equal employment opportunity legislation and the income of women and nonwhites. *American Sociological Review, 44,* 367–391.

Burstein, P. (1985). *Discrimination, politics, and jobs.* Chicago: University of Chicago Press.

Carnoy, M. (1994). *Faded dreams: The politics and economics of race in America.* New York: Cambridge University Press.

Carnoy, M., & Rothstein, R. (1996). *Hard lessons.* Washington, D.C.: Economic Policy Institute.

Catalyst. (1996). *Women in corporate leadership.* New York: Catalyst.

Clayton, S. D., & Crosby, F. J. (1992). *Justice, gender, and affirmative action.* Ann Arbor, MI: University of Michigan Press.

Collins, S. M. (1989). The marginalization of black executives. *Social Problems, 36,* 317–331.

Collins, S. M. (1997). *Black corporate executives: The making and breaking of a black middle class.* Philadelphia: Temple University Press.

Conk, M. (1981). Accuracy, efficiency and bias: The interpretation of women's work in the U.S. Census of Occupations, 1890–1940. *Historical Methods, 14,* 65–72.

Corcoran, M., Heflin, C. M., & Reyes, B. I. (1997). Latina women in the U.S.: The economic progress of Mexican and Puerto Rican women. In I. Browne (Ed.), *Race, gender, and economic inequality: African American and Latina women in the labor market.* New York: Russell Sage Foundation.

Cox, T. H., & Nkomo, S. M. (1986). Differential performance appraisal criteria: A field study of black and white managers. *Group & Organization Studies, 11,* 101–119.

Cunningham, J. S., & Zalokar, N. (1992). The economic progress of black women, 1940–1980: Occupational distribution and relative wages. *Industrial and Labor Relations Review, 45,* 540–555.

Deaux, K. (1984). From individual differences to social categories: Analysis of a decade's research on gender. *American Psychologist, 39,* 105–115.

Deaux, K. (1985). Sex and gender. *Annual Review of Psychology, 36,* 49–81.

Deaux, K., & Ullman, J. P. (1983). *Women of steel: Female blue-collar workers in the basic steel industry.* New York: Praeger.

DiTomaso, N. (1993). *Notes on Xerox case: Balanced work force at Xerox.* Unpublished.

Dobbin, F., Sutton, J., Meyer, J., & Scott, W. R. (1993). Equal opportunity law and the construction of internal labor markets. *American Journal of Sociology, 99,* 396–427.

Donohue, J. J., & Heckman, J. (1991). Re-evaluating federal civil rights policy. *Georgetown Law Review, 79,* 1713–1735.

Duncan, O. D., & Duncan, B. (1955). A methodological analysis of segregation indices. *American Sociological Review, 20,* 200–217.

Eagly, A. H., & Wood, W. (1982). Inferred sex differences in status as a determinant of gender stereotypes about social influence. *Journal of Personality and Social Psychology, 43,* 915–928.

Eagly, A. H., Makhijani, M. G., & Klonsky, B. G. (1992). Gender and the evaluation of leaders: A meta-analysis. *Psychological Bulletin, 111,* 3–22.

England, P. (1992). *Comparable worth: Theories and evidence.* New York: Aldine de Gruyter.

England, P., Chassie, M., & McCormack, L. (1982). Skill demands and earnings in female and male occupations. *Sociology and Social Research, 66,* 47–68.

England, P., Reid, L. L., & Kilbourne, B. S. (1996). The effect of sex composition on the starting wages in an organization: Findings from the NLSY. *Demography, 33,* 511–522.

England, P., Christopher, K., & Reid, L. L. (1997). How do intersections of race-ethnicity and gender affect pay among young cohorts of African Americans, European Americans, and Latinos/as? In I. Browne (Ed.), *Race, gender, and economic inequality: African American and Latina women in the labor market.* New York: Russell Sage.

Epstein, C. F. (1993). *Women in law.* Urbana: University of Illinois Press.

Erdreich, B., Slavet, B., & Amador, A. (1996). *Fair and equitable treatment: A progress report on minority employment in the federal government.* Washington, D.C.: U.S. Merit Systems Protection Board.

Farley, R. (1984). *Blacks and whites: Narrowing the gap.* Cambridge, MA. Harvard University Press.

Filer, R. (1989). Occupational segregation, compensating differentials, and comparable worth. In R. T. Michael, H. I. Hartmann, & B. O'Farrell (Eds.), *Pay equity: Empirical inquiries* (pp. 153–171). Washington, D.C.: National Academy Press.

Fiske, S. T., Bersoff, D. N., Borgida, E., Deaux, K., & Heilman, M. E. (1991). Social science research on trial: Use of sex stereotyping research in Price Waterhouse v. Hopkins. *American Psychologist, 46,* 1049–1060.

Fix, M., & Struyk, R. J. (Eds.). (1992). *Clear and convincing evidence. Measurement of discrimination in America.* Washington, D.C.: The Urban Institute.

Gera, S., & Hasan, A. (1982). More on returns to job search: A test of two models. *Review of Economics and Statistics, 64,* 151–156.

Gill, A. (1994). Incorporating the causes of occupational differences in studies of racial wage differentials. *Journal of Human Resources, 29,* 20–41.

Glass, J. (1990). The impact of occupational segregation on working conditions. *Social Forces, 68,* 779–796.

Glass, J., & Camarigg, V. (1992). Gender, parenthood and job-family compatibility. *American Journal of Sociology, 98,* 131–151.

Greenhaus, J. H., & Parasuraman, S. (1993). Job performance attributions and career advancement prospects: An examination of gender and race effects. *Organizational Behavior and Human Decision Processes, 55,* 273–297.

Greenhaus, J. H., Parasuraman, S., & Wormley, W. M. (1990). Effects of race on organizational experiences, job performance evaluations, and career outcomes. *Academy of Management Journal, 33,* 64–86.

Gross, E. (1968). Plus ca change: The sexual segregation of occupations over time. *Social Problems, 16,* 198–208.

Harrison, R. J., & Bennett, C. (1995). Racial and ethnic diversity. In R. Farley (Ed.), *State of the union: America in the 1990s.* Vol. 2: *Social trends* (pp. 141–210). New York: Russell Sage Foundation.

Heckman, J. J., & Payner, B. S. (1989). Determining the impact of anti-discrimination policy on the economic status of blacks: A study of South Carolina. *American Economic Review, 79,* 138–177.

Higginbotham, E. (1987). Employment for professional black women in the twentieth century. In C. Bose & G. Spitze (Eds.), *Ingredients for women's employment policy* (pp. 73–99). Albany, NY: SUNY Press.

Hirsch, B. T., & Schumacher, E. J. (1992). Labor earnings, discrimination, and the racial composition of jobs. *Journal of Human Resources, 27,* 602–628.

Holzer, H. J. (1996). *What employers want.* New York: Russell Sage Foundation.

Institute for Women's Policy Research. (1993). State pay equity programs raise women's wages. *News release,* May 20. Washington, D.C.: Institute for Women's Policy Research.

Institute for Women's Policy Research. (1996). *The wage gap: Women and men's earnings.* Washington, D.C.: Institute for Women's Policy Research.

Jacobs, J. A. (1989a). Long-term trends in occupational segregation by sex. *American Journal of Sociology, 95,* 160–173.

Jacobs, J. A. (1989b). *Revolving doors.* Stanford, CA: Stanford University Press.

Jacobs, J. A. (1995). Gender and academic specialties: Trends among degree recipients during the 1980s. *Sociology of Education, 68,* 81–98.

Jacobs, J. A., & Steinberg, R. J. (1990). Compensating differentials and the male-female wage gap: Evidence from the New York State Comparable Worth Study. *Social Forces, 69,* 439–468.

Jacobsen, J. P. (1997). Trends in workforce segregation: 1980 and 1990 Census figures. *Social Science Quarterly, 78,* 234–235.

Jencks, C., Perman, L., & Rainwater, L. (1988). What is a good job? A new measure of labor-market success. *American Journal of Sociology, 93,* 1322–1357.

Kahn, L. M. (1978). The returns to job search: A test of two models. *Review of Economics and Statistics, 15,* 496–503.

Kalleberg, A., & Reskin, B. F. (1995). Gender differences in promotion in the U.S. and Norway. *Research in Social Stratification and Mobility, 13,* 237–264.

Kalleberg, A., Marsden, P. V., Knoke, D., & Spaeth, J. L. (1996). Formalizing the employment relationship: Internal labor markets and dispute resolution procedures. In A. L. Kalleberg, D. Knoke, P. V. Marsden, & J. L. Spaeth (Eds), *Organizations in America* (pp. 87–112). Newbury Park, CA: Sage.

Kanter, R. M. (1976). The policy issues: Presentation VI. In M. Blaxall & B. Reagan (Eds.), *Women and the workplace* (pp. 282–291). Chicago: University of Chicago Press.

Kasinitz, P., & Rosenberg, J. (1996). Missing the connection: Social isolation and employment on the Brooklyn waterfront. *Social Problems, 43,* 180–196.

Kelley, M. R. (1984). Commentary: The need to study the transformation of job structures. In B. F. Reskin (Ed.), *Sex segregation in the workplace: Trends, explanations, remedies* (pp. 261–264). Washington, D.C.: National Academy Press.

Kern, L. (1996). Hiring and seniority: Issues in policing in the post-judicial intervention period. Unpublished paper, Columbus, OH: Ohio State University.

Kilbourne, B., England, P., & Beron, K. (1994a). Effects of individual, occupational, and industrial characteristics on earnings: Intersections of race and gender. *Social Forces, 72,* 1149–1176.

Kilbourne, B., England, P., Farkas, G., Beron, K., & Weir, D. (1994b). Returns to skill, compensating differentials, and gender bias: Effects of occupational characteristics on the wages of white women and men. *American Journal of Sociology, 100,* 689–719.

King, M. C. (1992). Occupational segregation by race and sex, 1940–88. *Monthly Labor Review, 115,* 30–36.

Kraiger, K., & Ford, J. K. (1985). A meta-analysis of ratee race effects in performance ratings. *Journal of Applied Psychology, 70,* 56–65.

Kraut, K., & Luna, M. (1992). *Work and wages: Facts on women and people of color in the workforce.* Washington, D.C.: National Committee on Pay Equity.

Lemons v. City and County of Denver, 17 FEP cases 906 (D. Col. 1978). 620 F. 2d 228 (10th Cir.) 1978.

Leonard, J. S. (1984a). The impact of affirmative action on employment. *Journal of Labor Economics, 2,* 439–463.

Leonard, J. S. (1984b). Employment and occupational advance under affirmative action. *The Review of Economics and Statistics, 66,* 377–385.

Leonard, J. S. (1994). Use of enforcement techniques in eliminating glass ceiling barriers. Report to the Glass Ceiling Commission, U.S. Department of Labor, April.

Lieberson, S. (1980). *A piece of the pie.* Berkeley, CA: University of California Press.

Major, B., McFarlin, D. B., & Gagnon, D. (1984). Overworked and underpaid: On the nature of gender differences in personal entitlement. *Journal of Personality and Social Psychology, 47,* 1399–1412.

Mare, R. D. (1995). Changes in educational attainment and school enrollment. In R. Farley (Ed.), *State of the Union: America in the 1990s.* Vol. I: *Economic Trends* (pp. 155–214). New York: Russell Sage Foundation.

Marini, M. M., & Brinton, M. C. (1984). Sex typing in occupational socialization. In B. F. Reskin (Ed.), *Sex segregation in the workplace: Trends, explanations, remedies* (pp. 192–232). Washington, D.C.: National Academy Press.

Marini, M. M., Fan, P., Finley, E., & Beutel, A. (1996). Gender and job values. *Sociology of Education, 69,* 49–65.

Markham, W. T., Harlan, S., & Hackett, E. J. (1987). Promotion opportunity in organizations. Research in *Personnel and Human Resource Management, 5,* 223–287.

Marsden, P. V. (1994). The hiring process: Recruitment methods. *American Behavioral Scientist, 7,* 979–991.

Marsden, P. V., Kalleberg, A. L., & Cook, C. R. (1993). Gender differences in organizational commitment: Influences of work positions and family roles. *Work and Occupations, 20,* 368–390.

Martin, S. E. (1991). The effectiveness of affirmative action: The case of women in policing. *Justice Quarterly, 8,* 489–504.

McGuire, G. M., & Reskin, B. F. (1993). Authority hierarchies at work: The impact of race and sex. *Gender & Society, 7,* 457–506.

Messick, D. M., & Mackie, D. (1989). Intergroup relations. *Annual Review of Psychology, 40,* 45–81.

Mishel, L., & Bernstein, J. (1994). *The state of working America, 1994–95.* Armonk, NY: M. E. Sharpe.

Moss, P., & Tilly, C. (1996). 'Soft' skills and race. *Work and Occupations, 23,* 252–276.

Neckerman, K. M., & Kirschenman, J. (1991). Hiring strategies. racial bias, and inner-city workers: An investigation of employers' hiring decisions. *Social Problems, 38,* 433–447.

Neumark, D., Bank, R., & Van Nort, K. (1995). Sex discrimination in the restaurant industry: An audit study. Working Paper No, 5024. Washington. D.C.: National Bureau of Economic Research.

Northrup, H. R., & Larson, J. A. (1979). The impact of the AT & T-EEO consent decrees. *Labor Relations and Public Policy Series,* No. 20. Philadelphia: Industrial Research Unit, University of Pennsylvania.

O'Neill, J., & Polachek, S. (1993). Why the gender gap in wages narrowed in the 1980s. *Journal of Labor Economics, 11,* 205–228.

Padavic, I. (1991a). The re-creation of gender in a male workplace. *Symbolic Interaction, 14,* 279–294.

Padavic, I. (1991b). Attractions of male blue-collar jobs for black and white women: Economic need, exposure, and attitudes. *Social Science Quarterly, 72,* 33–49.

Padavic, I., & Reskin, B. F. (1990). Men's behavior and women's interest in blue-collar jobs. *Social Problems, 37*, 613–628.

Peterson, T., & Morgan, L. (1995). Separate and unequal: Occupation-establishment sex segregation and the gender wage gap. *America Journal of Sociology, 101*, 329–365.

Pettigrew, T., & Martin, J. (1987). Shaping the organizational context for black American inclusion. *Journal of Social Issues, 43*, 41–78.

Polachek, S. (1981). A supply side approach to occupational segregation. Presented at the American Sociological Association meeting, Toronto.

Pulakos, E. D., White, L. A., Oppler, S. L., & Borman, W. C. (1989). Examination of race and sex effects on performance ratings. *Journal of Applied Social Psychology, 74*, 770–780.

Reskin, B. F. (1988). Bringing the men back in: Sex differentiation and the devaluation of women's work. *Gender & Society, 2*, 58–81.

Reskin, B. F. (1994). Segregating workers: Occupational differences by ethnicity, race, and sex. *Annual Proceedings of the Industrial Relations Research Association, 46*, 247–255.

Reskin, B. F. (1997a) Dimensions of segregation: An MDS analysis of occupational segregation by race, ethnicity, and sex. Paper presented at the University of Pennsylvania, March.

Reskin, B. F. (1997b). Gender, race, and economic vulnerability in nonstandard working arrangements. Paper presented at Northwestern University Institute for Policy Research, February 24.

Reskin, B. F. (1997c). Occupational segregation by race and ethnicity among female workers. In I. Browne (Ed.), *Race, gender and economic inequality: African, American and Latino women in the labor market.* New York: Russell Sage Foundation.

Reskin, B. F., & Cassirer, N. (1996). The effect of organizational arrangements on men's and women's promotion expectations and experiences. Unpublished manuscript. Columbus: Ohio State University.

Reskin, B. F., & Charles, C. Z. (1997). Now you see 'em, now you don't: Theoretical approaches to race and gender in labor markets. In I. Browne (Ed.), *Race, gender, and economic inequality: African American and Latina women in the labor market.* New York: Russell Sage Foundation.

Reskin, B. F., & Hartmann, H. I. (1986). *Women's work, men work: Sex segregation on the job.* Washington, D.C.: National Academy Press.

Reskin, B. F., & McBrier, D. B. (1998). Organizational determinants of the sexual division of managerial labor. Unpublished manuscript.

Reskin, B. F., & Padavic, I. (1988). Supervisors as gatekeepers: Male supervisors' response to women's integration in plant jobs. *Social Problems, 35*, 401–415.

Reskin, B. F., & Roos, P. (1990). *Job queues, gender queues.* Philadelphia: Temple University Press.

Reskin, B. F., & Ross, C. E. (1992). Jobs, authority, and earnings among managers: The continuing significance of sex. *Work and Occupations, 19*, 342–365.

Rollins, J. (1995). *Allis never said: The narrative of Odette Harper Hines.* Philadelphia: Temple University Press.

Roos, P. A., & Reskin, B. F. (1984). Institutionalized barriers to sex integration in the workplace. In B. F. Reskin (Ed.), *Sex segregation in the workplace* (pp. 235–260). Washington. D.C.: National Academy Press.

Sackett, P. R., DuBois, C. L., & Noe, A. W. (1991). Tokenism in performance evaluations: The effect of work group representation on male-female and white-black differences in performance ratings. *Journal of Applied Psychology, 76*, 263–267.

Schroedel, J. (1985). *Alone in a crowd.* Philadelphia: Temple University Press.

Schultz, V. (1991). Telling stories about women and work: Judicial interpretation of sex segregation in the workplace in Title VII cases raising the lack of interest argument. In K. Bartlett & R. Kennedy (Eds.), *Feminist legal theory* (pp. 124–43). Boulder, CO: Westview.

Segura, D. (1992). Chicanas in white-collar jobs: "You have to prove yourself." *Sociological Perspectives, 35*, 163–182.

Shaeffer, R. G., & Lynton, E. F. (1979). Corporate experience in improving women's job opportunities. Report no. 755. New York: The Conference Board.

Smith, J. P., & Welch, F. (1984). Affirmative action and labor markets. *Journal of Labor Economics, 2*, 269–301.

Smith, T. W. (1990). Ethnic images. *General Social Survey Report.* Chicago: National Opinion Research Center.

Sorensen, E. (1989). Measuring the effect of occupational sex and race composition on earnings. In R. T. Michael, H. I. Hartmann, & B. O'Farrell (Eds.), *Pay equity: Empirical inquiries* (pp. 49–69). Washington, D.C.: National Academy Press.

Spain, D., & Bianchi, S. M. (1996). *Balancing act: Motherhood, marriage, and employment among American women.* New York: Russell Sage Foundation.

Steinberg, R. (1987). Radical challenges in a liberal world: The mixed success of comparable worth. *Gender & Society, 1,* 466–475.

Subich, L. M., Barrett, G. V., Doverspike, D., & Alexander, R. A. (1989). The effects of sex-role related factors on occupational choice and salary. In R. T. Michael, H. I. Hartmann, & B. O'Farrell (Eds.), *Pay equity: Empirical inquiries* (pp. 91–104). Washington, D.C.: National Academy Press.

Swerdlow, M. (1989). Men's accommodations to women entering a nontraditional occupation: A case of rapid transit operatives. *Gender & Society, 3,* 373–387.

Szafran, R. F. (1982). What kinds of firms hire and promote women and blacks? A review of the literature. *Sociological Quarterly, 23,* 171–190.

Thurow, L. (1969). *Poverty and discrimination.* Washington, D.C.: The Brookings Institute.

Tomaskovic-Devey, D. (1993). *Gender and racial inequality at work: The sources and consequences of job segregation.* Ithaca, NY: ILR Press.

Tomaskovic-Devey, D. (1994). Race, ethnicity, and gender earnings inequality: The sources and consequences of employment segregation. Report to the Glass Ceiling Commission, U.S. Department of Labor.

Treiman, D. J., & Hartmann, H. I. (1981). *Women, work, and wages.* Washington, D.C.: National Academy Press.

Ullman, J. P., & Deaus, K. (1981). Recent efforts to increase female participation in apprenticeship in the basic steel industry in the Midwest. In V. M. Briggs, Jr., & F. Foltman (Eds.), *Apprenticeship research: Emerging findings and future trends* (pp. 133–149). Ithaca: NY State School of Industrial and Labor Relations, Cornell University.

U.S. Bureau of the Census. (1972). *U.S. census of the population, 1970. Subject Reports, 7C, Occupational characteristics.* Washington, D.C.: Census Bureau.

U.S. Bureau of the Census. (1981). Washington, D.C.: U.S. Government Printing Office.

U.S. Bureau of the Census. (1983). Washington, D.C.: U.S. Government Printing Office.

U.S. Bureau of the Census. (1988). Washington, D.C.: U.S. Government Printing Office.

U.S. Bureau of the Census. (1991). Washington, D.C.: U.S. Government Printing Office.

U.S. Bureau of the Census. (1992a). *Census of population and housing, 1990: Public use microdata samples U.S.* [machine-readable data files, prepared by the Bureau of the Census]. Washington, D.C.: Census Bureau.

U.S. Bureau of the Census. (1992b). *Detailed occupation and other characteristics from the EEO file for the United States. 1990 CP-S-1-1.* Washington, D.C.: U.S. Department of Commerce.

U.S. Bureau of the Census. (1995). Washington, D.C.: U.S. Government Printing Office.

U.S. Bureau of the Census. (1996a). Money income in the U.S., 1995. *Current Population Reports,* Series P-60. Washington, D.C.: Census Bureau.

U.S. Bureau of the Census. (1996b), *Statistical abstract of the United States: 1996* (116th ed.) Washington, D.C.: Census Bureau.

U.S. Bureau of Labor Statistics. (1961). *Employment and earnings 8 (January).* Washington, D.C.: U.S. Government Printing Office.

U.S. Bureau of Labor Statistics. (1995). *Employment and earnings 42 (January).* Washington, D.C.: U.S. Government Printing Office.

U.S. Bureau of Labor Statistics. (1996a). *Current population survey, February 1995: Contingent work supplement* [machine-readable data fuel]. Conducted by the Bureau of the Census for the Bureau of Labor Statistics. Washington, D.C.: Bureau of the Census [producer and distributor].

U.S. Bureau of Labor Statistics. (1996b). *Employment and earnings 43 (January).* Washington, D.C.: U.S. Government Printing Office.

U.S. Bureau of Labor Statistics. (1997). *Employment and earnings 44 (January).* Washington, D.C.: U.S. Government Printing Office.

U.S. Bureau of Labor Statistics. (1998). Web page www.bls.gov

U.S. Department of Labor. (1977). *Dictionary of occupational titles* (4th ed.). Washington, D.C.: U.S. Government Printing Office.

U.S. Department of Labor. (1996). Employment standards administration, Office for Federal Contract Compliance Programs. OFCCP egregious discrimination cases. Nov. 19. Washington, D.C.: U.S. Department of Labor.

U.S. Merit Systems Protection Board. (1992). *A question of equity: Women and the glass ceiling in the federal government.* A Report to the President and Congress by the U.S. Merit Systems Protection Board. Washington, D.C.: U.S. Merit Systems Protection Board.

U.S. Merit Systems Protection Board. (1996). *Fair and equitable treatment: A progress report on minority employment in the federal government.* Washington, D.C.: U.S. Merit Systems Protection Board.

Von Glinow, M. A. (1988). Women in corporate America: A caste of thousands. *New Management, 6,* 36–42.

Waldinger, R., & Bailey, T. (1991). The continuing significance of race: Racial conflict and racial discrimination in construction. *Politics and Society, 19,* 291–323.

Williams, C. L. (1989). *Gender differences at work: Women and men in nontraditional occupations.* Berkeley, CA: University of California Press.

Williams, C. L. (1995). *Still a man's world: Men who do "women's work."* Berkeley, CA: University of California Press.

Williams, J. B., & Best, D. (1986). Sex stereotypes and intergroup relations. In S. Worchel & W. G. Austin (Eds.), *Psychology of intergroup relations* (pp. 244–259). Chicago: Nelson-Hall.

Wilson, W. J. (1996). When work disappears: The world of the new urban poor. New York: Knopf.

V

Class, Status, *and* Party

INTRODUCTION

Whereas Marx emphasized class in explaining social inequality, Weber recognized multiple categories, including class as well as different forms of status and different kinds of political organizations. While Weber tended to talk about these forces in terms of discrete categories, he understood they would interact as well. The history of intersectionality is old and unending. If you pull on the thread of any identity, the whole sweater of race, class, gender, religion, nationality, and sexual orientation will unravel. No one is simply a worker, masculinity is never the only characteristic of a person, being Asian American is not an all-encompassing experience, and so on. In some cases, class, status, *and* party are all important at the same time. The idea that different sources of social identity are simultaneously consequential in terms of shaping access to resources was voiced by W.E.B. DuBois and Anna Julia Cooper even before Weber articulated his framework. Needless to say, the problems associated with multiple jeopardies are hardly resolved.

In contemporary research, scholars such as Barbara F. Reskin and Irene Padavic show how social forces associated with gender, race, ethnicity, occupation, and education lead to different kinds of social inequality. Their essay, "Sex, Race, and Ethnic Inequality in United States Workplaces," represents an analytical approach to identifying such connections. Overt discrimination in hiring and compensation is certainly part of the picture. But, as Reskin and Padavic demonstrate, more complicated processes related to socialization and segregation are at least as important. Another stream of research extending from the concerns of DuBois and Cooper and other pioneers recognizes more entanglement of social forces that cannot be reduced to additive oppression or dichotomous categories. In reality, privilege is never fixed or one-dimensional. The contemporary engagement among scholars of this important perspective can be dated, arguably, from 1993 when Patricia Hill Collins called for a new program in sociology (see her essay "Towards a New Vision: Race, Class, and Gender as Categories of Analysis and Connection") to 2009 when she served as President of the American Sociological Association and the agenda she helped lead was firmly established in the core of sociology.

Now the scholarship on these matters has blossomed. In an essay entitled "Intersectionality," Irene Browne and Joya Misra summarize the insights of mounting new research extending from Collins's "New Vision." The example of care chains and domestic labor illuminates global connections involving class, gender, race, ethnicity, and citizenship that are "mutually constituative and inherently intersectional."

In the final chapter of this section, Sharon Hays documents the lived reality of intersectionality in an excerpt from her book, *Flat Broke with Children*. This qualitative research illustrates the connections between personal "troubles" and social "issues," to borrow C. Wright Mills' useful terms. The socially constructed realities of class, race, and gender and bureaucratic challenges of welfare laws, Hays reveals, provide the context in which poor mothers and their children make their way through life.

33

"Toward a New Vision: Race, Class, and Gender as Categories of Analysis and Connection"

PATRICIA HILL COLLINS

"The true focus of revolutionary change is never merely the oppressive situations which we seek to escape, but that piece of the oppressor which is planted deep within each of us."

—Audre Lorde, Sister Outsider, 123

Audre Lorde's statement raises a troublesome issue for scholars and activists working for social change. While many of us have little difficulty assessing our own victimization within some major system of oppression, whether it be by race, social class, religion, sexual orientation, ethnicity, age or gender, we typically fail to see how our thoughts and actions uphold someone else's subordination. Thus, white feminists routinely point with confidence to their oppression as women but resist seeing how much their white skin privileges them. African-Americans who possess eloquent analyses of racism often persist in viewing poor White women as symbols of white power. The radical left fares little better. "If only people of color and women could see their true class interests," they argue, "class solidarity would eliminate racism and sexism." In essence, each group identifies the type of oppression with which it feels most comfortable as being fundamental and classifies all other types as being of lesser importance.*

Oppression is full of such contradictions. Errors in political judgment that we make concerning how we teach our courses, what we tell our children, and which organizations are worthy of our time, talents and financial support flow smoothly from

*Reprinted from Patricia Hill Collins, "Toward a New Vision: Race, Class, and Gender as Categories of Analysis and Connection," *Race, Sex, and Class,* Vol. 1, No. 1 (Fall 1993): 25–45, by permission of Patricia Hill Collins and the Center for Research on Women at the University of Memphis.

errors in theoretical analysis about the nature of oppression and activism. Once we realize that there are few pure victims or oppressors, and that each one of us derives varying amounts of penalty and privilege from the multiple systems of oppression that frame our lives, then we will be in a position to see the need for new ways of thought and action.

To get at that "piece of the oppressor which is planted deep within each of us," we need at least two things. First, we need new visions of what oppression is, new categories of analysis that are inclusive of race, class, and gender as distinctive yet interlocking structures of oppression. Adhering to a stance of comparing and ranking oppressions—the proverbial, "I'm more oppressed than you"—locks us all into a dangerous dance of competing for attention, resources, and theoretical supremacy. Instead, I suggest that we examine our different experiences within the more fundamental relationship of domination and subordination. To focus on the particular arrangements that race or class or gender take in our time and place without seeing these structures as sometimes parallel and sometimes interlocking dimensions of the more fundamental relationship of domination and subordination may temporarily ease our consciences. But while such thinking may lead to short term social reforms, it is simply inadequate for the task of bringing about long term social transformation.

While race, class and gender as categories of analysis are essential in helping us understand the structural bases of domination and subordination, new ways of thinking that are not accompanied by new ways of acting offer incomplete prospects for change. To get at that "piece of the oppressor which is planted deep within each of us," we also need to change our daily behavior. Currently, we are all enmeshed in a complex web of problematic relationships that grant our mirror images full human subjectivity while stereotyping and objectifying those most different than ourselves. We often assume that the people we work with, teach, I send our children to school with, and sit next to . . . will act and feel in prescribed ways because they belong to given race, social class or gender categories. These judgments by category must be replaced with fully human relationships that transcend the legitimate differences created by race, class and gender as categories of analysis. We require new

categories of connection, new visions of what our relationships with one another can be. . . .

[This discussion] addresses this need for new patterns of thought and action. I focus on two basic questions. First, how can we reconceptualize race, class and gender as categories of analysis? Second, how can we transcend the barriers created by our experiences with race, class and gender oppression in order to build the types of coalitions essential for social exchange? To address these questions I contend that we must acquire both new theories of how race, class and gender have shaped the experiences not just of women of color, but of all groups. Moreover, we must see the connections between these categories of analysis and the personal issues in our everyday lives, particularly our scholarship, our teaching and our relationships with our colleagues and students. As Audre Lorde points out, change starts with self, and relationships that we have with those around us must always be the primary site for social change.

How Can We Reconceptualize Race, Class, and Gender as Categories of *Analysis*?

To me, we must shift our discourse away from additive analyses of oppression (Spelman 1982; Collins 1989). Such approaches are typically based on two key premises. First, they depend on either/or, dichotomous thinking. Persons, things and ideas are conceptualized in terms of their opposites. For example, Black/White, man/woman, thought/feeling, and fact/opinion are defined in oppositional terms. Thought and feeling are not seen as two different and interconnected ways of approaching truth that can coexist in scholarship and teaching. Instead, feeling is defined as antithetical to reason, as its opposite. In spite of the fact that we all have "both/ and" identities, (I am both a college professor and a mother—I don't stop being a mother when I drop my child off at school, or forget everything I learned while scrubbing the toilet), we persist in trying to classify each other in either/or categories. I live each day as an African-American woman—a race/gender specific experience. And I am not alone. Everyone has a race/gender/class specific identity. Either/or, dichotomous thinking is especially troublesome when applied to theories of oppression because every individual must be classified as being either oppressed or not oppressed. The both/and position of simultaneously being oppressed and oppressor becomes conceptually impossible.

A second premise of additive analyses of oppression is that these dichotomous differences must be ranked. One side of the dichotomy is typically labeled dominant and the other subordinate. Thus, Whites rule Blacks, men are deemed superior to women, and reason is seen as being preferable to emotion. Applying this premise to discussions of oppression leads to the assumption that oppression can be quantified, and that some groups are oppressed more than others. I am frequently asked, "Which has been most oppressive to you, your status as a Black person or your status as a woman?" What I am really being asked to do is divide myself into little boxes and rank my various statuses. If I experience oppression as a both/and phenomenon, why should I analyze it any differently?

Additive analyses of oppression rest squarely on the twin pillars of either/or thinking and the necessity to quantify and rank all relationships in order to know where one stands. Such approaches typically see African-American women as being more oppressed than everyone else because the majority of Black women experience the negative effects of race, class and gender oppression simultaneously. In essence, if you add together separate oppressions, you are left with a grand oppression greater than the sum of its parts.

I am not denying that specific groups experience oppression more harshly than others—lynching is certainly objectively worse than being held up as a sex object. But we must be careful not to confuse this issue of the saliency of one type of oppression in people's lives with a theoretical stance positing the interlocking nature of oppression. Race, class and gender may all structure a situation but may not be equally visible and/or important in people's self-definitions. In certain contexts, such as the antebellum American South and contemporary South America, racial oppression is more visibly salient, while in other contexts, such as Haiti, El Salvador and Nicaragua, social class oppression may be more apparent. For middle class White women, gender may assume experiential primacy unavailable to poor Hispanic women struggling with the ongoing issues of low paid jobs and the frustrations of

the welfare bureaucracy. This recognition that one category may have salience over another for a given time and place does not minimize the theoretical importance of assuming that race, class and gender as categories of analysis structure all relationships.

In order to move toward new visions of what oppression is, I think that we need to ask new questions. How are relationships of domination and subordination structured and maintained in the American political economy? How do race, class and gender function as parallel and interlocking systems that shape this basic relationship of domination and subordination? Questions such as these promise to move us away from futile theoretical struggles concerned with ranking oppressions and towards analyses that assume race, class and gender are all present in any given setting, even if one appears more visible and salient than the others. Our task becomes redefined as one of reconceptualizing oppression by uncovering the connections among race, class and gender as categories of analysis.

1. *The Institutional Dimension of Oppression*

Sandra Harding's contention that gender oppression is structured along three main dimensions—the institutional, the symbolic, and the individual—offers a useful model for a more comprehensive analysis encompassing race, class and gender oppression (Harding 1986). Systemic relationships of domination and subordination structured through social institutions such as schools, businesses, hospitals, the work place, and government agencies represent the institutional dimension of oppression. Racism, sexism and elitism all have concrete institutional locations. Even though the workings of the institutional dimension of oppression are often obscured with ideologies claiming equality of opportunity, in actuality, race, class and gender place Asian-American women, Native American men, White men, African-American women, and other groups in distinct institutional niches with varying degrees of penalty and privilege.

Even though I realize that many . . . would not share this assumption, let us assume that the institutions of American society discriminate, whether by design or by accident. While many of us are familiar with how race, gender and class operate separately to structure inequality, I want to focus on how these three systems interlock in structuring the institutional dimension of oppression. To get at the interlocking nature of race, class and gender, I want you to think about the antebellum plantation as a guiding metaphor for a variety of American social institutions. Even though slavery is typically analyzed as a racist institution, and occasionally as a class institution, I suggest that slavery was a race, class, gender specific institution. Removing any one piece from our analysis diminishes our understanding of the true nature of relations of domination and subordination under slavery.

Slavery was a profoundly patriarchal institution. It rested on the dual tenets of White male authority and White male property, a joining of the political and the economic within the institution of the family. Heterosexism was assumed and all Whites were expected to marry. Control over affluent White women's sexuality remained key to slavery's survival because property was to be passed on to the legitimate heirs of the slave owner. Ensuring affluent White women's virginity and chastity was deeply intertwined with maintenance of property relations.

Under slavery, we see varying levels of institutional protection given to affluent White women, working class and poor White women, and enslaved African women. Poor White women enjoyed few of the protections held out to their upper class sisters. Moreover, the devalued status of Black women was key in keeping all White women in their assigned places. Controlling Black women's fertility was also key to the continuation of slavery, for children born to slave mothers themselves were slaves.

African-American women shared the devalued status of chattel with their husbands, fathers and sons. Racism stripped Blacks as a group of legal rights, education, and control over their own persons. African-Americans could be whipped, branded, sold, or killed, not because they were poor, or because they were women, but because they were Black. Racism ensured that Blacks would continue to serve Whites and suffer economic exploitation at the hands of all Whites.

So we have a very interesting chain of command on the plantation—the affluent White master as the reigning patriarch, his White wife helpmate to serve him, help him manage his property and bring up his heirs, his faithful servants whose production and reproduction were tied to the requirements of the capitalist political economy, and largely propertyless, working class White men and women watching from afar. In essence, the foundations for the contemporary roles of elite White women, poor Black women, working class White men, and a series of other groups can be seen in stark relief in this fundamental American social institution. While Blacks experienced the most harsh treatment under slavery, and thus made slavery clearly visible as a racist institution, race, class and gender interlocked in structuring slavery's systemic organization of domination and subordination.

Even today, the plantation remains a compelling metaphor for institutional oppression. Certainly the actual conditions of oppression are not as severe now as they were then. To argue, as some do, that things have not changed all that much denigrates the achievements of those who struggled for social change before us. But the basic relationships among Black men, Black women, elite White women, elite White men, working class White men and working class White women as groups remain essentially intact.

A brief analysis of key American social institutions most controlled by elite White men should convince us of the interlocking nature of race, class and gender in structuring the institutional dimension of oppression. For example, if you are from an American college or university, is your campus a modern plantation? Who controls your university's political economy? Are elite White men over represented among the upper administrators and trustees controlling your university's finances and policies? Are elite White men being joined by growing numbers of elite White women helpmates? What kinds of people are in your classrooms grooming the next generation who will occupy these and other decision-making positions? Who are the support staff that produce the mass mailings, order the supplies, fix the leaky pipes? Do African-Americans, Hispanics or other people of color form the majority of the invisible workers who feed you, wash your dishes, and clean up your offices and libraries after everyone else has gone home?

If your college is anything like mine, you know the answers to these questions. You may be affiliated with an institution that has Hispanic women as vice-presidents for finance, or substantial numbers of Black men among the faculty. If so, you are fortunate. Much more typical are colleges where a modified version of the plantation as a metaphor for the institutional dimension of oppression survives.

2. *The Symbolic Dimension of Oppression*

Widespread, societally-sanctioned ideologies used to justify relations of domination and subordination comprise the symbolic dimension of oppression. Central to this process is the use of stereotypical or controlling images of diverse race, class and gender groups. In order to assess the power of this dimension of oppression, I want you to make a list, either on paper or in your head, of "masculine" and "feminine" characteristics. If your list is anything like that compiled by most people, it reflects some variation of the following:

Masculine	*Feminine*
aggressive	passive
leader	follower
rational	emotional
strong	weak
intellectual	physical

Not only does this list reflect either/or dichotomous thinking and the need to rank both sides of the dichotomy, but ask yourself exactly which men and women you had in mind when compiling these characteristics. This list applies almost exclusively to middle class White men and women. The allegedly "masculine" qualities that you probably listed are only acceptable when exhibited by elite White men, or when used by Black and Hispanic men against each other or against women of color. Aggressive Black and Hispanic men are seen as dangerous, not powerful,

and are often penalized when they exhibit any of the allegedly "masculine" characteristics. Working class and poor White men fare slightly better and are also denied the allegedly "masculine" symbols of leadership, intellectual competence, and human rationality. Women of color and working class and poor White women are also not represented on this list, for they have never had the luxury of being "ladies." What appear to be universal categories representing all men and women instead are unmasked as being applicable to only a small group.

It is important to see how the symbolic images applied to different race, class and gender groups interact in maintaining systems of domination and subordination. If I were to ask you to repeat the same assignment, only this time, by making separate lists for Black men, Black women, Hispanic women and Hispanic men, I suspect that your gender symbolism would be quite different. In comparing all of the lists, you might begin to see the interdependence of symbols applied to all groups. For example, the elevated images of White womanhood need devalued images of Black womanhood in order to maintain credibility.

While the above exercise reveals the interlocking nature of race, class I and gender in structuring the symbolic dimension of oppression, part of its importance lies in demonstrating how race, class and gender pervade a wide range of what appears to be universal language. Attending to I diversity in our scholarship, in our teaching, and in our daily lives provides a new angle of vision on interpretations of reality thought to be natural, normal and "true." Moreover, viewing images of masculinity and femininity as universal gender symbolism, rather than as symbolic images that are race, class and gender specific, renders the experiences of people of color and of non-privileged White women and men invisible. One way to dehumanize an individual or a group is to deny the reality of their experiences. So when we refuse to deal with race or class because they do not appear to be directly relevant to gender, we are actually becoming part of some one else's problem.

Assuming that everyone is affected differently by the same interlocking set of symbolic images allows us to move forward toward new analyses. Women of color and White women have different relationships to White male authority and this difference explains the distinct gender symbolism applied to both groups. Black women encounter controlling images such as the mammy, the matriarch, the mule and the whore, that encourage others to reject us as fully human people. Ironically, the negative nature of these images simultaneously encourages us to reject them. In contrast, White women are offered seductive images, those that promise to reward them for supporting the status quo. And yet seductive images can be equally controlling. Consider, for example, the views of Nancy White, a 73 year-old Black woman, concerning images of rejection and seduction:

> My mother used to say that the black woman is the white man's mule and the white woman is his dog. Now, she said that to say this: we do the heavy work and get beat whether we do it well or not. But the white woman is closer to the master and he pats them on the head and lets them sleep in the house, but he ain't gon' treat neither one like he was dealing with a person. (Gwaltney 1980, 148)

Both sets of images stimulate particular political stances. By broadening the analysis beyond the confines of race, we can see the varying levels of rejection and seduction available to each of us due to our race, class and gender identity. Each of us lives with an allotted portion of institutional privilege and penalty, and with varying levels of rejection and seduction inherent in the symbolic images applied to us. This is the context in which we make our choices. Taken together, the institutional and symbolic dimensions of oppression create a structural backdrop against which all of us live our lives.

3. *The Individual Dimension of Oppression*

Whether we benefit or not, we all live within institutions that reproduce race, class and gender oppression. Even if we never have any contact with members of other race, class and gender groups, we all encounter images of these groups and are exposed to the symbolic meanings attached to those images. On this dimension of oppression, our individual biographies vary tremendously. As a result of our institutional and symbolic statuses, all of our choices become political acts.

Each of us must come to terms with the multiple ways in which race, class and gender as categories of analysis frame our individual biographies. I have lived my entire life as an African-American woman from a working class family and this basic fact has had a profound impact on my personal biography. Imagine how different your life might be if you had been born Black, or White, or poor, or of a different race/class/gender group than the one with which you are most familiar. The institutional treatment you would have received and the symbolic meanings attached to your very existence might differ dramatically from what you now consider to be natural, normal and part of everyday life. You might be the same, but your personal biography might have been quite different.

I believe that each of us carries around the cumulative effect of our lives within multiple structures of oppression. If you want to see how much you have been affected by this whole thing, I ask you one simple question—who are your close friends? Who are the people with whom you can share your hopes, dreams, vulnerabilities, fears and victories? Do they look like you? If they are all the same, circumstance may be the cause. For the first seven years of my life I saw only low income Black people. My friends from those years reflected the composition of my community. But now that I am an adult, can the defense of circumstance explain the patterns of people that I trust as my friends and colleagues? When given other alternatives, if my friends and colleagues reflect the homogeneity of one race, class and gender group, then these categories of analysis have indeed become barriers to connection.

I am not suggesting that people are doomed to follow the paths laid out for them by race, class and gender as categories of analysis. While these three structures certainly frame my opportunity structure, I as an individual always have the choice of accepting things as they are, or trying to change them. As Nikki Giovanni points out, "we've got to live in the real world. If we don't like the world we're living in, change it. And if we can't change it, we change ourselves. We can do something" (Tate 1983, 68). While a piece of the oppressor may be planted deep within each of us, we each have the choice of accepting that piece or challenging it as part of the "true focus of revolutionary change."

How Can We Transcend the Barriers Created by Our Experiences with Race, Class, and Gender Oppression in Order to Build the Types of Coalitions Essential for Social Change?

Reconceptualizing oppression and seeing the barriers created by race, class and gender as interlocking categories of analysis is a vital first step. But we must transcend these barriers by moving toward race, class and gender as categories of connection, by building relationships and coalitions that will bring about social change. What are some of the issues involved in doing this?

1. Differences in Power and Privilege

First, we must recognize that our differing experiences with oppression create problems in the relationships among us. Each of us lives within a system that vests us with varying levels of power and privilege. These differences in power, whether structured along axes of race, class, gender, age or sexual orientation, frame our relationships. African-American writer June Jordan describes her discomfort on a Caribbean vacation with Olive, the Black woman who cleaned her room:

> even though both "Olive" and "I" live inside a conflict neither one of us created, and even though both of us therefore hurt inside that conflict, I may be one of the monsters she needs to eliminate from her universe and, in a sense, she may be one of the monsters in mine. (1985, 47)

Differences in power constrain our ability to connect with one another even when we think we are engaged in dialogue across differences. Let me give you an example. One year, the students in my course "Sociology of the Black Community" got into a heated discussion about the reasons for the upsurge of racial incidents on college campuses. Black students complained vehemently about the apathy and resistance they felt most White students expressed about examining their own racism. Mark, a White male student, found their comments particularly unsettling. After claiming that all the Black people he had ever known had expressed no such beliefs to him, he questioned how representative the view points of his fellow students actually were. When pushed further, Mark revealed that he had participated in conversations over the years with the Black domestic worker employed by his family. Since she had never expressed such strong feelings about White racism, Mark was genuinely shocked by class discussions. Ask yourselves whether that domestic worker was in a position to speak freely. Would it have been wise for her to do so in a situation where the power between the two parties was so unequal?

In extreme cases, members of privileged groups can erase the very presence of the less privileged. When I first moved to Cincinnati, my family and I went on a picnic at a local park. Picnicking next to us was a family of White Appalachians. When I went to push my daughter on the swings, several of the children came over. They had missing, yellowed and broken teeth, they wore old clothing and their poverty was evident. I was shocked. Growing up in a large eastern city, I had never seen such awful poverty among Whites. The segregated neighborhoods in which I grew up made White poverty all but invisible. More importantly, the privileges attached to my newly acquired social class position allowed me to ignore and minimize the poverty among Whites that I did encounter. My reactions to those children made me realize how confining phrases such as "well, at least they're not Black," had become for me. In learning to grant human subjectivity to the Black victims of poverty, I had simultaneously learned to demand White victims of poverty. By applying categories of race to the objective conditions confronting me, I was quantifying and ranking oppressions and missing the very real suffering which, in fact, is the real issue.

One common pattern of relationships across differences in power is one that I label "voyeurism." From the perspective of the privileged, the lives of people of color, of the poor, and of women are interesting for their entertainment value. The privileged become voyeurs, passive onlookers who do not relate to the less powerful, but who are interested in seeing how the "different" live. Over the years, I have heard numerous African-American students complain about professors who never call on them except when a so-called Black issue is being discussed. The students' interest in discussing race or qualifications for doing so appear unimportant to the professor's efforts to use Black students' experiences as stories to make the material come alive for the White student audience. Asking Black students to perform on cue and provide a Black experience for their White classmates can be seen as voyeurism at its worst.

Members of subordinate groups do not willingly participate in such exchanges but often do so because members of dominant groups control the institutional and symbolic apparatuses of oppression. Racial/ethnic groups, women, and the poor have never had the luxury of being voyeurs of the lives of the privileged. Our ability to survive in hostile settings has hinged on our ability to learn intricate details about the behavior and world view of the powerful and adjust our behavior accordingly. I need only point to the difference in perception of those men and women in abusive relationships. Where men can view their girlfriends and wives as sex objects, helpmates and a collection of stereotypes categories of voyeurism—women must be attuned to every nuance of their partners' behavior. Are women "naturally" better in relating to people with more power than themselves, or have circumstances mandated that men and women develop different skills? . . .

Coming from a tradition where most relationships across difference are squarely rooted in relations of domination and subordination, we have much less experience relating to people as different but equal. The classroom is potentially one powerful and safe space where dialogues among individuals of unequal power relationships can occur. The relationship between Mark, the student in my class, and the domestic worker is typical of a whole series of relationships that people have when they relate across differences in power and privilege. The relationship among Mark and his classmates represents the power of the classroom to minimize those differences so that people of different levels of power can use race, class and gender as categories of analysis in order to generate meaningful dialogues.

In this case, the classroom equalized racial difference so that Black students who normally felt silenced spoke out. White students like Mark, generally unaware of how they had been privileged by their whiteness, lost that privilege in the classroom and thus became open to genuine dialogue. . . .

2. Coalitions around Common Causes

A second issue in building relationships and coalitions essential for social change concerns knowing the real reasons for coalition. Just what brings people together? One powerful catalyst fostering group solidarity is the presence of a common enemy. African-American, Hispanic, Asian-American, and women's studies all share the common intellectual heritage of challenging what passes for certified knowledge in the academy. But politically expedient relationships and coalitions like these are fragile because, as June Jordan points out:

> It occurs to me that much organizational grief could be avoided if people understood that partnership in misery does not necessarily provide for partnership for change: When we get the monsters off our backs all of us may want to run in very different directions. (1985, 47)

Sharing a common cause assists individuals and groups in maintaining relationships that transcend their differences. Building effective coalitions involves struggling to hear one another and developing empathy for each other's points of view. The coalitions that I have been involved in that lasted and that worked have been those where commitment to a specific issue mandated collaboration as the best strategy for addressing the issue at hand.

Several years ago, master's degree in hand, I chose to teach in an inner city, parochial school in danger of closing. The money was awful, the conditions were poor, but the need was great. In my job, I had to work with a range of individuals who, on the surface, had very little in common. We had White nuns, Black middle class graduate students, Blacks from the "community," some of whom had been incarcerated and/or were affiliated with a range of federal anti-poverty programs. Parents formed another part of this community, Harvard faculty another, and a few well-meaning White liberals from Colorado were sprinkled in for good measure.

As you might imagine, tension was high. Initially, our differences seemed insurmountable. But as time passed, we found a common bond that we each brought to the school. In spite of profound differences in our personal biographies, differences that in other settings would have hampered our ability to relate to one another, we found that we were all deeply committed to the education of Black children. By learning to value each other's commitment and by recognizing that we each had different skills that were essential to actualizing that commitment, we built an effective coalition around a common cause. Our school was successful, and the children we taught benefited from the diversity we offered them.

. . . None of us alone has a comprehensive vision of how race, class and gender operate as categories of analysis or how they might be used as categories of connection. Our personal biographies offer us partial views. Few of us can manage to study race, class and gender simultaneously. Instead, we each know more about some dimensions of this larger story and less about others . . . Just as the members of the school had special skills to offer to the task of building the school, we have areas of specialization and expertise, whether scholarly, theoretical, pedagogical or within areas of race, class or gender. We do not all have to do the same thing in the same way. Instead, we must support each other's efforts, realizing that they are all part of the larger enterprise of bringing about social change.

3. *Building Empathy*

A third issue involved in building the types of relationships and coalitions essential for social change concerns the issue of individual accountability. Race, class and gender oppression form the structural backdrop against which we frame our relationship— these are the forces that encourage us to substitute voyeurism . . . for fully human relationships. But while we may not have created this situation, we are each responsible for making individual, personal choices concerning which elements of race, class and gender oppression we will accept and which we will work to change.

One essential component of this accountability involves developing empathy for the experiences of individuals and groups different than ourselves. Empathy begins with taking an interest in the facts of other people's lives, both as individuals and as groups. If you care about me, you should want to know not only the details of my personal biography but a sense of how race, class and gender as categories of analysis created the institutional and symbolic backdrop for my personal biography. How can you hope to assess my character without knowing the details of the circumstances I face?

Moreover, by taking a theoretical stance that we have all been affected by race, class and gender as categories of analysis that have structured our treatment, we open up possibilities for using those same constructs as categories of connection in building empathy. For example, I have a good White woman friend with whom I share common interests and beliefs. But we know that our racial differences have provided us with different experiences. So we talk about them. We do not assume that because I am Black, race has only affected me and not her or that because I am a Black woman, race neutralizes the effect of gender in my life while accenting it in hers. We take those same categories of analysis that have created cleavages in our lives, in this case, categories of race and gender, and use them as categories of connection in building empathy for each other's experiences.

Finding common causes and building empathy is difficult, no matter which side of privilege we inhabit. Building empathy from the dominant side of privilege is difficult, simply because individuals from privileged backgrounds are not encouraged to do so. For example, in order fort those of you who are White to develop empathy for the experiences of people of color, you must grapple with how your white skin has privileged you. This is difficult to do, because it not only entails the intellectual process of seeing how whiteness is elevated in institutions and symbols, but it also involves the often painful process of seeing how your whiteness has shaped your personal biography. Intellectual stances against the institutional and symbolic dimensions of racism are generally easier to maintain than sustained self-reflection about how racism has shaped all of our individual biographies. Were and are your fathers, uncles, and grandfathers really more capable than mine, or can their accomplishments be explained in part by the racism members of my family experienced? Did your mothers stand silently by and watch all this happen? More importantly, how have they passed on the benefits of their whiteness to you?

These are difficult questions, and I have tremendous respect for my colleagues and students who are trying to answer them. Since there is no compelling reason to examine the source and meaning of one's own privilege, I know that those who do so have freely chosen this stance. They are making conscious efforts to root out the piece of the oppressor planted within them. To me, they are entitled to the support of people of color in their efforts. Men who declare themselves feminists, members of the middle class who ally themselves with anti-poverty struggles, heterosexuals who support gays and lesbians, are all trying to grow, and their efforts place them far ahead of the majority who never think of engaging in such important struggles.

Building empathy from the subordinate side of privilege is also difficult, but for different reasons. Members of subordinate groups are understandably reluctant to abandon a basic mistrust of members of powerful groups because this basic mistrust has traditionally been central to their survival. As a Black woman, it would be foolish for me to assume that White women, or Black men, or White men or any other group with a history of exploiting African-American women have my best interests at heart. These groups enjoy varying amounts of privilege over me and therefore I must carefully watch them and be prepared for a relation of domination and subordination.

Like the privileged, members of subordinate groups must also work toward replacing judgments by category with new ways of thinking and acting. Refusing to do so stifles prospects for effective coalition and social change. Let me use another example from my own experiences. When I was an undergraduate, I had little time or patience for the theorizing of the privileged. My initial years at a private, elite institution were difficult, not because the coursework was challenging (it was, but that wasn't what distracted me), or because I had to work while

my classmates lived on family allowances (I was used to work). The adjustment was difficult because I was surrounded by so many people who took their privilege for granted. Most of them felt entitled to their wealth. That astounded me.

I remember one incident of watching a White woman down the hall in my dormitory try to pick out which sweater to wear. The sweaters were piled up on her bed in all the colors of the rainbow, sweater after sweater. She asked my advice in a way that let me know that choosing a sweater was one of the most important decisions she had to make on a daily basis. Standing knee-deep in her sweaters, I realized how different our lives were. She did not have to worry about maintaining a solid academic average so that she could receive financial aid. Because she was in the majority, she was not treated as a representative of her race. She did not have to consider how her classroom comments or basic existence on campus contributed to the treatment her group would receive. Her allowance protected her from having to work, so she was free to spend her time studying, partying, or in her case, worrying about which sweater to wear. The degree of inequality in our lives and her unquestioned sense of entitlement concerning that inequality offended me. For a while, I categorized all affluent White women as being superficial, arrogant, overly concerned with material possessions, and part of my problem. But had I continued to classify people in this way, I would have missed out on making some very good friends whose discomfort with their inherited or acquired social class privileges pushed them to examine their position.

Since I opened with the words of Audre Lorde, it seems appropriate to close with another of her ideas. . . .

> Each of us is called upon to take a stand. So in these days ahead, as we examine ourselves and each other, our works, our fears, our differences, our sisterhood and survivals, I urge you to tackle what is most difficult for us all, self-scrutiny of our complacencies, the idea that since each of us believes she is on the side of right, she need not examine her position. (1985)

I urge you to examine your position.

References

Collins, Patricia Hill. 1989. "The Social Construction of Black Feminist Thought." *Signs.* Summer 1989.

Gwaltney, John Langston. 1980. *Drylongso: A Self-Portrait of Black America.* New York: Vintage.

Harding, Sandra. 1986. *The Science* Question *in Feminism.* Ithaca, New York: Cornell University Press.

Lorde, Audre. 1984. *Sister Outsider.* Trumansberg, New York: The Crossing Press.

——. 1985. "Sisterhood and Survival." Keynote address, conference on the Black Woman Writer and the Diaspora, Michigan State University.

Jordan, June. 1985. *On Call: Political Essays.* Boston: South End Press.

Spelman, Elizabeth. 1982. "Theories of Race and Gender: The Erasure of Black Women." *Quest* 5: 26–32.

Tate, Claudia, ed. 1983. *Black Women Writers at Work.* New York: Continuum.

34

"Intersectionality"

IRENE BROWNE AND JOYA MISRA

"At this particular juncture in gender studies, any scholar who neglects difference [by race and class] runs the risk of having her work viewed as theoretically misguided, politically irrelevant, or simply fantastical" (Davis 2008, p. 68).

1. What Is "Intersectionality?"

Intersecting oppressions by gender, race and class has become an important, if not crucial, concept among scholars studying inequality. In this essay, we present an overview of key debates and challenges in sociological research on intersectionality. We draw upon studies that focus on the workplace to illustrate our claims and provide examples of the range of approaches to research on intersectionality.

Intersectional perspectives grew out of research on gender. Gender scholars view studies of inequality that omit important dimensions of "difference" *among* women as suspect, arguing that gender, race and class are intimately connected as "intersecting oppressions" (Crenshaw 1989). From an intersectional perspective, studies of gender that omit differences by race and studies of race that omit considerations of gender stand as incomplete and therefore limit our understanding of inequality. In addition, their omissions can actually reproduce oppressive practices by omitting the experiences and perspectives of members of multiple disadvantaged groups, particularly women of color (hooks 1984).

Davis defines intersectionality as: "The interaction between gender, race and other categories of difference in individual lives, social practices, institutional arrangements and cultural ideologies and the outcomes of these interactions in terms of power" (Davis 2008: 67).

In Davis' definition, intersectionality operates at all levels of social life—from individual experience to entire social systems. This leaves open some important questions that scholars continue to hotly debate: *Which* "categories of difference" should social scientists highlight? Do social categories *always* intersect, or are there conditions under which one category becomes most salient in determining experiences of social inequality? *What are the mechanisms* through which gender, race, class and other categories of difference operate together to create inequality? How can we study these mechanisms? Below, we discuss some answers to these questions. As context, we first provide a background to the development of the concept of intersectionality.

Background

Black feminist scholars and multiracial feminist scholars have been at the forefront in developing a rich and sophisticated analysis of intersecting oppression. Accompanying the feminist movement and establishment of women's studies programs, gender scholarship exploded in the 1970s, and 1980s. In articles and books such as, *All the Women are White; All the Blacks are Men; But Some of Us are Brave* (Hull, Bell-Scott and Smith 1982), Black feminists critiqued feminist scholarship for basing analyses on White, middle class women, and they leveled critiques of race-based scholarship for focusing on Black men. Black feminist scholars argued that Black women's experience is simultaneously shaped by sexism, racism and class hierarchies. The experience of Black women cannot be understood by "adding" an analysis of gender inequality to an analysis of racism (hooks 1984). Instead, gender and race oppression need to be analyzed in combination, with an eye to how they mutually reinforce each other along with social class and other dimensions of difference (Deborah King 1988).

Multiracial feminists claim that the beliefs and practices associated with gender are inextricably interwoven with the beliefs and practices associated with race. Traditional definitions of femininity that include passivity and weakness describe the social norm for a White middle-class woman. Dominant culture has traditionally constructed Black femininity in juxtaposition to this image. According to Collins (2000), stereotypes of Black women have included the asexualized Mammy, the promiscuous Jezebel, and the profligate welfare queen. These images reinforce racial divisions by denigrating Black women in comparison with White women. At the same time, these images reinforce gender inequality among Whites by positing White women as weak and in need of White male protection. Thus, the experience of gender deeply reflects racial and ethnic meanings.

Intersectional perspectives emphasize that intersections of gender, race and class do not simply affect women of color; gender, race and class are relational systems of power and inequality that affect all people (Ken 2007). For instance, in Wingfield's study of Black men nurses, one respondent explained:

> Nursing, historically, has been a white female's job [so] being a Black male it's a weird position to be in. . . . I've, several times, gone into a room and a male patient, a white male patient has, you know, they'll say, "Where's the pretty nurse? Where's the pretty nurse? Where's the blonde nurse?". . . "You don't have one. I'm the nurse."

By referring to the "pretty blonde nurse," the patient re-creates racialized gender inequality for women as well as men—nurses are "pretty" (judged by a feminized physical appearance) and "blonde" (White). This demeans the skills necessary to nursing and excludes men as well as women of color from being seen as "pretty" or as nurses.

This example illustrates two other key points in intersectionality scholarship: individuals can experience *both* privilege and disadvantage, depending upon the combination of their gender, race and class. Therefore, a middle-class straight black woman may have a different set of privileges and disadvantages than a poor gay white man—yet both experience privilege and disadvantage. In addition, the configuration of privilege and disadvantage is specific to a particular time, place and situation (King 1988). So, for example, a middle-class straight black woman may experience privilege and disadvantage differently in 1950 versus 2010, or differently in New Orleans versus Detroit.

2. Debates

How Many Categories?

Intersectional scholars recognize dimensions of inequality beyond gender, race and class. Many scholars insist that sexuality should be included as a fourth dimension (Weber 2001). They argue that social institutions are organized around norms of heterosexuality, privileging particular forms of heterosexual identities and relations and ostracizing others (Battle and Ashley 2008). Jennifer Pierce discusses how the institutionally-enforced norms of heterosexuality, gender, class and race that she found in her study of law firms were also evident in her own Sociology Department. When she was an Assistant Professor, 80% of the Full Professors were White men, and there were no faculty of color in the Department.

> I realized that it wasn't just me and my intellectual style that irked people, but rather a combination of things—the dynamics of gender in the department, its top-heavy demographics, and my rank as assistant professor. Within this gendered context, I was not deferential to senior male scholars, as some expected I should be, but treated them as equals in intellectual debate. Nor was I the nurturing female type who bolstered their egos by flattering them and telling them how clever they were. I did not prepare elaborate dinners for them at my home or fuss over them as one of my female colleagues did. . . . But, most importantly of all, I was a young woman *and* a queer feminist who brought these facts to their attention . . . (Pierce 2003: 380, 381).

Pierce experienced hostility towards her sexuality and her work that was expressed in an explicitly racial way when she received a note in her mailbox. One side of the paper contained quotes from her book, *Gender Trials,* highlighting the terms she uses in the book, "Rambo litigator" and "feminized emotional labor." On the other side there was a Xeroxed passage about "Negroes taking care of their pickaninnies." The implication was that Pierce belonged to a supposedly disadvantaged group (female; queer) who "took care of their own."

Part of the antipathy that Pierce encountered arose from her colleagues' disrespect towards the qualitative, ethnographic method that Pierce employed and their privileging of quantitative work. Thus, in this particular institution, methodological approach combined with gender, race, sexuality and class to create an additional dimension of inequality with serious consequences for her career.

Some intersectional scholars advocate for always incorporating a wider array of dimensions of inequality beyond sexuality, such as ability/disability, citizenship status, religion and age (Davis 2008). The "how many categories?" question presents a dilemma for scholars: when designing a study taking an intersectional approach, a study that includes more than 3 or 4 dimensions of inequality can soon become unwieldy (McCall 2005).

In Miliann Kang's (2003) study of nail salons in New York, she studied one salon in a predominantly white and upper middle class neighborhood, another in a predominantly Black and lower class neighborhood, and a third in a mixed race middle class neighborhood. In addition to more than a year of participant observation in these salons, she conducted interviews with 10 Korean salon owners, 10 Korean salon workers, 15 Black customers, and 15 white customers. Through this research design, Kang is able to make insightful analyses of how nail salon workers' physical labor and emotional labor intersect with gender, race, and class to create:

> three distinct patterns of body labor provision: (1) high-service body labor involving physical pampering and emotional attentiveness serving mostly middle-and upperclass white female customers, (2) expressive body labor involving artistry in technical skills and communication of respect and fairness when serving mostly working-and lower-middle-class African American and Caribbean female customers, and (3) routinized body labor involving efficient, competent physical labor and courteous but minimal emotional labor when serving mostly lower-middle and middle-class racially mixed female customers. (Kang 2003: 827)

Her study design allows her to say less about how sexualities and age also shape body labor provision in these salons. In order to speak with authority regarding these "intersections," she would have had to make sure that she interviewed a certain number of customers of varying ages and sexualities. In addition, analyzing all of these intersections would have made the project even more complex.

Yet, focusing on race, class and gender "elevates" these categories of difference over others (Ken 2007). Including multiple dimensions of identities beyond gender, race and class becomes feasible—and necessary—for in-depth studies of specific groups. For instance, in her study of Mayan women who immigrated from Guatemala to Los Angeles, Menjívar (2006) demonstrates that being undocumented and speaking an indigenous language represent two important dimensions of inequality that combine with gender, race and class to severely restrict the women's family and work lives.

Omnipresent or Contingent Intersections?

Another challenge in intersectional research has to do with understanding *how* these dimensions of oppression "intersect." In her book, *Understanding Race, Class, Gender and Sexuality: A Conceptual Framework,* Weber (2001) stresses that race and gender intersect as "social systems" that "operate at all times and in all places." Given their inextricable and mutually constituting character, argues Weber, no one social category will ever eclipse the other (2001: 4).

> Race, class, gender, and sexuality are interrelated systems at the macroinstitutional level—they are created, maintained, and transformed simultaneously and in relation to one another. Therefore, they cannot be understood independently of one another. (Weber 2001: 104)

Weber's approach to intersectionality presumes that race, class, gender and sexuality are so interrelated that a researcher could not "tease out" one dimension, such as gender, from the other dimensions. From this perspective, intersectionality exists at all times and in all places (even if it changes forms). Some scholars disagree with this view of intersectionality, and argue that under some conditions, one category may supercede [*sic*] the other in determining experiences and outcomes (Browne and Misra 2003). For example, Kang (2003: 83) finds that in the nail salon located in a middle class neighborhood, "middle-class Black customers . . . mostly exhibited similar nail aesthetics to those of middle-class white women, suggesting the greater importance of class over race in influencing nail styles and expectations of body labor. . . ."

Some scholars see the question of the ubiquity and salience of gender and race disadvantage in the labor market as hypotheses to be tested (McCall 2001). For example, scholars may develop theoretical propositions that specify the conditions under which race or gender or class

may be salient in the labor market, and the conditions "under which they will inevitably interact" (Glass 1999: 420). This contingent perspective is more cautious in its assertions of intersectionality. For instance, Kilbourne et al. (1994) conceptualize gender and race as representing distinct stratification systems that might or might not be interrelated. They ask "Is the gender stratification system experienced differently depending on race and is the race stratification system experienced differently depending on gender?"

Aspects of the gender stratification system include the gender segregation of occupations and the devaluation of female-dominated jobs (Kilbourne et al. 1994; Reskin and Padavic 2002). Nursing, teaching and clerical work are "female dominated" jobs that pay lower wages than male-dominated jobs requiring similar skills (Kilbourne et al. 1994). The race stratification system also includes occupational segregation by race and ethnicity as well as residential segregation and unequal access to educational and training opportunities (Massey and Denton 1993; Bayard et al. 2003). As a result, both white women and women of color are more likely than men to become nurses due to gender stratification; but the race stratification system means that white women are more likely to become registered nurses, while women of color are more likely to become less well-paid and less autonomous licensed practical nurses. In this conceptualization, the gender and race systems of stratification are seen as distinct (although not necessarily unrelated), but the outcomes of these systems create unique experiences depending on the combination of gender and race.

Focusing on the finding that part of the wage inequality by gender and race arises from the segregation of individuals into different types of jobs (for example, women into positions as receptionists), Fernandez and Friedrich (2008) present evidence that illustrates the "contingent" perspective. The authors analyze gender and race differences in one step in the job segregation process. Men and women applying for a job in a single organization (a call center) listed the job that they most preferred among a list of openings. Primarily women "most preferred" stereotypically female jobs, such as receptionist, while men "most preferred" stereotypically male jobs, such as computer programmer. Yet, the patterns of job preference did not differ by race (they compared Whites, Blacks, Asians and Latinos). As the authors emphasize, "gender appears to be the master status guiding applicant's self expressions of interest and ability in these jobs" (11). Yet, although there were no differences in job preference by race/ethnicity, racial segregation did appear in the actual jobs held. This suggests that during the interviewing and hiring stage, individuals are steered to particular positions based on their race and ethnicity (and gender). These findings provide important leverage for an understanding of the mechanisms behind "intersecting systems of oppressions."

3. Studying Inequality from an Intersectional Perspective

Approaches to studying intersectionality are bound-up with assumptions about *how* intersectionality produces inequality. Sharp differences in research questions and research design reflect the disparate conceptualizations of the mechanisms through which gender, race, class and other categories of difference operate together. Leslie McCall (2005) identifies three distinct approaches to conducting research on intersections of gender, race and class: the anti-categorical approach; the single-group (intracategorical) approach; and the group comparison (intercategory) approach.

Anti-Categorical Approach

Advocates of the anti-categorical approach contend that inequality is generated through the creation of social categories such as race, class and gender. This perspective assumes that language creates social reality, so that identifying individuals as belonging to particular race, gender and class categories helps creates the "difference" that generates inequality. The categories are mutually constitutive and inherently intersectional: race is gendered and "classed," gender is "raced" and "classed."

From the anti-categorical perspective, categories are ongoing social constructions, not fixed positions. The categories are assumed to have fixed boundaries but are actually fluid and unstable. Gender is performed and constructed in ways that are circumscribed by race and class identities, and the performances change depending on the context.[1] Similarly, race is constructed situationally through interaction. For instance, when Belisa González

(2006) interviewed Latina and Black women engaged in cross-race organizing in Atlanta, the Latina respondents reported feeling that they did not fit into the U.S. categories of "race" at all. They responded to this "lack of fit" by adopting whichever category best fit the situation. As an illustration, a Puerto Rican teacher explained that she "passed" as "Black" in the workplace, asserted a "Latina" identity with the women in her activist group and identified as "Puerto Rican" with her family and close friends. In all of these contexts, the respondent's race/ethnic identity was intertwined with her gender identity and her middle class status. That is, when adopting a race identity at work, she was perceived as a "Black female professional (teacher)."

The anti-categorical perspective implies that scholarship that uses the categories separately for analyses (e.g., looking at the wage gap between men and women for different race groups, described below) reproduces the inequality by reifying the categories. The goal of scholarship and activism should be to challenge and "deconstruct" the categories. Some critique this approach for not offering practical tools for addressing inequality. That is, the critique of the "current system" of oppression is strong, but the practical steps to create a more just society are absent (Seidman 1993).

Single Group (Intra-Categorical) Approach

Scholars who use an intersectional perspective to study a single group also argue that categories are ongoing social constructions. Yet they use categories provisionally for one group to understand the intersections of gender, race, class, sexuality and other dimensions of identity for this group.

As noted above, Adia Wingfield studied a single group—Black male nurses to explore how race and gender operate. Nursing is a "female" profession in two important senses: the majority (over 85%) of nurses are women, and the nurturing and care tasks performed by nurses are "culturally feminized" as "women's work" (Wingfield 2009). Past research shows that men benefit from working in a female-dominated profession such as nursing; men are often assumed to possess traits that lead them into higher-status positions. Williams (1995) refers to this as the "glass escalator." In fact, men who enjoy their position in a female-dominated occupation often feel "pressure" from co-workers and administrators to advance into a supervisor position.

Yet Wingfield demonstrates that the "glass escalator" is a gendered *and* racialized phenomenon. While patients often mistake White male nurses for doctors, they are likely to assume that Black male nurses are orderlies. In addition, Black male nurses encounter gendered racial stereotypes that "emphasize the dangerous, threatening attributes associated with Black men and Black masculinity, framing Black men as threats to white women, prone to criminal behavior, and especially violent" (2009: 9–10). These stereotypes, held by White nurses, supervisors and physicians, prevent Black male nurses from moving up and gaining a position of authority. Thus, it is only White men who can ride the "glass escalator" in nursing.

Through the study of a single group, scholars can explore multiple social identities and the dynamic processes through which they are mutually constructed.

Group Comparison Approach

The group comparison perspective seeks to understand the structural relations between categories in order to ascertain *patterns* of inequality by gender, race and class that operate beyond a single group. According to McCall (2005), when analysis focuses on the *relationships* of inequality among already-constituted social groups, categorization is inevitable (2005: 1786). One very useful indicator summarizing the pattern of inequality between groups is the "wage gap." As Table 34.1 below

demonstrates, comparing wages by gender and race/ethnicity can produce at least 10 different cells (2 gender groups and 5 race/ethnic groups). This table presents clear evidence of important intersecting inequalities in wages: within race/ethnic groups, women consistently earn less than co-ethnic men. Yet white women earn more than African American men and Latino men, for instance.

Comparing groups to understand patterns of inequality comes with a trade-off: the number of intersections needs to be limited, and diverse individuals become collapsed into a single "category" (McCall 2005). Incorporating other dimensions of identity into the wage comparisons, such as citizenship status or religion, or even just categorizing race/ethnic groups further (e.g., Cuban American, Mexican American, Puerto Rican, etc.) would at least double the number of comparisons.

McCall demonstrates the usefulness of the comparative approach by using quantitative techniques to address the question: How does the "new economy" affect inequality between different groups? To answer this question, McCall looks at key features of the new economy for specific metropolitan areas. For instance, metro areas such as Detroit experienced a loss of manufacturing jobs and rise in service employment. In contrast, Miami saw a large increase in immigrant labor, while Dallas benefited from the development of high-tech industries. McCall (2000) investigates how these different changes in economic environments influenced wage inequality by gender, race and class. She finds that in Dallas, more high tech industries decreased the gap in wages between men

Table 34.1 The Gender Gap in Annual Earnings by Race/Ethnicity, 2007 Full-Time Wage and Salary Workers

	Men	Women	Gap (women's earnings as % of men's earnings)
White	$50,139	$36,398	.73
Black	$34,833	$28,837	.83
Asian	$51,174	$40,664	.79
Latino	$25,239	$25,454	.87

Note: "White" includes non-Hispanic Whites. "Black" includes only non-Hispanic Blacks. Whites, Blacks and Asians include only individuals who reported one race on the survey.

Source: U.S. Census Bureau. 2008. Income, Earnings, and Poverty Data from the 2007 American Community Survey. Table 7. http://www.bls.gov/cps/cpsaat37.pdf

and women (gender wage inequality) but increased the gap in wages between high school graduates and college graduates (class wage inequality). These findings bear important implications for economic policy; without careful forethought and attention to the multiple dimensions of inequality, attempts to reduce one type of inequality (e.g., gender inequality) may exacerbate other types of inequality (e.g., class inequality).

The group comparison approach thus allows researchers to document patterns of inequality, and uncover the conditions under which inequality by gender, race and class may intensify or diminish. This approach, however, may be derided by adherents of the anti-categorical perspective, who argue that group comparisons assumes "stable, fixed" categories and erases difference through placing individuals into those categories. However, as McCall (2005: 1800) stresses, ". . . reality is complexly patterned but patterned nonetheless." Documenting these patterns not only provides a stronger basis for developing policy or projects to combat inequality, but creates an arsenal of data to counter claims from elites and their constituencies that "discrimination" and unfair advantage no longer exist. McCall advocates for a more inclusive embrace of all methodological approaches.

Implications

The anti-categorical and intracategorical approaches to intersectionality correspond to the postmodern/interpretivist perspective in this volume, while the intercategorical approach is more likely to align with the "positivist" or "post-positivist" camps. Comparing across groups does not require quantitative methods, although a researcher needs sufficient number of cases from different categories to make comparisons.

4. Care Chains Ant Domestic Labor: Example of Richness and Indispensability of Intersectionality Research

Research on domestic labor examines intersections as relations between dimensions of inequality within a single occupation. It therefore combines the richness of the single group approach while understanding the structure of inequality from a comparative framework.

Scholarship on domestic work tends to be qualitative in nature, and emphasizes the intersections among gender, race/ethnicity, class, and nativity, language, and citizenship-status in the experiences of domestic workers *and* their employers (Rollins 1985; Glenn 1992; Romero 1992; Hondagneu-Sotelo 2001; Parreñas 2001). This research helps reconceptualize relations of power between employers and their workers, and show how race, gender, class, nationality, and citizenship inequalities are reproduced, maintained, and reinforced dynamically (Romero 1992).

For example, Pei-Chia Lan (2006) in *Global Cinderellas,* focuses primarily on migrant Filipino workers providing domestic labor for Taiwanese families, allowing Taiwanese women to pursue careers and upend traditional norms regarding filial piety. Though women employers are able to *stretch* traditional norms regarding Taiwanese women's behavior, in part through displacing "their" work on migrant women with fewer resources, they still face gendered burdens regarding their roles as mothers, daughters-in-law, and supervisors of domestic workers. Lan (2006: 69) also shows how Filipino and other Southeast Asian domestic workers are racially stereotyped by labor brokers and employers: "Filipino workers are 'smart yet unruly' while Indonesian workers are 'stupid yet obedient.' " At the same time, she shows how labor brokers present a particular defeminized and desexualized image of migrant workers (cutting the workers' hair and forbidding makeup), in order to meet the expectations of women employers. Ethnicity and gender are also experienced together, as in the way Taiwanese employers enact "ethnicized motherhood," to argue that *they* can mother their children more closely than their children's migrant caretakers.

Migrant domestic workers also illustrate the dynamic nature of class relations. Migrating requires a certain level of resources. Many migrant domestic workers are educated and may have worked in professional positions at home, yet can earn higher wages working abroad as migrants (Hondagneu-Sotelo 2001;

Parreñas 2001). Migrant domestic workers may also employ servants to care for their families in their home countries, creating complicated hierarchies of privilege (Parreñas 2001; Lan 2006). As Lan (2006: 145) reports:

> Several Filipina informants said to me, in a proud or embarrassed tone, "You know, I have a maid in the Philippines!" One of them is Christina, a college graduate and a former teacher . . . Despite holding a similar occupation now, Christina drew a clear distinction between herself and her maid: "My sister was laughing, you have a maid in the Philippines, but you are a maid in Taiwan! I said it's different. They are undereducated. Not everyone can work abroad. You have to be serious. You have to be very determined."

Scholarship on domestic work illustrates how both migrant workers and employers use intersecting ideologies of class, gender, race, ethnicity, citizenship, and gender to make sense of their choices and experiences. Migrant domestic workers and employers occupy a variety of positions that vary by context and moment. In part, this research has helped identify how gender, race, ethnicity, class, nationality, and citizenship are all relevant and interconnected in explaining the labor market experiences of domestic work. Class cannot be measured simply, as the class status of workers may vary, for example, depending on where they are. Similarly, measures of race and ethnicity, nationality and citizenship rely on specific contexts. This research reflects the complexity of analytically considering these intersections.

5.   Conclusion

Challenges for Future Research

If there is one key critique to be made of intersectional research, it is that in much of this research, class still remains undertheorized (for an exception, see Acker 2006). Unlike gender and race, class is based upon material factors such as income that can be measured and quantified. One individual can have more income and more education than another individual. However, this does not necessarily mean that the two individuals

occupy different class positions. What are the income and education levels that define where working class ends and middle class begins? Would an individual with a PhD who earns poverty-level income be considered "poor" or a member of the middle class? The "undertheorization" of class in intersectionality perspectives means that scholars have not provided clear criteria for the "cut-off points" to establish class boundaries. In addition, class is more than just income and education; class also encompasses knowledge about the world and tastes ("cultural capital"), social connections ("social capital"), and consumption patterns. Defining class position and class boundaries becomes even more complex when considering these multiple dimensions of class together. Studies of intersectionality that build upon fuzzy conceptualizations of class are difficult to interpret.

Yet, some intersectional works have taken a more thoughtful approach to class. Julie Bettie's (2000) study of the classed performances of white and Mexican-American teenage girls in one high school offers one such approach to reconceptualizing class identity, while attending to ethnicity, gender, and sexuality. Her work draws attention to how class is both dynamic and always experienced in specific racial/ethnic and gender constellations. That is, working class White girls enact and experience "class" differently from working class Mexican-American girls on the one hand and from middle-class White girls on the other hand (Bettie 2000). As Bettie describes:

> A whole array of gender-specific commodities were used as markers of distinction among different groups of girls who performed race/ethnic- and class-specific versions of femininity. Hairstyles, clothes, shoes, and the colors of lip liner, lipstick, and nail polish were key markers used to express group membership as the body became a resource and a site on which difference was inscribed. (Bettie 2000: 15)

Through intersectional research, we are able to understand the true complexity of social life, rather than focusing on only one axis of inequality, with little attention to how these processes are interrelated. This matters in order for us to understand social processes—as well as craft solutions to social problems.

Indeed, Kimberle Crenshaw (1989), considered the scholar to coin the term "intersectionality," used the concept to critique anti-discrimination policy. Crenshaw described a court case in which Black women's charges of discrimination against their employer was not covered by civil rights law. The law specified that they could sue for discrimination by race or discrimination by gender. But the appellants experienced discrimination as *Black women*. Because their complaint did not fit into either category exclusively, it was rejected by the judge.

Overall, intersectional understandings open up the study of inequality in society. By taking an intersectional perspective, authors more accurately map how class, race/ethnicity, gender, sexuality, and other statuses reflect and shape the experiences of all peoples. The complexity and richness of social identities makes taking an intersectional perspective a challenge—but one well worth embracing.

Note

1. The "performative" perspective of gender is consistent with theories of symbolic interaction and ethnomethology in Sociology.

References

Acker, Joan. 2006. *Class Questions: Feminist Answers.* Lanham, MD: Rowman & Littlefield.

Battle, Juan and Colin Ashley. 2008. "Intersectionality, Heteronormativity and Black Lesbian, Gay, Bisexual, and Transgender (LGBT) Families." *Black Women, Gender, and Families.* 2(1): 1–24.

Bettie, Julie. 2000. "Women without Class: Chicas, Cholas, Trash, and the Presence/Absence of Class Identity." *Signs.* 26: 1–35.

Bayard, Kimberly, Judith Hellerstein, David Neumark, and Kenneth Troske. 2003. "New Evidence on Sex Segregation and Sex Differences in Wages from Matched Employee-Employer Data," *Journal of Labor Economics.* 21(4): 887–922.

Browne, Irene and Joya Misra. 2003. "The Intersection of Gender and Race in Labor Markets." *Annual Review of Sociology.* 29: 487–513.

Cecilia Menjívar. 2006. "Global Processes and Local Lives: Guatemalan Women's Work at Home and Abroad." *International Labor and Working Class History.* 70(1): 86–105.

Collins, Patricia Hill. 2000. *Black Feminist Thought: Knowledge, Consciousness, and the Politics of Empowerment.* New York: Routledge.

Crenshaw, Kimberle. 1989. "Demarginalizing the Intersection of Race and Sex: A Black Feminist Critique of Antidiscrimination Doctrine, Feminist Theory and Antiracist Politics." *The University of Chicago Legal Forum,* 139–167.

Davis, Kathy. 2008. "Intersectionality as Buzzword: A Sociology of Science Perspective on What Makes a Feminist Theory Successful." *Feminist Theory.* 9(1): 67–85.

Fernandez, Roberto and Colette Friedrich. 2008. "Job Queues: Gender and Race at the Application Interface." Cambridge, MA: MIT Sloan School of Management.

Glass, J. 1999. "The Tangled Web We Weave." *Work and Occupations.* 26: 415–421.

Glenn, Evelyn Nakano. 1992. "From Servitude to Service Work: Historical Continuities in the Racial Division of Paid Reproductive Labor." *Signs.* 18: 1–43.

Gonzalez, Belisa. 2006. "Increasing Collaboration or Conflict: The Role of Similarities in Cross-Racial Organizing Between African American Women and Latinas in Georgia." Ph.D. Thesis, Emory University, United States—Georgia.

Hondagneu-Sotelo, Pierette. 2001. *Doméstica: Immigrant Workers Cleaning and Caring in the Shadows of Affluence.* Berkeley: University of California Press.

hooks, bell. *Feminist Theory from Margin to Center.* Boston, MA: South End Press, 1984.

Hull, Gloria T., Patricia Bell-Scott, and Barbara Smith. 1982. *All the Women are White, All the Blacks are Men, But Some of Us Are Brave: Black Women Studies.* New York: Feminist Press.

Kang, Miliann. 2003. "The Managed Hand: The Commercialization of Bodies and Emotions in Korean Immigrant-Owned Nail Salons." *Gender and Society.* 17: 820–839.

Ken, Ivy. 2007. "Race-Class-Gender Theory: An Image(ry) Problem." *Gender Issues.* 24(2): 1–20.

Kilbourne, Barbara, Paula England, and Kurt Beron. 1994. "Effects of Individual, Occupational, and Industrial Characteristics on Earnings: Intersections of Race and Gender." *Social Forces.* 72: 1149–1176.

King, Deborah K. 1988. "Multiple Jeopardy, Multiple Consciousness: The Context of a Black Feminist Ideology." *Signs.* 14(1): 42–72.

Lan, Pei-Chia. 2006. *Global Cinderellas: Migrant Domestics and Newly Rich Employers in Taiwan.* Durham, NC: Duke University Press.

Massey, Doug S. and Nancy A. Denton. 1993. *American Apartheid: Segregation and the Making of the Underclass.* Cambridge, MA: Harvard University Press.

McCall, Leslie. 2001. *Complex Inequality: Gender, Class, and Race in the New Economy.* New York: Routledge.

McCall, Leslie. 2005. "The Complexity of Intersectionality." *Signs: Journal of Women in Culture and Society.* 30(3): 1771–1800.

Parreñas, Rhacel Salazar. 2001. *Servants of Globalization: Women, Migration, and Domestic Work.* Stanford: Stanford University Press.

Pierce, Jennifer L. 2003. "Traveling from Feminism to Mainstream Sociology and Back: One Woman's Tale of Tenure and the Politics of Backlash." *Qualitative Sociology.* 26(3): 369–396.

Reskin, Barbara and Irene Padavic. 2002. *Women and Men at Work.* Thousand Oaks, CA; Pine Forge Press.

Rollins, Judith. 1985. *Between Women: Domestics and Their Employers.* Philadelphia: Temple University Press.

Romero, Mary. 1992. *Maid in the USA.* New York: Routledge.

Seidman, Stephen. 1993. "Identity and Politics in a Postmodern Gay Culture," in *Fear of a Queer Planet,* ed. Michael Warner. Minneapolis: University of Minnesota Press.

U.S. Census Bureau. 2008. *Income, Earnings, and Poverty Data from the 2007 American Community Survey.* Table 7. http://www.bls.gov/cps/cpsaat37.pdf

Weber, Lynn. 2001. *Understanding Race, Class, Gender, and Sexuality: A Conceptual Framework.* Boston: McGraw-Hill.

Williams, Christine. 1995. *Still a Man's World.* Berkeley: University of California Press.

Wingfield, Adia Harvey. 2009. "Racializing the Glass Escalator: Reconsidering Men's Experiences with Women's Work." *Gender & Society.* 23(1): 5–26.

Excerpts from
Flat Broke with Children

SHARON HAYS

A Nation's Laws Reflect a Nation's Values. The 1996 federal law reforming welfare offered not just a statement of values to the thousands of local welfare offices across the nation, it also backed this up with something much more tangible. Welfare reform came with money. Lots of it. Every client and caseworker in the welfare office experienced this. New social workers and employment counselors were hired. New signs were posted. New workshops were set up. In Arbordale and Sunbelt City, the two welfare offices I studied to write this book, every caseworker found a new computer on her desk.* In small-town Arbordale, the whole office got a facelift: new carpets, new paint, a new conference room, new office chairs, and plush new office dividers. The reception area, completely remodeled with plants and posters and a children's play area, came to resemble the waiting room of an elite pediatrician's office more than the entrance to a state bureaucracy. Sunbelt City acquired new carpets, a new paint job, and new furniture as well. And all the public areas in that welfare office were newly decorated with images of nature's magnificence—glistening raindrops, majestic mountains, crashing waves, setting sun—captioned with inspirational phrases like "perseverance," "seizing opportunities," "determination," and "success."

As I walked the halls of the Sunbelt City welfare office back in 1998, situated in one of the poorest and most dangerous neighborhoods of a western boom town, those scenes of nature's magnificence struck me as clearly out of place. But the inspirational messages they carried nonetheless seemed an apt symbolic representation of the new legislative strategy to train poor families in "mainstream" American values. Welfare reform, Congress had decreed, would "end the dependence of needy parents on government benefits by promoting job preparation, work, and marriage."[1] Welfare mothers, those Sunbelt signs implied, simply needed a *push—to* get them out to work, to keep them from having children they couldn't afford to raise, to get them married and safely embedded in family life. Seizing opportunities.

---

*Arbordale and Sunbelt City are pseudonyms for the two towns where I studied the effects of welfare reform. I gave them these ficticious names to protect all the clients and caseworkers who shared with me their experiences of reform.

States were awash in federal funds. And the economy was booming in those early years of reform. Everyone was feeling it. There was change in the air. A sense of possibilities—with just a tinge of foreboding.

The Personal Responsibility and Work Opportunity Reconciliation Act of 1996, the law that ended 61 years of poor families' entitlement to federal welfare benefits—the law that asserted and enforced a newly reformulated vision of the appropriate values of work and family life—provided all that additional funding as a way of demonstrating the depth of the nation's commitment to change in the welfare system. It provided state welfare programs with federal grants in amounts matching the peak years of national welfare caseloads (1992 to 1995)—even though those caseloads had everywhere since declined. This meant an average budget increase of 10 percent, before counting the tremendous amount of additional federal funding coming in for new childcare and welfare-to-work programs. Even though there was lots more money, most states did not pass it on to poor mothers in the form of larger welfare checks. In fact, only two states raised their benefit amounts, while two others lowered theirs at the inception of reform. . . .[2]

The Domino Effect

It's a Downward Spiral. And Once You Hit Bottom, You Hit Hard

The spiral for Sheila began just after she finished high school. Sheila is white and was 29 years old at the time I met her in the old and notoriously dangerous housing project where she lived, not far from the Sunbelt City welfare office. From a working-class background, she was raised in a small town "with small town values." She was engaged to be married to her high school sweetheart. The summer after they graduated he was killed in an auto accident.

I wish that then and there I had just said, "Okay, forward," instead of sitting and mourning and moping and weeping and thinking about what could have and should have and would have been. I should

have just gone on ahead to college like I had intended. And I didn't do it. But you know what they say, hindsight is 20-20.

She moved to Sunbelt City with her parents and took a part-time job. Less than a year later her father left her mother.

It was in February. He left a note on the kitchen table. It said, "I'm leaving you for good." And he left the keys to the car that was not paid for. He left one month owing in rent. My mom at the time was not working, and I was still mourning my boyfriend.

Shortly after that me and my mom found jobs at a dry cleaners. We opened it in the morning, and we worked for 15 hours a day. We'd come home, go to sleep, get up, and go right back there. Six days a week. And we were doing good. We had paid up the back rent, and the car was being paid for.

And then my mother got blood clots. She almost lost her leg. And the doctor said she shouldn't work any more. This meant we lost $1,500 a month in income and we were trying to make it on my little $1,200. With the medical bills and the car payments, I got a month behind on rent, and they evicted us.

We were homeless. In all the hoopla and everything, I lost my job. It just kind of dominoed. We were actually homeless, living with friends and things like that. And I mean we went hungry—we ate the throwaways from McDonald's.

A lot of people don't realize how close they live to being homeless. I mean, you're just one or two paychecks away from the street. And once you hit bottom you're gonna hit and you're gonna hit hard. But you have to remember that once you hit bottom you're as low as you can go. There's only one way to go, and that's up.

Unfortunately for Sheila, the downward spiral had not yet reached its lowest point. It was while she and her mother were homeless that she met the man who was to become the father of her daughter. He was, at that moment, her savior, but only a temporary one:

> I met Sam, and I thought he was a very nice gentleman. Sam was living with a friend, and they took the two of us in. I found another job. We were hopeful; even though my mom still couldn't work, we were beginning to get back on our feet.
>
> Sam had told me he was divorced. I was still young; I was 21 at the time. And, like I said, I come from a small community. Well, after we'd been together for almost a year, I got a phone call one morning—and it was his wife! So I used the money I had to put him on a bus back to his wife in Florida. And that's the last I heard of him.
>
> A month later I found out I was pregnant. Sam still doesn't know he's got a daughter. The child support people haven't found him yet.

Putting Sam on that bus meant that pregnant Sheila and her disabled mom were homeless again. And then Sheila was raped:

> For a while I wasn't sure if Sam was the father. There was the small issue of the fact that three weeks almost to the day after he left I was raped. That's a part of living on the street; that's a danger for women who live on the street.
>
> And that's how I came to find out I was pregnant—I went to the clinic to check a few weeks after the rape. So there were two possible identities to the father. I had a hard time knowing what to do. But as soon as she was born I saw what she looked like and I knew who she was; I knew who she belonged to. She looks too much like her dad.

Sheila was just 22 years old when she gave birth to her daughter. If things had gone as she had originally planned, she would have been starting her last year of college at that time.

Sheila first went to the welfare office in the last months of her pregnancy, hoping to get medical coverage for the birth.

> I was a high-risk pregnancy all the way through my pregnancy. I went down to the welfare office and applied for medical assistance. My mother and I were still homeless. I worked a part-time job until things [with the pregnancy] got too bad. My mother had gotten a job [against her doctor's advice] and we managed, with my first welfare check, to finally get our very own small studio apartment. Just two weeks later my daughter was born.

Sheila's daughter (who was busy with her homework during most of my visit) was seven years old when I met her.

From the time she gave birth to the time of our interview, Sheila had a string of jobs. She went back to work when her daughter was just three months old. That job she described as a "really good one," where she worked her way up to a management position in a fast-food restaurant. The rest of the jobs were temporary or low-paying jobs, mainly entry-level fast foods and unskilled clerical work. She left every one. She quit the good one after more than two years, and she's still sorry about it, even though she remembers well all the time she spent agonizing over that decision. She left because the hours and the bus rides were so long that she was spending over 12 hours a day away from home, and she never had a chance to see her daughter. "My daughter was nearly three years old and she was calling my mother 'mom' and calling me 'Sheila.' It was just too hard. I just wanted to get to know her, to do her ABCs and her 1-2-3s. I wanted to be there."

She went back on welfare and spent almost a year getting to know her daughter before again seeking work. She spoke nostalgically of that time with her three-year-old, but she also emphasized that leaving that job was her "third big mistake," alongside mourning rather than continuing on to college, and getting involved with a married man.

Sheila left subsequent jobs because she hurt her back, loading boxes ("the doctors say I'm not allowed to lift over 15 pounds now"), because the pay was too poor, because the jobs were only temporary (through a "temp" agency), and most recently, because her mother was diagnosed as terminally ill and needed to be cared for. Her mother suffered respiratory failure first, then a massive heart attack and, by the time I met her, Sheila was afraid to leave her alone most of the time. "That's my greatest fear, that I'll go to work, and I'll be at work, and something will happen to my mom. I don't know what to do."

Sheila's combined time on welfare, including the time when her child was born, between jobs, and since her mother's illness, added up to about three and a half years, including the last year and a half since welfare reform. She'd been using the resources offered by the welfare office to train herself on computers and in accounting skills. She told me about the contacts she'd made with state agencies that might hire her, and she was feeling somewhat optimistic, though still quite worried about her mom. Her primary goal was to find an employer flexible enough to allow her to care for both her daughter and her mother.

The sheer number of tragedies in Sheila's young life—her fiancé's death, her father leaving, her homelessness, her affair with a married man, her rape, her high-risk pregnancy, and now her mother's terminal illness—testify to the unique circumstances that led her to go on welfare. But every mother I talked to had a story of hardship to tell. And every mother I met had experienced some version of the domino effect: one problem leading to another and compounding it, until too many dominoes fall and the situation becomes impossible to manage. In this, Sheila's story represents the most prominent pattern in the road to welfare.

A second, partially hidden, pattern that Sheila shares with many welfare mothers who have children out of wedlock involves the issue of birth control. Most observers of Sheila's life would agree that she has had some very tough luck. Yet many would also want to know why she allowed herself to get pregnant. After all, it is clear from this vantage point that the last thing Sheila needed was a child to support. She answered, "I did use birth control, but it must not have worked. I don't know what happened."

The truth is, it could very well be that Sheila simply did not use birth control faithfully enough, or that the methods she and her partner used were not sufficiently foolproof. The crucial point here, however, is that a substantial number of sexually active young men and women do not use birth control faithfully enough. This fact does not appear to vary significantly by one's race or economic status. About 50 percent of female teens are sexually active. About 70 percent of those say they used birth control the last time they had sex. But this percentage is based on self-reporting—in which case Sheila, for instance, would be included as a "yes." And equally important, having used birth control recently is not the same thing as using it consistently. There tends to be a good deal of variation in answers to the questions "used at most recent sex," and "used at first sex," for example, which confirms that "recently" is not the same as "always."[3] Putting all this together, it becomes clear that a large number of sexually active young people do not use foolproof birth control every time they have sex. Sheila, in this sense, is a member of the majority.

The central factor separating poor and working-class youth from the middle and upper classes on this score is that financially privileged young women who find themselves pregnant before they are ready are more likely to get an abortion.[4] I asked Sheila if she had thought about having an abortion.

> Oh no, no. Well, I can't say it didn't cross my mind. But I'm a person who believes if you're gonna play, you're gonna pay. And it's not her fault. I'm the kind of person who thinks that, as soon as they have that heartbeat, which is like ten days after conception, then that's a live human being. I just couldn't do it. I love my daughter.

No matter what we might think of the consequences of this choice in the context of Sheila's life, the vast majority of Americans agree that she has a right to make this decision. And few would argue that her problem, in this instance, is a problem of bad values.

There is a third important pattern that Sheila shares with the majority of welfare mothers—the pushes toward work and the pulls toward home. The stress associated with those pushes and pulls is something welfare mothers have in common with parents of all classes and backgrounds. Sheila's desire to stay at home with her daughter is no different from all the other working moms who long to have more time to spend with their young children. Her longing for a job flexible enough to allow her to care for her child is shared by most working parents today. Her sense of regret over taking off those career-building years in order to be with her daughter mimics all the stay-at-home mothers who worry that they will never be able to recoup their lost time in the labor market.[5] And the fact that Sheila feels committed to staying at home with her terminally ill mother puts her in the same position as the millions of (mainly) women who care for their aging parents—many of whom suffer serious economic hardship because of it.[6] What makes Sheila's case distinct is solely that these realities landed her in the welfare office.

No matter what the edicts of welfare reform might mean to Sheila in the coming years, and no matter what we might think of the paths she chose at the multiple crossroads of her early adulthood, the difficulties she has faced speak to much larger social problems. To the extent that the Personal Responsibility Act is our collective cultural response, it is clear that this law has done little to address the underlying causes of the strains Sheila has experienced and the choices she was forced to make. . . .

Shared Values, Symbolic Boundaries, and the Politics of Exclusion

In responding to welfare reform, the welfare mothers I met often offered a perfect mirror of the complex mix of higher values, genuine concerns, exclusionary judgments, and cultural distortions that informed the Personal Responsibility Act. One mother, Denise, captured nearly all these elements in her response, offering the full range of the more prominent patterns I encountered and mimicking the words of welfare mothers you have heard throughout the book. A black woman with two daughters, at the time I met her Denise was recently employed at Mailboxes-R-Us for $6.50 an hour and was making ends meet with the help of welfare reform's (time-limited) income supplement, transportation vouchers, and childcare subsidy. This is what she had to say when I asked her for her overall assessment of reform:

> When I was younger, years ago, anybody could get on welfare. And I think that's what's good about welfare reform. People have to show some sort of **initiative**. Before, the welfare office didn't pressure you to find a job, but now they do. And I think that's a good system. They've really helped me out a lot.
>
> Plus, I think people are sick of having to pay their tax money. They say, "Look, I am out here working, and I don't make that much money, and I have kids of my own. I'm tired of having to take care of **your** babies." People are getting upset and it's rightly so. I think it's rightly so.
>
> And lots of people abuse the system. You see it every day. A lot of people that you run into and a lot of people that live in your neighborhood—I mean a lot of people do hair and get paid in cash. And I hear about these people who had children just to get a welfare check, just because they didn't want to go out and work. I've seen women that's on welfare, they're looking good and their children look poorly. I see that happening.
>
> Some of them are lazy and don't want to work. I think that some just want to stay home with their kids. But then they should have thought about that before they had the children.

At this point in her argument, Denise had hit upon nearly all the concerns of hardworking Americans who conscientiously pay their taxes, raise their children, and struggle to make it all work. She had also hit upon nearly all the well-worn stereotypes of poor mothers—implicitly labeling them as welfare cheats, lazy couch potatoes, promiscuous breeders, and lousy parents. But Denise wasn't finished.

> I think some people on welfare are being greedy—taking away from people that are homeless, people that really need the help.

I mean there are truly people out there living at the Salvation Army. I hear tell that there are people who can't get in those shelters because they're so full. And I think that's the sad part about it. Those women that don't really need welfare shouldn't be taking money away from the homeless.

But there are gonna be problems. Like, there are women that want to go out there and get a job, but who's gonna watch their kids? And there are people who will still need that little extra help to pay the bills. So that's a glitch in the system. And some of these women are already pregnant, and they're already poor, and they really do need the help. I think that we have to weigh things and maybe investigate a bit more. There are a lot of people that are disabled and need welfare; there are women who have been abused. Some of those people that are in a lot of trouble, you know, their kids are gonna be the ones you see on TV, shooting up the schools and everything.[7]

I know a lot of people say that this welfare reform is a good thing—and it is really gonna help a lot of people. But in the end things are probably gonna get worse. There's gonna be more crime 'cause people can't get on welfare and they're not gonna have any money and they're gonna go out and rob people, and kill people. And it happens, it happens. So that's a problem with the system.

If Denise had been responding to a national survey, "Do you approve of welfare reform?" her answer would simply be coded as a "yes." Yet you can't help noticing that she has a number of mixed feelings on this question.

This same sort of ambivalence is evident in Americans' response to welfare reform. Although most are positive about reform, the majority of Americans also say that they are "very" concerned about poverty. Most additionally believe that the national standards for poverty are set too low, stating that a family of four with an income of less than $20,000 is, in fact, "poor," even if the federal government does not label them as such.

More significantly, a majority of Americans are in favor of further aid to the poor—including the expansion of job opportunities, tax credits, medical coverage, subsidies for childcare and housing, and the provision of better schools. Still, Americans worry about the government's ability to appropriately and effectively provide that aid, and many don't want to have to pay higher taxes to subsidize the poor.[8]

Denise is also much like most Americans in that the central moral categories she uses to frame her response are work and family values, independence and commitment to others, self-sufficiency and concern for the common good. Women should take the "initiative," they should work, they should not rely on the help of others, they should support their own children, they should think twice before they give birth to children they cannot afford to raise. At the same time, people should not be "greedy," they should care for those who are more vulnerable than themselves, and they should consider the impact of their actions on the nation as a whole. All this makes perfect sense, and all this resonates perfectly with our nation's values. The trouble is that managing these commitments is hard enough if you have a spouse, a house in the suburbs, two cars in the garage, good health insurance, reliable childcare, a willingness to make compromises, a great deal of determination, empathy, and energy, and a household income of $60,000. The more items on this list that you lack, the tougher it becomes to live up to this demanding system of values. Denise, like most Americans, implicitly understands these "glitches." Yet her reasoning becomes a bit cloudy at this point—in large measure, I would argue, because of the loophole provided by the final significant element in her response to welfare reform.

It is hard to miss that Denise's support for the Personal Responsibility Act is predicated on the construction of a moral distinction between herself and all those "other" bad welfare mothers who fail to live up to social standards. Denise is making use of what Michèle Lamont has called "symbolic boundaries" to develop an implicit hierarchy of social worth. Like most people who use this strategy, she is not simply engaging in a mean-spirited attack on others or a self-interested attempt to highlight her own virtues. These symbolic boundaries also allow her to positively affirm shared values and specify the proper way to live one's life.[9]

Yet, given that many observers consider Denise herself a member of the deviant group she describes, the fact that she and other welfare mothers persist in this technique is curious. It testifies not just to the power and ubiquity of boundary making as a social strategy, it also speaks to the power and ubiquity of the demonization of poor single mothers. When welfare mothers distinguish themselves from those other "bad" women, they are calling on widely disseminated negative images of welfare mothers. These images seem to match all those strangers, those loud neighbors, those people who appear to spend their lives hanging out on street corners. The lives of the women they actually know, on the other hand, seem much more complex, their actions more understandable, their futures more redeemable.

The demonization of welfare mothers and the dichotomy between "us" and "them" can thus provide a dividing line that allows Denise and other Americans to say, if some welfare mothers can't make it, it's not because the problems they encounter in trying to manage work and family and still keep their heads above water are that bad or that widespread; it's because they didn't try hard enough or weren't good enough. Symbolic boundaries thus become *exclusionary* boundaries— simultaneously offering a means to affirm shared values and a means to think of "outsiders" in terms of individual blame. The obvious problem, in Denise's case, is that her own logic might ultimately leave her as one of the "accused." In broader terms, this exclusionary process means that all those Americans who are suffering from childcare woes, second shifts, inadequate health insurance, precarious jobs, unmanageable debt, and unstable communities are left to feel that their problems are *personal* problems for which no public solutions can be found. . . .

Winners and Losers

The extent to which the facts about the declining welfare rolls are read as a success ultimately depends on one's primary goals. If the goal of reform was solely to trim the rolls, then it has surely succeeded. If the goal was to place more single mothers in jobs

regardless of wages, that goal has been met. If we sought to ensure that more welfare mothers would face a double shift of paid work and childcare, placing them on an "equal" footing with their middle-class counterparts, then some celebrations are in order. If the aim was to ensure that poor men are prosecuted for failure to pay child support, then welfare reform has been relatively effective. If the goal was to make low-income single mothers more likely to seek out the help of men, no matter what the costs, there is some (inconclusive) evidence that this strategy may be working.[10] If the goal was to decrease poverty overall, there is no indication that anything but the cycle of the economy has had an impact. Beyond this, the answers are more complicated.

Thinking about losers, one can start with the families who have left welfare. One-half are sometimes without enough money to buy food. One-third have to cut the size of meals. Almost half find themselves unable to pay their rent or utility bills. Many more families are turning to locally funded services, food banks, churches, and other charities for aid. Many of those charities are already overburdened. In some locales, homeless shelters and housing assistance programs are closing their doors to new customers, food banks are running out of food, and other charities are being forced to tighten their eligibility requirements.[11]

Among the former welfare families who are now living with little or no measurable income, will those charities be enough? At ground level, Nancy, the supervisor in Arbordale's welfare office, told me more than once that she was deeply concerned about these families, particularly the children. Melissa, the supervisor in Sunbelt City, on the other hand, repeatedly responded to my questions regarding the fate of former welfare recipients with the simple statement, "They have other resources." Melissa was referring not only to all those (overloaded) charities, but also to all the boyfriends and family members who could help in paying the bills, and to all those unreported or underreported side jobs (doing hair, cleaning houses, caring for other people's children, selling sex or drugs).[12] Between these two welfare supervisors both of whom have spent many years working with poor mothers, who is right? And what about Denise, who both agreed with Melissa that many welfare mothers didn't really need the help, and predicted that welfare reform would result in frightening hardship, including a rise in crime?

Consider the "other resources" available to the women I have introduced in this reading. In the case of Sheila, the Sunbelt mother who was caring for her seven-year-old daughter and her terminally ill mother, the three of them might be able to survive somehow on her mom's disability check (about $550 per month) with the help of food stamps and local charities. If worse came to worst, she might be able to find some work on the graveyard shift so that she wouldn't have to leave her mom and daughter alone during the day (but she would be faced with leaving them alone at night in that very dangerous housing project). Diane, the Sunbelt mother with a three-year-old son and a long history of severe depression and domestic violence, could go back to operating that illegal flophouse and taking under-the-table housecleaning work (though it is not clear what impact this would have on her son, not to mention Diane). Nadia, the Arbordale mother with four children and no work experience, might rejoin her old friends in petty thievery and prostitution, or she could put further pressure on her employed aunt or the two unemployed fathers of her children, or she might consider turning her children over to relatives or to the foster care system (a worst-case scenario recognized by many of the mothers I talked to). Monique, the second-generation Arbordale recipient who'd had her first child at 17, could probably manage on her current job, though one might be a little concerned that her abusive ex-husband would return, force her to move, and throw the fragile balance of her life into chaos. Of course, there are also women like Sonya, the compulsive house re-arranger (and incest survivor), who have no family, no work experience, no marketable skills, and no idea about how to make use of local charitable institutions. Someone would surely notice such women eventually, if only because their children missed school or appeared too ill-kept or malnourished.

Most welfare mothers *do* have other resources. Yet many of those resources are only temporary, and many are, at best, inadequate. Most will likely add greater instability and uncertainty to the lives of these families. And nearly all these resources have their own price tags—practical, emotional, moral, and social.

As these negative effects begin to overburden ever-larger numbers of women, we can expect to see more crime, drug abuse, prostitution, domestic violence, mental health disorders, and homelessness. More children will end up in foster care, residing with relatives other than their parents, or living on the streets. These children will also be at greater risk for malnutrition, illness, and delinquency. At the same time, more sick and disabled relatives who once relied on the care of welfare mothers will find their way into state-supported facilities or be left to fend for themselves. Caseworkers in Arbordale told me that they were already noticing the rise in foster care cases and in child-only welfare cases (where mothers had relinquished their children to relatives—making those children eligible for welfare benefits until age 18).[†] In Sunbelt City, welfare clients told me they were already witnessing rising rates of hunger, drug abuse, prostitution, and crime among sanctioned or discouraged former welfare mothers they knew.

All this hardship will affect poor men as well as women. Not only are these men faced with a more rigid and unforgiving child support system, but they are also very likely to face pressure from the mothers of their children and from the recognition that their children may go hungry or become homeless.[13] The desperation of some of these men could result in a greater incidence of violence, crime, and drug abuse among a low-wage, chronically underemployed male population that is already suffering from severe hardship.

The long-term consequences of welfare reform will also place a tremendous burden on other working-poor and working-class families.

[†] According to the rules of reform, there are no time limits on welfare benefits to children who live with relatives (or other adults) who are not themselves receiving welfare. This policy thereby offers welfare mothers an *incentive* to give up their children to other family members, since it means continued financial assistance for those children. Among "streetwise" welfare recipients, this is already a well-known rule. And the number of child-only welfare cases has, in fact, been on the rise since reform (U.S. House of Representatives 2000, see also Bernstein 2002).

The upper classes can rest (fairly) assured that most desperately poor mothers won't come knocking on their doors, asking for cash, a meal, a place to stay, or the loan of a car. But many poor mothers will (reluctantly) knock on the doors of the working-poor and working-class people who are their friends and relatives. It is these people who will share their homes, their food, and their incomes and provide practical help with childcare and transportation. These good deeds won't appear on any income tax forms, welfare case reports, or analyses of charitable spending. But this burden on low-income working people will be one of the very real, and largely invisible, costs of welfare reform. And it will surely exacerbate existing income inequalities.

In the end, it is simultaneously true that most welfare mothers have other resources, many will face frightening hardship, and some proportion will turn to desperate measures. If nothing changes and welfare reform isn't itself reformed, by the close of the first decade of the twenty-first century, we will see the beginnings of measurable impacts on prison populations, mental health facilities, domestic violence shelters, children's protective services, and the foster care system.

This brings us to the goal of saving taxpayers' money. Given drastic cuts in food stamps and aid to legal immigrants as well as the declining number of welfare recipients, taxpayers are paying somewhat less in aid to the disadvantaged overall, though relative to the size of the welfare rolls, the 2002 per client costs are higher than they were in 1996.[14] Over the long haul, welfare reform is likely to become increasingly costly. Savings in welfare benefits will eventually be more than offset by the expenses associated with the social problems made worse as a result of reform. The average individual welfare recipient received approximately $1680 in cash and services annually in 1996; that same year, the annual cost of keeping one child in foster care was $6,000, and the cost of keeping one person in prison was $20,100.[15]

From this angle, the real winners in the story of welfare reform are all the restaurant, hotel, retail, and food service chains, and all the corporations, manufacturers, and small business owners across America who employ low-wage workers. These owners (and their stockholders) benefit not just from the availability of millions of poor women desperate to find work and willing to accept the lowest wages and the worst working conditions, they benefit not just from the additional availability of all those now more-desperate poor men, they also benefit because all this desperation creates more profitable labor market conditions overall. Welfare reform helps to convince all low-wage workers that they can be easily displaced by former welfare recipients and therefore makes them less likely to complain, change jobs, join unions, or demand higher wages. The logic of reform also means that low-wage employers can rest assured, for the moment at least, that no one will be calling into question the fact that their policies are less than family friendly and their workers are unable to support their children on the wages they take home.[16]

On a superficial level, the "end of welfare" appears to hold in place the symbolic messages that work is better than welfare and marriage is better than single parenthood. But by no stretch of the imagination could one argue that welfare reform brings with it anything resembling the triumph of "family values." And the practical reality of most low-wage employment no more offers "independence" and self-sufficiency to former welfare recipients than it does to all the middle-class teenagers who spend their summers working in fast-food restaurants and retail chains.

Although the negative results of welfare reform are dramatic, it is nonetheless quite possible that a substantial number of former welfare recipients will simply be "absorbed" into the society without a great deal of fanfare. In the larger scheme of things, after all, 12 million or so desperately poor people in a nation of 285 million are not that many. On the other hand, it's important to remember that those figures include the many millions of American children who were once supported by welfare checks. Further, such figures are inadequate to capture the reality that welfare poverty covers an ever-changing group of citizens: in coming decades, tens of millions will be affected by changes to the welfare system. But given class and race segregation in housing, work, and services, many middle Americans will not actually witness the daily hardships of poor families, at least not in a direct and immediate way.[17]

Of course, as I've suggested, there is also a real possibility that as conditions worsen, the nation will see higher levels of civil disobedience, especially in those locales with high concentrations of the poor—including New York City, Los Angeles, Baltimore, St. Louis, Philadelphia, Washington, D.C., and elsewhere. In any case, over the long haul the reform of welfare will be costly—in its human toll, its fiscal toil, and its moral and political toll. . . .

Notes

1. U.S. Congress (1996, PL104-193, Title I, Section 401).
2. Between July 1994 and January 2000, the real value of welfare benefits declined by 11 percent. Even though 16 states had raised their benefit amounts by 2000, most did not raise them enough to offset inflation. See U.S. House of Representatives (1998, 2000).
3. Terry and Manlove (1999); see also Luker (1996) and Waller (1999).
4. Luker (1996), Waller (1999), and Ventura and Bachrach (2000).
5. See, for instance, Hays (1996), Hochschild (1989, 1997).
6. See Arno et al. (1999) and Harvard School of Public Health (2000) on the number of women caring for disabled or aged family members.
7. Denise is referring to then prominent news stories on Columbine school shooting and the other shootings that followed.
8. See National Public Radio et al. (2001).
9. On symbolic boundaries, see Lamont (1992, 2000). For a connected, yet distinct treatment of "moral boundaries," see Tronto (1993). For an analysis of the construction of welfare mothers as the "other" in the division between "us" and "them," see Gans (1995) and Handler and Hasenfield (1997).
10. See Sorensen and Zibman (2000) and Cherlin and Fomby (2002).
11. See Loprest (1999), Boushev and Gunderson (2001), Sherman et al. (1998), and National Campaign for Jobs and Income Support (2001A, 2001B). A study of major U.S. cities found that from 2000 to 2001, requests for food had increased by 23 percent and requests for emergency housing were up by 13 percent (U.S. Conference of Mayors 2001).

12. See Edin and Lein (1997). . . .
13. See especially Waller (1999), Garfinkel et al. (2001), and McLanahan et al. (2001) on the ongoing ties between welfare children and their fathers.
14. This is actually more complicated, and the accountings are not always clear. For instance, I was unable to determine whether federal analyses of welfare costs since reform include the rising price of childcare subsidies and welfare-to-work programs. See U.S. House of Representatives (2000), Blau (1999), National Campaign for Jobs and Income Support (2001A).
15. For foster care, see Geen et al. (1999); for average welfare benefits, see Social Security Bulletin (2000); for prison costs, see Stephan (1999).
16. See, for instance, Newman (1988, 1999), Piven (1999), Blau (1999), Edin and Lein (1997), and Ehrenreich (2001). One might also note that a number of profit-making firms established quite lucrative state contracts for serving welfare clients. In some states, those operations profit directly from the number of welfare families they manage to delete from the welfare rolls (as was the case in Sunbelt City). For suggestive information on these operations, see Ehrenreich (1997) and the Wisconsin Joint Legislative Audit Committee (2001) report pointing out that some Wisconsin contracting agencies are under investigation for corrupt practices.
17. By 2000, there were still 2.2 million people living in desperate poverty, with incomes below 50 percent of the poverty level (Dalaker 2000); the comparable figure for 1996 (earlier on in the economic boom) was 14.4 million (Lamison-White 1997).

References

Arno, Peter, Carol Levine, and Margaret Memmott. 1999. "The Economic Value of Informal Caregiving." *Health Affairs* 18: 182–188.

Bernstein, Nina. 2002. "Side Effect of Welfare Law: The No Parent Family." *New York Times,* July 29: A1.

Blau, Joel. 1999. *Illusions of Prosperity: America's Working Families in an Age of Economic Insecurity.* New York: Oxford University Press.

Boushev, Heather and Bethney Gunderson. 2001. *When Work Just Isn't Enough: Measuring Hardships Faced by Families after Moving* from *Welfare to Work.* Washington, DC: Economic Policy Institute.

Cherlin, Andrew J. and Paula Fomby. 2002. *A Closer Look at Changes in Children's Living Arrangements.*

Welfare, Children, and Families: A Three-City Study, Working Paper 02–01. Baltimore, MD: Johns Hopkins University.

Dalaker, Joseph. 2001. *Poverty in the United States*. U.S. Census Bureau, Current Population Reports, Series P60-214. Washington, DC: U.S. Government Printing Office.

Edin, Kathryn and Laura Lein. 1997. *Making Ends Meet: How Single Mothers Survive Welfare and Low-Wage Work*. New York: Russell Sage Foundation.

Ehrenreich, Barbara. 1997. "Spinning the Poor into Gold." *Harper's Magazine* (August): 44–52.

Ehrenreich, Barbara. 2001. *Nickel and Dimed: On (Not) Getting By in America*. New York: Metropolitan Books.

Gans, Herbert J. 1995. *The War Against the Poor: The Underclass and Antipoverty Policy*. New York: Basic Books.

Garfinkel, Irwin, Sara S. McLanahan, Marta Tienda, and Jeanne Brooks-Gunn. 2001. "Fragile Families and Welfare Reform: An introduction." *Children and Youth Services Review* 23 (4/5): 277–301.

Geen, Rob, Shelley Waters Boots, and Karen C. Tumlin. 1999. *The Cost of Protecting Vulnerable Children: Understanding the Complexities of Federal, State, and Local Child Welfare Spending*. Washington, DC: Urban Institute.

Handler, Joel F. and Yeheskel Hasenfeld. 1997. *We the Poor People: Work, Poverty, and Welfare*. New Haven, CT: Yale University Press.

Hays, Sharon. 1996. *The Cultural Contradictions of Motherhood*. New Haven, CT: Yale University Press.

Hochschild, Arlie Russell with Anne Machung. 1989. *The Second Shift: Working Parents and the Revolution at Home*. New York: Viking.

Hochschild, Arlie Russell. 1997. *The Time Bind: When Work Becomes Home and Home Becomes Work*. New York: Metropolitan Books.

Lamison-White, Leatha. 1997. *Poverty in the United States: 1996*. U.S. Bureau of the Census, Current Population Reports, Series P60-198. Washington, DC: U.S. Government Printing Office.

Lamont, Michèle. 1992. *Money, Morals, and Manners*. Chicago: University of Chicago Press.

Lamont, Michèle. 2000. *The Dignity of Working Men: Morality and the Boundaries of Race, Class, and Immigration*. New York: Russell Sage Foundation.

Loprest, Pamela. 1999. *Families Who Left Welfare: Who Are They and How Are They Doing?* Washington, DC: Urban Institute.

Luker, Kristin. 1996. *Dubious Conceptions: The Politics of Teenage Pregnancy*. Cambridge, MA: Harvard University Press.

McLanahan, Sara, Irwin Garfinkel, and Ronald B. Mincy. 2001. *Fragile Families, Welfare Reform, and Marriage*. Welfare Reform and Beyond: Policy Brief No. 10. Washington, DC: Brookings Institution.

National Campaign for Jobs and Income Support. 2001A. *A Recession Like No Other: New Analysis Finds Safety Net in Tatters as Economic Slump Deepens*. Washington, DC: National Campaign for Jobs and Income Support.

National Campaign for Jobs and Income Support. 2001B. *Leaving Welfare. Left Behind: Employment Status, Income, and Well-Being of Former TANF Recipients*. Washington, DC: National Campaign for Jobs and Income Support.

National Public Radio, Kaiser Family Foundation, and Kennedy School of Government. 2001. *Poverty in America*. Washington, DC: National Public Radio.

Newman, Katherine S. 1988. *Falling from Grace*. New York. Free Press.

Newman, Katherine S. 1999. *No Shame in My Game: The Working Poor in the Inner City*. New York: Vintage Books.

Piven, Frances Fox. 1999. "Welfare and Work," pp. 83–99 in *Whose Welfare?* edited by Gwendolyn Mink. Ithaca, NY: Cornell University Press.

Sherman, Arloc, Cheryl Amey, Barbara Duffield, Nancy Ebb, and Deborah Weinstein. 1998. *Welfare to What? Early Findings on Family Hardship and Well-Being*. National Coalition for the Homeless. Washington, DC: Children's Defense Fund.

Social Security Bulletin. 2000. *Annual Statistical Supplement: 2000*. http://www.ssa.gov/statistics/supplement/2000.

Sorensen, Elaine and Chava Zibman. 2000. *Child Support Offers Some Protection Against Poverty*. Assessing the New Federalism, Series B, No. B-10. Washington, DC: Urban Institute.

Stephan, James J. 1999. *State Prison Expenditures, 1996*. U.S. Department of Justice, NCJ 172211. Washington, DC: U.S. Government Printing Office.

Terry, Elizabeth and Jennifer Manlove. 1999. *Trends in Sexual Activity and Contraceptive Use Among Teens*. Washington, DC: Child Trends.

Tronto, Joan C. 1993 [1994]. *Moral Boundaries: A Political Argument for an Ethic of Care*. New York: Routledge.

U.S. Conference of Mayors. 2001. *A Status Report on Hunger and Homelessness in America's Cities: A*

27-City Survey. Washington, DC: Conference of Mayors.

U.S. Congress. 1996. *Personal Responsibility and Work Opportunity Reconciliation Act of 1996.* Public Law 104–193, H.R. 3734.

U.S. House of Representatives, Committee on Ways and Means. 1998. *Green Book: Overview of Entitlement Programs.* Washington, DC: U.S. Government Printing Office.

U.S. House of Representatives, Committee on Ways and Means. 2000. *Green Book: Overview of Entitlement Programs.* Washington, DC: U.S. Government Printing Office.

Ventura, Stephanie and Christine A. Bachrach. 2000. *Nonmarital Childbearing in the United States,* 1940–99. U.S. Department of Health and Human Services, National Vital Statistics Reports 48 (16). Washington, DC: U.S. Government Printing Office.

Waller, Maureen R. 1999. "Meanings and Motives in New Family Stories: The Separation of Reproduction and Marriage Among Low-Income Black and White Parents," pp. 182–218 in *The Cultural Territories of Race: Black and White Boundaries,* edited by Michèle Lamont. Chicago: University of Chicago Press.

Wisconsin Joint Legislative Audit Committee. 2001. *An Evaluation: Wisconsin Works (W-2) Program, Department of Workforce Development.* Madison, WI: Legislative Audit Bureau.

APPENDIX

CLIFF BROWN

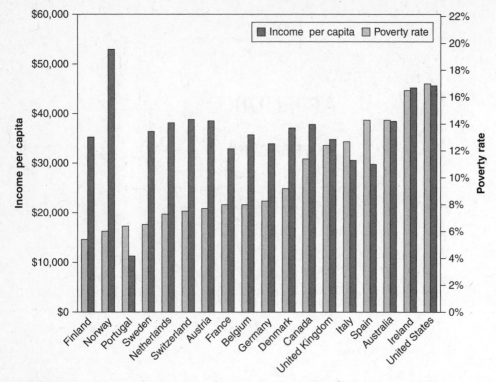

FIGURE A.1 International Comparison of Income Per Capita (2007$) and Poverty (2000).

Source: Mishel, Bernstein, and Shierholz 2008a.

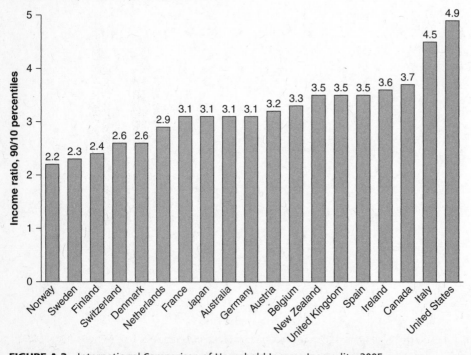

FIGURE A.2 International Comparison of Household Income Inequality, 2005.

Source: Mishel, Bernstein, and Shierholz 2008b.

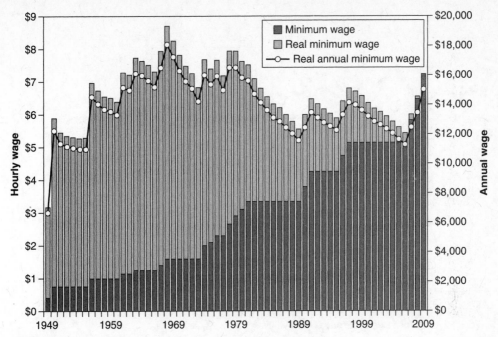

FIGURE A.3 The Minimum Wage in the United States, 1949–2009.

Source: Filion 2009.

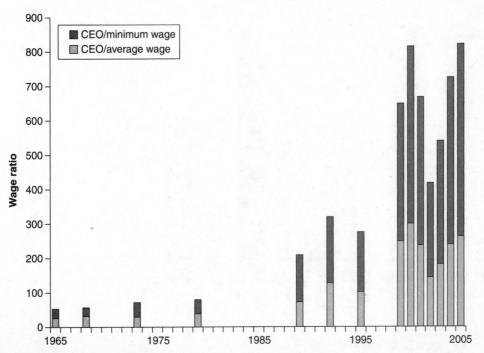

FIGURE A.4 Ratio of Average CEO Compensation to Average and Minimum Wages for U.S. Workers, 1965–2005.

Sources: Mishel 2006a and 2006b.

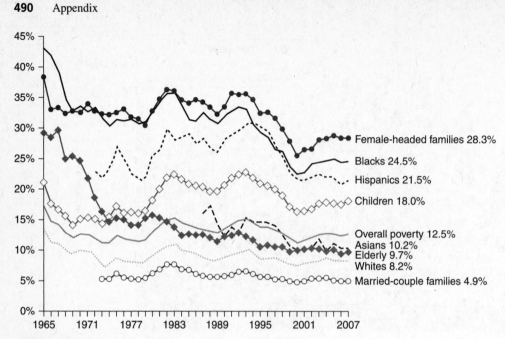

FIGURE A.5 Poverty Rates for Selected Groups, 1965–2007.

Source: DeNavas-Walt, Proctor, and Smith 2008.

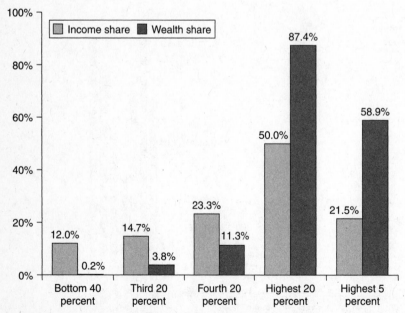

FIGURE A.6 Income and Wealth Distribution for U.S. Households.

Sources: U.S. Census Bureau 2009b and Wolff 2007.

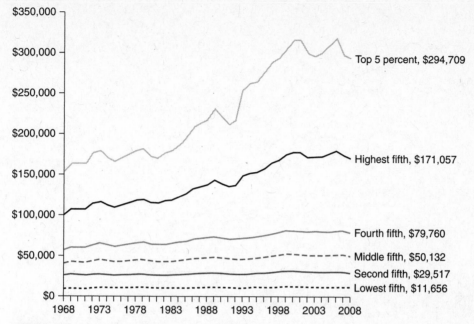

FIGURE A.7   Mean Household Income (2008$) by Quintile and for the Top 5 Percent, 1968–2008.
Source: U.S. Census Bureau 2009b.

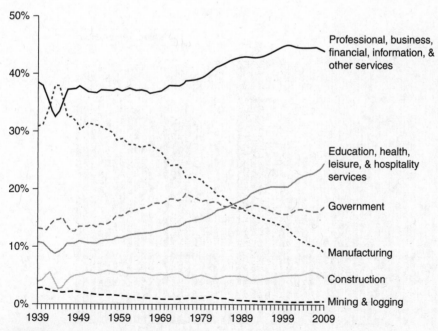

FIGURE A.8   Percent of U.S. Nonfarm Workers Employed by Sector, 1939–2009.
Source: Bureau of Labor Statistics 2010a.

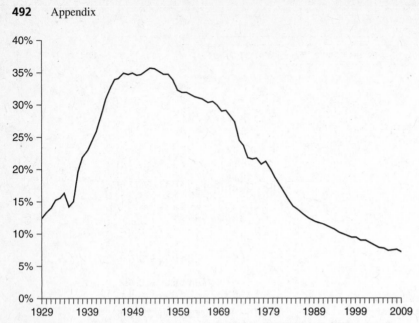

FIGURE A.9 Unionization Rates for Private-Sector Workers in the United States, 1929–2009.

Source: Hirsch 2008.

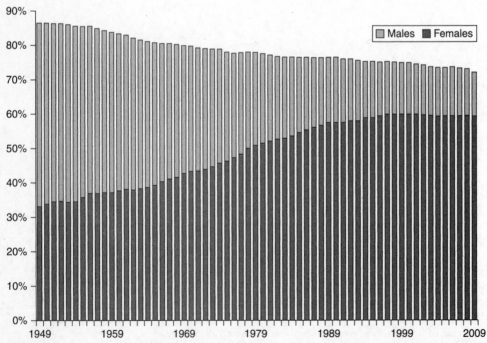

FIGURE A.10 Civilian Labor Force Participation Rates for Males and Females Age 16 and Over, 1949–2009.

Source: Bureau of Labor Statistics 2010b.

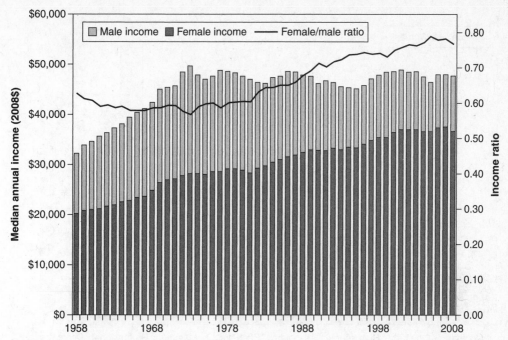

FIGURE A.11   Median Annual Income by Sex and the Female/Male Income Ratio for Full-Time, Year-Round U.S. Workers, 1958–2008.

Source: U.S. Census Bureau 2009a.

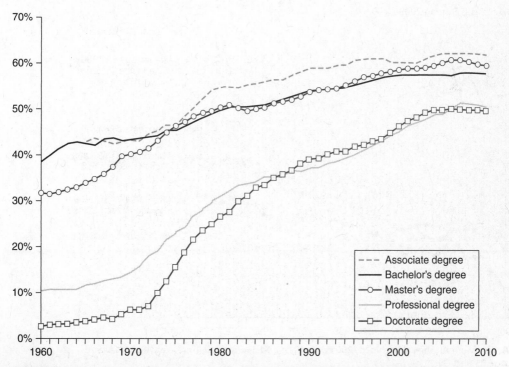

FIGURE A.12   Percentage of Degrees Earned by Women, 1960–2010. Data for 2009 and 2010 are projected.

Source: National Center for Education Statistics 2008.

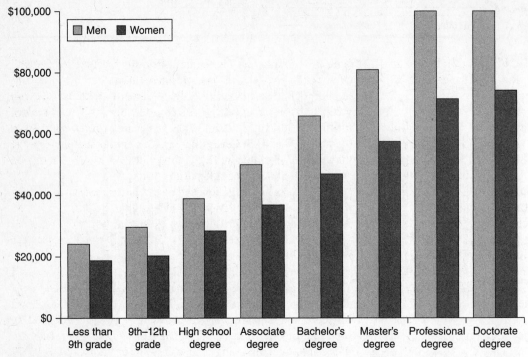

FIGURE A.13 Median Annual Earnings by Education for Full-Time, Year-Round U.S. Workers Age 25 and Over, 2008.

Source: U.S. Census Bureau 2009a.

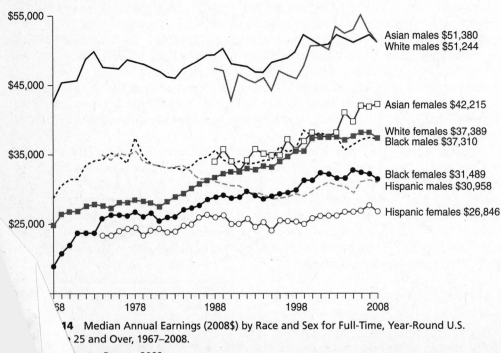

14 Median Annual Earnings (2008$) by Race and Sex for Full-Time, Year-Round U.S.
25 and Over, 1967–2008.

ensus Bureau 2009a.

REFERENCES

Bureau of Labor Statistics. 2010a. "Table B-1. Employees on Nonfarm Payrolls by Industry Sector." Retrieved January 20, 2010 (http://www.bls.gov/webapps/legacy/cesbtab1.htm).

Bureau of Labor Statistics. 2010b. "Labor Force Participation Rates." Series LNU01300001 and LNU01300002, retrieved January 26, 2010 (http://data.bls.gov/PDQ/servlet/SurveyOutputServlet).

DeNavas-Walt, Carmen, Bernadette Proctor, and Jessica C. Smith. 2008. "Income, Poverty, and Health Insurance Coverage in the United States: 2007." U.S. Census Bureau (Current Population Reports, P60-235), U.S. Government Printing Office, Washington, D.C. Tables B-1, B-2, and B-3 retrieved July 7, 2009 (http://www.census.gov/prod/2008pubs/p60-235.pdf).

Filion, Kai. 2009. "Minimum Wage Issue Guide." Economic Policy Institute. Data for Tables and Figures retrieved January 21, 2010 (http://www.epi.org/publications/entry/tables_figures_data/).

Hirsch, Barry T. 2008. "Sluggish Institutions in a Dynamic World: Can Unions and Industrial Competition Coexist?" *Journal of Economic Perspectives* 22 (1): 153–176. Data Appendix for Figure 1 retrieved January 21, 2010 (http://www.unionstats.com/).

Mishel, Lawrence. 2006a. "CEO-to-Worker Pay Imbalance Grows." Economic Policy Institute. Retrieved January 26, 2010 (http://www.epi.org/economic_snapshots/entry/ webfeatures_snapshots_20060621/).

Mishel, Lawrence. 2006b. "CEO-Minimum Wage Ratio Soars." Economic Policy Institute. Retrieved January 26, 2010 (http://www.epi.org/economic_snapshots/entry/webfeatures_snapshots_20060627/).

Mishel, Lawrence, Jared Bernstein, and Heidi Shierholz. 2008a. *The State of Working America 2008/2009*. Data for "Table 8.1: Per Capita Income Using Purchasing-Power Parity, 1950–2007" and "Table 8.16: Poverty rates, 2000," retrieved January 29, 2010 (http://www.stateof-workingamerica.org/tabfig_2008_08.html).

Mishel, Lawrence, Jared Bernstein, and Heidi Shierholz. 2008b. *The State of Working America 2008/2009*. Data for "Table 8.15: Household Income Inequality, 2005," retrieved January 29, 2010 (http://www.stateofworkingamerica.org/tabfig_2008_08.html).

National Center for Education Statistics. 2008. "Digest of Education Statistics." Data for Tables 249 and 268 retrieved January 26, 2010 (http://nces.ed.gov//programs/digest/d03/tables/dt249.asp and http://nces.ed.gov/programs/digest/d08/tables/dt08_268.asp?referrer=list).

U.S. Census Bureau. 2009a. "PINC-03. Educational Attainment—People 25 Years Old and Over, by Total Money Earnings in 2008, Work Experience in 2008, Age, Race, Hispanic Origin, and Sex." Retrieved January 20, 2010 (http://www.census.gov/hhes/www/cpstables/032009/perinc/new03_136.htm).

U.S. Census Bureau. 2009b. "Table H-3. Mean Household Income Received by Each Fifth and Top 5 Percent, All Races: 1967 to 2008. Retrieved January 20, 2010 (http://www.census.gov/hhes/www/income/histinc/h03AR.xls).

U.S. Census Bureau. 2009c. "Table P-38. Full-Time, Year-Round Workers by Median Earnings and Sex." Retrieved January 20, 2010 (http://www.census.gov/hhes/www/income/histinc/incpertoc.html).

Wolff, Edward N. 2007. "Recent Trends in Household Wealth in the United States: Rising Debt and the Middle-Class Squeeze." Levy Economics Institute Working Paper 502. Retrieved January 27, 2010 (http://www.levy.org/vtype.aspx?doctype=13).